Branding the Middle East

Studies on Modern Orient

Volume 38

Branding the Middle East

Communication Strategies and Image Building from Qom to Casablanca

Edited by
Steffen Wippel

DE GRUYTER

The present publication was funded by the Federal Ministry of Education and Research (BMBF, Merian Centre for Advanced Studies in the Maghreb/ MECAM).
For further information please visit: https://mecam.tn

Bundesministerium
für Bildung
und Forschung

ميكام
مركز ميريان
للدراسات المتقدمة
في المنطقة المغاربية

MECAM
Merian Centre
For Advanced Studies
In The Maghreb

ISBN 978-3-11-074062-2
e-ISBN (PDF) 978-3-11-074110-0
e-ISBN (EPUB) 978-3-11-074115-5
DOI https://doi.org/9783110741100

Library of Congress Control Number: 2023939557

Bibliographic information published by the Deutsche Nationalbibliothek
The Deutsche Nationalbibliothek lists this publication in the Deutsche Nationalbibliografie; detailed bibliographic data are available on the Internet at http://dnb.dnb.de.

Cover image: The Sailing Ship Monument on Al Wazarat Roundabout in Muscat, Oman
Photo: Steffen Wippel, 2009.
Printing and binding: CPI books GmbH, Leck

MIX
Papier | Fördert gute Waldnutzung
FSC® C083411

www.degruyter.com

Steffen Wippel

Branding a Seafaring Nation: The Sailing Ship Monument on Al Wazarat Roundabout in Muscat, Oman

The cover photo of this edited volume shows a ship monument that was displayed on the central Al Wazarat Roundabout at Al Khuwair in the Capital Area of Oman, when Muscat held the title of the Capital of Arab Culture for 2006 under the Arab League's cultural capital programme.[1] The monument physically reflects the logo of the festivities, as it was also reproduced on a special stamp edition, for instance. The simplified hull and the slightly twisted sail bearing the name of the city and the year of the event in Arabic script are intended to be reminiscent of a traditional dhow. This is part of national and local branding efforts in several respects: not only the honorary title served for one year to fuel local citizens' pride in their homeland and hometown, to attract international attention, and to make the city and its rich heritage known to foreign tourists, investors, and hauliers when its opening to the world and positioning as a destination was still in its infancy. The ship representation is also part of a conspicuously recurring number of roundabout monuments in Gulf cities that show idealised items of local culture and history and of the wide display of maritime motifs.[2] This is intended to construct continuities from past traditions and industries like sea pearl diving and trade to contemporary endeavours to develop global connections and demonstrate cosmopolitan openness. Oman is particularly eager to show its maritime heritage.[3] Like other Gulf states, the Sultanate wants to build a sustainable future, redirected from excessive hydrocarbon dependence to allegedly promising sectors like international trade and tourism. In particular, responsible actors strive to position the Sultanate as a country belonging to the economically emerging and pivotal Indian Ocean region and with centuries of experience in economic and cultural exchange with Asian, African, and Arab countries.[4] Repeatedly, Oman's glorious seafaring past has been praised: Sinbad is presented as a seafarer of Omani origin, who already crossed the waves of the Indian Ocean and adjacent seas to distant shores;

---

1 On this, see e.g. Oxford Business Group, 2007. For the cultural capital titles, cf. also the introductory part to this edited volume.

2 On Gulf roundabouts, cf. also Trenka-Dalton, 2016: 120–130.

3 More broadly on the twisting of branding and spatial planning in Oman, cf. Klinger, in this volume; see also Klinger, 2022: esp. 469–474.

4 Cf. in more detail, e.g. Wippel, 2014 and 2017.

https://doi.org/10.1515/9783110741100-001

museums display a broad range of old dhow types; coffee table books on traditional shipping are widely available; and enterprises from diverse sectors use ships as symbols in their corporate design. Since the 1980s, the media have widely featured the reconstruction of traditional vessels, their voyages along the historical maritime Silk Road to South and East Asia, and later their display on a roundabout in Muscat or in a museum in Singapore. Finally, the huge industrial and container ports that Oman has opened since the late 1990s and that are intended to become major global transhipment hubs advertise themselves as gateways to Indian Ocean rim countries.

Bibliography

Klinger, Thibaut. *L'Oman contemporain: Aménagement du territoire et identité nationale.* Berlin, Boston: de Gruyter, 2022.

Oxford Business Group. *Emerging Oman.* London, 2007.

Trenka-Dalton, Sophie-Therese. *Palms.* Hamburg: Textem Verlag, 2016.

Wippel, Steffen. "Port and Tourism Development in Oman: Between Economic Diversification and Global Branding." In *Under Construction: Logics of Urbanism in the Gulf Region*, edited by Steffen Wippel, Katrin Bromber, Christian Steiner, and Birgit Krawietz, 101–118. Farnham, Burlington: Ashgate, 2014.

Wippel, Steffen. "Sindbad the Sailor revived? Oman and its Indian Ocean Links." In *The Transnational Middle East: Places, People, Borders*, edited by Leïla Vignal, 122–147. Abingdon, New York: Routledge, 2017.

Acknowledgements

As always with such book projects, my thanks go first and foremost to my wife and friends who had to do without my intensive presence during the long editing period of this – again – very voluminous anthology. However, I would especially like to thank all the authors who, with passion for the subject and patience for my frequent suggestions for improvements, took up the book idea enthusiastically and have contributed to making this edited volume what it is – a well-rounded, multi-faceted, and richly documented and illustrated publication on branding in, of, and by the Middle East and the Arab world.

I want to thank the de Gruyter publishing house, namely its series editor in charge, Dr. Sophie Wagenhofer, who welcomed the extensive book project with openness and curiosity, enabled its free publication, patiently answered my constant queries, and intensively accompanied the publication process; in particular, she made the numerous colour illustrations in the book and the final formatting of the volume at the publishing house possible. At de Gruyter, I would also like to thank Eva Frantz, Katrin Hudey, and Matthias Wand for all their patient and cooperative fine-tuning in the final editing of the book for printing. As always, Mitch Cohen has provided accurate language proofreading of the contributions and helped to clarify the many subtleties of the content.

Originally, the anthology was planned for sale as a printed and online publication. I am all the more pleased that the board and the management of the German-Tunisian research platform Merian Centre for Advanced Studies in the Maghreb (MECAM) in Tunis, namely its German director Prof. Rachid Ouaissa (Philipps-Universität Marburg) and the academic coordinator Dr. Julius Dihstelhoff, supported an open access publication. In line with MECAM's guiding theme "Imagining Futures –Dealing with Disparity", this volume is also about attractive ideas, images, and visions that are widely communicated in order to ensure the lasting future success of the marketed objects; at the same time, branding must always deal with existing disparities, whether it seeks to bridge or blur gaps and boundaries, or in explicitly ignoring or dissimulating negative sides and consequences. Particularly, I thank the German Federal Ministry of Education and Research (BMBF), which provided the necessary funds in the framework of financing the MECAM's initial working phase.

https://doi.org/10.1515/9783110741100-002

Table of Contents

Part V: **Place Branding**

Abbreviations

3D	three-dimensional
AD	*Anno Domini*
ADNOC	Abu Dhabi National Oil Company
ADQ	Abu Dhabi Developmental Holding Company
AECOM	Architecture, Engineering, Consulting, Operations, and Maintenance, USA
AKP	*Adalet ve Kalkınma Partisi* (Justice and Development Party), Turkey
ALECSO	Arab League Educational, Cultural and Scientific Organization
AM	*Architecture du Maroc* (journal)
AMA	American Marketing Association
Aramco	Arabian-American Oil Company, now Saudi Aramco
APM	A.P. Møller-Mærsk (Terminals), Netherlands
BBC	British Broadcasting Corporation
BGSMCS	Berlin Graduate School Muslim Cultures and Societies, *Freie Universität Berlin*
BIBU	Tackling Biases and Bubbles in Participation consortium, Helsinki
BIE	*Bureau International des Expositions*
BMBF	*Bundesministerium für Bildung und Forschung* (Federal Ministry of Education and Research), Germany
BMW	*Bayerische Motoren Werke*
BOMU	Brand Oman Management Unit
CC	Coco Chanel
CE	Common Era
CEFREPA	*Centre français de recherche sur la péninsule arabique*, Kuwait
CEMAPI	*Centre Malien de Promotion de la Propriété Industrielle*
CEO	Chief Executive Officer
CER.ES	*Colecciones en Red* (*Red Digital de Colecciones de Museos de España*)
CHP	*Cumhuriyet Halk Partisi* (Republican People's Party), Turkey
CI	Competitive Identity or Corporate Identity
CIDOB	*Centro de Información y Documentación Internacionales en Barcelona*
CITERES	*Laboratoire Cités, TERritoires, Environnement et Sociétés*, Tours
CMA CGM	*Compagnie Maritime d'Affrètement – Compagnie Générale Maritime*, France
CNN	Cable News Network, USA
COP	Conference of the parties (United Nations Climate Change Conferences)
CRI	*Centre Régional d'Investissement*, Tanger–Tétouan
CUBES	Centre for Built Environment Studies, Johannesburg
DAVO	*Deutsche Arbeitsgemeinschaft Vorderer Orient für gegenwartsbezogene Forschung und Dokumentation* (German Middle East Studies Association for Contemporary Research and Documentation)
DED	Department of Economic Development, Dubai
DESS	*Diplôme d'études supérieures spécialisées*
DEWA	Dubai Electricity and Water Authority
DFG	*Deutsche Forschungsgemeinschaft* (German Research Foundation)
DIEDC	Dubai Islamic Economy Development Centre

https://doi.org/10.1515/9783110741100-003

DİSK	*Türkiye Devrimci İşçi Sendikaları Konfederasyonu* (Confederation of Revolutionary Trade Unions), Turkey
DKK	Danish krone
dmc	Dar Al-Mimar Construction, Egypt
DOI	Digital Object Identifier
DOT	*Deutscher Orientalistentag* (German Oriental conference)
dtdv	*Danimarka Türk Diyanet Vakfı* (Danish Turkish Islamic Foundation)
EA	*L'Écho d'Alger: Journal Républicain du matin*
ECSSR	Emirates Center for Strategic Studies and Research, Abu Dhabi
EGP	Egyptian Pound
EMAM	*Equipe Monde Arabe et Méditerranée*, Tours
ENCG	*Ecole Nationale de Commerce et de Gestion*, Settat
ESRC	Economic and Social Research Council, UK
ETA	Egyptian Tourism Authority
EU	European Union
EUR	Euro
FIFA	*Fédération internationale de football association*
FPT	Food Processing Technology
GaWC	Globalisation and World Cities Research Network, Loughborough
GCC	Gulf Cooperation Council
GDP	Gross domestic product
GIGA	*Leibniz-Institut für Globale und Regionale Studien*, Hamburg (German Institute for Global and Area Studies)
GMBA	Gibraltar and Morocco Business Association
GOPP	General Organization for Physical Planning, Egypt
GSLP	Gibraltar Socialist Labour Party
HDB	Housing and Development Bank, Egypt
HSSD	Hassad Foods, Qatar
İBB	*İstanbul Büyükşehir Belediyesi* (Istanbul Metropolitan Municipality)
ICESCO	Islamic World Educational, Scientific and Cultural Organization
IFSB	Islamic Financial Services Board, Kuala Lumpur
İGA	*İGA Havalimanı İşletmesi A.Ş.* (İstanbul Grand Airport Airport Operation Inc.)
IHC	International Humanitarian City, Dubai
IHS	Institute for Housing and Urban Development Studies, Erasmus University Rotterdam
İLAV	*İstanbul Lale Vakfı* (Istanbul Tulip Foundation)
ILF	Independent Liberal Forum, Gibraltar
ILKHA	*İlke Haber Ajansı* (Ilke News Agency), Diyarbakır
ILNA	Iranian Labour News Agency
INGO	International Nongovernmental Organisation
INRSP	*Institut national de recherche en santé publique*, Mali
IQNA	International Quran News Agency, Iran
IR	International Relations (theory)
IRES	*Institut Royal des Etudes Stratégiques*, Rabat
IS	Islamic State
ISDF	Informal Settlements Development Fund, Egypt
ISIS	Islamic State of Iraq and Syria
ITC	Integrated Tourism Complex

JWT	James Walter Thompson (advertisement holding company)
KAEC	King Abdullah Economic City, Saudi Arabia
KAUST	King Abdullah University of Science and Technology, Saudi Arabia
KIPCO	Kuwait Projects Company
KSA	Kingdom of Saudi Arabia
LADYSS	*Laboratoire Dynamiques Sociales et Recomposition des Espaces*, Paris
LGBTQ(+)	Lesbian, Gay, Bisexual, Transgender, Queer (and related communities)
MA	Master of Arts / Magister Artium
MAP	*Maghreb Arab Presse / Agence Marocaine de Presse*
MBS	Mohammed bin Salman (Crown Prince of Saudi Arabia)
MBZ	Sheikh Mohamed bin Zayed Al Nahyan (President of the UAE and ruler of Abu Dhabi)
MDG	Millennium Development Goal, United Nations
MECAM	Merian Centre for Advanced Studies in the Maghreb, Tunis
MENA	Middle East and North Africa
MHPV	*Ministère de l'Habitat, de l'Urbanisme et de la Politique de la Ville / Ministère de l'Aménagement du Territoire National, de l'Urbanisme, de l'Habitat et de la Politique de la Ville*, Morocco
MICE	Meetings, incentives, conferences and exhibitions (tourism)
MIT	Massachusetts Institute of Technology
MOE	Mall of the Emirates, Dubai
ndc-info	*Nouvelles du Continent*, Abidjan
NEOM	"New future," from *neo* (new) and *mustaqbal* (future), Saudi urban mega-project
NGO	Nongovernmental Organisation
NRK	Non-Residential Keralites
NTS	National Tourism Strategy, Oman
NUCA	New Urban Communities Authority, Egypt
NY	New York
OAPI	*Organisation Africaine de la Propriété Intellectuelle*, Yaoundé
OBG	Oxford Business Group
OCCI	Oman Chamber of Commerce and Industry
OCEC	Oman Convention & Exhibition Centre, Muscat
OFIC	Oman Food Investment Company
OIC	Organisation of Islamic Cooperation
OMRAN	Oman Tourism Development Company
ONMT	*Office National Marocain du Tourisme*
PERMANDU	Performance Management & Delivery Unit, Malaysia
PIF	Public Investment Fund, Saudi Arabia
PM	*Le Petit Marocain*
PR	Public Relations
QNFSP	Qatar National Food Security Programme
R&D	Research and development
SAPT	*Société d'Aménagement pour la Reconversion de la Zone Portuaire de Tanger*
SAR	Saudi Riyal
SDG	Sustainable Development Goal, United Nations
SGA	Strait of Gibraltar Association
SME	Small and medium-sized enterprises
SOAS	School of Oriental and African Studies, London

SWANA	South West Asia and North Africa
TA	Turkish Airlines (*Türk Hava Yolları*)
Tanfeedh	National Programme for Enhancing Economic Diversification, Oman
taz	*die tageszeitung* (German daily newspaper)
TGV	*Train à grande vitesse*
TMSA	TangerMed Special Agency
TMZ	Tanger Med Zones
TU	*Technische Universität* (Technical University)
U.AE	The United Arab Emirates' Government Portal
UAE	United Arab Emirates
UAR	United Arab Republic
UCLGA	United Cities and Local Governments of Africa
UK	United Kingdom
UN	United Nations
UN Comtrade	United Nations Commodity Trade Statistics Database
UNCTAD	United Nations Conference on Trade and Development
UNESCO	United Nations Educational, Scientific and Cultural Organization
UN-Habitat	United Nations Human Settlements Programme
UNHCR	United Nations High Commissioner for Refugees
UNOs	United Nations organisations
UNWTO	World Tourism Organization (UN agency)
URC	United Real Estate Company, Kuwait
US(A)	United States (of America)
USD	US dollar
VSBP	*Villes Sans Bidonvilles* programme, Morocco
WSJ	Wall Street Journal, New York
WTO	World Trade Organization
YGTV	Your Gibraltar TV
ZMO	*Leibniz-Zentrum Moderner Orient*, Berlin

Part I: **Introduction**

Steffen Wippel

Introduction: A Thoroughly Branded, but Little-Known Middle East

"Hello Tomorrow," "The Finest in the Sky," and "Fly Better." Few products and places from the Middle East and North Africa (MENA) are probably as well-known to a global public today as are the Dubai-owned Emirates airline, which is among the companies with a high brand value worldwide, and the city-state of Dubai itself. They are less known by their changing slogans[1] and logos (cf. Fig. 1a) than through a positive image of high quality, unlimited hospitality, and breath-taking urbanscape (Fig. 1b).

Fig. 1: The current Emirates logo and the Dubai skyline
Sources: a) Wikimedia Commons, 2022, author: Emirates, public domain; b) Photo Steffen Wippel, 2012.

In the MENA region since the turn of the millennium, it has been especially Dubai, the hypercapitalistic Gulf emirate, that has become a brandmark that succeeded in attracting worldwide attention and fascination. With its allure of speed and dynamics, its iconic architecture, grandiose infrastructure projects, hyperrealistic buildings, and landscaping urbanism, as well with its great shopping opportunities, its manifold festivals, and its widely advertised cosmopolitanism, it positioned itself at the forefront of place branding not only regionally, but also globally for at least a decade, before the Dubai boom came to a temporary standstill following

1 While Dubai did not excel by means of a specific slogan, Emirates has changed its tagline several times; cf. Wikipedia, 2022; Liaqat, 2016, including many of its advertising posters. Besides the written logo, Dubai very often also works with the shapes of its skyline and renowned solitary buildings like *Burj Al Arab* or *Burj Khalifa*.

https://doi.org/10.1515/9783110741100-004

the 2008/09 financial crisis.[2] Yet, other cities, regions, and nations in the Gulf and the MENA area also have high recognition value. In the past, some places had already acquired a well-established, widely radiating, yet meanwhile vanished reputation with certain ascribed characteristics, often linked to an Orientalising perception, such as Cairo, the "mother of the world" (*umm al-dunyā*) and the "Paris on the Nile," or Beirut as the "Paris of the Middle East" until the Lebanese civil war broke out in the mid-1970s. Pyramids, citadels, mosques, and churches in Cairo, Jerusalem, and Istanbul were long acknowledged landmarks, also beyond the region. Many places developed national tourism logos and slogans and, more recently, have endeavoured to follow the Dubai example, not only its admired economic and urbanistic model, but also its extensive branding policies.

Likewise, products have long become established brands in the MENA region through logos and slogans, but also by communicating of inherent values, qualities, and either ubiquitous advertisement or exquisite presentation. Local products and companies try to gain prestige and reputation in national and regional markets, and more and more also beyond, in the international realm, where some brand names and logos, for example of Arab and Turkish Airlines, are also more easily recognised today. However, even if oil is perhaps the product most associated with the Middle East in previous decades, one of the world's largest companies in the oil and gas sector, Saudi Aramco – the public Saudi Arabian Oil Company, formerly the Arabian-American Oil Company – is known only to a few specialists, rather than to a broader public. The same is true of other global brands from the region, like the Emirati telecom provider, Etisalat, with subsidiaries from South Asia to West Africa. Similarly, local brands, e.g. in the food industry, have developed, but are primarily known to the national or regional public. In contrast, international brands from the houseware, beverage, and automotive industries, were long ago introduced and massively advertised to the local consumers. Yet, sometimes they have been heavily disputed in public for their names, logos, or origin in the given cultural and political contexts;[3] sometimes, they have been so appealing that counterfeits and fakes are locally produced and distributed.[4] And finally, the region has many personalities who have become icons and who increasingly undertake explicit and effective self-branding policies, from the political area to the cultural field, including religious leaders and heads of extremist groupings, some of whom have achieved worldwide recognisability.

2 Cf., for instance, Bromber et al., 2014.

3 Cf. Kehrer, 2005.

4 On counterfeits, cf. Ermann and Hermanik, 2018: 4.

With that, especially during the last two decades, the contemporary branding boom that has become a rapidly expanding worldwide phenomenon since the 1980s/1990s also reached the MENA region, which wants to stand up to global competition and the worldwide attention economy. But while branding in the Western world and many emerging economies has been meticulously analysed, the MENA region, except for some Gulf countries, still remains underexplored.

Therefore, this present volume investigates and presents the unfoldings, manifestations, and expressions of this global phenomenon in an encompassing and conceptually framed manner, pertaining to the branding of places, products, and people in, through, and around the Middle East and North Africa, including some studies from adjacent regions and the wider Islamicate world. However, the main focus of this book is on branding cities, nations, and other places, from Qom to Casablanca. Going beyond simply presenting logos and slogans, it critically analyses processes of strategic communication and image building under the general conditions of globalisation, neoliberalisation, and postmodernisation and, from a regional perspective, of widespread, lasting authoritarian rule and increased endeavours for "worlding." In particular, it looks at the many actors involved in branding activities, their interests, and their motives, considers the great variety of addressees, and investigates tools, channels, and forms of branding. A major interest is in the entanglements of different spatial scales and in the (in)consistencies of the messages conveyed. Attention is paid to temporal reconfigurations of certain images and to the positioning of objects of branding in time and space. Historical case studies complement the focus on contemporary branding efforts.

With about 35 longer and shorter chapters, including a few "snapshots," the volume fills an important gap in the research on MENA countries. Its authors are of Western and Middle Eastern origin and represent a wide range of disciplines, which allows for a variety of topics and perspectives. The book consists of five parts: this introductory part; a part dealing with various aspects of branding in the fields of consumption, culture, and lifestyle, from beverages and fashion to preachers and queer brands; a part on the branding of premodern empires and modern nation states; one on the many facets of city branding; and, finally, further cases of branding specific places, such as mosques, neighbourhoods, new towns, and refugee camps, past and present, and their entanglements with political branding. The volume concludes with the biographical presentation of all the contributors.

After this brief lead, the introductory part is divided into three subsequent chapters.[5] The next chapter explores general theoretical and conceptual approaches to branding, which serve as the broader framework for this book. It includes a tour through the global, mostly Western, history of branding, a clarification of terminology, and a look at the global macro-contexts in which contemporary branding takes place. The second chapter presents a bird's-eye view of empirical developments and their interpretations in the MENA region, from product and personal branding to a *tour d'horizon* of place branding, starting from its hotspot along the Arab side of the Gulf, through West Asia and the Maghreb, to the region's peripheries. The final chapter provides the general outline of the present volume and explains its various parts and individual chapters.

Bibliography

Bromber, Katrin, Birgit Krawietz, Christian Steiner, and Steffen Wippel. "The Arab(ian) Gulf: Urban Development in the Making." In *Under Construction: Logics of Urbanism in the Gulf Region*, edited by Steffen Wippel, Katrin Bromber, Christian Steiner, and Birgit Krawietz, 1–14. Farnham, Burlington: Ashgate, 2014.

Ermann, Ulrich, and Klaus-Jürgen Hermanik. "Introduction: Branding the Nation, the Place, the Product." In *Branding the Nation, the Place, the Product*, edited by Ulrich Ermann and Klaus-Jürgen Hermanik, 1–13. Abingdon, New York: Routledge, 2018.

Kehrer, Michaela. "Transnationale Konsumgüterunternehmen in Ägypten: Lokale Kultur im globalen Marketing." In *Wirtschaft im Vorderen Orient: Interdisziplinäre Perspektiven*, edited by Steffen Wippel, 215–234. Berlin: Klaus Schwarz, 2005.

Liaqat, Khatija. "Taglines of Emirates Airline." 21 May 2016. https://khatijaliaqat.wordpress.com/2016/05/21/taglines-of-emirates-airline/. Accessed 7 January 2022.

Wikipedia. "Emirates (airline)." https://en.wikipedia.org/wiki/Emirates_(airline). Accessed 7 January 2022.

Wikimedia Commons. "File:Emirates logo.svg." https://commons.wikimedia.org/wiki/File:Emirates_logo.svg. Accessed 10 January 2022.

5 Special thanks go to Elke Friedrich and Birgit Krawietz for discussing the structuring of these introductory chapters with me.

Steffen Wippel

Branding as a Global Phenomenon: From Theory to Practice and Vice Versa

1 Introduction

This edited volume presents and investigates the still underexplored regional expressions and manifestations of the global branding phenomenon in a more encompassing, consistent, and conceptually framed manner. This first introductory chapter situates the contributions of the authors in the global debate on the phenomenon. It points to widespread empirical developments, relates to the elaboration of practical branding toolkits, and, most importantly, explores theoretical and conceptual approaches to branding that amount to the broader framework for this book.

The chapter starts with a short global, initially mostly Western, history of branding. An overview of conceptualisations of branding follows and first contrasts application-oriented literature with more critical studies and insights. It continues by presenting attempts to clarify terminology and discussing some important elements of the branding process, from the variety of its purposes, actors, and addressees to the proposed and employed tools and strategies. Another section pertains to the global macro-contexts in which contemporary branding is said to take place, including globalisation, neoliberalisation, and postmodernisation. Subsequently, some critical considerations relate to a range of political, social, and spatial aspects and consequences of branding. All this will be carried out with a certain bias in favour of place branding, corresponding to the main focus of the articles in the present volume. Most of the references used for this conceptual chapter were published from the late 1990s to the early 2010s, when, after the initiating works, the research field consolidated and provoked critical assessment before it ramified into ever more detailed issues.

2 A Short History of Branding

In general, the branding business has soared worldwide. Yet, branding is not a recent phenomenon, but has a long history. It is an old technique to demonstrate ownership and authorship and to singularise the respective object among others,

https://doi.org/10.1515/9783110741100-005

and it has been applied to creatures as well as artefacts.[1] Etymologically, the term goes back to an Old Germanic word root around the semantic field "to burn." In this sense, it refers to burning a mark of ownership with a hot branding iron on livestock, mostly cattle and horses, but also camels in arid Middle Eastern worlds; this practice has been proven since ancient Egyptian times.[2] Up to today, where and how to brand a camel continues to be a concern even in religious Islamic law.[3] Since ancient times, across many civilisations, hot iron branding and tattooing with indelible ink have been applied also to humans.[4] Its coercive use, as a sign of violence, shame, and domination, served the lifelong "stigmatisation" of persons, for penal but also religious, economic, or decorative reasons.[5] It monitored the ownership of slaves, punished escapees, helped to identify forced labourers, prostitutes, and prisoners of war, and served as a means to humiliate "outsiders." However, in some cultures and social groups, e.g. on Southern Pacific islands or among seamen, such body-marking, especially with tattoos, also provided ornamentation and demonstrated social belonging and pride or symbolised cultural rites of passage and these days has become re-fashioned, albeit to unprecedented degrees.

Trademarks imprinted on commodities are nearly as old. Already in China, the Indus Valley, Mesopotamia, and the circum-Mediterranean cultures, signs were stamped or painted as "proto-brands" on pottery, porcelain, and bricks, sometimes also on wooden products, precious metals, paper, baked products, and other material, to guarantee recognisability and to provide buyers along translocal and transregional trade chains with information on origin, quality, and status. Such pictorial symbols, names, or other wordmarks were put on goods either on their producers' initiative or were required by state authorities and professional guilds. Beyond such utilitarian purposes, these early physical forms of branding already served to promote an imaginary of the product, including the use of religion and sex (like the reproduction of gods of fertility, love, and beauty), to better promote its sales. It also served to differentiate products from competitors and the self-promotion of individual craftsmen. Sometimes, material of specific origin, like copper

---

1 On the origin and application of "branding" in early civilisations, cf. Bastos and Levy, 2012: 349–352; Rajaram and Stalin Shelly, 2012: 100–102; Moore and Raid, 2008. Cf. also Anttiroiko, 2014: 47–48; Pike, 2009: 623.

2 The terms "character" and "cauterisation" both stem from Old Greek designations for practices of branding animals; cf. Jones, 1987.

3 Cf. the legal opinions issued on the electronic *fatwā* site, Islamic fatwas, 2022.

4 Cf. also Ditchey, 2016.

5 From the Greek term *στίγμα* (etymologically close to "stick," "stitch") for such body-marking practices; cf. Jones, 1987.

from ancient Cyprus, was ascribed an inherent quality and value that assured a continuous and high demand. Sales shops and workshops were evoked by pictorial emblems, according to specialisation or owner, notably in societies of high illiteracy, and have survived until contemporary times.

Not only personal, associational, or regional origins of goods served as "brands"; places and spaces themselves were also "sold" and made distinguishable and attractive already very early in history for a broader public for economic, political, and sociocultural purposes.[6] Some authors refer to "Green"-Land as an early episode of place branding by name, which according to legend was deliberately coined by its explorer Leifur Eiríksson at the very beginning of the second millennium to attract the first settlers, whereas the country name for previously discovered "Ice"-Land can be considered a misnomer from a marketing perspective.[7] City branding, too, has distant historical roots, from competition among cities in ancient Greece to religious pilgrim destinations, among members of the Hanseatic League and medieval Italian city-states[8] or absolutist town foundations. We only have to recall that seats of rulership and power, in particular, were turned into impressive brands, notably with representative, highly symbolic buildings like cathedrals, palaces, and castles. Political and military powers and (proto-)nations branded themselves very early, especially on medieval battlefields, e.g. with heraldic banners and coats of arms, cravats, uniforms, and other signs of belonging to a certain rule.

According to Matthieu Adam, modern place branding resulted from the combination of emerging capitalism and imperialism.[9] That process started, when, from the 16th century onwards, global trading centres like Amsterdam and Antwerp and colonial trading societies, like the East India Company, developed strategies to attract settlers and merchants to the newly discovered and subjugated lands. The consolidation of the modern nation state since the 18th century provides a particular historical precedent to contemporary nation-branding practices.[10] As social artefacts and spatial containers, nation states have since sought to create dis-

6 Cf. Kavaratzis and Ashworth, 2005: 506, and 2008: 151.

7 See, e.g., Kavaratzis and Ashworth, 2008: 151; Ward, 1998b: 2; Pálsdottír, 2008: 183. In fact, it was Leifur's father Eiríkur Þorvaldsson, who is said to have named the country in the 980s. According to the sagas, it was his son who then, on his expeditions to North America, gave his most distant discoveries, probably Newfoundland, the likewise appealing name of "wine" or "pasture" lands (Vinland or Vínland).

8 Cf. Anttiroiko, 2014: 14; Ward, 1998b: 2; Harvey, 1989: 15.

9 Cf. Adam, 2020: 213.

10 On early nation branding, cf. Browning and de Oliveira, 2017: 483, 488–489. Cf. also Aronczyk, 2013: 3–5.

tinct identities and loyalties and have always paid attention to matters of image policy in their relations with others. For this, they relied on manifold symbols and sophisticated strategies – e.g., by using national flags, anthems, and constitutions, imposing new state names, and mobilising historical motifs – to mark their claim to sovereignty, to form a national citizenship, and to establish themselves as a kind of "brand," even if this terminology did not yet exist.[11] They staged national culture through artistic (re-)creations and other material and symbolic representations to impress international observers and gain recognition as equal members of the international community. Driven by a variety of objectives, they resorted to "state propaganda," "information policies," or "public diplomacy" as practices to influence their image and reputation.[12]

The phenomenon of modern commodity branding also goes back to the 18th century, based on the commercialisation of luxury goods, which were marked with signs of origin and quality.[13] Yet, it developed mainly in the liberal industrial age, in particular in the second half of the 19th century and early 20th century. It was propelled by the rapid expansion of mass markets for daily consumer goods, in combination with new production, transport, and communication technologies and the establishment of the modern nation states.[14] Industrial products, packaged in consumable quantities, were increasingly displacing traditional, locally grown or manufactured daily commodities, sold as bulk ware, especially in the sectors of food and household goods. The use of catchy labels, names, signs, and slogans helped to make these new products, fabricated in unprecedentedly great quantities, known and recognisable across great distances; they made it possible to distinguish them from similar ones in increasingly differentiated and competitive markets, in order to create confidence in their continuous quality and thereby to induce reliable product loyalty among consumers. For this, it was not enough to be merely informative; creating emotional bonds also seemed necessary.

The emergence of national newspapers and later communications media like radio and TV allowed for even more effective, far-radiating advertisement of products and their producers, which, in the globalisation phase of that time, soon also started to cross state borders and rapidly grew into multinational corporations.

11 Cf. van Ham, 2002: 259. Cf. also Jansen, 2008: 122; Dinnie, 2008: 20. On flags as the "real country logos," cf. Markessinis, 2011.

12 Cf. Browning and de Oliveira, 2017: 488–489. Yet, the differences from nation branding are not always really clear.

13 Cf. Hellmann 2005: 8.

14 On historical product branding, cf. Bastos and Levy, 2012: 354–355; Rajaram and Stalin Shelly, 2012: 102–103. Cf. also Anttiroiko, 2014: 48.

For international trade, "Made in" labels and "country-of-origin"[15] markings developed to promote national provenance linked with a positive country image based on seriousness, quality, reliability, industriousness, and ingenuity. At that time, many nationally and internationally renowned brands were created that still exist today and are highly valued in financial and emotional terms. Some brand names even turned into colloquial generic names for entire product categories (such as "Scotch," or "Tesa" in German, for adhesive tape).[16] With that, marketing that had long focused mainly on distribution techniques, slowly started to develop into a broader mix that included more sophisticated sales and logistics strategies, but also invested substantial advertising, promoting, and other sales efforts as essential dimensions in the attempt to individualise products against competitors.[17] Since the 1930s, psychological findings have informed marketing practices, while the market segmentation for mass products advanced further. However, the branding of single products, firms, and nations was still mostly oriented towards specific audiences along the value chain, mainly to particular groups of end consumers, whom it was hoped would buy the final product.

Similarly, several phases of modern place branding can be distinguished since at least the 19th century. Starting approximately in the 1840s with agricultural colonisation, it quickly spread in North America (but also in other settler colonies like Australia and South Africa), where "selling the frontier" became an interesting business, and new, relatively "empty" agricultural lands were described in glowing terms to lure potential settlers, workers, and investors.[18] This was particularly true of advancing railroad tracks, when railway companies promoted the newly created towns that were established partly as objects and arenas of speculation and were designed to keep their rail lines profitable. Growing urban functional differentiation pushed the marketing of specific sites and sectors further; "city boosterism" reacted to growing competition among places, caused by the nationalisation and globalisation of markets.[19] Thus, at the same time, health, mountain, and seaside resorts emerged, some of which were founded as completely new settlements, and also underwent targeted destination marketing in Europe and North America.

15 Country-of-origin designations spread particularly with post-World War II internationalisation and the definition of rules of origin in EU trade agreements in the 1970s and 1980s; cf. Pike, 2009: 625.

16 Cf. Bastos and Levy, 2012: 354.

17 Cf. especially Bastos and Levy, 2012: 354–355. On the distinction between marketing and branding, cf. below.

18 On place branding in the 19th to mid-20th century, cf. Ward, 1998a and 1998b; Kavaratzis and Ashworth, 2008: 154–155, 160; Adam, 2020: 213.

19 Cf. Kavaratzis and Ashworth, 2005: 506.

With the beginning of secular tourism, first for a limited social class but later as a growing mass phenomenon, stylish placards appeared, often designed by well-reputed artists.[20] While in the UK such place promotion was undertaken primarily by municipalities, in the USA and other countries, real estate, transport, and tourism business companies (hotels, casinos, etc.) were the main drivers; world exhibitions already helped to put their hosting towns on the map. In North America, the late 1870s saw the beginnings of the marketing of residential suburbs built outside polluted and crowded city centres. That development spread to the UK, where is peaked around the 1930s, while especially from the Great Depression until the 1970s, "Fordist" industrial towns were promoted with manifold incentives for a comparatively small number of investors to attract industrial companies and generate manufacturing jobs. But according to critics, place marketing remained superficial and ineffective, because it was restricted to pure sales promotion and image advertising.[21]

Branding experienced another boom after World War II, when the "consumer revolution" and the development of the welfare state increased demand, so that competition on commodity markets intensified and new brands challenged established ones.[22] From the consumer market, branding was extended to intermediate and investment goods; with services, it also reached immaterial commodities.[23] But since the late 1980s, and in particular after the turn to the third millennium, many consider branding is to have become a rapidly expanding, and in fact, all-pervasive and ubiquitous method and business.[24] According to Andy Pike, branding now seems to be a central feature of economic life and a core activity of contemporary capitalism, and he observes the development of an all-encompassing "brandspace."[25] Similarly, João Freire stated that, in the 1980s, the economy experienced a shift from the production of products to the production of brands.[26]

The branding concept has been strategically transferred to almost all spheres of human life. Concomitantly, the complexity of the branded objects and branding practices has increased. Hence, traditional practices evolved from branding material and immaterial products to branding corporations; the idea of brands was also extended to non-economic and non-profit sectors, including political and cultural

20 Cf. Vuignier, 2018: 21.

21 Cf. Kavaratzis, 2004: 59; Vanolo, 2017: 29.

22 Cf. Bastos and Levy, 2012: 355. On the post-WWII booms, cf. also Anttiroiko, 2014: 49.

23 Cf. Hellmann 2005: 8.

24 Many authors point to the 1970s/1980s boost; cf. also, for instance, Dinnie, 2008: 20; Pike, 2011: 4; Freire, 2005: 347; on place branding, Ward, 1998a: 48, and 1998b: 1.

25 Cf. Pike, 2011: 4.

26 Cf. Freire, 2005: 347.

realms. Also, individuals, including political leaders and artists, who have always been stylised as icons, are meanwhile increasingly turned into personal brands. The background to this was increased globalisation and neoliberalisation of the economy, which made inroads also into manifold social and cultural life spheres, which has led to the perception of fast-growing overall competition.[27] This intersected with a shift from modern to postmodern branding conditions and practices, which increasingly have emphasised service orientation, experiential qualities, simulations, and hyperrealities, as well as with a rapidly growing medialisation.

Advertising and branding places likewise received general acceptance and found systematic application in the last quarter of the 20th century.[28] Cities and regional entities also perceived tightened interurban, interregional, and international competition and felt the need to position themselves as attractive brands for potential investors, visitors, inhabitants, and workers. The beginning of contemporary city branding is often dated back to the famous 1977 "I ♥ NY" logo and campaign.[29] Its widespread popularity has been attributed to the new urban entrepreneurialism inspired by neoliberal ideologies and programmes, starting in the UK as a response to structural decline and the deindustrialisation of traditional economic centres.[30] In postmodern city branding, post-Fordist cities reinvented themselves as places of leisure and consumption and strategically developed into tourist and lifestyle destinations. At the same time, they experienced urban restructuring and regeneration – starting with the exemplary Boston case of waterfront refurbishment – that was enabled by the dislocation of former inner-city ports and industrial areas to the urban peripheries. Hence, those in charge built attractive museums and other urban flagship developments and organised festivals and other mass events.[31]

The same is true of nations, which are said to use branding primarily to pursue commercial ambitions, i. e. to support their exports and to compete for investment and tourism.[32] Moreover, in political terms, they strive for a good global reputation, based on images of political and social stability, peacefulness, respect for human rights, and the pursuit of sustainability; they do this in regard to other nations and international organisations, in order to realise political goals, create

---

27 For details on these macro-conditions, cf. below.

28 Cf. Kavaratzis, 2004: 59; Kavaratzis and Ashworth, 2005: 506.

29 Cf., e.g., Ward, 1998a: 31, and 1998b: 191; Govers 2013: 74; Ermann and Hermanik, 2018: 7.

30 Cf. especially Ward, 1998a.

31 Cf. Ward, 1998a: 46–48, and 1998b: 7, 186–208. Cf. also Kavaratzis and Ashworth, 2008: 155, 160; on waterfront development, e.g. Hoyle, 2000.

32 Cf., e.g., Jansen 2008: 122; and many others. For more on the purposes of nation branding, cf. below.

goodwill, obtain concessions, receive aid and credits under favourable conditions, etc. The end of the Cold War gave nation branding another push, when a considerable number of new nations, namely Central European countries and successor states of the Soviet Union, began to position themselves in the global arena.[33] The most recent example, at the time of writing, is Ukraine, which turned branding into a weapon to fight a war, with "bravery" as its new core image.[34]

3 From Application-Oriented to Critical Research

The rising importance of branding is reflected, and reciprocally strengthened, by a growing amount of literature. Yet, compared with the practical evolution of modern branding, thorough conceptualisation has lagged, on the part of both practitioners and academic scholars. First seminal work had already been published in the 1960s, but approaches have developed further since the late 1980s.[35] Marketing was long understood, first of all, as a logistical tool for providers and traders. Branding became part of a hands-on marketing mix, before it increasingly became conceived as a transcending strategy that needs closer reflection on its own. Under varying terms and designations, the conceptualisation of product branding initially prevailed and was only gradually extended to other objects. Likewise, place branding had already been put into practice before academic attention increased relatively late, particularly since the 1990s, and more nuanced theoretical concepts have been elaborated.[36] In both fields, the founding of special associations and topical journals contributed to the intensification of research. Today, the literature on branding is broad, fragmented, and multidisciplinary, so that publications often display conceptual vagueness and diverging definitions. Several authors have established literature surveys[37] and tried to categorise the different approaches.[38] For our purpose, we shall distinguish among three broad perspectives, which, however, largely overlap in practice.

---

33 Cf. van Ham, 2001: 5–6; van Ham, 2002 and Jansen, 2008 on Estonia; Aronczyk, 2013: 142, also on Georgia.

34 Cf. Kaneva, 2022.

35 Cf. Lucarelli and Brorström, 2013: 67.

36 Cf. Lucarelli and Berg, 2011: 12; Gertner, 2011: 91; Pike, 2011: 5.

37 Like Lucarelli and Berg, 2011; Gertner, 2011; Vuignier, 2017; Andersson, 2014. However, most of these studies are disciplinarily biased, limited to a few journals, and, in particular, restricted to English publications.

38 Cf. in the following, Lucarelli and Berg, 2011; Lucarelli and Brorström, 2013; Eggeling, 2020: 7–16, 37–40. Cf. also Vanolo, 2017: 21, 28–37; Vuignier, 2018: 33–34; Ward, 1998b: 4–6.

Most of the existing literature has been *application-oriented*, written mainly by and for professionals in marketing, business, administration, and consultancy or people coming from management and organisational studies or public diplomacy.[39] Protagonists who laid foundational work, such as Philip Kotler for branding in general since the 1960s and Wally Olins and Simon Anholt especially for nation branding in the 1990s, stimulated even further the exercise of branding in practice. Their contributions are primarily normative, advisory, and prescriptive, sometimes even "celebrative"[40] and still essentialist. Such "problem-solving" literature[41] postulates the need for branding in view of given macro-conditions, including rules, norms, and social and power relations, which lead to increasing complexity and competition. Such publications are primarily about how to create and manage a brand, and authors endeavour to develop general solutions to improve strategic communication, the marketing mix, and brand management and to provide toolboxes to optimise effects, for example on a country's international image, in order to "sell" their respective objects successfully and create the most positive overall impression possible by using a broad spectrum of instruments and historical, geographical, and sociocultural motifs.[42] As a rule, this literature advocates a consistent package of measures to be followed by all relevant actors to develop, manage, and communicate an image that is as homogeneous as possible; this approach is often still based on a rather deterministic understanding of human behaviour. Others plead in favour of a more participative approach that integrates different perspectives and varying interests, reflecting a multifaced reality.

Second, much of the literature consists of *descriptive and explanatory analyses*, mostly empirical studies of single cases, less often ones based on comparative research; the bulk of these writings seems to be predominantly qualitative. Such perspectives overlap in both directions: on the one hand, they want to assess the success of implemented branding strategies on the basis of predefined criteria and to support the development of new strategies and recommendations. On the other hand, such empirical studies are integrated parts of an increasing number of more critical studies in the broader field of social and cultural research.

Such a variety of academic *alternative and critical approaches* started to develop in the 1980s, associated with authors like David Harvey. They have proliferated since the late 1990s, but have still remained underrepresented far into the 2010s. As will be detailed in the following subchapters, these studies mirror a critical understanding of branding processes and ponder their time- and place-specific soci-

39 Cf. also Gertner, 2011: 96; Pike, 2011: 5.

40 Vanolo, 2017: 32.

41 Eggeling, 2020: 11.

42 On the mix of motifs, cf. also van Ham, 2001: 3; Govers and Go, 2009: 17.

etal contexts. In particular, they investigate the social production of brands, identify their producers, ask how they find and address their audiences, and explore which mechanisms and ideologies are working in the background. For this, critical cultural studies endeavour to decode promotional messages, to analyse branding discourses, and to understand the production of social meaning. Critical constructivists also examine influence and power struggles and look at the formation of interests, identities, norms, and values.[43] Considering branding a highly dynamic phenomenon, some authors stick to practice-, action-, and process-oriented approaches,[44] whereas others take longer historical perspectives.[45] They also situate the branding phenomenon in the political, economic, and cultural contexts of contemporary capitalist development, whilst again others challenge the allegedly given framework for action, ask how this order of the world itself came into being, and reflect on the mutual co-construction of branding and its environment. Moreover, critical research attempts to explain the economic, social, political, and cultural effects of the branding phenomenon. It investigates the commodification of places; links branding practices to identity politics and security policies; and scrutinises the use of branding to exercise and legitimise power. Some scholars examine place branding as a kind of public policy and evaluate it in terms of public interest and welfare criteria. Other authors research socio-spatial connotations and interactions and geopolitical implications. This wide diversity of concepts and methods corresponds to the broad range of disciplines. Thus, contributions to place branding come from several subfields of geography, from tourism and urban studies, in addition to planning and political sciences, including governance, public policy, International Relations (IR) theory,[46] and critical geopolitics, as well as sociology, social anthropology, and history.

4 Attempts to Define Branding

There is no single definition of "branding." Definitions vary considerably according to the authors' perspectives, approaches, and disciplines, as well as to the object that is to constitute the brand. Hence, the term remains ambiguous and fuzzy; many authors even renounce giving a clear or even any definition. Accordingly,

43 On the constructivist research agenda, cf. also van Ham, 2002: 260–262.
44 Such as Eggeling, 2020.
45 Cf. especially Ward, 1998a and 1998b.
46 On the intersection of PR and IR theory, see van Ham, 2002.

this is not the place to review all or even most existing definitions, but rather to synthesise them to find some common points and understandings.[47]

Beyond its original meaning of applying a physical mark to a body or artefact, branding is often understood as a practice, a process, or a strategy. Following an influential definition by the American Marketing Association (AMA), branding helps or explicitly serves to identify a particular object and to differentiate it from competitors;[48] this positioning in a competitive field of similar items makes it into a relational concept. Therefore, it deliberately selects attributes[49] that highlight a product's or place's advantages and positive characteristics, which in turn promise a certain economic, but also symbolic, experiential, and emotional value to addressees and attribute particular meaning to the object. In fact, many understand branding as the management, and at its best the control, of an object's reputation and image in the minds of a wider public by designing, planning, and communicating its nature and identity. Processually understood, it stands for building and further developing a brand. Essentially, senders try to influence people's mental images, perceptions, and connections in a favourable way. In this broad conception, branding still assembles all activities to "mark" a product (cf. *Marke* in German and *marque* in French). Hence, branding is a mode of (ideally, reciprocal) communication at the interface between firms (or other brand producers and owners) and stakeholders. However, besides being a strategic communication tool and symbolic construction process, branding is also a legal device related to protected trademarks and designations of origin.

The brand itself "embodies a whole set of physical and sociopsychological attributes and beliefs associated with a product."[50] It can be seen as a unique, multidimensional blend of elements that provide specific relevance for its target audiences. Vice versa, a brand reflects the whole set of perceptions, thoughts, feelings, and expectations that people attach to an object. Some understand it as part of the attractiveness of an object, especially consisting of its good name, while others insist on the importance of the manifold features that mirror its history, achievements, and aspirations.

47 For this synthesis, I consulted the works, most of them related to *place* branding, of Anttiroiko, 2014: 49–64; Vuignier, 2018: 37–61; Anholt, 2011: 289–290; Aronczyk, 2008: 42, and 2013: 29; Dinnie, 2008: 14; Govers, 2011 and 2013: 71; Govers and Go, 2009: 16–17; Kavaratzis, 2004; Kavaratzis and Ashworth, 2005: 507–508; Kotler and Gertner, 2002; Lucarelli and Berg, 2011: 21; Lucarelli and Brorström, 2013: 65–66; Kumar and Kumar Panda, 2019: 257. This review is based less on statements by outstanding practitioners than on reflections from more theorising and critical authors.

48 For the latest definition, cf. AMA, 2017. Other sources refer to the 1995 definition.

49 On the selection of attributes, cf. also Jansen, 2008: 122.

50 Kavaratzis and Ashworth, 2005: 508.

Since the 2000s, we can observe a shift in terms from "marketing" to a dominant use of "branding."[51] Some authors endeavour to distinguish "branding" from "marketing."[52] Historically, marketing is considered to have preceded the development of branding. Today, it is mostly conceived as a mix of techniques to position a product in the competition, to segment markets, and to target potential clients and consumers in order to satisfy specific, mostly commercial interests.[53] According to the AMA, marketing intends to influence and seduce its specific audience to react positively to the respective object.[54] Such efforts include processes of designing, promoting, selling, and distributing a certain offering.[55] Following this, branding can be regarded as a specific subfield or instrument of the broader marketing mix and as its qualitative extension.[56]

However, branding has been increasingly conceived as a distinct strategy that evolved from marketing and that still partly overlaps with it. Branding can be used to achieve a broader spectrum of economic, political, and other goals, and is much more oriented towards the society at large or an international audience, regardless of the markets to be served.[57] It consists of a wider set of practices and a more identity-based range of activities, and it communicates also less-tangible aspects of the object in question.[58] (Place) branding is also considered to be about larger assets, like overall reputation, trust, reputation, and soft power.

In fact, it is difficult to clearly distinguish between branding and other encompassing strategies for product and place attractiveness;[59] hence, many authors use the terms branding and marketing more or less interchangeably.[60] Accordingly, for places, they resort to a plethora of further terms and concepts to describe and comprehend similar processes, like "place promotion" as another subfield of mar-

51 Cf., especially on places, Vanolo, 2017: 28; Lucarelli and Berg, 2011: 19; Gertner, 2011: 97–98. In French, there is a general preference for the term "marketing territorial" to designate place branding.

52 See, for instance, Lucarelli and Berg, 2011: 21; Lucarelli and Brorström, 2013: 66; Gertner, 2011: 91; Anholt, 2008a.

53 Cf. also Govers and Go, 2009: 19. Yet, Kavaratzis, 2004: 70 emphasises that marketing serves to achieve several aims, not all of them economic.

54 Cf. Govers, 2011: 228.

55 This corresponds to the famous four pillars (4 P's) of the marketing mix, namely price, product, place, and promotion; cf. AMA, 2022; Anttiroiko, 2014: 49–50.

56 Compare in this sense, e.g., Anttiroiko, 2014: 49, 64; Vuignier, 2018: 37–38. Cf. also Kavaratzis, 2004: 58.

57 Cf., e.g., Anholt, 2008a: 1.

58 Cf. also Vanolo, 2017: 29, 54.

59 Cf. Vuignier, 2018: 23.

60 Cf., similarly, Vanolo, 2017: 28, 30; Lucarelli and Brorström, 2013: 70.

keting,[61] or "place selling" as a long-standing historical exercise, which, in turn, goes beyond pure "place advertising."[62] Anholt refined the nation-branding concept towards a more encompassing "competitive identity" as a blend of brand management, public diplomacy, and economic promotion.[63]

Hence, for our purposes, the essence of branding – irrespective of the specific kind of branded objects – consists in the purposeful construction of a broader, fundamentally positive and attractive image of the object under scrutiny and its strategic communication, for a variety of reasons, to a broad, *in extremis* global, public. It turns objects into distinguishable and attractive "brands" for the addressees and intends to evoke favourable and helpful connotations, associations, and attitudes. In this context, we do not understand "image" in its literal sense as a solely visual representation (picture), but as a mental representation (imagination). Yet, this rough definition of branding still needs gradual modulation, as the following explanations demonstrate. Moreover, given the vagueness of existing definitions, the widespread imprecise use of terminology, and the different approaches in the present book, this introduction and the various authors throughout this edited volume cannot be expected to consistently distinguish between the "branding" and "marketing" of products, persons, and places.

5 Branding Purposes, Actors, and Addressees

Reviewing its history and definitions demonstrates that branding serves a great variety of goals, addresses a broad range of publics, and encompasses many acting persons and institutions. Mainly, it has to do with generating and increasing overall economic and political competitive advantages.[64] In general, both externally and internally, branding is about instilling identification with the branded object and its main internal stakeholders, inducing addressees to engage in some kind of favourable behaviour.[65] In the present condition of widespread social upheaval and increasing distrust in institutions, brands are taken as guarantees of trustworthiness.[66] Brands are expected to guide today's consumers and citizens who face

61 Cf., for instance, Anttiroiko, 2014: 63–64. According to the AMA, 2022, promotion is tactical advertising and PR to encourage short-term purchase decisions. Cf. also Kotler, Haider, and Rain, 1993: 99.

62 Cf. Ward, 1998: 3–4.

63 Cf. Anholt, 2008a and 2008b: 22. Cf. also Gertner, 2007: 5; Anttiroiko, 2014: 63; Dinnie, 2008: 251.

64 Cf. van Ham, 2002: 252. Cf. also Kavaratzis, 2004: 70.

65 Compare van Ham, 2002: 250.

66 Cf. Hellmann, 2005: 12.

increasing indigestible complexity and information overload.[67] Manifestly, for goods and services, commercial goals are of the utmost centrality, i. e. the maximisation of sales figures and the optimisation of profits for their producers. Similarly, for nation branding, this includes the promotion of exports, based on a good country-of-origin reputation. Many of its protagonists consider place branding to be an economic endeavour and as decisive for a place's prosperity and competitiveness.[68] In the alleged contemporary "flow economy," a concept made popular by Manuel Castells,[69] places are said to have to compete to capture, partake in, and benefit from a variety of circuits and attract a maximum of material and immaterial resources, particularly on transnational and transregional, if not on global scales. Hence, they try to lure direct investment or other businesses to an economically appealing and supposedly politically safe location; to convince a very demanding clientele of the quality of products; to recruit needed competencies and qualifications; or to attract tourism to pleasing destinations.[70] More and more attention has been given to the consumers' perceptions and their aspiration for conspicuous consumption, distinction, and social status enhancement.[71] Yet, place branding in particular is also undertaken for wider political and strategic motives – e. g. expanding political influence or collecting political goodwill – and is considered an essential element of policy-making.[72]

Historically, individualisation, increasing product differentiation, more sophisticated consumer research, and digitalisation have permitted practitioners to address an extended target group as well as a more specific targeting of addressees; new technological devices have made it possible to use e-commerce and social media to place brands. Accordingly, the intended audience of effective branding can be defined as a wide range of different target groups or the wider public, be it local, national, or global. In its predominantly economic understanding, place branding addresses the actors behind the flows that the branders and their clients want to capture: among the different organisations and individuals repeatedly named, we find (potential new) companies and factories, investors, busi-

67 Cf. van Ham, 2001: 2, and 2002: 252.

68 Cf., e. g., Gertner, 2007: 5; Anholt, 2008b: 22; Anttiroiko, 2014: 1.

69 According to Castells, esp. 1996: 376–428, with the constitution of the contemporary "network society" and the global "information economy," the "space of flows" has increasingly replaced the "space of places" as the predominant spatial and social logic.

70 For example, cf. Dinnie, 2008: 21; Anttiroiko, 2014: 1, 70; Kotler and Gertner, 2002: 249; Kavaratzis, 2004: 59; van Ham, 2001: 2.

71 Cf. Bastos and Levy, 2012: e. g. 360–362. Thorstein Veblen highlighted conspicuous consumption, which serves to signal social status, particularly in modern societies; see e. g. von Scheve, 2017.

72 Cf. van Ham, 2001; Anttiroiko, 2014: 70; Anholt, 2008b: 23.

nessmen, industrialists, manufacturers, exporters and importers, corporate headquarters, purchasers, users, conventioneers, tourists and other visitors, residents, foreign students, a skilled workforce, and talented people.[73] For the latter, attracting the highly qualified and innovative, but also demanding and mobile "creative class" and luring it into a "creative city" that offers them a vibrant cultural life and corresponding infrastructural amenities has become a powerful concept, pushed by Richard Florida since the early 2000s, in order to promote urban (or regional or national) development.[74] Even though the relevance of his ideas is highly controversial, this utopian imaginary of the city is also reflected in place branding: the depiction of scenes with people meeting and talking, displaying cosmopolitan diversity and multicultural tolerance; the presentation of a local art scene, nightlife, and landmarks; and reference to educational and consumption opportunities as well as mega-events are considered characteristic.[75] Likewise, those responsible for the further circulation of brand messages (such as journalists, bloggers, followers, marketers, and other media people), but also the regulators, facilitators, and donors (such as state authorities; government officials; local representatives; trade, investment, and tourism agencies; business associations; diplomatic missions; and international organisations) are targets of this kind of communication.[76]

The strong external orientation of branding is complemented by an inward-oriented function: in the case of corporations, it turns to the workers and employees and to other internal stakeholders; for places, it is directed towards citizens, inhabitants, and other societal actors, in order to build and strengthen the sense of a place and feelings of belonging, confidence, and wellbeing, to induce loyalty or stabilise (political) legitimacy, to form and reinforce organisation- or place-related identity and identification, and to activate civic pride, local harmony, social cohesiveness, and responsibility.[77]

For states, nation branding is primarily about broadcasting national interests to an audience at large. However, authors often state that it is not primarily directed towards domestic addressees, as was traditional nationalistic rhetoric, but to an

73 For such enumerations, cf., e. g., Kotler, Haider, and Rain, 1993: 19, 24; Kotler and Gertner, 2002: 254–258; Gertner, 2007: 4; Govers and Go, 2009: 5; Dinnie, 2011: 4–5; Anttiroiko, 2014: 70; Adam, 2020: 214, 217.

74 On the concept, cf., e. g., Florida, 2003. On the Saudi city project of NEOM, cf. already Aly, 2019: 99–101; on attracting the creative class by branding, Dinnie, 2011: 4; Andersson, 2014: 151.

75 Cf. Vanolo, 2017: 119–122.

76 Cf. esp. Pike, 2018: 18.

77 On nation branding, cf. van Ham, 2002: 252–255; Govers, 2011: 230; Aronczyk, 2013: 64; on city branding, Dinnie, 2011: 5; Kavaratzis, 2004: 70; Anttiroiko, 2014: 70; also Vanolo, 2017: 11.

international public, considered to consist mainly of investors.[78] Others underline the importance of a strong internal branding directed at public, private, and civil society actors, who should be activated to "live the brand."[79] Yet, national identity building can be an international marketing asset as well as a domestic propaganda tool.[80] In any case, product as well as place branding have to take into account diverse, often highly contradictory value systems, lifestyles, and preferences, especially since branding has expanded from the national into the global market.[81]

Traditional application-oriented approaches have often started from the assumption that a uniform, comprehensive communication strategy is needed, with a central direction – be it via a brand manager in a firm or a public authority, a private agency, or a public-private partnership – to develop, manage, and communicate a homogeneous, consistent, and clearly recognisable brand. But, as with addressees, there is in fact a plurality of "makers" involved in branding policies. The coproduction perspective has already developed a more relational approach to the actors' role and influence and perceives place branding as a dynamic process.[82] For place marketing, Kotler enumerates actors from local and regional to national and international spatial and hierarchical scales.[83] This includes brand owners, designers, and manufacturers from the public and the private sector, as well as advertisers, but also many of the regulatory actors already mentioned.[84]

However, producers and addressees of branding are sometimes difficult to distinguish, as the latter can also be active contributors to the branding process. A more participative understanding integrates different perspectives and varying perceptions, attitudes, and interests of the population and of other stakeholders.[85] Branding is implemented not only top-down: consumers also actively participate in producing and conveying brands, especially with the rise of social media; but also authorities endeavour to include citizens in the coproduction of brands.[86] So, at its best, branding is a two-way communication process,[87] and citizens can become,

78 Cf. Aronczyk, 2008: 44. Cf. also Bolin and Ståhlberg, 2010: 80, 94.
79 Cf. Govers, 2011: 230.
80 Cf. Jansen 2008: 129, on the Estonian case.
81 Cf. Fırat, Dholakia, and Venkatesh, 1995: 44.
82 Cf. Lucarelli and Brorström, 2013: 73–76. Cf. also Aronczyk, 2013: 114, on the fragmented nature of branding efforts.
83 Cf. Kotler, Haider, and Rein, 1993: 34.
84 Cf. Pike, 2018: 18.
85 Cf. Lucarelli and Brorström, 2013: 74–76; Lucarelli and Berg, 2011: 18. On citizens' "right to brand," cf. Vanolo, 2017: 106–108.
86 Cf. Vanolo, 2017: 68, 73–74.
87 Cf. Kavaratzis and Ashworth, 2005: 508.

consciously or unconsciously, "brand ambassadors" to the outside world.[88] However, subjectivist approaches have rarely tackled bottom-up appropriation, counter-discourse, conflict, and resistance, e.g. among residents and social agents, related to brands.[89]

6 Branding Tools and Strategies

To elaborate the means and strategies for effective and successful branding is a task of application-oriented authors, including branding agencies and consultants. In particular, branding also has to address values and emotions.[90] Practitioners still favour wordmarks, slogans, signs, logos, and other graphic elements as the means to advertise the objects of branding.[91] As a communication tool, these means are regarded as the symbols that constitute the brand. They help to establish a clear and consistent image that allows for a quick recognition and buying decision, especially in commercial branding, and to facilitate the introduction of new products and businesses.

Thus, for instance, for product branding, the slogan "delicious and refreshing," coined for Coca Cola's first advertisement campaign in 1886, remained an integral part of the brand for decades; the lettering and bottle shape, which were soon created, too, have become globally familiar characteristics; early on, the producer also used music with popular melodies and lyrics. Simple slogans like the early "Drink Coca-Cola" and the more recent "You can't beat the feeling" have become classics.[92] For non-profit organisations, the Red Cross and, in Muslim countries, the Red Crescent have become worldwide immediately recognised symbols that stand for its reputation and untouchability. They are based on the inverted national symbol of Switzerland, where the international federation is headquartered, respectively a colour-reversed derivative from the Ottoman imperial and Turkish national emblem, which in itself is a strong and enduring symbol. As already mentioned, in place branding, the "I Love New York" logo and slogan are considered prototypes. Some slogans have rather unintentionally branded countries: thus, "Cool Britannia," initially coined for ice cream advertising in the mid-1990s, rather than being officially used, soon became very popular in the media, for it gave the coun-

88 Cf. Vanolo, 2017: 76; Anttiroiko, 2014: 79; Adam, 2020: 219–220; on corporate identity and workers, Aronczyk, 2013: 27.

89 Cf. Lucarelli and Brorström, 2013: 73, 76; similarly, Anttiroiko, 2014: 154–157.

90 Cf., e.g., Pike, 2009: 624.

91 Cf. Govers, 2013. Cf. also Vuignier, 2018: 48–49; Pike, 2009: 624; Ward, 1998b: 5–57, 164–170.

92 Cf. Coca-Cola Deutschland, 2022; Wikipedia, 2022.

try a fresh new look after years of decay and reflected a certain cultural boom, optimism, and pride in the New Labour era.[93] As already mentioned in the previous chapter, in the Middle East and North Africa (MENA), Dubai's Emirates airline logo, based on a wordmark in Arabic and Latin script, has also become a widely known, pervasive sign of a reputed company.

In contrast, many authors contest the effectiveness of concentrating exclusively on such catchy textual and graphical elements, or even describe them as useless.[94] They claim that branding is "much more than merely creating a logo and a slogan,"[95] especially for place and nation branding. The focus then is on broader consistent communication strategies that convey clear messages and are based on evident substance. For city branding, material artefacts like signature buildings and landmark architecture as well as special events, especially in the fields of sports and culture, and in general, a rich cultural life, are regarded as further central features that help to spread appealing messages.[96] Scholars also underline that urban branding is not only a discursive practice to establish bright representations; they also point to effective corporate or public policies that produce actual progress and tangible improvement, e. g. in areas such as competitive positioning, social responsibility, and urban regeneration.[97] However, also for places, logos and slogans remain important tools. Since their introduction, coin money, banknotes, and stamps have been widely circulating, mostly state-controlled tools with highly symbolic representations, whose effigies have changed with the passage of time.[98] For conveying key textual and visual elements, especially PR events, factsheets, brochures, videos, and websites have become increasingly prominent devices.[99] Moreover, companies and product families have become influential "umbrella brands" for a range of goods. This is also true in place branding, where national

---

93 See e. g. van Ham, 2001: 4, and 2002: 251–252. Cf. also Browning and de Oliveira, 2017: 481; Bolin and Ståhlberg, 2010: 82. The slogan was a play on words with the title of the unofficial anthem "Rule, Britannia!"

94 Cf. Govers, 2013.

95 Govers and Go, 2009: 13. Similarly, cf. Pike, 2009: 624; Vuignier, 2018: 52, 59; Kumar and Kumar Panda, 2019: 257; Ermann and Hermanik, 2018: 7; Anholt, 2008a: 1; van Ham, 2002: 252.

96 Cf. examples given by Ward, 1998b: 186–208; Kavaratzis, 2004: 70; Kavaratzis and Ashworth, 2005: 513; Dinnie, 2011: 4. On architecture, cf. also, e. g., Crilley, 1993; Grubbauer, 2011. Klingmann, 2007 relates the use of architecture to personal, residential, urban, and corporate branding.

97 Cf., e. g., Anholt, 2008a: 2, who says he represents the "action not words" school, and 2011: 289; Gertner 2007: 5; Vanolo, 2017: 10, 54.

98 Cf. Hymans, 2010; Penrose, 2011; Brunn, 2018.

99 Cf. Ward, 1998b: e. g. 200–207.

brands can serve as strong umbrellas for regional and urban sub-brands;[100] an overall state or city brand can cover a wide range of segments (tourism, investment, etc.) and speak to various audiences simultaneously.[101] Yet, such subordinated places and products can also be branded independently, but can also either compete with superbrands[102] or be infected adversely by these umbrella brands' bad reputation.

For a comprehensive approach to branding, scholars developed multidimensional models. To refer to but a few of them, Melissa Aronczyk, for instance, summarises four distinct essential steps to prepare a nation brand, namely evaluation (by measuring and ranking); training (with improvement and refinement of tools); identification (of the core idea and message); and implementation and communication (including living the brand).[103] Renaud Vuignier points to four components for a brand as a marketing tool, which relate to construction, exchange, perceptions, and influence.[104] Mihalis Kavaratzis proposes a tiered model of image communication that includes indirect ("primary") communication, e. g. through infrastructure, administration, and services that reflect a place's qualities; intentional ("secondary") communication via marketing practices, like PR, design, advertisement; and tertiary channels that are difficult to control, such as word of mouth and public and social media.[105] Robert Govers and Frank Go developed a place branding model that focuses on closing three major gaps, namely the "strategy gap" between identity and projected image; the "performance gap" contrasting strategic image projection and actual place experience; and the "satisfaction gap" that exists between the visitors' experience of a place and the perceived place image.[106]

The modern concept of branding, irrespective of its historical predecessors, has been increasingly expanded to cover objects other than material, manufactured products.[107] As described above, it started to include services, corporations, organisations, and finally a broad range of places, from cities to regions, countries,

---

100 Cf. Dinnie, 2011: 5, 95, 195; Anttiroiko, 2014: 74–76, 93; similarly, Browning and de Oliveira, 2017: 484; Ward, 1998b: 211, on positioning cities and resorts in larger spatial units, from sub- to supranational regions.

101 Cf. Kavaratzis 2004: 71; Kavaratzis and Ashworth, 2005: 512.

102 Cf. van Ham, 2001: 6, referring to spatial and other entities such as the EU, CNN, the Catholic Church, and multinational corporations.

103 Cf. Aronczyk, 2008: 49–55, and 2013: 68–77.

104 Cf. Vuignier, 2018: 50.

105 Cf. Kavaratzis, 2004: 67–69.

106 Cf. Govers and Go, 2009: 40–42, 245–249.

107 On this expansion process, cf., e. g., Dinnie, 2008: 22; Kavaratzis, 2004: 60; Kavaratzis and Ashworth, 2008: 156; Hellmann 2005: 7–9. See also Kumar and Kumar Panda, 2019: 258.

and supranational entities. While branding has historically been more about products than companies, corporate brands have by now become equally present and powerful. Their development was strongly based on the evolving concept of "Corporate Identity" (CI). It developed from about the 1970s as a key strategy for enhancing corporate competitiveness and instilling a sense of loyalty, commitment, and pride to the internal audience.[108] A coordinated "identity mix" conveys and shapes the CI through "corporate communications," "corporate behaviour," the "corporate design," and an "organisational philosophy."

The idea of branding was also extended to social and non-profit purposes, to encompass charitable, cultural, religious, and educational institutions; media houses; sport clubs; and cultural and sports events.[109] Lastly, we should not forget strategic self-branding by individuals, to support the formation of the desired perception by others. Especially in professional life, it is directed at employers, clients, and peers as further categories of addressees.[110] But personality branding is not limited to business, it also extends to political and cultural spheres. More and more people move in largely saturated markets where they feel they have to vigorously profile their brand image in the struggle for attention; this includes artists in the entertainment market and athletes in the sponsorship market.[111] Historically, Albrecht Dürer (1471–1528) is considered an early personal brand, as the first painter to sign his works and to use his own distinctive logo with his initials as a mark of quality, as well as being an early adopter of letterpress printing to publicise his works, which he was the first to sell in large editions to a wide audience; he is even said to have received an imperial privilege to trademark his products.[112] In the political realm, brands have also been developed by politicians and political parties, to facilitate identification and provide orientation in the opinion market. Occasionally, therefore, parallels are seen between buying decisions and voting decisions.[113]

Many marketing and branding specialists did not see any practical problems in transferring the definitions, methods, and approaches applied to products, and

108 Cf. Kavaratzis, 2004: 63–64; Kavaratzis and Ashworth, 2005: 509; Aronczyk, 2013: 83. On the concept, see, e. g., Birkigt and Stadler, 1986; on the analytical application to Egypt's Islamic economy, Wippel, 1995.

109 On sports and clubs, cf. Sasserath, 2005; Rein and Shields, 2007.

110 Cf. Evans, 2017.

111 Cf. Herbst, 2005, also on the transferability of the concepts from other marketing fields.

112 Cf. Ebeling, 2013.

113 Cf. Schneider, 2005.

especially to corporations, to the promotion of territories and places.[114] This has increasingly changed, and place branding is mostly regarded as a separate domain with its own techniques. While a few authors absolutely denied the possibility to treat countries like commodities,[115] most point out some fundamental discrepancies between place branding and conventional product marketing and emphasise that this transfer needs careful adaptation.[116] In particular, they underline the much higher degree of complexity and the multifaceted nature of places, which resist simple categorisation. Places reflect long complex histories of internal evolution and external relationships. They show multiple identities and have to deal with and address multiple groups of stakeholders. In economic terms, places are not limited to a particular industry. While marketing and branding products is done by commercial entities and for economic purposes, places are promoted primarily by public bodies and for a wider array of interests and goals.[117] Finally, places already have a name by which they are known, to which people attach meaning, and that is not so easy to change. Hence, the images of places are much harder to control than those of products or companies.[118]

Brands are also associated with value and valuation.[119] The value of a brand is considered "brand equity." This brand value is generated in relationship with individuals: it is positioned in the consumers' minds and reflected in their brand awareness, quality associations, and subjective judgements, and it evokes psychological and emotional ties with the product, service, or place;[120] a broader perspective encompasses the perceptions of investors, shareholders, and the general public.[121] For products and firms, the brand and its reputation are considered an important asset. Brand equity translates into customers' preferences and loyalty and generates economic benefits.[122] Successful branding promotes symbolic

114 In the following, cf. on transfer from product branding, Kavaratzis and Ashworth, 2008: 152; Anttiroiko, 2014: 61–64; Vanolo, 2017: 28; Freire, 2005: 348; on its vicinity with corporate branding, Anholt, 2008b: 22; Vuignier, 2018: 37–45; on both, van Ham, 2002: 250.

115 Cf. Gertner, 2007: 3.

116 On these differences, cf. esp. Govers and Go, 2009: 13, 68–70; Kavaratzis, 2004: 58, 66. Cf. also Anholt, 2008b: 22; Jansen, 2008: 125; Kavaratzis and Ashworth, 2005: 510–513; Govers, 2013: 72; Dinnie, 2008: 42, 49, and 2011: 3–4; Kumar and Kumar Panda, 2019: 258.

117 Cf. also Anholt, 2008a: 1–2; Dinnie, 2008: 19.

118 Referring to corporations, cf. Govers, 2011: 228.

119 On brand equity, cf. in the following Anttiroiko, 2014: 52, 56–59; Dinnie, 2008: 61–74; Pike, 2009. Cf. also Govers, 2013: 71; Govers and Go, 2009: 15–17; Vuignier, 2018: 50–52.

120 Cf. also van Ham, 2001: 250; Kavaratzis and Ashworth, 2005: 509; Kumar and Kumar Panda, 2019: 257.

121 Cf. Aronczyk, 2013: 24.

122 Cf. also Kotler and Gertner, 2002: 250; on economic benefit, AMA, 2017.

rents by creating reputational monopolies. Especially under conditions of imperfect and asymmetric information, customers will be willing to pay a price premium for highly esteemed and reputed brands. Similarly, in the case of nations, this translates into greater willingness to buy products from a specific country. Hence, brand equity also indicates the actual financial worth of a brand and has started to be quantified in corporate accounting. Accordingly, firms, and by extension places, try to build up, manage, and increase their brand equity.[123] However, especially the intangible elements of a brand are difficult to operationalise to measure its effects.[124]

This valorisation of a brand is also linked to reflections about the qualification and singularisation of products.[125] With regard to the late modern economy and society, the "singular" and the "unique" have increasingly become the focus of scientific considerations in recent years. The production of quality at various stages of product processing, from cultivation to refinement to sale to the end consumer, is at the core of these reflections. Marketing or branding, which turns a product into a brand, plays a prominent role, especially at the final stage. According to Michel Callon and his colleagues, in an "economy of qualities," economic agents are concerned with the continuous (re-)qualification of the goods and services they design, produce, distribute, and consume and with their positioning in relation to other products in the market.[126] In relation to contemporary society at large, singularities have shaped more and more areas since the 1970s, promoted by individualisation and digitalisation.[127] This not only goes hand in hand with individuals' striving for self-realisation and authenticity, but also extends to things, places, events, and human collectives, each with their own identities. In a post-industrial "economy of singularities,"[128] uniform mass production gives way to events and objects that are characterised, e. g. by narrative, aesthetic, creative, and ethical qualities. Accordingly, the commodity-consumer relationship is less controlled by prices and more by the particular quality attributed to the respective products. Social mechanisms contribute to the formation of individual judgements. Competitive strategies primarily aim at visibility, recognition, attention, and attractiveness. Socio-cognitive arrangements (including the display, packaging, and promotion of the

---

123 Cf. also Kotler and Gertner, 2002: 253; Anholt, 2008a: 3; Kavaratzis and Ashworth, 2005: 509–510. On places and states, cf. Govers and Go, 2009: 12; van Ham, 2002: 253–254; Eggeling, 2020: 8.
124 Cf. Vuignier, 2018: 74.
125 Cf. Pike, 2009: 625.
126 Cf. Callon, Méadel, and Rabeharisoa, 2002.
127 Cf. Reckwitz, 2017.
128 Cf. Karpik, 2010.

goods, the brand, etc.) are also significantly involved in the creation of quality.[129] Places that want to attract buyers, tourists, or investors are characterised by uniqueness, too, just like architecture.

7 Global Macro Contexts

Globalisation, neoliberalisation, and postmodernisation are counted among the main processes that favour the enormous acceleration and spread of branding activities in recent decades. They shall be succinctly dealt with in this section.

7.1 Globalisation

The contemporary wave of globalisation has been both a strong narrative underlining the need for branding in proscriptive approaches and an ongoing process, in which, according to more descriptive and analytical studies, the surge of branding since the late 1980s is embedded and with which it mutually interacts. The term "globalisation" has often been used as a shorthand for processes in which flows and networks play at least as important a role as national institutions as a framework for social and economic life. The idea that we live in such a space of flows instead of a space of places has become pervasive.[130] In a globalised world in which capital, goods, and people move freely around the globe and can choose to settle in the most attractive places for their businesses and residencies, attractiveness is considered key to economic success.[131]

Opening borders for free trade between national markets on regional and global scales has increased competition between products and companies, which calls for their more proactive positioning. But cities, regions, and states are also considered to have entered considerable immediate interurban, interregional, and international competition for resources and flows of values and hence feel obliged to market themselves to promote their development in a globalised world.[132]

129 In branding wine, for instance, the design of bottles and boxes, tastings, and participation in events such as trade fairs, stories about the production process, the region of origin, and the company tradition are part of the further qualification; cf., e.g., Rainer, Kister, and Steiner, 2019.

130 Cf. again Castell's 1996 seminal work.

131 Compare Anttiroiko, 2014: 17, 34–42.

132 Compare, for instance and on different scales, Anttiroiko, 2014: 1, 61–96; Govers, 2011: 228; van Ham, 2001: 3; Anholt, 2008a: 6; Jansen, 2008: 121.

To be able to stand up to global competition, first, nation branding surged as a means that merges traditional national identity politics and economic country-of-origin marketing; thus, in predominantly economically oriented branding, national identity becomes mobilised as a competitive resource.[133] An important research milestone in this respect was Michael Porter's work, according to which, just like organisations and firms, states strive to achieve competitive advantages over their rivals by playing on the costs and the differentiation among products and supporting productivity and innovation among national corporations.[134] At the same time, globalisation is said to have enormously defied the role of the state, leading to a great loss of state power and control over economic and political affairs.[135] With that, authorities have turned to nation branding as an updated and soft-power version of nation building and nationalism.[136] This was paralleled by claims, made by Edward Luttwak and Pascal Lorot also in the 1990s, of a contemporary shift of interstate conflicts from traditional strategic geopolitics and "hard" (military) power to geoeconomics striving for technological and economic superiority and securing the highest possible welfare and employment for the national population.[137] Accordingly, after the end of the Cold War – at least in the Global North and before Ukraine was attacked in 2022 – markets replaced war, and performance in the marketplace has become more relevant than on the battlefield.[138]

Second, on an urban level, responsible actors also perceive the need to enter unprecedented interurban competition for resources, influence, and recognition. In particular, we can observe the rise and conceptualisation of worldwide dominating and radiating urban places in an emergent hierarchical network of cities.[139] Such "global" or "world cities" are directly connected to the world economy, stand out as basing points for international capital, and house the headquarters of worldwide leading industries, media, and political and cultural institutions.

133 Cf. Dinnie, 2008: 21; Aronczyk, 2013: 15. Cf. again Anholt's idea of "competitive identity," e.g. 2008b.

134 Cf. Porter, 1990. On the impulse for place branding, cf. Ward, 1998b: 4.

135 Cf. Pike, 2011: 10; Jansen, 2008: 125.

136 Cf. Browning and de Oliveira, 2017; Aronczyk, 2013: 16; Bolin and Ståhlberg, 2010: 80–83.

137 Cf. Luttwak, 1990; Lorot, 1999. While the US approach is a more normative, strategic kind, the French approach is primarily analytic. On a branding perspective on this, cf. Browning and de Oliveira, 2017: 483. For a critical discussion, cf. below.

138 Cf. Jansen, 2008: 125.

139 Cf. Sassen, 2001; Taylor, 2004. Increasingly, the samples under study extended to a larger range of places of global standing, and tiered categorisations of globalness developed. In fact, world cities have also been a historical phenomenon, with many of them placed in the MENA region, Constantinople/Istanbul being the most prominent case, besides Cairo, Damascus, Baghdad, Tabriz, and others; cf., e.g., Taylor, 2004: 8–10.

They also resort to branding as a means of presence on the world stage, notably in the Western world and East Asia.[140] Hence, starting from this attractive narrative, cities struggle to be recognised as nodes in global networks and for their cosmopolitanism. Yet, metropolises in the Global South have also begun to turn to "worlding" strategies, which include intense branding processes, for a favourable position in the global (attention) economy and recognition as being "world-class."[141] Moreover, branding is not only a device for recognised global cities and major countries, but has also become an important tool against the political, economic, and cultural marginalisation of small states and "secondary cities" in the North and the South, which endeavour to gain visibility as global players in selected fields and central hubs in specific far-reaching networks.[142]

7.2 Neoliberalisation

Globalisation is also understood as closely interrelated with far-reaching neoliberalisation, as the latter's mutual driver, pretext, and consequence.[143] Since the early 1980s, the rise of branding paralleled the fast-growing application and global circulation of neoliberal development policies as well as the rapid spread of an omnipresent economic discourse, both of which privilege market relations.[144] The neoliberal economic logic did not remain confined to the commercial realm, but has meanwhile pervaded almost all spheres of human life.[145] Thus, place branding in particular became oriented primarily towards economic ambitions, so that nations and cities have become increasingly regarded as being (and needing to act) like commercial enterprises. According to Göran Bolin and Per Ståhlberg, nation branding, for instance, became a form of producing images of the nation quite different from the imagined communities of previous times.[146] As market logic has increasingly underpinned state policies,[147] the nation is nowadays branded less for achieving a favourable political standing and more for its value in the market.

---

140 Cf. Anttiroiko, 2014: 2 et passim; Vanolo, 2017: 132–134.

141 Cf. Roy and Ong, 2011; on MENA cities, Beier, 2019.

142 On states, cf. Jansen, 2008: 131; on cities, Anttiroiko, 2014: 71, 164; Alaily-Mattar, Dreher, and Thierstein, 2018; on the MENA region, Wippel 2021: esp. 52, 75–76.

143 Following Peck and Tickell, 2002, I mostly prefer the term "neoliberalisation," designating an open, recurrent, multiplex process, to the more static "neoliberalism."

144 On global circulation, cf. Vanolo, 2017: 68; on market relations, Jansen 2008: 121.

145 Cf. Vanolo, 2017: 28.

146 Cf. Bolin and Ståhlberg, 2010: 79, 94.

147 Cf. Aronczyk, 2008: 45.

The nation is considered to have become a marketable product, and national identity has been transformed into a market asset.[148]

Neoliberalisation has also reached cities: it effectuated important economic and political changes and deeply affected urban life, even if its implementation differs in detail from one city and one part of the world to the other.[149] Neoliberal understanding of development regards cities as engines of economic growth; at the same time, cities have been more and more made responsible for their own development and their self-promotion. In this context, the rise of the "entrepreneurial city" since the 1970s, which, according to Harvey, surrendered to market rationality and interurban competition, has considerably transformed urban governance.[150] Place marketing and branding are being regarded as one of the most visible and powerful expressions of this entrepreneurialisation of urban policies, when cities have to try to find a position in the market and compete for private investment.[151] Simultaneously, cities, and places in general, are subject to ongoing commodification.[152] They become an experience to be consumed. This goes hand in hand with a growing proliferation of spaces of consumption. Large parts of cities have been turned into arenas for tourism, leisure, cultural events, and spectacles. Under conditions of globalisation and the neoliberal transformation of the urban, namely branding cities together with large urban development schemes, infrastructural megaprojects, and urban renewal and revitalisation have become important tools to draw international attention.

In this context, the role of the state has changed considerably. State agency is largely substituted by the blurring of public and private interests from different spatial scales. Private sector logics and interests have been increasingly integrated in public sector settings; public-private partnerships and outsourcing tasks to private companies have also reached public place and institution branding efforts.[153] According to Ari-Veikko Anttiroiko, "City branding has been associated with proactive operations of the neo-liberal city or entrepreneurial city (...) to promote the interests of the business and especially property owners (...)."[154] There is also a strong presence of international actors (investors, developers, donor organisations,

148 Cf. Jansen, 2008: 121–122, 129.

149 On the neoliberal city more generally, see e.g. Brenner and Theodore, 2002; Swyngedouw, Moulaert, and Rodriguez, 2002.

150 Cf. Harvey, 1989. For reference to urban entrepreneurialism, see, among others, also Vanolo, 2017: 21 et passim; Kavaratzis, 2004: 59; Aronczyk, 2008: 44; Anttiroiko, 2014: 154 et passim.

151 Cf. also Ward, 1998a: 47, and 1998b: 5.

152 See also Medway and Warnaby, 2014, on the commodification of place names.

153 Cf. Jansen, 2008: 122, 129; Aronczyk, 2013: 163; Harvey, 1989: 7.

154 Anttiroiko, 2014: 154.

operators, etc.), including the branding business. But against widely held assumptions, state institutions are still strong actors, which massively help enforce neoliberal principles, frequently by means of anti-liberal policies, and have even started to act like private businesses, e. g. by handing over activities to public agencies that can act beyond bureaucratic regulations.[155] In the end, branding has become a part of the production of new urban elites and new positions of power.[156]

7.3 Postmodernisation

Authors also see marketing and branding as a part and reflex of postmodernisation. Among the characteristics of the postmodern era are fragmented experiences and juxtapositions in style, imagery, and discourse and a high degree of openness to difference, plurality, and diversity.[157] Under increasing individualisation and mobility, people become less attached to (and determined by) social classes, traditional ties, and given places. Not least, postmodernity is associated with the rise of post-industrial societies, including the shift from material production to providing and circulating services, knowledge, and information. Another characteristic of the transition from modernism to postmodernism is the central significance of consumption. With the saturation and sophistication of Western consumer markets[158] and the emergence of new affluent, aesthetically and emotionally sensitive middle classes, consumption has itself turned into a central means of producing identity, meaning, and substance in life. Products are less often "finished," but evolve in a process into which consumers can immerse und provide inputs. For the postmodern consumer, experience has replaced material benefit. Tourism in particular is considered a postmodern phenomenon. Politically, the citizen has been increasingly substituted by the consumer.

In particular, postmodern theory concedes a greater role to symbolic than to material conditions. Several authors working on branding point to the importance

155 Cf. also Amarouche and Bogaert, 2019 on the "agencification" of urban policies in Morocco.
156 Cf. Vanolo, 2017: 68.
157 On the postmodern era, including the role of consumption, cf. in this paragraph, Fırat and Dholakia, 2006: 129–130; Fırat, Dholakia, and Venkatesh, 1995; Featherstone, 2007. Cf. also Govers and Go, 2009: 5; Freire, 2005: 351–355. While, depending on disciplines, postmodernism emerged as an intellectual field in the 1970s and 1980s, concrete manifestations already came up earlier, for example in the arts and urbanism, mainly in the 1960s. Similar to globalisation and neoliberalisation, "postmodernisation" emphasises the processual character of the phenomenon.
158 Cf. Pike, 2009: 624.

of symbols, icons, and simulacra.[159] Postmodern branding and marketing can be notably related to conceptual ideas of hyperrealities. In Umberto Eco's understanding, hyperreality means that something "more real" than its archetype is being constructed, though it still refers to some social "reality."[160] In contrast, Jean Baudrillard noted that advancing orders in the system of signs increasingly lack reference to any independent spatial, historical, or social reality – from simple, equivalent imitations of "reality" and serial (re)productions to simulation, characterised by the autonomisation of signs.[161] This last, self-reproducing and self-referential system creates hyperrealities that can still have real consequences (cf. below). In such a simulational world, it is through media rather than social interaction that symbols are communicated. Mass media and information technologies generate their own new realities – and events have to adapt to the mediated reality.

In line with this, Fuat Fırat and his colleagues stated that "the postmodern age is essentially a marketing age."[162] In the postmodern global branding revolution, the brand itself became the focus of promotional efforts.[163] The main importance of an object is its associated sign, which gives meaning to consumption in contemporary society and adds value to it.[164] People consume less the physical products than the meaning incorporated in a brand, which helps them to define their self-images and to become identified and placed in society.[165] On the individual level, in a "society of singularities,"[166] the need to promote oneself by performing, competing, and self-optimising is as much part of the neoliberal as of the postmodern age.

Marketing and branding are also considered central to the establishment and propagation of hyperrealities.[167] Branding demonstrates that the image takes precedence over the original.[168] The predominance of aural, visual, and figural sensations over written and discursive forms[169] parallels the focus on logos, images, and

159 See, among others, Vanolo, 2017: 145–176; Fırat and Dholakia, 2006: 129; Freire, 2005.
160 Cf. Eco, 1995: 3–58.
161 Cf. Baudrillard, 1988: esp. 119–148, 166–184; for an interpretation of Baudrillard's work, Blask, 2005. See also Featherstone, 2007: 3, 66–68, 97; Schmid, 2006: 347; on the application of Baudrillard's thoughts to Middle East urbanism and branding, e.g. Steiner, 2010 and 2014; Wippel, 2016.
162 Fırat, Dholakia, and Venkatesh, 1995: 48. According to Freire, 2005: 354, Baudrillard already acknowledged the importance of branding.
163 Cf. Jansen, 2008: 125.
164 Cf. Freire, 2005; similarly, Vuignier, 2018: 41–42.
165 Cf. Fırat, Dholakia, and Venkatesh, 1995: 42; Kavaratzis and Ashworth, 2005: 510.
166 Cf. again Reckwitz, 2017.
167 On this, cf. especially Fırat, Dholakia, and Venkatesh, 1995.
168 Cf. Freire, 2005: 355. Harvey, 1989: 14 also conceded a triumph of image over substance.
169 Cf. Featherstone, 2007: 68, 96–97.

advertising spots in practical branding. But it also has to adapt to inconsistent consumer behaviour and the diverse, sometimes incompatible lifestyles of the multitude of publics.[170] In postmodern marketing, images precede the final products and products strive to fulfil the provided image. Thus, the product is increasingly becoming a process that interplays with its merchandising. A brand can even develop its own life independent from the product to which it was initially attached.[171] The political process, too, has progressively become a marketing process. Suitability for media and promotional fitness have become essential for political personalities.

Place marketing in particular is seen as exemplary of postmodernity.[172] This links to reflections on the form and structure of contemporary cities. Edward Soja presented six intertwined interpretations of their "restructurings" and resulting "new geographies" generated by political and economic crises since the late 1960s.[173] This starts with the transformation of their economic base, towards a post-Fordist production mode that embraces finance, real estate, and entertainment industries.[174] In parallel, these "postmetropolises" have experienced processes of globalisation and integrated worldwide urban networks, too. Their highly diverse and segregated population does not allow for a clearly defined collective identity anymore. Other authors include the eclectic architecture and greater aestheticisation of the urban fabric in the appearances of postmodern cities: building on more playful and experiential designs, they are characterised by stylistic collages, citations of historical references, and the use of decorative, ornamental forms.[175]

Finally, Soja underlines the growing power of simulations in shaping postmodern cities. More and more, entire settlements, shopping malls, festival marketplaces, resort hotels, leisure parks, and other fantasy-made hyperreal spaces are conceived in accordance with mottos and themes.[176] Postmodern cities have become centres of consumption, amusement, and entertainment, soaked with images and signs, in which everything can be staged and made an object of interest, par-

---

170 Cf., similarly, Govers and Go, 2009: 6–7.
171 Cf. Klingmann, 2007: 58–61, e.g. on the Absolut and Nike trademarks.
172 Cf. Ward, 1998b: 5; similarly, Harvey, 1989.
173 Cf. Soja, 2000. See also Dear and Flusty, 1998; Schmid, 2006.
174 On the turn to cultural and creative, technology-based "smart" cities, cf. also Vanolo, 2017: 115–122, 126–128.
175 Cf. also Featherstone, 2007: 96–103.
176 In the following, cf. especially on the MENA region, Steiner and Wippel, 2019: 10–12; Steiner, 2010 and 2014.

ticularly for the "tourist gaze."[177] Numerous tourism complexes assemble various architectural styles to attract visitors with an "authentic" impression of "traditional" architecture. As simulacra, they are exact and spectacular copies of an original that never existed. Alberto Vanolo also points to the role of architectural replicas, as well as to that of skyscrapers, as distinctive landmarks, designed by globally reputed starchitects, in contemporary urbanism.[178] They have become highly visible, easily readable, and powerful symbols of urban success and attractiveness; the verticality of skyscrapers, in particular, serves as visual proof of having entered the upper ranks of global cities. Cultural icons, like brand-new museum buildings, likewise, carry positive images. Already Baudrillard assumed that, in the age of hyperrealities, the territory no longer precedes the map that tries to reproduce and represent it; rather, maps and simulations like 3D models and virtual animations, which gained a central role in planning and staging the urban, now precede, generate, and sometimes even replace material development on the ground.[179] Fierce communication strategies have sometimes become more important than the erection of real buildings and infrastructure. Social media, movies, music, and other cultural channels give "reality-like" insights into place experience and identity.[180]

Not surprisingly, the postmodernisation of cities has drastic consequences for city branding. According to Stephen Ward, linked with the structural decline of the modern industrial city in the late 20th century, selling the reinvented post-industrial city started to boom.[181] The use of iconic architecture and postmodern aesthetics has certainly become one of the most successful means to make places attractive to investors, tourists, and visitors. Such architectural dreamscapes can be easily converted into marketable commodities, to satisfy the fantasies of their clienteles. The fact that simulations can attribute to places any meaning whatsoever allows developers to intentionally invent new place identities, in places where identity is inherently absent. Symbolism helps to create comparative advantages, to shape consumers' needs, and to generate fascination, as demonstrated by Heiko Schmid for Las Vegas and Dubai.[182] For Vanolo, any physical urban element can be mobilised, via its iconicity, impressiveness, and size, to enable any place to foster its recognisability, provoke positive associations, and trigger curiosity.[183] In

177 Cf. Featherstone, 2007: 99; similarly, Govers and Go, 2009: 135–150.

178 Cf. Vanolo, 2017: 145–165. On the role of postmodern architecture, cf. also Crilley, 1993.

179 Cf. Baudrillard, 1988: 166–167.

180 Cf. Govers and Go, 2009: 142.

181 Cf. Ward, 1998a: 46–48, and 1998b: 186–194.

182 Cf., for example, Schmid, 2006, on a shift from the "economy of attention" to the "economy of fascination."

183 Cf. Vanolo, 2017: 164.

this regard, Christian Steiner already affirmed that the hyperreal character of many (especially tourist) places nowadays ideally fits postmodern marketing requirements and consumer demands before displaying functionality. Referring to Pierre Bourdieu, he also points to the symbolic capital and political value of hyperrealities.[184] The establishment of hyperreal iconic spaces can be understood as a way to accumulate materialised symbolic capital in a global competition for distinction and recognition; in turn, it can be transformed into economic and political surpluses for its holders, namely the ruling elite who created and owns them, and can enhance their political legitimacy. For them, visions of urban and national economic and societal futures are another important place branding tool.[185] Not least, "cool" nation brands are associated with certain lifestyles and images.[186] In particular, nation brands pass for a postmodern variety of identity formation.[187]

8 Some Critical Considerations of Branding

Critical reflections question many of the assumptions of conventional branding approaches and point to the downsides of pervasive branding efforts. In the following, I point out only some of the observations that seem to be the most relevant for the present publication.

8.1 The Social Construction of Brands

More functional, application-oriented approaches often claim that branding aims to capture a brand's essence and make its "real" identity visible.[188] Nation branding, for instance, is said to represent and communicate given characteristics of a country. Yet, from a more constructivist position, critical approaches point out that branding first makes the brand. It comes into being through socially meaningful interpretations. Following Vanolo, brands are nothing pre-specified, but social constructions emerging from a multitude of active contributions, subjective voices,

184 Cf. Steiner, 2014. Cf. also Adam, 2020: esp. 214; on objectivated "cultural capital," Vanolo, 2017: 148.
185 On the MENA region, cf. Bromber et al., 2014: 7–8; Steiner and Wippel, 2019: 8–9. For more, cf. the next chapter.
186 Cf. van Ham, 2001: 3–4. For an example, compare above the slogan "Cool Britannia."
187 Cf. van Ham, 2002: 265.
188 Cf., e.g., Govers, 2011: 227, 230; Anttiroiko, 2014, 62; Dinnie, 2008: 14–15; Eggeling, 2020: 9–10. On this identity-basis, cf. also Govers and Go, 2009: 16.

and individual life experiences.[189] Besides being an economically motivated instrument, place branding and especially nation branding in fact constitute a truly political practice, contributing to the fabrication and spread of political meaning. This parallels, e. g., the conception of the "nation," which is nothing primordial or naturally given, either, but a continuously reproduced historical construction and social artefact. Benedict Anderson, who conceived nations as "imagined communities," and Eric Hobsbawm and Terence Ranger, who underlined the role of "invented traditions," contributed enormously to this understanding.[190] Hence, brands are complex, relational, and path-dependent, but they also cannot be freely "invented," as suggested in some early manuals, if they are entirely incongruent with prevailing popular perceptions.[191] Scholars like Kristin Anabel Eggeling therefore plead for a non-essentialist, processual understanding and an approach oriented towards material and discursive practices to investigate, why, how, and by whom the brand and the story behind it are being produced and how branding becomes (politically) productive.[192]

Evidently, urban and other marketing campaigns are always idealised and sanitised representations.[193] In striving to sell a product or place and to present it in the best possible light, branding is very selective and highlights the positive and most appealing elements, meanings, and myths that enhance the marketability of the branded object. In contrast to these messages that seek hypervisibility, other, less positive aspects are deliberately ignored, elided, or eliminated.[194] Representational strategies try to combat and reshape adverse perceptions, such as a negative country-of-origin bias or remnant images of a problematic past in nation branding.[195] Further objects of such a conscious "politics of forgetting"[196]

---

189 Cf. Vanolo, 2017: 108.

190 Cf., e. g., Eggeling, 2020: 4–5, 43–44; Jansen, 2008: 124; van Ham, 2002: 259; Aronczyk, 2013: 83–84; Dinnie, 2008: 116–188; with references to Anderson, 1983 and Hobsbawm and Ranger, 1983.

191 Cf. Vanolo, 2017: 54.

192 Cf. Eggeling, 2020: esp. 10–16, 36–59. For a primordially discourse analysis approach, cf. Mattissek, 2010.

193 In the following, cf. especially Vanolo, 2017: passim; Ermann and Hermanik, 2018: 7–8. In his book, Vanolo illustrates selective and partial visibility versus invisibility with the metaphor of the spectre and the ghost. Here, cf. also Ward, 1998b: 54; Jansen, 2008: 122; Eggeling, 2020: 7, including on endeavours to rewrite and brighten national history in nation branding; Aronczyk, 2013: 34, specifically for Spain.

194 Cf., e. g., Aronczyk, 2013: 31, 138; similarly, Andersson, 2014: 151; Jansen, 2008: 134, on hypervisibility.

195 Cf. Dinnie, 2011: 4, and 2008: 96; Gertner, 2007: 4. Cf. also van Ham, 2002: 254; Aronczyk, 2013: 138, e. g. in the case of Chile.

196 Vanolo, 2017: 104.

are disturbing homeless people, poor urban neighbourhoods, slums, abandoned and deindustrialised landscapes, and political activism. Other aspects oscillate between the visible and the invisible, depending on social, cultural, and political contexts, such as the presence of mosques, mostly ignored in Western cities, but a key element of branding in Muslim societies, and the presence of gay/LGBTQ people, which only in recent years and mostly only in the Western world have become unique selling points. More generally, advertisements for project sites and cities often feature either stereotyped "typical" locals, or very few or no "real" people at all, in the smoothened and stylish aesthetic and utopian renderings of places.[197]

However, a brand is not only the result of an intentional, strategically planned process under the full control of those who formally conceive it; it also emerges in many unintended and contradictory ways. Beyond what is officially shown, certain things made invisible can still (re-)enter subjective and personal imaginaries and be difficult to make disappear. Imbalanced exaggerations and exclusions in branding can also be counterproductive, when counter-discourses arise, triggered by certain events, like coups and terror attacks, the destruction of cultural heritage, or media images that foreground decadence, misery, poor labour conditions, or bad treatment of migrants or minorities.[198]

8.2 Race for Ranks and Imitation Effects

Measuring and evaluating also plays an increasing role in branding endeavours.[199] As an evaluation tool, for example, Anholt developed the City Brand Index, which is among the most popular rankings; various other international indices and listings received growing attention. Such benchmarking and ranking, e.g. on economic performance, world-citiness, liveability, creativity, and sustainability, disclose strategic information about cities and nations. Today, this is supplemented by user-generated classifications on social media. Widely published top rankings not only help to improve the international image of places, but also build representations that are catchy and easily communicable – either as a sales argument in advertisements or as an impulse for responsible actors to strengthen branding ef-

197 Cf. also Freire, 2009: 420, on typical locals.

198 Exaggerations and special forms of deliberate obscuring, such as greenwashing, pinkwashing, and more recently sportswashing, which can also prove counterproductive, are dealt with in the next, empirical chapter of the introductory part of this book.

199 On the establishment of city rankings, cf. Vanolo, 2017: 177–190; Anttiroiko, 2014: 109–141 et passim; on nations, Aronczyk, 2013: 69–75 et passim; Eggeling, 2020: 6, 38–39; on the objectivating use of statistics, Adam, 2020: 219.

forts. However, they also contribute to the excessive use of superlatives ("best," "leading," "world-class") and instigate a not always productive race to the top for better positioning in the competition among places.

But successful symbolic and iconic elements of branding risk replication and plagiary. The quick imitation, e.g. of product or architectural innovations, leads to the rapid loss of comparative advantages.[200] Not only are commodities increasingly standardised to garner widespread trust and acceptance;[201] urban renewal and transformation programmes that accompany inter-city competition also risk leading to the standardisation and confusability of cityscapes and the loss of place identity.[202] Vanolo therefore warns against mimicking urban policies and architecture with similar types of waterfronts, marinas, skyscrapers, and skylines, as well as against branding material featuring nearly the same visual images, messages, and logos; the repeated use of always the same adjectives – such as "global," "cosmopolitan," "vibrant," "exciting," "creative," "dynamic," "smart," "green," "sustainable," and other buzzwords from the neoliberal catalogue – is notorious.[203] Similarly, nations make repeated references to established global discourses of recognised economic and cultural achievements, efforts, and aspirations.[204] For products and places, aspects like social responsibility, fair trade, and ecological awareness have been growing in importance for the image of a brand and also tend to be widely evoked. Thus, uniform commercial "brandscapes" emerge, when the few same global brands dominate everywhere.[205]

8.3 Fragmentation Effects and Uneven Development

Globalisation and neoliberalisation led to the dominance of economic discourses. In particular, branding strategies show a tendency to erase the visibility of the effects that globalisation, neoliberalisation, and postmodernisation have on cities.[206] Soja describes the postmodern transformations of the metropolitan structure as a process of increasing spatial, economic, and social segregation, fragmentation, and

200 Cf. Harvey, 1989: 12.

201 Cf. Ermann and Hermanik, 2018: 5–6.

202 Cf. Andersson, 2014: 145, who also mentions the "paradox of similarity." Cf. also Jansen, 208: 131; Adam, 2020: 221.

203 Cf. Vanolo, 2017: 94–95, especially with reference to Asian cities, 117–144.

204 Cf. Eggeling, 2020: 49–50.

205 Cf. Pike, 2011: 10; on brandscapes, Klingmann, 2007. For Anttiroiko, 2014: 17, likewise, the race for ranks risks assimilation.

206 Cf. Vanolo, 2017: 134.

polycentralisation, due to which urban agglomerations have clearly become more amorphous, diverse, and less tangible – a mixture increasingly difficult to be held together.[207] Besides its creative aspects, an extremely heterogeneous and multicultural population also shows destructive dynamics. New patterns of polarisation and uneven development have arisen and create new landscapes of despair, poverty, conflict, and violence, reinforced by urban branding in the interest of the capitalist class.[208] In consequence, there is an obsessive demand for security, leading to a steep rise in spatial surveillance, social control, and fortified areas of exclusion, which in turn are preferentially marketed. Also, spatial planning has become less inclusive and more fragmentary, concentrating on the lucrative and appealing parts of the city devoted to leisure, consumption, and simulation, while it turns to social issues only with the aim of halting the spread of unrest and of pacifying certain neighbourhoods.[209] The physical "cleansing" and "redeveloping" of stigmatised and marginalised places in neoliberal and postmodern urbanism parallels their being ignored in branding.[210] The accessibility of the many hyperreal projects, in particular, is often at least partially restricted by security guards, entrance fees, or exorbitant prices.[211] Negative externalities ascribed to excessive destination branding include excessive tourism, pollution, precarious jobs, and rising prices and rents.[212] Another result of interurban competition is said to be the formation of asymmetrical global hierarchies, in which a few cities and regions assume a pivotal role in the contemporary globalised economy.[213] The omnipresent "space of flows," which all strive their best to integrate into, does not lead to spatial homogeneity: flows bypass organisations and territories considered uninteresting or merely ordinary, thereby leading to uneven geographies, which in turn demand even more activities to attract attention.

In connection with the preceding explanations, various scholars also critically scrutinise branding's focus on the "creative class" as a component of the neoliberal agenda.[214] According to Anttiroiko, the contest for the creative class and the creative city legitimises urban restructuring and the use of starchitecture against

207 Cf. Soja, 2000; Dear and Flusty, 1998. Featherstone, 2007: 107, likewise contrasts the aestheticisation, primarily of Western cities, in recent decades with the persistence of classification, hierarchies, and segregation within urban areas.

208 On branding effects such as marginalisation, polarisation, and gentrification, cf. also Andersson, 2014: 150.

209 On the MENA region, cf. Steiner and Wippel, 2019: 9–10; Wippel, 2021: 51.

210 Compare also Vanolo, 2017: 125.

211 Cf. also Steiner, 2014: 26; Wippel, 2021: 77–78.

212 Cf. de Losada, 2019: 1–2.

213 Cf. Anttiroiko, 2014: 26–33.

214 Cf. in the following Aly, 2019: esp. 101, with regard to the new Saudi town of NEOM.

emerging social tensions and identity conflicts.[215] Innovation- and talent-oriented branding offers this narrow class of people a better quality of life at the expense of the rest; it risks increasing tensions in job markets and higher prices and rents.[216] Other groups that actually exist are intentionally kept invisible. Also, the assumption has been challenged that these creatives are exceptionally spatially mobile and prefer soft factors like the event quality of a place over hard factors such as job opportunities. Another criticism of the concept has been directed at the missing causal link between attracting the creative class and fostering economic progress.

8.4 Political and Societal Consequences

From a critical perspective, place branding and especially nation branding also raise issues of democracy, participation, and governance.[217] The shift of decision-making and implementation from (elected) state representatives and public actors to the corporate sphere reflects and further fuels the neoliberal restructuring of the economy and society and entails serious dangers for democratic procedures and civic participation. A major impetus for branding is to control the communicated and perceived image of a nation. But according to Peter van Ham, when protagonists ask for high-level coordination and consistency, as well as for internal cohesion and commitment, this may result in a disciplined society.[218] He warns that strict implementation of established branding methodologies is difficult to realise in democratic countries; in contrast, authoritarian regimes feel free to act as they want. As a depoliticising practice, nation branding is a particularly attractive, persuasive instrument of legitimation for leaders and elites in undemocratic contexts. Therefore, critical research also looks at the ideological work behind branding. It investigates links of branding practices to identity politics and security policies and their use to legitimate political power. Moreover, it analyses the work and influence of private consultancy firms and regards branding as a form of spectacle that reinforces depoliticisation trends.

Decision-making in this process often remains opaque and exclusive, and no input from civil society and citizens is desired or expected. Contemporary brand-

215 Cf. Anttiroiko, 2014: 142–152.

216 Cf. De Losada, 2019: 2–3.

217 In the following, cf., for instance, Jansen, 2008: 121–124, 134–135; Aronczyk, 2008: 43, 45, 55, and 2013: 64–65, 85. Cf. also Andersson, 2014: 145, 150; Eggeling, 2020: 36–40 et passim; Browning and de Oliveira, 2017: 487.

218 Cf. van Ham, 2002: 266–268.

ing also favours certain elites' visions and knowledge and, for instance, advances a specific vision of globalisation and presents it as unavoidable and compulsory. At the same time, this changes the context in which national identity is developed. Authorities tend to establish a "monologic, hierarchical, reductive form of communication"[219] that allows for only one particular kind of message and collective representation, ignores pluralities, dissent, and resistance, and eliminates alternative ideas and imaginaries of the state and society. Similarly, cities are conceptualised as single, homogenous collective actors.[220] Their branding is conceived as a predominantly technical issue, leaving little opportunity for local protest, grassroots action, or political struggle. Accordingly, practitioners and researchers increasingly have asked to integrate the broader public's ideas and views in more open, participatory processes, also to ensure that a place's population will consequently "live" the brand.[221] Yet, this obviously clashes with the manifold restrictions in authoritarian (and profoundly neoliberal) regimes, as prevail notably in the MENA region that is the focus of this volume.

8.5 (Socio-)Spatial and Temporal Entanglements

While place branding very obviously is based on geographical references and reflects asymmetric geographies that cities try to cope with, other forms of branding, too, are intrinsically linked to space and place. Andy Pike, a key author in critical research, points in particular to the deep and still-growing spatial entanglements of brands for commodities and services.[222] First of all, the geographies of brands refer to the entanglement of product brands and place brands. Product brands are closely linked to spatial provenance and connotations that help to affirm their value and meaning; however, these associations may also lower the value of the object if linked to negative images, e. g. of quality. As we have seen above, already very early in world history, branding was used to guarantee geographic origin; later, in the mass industrial age, "Made in" labels emerged in tandem with the consolidating territorial nation state. As a next step, country-of-origin proofs were demanded by rules-of-origin clauses in trade agreements in a both liberalising and regionalising world economy. More recently, local or regional "geographic indica-

219 Jansen, 2008: 134.

220 Cf. Vanolo, 2017: 129, 189; Eggeling, 2020: 7.

221 Others criticise the transfer of responsibility to "live the brand" to the citizens; cf. Browning and de Oliveira, 2017: 487.

222 In the following section, cf. Pike, 2009 and 2011. Cf. also Anttiroiko, 2014: esp. 26–33; Vanolo, 2017: 36; Andersson, 2014.

tions" and "protected designations of origin" have proliferated to warrant a product's source and qualities, related to methods and reputation, and are protected by international conventions or national legislation. Geographic nomenclature can also be part of a brand name and a protected trademark, which serves as primary product identification.[223] Socio-spatially entangled histories, national stereotypes, and other place-related connotations play a considerable role in consumers' valuation of brands. In the case of intertwined "place-product co-branding," certain places are associated with certain products and, vice versa, products with certain symbolic qualities are ascribed to places (like for Detroit and Ford and for chocolate or watches and Switzerland).[224]

We can also find geographic markers in branding that connect with prominent distant places, such as "Paris," "Venice," or "Switzerland" for a city's or region's atmosphere, architecture, or landscape.[225] Places themselves are repeatedly spatially positioned, with spatial metaphors, such as regional or civilisational "bridges," "gateways," "crossroads," "hearts," and "hubs," to represent key strategic locations on the global map.[226] Such efforts are particularly enormous when places from the periphery of international politics, economics, and attention attempt to move into more central positions of perception. Betweenness then becomes a particular geopolitical asset and an opportunity to emphasise cosmopolitan traits of identity. Vice versa, attempts are being made to give negative geopolitical associations a positive twist, such as with the continental marker "Africa."[227]

However, the resonance of brands may be geographically uneven and nuanced, e.g. due to varying cultural responsiveness and sensitivity, nurtured by and further nurturing spatial differences and unequal geographies of power.[228]

---

223 Cf. also Kavaratzis and Ashworth, 2005: 511, and 2008: 152–153. This is done especially for food (e.g. *Jamón ibérico*, parmesan, champagne, etc.), but also for other products and companies (such as, in an arbitrary list, *Eau de Cologne*, *Deutsche Bank*, American Airlines, Kentucky Fried Chicken, the *Jysk* retail chain, and *Bayerische Motoren Werke*/BMW).

224 Moreover, cf., similarly, Anttiroiko, 2014: 50.

225 Cf. Ermann and Hermanik, 2018: 8, on Budapest as the "Little Paris of Middle Europe." In the MENA region, Beirut, for example, was the former "Paris of the Middle East" and strove to become "Hongkong on the Mediterranean" in the 1990s; cf. Schmid, 2001.

226 Cf. Browning and de Oliveira, 2017: 496; Adam, 2020: 218; Vanolo, 20017: 11; Eggeling, 2020: 49. Kazakhstan and Turkey are examples of states that want to leave peripheral situations in favour of more central positions.

227 Cf. Browning and de Oliveira, 2017: 497. We can add practices of reference to (re)emerging and (re)invented regional contexts, like the "Indian Ocean," instead of the "Arab world" or the "Middle East;" cf. Wippel, 2013.

228 Cf. also Andersson, 2014: 150; Vanolo, 2017: 36–37; Govers and Go, 2009: 11; Medway and Warnaby, 2014, on the linguistic, ethnical, and political contestations of place names.

The progressively hybrid, multi-country origin of products in transnational value chains and the existence of truly global brands render associations more complex and multiscalar. With the pluralisation and globalisation of media, brands have been increasingly communicated across territorial borders; e-branding has de-territorialised brands even more. At the same time, market segmentation and differentiation in search of niche markets and premium payments by exploiting economic and social disparities lead to branding practices that vary among places and contribute to the perpetuation of uneven development and socio-spatial inequalities; the same is true, on the production side, for the division of labour across the globe by big brands. Moreover, the geographic positioning of places may also reinforce geopolitical hierarchies, when they are associated with the sphere of a strong country or world region (such as "Europe").[229]

References are not only spatial, but also temporal – to past, present, and future.[230] While branding regularly silences problematic historical aspects, allusions to a distant history can also be made explicit and serve to link the present to the myths of a vital and continuing glorious past, an ancient civilisation, or long-lasting "traditions"[231] and can help to legitimise current economic orientations or retain a political order (particularly important for dynastic lineages of monarchies), but also to distance a new political regime from dark previous ones (such as in the post-Soviet era). Vice versa, besides emphasising current strengths, temporal references can be "revolutionary" and point to change, progress, and visions and promise a bright, prosperous, and peaceful future.[232] At the same time, such future-oriented outlooks can serve to manage and control the future by limiting or even ruling out the possibility of alternative conceptions from the outset.[233]

8.6 Geopolitical Aspects and International Relations

The debate on nation branding partly blends with current conceptual thinking about geopolitics, international relations (IR), and national identity. As we have seen, authors like van Ham think that a fundamental transformation has occurred in recent decades from traditional geopolitics characterised by the logic of hard

229 Cf. Browning and de Oliveira, 2017: 496.
230 Cf. Eggeling, 2020: 6–7, 49–50.
231 Cf. Ermann and Hermanik, 2018: 8. Cf. again Wippel, 2013, on Oman as an old "trading empire."
232 On the role of visions in Gulf cities and nations, cf. also Bromber et al., 2014; on the future orientation of branding, Bolin and Ståhlberg, 2010: 94.
233 Compare also Eggeling, 2020: 30.

power relating to territorial claims, border control, and warfare to postmodern soft and competitive expressions of power based on the use of intangible assets of influence, status, and prestige and the formation and spread of images in world politics.[234] In this widely perceived shift, factors like culture, values, moral authority, and legitimate policies and institutions have increasingly been integrated as tools of power; visibility and attractiveness have come in the focus of the contemporary attention economy. In the logic of neoliberal globalisation, national identity becomes central to national competitiveness and serves as a potential resource of added value. While nation-building was traditionally conceived as a concept and practice turned to the domestic context to generate collective identification, strengthened globalisation has extended national identity into the international sphere. Market-oriented nation branding is understood as a device to increase a state's soft power and global recognition of its importance and is interpreted as the updated and more benign, even peace-promoting form of (a commercial) nationalism.[235] This also entails a reconceptualisation of states from ends to means of political action.

Yet, against the postulated shift from geopolitics to geoeconomics, more critical authors see a less categorical contrast and point to the persistence of traditional forms of geopolitics and state power. Accordingly, nation branding remains deeply entangled with rather traditional geopolitical scripts, and emerging geoeconomic forms tend to recast conventional geopolitics in light of market logics, i. e. when boundaries between public and private, state and market, domestic and international become more blurred. States always paid attention to matters of image and identity (and their manipulation) in relations with others, in order to achieve influence. As the state as such is invisible, it has always needed to be personalised, symbolised, and imagined. Vice versa, not all moves in contemporary international policy are only about image-making and subordinated to economic ends. Diplomatic logics (i. e. a secure position in the international system), economic logics (seeking an advanced competitive standing in globalised markets), and cultural logics (seeking the construction of a collective identity) do not necessarily oppose, but can reinforce each other. Nevertheless, the divergence of branding messages to the inside and the outside can still obstruct domestic nation-building, but can also have a disciplining function. Likewise, instead of emphasising peace, conflict resolution, and intercultural understanding, nation branding can be used to glob-

---

234 In connection with this paragraph, cf. in particular van Ham, 2001 and 2002; for more critical perspectives and in connection with the entire subsection, Eggeling, 2020: esp. 4–9, 38; Browning and de Oliveira, 2017.

235 Cf. also Jansen, 2008: 133.

ally less inclusive and cosmopolitan ends, representing instead aggressive nationalisms, as demonstrated by cases like North Korea, Russia, and ISIS (the latter voicing a quasi-state claim and exhibiting a branding strategy of its own), or a still strongly discriminating geoeconomic logic.

Moreover, for Sue Jansen, neoliberal branding is a kind of privatisation of foreign policy.[236] It finally also perpetuates and legitimises the nation state as a frame of identity, allegiance, and belonging in the context of advancing globalisation.[237] In practice, especially in authoritarian contexts, branding increasingly serves less to brand the nation than the state and the ruling regime, e. g. by promoting the image of a benevolent ruler.[238]

9 Outlook

This chapter has shown the deep historical roots of branding and how it has gained considerable momentum in recent decades in interaction with the rapid changes in macroeconomic, social, and political conditions. This went hand in hand with the development of application-oriented publications that designed rather schematic, ready-made toolkits. However, the phenomenon was gradually subjected to explicitly critical and reflexive conceptualisation and assessment. Likewise, the manifold forms of the branding phenomenon, including the object areas to which it has increasingly extended, and the multiple, interdisciplinary sources, questions, and perspectives of the theoretical approaches that have developed in the meantime, have been identified and demonstrated in the preceding sections. An immense number of ensuing publications could have been integrated into the conceptual part of this introduction. However, they have mostly only branched out into more specific aspects and sub-fields of branding theory and concepts, or have merely further elaborated on many of the aspects already dealt with here without adding much of significance to these explanations. In addition to this chapter's overall framing of this edited volume, the authors' individual book contributions repeatedly take up partial aspects of the general ideas on branding addressed in this conceptual introduction. But first, the next chapter turns to the MENA region and provides a literature-based overview of the regional unfolding and varieties of the global branding phenomenon, which have been repeatedly tied back to the various conceptualisations of branding as presented here.

236 Cf. Jansen, 2008: 124.

237 Cf. Aronczyk, 2008: 43, and 2013: 64.

238 Cf. Eggeling, 2020: 39, 51, on Kazakhstan and Qatar.

Bibliography

Adam, Matthieu. "Marketing: La quête du capital symbolique." In *Le capital dans la cité: Une encyclopédie critique de la ville*, edited by Matthieu Adam and Emeline Comby, 211–223. Paris: Editions Amsterdam, 2020.

Alaily-Mattar, Nadia, Johannes Dreher, and Alain Thierstein. "Repositioning Cities through Star Architecture: How Does it Work?" *Journal of Urban Design* 23.2 (2018): 169–192.

AMA (American Marketing Association). "What Is Marketing? The Definition of Marketing." 2017. https://www.ama.org/the-definition-of-marketing-what-is-marketing/. Accessed 9 November 2022.

AMA. "The Four Ps of Marketing." 12 July 2022. https://www.ama.org/marketing-news/the-four-ps-of-marketing/. Accessed 9 November 2022.

Amarouche, Maryame, and Koenraad Bogaert. "Reshaping Space and Time in Morocco: The Agencification of Urban Government and its Effects in the Bouregreg Valley (Rabat/Salé)." *Middle East–Topics & Arguments* 12.1 (2019): 44–54. https://archiv.ub.uni-marburg.de/ep/0003/article/view/7934. Accessed 22 November 2022.

Anderson, Benedict. *Imagined Communities: Reflections on the Origin and Spread of Nationalism.* London: Verso, 1983.

Andersson, Ida. "Placing Place Branding: An Analysis of an Emerging Research Field in Human Geography." *Geografisk Tidsskrift-Danish Journal of Geography* 114.2 (2014): 143–155.

Anholt, Simon. "Editorial. Place Branding: Is it Marketing, or isn' t it?" *Place Branding and Public Diplomacy* 4.1 (2008a): 1–6.

Anholt, Simon. "From Nation Branding to Competitive Identity: The Role of Brand Management as a Component of National Policy." In *Nation Branding: Concepts, Issues, Practice*, edited by Keith Dinnie, 22–23. Oxford, Burlington: Butterworth-Heinemann, 2008b.

Anholt, Simon. "Beyond the Nation Brand: The Role of Image and Identity in International Relations." In *Brands and Branding Geographies*, edited by Andy Pike, 289–301. Cheltenham, Northampton: Edward Elgar, 2011.

Anttiroiko, Ari-Veikko. *The Political Economy of City Branding.* Abingdon, New York: Routledge, 2014.

Aronczyk, Melissa. "'Living the Brand': Nationality, Globality and the Identity Strategies of Nation Branding Consultants." *International Journal of Communication* 2 (2008): 41–65.

Aronczyk, Melissa. *Branding the Nation: The Global Business of National Identity.* [Oxford]: Oxford Scholarship Online [Oxford University Press], 2013.

Bastos, Wilson, and Sidney J. Levy, "A History of the Concept of Branding: Practice and Theory." *Journal of Historical Research in Marketing* 4.3 (2012): 347–368.

Baudrillard, Jean. *Selected Writings.* Edited and with an Introduction by Mark Poster. Stanford: Stanford University Press, 1988.

Beier, Raffael. "Worlding Cities in the Middle East and North Africa: Arguments for a Conceptual Turn." *Middle East–Topics & Arguments* 12.1 (2019): 28–34. https://archiv.ub.uni-marburg.de/ep/0003/2019/230/7828/. Accessed 22 November 2022.

Birkigt, Klaus, and Marinus M. Stadler, eds. *Corporate Identity: Grundlagen, Funktionen, Fallbeispiele.* Landsberg/Lech: Moderne Industrie, 3rd ed., 1986.

Blask, Falko. *Jean Baudrillard zur Einführung.* Hamburg: Junius, 3rd ed., 1995.

Bolin, Göran, and Per Ståhlberg. "Between Community and. Commodity: Nationalism and Nation Branding." In *Communicating the Nation: National Topographies of Global Media Landscapes*, edited by Anna Roosvall and Inka Salovaara-Moring, 79–101. Göteborg: Nordicom, 2010.

Brenner, Neil, and Nik Theodore. "Cities and the Geographies of 'Actually Existing Neoliberalism'." *Antipode* 34.3 (2002): 349–379.

Bromber, Katrin, Birgit Krawietz, Christian Steiner, and Steffen Wippel. "The Arab(ian) Gulf: Urban Development in the Making." In *Under Construction: Logics of Urbanism in the Gulf Region*, edited by Steffen Wippel, Katrin Bromber, Christian Steiner, and Birgit Krawietz, 1–14. Farnham, Burlington: Ashgate, 2014.

Browning, Christopher S., and Antonio Ferraz de Oliveira. "Introduction: Nation Branding and Competitive Identity in World Politics." *Geopolitics* 22.3 (2017): 481–501.

Brunn, Stanley D. "The State Branding of US Postage Stamps for State Commemorative Years: From Heritage, Iconography and Place to Placelessness." In *Branding the Nation, the Place, the Product*, edited by Ulrich Ermann and Klaus-Jürgen Hermanik, 29–51. Abingdon, New York: Routledge, 2018.

Callon, Michel, Cécile Méadel, and Vololona Rabeharisoa. "The Economy of Qualities." *Economy and Society* 31.2 (2002): 194–217.

Castells, Manuel. *The Rise of the Network Society. The Information Age: Economy, Society and Culture, Vol. I.* Cambridge, MA, Oxford: Blackwell, 1996.

Coca-Cola Deutschland. "Eiskalte Klassiker: Coca-Cola Werbung von 1886 bis heute." https://www.coca-cola-deutschland.de/unterhaltung/fans-und-sammler/coca-cola-werbung-1886-bis-heute. Accessed 14 November 2022.

Crilley, Darrel. "Architecture as Advertising: Constructing the Image of Redevelopment." In *Selling Places: The City as Cultural Capital, Past and Present*, edited by Gerry Kearns and Chris Philo, 231–252. Oxford, New York, et al.: Pergamon Press, 1993.

Dear, Michael, and Steven Flusty. "Postmodern Urbanism." *Annals of the Association of American Geographers* 88.1 (1998): 50–72.

de Losada, Agustí Fernández. *The Downside of the International Impact of City Branding.* Barcelona: Centro de Información y Documentación Internacionales en Barcelona, 2019. https://www.cidob.org/en/content/download/73958/2364662/version/6/file/594_OPINION_AGUSTI%20FERNANDEZ%20DE%20LOSADA_ANG.pdf. Accessed 25 July 2020.

Dinnie, Keith. *Nation Branding: Concepts, Issues, Practice.* Oxford, Burlington: Butterworth-Heinemann, 2008.

Dinnie, Keith, ed. *City Branding: Theory and Cases.* Basingstoke, New York: Palgrave Macmillan, 2011.

Ditchey, Mallory. "Body Language: Tattooing and Branding in Ancient Mesopotamia." *Journal of Ancient Near Eastern History,* 3.1 (2016): 1–24.

Ebeling, Friederike. *Albrecht Dürer als Marke: Zur Archäologie von Markenbildung am Beispiel eines Renaissancekünstlers.* BA thesis, Faculty of Media, Hochschule Mittweida, 2013. https://monami.hs-mittweida.de/files/3817/Bachelorarbeit_Duerer_Ebeling.pdf. Accessed 7 December 2022.

Eco, Umberto. *Faith in Fakes: Travels in Hyperreality.* London, Auckland, et al.: Minerva, reprint, 1995.

Eggeling, Kristin Anabel. *Nation-branding in Practice: The Politics of Promoting Sports, Cities and Universities in Kazakhstan and Qatar.* Abingdon, New York: Routledge, 2020.

Ermann, Ulrich, and Klaus-Jürgen Hermanik. "Introduction: Branding the Nation, the Place, the Product." In *Branding the Nation, the Place, the Product*, edited by Ulrich Ermann and Klaus-Jürgen Hermanik, 1–13. Abingdon, New York: Routledge, 2018.

Evans, Joel R. "A Strategic Approach to Self-Branding." *Journal of Global Scholars of Marketing Science* 27.4 (2017): 270–311.

Featherstone, Mike. *Consumer Culture and Postmodernism.* London, Thousand Oaks, et al.: Sage, 2nd ed., 2007.

Fırat, A. Fuat, and Nikhilesh Dholakia. "Theoretical and Philosophical Implications of Postmodern Debates: Some Challenges to Modern Marketing." *Marketing Theory* 6.2 (2006): 123–162.
Fırat, A. Fuat, Nikhilesh Dholakia, and Alladi Venkatesh. "Marketing in a Postmodern World." *European Journal of Marketing* 29.1 (1995): 40–56.
Florida, Richard. "Cities and the Creative Class." *City & Community* 2.1 (2003): 3–19.
Freire, João R. "Geobranding, Are We Talking Nonsense? A Theoretical Reflection on Brands Applied to Places." *Place Branding* 1.4 (2005): 347–362.
Freire, João Ricardo. "'Local People' a Critical Dimension for Place Brands." *Journal of Brand Management* 16.7 (2009): 420–438.
Gertner, David. "Unfolding and Configuring Two Decades of Research and Publications on Place Marketing and Place Branding." *Place Branding and Public Diplomacy* 7.2 (2011): 91–106.
Govers, Robert. "Guest Editorial: From Place Marketing to Place Branding and Back." *Place Branding and Public Diplomacy* 7.4 (2011): 227–231.
Govers, Robert. "Editorial: Why Place Branding is not about Logos and Slogans." *Place Branding and Public Diplomacy* 9.2 (2013): 71–75.
Govers, Robert, and Frank Go. *Place Branding: Glocal, Virtual and Physical Identities, Constructed, Imagined and Experienced.* Basingstoke, New York: Palgrave Macmillan, 2009.
Grubbauer, Monika. *Die vorgestellte Stadt: Globale Büroarchitektur, Stadtmarketing und politischer Wandel in Wien.* Bielefeld: Transcript, 2011.
Harvey, David. "From Managerialism to Entrepreneurialism: The Transformation in Urban Governance in Late Capitalism." *Geografiska Annaler, Series B, Human Geography* 71.1 (1989): 3–17.
Hellmann, Kai-Uwe. "Ausweitung der Markenzone: Zur Einführung." In *Ausweitung der Markenzone: Interdisziplinäre Zugänge zur Erforschung des Markenwesens*, edited by Kai-Uwe Hellmann and Rüdiger Pichler, 7–18. Wiesbaden: VS Verlag für Sozialwissenschaften, 2005.
Herbst, Dieter. "Der Mensch als Marke." In *Ausweitung der Markenzone: Interdisziplinäre Zugänge zur Erforschung des Markenwesens*, edited by Kai-Uwe Hellmann and Rüdiger Pichler, 99–118. Wiesbaden: VS Verlag für Sozialwissenschaften, 2005.
Hobsbawm, Eric, and Terence Ranger, eds. *The Invention of Tradition.* Cambridge MA, New York: Cambridge University Press, 1983.
Hoyle, Brian. "Global and Local Change on the Port-City Waterfront." *Geographical Review* 90.3 (2000): 395–417.
Hymans, Jacques E.C. "East is East, and West is West? Currency Iconography as Nation-branding in the Wider Europe." *Political Geography* 29.2 (2010): 97–108.
Islamic Fatwas. "Branding and Castrating Cattles [sic!]." Collection of *fatwās*. https://www.al-feqh.com/en/category/branding-and-castrating-cattles. Accessed 27 January 2022.
Jansen, Sue Curry. "Designer Nations: Neo-liberal Nation Branding – Brand Estonia." *Social Identities: Journal for the Study of Race, Nation and Culture* 14.1 (2008): 121–142.
Jones, Christopher P. "Stigma: Tattooing and Branding in Graeco-Roman Antiquity." *The Journal of Roman Studies* 77 (1987): 139–155.
Kaneva, Nadia. "With 'Bravery' as its New Brand, Ukraine is Turning Advertising into a Weapon of War." *The Conversation* 19 August 2022. https://theconversation.com/with-bravery-as-its-new-brand-ukraine-is-turning-advertising-into-a-weapon-of-war-188408. Accessed 14 November 2022.
Karpik, Lucien. *Valuing the Unique: The Economics of Singularities.* Princeton: Princeton University Press, 2010.
Kavaratzis, Michalis. "From City Marketing to City Branding: Towards a Theoretical Framework for Developing City Brands." *Place Branding* 1.1 (2004): 58–73.

Kavaratzis, Mihalis, and Gregory J. Ashworth. “City Branding: An Effective Assertion of Identity or a Transitory Marketing Trick?” *Tijdschrift voor Economische en Sociale Geografie* 96.5 (2005): 506–514.

Kavaratzis, Mihalis, and Gregory Ashworth. “Place Marketing: How Did We Get Here and Where Are We Going?” *Journal of Place Management and Development* 1.2 (2008): 150–165.

Klingmann, Anna. *Brandscapes: Architecture in the Experience Economy.* Cambridge MA, London: The MIT Press, 2007.

Kotler, Philip, and David Gertner. “Country as Brand, Product, and Beyond: A Place Marketing and Brand Management Perspective.” *Brand Management* 9.4–5 (2002): 249–261.

Kotler, Philip, Donald H. Haider, and Irving Rein. *Marketing Places: Attracting Investment, Industry, and Tourism to Cities, States, and Nations.* New York, Don Mills: The Free Press, 1993.

Kumar, Navin, and Rajeev Kumar Panda. “Place Branding and Place Marketing: A Contemporary Analysis of the Literature and Usage of Terminology.” *International Review on Public and Nonprofit Marketing* 16 (2019): 255–292.

Lorot, Pascal, ed. *Introduction à la Géoéconomie.* Paris: Economica, 1999.

Lucarelli, Andrea, and Per·Olof Berg. “City Branding: A State-of-the-art Review of the Research Domain.” *Journal of Place Management and Development* 4.1 (2011): 9–27.

Lucarelli, Andrea, and Sara Brorström. “Problematising Place Branding Research: A Meta-theoretical Analysis of the Literature.” *The Marketing Review* 13.1 (2013): 65–81.

Luttwak, Edward N. “From Geopolitics to Geo-Economics: Logic of Conflict, Grammar of Commerce.” *The National Interest* 20 (1990): 17–23.

Markessinis, Andreas. “National Flags: The Real Country Logos.” *Nation Branding: Everything about Nation Branding and Country Brands* 11 May 2011. http://nation-branding.info/2011/05/11/national-flags-real-country-logos/. Accessed 28 September 2012 (link expired).

Mattissek, Annika. “Analyzing City Images: Potentials of the ‘French School of Discourse Analysis’.” *Erdkunde* 64.4 (2010): 315–326.

Medway, Dominic, and Gary Warnaby. “What’s in a Name? Place Branding and Toponymic Commodification.” *Environment and Planning A* 46 (2014): 153–167.

Moore, Karl, and Susan Reid. “The Birth of Brand: 4000 Years of Branding.” *Business History* 50.4 (2008): 419–432.

Pálsdóttir, Inga Hlín. “Country Case Insight – Iceland: The Case of ‘Iceland Naturally’ – Establishing an Umbrella Brand to Increase Country Image Impact and Coherence.” In *Nation Branding: Concepts, Issues, Practice*, edited by Keith Dinnie, 183–186. Oxford, Burlington: Butterworth-Heinemann, 2008.

Peck, Jamie, and Adam Tickell. “Neoliberalizing Space.” *Antipode* 34.3 (2002): 380–404.

Penrose, Jan. “Designing the Nation: Banknotes, Banal Nationalism and Alternative Conceptions of the State.” *Political Geography* 30.8 (2011): 429–440.

Pike, Andy. “Geographies of Brands and Branding.” *Progress in Human Geography* 33.5 (2009): 619–645.

Pike, Andy. “Introduction: Brands and Branding Geographies.” In *Brands and Branding Geographies*, edited by Andy Pike, 3–24. Cheltenham, Northampton: Edward Elgar, 2011.

Pike, Andy. “Origination: The Geographies of Brands and Branding.” In *Branding the Nation, the Place, the Product*, edited by Ulrich Ermann and Klaus-Jürgen Hermanik, 15–28. Abingdon, New York: Routledge, 2018.

Porter, Michael E. *The Competitive Advantage of Nations.* New York: Free Press, 1990.

Rainer, Gerhard, Jutta Kister, and Christian Steiner. “Qualifizierungsstrategien in regionalen Restrukturierungsprozessen: Die Neuerfindung Südtirols in einem globalen Weinmarkt.” *Geographische Zeitschrift* 107.2 (2019): 130–156.

Rajaram, S., and Stalin Shelly, C. “History of Branding.” *International Journal of Social Sciences and Interdisciplinary Research* 1.3 (2012): 100–104.

Reckwitz, Andreas. *Die Gesellschaft der Singularitäten: Zum Strukturwandel der Moderne.* Berlin: Suhrkamp, 2017.

Rein, Irving, and Ben Shields. “Place Branding Sports: Strategies for Differentiating Emerging, Transitional, Negatively Viewed and Newly Industrialised Nations.” *Place Branding and Public Diplomacy* 3.1 (2007): 73–85.

Roy, Ananya, and Aihwa Ong, eds. *Worlding Cities: Asian Experiments and the Art of Being Global.* Chichester, Malden: Wiley-Blackwell, 2011.

Sassen, Saskia. *The Global City: New York, London, Tokyo.* Princeton, London: Princeton University Press, 2nd ed., 2001.

Sasserath, Marc. “Fußball ist unser Leben und König Fußball regiert die (Marken-)Welt! Oder vom Sinn und Unsinn der Verbindung von Fußball und Marken.” In *Ausweitung der Markenzone: Interdisziplinäre Zugänge zur Erforschung des Markenwesens*, edited by Kai-Uwe Hellmann and Rüdiger Pichler, 121–139. Wiesbaden: VS Verlag für Sozialwissenschaften, 2005.

Schmid, Heiko. “Economy of Fascination: Dubai and Las Vegas as Examples of Themed Urban Landscape.” *Erdkunde* 60 (2006): 346–360.

Schneider, Helmut. “Political Brand Matters: Ansatzpunkte für das Management von Marken in der Politik.” In *Ausweitung der Markenzone: Interdisziplinäre Zugänge zur Erforschung des Markenwesens*, edited by Kai-Uwe Hellmann and Rüdiger Pichler, 140–165. Wiesbaden: VS Verlag für Sozialwissenschaften, 2005.

Soja, Edward W. *Postmetropolis: Critical Studies of Cities and Regions.* Oxford, Malden: Blackwell, 2000.

Steiner, Christian. “From Heritage to Hyper-reality? Tourism Destination Development in the Middle East between Petra and the Palm.” *Journal of Tourism and Cultural Change* 8.4 (2010): 240–253.

Steiner, Christian. “Iconic Spaces, Symbolic Capital and the Political Economy of Urban Development in the Arab Gulf.” In *Under Construction: Logics of Urbanism in the Gulf Region*, edited by Steffen Wippel, Katrin Bromber, Christian Steiner, and Birgit Krawietz, 17–30. Farnham, Burlington: Ashgate, 2014.

Steiner, Christian, and Steffen Wippel. “Urban Development in the Middle East and North Africa: Deconstructing Visions, Politics, and Identities.” *Middle East–Topics & Arguments* 12.1 (2019): 5–16. https://archiv.ub.uni-marburg.de/ep/0003/article/view/8022. Accessed 22 November 2022.

Swyngedouw, Erik, Frank Moulaert, and Arantxa Rodriguez. “Neoliberal Urbanization in Europe: Large-Scale Urban Development Projects and the New Urban Policy.” *Antipode* 34.3 (2002): 542–577.

Taylor, Peter J. *World City Network: A Global Urban Analysis.* London, New York: Routledge, 2004.

van Ham, Peter. “The Rise of the Brand State: The Postmodern Politics of Image and Reputation.” *Foreign Affairs* 80.5 (2001): 2–6.

van Ham, Peter. “Branding Territory: Inside the Wonderful Worlds of PR and IR Theory.” *Millennium: Journal of International Studies* 31 (2002): 249–269.

Vanolo, Alberto. *City Branding: The Ghostly Politics of Representation in Globalising Cities.* New York, Abingdon: Routledge, 2017.

von Scheve, Christian. "Thorstein Veblen: The Theory of the Leisure Class." In *Schlüsselwerke der Wirtschaftssoziologie*, edited by Klaus Kraemer and Florian Brugger, 55–63. Wiesbaden: Springer VS, 2017.

Vuignier, Renaud. "Place Branding & Place Marketing 1976–2016: A Multidisciplinary Literature Review." *International Review on Public and Nonprofit Marketing* 14.4 (2017): 447–473.

Vuignier, Renaud. *Attractivité des territoires et place branding: Etude exploratoire de la sensibilité des décideurs d'entreprise à la marque territoriale.* PhD thesis, Faculté de droit, des sciences criminelles et d'administration publique, Université de Lausanne, 2018.

Ward, Stephen V. "Place Marketing: A Historical Comparison of Britain and North America." In *The Entrepreneurial City: Geographies of Politics, Regime and Representation*, edited by Tim Hall and Phil Hubbard, 31–53. Chichester: John Wiley & Sons, 1998a.

Ward, Stephen V. *Selling Places: The Marketing and Promotion of Towns and Cities, 1850–2000.* London, New York: E & FN Spon, Routledge, 1998b.

Wikipedia. "List of Coca-Cola Slogans." https://en.wikipedia.org/wiki/List_of_Coca-Cola_slogans. Accessed 14 November 2022.

Wippel, Steffen. *Islam als "Corporate Identity" von Wirtschafts- und Wohlfahrtseinrichtungen: Eine Fallstudie aus Ägypten.* Berlin: Das Arabische Buch, 1995.

Wippel, Steffen. "Oman and the Indian Ocean Rim: Economic Integration Across Conventional Meta-Regions." In *Regionalizing Oman: Political, Economic and Social Dynamics*, edited by Steffen Wippel, 159–183. Dordrecht, Heidelberg, et al.: Springer, 2013.

Wippel, Steffen. *The Reality and Hyperreality of Other Places: Integrated Tourism Complexes and Container Ports in Oman.* Berlin: Klaus Schwarz, 2016.

Wippel, Steffen. "The Globalisation of 'Secondary Cities' in the Middle East and North Africa: Conceptual Considerations and Empirical Findings." *Hespéris-Tamuda* 56.4 (2021): 47–95. https://www.hesperis-tamuda.com/Downloads/2021/fascicule-4/3.pdf. Accessed 2 December 2021.

Wippel, Steffen, Katrin Bromber, Christian Steiner, and Birgit Krawietz, eds. *Under Construction: Logics of Urbanism in the Gulf Region.* Farnham, Burlington: Ashgate, 2014.

Steffen Wippel

Branding the Middle East: A Review of Regional Manifestations of a Global Phenomenon

1 Meandering in a Bird's Flight through the Middle East and North Africa

Branding has its ancient roots in the wider Mediterranean and the Middle East, as we have seen in the preceding conceptual chapter. Throughout history, branding products, persons, and places – even if the concept did not yet exist by this name – has been practised in the Arab, Ottoman, and Islamic realms. Especially with increasing contemporary globalisation and implementation of neoliberal agendas, the pressure on nations and cities for competitive positioning and worlding has dramatically increased everywhere in the Middle East and North Africa (MENA). In particular, the hydrocarbon-based ascension of the Arab Gulf countries and their quest to prepare for a post-oil and post-gas era, with Dubai clearly at the forefront, has given pervasive branding endeavours a particular push. Supported by technological advances and in a world of growing postmodern experiments, these places excelled in constructing hyperreal worlds and preparing virtual presentations, which perfectly fit the global attention economy. This allowed Christian Steiner and Steffen Wippel to define place branding as one of "four – overlapping and interpenetrating – regional and transregional megatrends" in MENA urbanism, which is used "to perform a double task, one outward-oriented to create and disseminate politically, economically, and culturally appealing images, but another directed toward the local population to (re)shape urban and national identities and legitimate political action."[1] Yet, they also concluded: "The strengthened attempts at place branding, which means transforming cities' characters from a socio-political arena into an easily readable object of investment and consumption, have not gained as much academic attention as could be expected."[2]

Last but not least, this coincides with the fact that the world's largest contiguous, densest, and longest-lasting cluster of neopatrimonial-authoritarian regimes is to be found in the MENA region. With few exceptions, its political systems can be

1 Steiner and Wippel, 2019: 7.
2 Steiner and Wippel, 2019: 6.

https://doi.org/10.1515/9783110741100-006

characterised as relatively consistently non-democratic for many decades, despite the temporary upheavals in the wake of the Arab Spring. The broad spectrum of authoritarian regimes includes autocratically run republics, some of them currently engaged in (civil) wars or having become "failed states."[3] Among Arab monarchies in the Gulf states, a family-dynastic, rentier-state-based form of political rule prevails, based on traditional (in Saudi Arabia: also religious) legitimacy. In contrast, in highly personalised monarchies such as Jordan and Morocco, power is concentrated in the hands of the individual ruler. At the same time, these countries present economically different degrees of neoliberalisation.[4] In authoritarian regimes, political legitimacy is primarily achieved through the personal origins, merit, and charisma – i.e. the personal brands – of the respective rulers, who see themselves as protectors of their subjects. Spectacular urbanism, in combination with royal or presidential visions, is particularly helpful to distract citizens' attention from omnipresent economic, social, and political grievances and to build up positive external reputation.

Regionally, this volume is confined to the Middle East and North Africa. Generations of authors have attempted to define this part of the world, which is characterised by contrasting natural and human traits and, at the same time, by strong transregional entanglements.[5] Hence, definitions vary, largely by historical time, geographical position, research question, and even the language used. In a pragmatic way, the region under study in this volume is understood as the mostly uncontested core of the Arab world, from the Arabian Peninsula through Mesopotamia and the Levant to the North African countries that have a Mediterranean shore, even if all these designations might also be debatable.[6] Added to this are the modern states of Turkey and Iran and their imperial predecessors. Countries like Mauritania and Sudan form linguistic, cultural, and political interstices at the region's periphery. To accommodate larger regional understandings and strong historical and contemporary influences and ties, some adjacent areas of the "Islamicate world," from Europe, the Sahel, and West Africa to South and Central Asia, are taken into account.

For a long time, branding studies concentrated on the Western world and emerging economies, notably in eastern parts of Asia. Diverse samples of urban

3 On the various regime types, see, e.g. Derichs and Demmelhuber, 2014; Bank, Richter, and Sunik, 2014.

4 Compare, as a hint, e.g. Bertelsmann Stiftung, 2020.

5 On shifting definitions of the Middle East, cf., e.g., Scheffler, 2003; on transregional entanglements, Wippel and Fischer-Tahir, 2018.

6 As an adjective, "Middle Eastern" is sometimes used as a shortcut for the entire MENA region, and sometimes only refers to its actually designated Eastern parts.

and place branding studies up to the late 2000s/early 2010s showed that only a negligible number of case studies were devoted to the Middle East and Africa.[7] However, all these studies are based in a narrow base of pertinent specialised journals, limited with respect to the disciplines studied, and, in particular, biased in favour of publications exclusively in the English language. But voluminous handbooks that allude to a considerable number of case studies also usually neglect MENA cities and nations.[8] Only in recent years has the range of case studies been extended to more parts of the Global South, including the Middle East and North Africa, following efforts there to enter the branding business more eagerly. Quite early, already in the late 2000s, Dubai, but only it, played a prominent role in empirical, and increasingly critical, branding studies; other parts of the region followed, especially other Gulf places, and the entire region, from Turkey to Morocco. Approaches to empirical cases are not only descriptive, they also reflect both application-oriented and critical investigations of the images conveyed, the relevant actors, and larger economic and political contexts. However, in its width and breadth, the region remains underrepresented compared with the entire array of empirical branding research; encompassing overviews and anthologies are still missing, as are thoroughly critical analyses. Many indications of branding strategies in the MENA region can be found only in other academic publications, e.g. on local consumption, Islamic lifestyle, urban development, and regional geopolitics, where they do not constitute the actual focus, are part of larger studies, or can merely be distilled by reading between the lines of certain marginal notes and remarks.

The following empirical overview of branding Middle Eastern products, persons, and places, which is based on a variety of publications, attempts to be as encompassing as possible, but remains exemplary, selective, and subjective. Given the variety of cases and sources, the presentation is not as redundant as it could be. In the following, this chapter starts with a few tables and illustrations pointing to pertinent rankings, major international events, and general trends in branding in and of the MENA region. Commodity and company brands as well as the branding of certain personalities and political groups are discussed in separate subsections. As most of the chapters in this book have to do with places, even if not only with place branding in the proper sense, the major part of this chapter consists of a meandering bird's-eye view of the region, which gives details on previous work on and general impressions of the branding of countries, regions, cities,

7 Cf. Lucarelli and Berg, 2011: 17; Andersson, 2014: 149.

8 Compare Dinnie, 2008, who addresses only Egypt among more than 20 country cases; or Dinnie, 2011, who mentions no MENA city among nearly 20 case studies.

and project sites. This starts with the outstanding case of Dubai, then extends to other Arab Gulf places, and crosses the rest of West Asia and North Africa, before catching a glimpse of more peripheral places. However, it sometimes proves difficult to distinguish between the various objects of branding, as especially the branding of places and (political) persons, and of products or events and places is often closely intertwined. Implicit or explicit reference to the previous chapter that presents global developments in the branding business, diverse conceptual approaches, and the main research questions is included in these sections. A short conclusion summarises the findings, gives an outlook on research gaps, and links with the next chapter that presents the contributions to this volume.

2 A Few Glimpses: In the Race for Rank and Recognition

As we know, rankings and statistical figures are highly esteemed tools in branding, and placement in these lists incites increased efforts to brand a product, corporation, nation, or city. Initially, these rankings concentrated on the Western world and sometimes objects of East Asian origin. Progressively, other parts of the Global South have been included, even if Middle Eastern and African countries have appeared only in fits and starts. Despite all methodological problems, these quantifications indicate a gradual or sometimes rapid progress in the branding business, and hence of the value of brands, not only of Gulf states, but also in the rest of the MENA region.

First, several consulting firms and other institutions have established worldwide, regional, and national rankings of corporate brands, sometimes corresponding to sectors. According to BrandFinance, there was a shift over the course of the 2010s from firms from Western, namely Anglo-American countries, to firms in the USA and China in the global brand value top ranks.[9] In 2021, Saudi Aramco was the Middle East's most valuable brand, equivalent to world rank 33 (2020: 24), followed by ADNOC, another oil and gas company, this one from the UAE (Table 1). Telecoms, banks, and airlines have also been strongly present among regional top brands.

9 Cf. BrandFinance, 2022, which defines the six GCC states plus Iraq, Jordan, and Lebanon as the "Middle East." Most other rankings of "global brands" do not include any MENA countries or companies.

Table 1: Top 20 corporate brands in the Middle East and Gulf region 2021
Source: BrandFinance, 2022.

Regional rank*	Company name	Country	Sector	Global rank (Top 500)	Global sectoral rank°	Brand value in bn USD**
–	Apple	USA	*Tech*	*1*	*1*	*263.4*
1	Saudi Aramco	KSA	Oil & gas	33	2	37.5
2	ADNOC	UAE	Oil & gas	163	10	10.8
3	STC	KSA	Telecom	189	13	9.2
4	Etisalat	UAE	Telecom	208	15	8.5
5	QNB	Qatar	Banking	321	48	6.1
6	Emirates	UAE	Airlines	421	4	4.7
7	SABIC	KSA	Chemicals	495	2	4.0
8	Emirates NBD	UAE	Banking		74	3.7
9	FAB	UAE	Banking		77	3.6
10	Al-Rajhi Bank	KSA	Banking		81	3.4
11	Ooredoo	Qatar	Telecom		40	3.2
12	NCB	KSA	Banking		110	2.4
13	Almarai	KSA	Food		33	2.2
14	Zain	Kuwait	Telecom		54	2.1
15	ADCB	UAE	Banking		120	1.8
16	du	UAE	Telecom		62	2.3
17	Qatar Airways	Qatar	Airlines		12	1.6
18	Dubai Islamic Bank	UAE	Banking		145	1.6
19	Emaar Properties	UAE	Real Estate		23	1.4
20	Enoc	UAE	Oil & gas		–	1.6

* The "region" includes only GCC members, Jordan, Lebanon, and Iraq. For information purposes, I added rank 1 worldwide. ** Data is freely available only for the regional Top Ten, supplemented by national rankings. ° From the global Top 50 oil & gas; Top 150 telecoms; Top 500 banks; Top 25 chemicals; Top 100 food; Top 50 airlines; Top 25 real estate services. °° In 2020. KSA: Kingdom of Saudi Arabia.

As more and more firms have been included in the rankings, the well-reputed Emirates airline declined to regional place 6 (2021) from place 1 (2010), when oil companies were not yet included – its logo also serves to brand other amenities in South India, as Sophie-Theresa Trenka-Dalton demonstrates in her photo essay in this volume. Since 2021, the Covid pandemic, too, contributed to downscaling economically affected firms, like airlines and banks. Moreover, in the global top

500 ranking, nearly exclusively Gulf brands dominate, with Turkish Airlines and *Maroc Télécom* being temporarily among the few exceptions.[10]

Table 2: Nation brand indices (global ranks)
Sources: BrandFinance, 2022; FutureBrand, 2020; Bloom Consulting, 2019a, 2019b.

BrandFinance Nation Brands 2020		**BrandFinance Global Soft Power Index**		**FutureBrand Country Index 2020**		**Bloom Consulting Country Brand Ranking 2019/20**			
Top 100 most valuable nation brands		Top 100 Countries		Top 75 Countries		Tourism edition		Trade edition	
Country	Rank	Country	Rank	Country	Rank	Country	Rank	Country	Rank
USA	*1*	*Germany*	*1*	*Japan*	*1*	*USA*	*1*	*USA*	*1*
India	*7*	UAE	17	UAE	9	Turkey	12	*India*	*4*
UAE	18	KSA	24	Qatar	18	Israel	13	Turkey	19
KSA	20	Israel	25	Israel	22	*India*	*18*	UAE	29
Turkey	30	Qatar	26	Oman	25	Egypt	27	Israel	32
Israel	37	Turkey	27	Kuwait	27	Morocco	40	KSA	35
Iran	38	Egypt	34	KSA	28	KSA	63	Egypt	46
Qatar	41	*India*	*36*	Algeria	34	Qatar	68	Morocco	48
Egypt	51	Kuwait	42	Turkey	51	UAE	72	Iran	50
Kuwait	53	Morocco	48	Egypt	54	Jordan	75	Jordan	65
Algeria	58	Jordan	50	Morocco	64	Oman	77	Iraq	68
Iraq	60	Oman	51	*India*	*67*	Tunisia	81	Qatar	75

The table shows the regional Top Ten countries, plus the world's no. 1 and India. Non-MENA countries are named in italics.

In sectoral brand listings, Aramco and ADNOC have taken ranks 2 and 10 worldwide in the oil and gas sector, but remained the only two from the Middle East in the global Top 50 as of 2021. Seven companies from the MENA region are represented in the Top 150 telecom ranking, starting at place 13 and below. In the Top 200 banking list, 15 MENA brands, all below rank 48, are included. Among airlines, five are among the Top 50, with Emirates taking global rank 4. Yet, the well-known real estate company and developer *Emaar* from Dubai ranked only 23rd in the 2020 worldwide real estate sector list, while a dairy company like Almarai from

10 Turkish Airlines ranks 15th and *Maroc Télécom* 101st on the respective global sectoral lists. Among African brands, *Maroc Télécom* is the first non-South African company, in place 13.

Saudi Arabia, which Natalie Koch describes in more detail in this volume, appears at global place 33 in the food sector.

Second, *nation brands* are evaluated, based on different methodologies using brand strength and value, brand scores, and brand reputation. According to the Nation Brands index established by BrandFinance, the UAE has regularly turned up as the top-value regional brand in recent years; it has advanced from global place 27 (2015) to 17 (2021), with a brand value of 749 bn USD, beating Saudi Arabia and Turkey (Table 2).[11] Besides other Gulf states and Israel, Egypt and Iran have been among the upper regional ranks. Yet India, on which this edited volume includes another case study, has been constantly ranked much higher than MENA countries. BrandFinance also published the Global Soft Power Index, reflecting how national brands were perceived by the general public and specialists: it shows a similar order of MENA countries, with most of them doing (slightly) better than in the Nation Brand index. Similarly, the FutureBrand Country Index ranks the UAE first among MENA countries on its global lists, where it advanced from place 23 (2009) to 9 (2020).[12] Other Gulf countries progressed even more during the same period (e.g., Qatar from 70 to 18, Oman from 57 to 25). They closed ranks with Israel, which remained in the regional top, whereas Turkey first gained and then, from 2019 to 2020, lost rank again.

The East-West Communications Nation Brand Index 2008–2011 already ranked Gulf countries high among countries worldwide.[13] However, it also shows the UAE's heavy drop in score mentions in 2010 (from place 5 in 2008 to place 111) following the financial crisis, unlike other small Gulf states, before it rapidly recovered again in 2011 (to place 9). During the period covered, relatively stable Morocco advanced from place 154 to 73, while Tunisia, in the aftermath of the "Jasmine Revolution," dropped from rank 64 to 185. Hence, these rankings also reflect changing political and economic conditions. In addition, Bloom Consulting published two Country Brand Ranking indices: while Turkey and Israel both ranked high in tourism in 2019/20, but also had a relatively advanced position in trade, there is a striking difference in the UAE's trade position (29) vs. its rank in the tourism edition (72).[14] Finally, the 2015 Global Creativity Index, based on Richard Florida's "creative class" concept, considers Israel high on the list (place 30), followed, at a distance, by Iran, Syria, and Jordan, which clearly advance the Gulf countries. However, the

11 Cf. BrandFinance, 2022. In recent years, the same evaluation placed the UAE in places 6 (2019) and 3 (2017–2018) of the global Top Ten of the *Strongest* Nation Brands.

12 Cf. FutureBrand, 2020.

13 Cf. East West Communications, 2021.

14 Cf. Bloom Consulting, 2019a, 2019b.

publication shows huge divergences concerning subindices related to technology, talent, and especially tolerance, where MENA countries rank particularly low.[15]

Table 3: MENA cities in the GaWC world cities ranking
Source: GaWC, 2022.

1998 (n = 55)		**2010** (n = c. 525*)		**2020** (n = 707)
Alpha world cities		**Alpha-level cities**		
12	*London, New York, Paris, Tokyo*	α++	*London, New York*	*London, New York*
		α+	Dubai	Dubai
11		α	*Mumbai*	*Mumbai*
10		α-	Istanbul	Riyadh, Istanbul
Beta world cities		**Beta-level cities**		
9		β+	Cairo, Tel Aviv	Tel Aviv, Doha, Cairo, Beirut
8		β	Beirut, Riyadh	Abu Dhabi, Casablanca, Manama
7		β-	Abu Dhabi, Amman, Casablanca, Kuwait, Manama, Tunis	Kuwait, Tunis, Amman, Muscat, Jeddah
Gamma world cities		**Gamma-level cities**		
6		γ+	Jeddah, Doha,	Algiers
5		γ		Ankara
4	Istanbul	γ-	Muscat	
Evidence of world city formation		**Cities with sufficiency of services**		
3	Tel Aviv, *Mumbai*	hs	Algiers, Ankara	Dammam
2	Abu Dhabi, Cairo, Dubai, Riyadh	s	Alexandria, Haifa, Izmir, Jerusalem	Izmir, Alexandria, Bursa, Jerusalem, Haifa, Baghdad, Sana'a
1	Tehran			

* If the same size as 2008 and 2012 applies. Hs: High sufficiency; s: Sufficiency.
Besides MENA cities, this table also gives all cities worldwide in the respective top category and the first Indian metropolis (in italics). Note: There was an important change of evaluation criteria between 1998 and 2000.

Widely used and perceived rankings have also been produced for *urban brands*. As in academic research, the range of cities covered was initially slow to expand to

15 Cf. Florida, Mellander, and King, 2015: 40–60. The UAE is not included in this ranking.

include the Global South. Moreover, these listings are less regularly released and less comprehensive than for nation branding. The samples of cities by number and geographic coverage vary considerably from one index to another. As elsewhere in the world, MENA cities are strongly globalising and attempting to close ranks with other global cities. Whereas around the year 1300, Middle Eastern cities featured prominently in the "transcontinental archipelago of cities" from Eastern Asia to Western Europe,[16] John Friedmann's early contemporary "hierarchy of world cities" from 1986 did not include any African or West or South Asian city (except for Johannesburg, in the lowest tier).[17] Yet, the world city ranking of the Globalization and World Cities (GaWC) Research Network at Loughborough University, which measures connectivity in the field of advanced producer services, demonstrates that, since then, more and more MENA cities have appeared in these lists and advanced to upper ranks (Table 3).[18]

This is particularly evident for Dubai, which in the first 1998 edition still only showed a certain "evidence of world city formation," but quickly appeared on the alpha level of highly integrated, very important world cities, immediately below the global top dyad of London and New York. Well-established metropolises like Istanbul, Cairo, and Beirut, as well as relative newcomers such as Tel Aviv and Riyadh, have persistently held on to the regional lead, but Gulf cities like Abu Dhabi and Doha have also caught up.

Yet, few MENA cities are by now included in the evaluations of global urban brands. In 2017, the Top 100 of the Resonance World's Best City Brands considered only four MENA cities; Dubai ranked highest in the region, in place 22 worldwide, followed by Istanbul, Tel Aviv, and Doha (Table 4).[19] Ranks diverged considerably in the sub-categories: so Dubai was placed first among the City Brands for People, ninth among the City Brands for Prosperity, but only in places 58 and 63 in the Programming and Promotion categories, respectively. Dubai and Doha notably excelled for their prosperity (global ranks 1 and 2), while additional Middle Eastern cities (including Kuwait, Muscat, and Amman) were among the Top Ten places for people. FutureBrand also ranks the world's most influential cities.[20] Here, in the global Top 20 of the years 2014, 2019, and 2020, it names, first, Dubai again (oscillating around place 10), seconded by Istanbul, which advanced from rank 21 to 12 over the period. In addition, based on the work of the pioneer of place branding, the 2020 Anholt-Ipsos City Brands Index, ranked Dubai as the only Middle Eastern

16 Cf. Taylor, 2004: 8–10.

17 Presented in Taylor, 2004: 22–24.

18 Cf. GaWC, 2022.

19 Cf. Resonance, 2017.

20 Cf. FutureBrand, 2020.

and African city in the third tier (places 21–30) and Cairo, Doha, and Riyadh in the final tier of 50 metropolises worldwide.[21]

Table 4: Top city brands (global ranks)
Sources: Resonance, 2017; FutureBrand, 2020; Michael and Sedghi, 2014.

Resonance World's Best City Brands		**FutureBrand Most influential cities**		**Anholt-Ipsos City Brands Index**		**The Guardian/ Saffron**	
Top 100, 2017		Top 20, 2020		Top 50, 2020		57 cities, 2014	
City	Rank	City	Rank	City	Tier	City	Rank
London	*1*	*New York*	*1*	*London*	*1*	*Los Angeles*	*1*
Dubai	22	Dubai	9	Dubai	21–30	Dubai	10
Istanbul	49	Istanbul	12	Cairo	41–50	Istanbul	11
Tel Aviv	64			Doha	41–50	*Mumbai*	*19*
Mumbai	73			Riyadh	41–50	Mecca	21
Doha	79					Riyadh	29
						Abu Dhabi	34
						Doha	45
						Marrakech	47
						Tel Aviv	49
						Algiers	50

Includes global top city and the first-placed Indian city (in italics).

In 2014, *The Guardian* published the results of another assessment, which included nine MENA cities among 57 metropolises studied worldwide.[22] This survey ranked Dubai tenth, closely followed by Istanbul in place 11; as a noticeable up-and-comer, Mecca arrived in place 21. Whereas for Dubai and Istanbul the "buzz strength," based on conventional and social media mentions, exceeded "asset strength," which captures infrastructure, prosperity, safety, climate, and attractions, this reverses for most cities in lower ranks, such as Doha, Marrakech, and Tel Aviv, where tangible assets contributed the most by far to their rating.

One measure to promote cities beyond borders is labelling them cultural capitals; besides self-proclamation, the regular nomination of cultural cities by regional entities expanded from the European context across other parts of the world.[23] Each year since 1996, the League of Arab States nominates an Arab Capital of Cul-

21 Cf. Ipsos, 2020.
22 Cf. Michael and Sedghi, 2014.
23 On the European initiative's role in branding, cf. Vanolo, 2017: 34.

ture "to promote and celebrate Arab culture and encourage cooperation in the Arab region."[24] In a similar vein, the Islamic World Educational, Scientific and Cultural Organization (ICESCO) presents three annual Capitals of Islamic Culture, one each in the Arab, African, and Asian subregions.[25] Since 2005, numerous metropolises throughout the MENA region, as well as other renowned second-tier cities, have been awarded these distinctions (Fig. 1). Sporadically, MENA cities have also been selected European or African Capitals of Culture (respectively: Istanbul 2010; and Rabat 2021, replacing initially nominated Marrakech).[26]

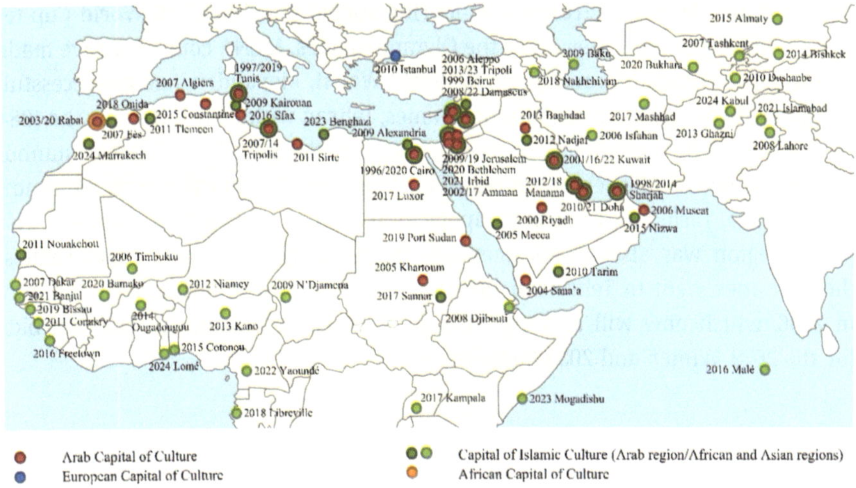

Fig. 1: Capitals of culture in the MENA region
Sources: Wikipedia, 2021a, 2021b, 2021c; ALECSO, 2019; ICESCO, 2021; UCLGA, 2023. Map: Wikimedia, 2010. Work released into the public domain. Reworked by Steffen Wippel, January 2022.
Borders on this map are not politically authoritative.

Organising a World's Fair has a similar effect on worldwide attention. Since the inception of the World's Fair in 1851, Dubai was the first in the Arab world to host one – Expo 2020 (postponed to 2021/22 due to the covid crisis), under the motto "Connecting Minds, Creating the Future."[27] For this event, Izmir, which

24 Cf. Wikipedia, 2021a; ALECSO, 2019.
25 Cf. Wikipedia, 2021b; ICESCO, 2021. Recently, compared with the map in Fig. 1, smaller changes occurred: Abidjan is now the African capital for 2023, while Mogadishu will hold the 2025 award; Aşgabat will be the Asian Capital of Islamic Culture in 2025.
26 Cf. Wikipedia, 2021c; UCLGA, 2023; Wüst and Nicolai, 2022: 13.
27 For a list of expos, cf. Wikipedia, 2022b; see also BIE, 2022.

had beaten Ankara at the national level, was a contender in the last round, whereas Tangier, as mentioned in Steffen Wippel's chapter in this volume, was a candidate in the final round for the World's Fair 2012. For Expo 2030, Riyadh is one of the current candidates. Besides, specialised world exhibitions took place in the region, namely twice in Israel in the 1950s (on desert conquest and citriculture), in Antalya (2016, on horticulture), and in Doha (2023, also on horticulture).

Sporting events have a similar prestige benefit. Among the highest-profile competitions, Qatar hosted the MENA region's first FIFA Football World Cup in 2022. Morocco has unsuccessfully bid for the World Cup five times.[28] According to recent reports, Saudi Arabia is strongly considering applying for the 2030 World Cup together with Egypt and Greece. For the Olympic Games, MENA countries have made it only to the elimination round: up to World War II, Alexandria had unsuccessfully applied three times for the Summer Games; Tehran withdrew its bid for the 1984 Games during the selection process (Table 5). For the post–2000 Games, Istanbul applied unsuccessfully several times; other bids were not shortlisted to the candidature stage, including Erzurum's application for the 2026 Winter Games.[29] The MENA region was also a latecomer for the similarly prestigious Asian Games: the first ones went to Tehran in 1974, while the next were hosted by Doha only in 2006, which now will also organise the 2030 edition. Saudi Arabia won bids for the 2029 Winter and 2034 Summer Games.

Table 5: High-profile sport events in MENA cities
Source: Wikipedia, 2023a and 2023b.

City	Candidate cities for the Olympic Games			Host cities of the Asian Games
	Unsuccessful bid	Bid not shortlisted	Bid withdrawn	
Alexandria	1916, 1936, 1940			
Tehran			1984	1974
Istanbul	2000, 2008, 2020	2004, 2012		
Erzurum		2026 (Winter)		
Cairo		2008		
Doha		2016, 2020		2006, 2030
Riyadh				2034
Trojena (NEOM)				2029 (Winter)

The general understanding is that brands are primarily transmitted by catchy slogans and logos. Logos of iconic product and company brands, such as Emirates air-

28 Cf. Wikipedia, 2023c.
29 Cf. Wikipedia, 2023b.

lines, were already mentioned in the lead introductory chapter. Most, but not all MENA countries and some cities have also started to use tourism logos and slogans for destination branding on a regular basis.[30] Few have acquired such a presence in general perception as the "Incredible !ndia" slogan and logo, which is perhaps one of the most pertinent destination brands in the Global South. While countries like Egypt and Tunisia have changed and further developed their textual and visual marks, the brands of other countries, such as Syria's "Always Beautiful," seem to be quite outdated given their political situation. Symbols often integrate the respective place names. Among the more striking symbols, the Turkish tourism logo plays with the historical tulip motif (Fig. 2a), which Birgit Krawietz presents as an important branding item in this volume. Egypt, on which Karin Ahlberg reports in more detail, delves even deeper into its past as a country "where it all begins" and features a name tag with a final t recalling the ancient Egyptian hieroglyph *ankh* (key of life) (Fig. 2b), which, in the early 2010s, replaced the Pharaonic sun disk and the slogan "Nothing Compares!"[31] Tourism logos developed for countries like Jordan, Qatar, and the city-state of Dubai play with wordmarks in both Arabic and Latin script (Fig. 2c, 2d).[32] The same is true of the logo of Oman, where "Beauty has an address", as Thibaut Klinger describes in this book.[33] Israel, in contrast, after a series of earlier advertising slogans, has promoted the "Land of Creation" since 2013, which can be read historically and religiously, as well as with regard to its contemporary cultural and economic creativity, and a logo referring to its diversity that contrasts with neighbouring countries. Similarly, Lebanese campaigns, "Live Love Lebanon," "Passion for Living" (2018), and "A crazy love," to reinvigorate tourism during the covid crisis (Fig. 4b), hint at its reputation as an uncommon, open-minded lifestyle destination, a motif Ghassan Moussawi takes up in a later chapter. Besides many slogans lacking real content, some countries also play on words with their country names such as Djibouti ("Djibeauty") and Morocco ("Much Mor").

4 Branding Commodities and Corporations

The branding of commodities and corporations in and from the MENA region is certainly the least systematically considered in the academic literature. According-

30 Cf. among other publications and blogs, Schaffrinna, 2022; Laura, 2022; Homes & Leisure, 2022.

31 Cf. also Nation Branding, 2011.

32 On Dubai, cf. Thorton, 2015. The wordmark also exists in other colour combinations. Its interwoven scripts represent Dubai's "fusion of cultures and nationalities."

33 Cf. also Wippel, 2013: 177–178.

Fig. 2: Examples of MENA destination brand logos
Promotional logos of a) Turkey; b) Egypt; c) Jordan; d) Dubai.
Sources: Schaffrinna, 2022 (Turkey, Egypt, Jordan); Thornton, 2015 (Dubai).

ly, the following explanations are also rather eclectic insights into the subject. In the ancient history of branding, our area of study already played a special role: branding practices on animals, bodies, and handicrafts can be traced back to the larger West Asian and Mediterranean regions from the Indus valley through Mesopotamia, the Levant, Arabia, and the Nile Valley to the Carthaginian, Greek, and Roman realms.

In more recent times, if we skip the colonial era, in particular since the *infitāḥ*, the economic Opening Policy, inaugurated in the 1970s first in Egypt, transnational companies and their products have entered the Middle Eastern markets. Yet, market penetration was not always easy. Sometimes, these foreign brands were regarded with suspicion and, especially in times of crises, had to struggle with perfidious rumours. Notorious cases have been Coca Cola, which was criticised in 2000 because the mirror-image of its Arabic signature can be read as “lā Muḥāmmad, lā Makka” (there is no Muhammad and no Mecca); the detergent Ariel was blamed for the similarity of its name with that of Israeli prime minister Ariel Sharon and of its logo depicting the path of an atom with the Star of David.[34] Such allegations could be countered only by the issue of a religious *fatwā* (legal opinion), branding as a local product, and the replacement of the logo. Gradually, such global corporations adapted their centralised, Western marketing concepts to culturally more sensitive promotion strategies: they tried to convince addressees of their local rootedness, established local marketing departments with a domestic workforce, translated global campaigns for the national markets, adjusted their products to fit local consumption patterns, and communicated socially responsible activities. Thereafter, advertising billboards pervaded the urbanscape,[35] and many international brands representing a particular way of life became present in peo-

34 Cf. Kehrer, 2005.
35 Cf. Abotera and Ashoub, 2020.

ple's minds, even if most cannot afford them.[36] But sometimes international brands appeal to the extent that counterfeits are imported, often from China, or locally produced and distributed. Fake brands, using (slightly altered) famous global names and logos are found across shops and markets in the region and are, in principle, subject to legal prosecution.[37]

Brands across all sectors have also emerged from local producers since the industrial era has arrived in the MENA region. A few renowned brands have already been mentioned (Table 1). While Arab oil companies needed much less vigorous promotion and positioning in the market, significant branding campaigns have pushed forward Gulf companies, in particular, which have boomed in recent decades in sectors such as transport, tourism, and real estate. In a highly competitive and globalised environment, constant (re)positioning is necessary, e.g. of airlines that also serve as national icons. Oman Air's "The Soul of Arabia" campaign has been a prominent co-branding case that promoted the company and the country simultaneously.[38] The airline needed a revamp when it wanted to develop from a regional short-haul carrier into a full-fledged international airline competing with companies from the Arabian Peninsula and the Indian subcontinent. With the help of the German Shanghai Berlin agency, it launched an attention-grabbing cross-media campaign to create awareness of a destination that had been virtually unknown to most Europeans until then. To position the country in contrast to spectacular emirates such as Dubai as a still pristine country with a lot of history and culture, the campaign featured high-quality photographs with exotic sceneries and faces. The sovereign wealth funds of Dubai, Abu Dhabi, Qatar, and Bahrain, which are among the largest in the world, also engage in intense brand competition, seeking to position themselves in certain niches (such as insurance, Islamic finance, asset management, etc.).[39]

A comparative study demonstrates that in the late 1990s, the intention to buy locally produced goods was much stronger in Arab than in Asian and Western communities living in the UAE; however, this consumer nationalism was still weak compared with the general preference for international brands and was not necessarily reflected in actual purchasing behaviour.[40] Another article shows that almost half of studied Saudi TV ads used a foreign language, mostly English, which is connotated with prestige, sophistication, and modernity and can be un-

36 Cf., e.g., also Adham, 2004.

37 Among the abundant literature, cf. for instance on Chinese-North African trade, consisting mostly of fakes, Belguidoum and Pliez, 2015.

38 Cf. Rajasekar and Moideenkutty, 2007; Karl, 2012. Cf. also Wippel, 2014: 107, 112.

39 Cf. Ali and Al-Aswad, 2012.

40 Cf. Uncles and Saurazas, 2000.

derstood as a kind of symbolic capital.[41] The defence of national products takes place in a context of increasing "war on brands" and origins and of rising political tensions.[42] The country-of-origin effect played a role, e.g., in the widespread boycott of Danish brands after emotions in the Arab and Islamic world had boiled over in 2015 because of the Mohammed cartoons in the newspaper *Jyllands-Posten.*[43] Similar calls were raised against France in 2020, after the publication of other caricatures in French media; in part, the same political rejection targeted the USA and its products. Other countries can benefit from positive perceptions, such as Switzerland, at least before its ban on building mosques. In Morocco, a social networks campaign in 2018 called on national consumers to boycott products of the *Centrale Danone* brand, known for its dairy products, but also a well-known Moroccan mineral water and major petrol station chain, with the stated aim of protecting consumers' rights and purchasing power from the greed and high profit margins of manufacturing companies. While some celebrities joined the campaign, authorities opposed it, calling it sabotage of consumer goods produced in Morocco and a betrayal of the nation and its farmers.[44]

On a regional level, in the 2010s, traders, industrial leaders, and business associations in Morocco – as in Algeria, Tunisia, and Jordan – increasingly complained that cheap Turkish products inundated Moroccan markets. An amendment of the bilateral free trade agreement in 2020 allowed the Moroccan government to re-establish custom duties on Turkish textiles and to exclude a long list of commodities from free trade, in order to attenuate the effects of covid on the pandemic-plagued country.[45] Some experts, however, linked this action also to persisting bilateral political tensions and, especially, to pressures from Saudi Arabia and the UAE, two important partners in Morocco's economic diversification strategy, to boycott Turkey. Saudi Arabia had already started an informal embargo on brands of Turkish origin, and the Saudi Chamber of Commerce called on citizens to shun "everything that is Turkish" in answer to the Turkish government's "hostilities" towards the kingdom. This was due to its political role, especially during the Qatar boycott, which Natalie Koch considers more closely in her chapter, but also in supporting unwelcome Islamist movements.

---

41 Cf. Olwi, 2022. Most of these advertisements were in a mix of English and Arabic, and only a small percentage were exclusively in English or, for perfumes, mixed with Italian.

42 On economically motivated nation branding and "made in" promotion, cf. also below.

43 Cf., e.g., Alserhan, 2010a: 45.

44 Cf., e.g., Berrada, 2018.

45 Cf. Pérez, 2020; Allouche, 2020.

"Islamic branding"[46] has become a field of its own. It accompanies the booming economic and social sector that proclaims that it follows Islamic rules and values and provides, in particular, *šarīʿa*-compliant *ḥalāl* brands that are consistent with religious principles of permissible behaviour and products. Branding such commodities and services has developed into a growing business; because of their assumed quality, Islamic products are also widely consumed by non-Muslim customers. On the academic side, numerous specialised conferences have taken place, and journals, research groups, and institutions were founded to develop "the theory and practice of marketing in the Muslim world and beyond"[47] and to meet the enormous demand for experts. Application-oriented research and empirical evaluation seem to dominate, while far fewer critical analyses with a social or cultural sciences background exist. Research topics start from how to advance Islamic branding, the possibilities and limits of Islamic advertising, and commitment to social responsibility and economic development; and they extend to studies of specific sectors, consumption patterns, and users' brand perceptions.[48]

Sectors that get particular attention from Islamic branding are food and beverages (e.g. excluding pork and alcohol), pharmaceuticals, cosmetics (no alcoholic ingredients or animal fats), clothing and other lifestyle products, and services, particulary in the fields of finance (usury-free transactions), hospitality (no serving of alcohol, ban on gambling), and logistics (especially the prevention of contamination with impure products).[49] In the latter field, many places within and outside the Islamic world are striving to develop into *ḥalāl* hubs and logistic centres (e.g. with their own warehouses and slaughterhouses), where Islamic products can be adequately processed, stored, and transhipped – compare Heiko Schuss in this volume for Dubai's various endeavours to become the Capital of the Islamic Economy. Also, well-known and well-reputed multinational corporations want to participate in the promising business. Their strategies of "branding to Muslims" started in the 1970s and included differentiating and converting their product portfolio to fit the needs of Muslim markets, as well as developing and introducing new brands. Especially in the food sector, firms from non-Muslim countries still dominated in 2010, while the Muslim-owned large- and small-scale local brands had not yet penetrated international markets. Vice versa, the Islamic banking segment was

46 In the following, cf. especially Shirazi, 2016; Alserhan, 2010a and 2010b.

47 International Islamic Marketing Association, 2023.

48 Cf., e.g., the list of articles and topics covered in the *International Journal of Islamic Marketing and Branding*, 2015–2017.

49 According to Fischer, 2012, in the Middle East, *ḥalāl* primarily relates to meat, while in South East Asia it encompasses all consumable goods.

primarily a Muslim business, although Western and Far Eastern interest in the sector was also growing.

Scholars call for an Islamic branding "to change the way goods and services are sold to Muslim consumers."[50] With certain restrictions, marketing and branding are considered to be in line with Islamic values, since according to the *Qur'ān* and *ḥadīṯ*, the Prophet Muhammad himself gave new names to persons close to him to honour them and renamed personal property to avoid unethical connotations; specific colours were chosen for special occasions, and signet rings served to "brand" letters in Islamic history.[51] But branding techniques should respect the motivations and spiritual needs of target consumers and make marketing decisions in accordance with religious guidelines. Baker Ahmad Alserhan distinguishes three modes of Islamic branding: compliance with religious Law (*ḥalāl* brands); reference to Muslim-country origin (independent of factual *šarīʿa* compliance); and Muslim-customer target groups (regardless of their devoutness). "True" Islamic brands then result if all three characteristics come together. Indeed, certification with *ḥalāl* labels and logos that confirm their accordance with Islamic rules plays a central role in Islamic branding: it generates trust in the products and can be regarded as a qualification tool.[52] Accordingly, since the 1970s, certification agencies have developed all over the world, across Southeast Asia and the Arab world to Western countries. However, there is no universally authoritative accreditation body, and reputations and qualifications fluctuate, with Malaysian, Saudi, Emirati, and Sudanese labels considered the most trustworthy.

Due to its early development and great importance, the banking system has attracted particular consideration. Ishtiaq and Siddiqui show that for Islamic banks in Pakistan, Arabic script, emblems like minarets, crescents, and historical coins, the green colour associated with Islam, religious terms, addressing religious sentiments, and avoiding images of living creatures and women in particular are characteristic of their public appearance.[53] Using the Corporate Identity approach, Steffen Wippel examined the degree to which Islamic features were used by various allegedly Islamic economic and social institutions in Egypt in the 1980s and '90s.[54] Across the entire sector, the most pronounced feature was the will to follow detailed rules of conduct, the use of corresponding self-designations, and the linguistic and visual content of communication. However, there were also large differences in the manifestation of Islamic identity characteristics between, but also

---

50 Doherty, 2015: 1, 3.
51 Cf. Ishtiaq and Siddiqui, 2016: 34–35.
52 For *ḥalāl* certification, cf. also Fischer, 2012.
53 Cf. Ishtiaq and Siddiqui, 2016.
54 Cf. Wippel, 1995.

within, the various sub-sectors. Islamic banks and welfare institutions used the most "Islamic" identifiers. An Islamic corporate design (consisting of graphics, architecture, and clothing) was only moderately developed; graphic elements associated with Islam (logos, calligraphy, decor, symbols, colours) were most likely to be applied by banks, whereas clothing considered to be in conformity with Islam played virtually no role in their daily work. Intense corporate communication was mainly practised by banks, investment companies, and welfare associations. In some cases, the personal identity of the owners, chairmen, and founders of the institutions played a major role. In addition to Islamic aspects, they also repeatedly emphasised their openness to the world, national responsibility, and conformity with state rules and could be regarded as typical phenomena of the *infitāḥ* period.

Alina Kokoschka shows how everyday products have increasingly become significant for Muslim religious practice.[55] In pre-war Syria in the 2000s, the Islamisation of society and neoliberal globalisation led to visible changes in the field of consumer culture, such as wearing and using symbols of faith. Syrian and international companies increasingly discovered "Muslims" as a target group. Islamic-influenced images, signs, and things proliferated in the public sphere and were consciously used by producers to market their merchandises. Historical references were made, but the aesthetics of these brands were also suitable for a lived critique of existing political and economic conditions, whereas Islamic utopias were designed on packaging and in fashion. Comparable changes can be observed from Lebanon and Turkey to Muslim neighbourhoods in Northern metropolises. In her contribution to this volume, Kokoschka discusses how international brands are "Islamised" and how fakes gain reputation, when "Islamic Garments Meet French *Haute Couture.*"

Drinking studies are a specific area of research that turned to the branding of the beverage industry. The "Cola Wars" that are being fought in the Middle East demonstrate how brands can become ideological symbols. Following the second Palestinian *intifada*, the 9/11 attacks, and the invasion of Iraq, in the early 2000s anti-American resentment soared in the Middle East, but also in parts of Europe. This included the rejection of American brands like Coca Cola as a worldwide-established symbol of the "American way of life."[56] Several competitors attempted to challenge the multinational producer and to open a niche market by launching "Muslim-friendly" drinks. The most prominent brand was perhaps Mecca Cola, cre-

55 Cf. Kokoschka, 2019.

56 Cf. Aggarwal, Knudsen, and Maamoun, 2009; Ram, 2005. In 2021, Coca Cola ranked 39 among the most valuable brands worldwide (but took first place on the list of non-alcoholic drinks); cf. Brand-Finance, 2022.

ated in France, whose tagline “Ne buvez plus idiot, buvez engagé” called for “committed” drinking. The producer did not spend much money on advertising, but developed by word of mouth. Although there was some criticism from the clergy about the “misuse” of the name of a holy place, the brand expanded rapidly from small shops into supermarkets and into other European, Arab, and Asian countries. According to Uri Ram, in the end, the product tried to unite apparently opposing aspects, such as cultural authenticity with capitalistic commercialisation and symbols like the bottle design, lettering, and colours, which emulate those of its great model, but using Muslim rhetoric. Other brands were *Qibla Cola* from the UK, which also successfully expanded beyond its original place, and *Zam Zam Cola*, in fact a former Iranian partner of Pepsi, which was nationalised during the Iranian revolution, but in 2002 expanded beyond its home market to the Middle East and Europe.

The example of alcohol demonstrates branding in a culturally difficult environment. Historically, beer was introduced to the Ottoman Empire in the 1830s, and from the beginning it was an object of social and cultural struggles.[57] The cleavages were mostly between the acceptance and appeal of Western products and lifestyles as signs of modernity and cosmopolitanism and the denouncement of beer as a symbol of foreignness and Europeanisation. Nationalists promoted the conspicuous consumption of *rakı* as a national, yet alcoholic drink. The young Turkish Republic indigenised beer by nationalising production; brands’ and beer houses’ names were also Turkified. Today, the Islamist-led governments have passed increasingly draconic rules against the sale, advertisement, consumption of alcohol. This goes hand in hand with promoting the salted yoghurt drink *ayran* as a “true” Turkish alternative to beer. Wine has to struggle, too, with these contemporary constraints; yet, authors still point to the need to purposefully develop strong and innovative brands to improve national and international market positions and continue the growth of Turkish wine production that began with the turn of the century.[58] Yet, alcohol drinking and marketing is an issue also in other MENA countries. Partly based on extended previous work,[59] in this volume, short snapshots touch upon the historical and contemporary branding of alcoholic beverages, from building a brand in colonial North Africa (Nina Studer) to the qualification of Moroccan wine (Steffen Wippel) and advertising in Lebanon (Marie Bonte).

57 Cf. Fuhrmann, 2014.

58 Cf. Oraman, Yılmaz, and Abdikoğlu, 2017.

59 Cf., e.g., Bonte, 2021.

Last but not least, rising incomes and the globalisation of lifestyles and tastes have fostered a sustained demand for gourmet products, which cater to the pursuit and display of luxury consumption.[60] Thus, in recent years, the Middle East/Africa sales region has been among the world's fastest-expanding chocolate markets; demand in Arab Gulf states in particular is booming. In the past, chocolate, especially of the premium variety, was exclusively imported, but since the turn of the millennium, a regional confectionery industry, in particular in the high-end luxury segment, has gradually developed. For reasons of reputation, these chocolate and praline producers often refer to European traditions; local authenticity is partly given through regional ingredients or special spice notes. Presentation and the art of packaging – e. g., high-class shop interiors, jewel-like displays, and treasure-imitating chocolate boxes – play a central role in the "preciosisation" of their products. By establishing special chain shops and participating in sales exhibitions and trade fairs, manufacturers try to gain recognition and enter the export market, in and beyond the region. In this way, the UAE itself has become one of the largest chocolate producers and exporters in the world. Especially in Dubai, exquisite chocolate shops have spread, fulfilling the city's claimed luxury dimension in often less noticed ways. In the Dubai Mall, a central element of its urban branding, this segment even occupied its own shopping "street." The spatially concentrated, noble presentation, in turn, upgraded the factual mass shopping centre. The spectrum of renowned brands from the chocolate industry ranges from well-known Western luxury brands to products from high-quality Arab confectioners of Syrian-Lebanese and increasingly Saudi and Emirati provenance. But despite all its resonant cosmopolitanism, the assortment obviously contains no or hardly any alcohol, even if its *ḥalāl* quality is rarely openly advertised.

5 Branding Personalities and Political Groups

Especially in countries where family businesses still play an important role, the personalities of their founders or owners are crucial in constituting the enterprise brand. Notably in authoritarian regimes, political rulers have a tendency to personal self-promotion; the long list in contemporary Middle East and North Africa includes monarchs, leaders, and presidents known around the world, from the first president of modern Turkey, Mustafa Kemal Atatürk (r. 1923–1938), and Egyptian presidents Gamal Abdel Nasser (r. 1952–1970) and Anwar al-Sadat (r. 1970–1981) to the Libyan revolution guide Muʿammar al-Qaddhafi (r. 1969–2011) or more re-

60 Cf. Wippel, 2024.

cently Saudi crown prince Mohammed bin Salman Al Saud (* 1985), who is an outstanding example of using manifold personal branding strategies. As demonstrated in the subsequent section and, in more detail, in several empirical studies in this volume, e.g. in the chapters by Annegret Roelcke on the Istanbul Eyüpsultan quarter and by Hend Aly on the Saudi NEOM project, also a strong co-branding of nations, cities, or projects goes along with the ostentatious self-advertisement of these rulers.

Typical of the region is also the branding of personalities connected with Islam. Among them, Yūsuf ʿAbdallāh al-Qaraḍāwī (1926–2022), born in Egypt and based in Qatar since 1961, was an authoritative scholar, important activist, and perhaps one of the best-known representatives of contemporary Sunni Islam. As a "global mufti," he became a highly popular and at the same time controversial figure of the Islamic movement worldwide and leveraged his acknowledged religious authority to intervene in political debates.[61] To disseminate his views and visions of a worldwide Islamic community, al-Qaraḍāwī made intensive use of all available media technologies. He skilfully knew how to benefit from the political rise of Qatar (see below) and its media activism, especially the founding of the satellite TV station *Al Jazeera* in 1996, to promote himself and his activities. Until 2013, his weekly religious programme on *Al Jazeera* attracted a worldwide audience. He was the first Muslim scholar to publish *fatwā*s online, answering ordinary people's questions. Al-Qaraḍāwī also got involved in the transformation of the legal opinion practice from a religious advisory institution, directed primarily at individuals, into an instrument that publicly addresses social issues and contributes to public opinion. In parallel and subsequently, similar preachers who have become renowned through the Internet and social media have emerged at local, national, and regional levels throughout the MENA region. Liza Franke contributes on this aspect with a case study on the spiritual brand of an Egyptian television guide.

Islamic brands can also be used for national co-branding. Mauritania is an example of a state in search of its national identity and regional belonging, which are difficult to define because of the country's particular historical and contemporary legacies. Trends towards a strengthened Arab brand have regularly conflicted with the self-identification of non-Arabophone groups and sub-Saharan orientations.[62] In this respect, Islam can serve as a common reference point for national unity and help to hold the ethnolingually plural and socially stratified society together.

61 Cf. Gräf, 2003 and 2009.

62 Cf. Frede, 2021. On the country's inner conflicts and regional orientation options, cf. also Wippel, 2012.

Thus, an Islamic brand like the *maḥḍara*, a "traditional" yet highly dynamic institution of Islamic education, has been promoted by politicians and *'ulamā'* as part of the national educational system since the late 1970s, to support social peace and national cohesiveness. Vice versa, to promote its international standing and tranquilise fears abroad that have considered these schools as breeding grounds for radicalism, Mauritania has initiated a discourse about good local Islam vs. the Islamic extremism intruding from outside and presents itself as a regional leader of counterterrorism in the Sahel zone.

Personal and corporate branding is also practised by radical activists and terrorists. Militant Islamist organisations and Jihadist networks, which among their adherents built on an identity of resistance to the depravity of national leaders, Islamic societies, and the West, established themselves as brands.[63] The extensive propaganda used mainstream media and the groups' own news agencies, social media platforms, and online magazines to spread their ideologies and messages; the reporting that accompanied their activities and visual uniformity, e.g. of logos and letterheads, also contributed to the promotion of a visible and appealing brand. This is also how *al-Qāʿida* (*1988) was able to become one of the most successful virtual communities and rose to global notoriety. Especially its leader Osama bin Laden (1957–2011) was an easily recognisable "face" and "poster boy."[64] He was a strategic architect of effective communication, propaganda, and self-promotion and applied the management techniques he had learned in his business studies and in the family construction business to maintain a long-lasting "stock value" of his organisation.[65] Yet, he did not fully control the brand: after 11 September 2001, his negative public image served as an adverse umbrella brand that fed widespread Islamophobia and resulted in a loss of reputational capital for Muslims. In branding the "Islamic State" (IS; *1999), three elements were essential to attract millennials: story creation around the historical significance of Islamic prophecies; the symbolisms linked with the brand, such as a flag, a leader, a logo, and a caliphate; and the actions and the sense attached to the IS through practised ideology.[66] By advertising death adventurously with heroism and martyrdom, it succeeded in consolidating its followers' allegiance and persuading them to commit the ultimate self-sacrifice.

In a processual perspective, also rebranding took place.[67] Bin Laden already considered renaming *al-Qāʿida*, as he was concerned about the organisation's

63 For general branding literature, cf. Brückerhoff, 2004. Cf. also Govers and Go, 2009: 2.

64 Brückerhoff, 2004.

65 Cf. Amour, 2018; Hoffmann, 2006.

66 Cf. Bandopadhyaya, 2019.

67 Cf. Wilson, 2014.

image in the eyes of Muslims and its ability to recruit followers. The Islamic State of Iraq and Syria (or the Levant) was a successor of *al-Qāʿida* in Iraq and changed its name in 2014 to IS only, to underline its claim to statehood, control of conquered territories, and imperial reach beyond. Jihadist movements extended their geographical reach by establishing whole brand families.[68] This was the case with *al-Qāʿida*, which expanded from Afghanistan as far as Algeria and Somalia by building up branches and merging with existing organisations. The IS widened its brand by establishing affiliates and franchise groups, which extended to Nigeria, Russia, and the Philippines, especially when its Caliphate began to collapse. This helped the groups to increase legitimacy under conditions of lasting conflicts, to appear more powerful than they actually were, and to gain local expertise. However, brand management problems arose when subgroups' objectives and actions conflicted with the umbrella brand and tensions between local and global agendas emerged. Positioning themselves in a competitive market and striving for "Jihadist supremacy," the two groups answered with different strategies to the 2011 political unrest in the Middle East.[69] *Al-Qāʿida* attempted to improve its image by slowing down the implementation of *šarīʿa* law and by rebranding some of its affiliates at the cost of its central authority. In contrast, IS focused on the violent conquest of territory and began its own state-building. So while *al-Qāʿida* was better positioned locally and successfully expanded its impact on a series of Middle Eastern internal wars, IS lost credibility with the local population, but remained popular with younger jihadists. Even though it lost most of its territory, it retained the ideological power to inspire attacks abroad.

6 Dubai as the Signature Case of Place Branding

The surge in the contemporary place branding business in the Middle East and North Africa is strongly linked to the ascendance of Dubai as a known and reputed brand worldwide. As reflected in the global and regional rankings, Dubai is *the* "signature case"[70] of branding in the MENA region (and beyond). It is by far the best-examined case, and critical analyses prevail. It has even found its way into foundational works on branding; likewise, the nascent literature on branding in the region started with a focus on Dubai, to the extent that this section allows us to summarise only some of these findings exemplarily. Most of this was written

68 Cf. Clarke, 2018.

69 Cf. Lister, 2017.

70 Govers and Go, 2009: 4.

in the late 2000s, when Dubai approached the peak of its boom, and in the early 2010s, taking stock of the same period before the financial crisis took place. Like for the subsequent, mostly geographically ordered *tour d'horizon* that starts in the Gulf region and ends in the Maghreb and at MENA's periphery, many of the cited works are often less explicitly, but more implicitly or only cursorily about branding.

Already as of 1989, Dubai had created a number of special institutions to promote the city internationally.[71] In the course of the 2000s, it excelled as a shooting star brand in the global attention economy and attracted tourists, buyers, investors, stars, etc. Dubai's branding helped make it a global city, and conversely, the branding reflected its becoming a world city.[72] Nevertheless, Robert Govers and Frank Go stated that, at that time, the emirate "had not yet developed an orchestrated brand strategy in terms of the use of symbols (logos, slogans)."[73] Among these classic instruments, there was a series of differing slogans, and different institutions used different types of logos. Branding was fragmented and product-oriented and failed to coherently reflect the place identity to be communicated across sectors. Too many images associated with the city were circulating.[74] Potential addressees had difficulties describing the city's identity, while the perceived image also contained many stereotypes based on generalisations about the Middle East and Islam.[75] Moreover, Dubai was among the places in the region hardest hit by the rapidly spreading global financial and economic crisis in 2009 and had to suspend, at least temporarily, many of its construction projects. In the following years, it slowly recovered and continued to develop its brand. Only in the mid-2010s was an umbrella logo developed for multifunctional use (Fig. 2d).

Instead, Dubai built its place brand mainly by means of vigorous and well-communicated actions. In particular, there was an intense, mutually reinforcing co-branding of the city, project sites, firms, and products.[76] Already since the 1960s–'70s, Dubai's planned transformation through spectacular architecture

71 Cf. Stephenson, 2014: 725. Cf. also Govers and Go, 2009: 96–97.

72 Cf. Ooi, 2011: 56.

73 Govers and Go, 2009: 74.

74 On the brand images and perceptions, cf. Govers, 2012; Govers and Go, 2009: passim. Cf. also Balakrishnan, 2008: 81–82.

75 On the negative country-of-origin effect for DP World's envisaged investment in North American ports, cf. Balakrishnan, 2008: 68; on the effects of 9/11 and unrest in the Middle East on tourism, Steiner, 2009.

76 Compare the example given by Schmid, 2006: 357: marketing new Emirates flight routes involved the Department of Tourism and Commerce Marketing, hotels, and real estate companies, which simultaneously woo passengers, tourists, and investors. Cf. also Burs, 2016: 183.

made it a "showpiece city."[77] Its physical appearance, above all, turns it into an "instantly recognizable"[78] place and a symbol of modernity, human endeavour, and success.[79] Many constructions have the city's toponym in their brand name, thereby equating the project and the city and vice versa.[80] Branding through the continuous construction of new, attention-grabbing megaprojects scattered across the city seems particularly suitable to meet global marketing requirements, can be economically valorised, and promises the ruling elites a considerable gain in political legitimacy.[81] This encompasses extensive landscaping, including large urban revitalisation and extended waterfront development, as well as highly impressive standalone landmark buildings designed by global "starchitects" and lavishly presented in the media.[82]

In addition, hosting events has become an important instrument. The field of culture, in particular, is another means for branding Dubai; it endows the city with an image of openness and creativity. With events such as the Dubai Art Fair, Dubai seeks to gain recognition in a regional and global network of competing venues.[83] For example, it has become a platform for Iranian artists from all over the world to showcase and market their work internationally across the political divide of the Persian Gulf. Together with extravagant malls, widely marketed annual shopping festivals where hundreds of reputed international brands are present cater to shopping purposes, for which visitors are lured to "Do-Buy."[84] In parallel, Dubai has succeeded in establishing many reputed home brands that are active all over the world and simultaneously serve as brand ambassadors, like the property developers *Emaar* and *Nakheel*, the Emirates airline, and DP World for port management. In addition to hosting the Expo 2020, which again allowed Dubai to stage its global position, the city had already "expo-ised" itself as a site where enterprises from all over the world seek to outdo each other in their external presentation, just like corporate micronations in an enormous real-world exhibition.[85]

---

77 Cf. Reisz, 2020.

78 Bagaeen, 2007.

79 Compare Elsheshtawy, 2010: 161.

80 Cf. Acuto, 2010: 278.

81 Cf. Steiner, 2017: 7.

82 On "blue" waterside projects, cf. Brorman Jensen, 2007: 44–57; Bolleter, 2009; for the manmade channel that reconnects the creek, where the city originated, to the sea, Semple, 2017. On the media presentation of contemporary architecture, also generally in the UAE, cf. Burs, 2016.

83 Cf. Moghadam, 2018 and 2021.

84 Cf., e.g., Sangeeta, Anandkumar, and Peter, 2013; Brorman Jensen, 2007: 98; Balakrishnan, 2008: 80 (also on home brands); Haines, 2011: 169.

85 Cf. Brorman Jensen, 2007: 44–57.

The place image of Dubai is transported via the visual and textual content of brochures and other information media.[86] Yet, direct advertisement campaigns seem to have had only limited impact in the past. In contrast, intense global media coverage of all the iconic buildings and outstanding events had an important role in conveying and building Dubai's global brand. Personal experiences were also much-used information sources. Across the city, huge billboards announced the emergence of new projects – even if they sometimes found no reflection on the ground, but were put on hold or never realised. Literature cursorily mentions that, in contrast, people were largely absent in these images; in this volume, Philip Geisler elaborates in depth on the sanitised and immaculate images that are being created. With the growing presence of the Internet, the place image early began to be largely projected online by all available means. This includes the massive use of global social media, up to the recent trend to attract influencers to live in the city and deploy their clips in front of alluring sceneries from there – at the cost of avoiding any critique of Dubai.

The branding initiatives were conceived and driven by a small elite. The emirate's ruler Sheikh Mohammed bin Rashid Al Maktoum, in particular, was associated with several strong urban visions and statements to the wider public.[87] Strategic visions for the mid-2010s claimed to make Dubai a "globally leading Arab city;"[88] according to the emir, Dubai had to be "number one in the world, in everything."[89] In fact, many different actors were involved. In particular, the private sector was instrumental in the success of branding Dubai. Numerous architecture and landscape designers and property and city developers have contributed to building the place's worldwide image. But, in the dominating political and economic system that characterises Dubai, with a mix of the sheikh's private property, formally public entities, and private corporations owned by clan members and personalities close to the ruler, the boundaries between different actors blurred.[90] However, these actors are not able to completely control the brand, given the role of, e.g., international journalists and activists.[91]

---

86 On the media of branding Dubai, cf., e.g., Govers and Go, 2009: 151–167 et passim; Coombe and Melki, 2012. On media coverage and billboards, cf. also Elsheshtawy, 2010: 161–162; on the use of social media, Govers, 2012: 51. On the absence of people in and the decontextualisation of images of buildings, cf. also Nastasi, 2019.

87 For the key actors, cf. Govers and Go, 2009: 95, 98; Acuto, 2010: 278; Hashim, Irazábal, and Byrum, 2010: 218; especially on the ruler and his visions, Schmid, 2006: 357; Bromber et al., 2014: 7.

88 Quoted in Balakrishnan, 2008: 70.

89 Quoted in Acuto, 2010: 278.

90 Cf. Steiner, 2014: 18–20.

91 Cf. Haines, 2011: 167.

Dubai is to be a hypercentre of neoliberal development and a site of the techno-utopic future of the 21st century, where everything is possible.[92] According to Samer Bagaeen, Dubai also perfectly fits Edward Soja's description of the postmodern city.[93] The splintering of the city, and namely the division of previously empty desert land into numbered plots like a bingo game board, available for unconnected and monocultural uses, made Dubai an exemplary case of postmodern "bingo urbanism."[94] Everything is designed for staging and visibility in order to be able to serve as a symbol. Many projects lack any spatial, historical, or social embeddedness. In particular, Dubai is a city of hyperreal experiences. Its development is strongly linked to the creation of simulacra and replicas.[95] Uniqueness is a major aspect of the branding strategy, which intends to create an image of fascination.[96] As is characteristic of the postmodern city, the distinction between the city and a theme park vanishes and even finds its global apotheosis in Dubai.[97] Such creations of hyperrealities meet marketing purposes and grant prestige, recognition, and legitimation to their holders and owners. Simultaneously, due to their lack of ties to their immediate environment, such projects are ideally suited to be filled with symbolic significance within urban branding campaigns. Intangible emotional and experiential aspects are central for making the place consumable. With this, Dubai sells "a global dream of high-class consumption and luxurious lifestyles."[98]

Shopping malls have become outstanding examples of the citywide display of "theme-scapes."[99] Eclectically combined architectural elements of Arab, South Asian, Mediterranean, and other decors are almost non-functional.[100] At the same time, some logo-like structures, such as the Palm and World Islands, can be transmitted only by maps or views from the air or outer space, like the ground plan of *Burj Khalifa* in the form of a desert flower.[101] It is here where the primacy of the map and of branding requirements over the realisation of the projects and their relevance to daily life becomes the most apparent. Hotels also became desti-

---

92 Cf. Hashim, Irazábal, and Byrum, 2010: 211 et passim.

93 Cf. Bagaeen, 2007.

94 Cf. Brormann Jensen, 2007.

95 Cf. especially Steiner, 2010, 2014, and 2017; Bromber et al., 2014. Cf. also Govers and Go, 2009: 11; Vanolo, 2017: 162.

96 On Dubai in the global fascination economy, cf. Schmid, 2006.

97 Cf. Bolleter, 2009: 8.

98 Haines, 2011: 161.

99 Cf. Bolleter, 2009: 10.

100 Cf. Steiner, 2010: 246.

101 Cf. Brorman Jensen, 2007: 70–72; Bolleter, 2009: 10; Elsheshtawy, 2010: 151, 166; Steiner, 2010: 247, and 2014: 25.

nations in themselves, sometimes tied to other well-known brands like fashion trademarks (Armani Hotel) or celebrities (e.g., top golfers playing on the *Burj Al Arab* helipad).[102] Touring these new themed sites, which their visitors often understand as museums (Ibn Battuta Mall) and actual historical remnants (Souk Madinat Jumeirah), is at the core of the emirate's travel business. Julian Bolleter conceives Dubai's landscape architecture as "para-scapes," which serve the *para*disiacal image of the city.[103] They are derived both from Quranic descriptions of paradise, which is symbolically recreated, and from the first president of the UAE's vision of greening the desert, which Gergana Alzeer and Tilde Rosmer explore in their later chapter. But as this hybridised landscape architecture is entirely artificial and beyond all ecological requirements, "para" also refers to Dubai's state of *para*lysis.

Already in the 2000s, Dubai had "almost more than any other city, made the spectacular its *raison d'être!*"[104] It used superlatives to build and mark its distinctiveness; many urban projects were – in the word's double sense – "exclusive" in nature. The artificially developed hospitality, office, residential, and shopping complexes had nearly no comparison in scale and volume worldwide.[105] Qualifiers, for instance in the promotion of "seven star" hotels or in claims to be or have the (preferably: world's) "highest," "tallest," "fastest," or "biggest" structures, all of which are "unique" and "ground-breaking," proliferated, with the inherent risk of being quickly outpaced in the global race for supremacy. Height like that of the *Burj Khalifa* was also a symbol of power.[106] Accordingly, storytelling is closely linked to the material constructions and can be regarded as a central feature of branding. Given that these narratives need to be constantly varied and recreated in order to avoid the effects of fatigue and to maintain a unique selling position, the metaphor of the "Scheherazade Syndrome" suggests that, as in the 1001 Nights, survival depends to a large extent on the endless stretching of a story.[107]

Furthermore, contemporary projects in Dubai intend to demonstrate the power of "making history" and represent a place "where the future begins."[108]

---

102 Cf. Elsheshtawy, 2010: 140–141; Burs, 2016: 206 (and 214–215, on the planned Tiger Woods hotel).

103 Cf. Bolleter, 2009.

104 Elsheshtawy, 2010: 137.

105 Cf. Elsheshtawy, 2010: 134, 165; Steiner, 2010: 241, 247; Balakrishnan, 2008: 80–81.

106 Cf. Elsheshtawy, 2010: 152, 164; Acuto, 2010: 272–273; Burs, 2016: e.g. 250–255. Initially named *Burj Dubai*, the tower's name was changed in the aftermath of the financial crisis, when Abu Dhabi had supported Dubai and used this opportunity to strengthen its position within the UAE.

107 Cf. Hashim, Irazábal, and Byrum, 2010.

108 Haines, 2011: 165.

Yet, the temporal aspects of Dubai's brand are also reflected in the felt need to contextualise buildings in local and broader Arab-Islamic history and traditions.[109] Especially in a place without a pronounced urban history, suggesting deep cultural roots should help to realise the vision of a modern Arab and Muslim society. For this, the few historical buildings started to be diligently preserved and act as a form of staged authenticity to create awareness of the one's own cultural origins, contribute to building national identity, and generate some sense of place. Heritage planning serves to improve the past; the city's own history on display, e.g. in museums and heritage villages, shows the successful rise from a poor Bedouin society to a prosperous world centre; and early-flourishing fields of activity, such as pearl fishing and translocal trade, should demonstrate continuity with the city's present-day centrality and cosmopolitanism. New constructions also go along with narratives and motifs that link them to cultural traditions and natural conditions, be it the repetitive palm-tree motif, for instance the artificial islands in front of the coastline; the *dhow*-like iconic shape of *Burj Al Arab*; or the ground plan of the *Burj Khalifa*, which is supposed to represent an endemic desert rose.[110]

Simultaneously, Dubai's success, both as a brand and in economic development, has further deepened profound paradoxes and discrepancies. First, there was great unevenness in the uses and achievements of branding: while the state leadership, public authorities, and multinational businesses were very successful in their personal, urban, and corporate branding endeavours, in the mid-2010s, small and medium enterprises still experienced major barriers to brand building.[111] However, there have also been exceptions, as shown for example by the recent branding efforts in the local confectionery industry. Second, the promising present and future marketed by Dubai also attracted a rapidly growing number of migrants. But the impressive economic and touristic development is contrasted by adverse social and environmental conditions that long remained overlooked by many incoming tourists and businessmen and disregarded in the selective representations of the brand.[112] Hence, for migrants, going to Dubai to earn a living is an ambivalent pleasure: on the one hand, the glittering face of Dubai that is stag-

---

109 On the issues in this paragraph, cf., for instance, Govers and Go, 2009: 103–107 et passim; Elsheshtawy, 2010: 161; Bromber et al., 2014; Haines, 2011: 167–169; Stephenson, 2014: 8–9. On traditional sports, cf. below.

110 On the two *burjs*, cf., e.g., Schmid, 2006: 356; Elsheshtawy, 2010: 138–139, 161; Steiner, 2014: 24–25.

111 Cf. Gundala, Jack, and Khawaja, 2014.

112 Many authors point to this downside; cf., e.g. Haines, 2011; Bolleter, 2009; Hashim, Irazábal, and Byrum, 2010: 222–227. On hiding, cf. also Bagaeen, 2007: 187; Nastasi, 2019: 126; similarly on art and culture, Moghadam, 2021: 4, 6.

ed for the world has its important dark underbelly of absolutely deplorable living and working conditions for those who construct these fairy-tale illusions; on the other hand, they are attracted not only by material gains, but also by the possibility of participating in Dubai's special aura as a global, cosmopolitan, and ultra-modern city, which holds the prospect of raising their own status.[113] The identities and images imposed from above also have provoked conscious appropriation as well as circumventing counter-strategies from below. In a city full of para-, logo- and theme-scapes, the less wealthy parts of society and notably migrant workers often occupy space left over in planning on the margins of road arteries and other infrastructural developments for meeting, chatting, relaxing, and picnicking.[114] For national citizens, local entrepreneurs with their specific cultural knowledge of the place have been able to create and market refuges where, for example, local eateries offer typical Emirati food away from the glitzy ambience in most of the city.[115]

7 Branding other Gulf Cities and Nations

While Dubai began to establish itself as a globally perceived brand around the turn of the millennium, elsewhere in the region efforts to strategically communicate an attractive image have emerged more recently. As the debate conducted under keywords such as "Dubai elsewhere," "Dubaization," and "Dubaification"[116]demonstrates, the model of economic and urban development that appeared quite successful, despite the interim setbacks, began to be exported and imitated, including the associated attention strategies, as a kind of "travelling practice."[117] Dubai's example was first taken up in other Arab Gulf metropolises and small nations. Here, contemporary architecture in the Gulf region is also lavishly presented in the media, and, in particular, hyperreal tourist resorts and shopping malls likewise contribute centrally to image construction.[118] Nevertheless, different nuances can be discerned in the strategies adopted: while some places shine in intense brand competition through cultural and sport facilities planned by star architects,

113 Cf. Haines, 2011: 172–176. Cf. also Vanolo, 2017: 67.

114 Cf. Bolleter, 2009: 11–12. Cf. also Brorman Jensen, 2007: 33.

115 Cf. Reichenbach and Ibrahim, 2019.

116 Cf., e.g., Wippel et al., 2014; Elsheshtawy, 2010: 249–279; Adham, 2011: 247. Cf. also Steiner, 2010: 249.

117 Related to nation branding, cf. Eggeling, 2020: 229. On travelling projects of similar design and mobilities of the spectacular, cf. Ponzini, 2019.

118 Cf. Burs, 2016; Steiner, 2010.

others present themselves primarily as ecological pioneers, business-friendly locations, or international event venues. All have founded agencies for commercial and tourism marketing, which are working within an entire ecosystem of institutions – national tourism and investment authorities, local developers, national carriers, etc. – to promote the respective place. At the same time, urban and national future "visions" with precise target years, often announced by the national or local ruler himself, have been comprehensively integrated into marketing activities in many places, too, but so far have only briefly been touched upon in academic literature.[119] They combine strategic targets for economic, touristic, and infrastructural progress with catchy images and slogans. Moreover, historical-tribal references and spectacles – including custom-fit pre-national genealogies, fantasy architectures, national museums, neo-traditional sport, dress codes, and poetry contests – have been selectively incorporated into the branding of the young nation states of the Gulf, erasing the cultural ambivalences and hardships of the past.[120] Among the many political rivalries that run across the region, geographical naming has become a central branding device, as in the dispute over the correct designation of the Gulf as "Persian" or "Arabic," which has even led to restrictions on postal and freight traffic.[121]

7.1 Establishing Abu Dhabi as a Cultural and Green Brand

The other UAE emirates strongly feel the need to position themselves against Dubai's globally outshining role. While the UAE has been consistently at the top, e.g. of the BrandFinance nation ranking (probably largely based on Dubai's reputation), as an amalgam of federal emirates, each with its own identity, history, and dynasty, it is still in process of nation building. The spirit of belonging together has long been underdeveloped.[122] In recent years, there have been efforts to strengthen the collective identity of the UAE. In this volume, Moritz Mihatsch and Richard Gauvain present recent endeavours to forge a more solid overarching

119 Cf. Hvidt, 2012; Bromber et al., 2014. Such visions are particularly conspicuous in the Gulf region, namely Abu Dhabi Economic Vision 2030 (launched 2006); Sharjah Tourism Vision 2021 (2015); UAE Vision 2021 (2010) and "We the UAE" Vision 2031 (2022); UAE Centennial 2071 (2017); Qatar National Vision 2030 (2008); Bahrain Vision 2030 (2008); New Kuwait Vision 2035 (2010); Saudi Vision 2030 (2016); Oman Vision 2040 (2020), following Vision Oman 2020 (1995); etc.

120 Cf. Cooke, 2014. Even Orientalist art serves as a means to confirm purged images of the past.

121 On the naming dispute, cf. Medway and Warnaby, 2014: 163. In more detail, see, e.g., Krause, 2001.

122 Cf., e.g. from the perspective of destination marketing, Stephenson, 2012: 10–11.

identity and present the federation collectively to its citizens and the outside world by creating a logo that simultaneously symbolises unity and diversity. But to a large extent, the different emirates brand themselves individually.

Compared to Dubai, Abu Dhabi was a relative latecomer in economic diversification, urban transformation, tourism development, and, with that, branding.[123] Endeavours in these directions were particularly strengthened when Sheikh Khalifa (r. 2004–2022), the son of the UAE's founder Sheikh Zayed bin Sultan Al Nahyan (r. 1966–2004), came to power. As the federal capital and presidency, Abu Dhabi aspires for a stronger centralisation of the UAE, especially since the financial crisis, when the extent to which it has to finance the rest of country, including Dubai, became obvious. The first concern has been the development of a brand easily distinguishable from its neighbour and dynamising the somewhat boring image of the city. Still, the emirate builds on a smoother transition and a more heritage- and tradition-inspired development and image. In the travel segment, the focus is on cultural and event tourism. Culture, sport, and sustainability can be considered the buzzwords of the branding strategy and are linked to the major attention-drawing projects. Since 2007, an explicit Office of the Brand of Abu Dhabi has been developing and implementing a comprehensive brand from the beginning.[124] The logo in the shape of a local *dhow* sail in which the emirate's calligraphic name is inscribed is widely used across the different sectors and regions of the emirate. The brand story centres on a small fishing village turned into a hospitable and exciting metropolis and on heritage, nature, and people. There is a strong effort to ensure the public and private entities' firm commitment to the brand and its respect in the behaviour of citizens.

Inside the city, a major urban transformation was the building of the Corniche, which embodies a modern and paradisaic place, serves as a scene where most local events resonate, and enhances the visibility of the city to its inhabitants and the foreign public.[125] In competition with Dubai, Abu Dhabi stablished its own world-class flagship carrier and more recently a container mega-port. Like other emirates, Abu Dhabi has invested in higher education as another reputational means and attracted branches of international university brands. In the field of culture, it is trying to catch up with international standards and become a world leader. Since the late 2000s, the focus has been on developing Saadiyat Island into a

---

123 On the branding strategy, cf. in the following Hazime, 2011; Westwood, 2011; Bani Hashim, 2012. Cf. also Scharfenort, 2010.

124 In 2023, the new ruler of Abu Dhabi, Sheikh Mohamed bin Zayed, instituted the Abu Dhabi Media Office to establish guidelines for the coherent use of the emirate's promotional brands; cf. Abu Dhabi Media Office, 2023.

125 Cf. Assaf, 2013.

"Cultural District" with numerous museums.[126] To attract attention, institutional and nominal links are made to Western brands; we find branches of the Louvre (opened in 2017) and Guggenheim museums (to be completed in 2025), in addition to museums, still under construction, displaying national history and ecology. Perhaps even more starchitects designed iconic buildings in this concentrated space than in Dubai; to balance between alleged global culture and local traditions, they evoke local building techniques and forms, such as wind towers, Bedouin tents, narrow alleyways, and mosque domes. The island encompasses also exclusive residential compounds, tourism resorts, shopping facilities, the unavoidable golf courses, and an eco-reserve; it sells the fascination of a tropical island, a paradise, and an Oriental dream, but can again be considered the spatial manifestation of harsh inequalities between a transnational creative and affluent class and the global marginalised and poor. Yas Island is a second island development that includes a motor racing course and theme park and integrates top-level sport as a separate field of the local brand, similar to Qatar (cf. below). Its form-finding and design directly followed a simulated 3D model.[127]

The third area that is expected to contribute exceptionally to Abu Dhabi's brand image is the pursuit of environmental sustainability. Part of its massive (re)branding since the mid-2000s has been the attempt to transform its international image from a major oil and gas producer into an energy giant relying on a broad portfolio including alternative resources; at the same time, this is meant to be a clear marker of distinction from its regional competitors.[128] Hoped-for effects are to accelerate the diversification of the emirate's economy and strengthen the ruler's political legitimacy at home and abroad. Its advocacy of renewable energies, in particular, has produced much fascination. After it was able to organise the World Future Energy Summit in 2008, it won the bid for the headquarters of the new International Renewable Energy Agency in 2009. The "jewel in the crown of the new strategy"[129] was the Masdar initiative, launched in 2006 in a joint effort of several public institutions. Its core project was Masdar City, branded as a "smart city," fully self-sufficient in renewable energies, served by an automated transport system, and following climate-adapted traditional building patterns. The Masdar Institute of Science and Technology was established in collaboration with the MIT brand to serve as a showcase for high-profile research and education and to market Abu Dhabi as a surging knowledge economy. The project was promoted as a future-oriented utopia making it possible to explore a new frontier in the des-

126 Cf. also Dumortier, 2014; Burs, 2016: 221.

127 Cf. Burs, 2016: 211–213.

128 On Masdar, cf., e.g., Sim, 2012; Günel, 2019; Rietmann, 2021.

129 Mahroum and Alsaleh, 2012.

ert. Politically, it was said to preserve the legacy of Shaykh Zayed and his engagement for a green environment. But several setbacks already during the 2008/09 financial crisis meant that the Masdar project had to be downscaled in size and ambition. Masdar City no longer claims it will be "zero-carbon" when it is finished one day, but now aims to be "carbon-neutral" instead.

Subsequently, more and more projects, and finally cities and states in the MENA region, have been branded as "green" and "sustainable" (and in combination with that, as "smart") as an essential element in their global image-building strategy during the last decade. Other places in the Gulf region established similar projects that wanted to be vanguard, but often failed or showed limited progress.[130] According to Agatino Rizzo, "Governments in the Gulf seek to compete with one another for the title of creating the 'greenest', 'eco-friendliest', or 'most sustainable' city in the region."[131] In the UAE, this includes the Dubai Expo 2020 venue, which aimed "to go green;"[132] in Qatar, for instance, the 2022 FIFA World Cup was announced as an eco-friendly, carbon-neutral event. Like Abu Dhabi, Qatar prefers large-scale "green" projects, while Dubai displays a number of smaller scattered institutions and neighbourhoods.[133] Qatar pushes the "climate change brand" in contrast to Abu Dhabi's "renewable energy brand."[134] In 2012, Doha hosted the first United Nations Climate Change Conference (COP 18) in the Middle East, which also added to its global visibility.[135] Saudi Arabia established the private King Abdullah University of Science and Technology (KAUST), including specialisations in water, energy, and environment issues, and organised many campaigns, such as beach cleaning and afforestation; Kuwait has undertaken many environmental protection measures. Other countries followed suit, yet most often in smaller dimensions and less globally publicised, such as with the New Borg El Arab EcoCity in Egypt or the latest generation of planned new towns and settlements branded as "green" in Morocco (cf. below).

Abu Dhabi approached the ecological reorientation of its brand primarily to proactively pre-empt the tarnishing of its international image.[136] Consequently,

---

130 Cf., e.g., De Jong, Hoppe, and Noori, 2019 on projects in Qatar, Abu Dhabi, and Dubai; Zumbrägel, 2020 with a focus on Qatar, Saudi Arabia, and Kuwait. On Qatar's green policies, cf. also Koch, 2014; Eggeling, 2020: 170–172. For more details, cf. also below.

131 Rizzo, 2017: 86.

132 Cf. Koch, 2014: 1118.

133 Cf. De Jong, Hoppe, and Noori, 2019: 1–2.

134 Cf. Makdisi, 2012: 6.

135 Other venues in the MENA region were Marrakech (COP 7, 2011; COP 22, 2016) and Sharm El Sheikh (COP 27, 2022); the 2023 COP 28 is scheduled in Dubai. Cf. Wikipedia, 2023d.

136 Cf. Sim, 2012: 87; Brorman Jensen, 2014: 51. Cf. also Rietmann, 2021: 48.

the Masdar project has attracted much public sympathy, but also a lot of criticism, exemplarily for similar projects. It is regarded as a decontextualised import with limited local implications, an elitist exclave contributing to the further fragmentation of the existing urban space.[137] Its promotional budget is considered its largest investment. While some authors admit that the project contributes to raising awareness of the importance of sustainability in people's minds, others underline that exactly this has failed and that urban sustainability is largely reduced to technological solutions. In the local understanding, "green" does not always equate with "sustainable," as it may primarily be about planting and supplying green spaces as an important aspect of quality of life – e. g. among students in Qatar, but also in Dubai as Gergana Alzeer and Tilde Rosmer highlight in their article in this volume. Sometimes, environmental issues are also framed in religious terms or linked to national heritage. The main concern of the branding strategy seems to be to use such projects as a political (soft power) instrument for domestic nation building and national pride; as a way to forestall external and internal pressure; and as another spectacular umbrella brand to address various important players in the field of sustainability. In fact, the Masdar project greatly resembles a theme park; it exists primarily on paper and in PowerPoint presentations, making it a hyperreal simulacrum. As an "empty signifier," it can be deliberately filled with content and shaped by the ruler.

Occasionally, the sustainability label has been attached to projects only in their latter stages of advancement. In particular, economic success prevails over the ecological achievements of sustainable projects. The official rhetoric in line with the global debate contrasts with the actual continuation of unsustainable practices, which challenge the credibility of the branding story and risk generating "science fiction"[138] projects. Martin De Jong et al. affirmed that "the branding of these [ambitious] policies is decidedly more effective than their implementation."[139] Many therefore consider such green branding schemes to be outstanding cases of window dressing and "greenwashing." This term, first used in the 1980s for greening consumer goods and later extended to governments, points to discrepancies between high-flying announcements and poor realisations, to misleading information and narratives, to dubious labels on brands, and to the manipulation and de-

137 In view of such unsuccessful urban experiments, Cugurullo, 2018 considers this an exemplary case of "Frankenstein urbanism." For subsequent analyses and criticisms, cf. Mahroum and Alsaleh, 2012; Brorman Jensen, 2014; Koch, 2014; Rizzo, 2017; Cummings and von Richthofen, 2017; Elsheshtawy, 2018; Günel, 2019; Zumbrägel, 2020.

138 Günel, 2019: 38.

139 De Jong, Hoppe, and Noori, 2019: 23.

ception of consumers.[140] Such allegations have been explicitly formulated for some megaprojects with an intensely communicated green touch, such as the Dubai Water Canal, where in fact environmental aspects are often relegated to second rank.[141] For other Dubai "para-scape" projects, "green" is rather an exotic attribute in an originally desertic environment and stands much more for luxury than for the ecological realities of the place.[142] Yet, more nuanced positions prevail in academia, which struggles to uncover the various rationalities and motivations behind such green branding programmes.

Among the small emirates, perhaps Sharjah and Ras Al Khaimah have the most potential for "'catching up' in comparison with Dubai and Abu Dhabi, their wealthier and more high-profile siblings."[143] In the 2000s, high-rise buildings were erected also in Sharjah, which benefitted much from Dubai's spatial and economic expansion, but at the risk of being swallowed up by the growing agglomeration.[144] Building on its past as the most important port in the wider area, it wants to become again an important regional trade centre and, in particular, the trade "gate" to the northern emirates. Like other cities on the Arabian Peninsula, it has established its own shopping festival;[145] it has also attracted attention as the promoter of the region's first low-cost carrier. This emirate, which has a more conservative image, is consciously branded as a Muslim space that contrasts with its immediate neighbour[146] and banks heavily on culture and heritage. Its de facto status as *the* cultural capital of the UAE is reflected by its nomination as the Arab and Islamic Capitals of Culture (Fig. 1). Several cultural events, including the arts Biennial, museums, and heritage sites, are based there; the main landmarks early excelled with their reference to traditional, Arabic style. The ruler, Sultan bin Muhammad al-Qasimi (since 1972), has authored plenty of historical and literary works. The emirate wants to be not only a cultural, but also an educational and sport hub (especially in the discipline of cricket). Yet, despite initial modest efforts, in the early 2010s, Sharjah still needed more serious branding, especially as its important cultural attractions remained marginal in its tourism offer.

Ras Al Khaimah, the capital of the northernmost emirate, experienced a more recent boom.[147] The place is also proud of a glorious past based on pearl diving and

140 Cf., e.g., Skey, 2022: 3–4.
141 Cf. Semple, 2017.
142 Cf. Brorman Jensen, 2007: 129; Bolleter, 2009: 7–9.
143 Madichie and Madichie, 2013: 81.
144 Cf. Madichie and Madichie, 2013.
145 Cf., e.g., Sangeeta, Anandkumar, and Peter, 2013.
146 Cf. Haines, 2011: 170.
147 Cf. Dumortier, 2013.

trade, but unlike other UAE cities, it only lately showed enhanced ambitions for greater development projects accompanied by image and marketing campaigns in trade and tourism. Yet, several projects adapted to the requirements of a post-modern fascination economy failed, such as an artificial island emulating the Dubai Palms and the Gateway Eco City, resembling Masdar.

7.2 Qatar as the Rising Brand between Sport and Culture

While research literature intensely focused on Dubai's worldwide-perceived branding endeavours up to the early 2010s, this focus has greatly shifted to Qatar and its capital Doha as an emerging "brand state par excellence."[148] Since the late 2000s, Qatar has embarked on a branding strategy similar to that of Dubai, in a mix of a catch-up race and the search for specific niches, but with a clearer set of actions. This was again instigated by a generational change, when the current ruler, Hamad bin Khalifa Al Thani (r. 1995–2013), ousted his father. He began Qatar's international branding by positioning the country as a diplomatic mediator and dialogue partner for all sides in the multiple conflicts of the Middle East and by maintaining simultaneous relationships with the USA, Saudi Arabia, Israel, Iran, and radical Islamist groupings.[149] It hosted international political meetings, from the WTO Doha Round 2001 to the COP 18 in 2012. In a media offensive, Qatar established *Al Jazeera* as a regional and global broadcasting station and opinion maker that challenged the Anglo-American monopoly and served as the mouthpiece of Qatari storytelling. In terms of geography and demography a micro-state, its policy-based branding and soft power approach appeared as an essential survival strategy to gain international legitimacy and awareness and to convince other international actors of its uniqueness and indispensability.

However, since its founding, the *Al Jazeera* news station has repeatedly been accused of interference in internal affairs and overly anti-Western stances, even though the opening of its English service in 2006 improved the image of the brand as a credible source.[150] The strategy failed, especially when, in 2011, Qatar took a position in favour of revolutionary Islamist movements, in the hope of gaining some moderating influence. Other states, in particular the Saudi monarchy, re-

148 Eggeling, 2020: 95.

149 For Qatar's branding through foreign policy, including *Al Jazeera*, cf. Peterson, 2006; Windecker and Sendrowicz, 2014. On some aspects, cf. also Koch, 2014: 1119–1121; Alraouf, 2018; Eggeling, 2020: 91–94; Sons, 2022: 22; Beck, 2022: 6.

150 Cf. also King and Zayani, 2008. Compare the earlier passage on the prominent al-Qaraḍāwī show on *Al Jazeera*.

garded this as a menace to their interests. In 2013, the ruling emir handed over power to his son, who again tried to be more cautious in foreign policy and shifted international image-building more to implementing the numerous large-scale projects for economic development and diversification. Yet, this did not prevent the emirate's multi-year diplomatic, trade, and transport blockade, led by Saudi Arabia and its allies, between 2017 and 2021. How Qatar resisted and developed its own dairy industry, which became a national symbol and then sparked an accelerating "milk brands" race among neighbouring countries, is explored by Natalie Koch in her separate chapter in this book.

A second branding motive for Qatar was to demonstrate competitiveness in specific niches as a world-class performer.[151] Prominent ways to spread its name were the establishment of recognised national firm brands and direct investment in reputed companies abroad. Like other Gulf countries, it created its own successful international airline in 1993, which helps to increase national visibility by carrying its brand all over the world.[152] Qatar likewise has entered the age of "sign wars," "brand icons," and an "urbanism of spectacle" by making architecture and themed districts again a primary source of communication.[153] Doha constructed an impressive skyline of impressive high-rises, sometimes with pseudo-Arabic details. It built hyperreal shopping centres like the *Villagio Mall* with a Venetian-style gondola-lined *Canal Grande* and the artificial mixed-style island The Pearl, marketed as "The Riviera Arabia." The nearby *Katara Cultural Village* provides a stage for displaying arts and crafts from various world regions. The renovated *Souk Waqif* is a major tourist attraction, but in this form had never existed before.[154] The Msheireb Downtown quarter flagship project that is nearing completion claims attachment to a traditional Arab city layout and to principles of sustainability, like the Lusail City development, which is still under construction. Moreover, Education City attracted a number of reputed international university and research institutions. With knowledge- and technology-based development, the city wants to lure foreign experts and the much-vaunted creative class. Qatar also embarked on the cultural track, in particular by building a series of flagship museums, starting with the distinctive Museum of Islamic Art (inaugurat-

151 Cf., among others, Hazime, 2011: 4739; Scharfenort, 2014: 74; Eggeling, 2020: 95.

152 Cf. Peterson, 2006: 747; Lebel, 2019.

153 Cf. Adham, 2011: esp. 236–251. On the large urban projects, cf. also Salama and Wiedmann, 2013; Scharfenort, 2014; Koch, 2014: 1127–1133; Eggeling, 2020.

154 Cf. in addition Cooke, 2014: 84–97.

ed in 2008) and followed by the *Mathaf: Arab Museum of Modern Art* (2010).[155] In contrast to Abu Dhabi, its main regional challenger in this field, it focuses more on historical and modern Islamic artefacts and regional works that greatly cohere with its inward-looking nation-building narratives. But here too, many urban megastructures are exclusive urban enclaves built to serve branding purposes and the interests of a certain elite, rather than the broader population.

Thus, in the mid-2000s, the country had been "put on the map." Whereas it appeared more prominently in the Western press, it was portrayed significantly more positively in Asian, Middle Eastern, and African newspapers.[156] Doha strives to become a global hub with deep cultural roots balancing past and future and pushes the narrative of its successful rise from a former small fishing port and uninspiring provincial town.[157] Reference is often made to local history and nature, such as to certain desert flowers in the shape of the new National Museum and the name of the "Lusail" project, the pearl as a symbol of the past, and the Al-Bayt football arena that resembles a Bedouin tent; the city's development is presented "as a linear (…) trajectory from a modest past into a rich present and an even brighter future."[158] All this has been well branded, including widespread tourism campaigns, with the oryx as a widely-used logo and mascot. Yet, the branding has still tended to refer to individual spectacular projects than to the city as a whole. While the former emir was particularly eager to push sport issues, one of his wives and his daughters were engaged in promoting mainly the education and cultural sectors, respectively.[159] Branding particularly highlights the paternalistic leadership of the royal elite and ties urban development to the national visions and wise foresight of the ruler.[160] Even if numerous actors participate in establishing the brand, the distinction between emir's, public, and private entities is difficult to make, as in Dubai.[161] In this multitude of actors, Jérémie Molho underlines the central role played by star curators acting in a field of tension between ambitious top-down strategies to design world-class collections, on the one hand,

155 On education and culture brands, cf. also Peterson, 2006: 747; Alraouf, 2018; Dumortier, 2014: 181; Molho, 2021; Sons, 2022: 22. Cooke, 2014: 79–84, describes the task of National Museums in the Gulf to build and promote distinct national brands.

156 Cf. King, 2008.

157 Cf. Eggeling, 2020: 96, 168–170; Molho, 2021: 461; Adham, 2011: 237, 251.

158 Eggeling, 2020: 170.

159 Cf., e.g., Windecker and Sendrowicz, 2014: 93; Salama and Wiedmann, 2013: 93.

160 Cf. Eggeling, 2020: 173, 227–228.

161 Cf. Koch, 2014: 1121–1124.

and cumbersome state bureaucracies and official restrictions on civil society, on the other.[162]

One specific field in which Qatar brands itself is sport, which is also prominently present in the branding portfolio of other Gulf states. First, promoting competitive sport has become a major activity integrated into place branding. Qatar founded the Aspire Academy in 2004 as a central institution behind its international ambitions; the Academy is one of the world's largest training centres for top national and international athletes in several disciplines.[163] It is part of the Aspire Zone, or Doha Sports City, which includes one of the world's largest indoor sport stadiums, Qatar's first major international football stadium, and the iconic, torch-shaped Aspire Tower. Similarly, Dubai Sports City, partially opened in 2011, is a multi-use complex that is set to become a high-profile venue with several stadiums and academies. In the international realm, ownership especially of prestigious football clubs and sponsorship by major national enterprises has also attracted much attention.[164] Beyond elite sport, Gulf states also endeavour to promote amateur sport, especially to cope with widespread diseases like diabetes and obesity. Not least, *Al Jazeera* has had an eminent role in promoting sport. Moreover, across the region, traditional disciplines associated with desert life, such as falconry and horse and camel racing, have been reinvigorated if not reinvented and sometimes exhibited in national museums, as were pearl diving and fishing, which in fact were once hard subsistence labour.[165] In addition, motifs like falcons, which refer to local history and nature, have been employed as important visual symbols and brand names for sporting events and facilities, especially those frequented by a Gulf public.

Even more important is the organisation of major international sport competitions that are also broadcast on TV screens to the broad masses worldwide.[166] Across the region, winning bids to host major sporting events has become particularly welcome (cf. Table 5). Forerunners of such global presence have been Bah-

---

162 Cf. Molho, 2021.
163 On sports promotion in Qatar and partly in Dubai, cf. Eggeling, 2020: 120–122; Ginesta and de San Eugenio, 2014; Salama and Wiedmann, 2013: 77; Bromber and Krawietz, 2013: 193–196; Bromber, 2014: 120–124; Sons, 2022: 20–23; Windecker and Sendrowicz, 2014: 90, 94; Ibahrine, 2016.
164 For an entire list of Qatar's sponsorships, partnerships, and TV rights across all disciplines, cf. Blichfeldt Olsen, 2022.
165 Cf. Krawietz, 2014; Sons, 2022: 23; Cooke, 2014: 103–111.
166 On international sport events, cf. Eggeling, 2020: 122–125; Ginesta and de San Eugenio, 2014; Westwood, 2011; Windecker and Sendrowicz, 2014: 94. Cf. also Salama and Wiedmann, 2013: 77; Peterson, 2006: 747; Sons, 2022: 19–20, 23; Scharfenort, 2010 and 2014: 71–73, 83; Bromber, 2014; Bromber and Krawietz, 2013; Beck, 2022: 7; Hazime, 2011: 4741; Ibahrine, 2016: 105–107; Adham, 2011: 242–243.

rain and Abu Dhabi, which established world-class motor racing circuits and hosted regular Formula I Grand Prix from 2004 and 2009 onwards.[167] These events allowed them to attract more media "buzz," at least temporarily, than Dubai at that time.[168]

In Qatar, the first major sport event was the Qatar Open in tennis in 1993. In 2000, Qatar was the first Arab country to win the bid to host the Asian Games 2006. This was perhaps the most important turning point on the emirate's path to becoming an acknowledged sport hub, as it enabled it to stage its talent and reliability vis-à-vis its international partners. International championships in other disciplines followed, but the award of the FIFA World Cup for 2022 was the culmination of Qatar's national image strategy.[169] Related to this mega-event, it built a series of landmark stadiums and pushed the progress of several large urban development projects, comparable to the 1992 Barcelona Olympics. This reveals a kind of regional functional division: while Abu Dhabi focuses primarily on motor, air, and water sport of the highest calibre, Dubai and Doha are home to prime tournaments, for example in tennis, golf, and equestrian sport. Since winning the FIFA Cup, Qatar has clearly set itself apart from Dubai in its quest for speed, hypermodernity, and luxury. Similarly, Oman's more modest, but no less prominent sport activities allow it to distance itself further from its glamourous northern neighbour: cycling and sailing have become integral elements of the comprehensive Brand Oman campaign; especially water sport has been closely linked to the purposefully emphasised seafaring traditions of the nation (see below) and, in close cooperation with tourism marketing, to its natural maritime assets. With the Asia Games in Riyadh, Saudi Arabia will hold its first major athletic event in 2034, but has now submitted an application for the Olympic Winter Games and is considering doing the same for the Summer Games.

In line with overall interpretations of projects and urbanism in the Golf region, facilities like the Dubai and Doha Sports Cities and the architectures for racetracks and stadiums represent artificial sport worlds and exhibition theme parks that function as hyperreal attractions, entirely master-planned and lacking historical and temporal embedding.[170] According to Kristin Anabel Eggeling, "[R]ather than representing an existing reality, the projects in this sector help *make* the realities of which they speak, thereby *fixing* a certain interpretation of social reality."[171] Motives for such sport-related branding are very consistent with other fields

167 Jeddah was added to the Grand Prix in 2021.

168 Cf. Govers, 2012.

169 While bids for the Summer Olympics failed, Qatar will host the Asian Games again in 2030.

170 Cf. Bromber and Krawietz, 2013; also Bromber, 2014: 123–124.

171 Eggeling, 2020: 138–139.

of nation and city branding. The multifaceted image that is communicated speaks to different audiences. Domestically, sport is used to strengthen cultural identity, social cohesion, and patriotism and to secure the power of the political system.[172] It serves as a vehicle for economic, infrastructural, and urban development and to make the country a healthy sporting nation. Top-down branding and royal patronage of the high-profile projects link the sport-state closely to the visions and positions of the regime. Stadiums, for instance, combine up-to-date technology and design with shapes, symbols, and motifs referencing local history and heritage.

In the global arena, sport is all about improving a country's image, showing international presence, and overcoming clichés of backwardness and conflict. It serves to make the small Gulf sheikhdoms, in particular, bigger than they are. Besides, it is very concretely about attracting investment and tourism to national economies; for corporations and organisations involved in sponsoring events and clubs, it can enhance their own brand value through co-branding effects.[173] It can help to bolster diplomatic partnerships, alliances, and support, especially when a state like Qatar is surrounded by hostile neighbours. This did not prevent the blockade in 2017, which was assumed to aim also at undermining the organisation of the football competition; conversely, the latter may have contributed to the lifting of the boycott in 2021, as the initiators did not want to suffer any damage to their own image. Ultimately, it is not just individual cities or nations that position themselves in and through the sport segment, but the entire Gulf region that benefits from increased awareness and reputation.[174]

But such strong self-portrayals can easily turn into their opposite and provoke strong criticism. Thus, already in the early 2010s, Bahrain suffered an image setback, when the very positive reputation it had generated in the media with Formula I was seriously damaged by the harsh persecution of protesters during the "Pearl" uprising.[175] In particular in connection with the 2022 World Cup, "sportswashing" has become an important catchword. Similar to allegations of greenwashing, this neologism points to the calculated staging of sport for proactive international reputation management, by hiding and silencing harmful policies and

---

172 On diverse domestic, regional, and global ambitions and effects, cf. Eggeling, 2020: 132–139; Sons, 2022: 20–23; Bromber and Krawietz, 2013: 190; Bromber, 2014: 120–125; Windecker and Sendrowicz, 2014: 90, 103; Scharfenort, 2014: 71.

173 On this co-branding effect, cf. Ginesta and de San Eugenio, 2014: 226. Cf. also Scharfenort, 2010: 5; Ibahrine, 2016: 108–109.

174 Cf. especially Scharfenort, 2010: 6.

175 Cf. Govers, 2012: 52–56.

impacts that run counter to proclaimed objectives.[176] Accordingly, the event drew attention to social issues that appeared important in the eyes of the (Western) world public, although this viewpoint was often marked by orientalising clichés and hypocrisy. Its scandalisation clearly went beyond the politicisation of similar earlier major international sporting events.

The main criticisms were of violations of essential human and social rights and the miserable living and working conditions of the migrants who built the stadiums. Consequently, the Qatari government improved some labour rights. Strong reservations also arose about massive corruption in the process of awarding the games and the relatively fruitless attempts to promote women's football, as provided for in FIFA's award statutes. Health and environmental concerns about matches in the summer heat were countered by moving them to the cooler season and using modular constructions, combined with the idea of later altruistic donations to poorer countries.[177] Shortly before the opening of the Games, the focus turned to how the Games would be run, from the potential harassment of LGBTQ visitors to restrictions on alcohol consumption on site. Moreover, fans have questioned advertising partnerships with their clubs; and the granting of Qatari citizenship, which is otherwise almost unobtainable, to recognised international athletes in order for them to join the national team has also come in for criticism from time to time.[178] In official circles, large parts of the Qatari population, and beyond that the Arab world, this criticism was perceived as Eurocentric and Arabophobic, especially since the critics themselves were far from meeting their own standards; rather, the Games were presented above all as a reason for national and regional pride.

7.3 Branding Endeavours in Other Arab Gulf States

Bahrain, benefitting from the regional boom and Beirut's decline, has since the mid-1970s developed its brand as an offshore banking hub and, despite emerging competition from other Gulf countries, is today still one of the most important financial services centres in the Middle East. Intra-Arab tourism also became an im-

176 On the term, cf. Skey, 2022. The notion came up in 2015 in connection with the European Games in autocratic Azerbaijan; it was used again, when Russia hosted the football cup in 2018. But many antecedents exist, such as the propagandistic use of the 1936 Olympics in the Third Reich and the 1934 and 1978 World Cups in fascist Italy and military-ruled Argentina, respectively. On the FIFA 2022 controversy, cf. Reuß, 2022; Beck, 2022; Sons, 2022: 20–21; Fruh, Archer, and Wojtowicz, 2023; Ibahrine, 2016: 113.

177 Cf. Koch, 2014: 1120; Eggeling, 2020: 135–136.

178 On this, cf. already Peterson, 2006: 747.

portant factor, mainly because of more liberal customs in proximity to Saudi Arabia. Since the early 2000s, location marketing, based on established strategies, has been a fundamental instrument to further diversify its economy and attract foreign investment.[179] Competitiveness, sustainability, and justice have been the guiding principles of Bahrain's national Vision 2030 variant. The public-private Economic Development Board conducted a successful global "Business Friendly Bahrain" advertising campaign. But the country's positive reputation was tarnished considerably following the violent suppression of the 2011 uprisings, mostly led by protesters from the less affluent Shiʿi population majority. This also revealed the limited identification potential of the brand for this part of the population. As a result, international conferences moved to Doha, the annual Bahrain Grand Prix was cancelled, new foreign investment was postponed, and tourists stayed away.

In Bahrain, too, large-scale urban projects were to become image carriers and point the way to the country's future.[180] Among the first to emulate Dubai, it developed two major artificial island projects. The reconstruction of Manama's old town, which had been increasingly abandoned by its established population because of its dilapidated infrastructure, is also a means of city marketing. The redesigns were each placed under a motto, for example as a "Pearling Trail," which refers to the historically important pearl fishing and trade and serves to positively portray the ruling dynasty. Decisions are usually made without transparency by the most influential members of the royal court. Thus, the historical souk was demolished and replaced by a more attractive shopping centre, which, however, led to segregation processes between different income groups.

In contrast, Kuwait, probably long one of the most economically advanced Gulf states, seems to be the region's least-studied case of branding – perhaps due to the heavy setback it experienced during the 1990/91 Gulf War that drew attention to other, ostensibly more pressing issues. Accordingly, in this volume, two colleagues investigate the emirate, focusing on issues that also concern the wider Arab Gulf area. In line with the explanations in the previous chapter, Laura Hindelang demonstrates the long-lasting adoption of stamps with deliberate designs for nation branding in Kuwait and other Gulf countries. This is based on her book, in which she studied the aesthetic staging of petro-modernity in Kuwait's urban and national visual culture since the 1950s. In contrast to arguments that city branding follows the establishment of a basic infrastructure, already in times of high modernity, visual representations of the city advanced development projects

179 Cf. Moock, 2012.
180 Cf. Margraff, 2019. Cf. also Margraff and Scharfenort, 2017.

and sometimes remained images only.[181] With the takeover of the postal system, the Kuwaiti government issued its own postage stamps that manifested a new visual presence and challenged the national oil company's predominance in branding the state and the city. The first set of stamps depicted sites of architectural and infrastructural development that were considered the most attractive for the country's self-promotion. This contrasted with stamps from other Arab countries at that time, which still corresponded to the colonial gaze. In his text-cum-photo essay, Roman Stadnicki continues in this line under postmodern post-oil conditions in Kuwait and other Gulf states, where billboards dominate the urban scene with images that tend to become independent of the projects they advertise – and that even survive when projects have long been abandoned.

Saudi Arabia and its rulers already have a brand core identity as the Custodian of the Two Holy Mosques, which attract a huge number of pilgrims every year. In addition, the country is certainly the best-known oil exporter and home to the company with MENA's highest brand value (Table 1). In contrast to its conservative and illiberal image, the Kingdom is now increasingly seeking to distinguish itself through economic diversification, socio-cultural modernisation, and political moderation. Already the foundation of the KAUST symbolised the government's technology- and environment-related ambitions.[182] The programmatic Saudi Vision 2030, announced in 2016, is a central branding tool to convey the image of a progressing and modern nation. Economically, the programme anticipates a boost in investment and diversification in the long run, but also includes important promises of transparency, consultation, and social freedoms, which should help to rebrand the perception of the country.[183] A special target is to promote the country "as a new frontier for world-class tourism"[184] by creating large-scale entertainment and theme parks, upscale vacation resorts, heritage areas (including the promotion of pre-Islamic sites), and cultural institutions. This involves the use of cutting-edge social media and a "Gateway" travel programme for bloggers and influencers. Mega-events have started to play an important role: this includes well-marketed cultural activities arranged by the specially established General Entertainment Authority, as well as sport championships, which again provoked allegations of green- and sportswashing.[185]

Among cities, only Jeddah long benefited from its image as a relatively open and liberal place with centuries-old trade connections; "Jeddah is Different"

181 Cf. Hindelang, 2022.

182 For Saudi Arabia's green policies, cf. Zumbrägel, 2020: esp. 167–221.

183 Cf., also in the following, Klingmann, 2021: 41–44.

184 Klingmann, 2021: 42.

185 Cf. Tagesschau, 2022c and 2023.

(*Ǧidda ġayr*) has been the motto of its annual summer festival.[186] Although in principle Mecca does not need an ambitious active branding to attract people, since the 2000s it has embarked on an urban renovation programme to rise from a religious destination to a model world city for development and modernisation.[187] In fact, the construction of new skyscrapers, including the hyperreal *Abraj Al Bait* Clock Tower, the fourth-tallest building in the world and simulating London's Big Ben, shopping malls, and accommodation and leisure facilities in immediate proximity to the Great Mosque, has in the eyes of national critics obscured the city's holy centre, instigated feelings of alienation, and forced the relocation of many local residents. The 2030 Vision also encompassed a programme for improving Saudi cities' national and international attractiveness and provides a framework for sustainable, future-oriented urban development meeting international standards.[188] A special focus of urban and architectural branding strategies is on Riyadh, in the attempt to make the national capital, reputed for its tediousness and car-orientation, a globally recognised city. To create a positive image directed at international travellers and an affluent local clientele, dimensions such as culture, leisure, lifestyle, public transport, and greening drew special attention. However, participatory and inclusive elements are still missing in the urban development and branding strategies. Similar to megaprojects in other MENA countries, the high dependency on fluctuating oil revenues and the imponderabilities of global crises challenge the extent to which these widely communicated dreams will be realised one day.

The programme of six New Economic Cities announced in 2005 has become perhaps the most important rebranding asset. In fact, by now, only King Abdullah Economic City, established as a logistical and manufacturing platform, has made some still-limited progress. Most branding initiatives for it have been undertaken by local agencies and developers instead of by national authorities.[189] In the city's initial development phase, branding focused on economic and social progress, urban development, attachment to the Saudi Vision, and national pride; different identities were used to target prospective domestic and international clients. However, the weak performance and low transparency in the city's development endangered its overall public image. As an exemplary case, its built urban form and physical fabric developed in mutual interaction with place branding. In 2014, a management change stabilised the megaproject, a new visual identity was developed, and branding turned to a more global audience, underlining luxu-

186 Cf. Shoaib, 2017: 56–57.

187 On Mecca, cf. Al Amoudy, 2014; Bsheer, 2010.

188 Cf. Klingmann, 2021.

189 Cf. Shoaib, 2017. Cf. also Shoaib and Keivani, 2015.

ry, affluence, and exclusivity. Media increasingly took notice of the project, and the number of articles in Arab newspapers steadily grew.

Probably the most acclaimed project in the international media is NEOM, presented for the first time in 2017 as part of the Saudi Vision. This vast complex, fully automated and powered exclusively by renewable energies, envisages a series of urban projects, including an industrial city and a luxury seaside resort. In particular, the 170-kilometre-long, car-free linear city The Line has become prominent since its announcement in early 2021; the Trojena skiing resort, declared 100 % sustainable, too, appeared in the media together with the award of the Asian Winter Games in 2029. NEOM's branding has served to position the to-be-built city within the global competition of places, make it a global hub for trade, innovation, and knowledge, and attract the desired investors and creative class of "dreamers." The vision behind it is giving birth to a new kind of a "PowerPoint city" that for now exists only virtually; accordingly, the question arises whether the object of its marketing is actually the city, or rather a start-up, the country, or its initiator's personal dream.[190]

Politically, the Kingdom endeavours to position itself in competition especially with other Gulf countries that are more active on the diplomatic front; economically, since it penetrates in sectors like tourism and entertainment, it is in competitive rivalry with them.[191] International events, such as sport meetings, political summits, and environmental conferences started to be used to politically brand the country and its current leadership. A large number of environmental and research institutions have been named after the late and the current kings and support their personal image and power legitimacy.[192] Especially the de facto ruler Mohammed bin Salman Al Saud is a master of self-marketing. It was he who, a year before his nomination as a Crown Prince in 2017, launched the Vision 2030, which, at both the domestic and the international level, branded him as a forward-thinking ruler; he pushed several policies related to greater social and cultural liberties, mostly for economic motives, while at the same time he is eager to maintain his authoritarian rule. He also prominently announced most of the country's new urban megaprojects.[193] As Hend Aly has already shown in her recent article[194] and details further in this volume, NEOM was above all an instrument of his personal branding. After his star-like rise as a young, progressive leader, his international image experienced a series of setbacks, due to his role in the

190 Cf. Aly, 2019. Cf. also Farag, 2019.
191 Cf. Ulrichsen, 2021.
192 Cf. Zumbrägel, 2020: 204–205.
193 Cf. Klingmann, 2021: 41, 43.
194 Cf. again Aly, 2019.

Yemen war, the Qatar blockade, and the murder of the Saudi journalist Jamal Khashoggi. He now attempts to position himself and his country as the inevitable pivot in regional policy at the GCC level and to recast himself from an impulsive, destabilising leader into a moderate and responsible statesman and Saudi Arabia's diplomatic face.[195]

Compared with Dubai, two decades ago, Oman was still virtually unknown to the wider world.[196] Yet, preceding Qatar, the Sultanate had already acquired a reputation as a mediator in regional conflicts that is on good terms with all sides.[197] In the immediate vicinity of the UAE, Oman is under its considerable economic, politic, and social influence, but insists on its own independent, more moderate development path. It was not until the mid-1990s that Oman, based on its Vision 2020, began to diversify its economy and to orient itself towards international markets. Since then, it has made great efforts, in particular, to attract high-end tourism and to establish itself as a trade and transport hub in global networks. Gradually, large infrastructure and urban development projects were initiated. In particular, often with the help of project developers from other Gulf states, it began to build "Integrated Tourism Complexes" (ITCs) that include residential, shopping, and sometimes educational and medical facilities. The growing similarity of such resorts has required huge marketing efforts, which also serve to put Oman on the world map as a tourist destination and a place to live. At the same time, urban space has been increasingly festivalised. For trade development, Oman established a series of big ports, rivalling other Gulf cities, and combined them with adjacent free economic and industrial zones.

Its current tourism branding wants to contrast the Sultanate to its bustling neighbour as a quiet destination with deep historical roots and a varied landscape. On the brink of the 2010s, the tourism slogan changed from Oman as "The Essence of Arabia," with a certain Orientalist undertone, to "Beauty has an address," marking the difference from the other nearby sheikhdoms. As a brand ambassador, the national carrier's logo then shifted from the traditional dagger to a symbol reminiscent of frankincense smoke, and the airline's co-branding campaign pointed to Oman as "The Soul of Arabia" (cf. above). The Oman Brand Management Unit was established to promote products of Omani origin and a trademark logo was introduced, which was primarily for domestic use; later, a "Brand Oman" campaign and logo served to promote Oman internationally. However, its umbrella character pertaining to diverse sectors like tourism, business, IT, and education seemed to be

195 Cf. Ulrichsen, 2021.

196 On Oman's branding, cf. in the following especially Wippel, 2014 and 2016a; for a more recent and encompassing work, Klinger, 2022: esp. 362–412.

197 Cf., e.g., Kechichian, 1995.

confusing and losing focus.[198] Moreover, many interviewed local citizens either did not know or did not care about these branding efforts.[199] In his paper following later in this volume, Thibaut Klinger elaborates in more detail nation branding's interaction with spatial planning and its contributions to shape national identity and to legitimate the ruler in power.

Branding is a key tool in the redevelopment of the Omani capital, as well. Muscat presented itself as the Arab "cultural capital" (2006) and "tourism capital" (2012). Urban revitalisation and reconstruction in the metropolitan area are geared towards skilful marketing to increase recognisability and to position the city in local, regional, and international contexts.[200] In addition to attracting attention, investment, tourists, and a highly skilled workforce, urban development projects, which are usually built in the most attractive and central urban locations, aim to impress the local population, foster national unity, and, via personal branding, secure the power position of the caring Sultan Qaboos (r. 1970–2020). In the process, the attempt to develop Muttrah, one of the two old city centres, into the most important tourist destination of the capital agglomeration is a beacon within the country's marketing strategy and has resulted in far-reaching social, functional, and spatial restructuring, including conversion of the country's former main port into an attractive world-class waterfront. Old Muscat, which has largely lost its importance as the seat of government, has been rebranded as a cultural flagship, but without urban life away from the tourist crowds. To cater for mass cruise tourism, the Muttrah Souk was visually "beautified" for the tourist gaze and branded with stories from the Arabian Nights as an authentic Oriental market in a fairy tale country.[201] This fits well with Oman's self-Orientalisation when it situates itself within a Western-centric discourse of tourism promotion. National history and culture are thereby transformed into assets to be traded on the international tourism market and at the same time authorise the regime's understanding of the past and vision of the future.[202] Cultural and climatic features make the southern region of Dhofar another tourist attraction.[203] Instead of a specific local marketing campaign, Dhofar's image, which refers to the area's fertility and its frankincense tradition, is part of the national branding and immediately contributes to it. Local ITCs are advertised mainly by their seclusion and the attractive combination of

198 Cf. also Alzadjali, 2010; Klinger, 2022: 369–370.

199 Cf. Al Balushi, Butt, and Al Siyabi, 2013.

200 Cf. in comparison with Manama, Margraff and Scharfenort, 2017; Margraff, 2019.

201 Cf. Gutberlet, 2019.

202 Cf. Feighery, 2012, discussing a tourism promotional film.

203 On Salalah, cf. also Wippel, 2015 and 2016b: 88–96.

new and old; their eclectic style symbolises an invented hybrid "Orient," and their marketing presents them as an "effectively enacted utopia."[204]

Nation branding includes issues of regional orientation and belonging. Internally, this serves self-identification and nation-building; externally, the Sultanate tries to position itself as a site for production, trade, and tourism. In connection with, e.g., the new port of Salalah that is to become a central hub of world trade, and to link past and present, reference is made to historical glory and prosperity and continuous or renewed traditions and know-how, to deeply entrenched openness to the outside world, and to inherited cosmopolitanism based on Oman's trans-oceanic empire and trade connections.[205] This includes its self-image as an experienced seafaring nation. Therefore, national narratives repeatedly allude to the legend of Sindbad as a son of the country who sailed the seas of the world at a very early time. This has been enacted with symbolic and highly mediatised events, such as rebuilding traditional vessels and sending them on expeditions along the maritime Silk Road to Venice or Singapore, which aimed to reflect the early basis for today's orientation towards tourism and trade. The wooden *dhow* is a ubiquitous motif embodied by countless logos, pictures, and monuments (cf. the cover of this book and my precursory explanation). The country's historic role as an *entrepôt* for trade and its strategic location are repeatedly emphasised, which translates into a geoeconomically favourable position at the crossroads between Asia and Africa and East and West and as a gateway to the Indian Ocean. Accordingly, its nation branding positions the country less at the periphery of the conflict-driven Arab world than in the centre of a transregional and transcultural maritime region, which is simultaneously located at geographical, temporal, and cultural interfaces.

Ports in general are objects of branding. A study of the website branding of the largest seaports in the Middle East and along the Arabian Peninsula showed that Jebel Ali in Dubai, the most important transhipment hub in the region and long among the Top Ten by throughput worldwide, was the only one that had developed a distinctive brand personality.[206] In Oman, the establishment of the Port of Sohar was accompanied by an aggressive branding campaign, even up to placing promotional material in front of the Jebel Ali port entrance to entice transhippers. For countries such as Qatar, Oman, and the UAE, infrastructure branding was part of the enhancement of their country's images. In ports, "competence" was generally the most frequently used semantic field, pointing to technical superiority, ef-

204 Cf. Wippel, 2014: 107, following Michel Foucault's concept of "heterotopias."
205 Cf. especially Wippel, 2013 and 2017.
206 Cf. Rutter et al., 2018.

ficiency, and safety. The similarity of images displayed by ports within the same country indicates important country-of-origin effects. Thus, the Omani ports of Salalah and Sohar both made strong connections to the national sovereign.

8 Place Branding in the Middle East and its Entanglements

The current wave of place branding has also spread beyond the Arab Gulf countries to other parts of the MENA region. Accordingly, this subsection tours across the Middle East, from Iran at the opposite side of the Persian Gulf to the Levant and Turkey. This is followed by another subsection on Northern Africa, from Egypt to Morocco at the Western end of the Arab world.

8.1 Timid Branding Efforts in the Islamic Republic of Iran

Across the Persian Gulf, branding in Iran has been much less investigated. Since its establishment, the Islamic Republic had an overwhelmingly negative reputation as a "rogue state" in large parts of the world. Obviously, in the political and religious realm, leading figures like Ayatollah Ruhollah Khomeini (r. 1979–1989) have been well-known, controversial personal brands. However, as in many authoritarian regimes, cultural diplomacy has been used to soften tensions over the last decades.

Through its widely acclaimed cinema, poetry, theatre, and fine arts, Iran has been able to maintain an image as a distinct cultural hotspot. Although these cultural activities are often dissident, they support the country's image, especially compared with the Arabic Gulf states, which have not been culturally active for nearly as long. Iranian cinema, in particular, including films from the diaspora, after benefitting from some relief from censorship, have gained international recognition and obtained numerous awards in international film festivals.[207] Vice versa, these films also assisted these festivals to develop a distinct brand. The *Berlinale*, in particular, used its focus on Iranian cinema since the mid-2000s to co-brand itself as a politically engaged festival in a city, where it was founded in the early 1950s as a showcase of the "free world" and that also helped to stage non-conformist movies and to highlight the personal brands of persecuted filmmak-

207 Cf., for instance, Strohmaier, 2019.

ers.[208] As already mentioned, Dubai has developed as a global centre for showing and selling Iranian artwork and a meeting point for Iranian artists from home and exile, among themselves and with their critics and buyers.[209] Domestically, Tehran's art scene, in particular, has developed, too, and has drawn increasing interest from foreign observers.[210] This includes the many murals on buildings that are a feature of the capital's cityscape. Such public art installations, either tolerated or commissioned by the municipality, can be seen as part of a branding-like campaign. Modern public murals, billboards, and tile works not only serve as identity markers for the country's own citizenry, but also aim to counter the negative outside image of the country.[211]

Although a comprehensive strategy of nation branding has not been pursued yet by Iranian authorities, place branding nevertheless has occurred in tourism and other sectors. In an application-oriented approach, some authors thought about how to improve the positioning of big entertainment, residential, and sport projects in the country, particularly by defining a brand that respects Persian cultural and historical identity.[212] In a phase of relative détente in the 2000s, big cities in Iran also started profiling themselves and made attempts to develop into attractive and liveable places.[213] In the self-images promoted in their masterplans and on their websites, religious, cultural, historical, and natural dimensions featured more prominently than in comparable cities in Germany or China. A focus on future economic development, smartness, and knowledge-orientation, as well as the most professional branding strategies, appeared mainly in cities that had already experienced some economic progress. Tehran showed the strongest global ambitions as a "world-class" city, while Mashhad, Isfahan, Tabriz, and Qom were the most eager to demonstrate the links between past, present, and future. Yet, this did not fully overlap with the set of cities that stood the most firmly behind their policy choices and were therefore accredited the highest brand credibility.

For a few years now, the city of Qom, which is widely reputed the religious capital of Iran and had a key role in the Iranian Revolution, has experienced a

208 Cf. Ullmann, 2020. In 2021, Viktor Ullman successfully defended his (as yet unpublished) PhD thesis "Staging Iranian Cinema at the Berlinale" at the *Freie Universität Berlin.* Compare also his presentation "Buddy-Bears: Discursive Branding of Iranian Cinema at the Berlinale" at the *Deutsche Orientalistentag* 2017 in Jena.

209 Cf. again Moghadam, 2018 and 2021.

210 Cf., e.g., newspaper articles such as Krüger, 2017.

211 Cf. Walter, 2016.

212 See, e.g., Divandari, Ekhlassi, and Rahmani, 2014.

213 Cf. Noori and De Jong, 2018.

sweeping rebranding.[214] Based on its well-known Islamic architecture, it wants to boost its tourism profile, but also intends to become a smart and green city. Compared with other big Iranian cities, it scored high in displaying an overarching strategy.[215] While municipal authorities aspired to conserve the city's historical image, recent trends in urban formation and policy made Qom enter the path of "Islamicised capitalism," neoliberal urbanism, and middle-class consumerism. Shopping centres, luxurious shops selling international brands, and leisure facilities have popped up across the city. Fashionable neoclassicist villas present a post-modern architecture of Western origin. Many of the mushrooming buildings in the better parts of Qom belong to religious seminaries competing to have the most spectacular and luxurious ones. The prosperity of the richer neighbourhoods contrasts with the disregard for poorer parts of the city, and social protests have erupted time and again. In this volume, Kamaluddin Duaei demonstrates the role of the new social media and of Qom's closeness to Tehran, making it a kind of wider suburb in its factual rebranding.

8.2 Branding the Levant between High-Tech, Pinkwashing, and the Conditions of War

In the Levant, beyond being a nation rich in historical and religious places, Israel, since its founding, has endeavoured to position itself as an innovative high-tech superpower and to transform this into a strong nation brand. It developed from a small-country model in agricultural and irrigation technologies resisting a naturally and politically inhospitable environment into one of the most important centres for information and security technology and a pioneer in areas such as medical technology, biotechnology, and nanotechnology, and today not least in artificial intelligence.[216] Beyond this reputation as a "start-up nation" and "Silicon Wadi," since the early 2000s, Israel also recognised the need to rebrand the country and overcome detrimental images that trigger antisemitism, anti-Israeli rhetoric, and divestment campaigns. For this, led by the Ministry of Public Diplomacy and Diaspora Affairs (with the Jewish diaspora playing an essential role as brand ambassadors), the government invested in *hasbara*, approximately "soft power," to counter the negative perceptions and to discredit sceptics of Israeli pol-

214 On Qom, cf. Duaei, 2019.
215 Cf. Noori and De Jong, 2018: 10–14.
216 From a political economics perspective, cf., e.g., Hofmann, 2020.

icy.[217] As part of this operation, US supporters, such as the Brand Israel group, launched initiatives to turn existing brand awareness into a more controlled, positive direction of a sympathetic nation and multicultural melting pot.[218]

Hence, much of the nation's branding has been done in large part to conceal controversial dimensions of the Israeli state. Culture ranked high in these endeavours, including promoting Israeli writers and artists abroad and inviting foreign celebrities to tour Israel. First, what Rhys Crilley and Ilan Manor call "un-nation branding," promotion, e.g. as a destination, has avoided (too much) reference to the nation state, but has represented Israel through its regions and cities, such as Jerusalem and Tel Aviv. Vice versa, cities obviated being associated with the state of Israel in their branding.[219] Second, a particular strategy was to stage Israel as liberal and open-minded towards gay and LGBTQ life and rights.[220] Tel Aviv, in particular, is presented as a hotspot for leisure, a meeting point of the youth of the world and in particular for the larger LGBTQ community. The pride festivities in the "Gay Capital of the Middle East" soon attracted a lot of visitors, many of whom returned to their home countries with positive impressions, including the "safety" provided by Israeli forces at such events. At the same time, disseminated images of Western modernity and progressivity contrast with exoticising Orientalist ones and make Tel Aviv a symbol of the "Progressive Orient." Yet, soon critical voices, including opposition from the queer community itself, accused this branding of "pinkwashing" and inherent homonational aspects.[221] The festivalisation of basically political concerns was opposed as commodifying and consumeristic. In particular, it is criticised that the positive, gay-friendly image is exploited by Israeli foreign policy to divert attention from the continuing occupation of Palestinian territory and violations of Palestinians' human rights. White gay people feel misused by this brand strategy for anti-Arab and anti-Muslim sentiments, while LGBTQ people from other ethnic backgrounds still face many problems in and from Israeli politics and society. Simultaneously, this was also an opportunity for a local *Mizrahi* ("Oriental" Jewish) gay culture to develop.

In a similar direction, accusations of greenwashing are directed, e.g. against a large-scale wind turbine farm project on the Golan Heights.[222] The project is part of a decades-long campaign by the Israeli state to boost its image as green and eco-

217 Cf. Dart, 2016: 1406–1408.
218 Cf. Popper, 2005; Cravatts, 2007.
219 Cf. Crilley and Manor, 2020.
220 Cf. Kama and Ram, 2020; Hartal and Sasson-Levy, 2021.
221 Cf. also Schulman, 2011; Ritchie, 2015; Dart, 2016: 1408. Moreover, see Skey, 2022: 4 on the concept, compared with greenwashing and sportswashing.
222 Cf. Dajani, 2020.

friendly. This not only contrasts with its enormously high per capita ecological footprint; the country's image is further tarnished by environmental rights violations in the occupied territories. Considered part of Israel's green colonialism, the project stands against the interests of the local inhabitants. Finally, small sport events were used to project a positive image of the country.[223] Yet, critical Palestinians and their European supporters denounced this and asked for the, at least symbolic, exclusion of Israel from international institutions and tournaments.

In contrast to Israel, it has proved difficult for the Palestinian community to keep up by pursuing an equally positive image building. Its situation is perhaps best characterised as being "[t]he newest country probably with the oldest nation brand in the world."[224] Even if cities such as Bethlehem and Jerusalem were important pilgrimage destinations for centuries, Palestine suffers from having an undefined state brand. Developing a nation brand has not really been a priority since the establishment of the Palestinian Authority in 1993, except for a few initiatives to brand exports. Accordingly, two papers discuss fundamental questions of the development of a successful image via nation branding and public diplomacy on a theoretical basis. In general, it is proposed to integrate a wide spectrum of stakeholders to ensure that all critical building factors are being considered.[225] It is suggested, for example, that governmental bodies involve Palestinian writers who could market the story of the Palestinian refugees better and more convincingly than the official story delivered by diplomats.[226] In contrast, reference to history and religion is considered too sensitive, as it collides with the Israeli narrative of having been the first in previously empty lands. To counter the image of victimhood and statelessness, Dalal Iriqat proposes to concentrate on the human capital of its heroes, from iconic political leaders such as Yasser Arafat to contemporary artists, poets, singers, and musicians; other identifiable unique selling points could be the high number of world heritage sites and cultural aspects, from traditional dress[227] to cuisine and hospitality.

The capital of Israel's northern neighbour has an old reputation as the "Paris of the (Middle) East," while the country had the byname of the "Switzerland of the

223 For a soft power perspective, cf. Dart, 2016.

224 Abdalmajid and Papasolomou, 2018: 189.

225 Cf. Abdalmajid and Papasolomou, 2018.

226 Cf. Iriqat, 2019.

227 In line with this, Nagla Abed, who presented a paper "Palestinian Women: Preservers of History, Culture and Identity through Tatreez [i.e. embroidery]" at the 27th International DAVO Congress 2021 in Osnabrück, originally proposed an (unfortunately not realised) article for this volume on "No Nation Branding for Palestine: Changing the Image of Palestine through Women-led Social Media Initiatives to Preserve Cultural Heritage."

Middle East," stemming from its banking and entertainment industries, art scene, tourism potential, and variegated landscapes.[228] This image already singled Lebanon out as an exceptional Arab nation, but was repeatedly tarnished by periods of war and unrest. With its immense downtown reconstruction project after the civil war (1975–1990), Beirut aspired to modernise and develop into a "Hongkong on the Mediterranean."[229] The city recovered, was in large parts remodelled according to neoliberal urban planning, and has become another paradigmatic case of post-modern urbanism. While its cosmopolitanism and Westernisation are promoted by entrepreneurs and the state to attract business and, in particular, tourism, this contrasts with the image of sectarian strife that still marks post-war Beirut, as it is publicly reflected in the personality cult around sectarian leaders and in public rallies that brandish portraits of martyrs, flags, and insignia as emblems of collective identities. In the 2000s, the Ministry of Tourism made great efforts to rebrand the country and to encourage Arabs and Westerners to fly in for visits. New large urban development projects were widely advertised with slogans such as "Beirut is back on the map" or "The World is Beiruting Again" (Fig. 3a).

Fig. 3: (Re-)branding Beirut
Sources: Photo Ghassan Moussawi, 2010; Rasool, 2021. The first image is courtesy of the photographer.

Above all, over the past century, Beirut acquired a reputation as the nightlife destination of choice in the region – from the era of the grand ball during the Mandate period to informal underground nightlife during the civil war.[230] Nowadays, Beirut has regained this former reputation for lifestyle and entertainment.[231] This concurs with its widely perceived image as a liberal and tolerant place,

228 Cf. Seidman, 2012; Abdallah, 2015.
229 On this label, cf. Schmid, 2001.
230 Cf. Buchakjian, 2015.
231 Cf. Abdallah, 2015.

where consuming alcohol poses no problems, gambling is allowed, women can move and dress freely, men find their – also sexual – pleasures, and people of all classes, beliefs, and countries can meet and mix. This has resulted in another label, that of "Sin City," especially in the eyes and minds of many Arabs. Photography plays a major role in the global image of Beirutas the capital of nightlife fun. It constitutes a kind of grassroots place branding, which is also an implicit resource for state authorities seeking to promote the "Brand Beirut." Decadent parties became the pride of the city and a showcase for the whole country. Certain quarters such as Hamra, in particular, benefit from a collective representation as especially secular and diverse, catering to the various needs of its visitors.[232] The assumed geopolitical exceptionality in the Middle East, which is part of the original national myth, is thereby paralleled by similarly conveyed images of differentiation inside Lebanon and within the capital of modern and globalised vs. conservative and communitarian places. Inherent in these narratives is a normative claim that these progressive territories and places should serve as a model for other parts of the region, nation, or city. Certain quarters emerged as new hotspots of alcohol consumption with a reputation for fashionable brands of liquor and spirits. [233] In this volume, Marie Bonte discusses alcohol branding and how it becomes connected with growing demands for more liberties under still sectarian religious law.

In particular, the city experienced a "queering" of its exceptionalism. It acquired a reputation as a place and "safe haven" where the LGBTQ communities and visitors from East and West can freely meet and party, similar to Tel Aviv, less than 250 kilometres to the south, but barred by an impermeable border.[234] Academia, too, has started to critically analyse the complexities and incongruities of these ascriptions, the gaps between the brand and lived realities, on the one hand, and inherent Orientalisms, on the other. Nightlife in general, and queer life in particular, are characterised by many exclusive moments, mainly with regard to possibilities of access, based on income, race, gender, and nationality, which the inclusive branding avoids mentioning. Ghassan Moussawi interprets his work on "Fractal Orientalism" further in the direction of branding distinctiveness at various spatial scales in his chapter of this book. The current multiple crises of economic collapse, political unrest, covid pandemic, and the mega-explosion in the harbour make it difficult to maintain Beirut's polished image; generally speaking, Gregory Buchakjian considers the rise and fall of Beirut as a nightlife

---

232 Cf. Seidman, 2012; Abdallah, 2015: 9.

233 Cf. Bonte, 2016.

234 Cf. Bonte, 2013; Moussawi, 2013, 2018, and 2019.

destination a paradigm for the failed state.[235] Consequently, in 2021, the (Maronite) tourism minister launched a new promotional campaign "I love you in your madness" (English version: "A crazy love"), alluding to the recent turbulences as well as to the country's exceptionalism (Fig. 3b). The "bold" slogan to be carried into the world by the national airline and social media instantly triggered criticism, especially from the (Sunni) prime minister, for turning instability into a reason for pride.[236]

Other countries in this part of the Middle East, for example Syria and Iraq, currently have much bigger problems branding themselves positively. Correspondingly, few studies consider branding issues in these countries. As mentioned above, despite the ongoing war, Syria has continued to sell itself in an outdated way as a tourist destination. In the late 2000s, Damascus was characterised by a mix of frozen socialist appearance (from its architecture to the ubiquitous slogans) and a "new architectural philosophy" that reflected the economic opening and the atmosphere of new beginnings; this was mirrored in newly opened hotels, shopping malls, and cultural institutions – the image of the "Beirutisation" of the capital was certainly a welcome side effect that found its way also into Western newspapers.[237] The introduction of the Dubai model in Damascus, manifested in (a limited number of) high-end residential, commercial, and office projects – cancelled or put on hold soon after the outbreak of war in 2011 – served as a modernisation narrative for private interests. This policy resulted from a "combination of the local authorities' need for a 'quick fix' to solve multiple internal urban issues, the Syrian state's desire to attract new investments and the investment strategies (mainly) from big Gulf property developers."[238]

Important changes also happened in the brandscape of consumer products, imported or manufactured under licence (notably fashion, food, health and beauty products, technical items), since the country's cautious *infitāḥ* in the 1990.[239] Simultaneously, this contributed to the transformation of the urban landscape, from the mushrooming large advertising posters to the emergence of new distribution cen-

---

235 Personal communication. Last but not least, this accumulation of adverse circumstances has prevented two scholars who had already agreed to participate in this edited volume from completing their contributions, one by Gregory Buchakjian on "The Rise and Fall of Beirut as Nightlife Destination: Paradigm for a Failed State," the other by Sally Zakhia, "Territorial Branding and Local Development in Ehden, Lebanon: An Economic Factor Facing the 2020 Crisis in Rural Areas," on efforts to brand smaller communities in the countryside.

236 Cf., e.g., Sheikh Moussa, 2021; Rasool, 2021. The slogan is taken from a song by the star singer Fairuz, another component of the national brand.

237 Cf. Nüsse, 2008; Vignal, 2014.

238 Vignal, 2014: 259.

239 Cf. Vignal, 2006.

tres and consumption-related places, like shopping centres, boutiques, Internet cafés, and trendy bistros. At the same time, Syria and Jordan alike rediscovered and rebranded their urban heritage, which contests and competes with hitherto dominant Western-centric (and nationalist) imaginations of local history, relating to Antiquity, the biblical Levant, and colonial nostalgia (as well as ideas of the early Golden Age of Islam).[240] This resulted in a restoration and building boom in Damascus as a central locus of Arab-Levantine heritage, which was reappropriated by an urban bourgeoisie that the socialist regime had pushed aside. Since King Abdullah's accession to the Jordanian throne in 1999, downtown Amman, reflecting a more recent Levantine modernity, was reconceived as an attractive traditional Arab city. This process included a reappraisal of the Ottoman heritage, often left out of previous historical narratives, and also catered to the increasing number of tourists and investors from the Arab Gulf countries and their growing interest in regional history. In contrast, the huge refugee camps that appeared in recent years experienced their own strategic brand placements from donor states and organisations, as Melissa Gatter demonstrates in her contribution to this book.

Despite enduring war and crises, people endeavour to change the brand of their respective cities. For instance, in Mosul, until 2017 the capital of the IS in Iraq, the local "Green Mosul" initiative has been trying to give the city a more favourable image, albeit large parts are still in ruins.[241] The quasi-state of Iraqi Kurdistan wants to broadcast to the wider world an image of relative peace, stability, and progress in turbulent surroundings, notably to attract foreign investment. Its capital Erbil, in particular, has rapidly expanded in the last two decades. Building on a prosperous and cosmopolitan past and emulating Dubai's urban role model to become a "new Dubai," it wants to be present in the world's mind as a booming and attractive metropolis.[242] Mushrooming shopping malls became the material symbols of neoliberal transformation, socioeconomic progress, successful integration in the global economic system, and the overcoming of past oppression. Many other large urban development projects were started, including the spread of skyscrapers and gated communities. Yet, falling oil prices and the war with IS brutally halted the economic boom in 2014, and many development projects have been abandoned.

---

240 Cf. Jacobs, 2010.

241 Cf. Musharbash, 2021.

242 Cf. Sama, 2015; Boissière and Morvan, 2019; Champigny, 2020.

8.3 Branding Turkey between Past and Present, East and West

North of the Levant, in Turkey, branding has become a widespread practice in the production and tourism sectors. This serves to promote the many well-known holdings, which are also expanding beyond national borders, and, vice versa, to lure international investors as well as foreign travellers, who arrived in rapidly growing numbers particularly since the late 1990s. In the meantime, Turkey has been among the Top Ten destinations in the world and has become by far the most frequently visited MENA country (cf. Table 6), even if growth in this sector was temporarily stalled by several geopolitical incidents and the recent health crisis.

Table 6: MENA top tourism destinations

Ranks	**Country**	**International tourist arrivals (2019)**
Global 6; Europe 4	Turkey	51.2 million
Middle East* 1	Saudi Arabia	17.5 million
Middle East* 2	UAE	16.7 million
Africa 1; Middle East 3*	Egypt	13.0 million
Africa 2	Morocco	12.9 million
Africa 4	Tunisia	9.4 million
Global rank	**City**	**Arrivals (2018)**
7	Dubai	15.9 million
10	Istanbul	13.4 million
12	Antalya	12.4 million
21	Mecca	9.6 million
24	Medina	8.6 million
43	Cairo	5.8 million

* UNWTO “Middle East” definition without Turkey.
Differing methodologies make it difficult to compare country and city figures.

Nation branding is not a practice as new as most of the literature supposes and is linked not only to postmodern capitalist development emanating from the global West, as Philip Geisler demonstrates in his chapter on architectural “imperial branding.” Today, as the successor state of the Ottoman Empire, Turkey can avail itself of an ample foundation for historical nation branding. Birgit Krawietz shows how a central symbol of Ottoman times, the tulip, has been integrated as a history-laden emblem into contemporary nation branding and destination marketing. This simultaneously alludes to the fact that place branding is sometimes multi-scalar, using symbols that refer to nations, cities, and specific places within cities simultaneously.

In geographical and cultural terms, Turkey suffered repeatedly from an image of being situated between East and West.[243] After the Empire's disintegration, the young Turkish Republic pursued an ambitious Westernisation programme lured by the Western world's perceived progressiveness and modernity in contrast with the negative view of the (lost) Arab world as backward and untrustworthy. Since the 1990s, Turkish political and economic elites have tried to transform this double liminal situation into an attractive asset in foreign policy, trade and investment promotion,[244] and cultural diplomacy. This started with positioning Turkey as a "Eurasian" state, underpinning its orientation towards the post-Soviet Turkic Republics in the early 1990s, and continued later with its efforts for EU accession and more recently with its self-labelling as "Afro-Eurasian" in its quest to conquer African markets. In the aftermath of 9/11 and of debates on the "clash of civilisations," Turkey represented the Eastern (and Spain the Western) pillar in the UN-sponsored Alliance of Civilisations.[245]

Especially under the governments led by the Justice and Development Party (AKP) since 2002, when neoliberal economic policies married political authoritarianism, nation branding has become an essential governance tool. The party's Political Academy prepares its trainees to take an explicit brand approach to Turkey and to pay attention to improving its various international rankings.[246] A central aim is to spur economic growth and to attract international investment by emphasising political stability in difficult regional environments. Its dual belonging allowed Turkey to speak to different audiences with different economic and political agendas.[247] Directed at its Western allies, officials presented Turkey as committed to Western norms and standards and working towards peaceful conflict solutions; they sponsored large exhibitions and established cultural centres abroad. Particularly as rapprochement with the EU became increasingly difficult, the AKP embraced a policy of "Neo-Ottomanism," not only expressed in a historicising architectural style and urbanism, but also by reframing Turkey's history as anchored in a multi-oriented and multi-ethnic Ottoman Empire and propagating the image of a

243 Cf. Al-Ghazzi and Kraidy, 2013; Rumelili and Suleymanoglu-Kurum, 2017.

244 The parallel 2005 "Turquality" program expected to establish ten Turkish brands as international trademarks in the next ten years and served as a mutual co-branding strategy of state and products.

245 Cf. Iğsız, 2014. In fact, according to the author, these discourses at least implicitly perpetuated existing Orientalisms.

246 Cf. Iğsız, 2013 and 2014: 698. Cf. also Rumelili and Suleymanoglu-Kurum, 2017: 551.

247 Cf., again, Rumelili and Suleymanoglu-Kurum, 2017.

politically influential, economically successful, culturally attractive, and morally powerful nation.[248] Vis-à-vis its Middle Eastern and Muslim partners, the state-guided strategic communication pointed to the country's civilisational compatibility, historical ties, and cultural proximity. In particular, this reorientation towards the East and South was supported by performing again as a mediator in conflicts, concluding cooperation agreements, opening diplomatic missions, and expanding the Turkish Airlines network. Turkey's cultural policy has used popular culture and media broadcasting, especially Arabic language satellite TV channels that show sentimental drama series. All this resulted, by the early 2010s, in the successful construction of a powerful, integrated "Neo-Ottoman Cool" brand and a spectacular rise of popularity among Arabs.[249]

However, these rebranding efforts also experienced a series of limitations that constrained the presentation of a coherent image to the world. First, domestic controversies about national Western or Islamic identity were fuelled even further and, second, hegemonic global discourses continued to consider East and West incompatible and mutually exclusive. After the Arab upheavals in 2011 and the Istanbul Gezi protests in 2013, the country's brand lost much of its international credibility; in the Middle East, Turkey was often considered an unwelcome interventionist in domestic affairs.[250] Here, its role in recent geopolitical conflicts even ended with the threat to boycott Turkish products (see above). In the West, its image was further damaged by the strengthening of authoritarian rule and its ill-regarded foreign policy decisions. The authorities' first concern seems to be to safeguard foreign investors' interests, which led to accusations during the Gezi protests that the international press' coverage of the events was jeopardising Turkey's brand value.[251] A final move to rebrand the country was its renaming in 2022 in all languages as "Türkiye," mainly to avoid mockery based on the other meaning of the English name.[252]

The tension between a secular and religious modernity is also reflected on the urban stage. This has become evident, for instance, in the long-lasting controversy

---

248 Cf. Al-Ghazzi and Kraidy, 2013. Cf. also Iğsız, 2014: 692–693.

249 Cf. Al-Ghazzi and Kraidy, 2013: esp. 2346–2350. For TV broadcasts, cf. also Rumelili and Suleymanoglu-Kurum, 2017: 560–561. Compare brand coolness with the "Cool Britannia" brand, as mentioned in the previous chapter.

250 Cf. Rumelili and Suleymanoglu-Kurum, 2017: esp. 561–563. For Turkey's image loss in the Middle East, cf. also Al-Ghazzi and Kraidy, 2013: 2351–2353.

251 Cf. Iğsız, 2013 and 2014: 698.

252 Cf. Nüsse, 2022; Tagesschau, 2022b. Already earlier, exports were marked "Made in Türkiye" and Turkish Airlines advertised with the promotion slogan "Hello Türkiye"; cf. Tagesschau, 2022a.

about Ankara's urban emblem.[253] In the course of this conflict, a broad range of stakeholders started to discuss the historical, political, and cultural identity of the national capital and expressed their claims to brand ownership, legitimacy, and authority. The metropolitan mayor, affiliated with the AKP and its predecessors, argued that the pre-Islamic Hittite Sun that was used before did not adequately reflect the city's identity; in 1995, he replaced it with a logo depicting an urban scenery that included the minarets of the biggest mosque in Ankara. In 2010, in the course of the heavy debate, he changed the logo again into a more innocuous smiling Angora cat, intended to symbolise the capital's hospitality and its young and dynamic population.

Even more than Ankara, Istanbul is in the focus of current city branding strategies. Turkish destination branding long concentrated on tourism to the country in general or to seaside resorts and heritage sites outside the big cities. Hence, branding efforts in Istanbul to promote urban tourism developed only slowly, in parallel with its ascending global economic position.[254] Until 2007, the city's promotion was part of centrally administered tourism policies, which strongly relied on a self-orientalising discourse reflecting Western representations of basic civilisational differences. Only when Istanbul had won the bid for the 2010 European Capital of Culture (cf. Fig. 1) and EU accession seemed at hand did the metropolitan municipality activate its own branding process and develop a coherent communication strategy to present the metropolis as an open, tolerant, and multicultural "City of Religions." This changed again with the city's candidature for the 2020 Summer Olympics (Table 5), submitted in 2012.[255] A variety of themes and motifs introduced Istanbul as a "cool," dynamic and creative, multifaceted place that addresses multiple lifestyles and interests, including potential visitors from Russia and the Middle East, according to the government's geopolitical reorientations.

Already before 2012, project megalomania inspired by Dubai had made itself felt in Istanbul, in particular in the field of infrastructure. This was part of a global city-making project to catapult the largest Turkish city into the top league of various rankings. In this worldwide competition, its rapidly changing appearance, its central intercontinental location, its economic dynamism, and its rich human cap-

253 Cf. Hayden and Sevin, 2012.

254 Cf. Uysal, 2017. The first GaWC inventory in 1998 categorised Istanbul as a global city that had just arrived at a minor ("gamma") status; in the meantime, it has ascended to an "alpha" world city profile since 2016, second in the MENA region only to Dubai; cf. GaWC, 2022 (compare Table 3). It is also the second-most frequently visited MENA city after Dubai and the tenth most frequently visited city worldwide (Table 6).

255 Baş and Delaplace, 2023, show that even this unsuccessful bid has helped to boost the city's reputation and develop its infrastructure.

ital have been fervently branded.[256] This cosmopolitan claim contrasts with the marketing of gated communities aiming at a religiously oriented, if not Islamist-friendly middle class, which have gained momentum as shelter against the moral threats of the rapidly changing metropolis. In the case of the Başakşehir community, however, this led to negative propaganda in the mainstream media and secular investors' reluctance to engage in the housing project; instead, supporters of Islamist parties stepped in.[257] More recently, promoting new real estate projects as "green," "ecological," and "sustainable" has also become fashionable. Advertising the sustainability of high-rise buildings, in particular, which have special brand value, is often contested as greenwashing.[258] Additionally, to enhance their prestige, contemporary projects like the Bio-Istanbul smart and sustainable city use references to the historical urban landscape in accordance with the AKP's ideological ideas, like the traditional *mahalle* (neighbourhood) offering refuge and social and physical proximity, even if, in the end, this only advances neoliberally inspired speculation and segregation.[259]

Also, urban quarters and their branding have become objects of political struggle, as demonstrated by two examples from Istanbul presented in this volume. The historical quarter of Eyüp is a prime example in its use for political ends and demonstrates the interplay between personal and place branding. The municipality, governed by the AKP and its predecessors since 1994, has considerably modified its branding strategies for the neighbourhood several times in accordance with shifting political contexts.[260] Initially, Eyüp was described as a significant place for the Ottoman state and society in the context of the party's Islamic and neo-Ottoman activism and as an attractive, modern place to live for higher-status residents. After consolidating power, the municipality promoted Eyüp as one of the most important spiritual centres of the Islamic world to attract religious tourism. In contrast, since 2014, Eyüp has been branded the "Capital of Inner Peace," aiming at visitors from various backgrounds. The shifting branding activities indicate the constructed nature of a place's identity and demonstrate the quintessentially political nature of tourism marketing. By portraying itself as the protector of Eyüp's heritage and, by extension, of the larger Islamic-Ottoman community's identity, the AKP seeks to legitimise its grip on power. The use for the personal branding of politicians is exemplified further in Annegret Roelcke's contribution to this book, in which she demonstrates that members of secular parties have likewise

256 Cf. Adanali, 2011.
257 Cf. Çavdar, 2016.
258 On the case of the Bayraklı Towers in Izmir, cf. Öner and Pasin, 2015.
259 Cf. Arik, 2015.
260 Cf. Roelcke, 2019.

entered this battlefield. In contrast, Pekka Tuominen's chapter explores the question how the local population conforms with, resists, or appropriates official urban brands in a more central and more secular neighbourhood.

Fig. 4: Welcome Edirne city logo with the Selimiye Mosque in the background
Photo: Birgit Krawietz, 2017. Courtesy of the photographer.

In the shadow of global cities, secondary cities also endeavour to brand themselves and to communicate a favourable image to their citizens and the world. Among them, Edirne has recently attracted much scholarly attention. The city was already an early example of architectural branding. Namely, the iconic Selimiye Mosque was used to brand the 16th-century Ottoman Empire, challenging the role of Istanbul's Hagia Sophia, which represented the Byzantine past.[261] The extreme visibility of the Selimiye not only transformed Edirne's urban space, but also branded the city with an Ottoman imperial image (for a comparison with other Ottoman iconic practices, see Philip Geisler in this volume). Today, the promotion of Edirne as the "City of Sultans" is nearly exclusively oriented towards its glorious past and hints at the precious historical buildings.[262] The iconic Selimiye clearly stands in the centre of these efforts and visually dominates the official logo of the city (Fig. 4). Its

261 Cf. Geisler, 2020.
262 Cf. Krawietz, 2020, including wrestling; Wippel, 2020; Krawietz and Riedler, 2020.

importance has grown even more with its international recognition as a UNESCO World Heritage site. In the meantime, the sheer number of UNESCO-branded tangible and intangible heritage items helps to draw attention to the town and province of Edirne, which can compete in this respect with the Istanbul metropolitan area. In particular, the tradition of oil wrestling is not merely staged as a regular event that contributes to a temporally limited urban festivalisation, but also maintains its visual presence all year round. The ubiquitous presence of Turkish flags and municipal emblems at the annual festivities contributes to both national and local branding. The encompassing reappraisal of the Ottoman past has also a specific regional component, with a certain nostalgia for Rumelia, the historical European part of the Empire. However, the (re)opening of the City Museum and the Synagogue attest to different versions of history presented to different audiences. Nevertheless, branding the city is not exclusively backward-looking: the national tourism office also introduces Edirne as an open "border city," a "gateway to the West," and a "cultural mosaic." But in the end, Edirne's brand promotion is still limited, especially if compared with the top image enjoyed by nearby Istanbul.

9 Branding North Africa

9.1 Place Branding from the Nile to the Maghreb

Turning to North Africa, comparatively little seems to have been written explicitly about branding (in) Egypt, despite (or perhaps because of) the widespread history-packed images of the country. First, Egypt is considered a "must see" destination in tourism, which is a major source of national revenue. For this, its historical roots and continuity since ancient times are widely used in national destination branding. However, domestic and regional crises, such as wars, unrest, and attacks, as well as growing authoritarianism and Islamism, have resulted in negative perceptions among potential visitors regarding safety, but also sanitation and nightlife.[263]

Therefore, especially since the 2011 "revolution" and the 2013 restorative move, international nation branding specialists and PR consultants have worked hard for a global repositioning of the country and to reshape its image in the world.[264] To attract investors and tourists, the brand strategy has focused on president Abdel-Fatah al-Sisi as a leader stabilising the country against extremism and insecurities

263 Cf. Avraham, 2016. On transmission effects on tourism from events abroad, ascribed to the entire Middle East region, cf. Steiner, 2009.
264 Cf. Shenker, 2017.

and making its resources available to the world. A qualitative content analysis of branding material demonstrates that marketers employed three types of strategies to counter negative perceptions; these strategies aim at international opinion influencers, try to influence the audience itself, and endeavour to correct stereotypical messages.[265] In this volume, based on her unpublished PhD thesis on strategies to present a "Brand New Egypt" to the global public, Karin Ahlberg analyses Egypt's official promotion in the late 2000s, which separately targeted the two main source markets, the Arab and the international market, and made use of diverging symbolisms. Beyond tourism, one high-quality export product, namely cotton, was long in the focus of national branding efforts. As this proved too narrow and was no longer considered representative, the government tried to rebrand the country as a business destination.[266] Still in the era of President Hosni Mubarak (r. 1981–2011), a service company group proposed a strategy to increase buyers' and investors' awareness of Egypt as a business partner and, in line with application-oriented literature, suggested a central office that would guarantee a consistent message focusing on transparency and reform.

On the urban level, Cairo, nicknamed "Mother of the world" (*umm al-dunyā*), is not only a historically important city, but has also been reputed an urban Moloch and acquired an image as a favourite place of entertainment and pleasure to the point of becoming an unofficial sex tourism destination, mainly for Arab tourists from the more restrictive Gulf states, who thronged the city from the 1980s on.[267] Already in the 19th century, Egypt's capital experienced several spatial reconfigurations aimed at a more modern image of the city. This included a first "new town," Heliopolis, built in 1907 at the city's desert fringe, which required a specific marketing strategy to target foreign residents as well as certain segments of the local population.[268] Like other quarters, the settlement's architecture mimicked a pretended historical Arabian style and stereotyped Oriental atmosphere reflecting colonial visions of the Orient. Similarly, contemporary real estate projects, such as the more recent "desert cities," luxurious residential compounds, shopping malls, and theme parks, are widely advertised today. While huge billboards feature architectural elements of gated communities built recently or in the near future and praise again the conquest and the greening of the desert, they physically hide and even replace existing buildings and green spaces, making the latter

265 Cf., again, Avraham, 2016.

266 Cf. Dinnie, 2008: 29; ZAD Group, 2008. On the intense branding of products in Egypt and of Egyptian origin, cf. earlier passages in this text.

267 Cf., e.g., el-Gawhary, 1995.

268 Cf. Adham, 2004: esp. 144–151; also mentioned by Stadnicki, 2017.

even more scarce and the city more crowded.[269] According to visions already developed under the former Mubarak administration, Cairo was to have been largely reconfigured with new high-end real estate megaprojects and attention-drawing starchitecture following the fashionable Dubai model in order to attract more international tourists and investors.[270] Promotional videos showed an immaculate city, cleansed of its inhabitants and with polished streets, in which Gulf visitors stroll around and are served by Egyptian celebrities. "The proposal was replete with eye-catching perspectives of architectural and urban design solutions that promised a rebranded Cairo that by 2050 would be totally transformed into a truly global city."[271]

After the 25 January Revolution, the new governments' strategies first tended towards a few socially more inclusive showcase projects, the provision of social housing, and an appeasing policy towards informal settlements.[272] At the latest with the consolidation of al-Sisi's power in the mid-2010s, the strategy changed again towards more control and repression. The neoliberal worlding projects, which had been hesitantly remodelled to meet some social concerns, were deftly put into operation again. To circumvent earlier criticism of incommensurability and forced evictions, a number of less all-encompassing sub-projects were announced. New sites for visits continue to be built, such as the Grand Egyptian Museum in outer Giza, where the planned installation of "true copies" of the most threatened Pharaonic tombs from Luxor constitute examples of second-order simulacra.[273] The most spectacular component of the intense efforts to establish a "modern" image of the city is the construction of a New Administrative Capital at the megalopolis' periphery. The megalomanic project helps the Egyptian president present a strenuously implemented strategy of innovation and modernisation to the world and reflects its decision-makers' ambition to place Cairo on the map of global cities.[274] Yet, with the slow progress of the project, the huge number of images that initially circulated on billboards and in the media rapidly stopped; in particular, promotional brochures and films have avoided highlighting the centrepiece of this "Sisi City," the immoderate Presidential palace.[275] Khaled Adham's essay in this volume takes a closer look at the political economy behind such large-

269 Cf. Abotera and Ashoub, 2020.
270 Cf. Adham, 2004, 2014, and 2017.
271 Adham, 2014: 239–240.
272 Cf. Beier, 2016: esp. 12–15, 20–22.
273 Cf. Steiner 2010: 246. For Jean Baudrillard's concept of simulacra, cf. the previous conceptual chapter.
274 Cf. Stadnicki, 2017.
275 Cf. Loewert and Steiner, 2019.

scale urban advertising, showing how this constructs a memory of the future and transforms it into present political and economic wealth. In contrast, Raffael Beier and Hassan Elmouelhi demonstrate how legitimation-seeking politicians, modernist urban planners, and international organisations brand "slum-free" metropolises and subsequently eradicate neighbourhoods that consist of precarious housing conditions.

On the countries west of Egypt except for Morocco, only a limited number of publications specific to branding have emerged within the bulk of literature on economic and political transformation and contemporary urbanism; most of the few cases in Tunisia and Algeria are studied in comparison with Morocco. In the case of Libya, the revolutionary leader Mu'ammar al-Qaddhafi was a strong personal brand in his own right until the collapse of his regime. In the mid-2000s, a US consultancy developed a branding project for a "New Libya" after economic sanctions had been lifted to counter existing perceptions as a pariah state.[276] This aimed at encouraging trade and investment and improving the country's political standing and included a vision for the 50th anniversary of the Revolution in 2019. A programme directed at the domestic audience sought to convince it to "live the brand"; other measures were designed to encourage international academics and media to publish positive reports – to the extent that some articles portrayed Libya as the future Norway of Africa – and convey a positive brand image of al-Qaddhafi as a responsible and recognised leader.

In the Maghreb, too, the 21st century has become an age of urban megaprojects, which cater primarily to branding issues. According to Raffaele Cattedra, we are witnessing the staging of gleaming models that reproduce images of future or futuristic developments, disseminated through various channels.[277] Sophisticated marketing strategies often promoted projects only for their performative efficiency, creating a kind of "mirage effect." The image serves as a political device to legitimise the project in society. However, in Tunisia, the capital's central axis Avenue Habib Bourguiba has been a case of continuous spatial rebranding since its construction in the 1860s: while the French administration established it as a "Parisian Colonial" boulevard, after independence, it could be labelled an example of "Tunisian Modernity" and was refurbished under the Ben Ali regime as a "Parisian Global" streetscape and historicist showcase of globalisation ambitions.[278] In and after the 2011 revolution, it became emblematic as a meeting place and demonstration arena of civil society and could capitalise on images of an open and tol-

276 Cf. Aronczyk, 2013: 153–156. The consultancy was headed by Michael Porter, the protagonist of the "competitive advantage of nations"; cf. previous chapter.
277 Cf. Cattedra, 2010.
278 Cf. Coslett, 2017.

erant identity. In each historical era, the avenue was a component of staged authenticity in which diverse actors, from planners and architects to preservationists and public authorities, strategically condensed and simplified history into a thematic brand. Today, it is charged with complex images and reflects Tunisia's hybrid postcolonial identity.

Especially under the rule of then-President Zine El Abidine Ben Ali (r. 1987–2011), Tunisia undertook strong worlding endeavours. Here, another example of postmodern simulation was built to feed visitors with illusions: the themed *Medinat Hammamet* project, at the artificial Yasmine Hammamet tourism complex, pretends to represent an authentic (and by the way, cleansed) old city with various shopping and leisure areas, each in a distinct architectural style.[279] In both Morocco and Tunisia, the concept of waterfront development and the role of territorial marketing have become essential in contemporary urbanism, given cities' claimed interurban competition and aspired internationalisation. In Tunisia, the most notable project was the clean-up of the Lac de Tunis lagoon in the 1980s and the subsequent plans to develop a new urban waterfront to stage the city.[280] According to Pierre-Arnaud Barthel, the extensive rhetoric that accompanied the land-use scheme for the Southern Lake's shore and the Tunis Sports City project on the Northern Lake since the mid-2000s had, on the one hand, a performative function to increase the visibility and legitimacy of the transformation of a hitherto neglected urban area. On the other hand, its ideological function was to mobilise and to insinuate continuities with prestigious city models, from Dubai to Miami. The presentation as "presidential projects" aimed to consolidate the position of the state leader. The claimed sustainability of these large urban development schemes was seen as window dressing, especially as it lacked any participatory approach, social inclusion, or spatial integration. While the *Berges Nord du Lac* development was accomplished with a 30-year alcohol-free Saudi concession, the other megaprojects failed mainly because Gulf developers withdrew after the economic crisis and the Arab Spring. Not least, the accusation of corruption and having ceded the "jewels" of the city for these urban prestige projects contributed to Ben Ali's ouster. In contrast to these showily branded projects, shortly after the Jasmine Revolution, the Tunisian government endeavoured to lay the foundations for a more decentralised and inclusive urban policy to reduce disparities within and between cities.[281] Yet, a few years later, the regime was torn again between social responsible urbanism and revitalised worlding endeavours: megaprojects re-emerged in public de-

279 Cf. Steiner, 2010: 244–245.

280 Cf. Barthel, 2006 and 2014; Gaillard, 2016.

281 Cf. Beier, 2016: esp. 15–17, 23–24, and 2017.

bates, as they were considered an opportunity to boost attractiveness for tourists and to demonstrate the country's global economic ambitions, but they made hardly any progress.[282]

In Algeria, branding is particularly discussed in connection with the widely advertised construction of "New Towns" intended to provide housing and relieve existing urban agglomerations. Compared with Tamansourt near Marrakech, the Algerian *ville nouvelle* of Ali Mendjeli on the outskirts of Constantine is better equipped, which gives the project a rather positive image and makes it more attractive for residents to stay.[283] However, those who wish to leave essentially attribute this to the gap between the cajoling projected images of a kind of ideal urban utopia, on the one hand, and still less-illustrious life realities, on the other. As part of neoliberal urbanism and in much harsher competition with other residential projects, Moroccan branding is more opulent, but disillusion over project implementation much greater. Especially in Tamansourt, "outre l'objectif de vendre la 'ville nouvelle', [le marketing urbain] vise aussi une territorialisation du projet par l'image, à défaut de pouvoir se prévaloir, comme dans le cas d'Ali Mendjeli, d'une territorialisation par la pratique."[284] The term "new town" lends itself to two different readings. One refers to the future town, conveys the image of a town (perhaps) to come, and distorts the reality that users will have to live with in practice.[285] The second reading points to the town of the future, a fantasy city, which by its very existence enables a leap into a new era. Such urban megaprojects mobilise all the vocabulary that urban marketing has at its disposal to disseminate the image of their modernity: competitiveness; excellence; green, sustainable, and zero-emission towns; and intelligent and smart cities.

9.2 Morocco as Another Case of Intense Product and Place Branding

Morocco has perhaps become one of the Arab countries beyond the Gulf most active in nation and product branding. Constitutional preambles can also constitute a kind of nation brand marker by defining the fundamentals of political regimes and especially the regional and civilisational belonging and orientation of the nation. Accordingly, as reflected in the Moroccan constitution, the kingdom today brands

282 E.g., the Sports City project has been reconsidered recently; cf. Galtier, 2022.
283 Cf. Ballout, 2015.
284 Ballout, 2015.
285 Cf. Sidi Boumedine and Signoles, 2017.

itself as an ethnically, religiously, and linguistically pluralistic country that possesses multiple transregional historical and cultural roots and ties. In contrast, in the first post-colonial decades, its unity and homogeneity were emphasised and alternative narratives were largely ignored or forcefully suppressed.[286] This already started to change in the 1970s, when King Hassan II (r. 1961–1999) wanted to present the country as a predestined mediator in political conflicts, based on the image of a cultural melting pot and a bridge between different world regions. Given Morocco's difficult relations with Europa and within the Maghreb, the preamble today situates the whole country between the Mediterranean, the Arab, and the African worlds, which allows it to have several geostrategic orientations simultaneously.[287] Morocco's affiliation with the encompassing Berber lands between the Maghreb and the Sahel and with *Al-Andalus*, stretching from the Iberian Peninsula to Northern Morocco, with its Sahrawi-Hassani component, and with the artistic and architectural legacy of the Islamic Golden Age has all been rediscovered relatively recently. In particular, on a microregional level this also includes the newly branded Strait-crossing bonds between the Tangier Peninsula and Gibraltar, which Dieter Haller discusses later in this book.

The current King Mohammed VI, who acceded to the throne in 1999, has repeatedly emphasised the promotion of the *Label Maroc*, the Moroccan nation brand.[288] Together with government authorities, he has worked hard in international arenas to make his country recognised as an equal and reliable partner sharing universal values and constituting a haven of safety, peace, and tolerance. These nation branding endeavours not only serve as a strategic tool of foreign policy, but are also directed at the national citizens to promote an alternative image and vision against radical Islamist movements. A state think tank has repeatedly evaluated Morocco's domestic and international reputation.[289] The latest report positioned Morocco in the mid-tier among the 72 nations under study; its image has improved over the long term, but suffered a short-term decline internally and among Western observers. Among several dimensions, living conditions are rated the best, outdistancing institutional quality and the level of development.

To pursue its foreign policy goals, the Moroccan regime has increasingly employed economic and cultural soft power. This public diplomacy that has politicised art and culture from above has helped Morocco to gain more support for its claim to sovereignty over the Western Sahara, especially among African governments,

286 Cf. Wagenhofer, 2021.
287 Cf. Wippel, 2018: 283–284.
288 Cf. Wüst and Nicolai, 2022: 7.
289 For the latest report, based on opinions in 25 countries, cf. IRES, 2021.

while it also seems to have been appealing to foreign investors. In particular, the kingdom has capitalised on its considerable cultural treasure to improve its image and influence abroad.[290] Cultural policy conveys a specific Moroccan brand of Islam, folklorises and commercialises immaterial heritage, and invests massively in cultural infrastructure, namely a modern museum landscape. Host cities have been profiled, but urban film, music, and art festivals that have widely proliferated over the years have also become vehicles to transmit to the world a decidedly positive image of a modern, open, and dynamic country. Specific festivals intend to demonstrate the position of cities like Rabat as an "African capital" and the country's role as a bridge to the continent.[291] Museums in particular strongly reflect this shift in self-understanding and have become an important tool to display images of diversity. Among them, we find newly established museums dealing with "minorities," such as the those for Moroccan Judaism in Casablanca (opened in 1997), Saharan Art in Laayoune (founded in 2001), and Amazigh Culture in Agadir (2005). In contrast to other Jewish museums worldwide, which often emphasise differentness, the Moroccan one promotes the sameness of Jews and Muslims and the historical integration of Jews in Moroccan society.[292] While conveying the image of peaceful coexistence, the museum maintains silence on sensitive issues such as their situation during World War II, their later mass emigration, and contemporary antisemitism. Morocco is presented to the outside as an outstanding example in the Arab world and a potential mediator in the Middle East conflict. Within the country, the positive picture of Jews fits well into the new image of a plural society, promoted by state representatives, but also among the younger generation.

Sport, and football in particular, is of course also a key means of branding the country internally and externally, including in terms of regional affiliations. The royal announcement of a tri-national bid together with Spain and Portugal for the 2030 World Cup is presented to the world as historically unprecedented in its Euro-African, trans-Mediterranean, and Arab components.[293] Likewise, the recent advance to the semi-finals of the Qatar World Cup 2022 is declared the first "Muslim," "African," and "Arab" success, which also contains an anti-/post-colonial dimension in the victory against Spain, even if this actually ignores other aspects,

290 Cf. Wüst and Nicolai, 2022.

291 Cf. Dines, 2021. On similar cultural activities to demonstrate Tangier's role as a springboard towards sub-Saharan Africa, cf. also Wippel, 2021.

292 Cf. Wagenhofer, 2014. When it opened, the museum was the first officially recognised of its kind in the Arab world. In Istanbul, a museum on Turkish Jewry opened in 2001.

293 Cf. Le Matin, 2023.

such as the strong Amazigh and European identities of the country and the majority of its players, as well as the earlier successes of Turkey and Senegal.[294]

At the same time, in the course of its economic opening, the country is trying to attract international investors and establish itself as a trade hub. The collective origin of product branding in Arab countries often is quite recent. For example, a 2016 study found that Moroccan efforts in this regard are mostly sectoral, and each public company or agency promotes its own individual brand.[295] A non-profit association of companies did not establish a "Made in Morocco" label to promote national products until 2014 (Fig. 5a).[296] In 2015, a national strategy with a common umbrella label for the handicrafts sector was launched.[297] Even more recently, Morocco has developed a new official business brand to sell the country as an exporter and to place itself as a valuable and attractive destination for investment, close to European and Mediterranean markets. The multi-coloured "Morocco NOW" word sign logo (Fig. 5b) has been widely displayed, from its official launch at the Dubai Expo through its web presence to diverse national and international media.[298] As part of its "Restart" strategy in the covid crisis and in the course of refreshing its tourism promotion campaign, the Moroccan National Tourist Office (ONMT) also introduced a new visual identity with a more vivid word logo (Fig. 5c).[299]

Fig. 5: Moroccan national promotional logos
Sources: Made in Morocco, 2014; Morocco Now, 2021b; ONMT, 2021.

Morocco is above all an established and much-studied tourist destination. It aims to become one of the 20 largest tourist destinations in the world (cp. Table 6). Some

294 Cf. Warshel, 2023.
295 Cf. Ghannam and Ghoufrane, 2016.
296 Cf. Made in Morocco, 2022. For the struggles accompanying international and regional trade, cf. earlier passages in this chapter.
297 Cf. Ministère de l'Artisanat, de l'Economie Sociale et Solidaire, 2015.
298 Cf., e.g., Morocco Now, 2021a.
299 Cf. Menara, 2021; El Rhazi, 2022.

of the numerous publications on Moroccan cities also analyse their external perception, especially as top tourist destinations. The perception of tourism advertising among emigrants, considered key in transmitting country images, has also been studied: often they regard existing destination branding as insufficient and inadequate, and gaps exist between images conveyed by official websites and by emigrants.[300] The few focused empirical or critical, theoretically grounded appraisals of urban branding contrast with numerous papers that, since the mid-2010s, present general explanations and application-oriented suggestions how to enhance the brands of Moroccan cities, which I mostly ignore here. Yet, many analyses of contemporary urban development reserve some remarks on issues of "territorial marketing" and image-building.

Especially the two decades since Mohammed VI took power have been characterised by mushrooming urban megaprojects throughout the country as part of growing worlding ambitions. Such iconic projects (often playing again with superlatives) reflect the neoliberal and postmodern shift in urban management towards strategies of branding and communication and are based on practices of exemption from urban planning. Political decentralisation increased local political actors' interest in having their "own" prestigious large-scale projects built. In parallel, geopolitical change led Morocco to open up to capital and expertise from the Gulf states, especially in the real estate sector. Initial admiration of the Dubai model gave way to a clear distancing, while French influences, for instance, continue to have an impact.[301] Except for some projects that were delayed (or cancelled) after the 2008/09 financial crisis, these constructions continued after the 2011 uprisings, and even new projects have been launched to signal stability in a regional environment of political turbulence.

In particular, Casablanca, the country's economic centre, endeavours to overcome its bad reputation as a congested and run-down metropolis. Instead, it wants to establish itself as a world-class city with new attractive business and residential quarters. To this end, several metropolitan visions and strategies have been launched. In particular, Casablanca strives to excel with a series of megaprojects.[302] The first contemporary project, which dominates the urban coastline, was the construction of the Hassan II Mosque, completed in 1993, with the then-tallest minaret worldwide. Other big projects ensued, most of them still under construction, among them Anfa City, including Casablanca Finance City, whose ambition is to become Africa's financial hub; the Morocco Mall, the largest African shopping cen-

300 Cf. El Aouni, Cascón-Pereira, and Hernández-Lara, 2012.
301 Cf. Barthel, 2014 and 2015b.
302 Cf. Beier, 2016: esp. 22, and 2017; Aljem and Strava, 2020.

tre;[303] the new *Grand Théâtre*, which will be the biggest one in Africa; and the *Avenue Royale*, an ongoing vast urban renewal programme in the city centre. The high-end Casa Marina project, conceived in the late 2000s, in particular has been intensely marketed for international investors and purchasers, but also contributed to the evolution of the brand of its Moroccan development holding, which kept power over the project's management vis-à-vis its Gulf partners, in contrast to Tunis' experience at that time.[304] Transport infrastructure is also to back the image of aspired world city status: accordingly, Casablanca's tramway network, opened in 2012, has become an important part of the local marketing mix that points to aspects like speed, progress, and environmental concerns.[305] The project helps to promote the image of a socially more inclusive city; however, it has instead made the ruptures in the urban fabric even more visible. Throughout the MENA region, such mass transit projects also contribute to the prestige and political legitimacy of the mostly authoritarian rulers, who preen as initiators and promoters of ecologically and technologically pioneering means of transport.[306] However, there is a huge gap between local needs and the neoliberal and worlding logics behind these megaprojects.[307] They greatly impede the population's right to the city and displace residents to poorly developed outer districts. To eliminate informal settlements, viewed as hardly controllable, a nationwide "Cities without Slums" programme was proclaimed in the early 2000s.[308] In a separate chapter of this book, Raffael Beier and Hassan Elmouelhi compare Cairo and Casablanca to demonstrate how these processes are being used to upgrade the cities' current brand images.

Finally, in 2016, Casablanca was the first Moroccan and allegedly the first African city to initiate an encompassing urban branding strategy. The strategy was based on a preceding survey of inhabitants and visitors to carve out the city's "identity" and to identify gaps between the perceived and the desired images. As a coherent umbrella brand, the newly created logo and slogan "WeCasablanca" and related promotional materials and activities can be adapted as sub-brands to various target sectors (e. g., housing, transport, tourism, business).[309] It is piloted by a local agency that represents regional, prefectural, and municipal authorities.

---

303 Developers envisioned that the shopping centre would turn Casablanca into a kind of Dubai in Africa or at least for the Western Mediterranean; cf. Elsheshtawy, 2012.

304 Cf. Barthel, 2014.

305 Cf. Strava, 2018; Beier, 2019. The similar Rabat-Salé tramway opened in 2011.

306 Cf. Wippel, 2022.

307 Compare Aljem and Strava, 2020: 12.

308 Cf. Beier, 2016: 17–20, and 2017.

309 Cf. Sedra and El Bayed, 2022; Echattabi and Khattab, 2021: 51–52.

A few studies investigated residents' perception of the city before the brand was created and of the brand's adoption shortly after its launch.[310] This hints at the need to improve the quality of life and public services before such a strong branding strategy is implemented. In their article in this volume, Dounia Sedra and Hicham El Bayed provide insight into the genesis of the branding strategy and an evaluation of its reception by the local population at a greater temporal distance, with a view to preparing its updating.

In other major cities, construction of numerous emblematic large-scale projects with new landmarks has also begun. In Rabat, prime examples are the slowly progressing conversion of the seafront road into a luxurious corniche and the ambitious Bouregreg Valley project, including a new marina; the Zaha Hadid-designed opera; and the Mohammed VI Tower, which will be the second tallest one in Africa.[311] They aim to convey a new image of the capital, making it a city by the water, which it never was historically. Here, too, prestigious Gulf partners are often involved in project development. These projects especially benefit the better-off classes and are intensely promoted with the help of targeted ad hoc structures. In fact, the Bouregreg project is not just a wasteland development, as it is often presented, but represents the creation of a globalised space, at the expense of small-scale farmers and private landowners. As in the case of the Rabat Corniche, the failure to consult the population parallels challenging environmental and sustainable effects. A special case is the extended new suburb of Hay Ryad, which was the object of intense marketing operations that led to an elitist image of the area as a ghetto for the rich and wealthy.[312] Furthermore, a series of "Rabat Ville Lumière" projects valorise Rabat's new World Heritage status from 2012 and seek to make the hitherto undistinctive administrative city a more vibrant national capital of culture able to compete, especially with Mediterranean cities.[313] Moreover, in order to also increase its reputation as a continental centre, the newly created title, African Capital of Culture, has been first awarded for 2020 to Rabat.[314]

Tangier also suffered for a long time from its political neglect and deteriorated image; for two decades now, strategies promoted by the king have endeavoured to develop the northern metropolis into a showcase city and a supra-regional commercial hub whose favourable location is sold to the world. Steffen Wippel points

310 Cf. Belkadi, 2015 and 2019.

311 On the Bouregreg project, cf. Amarouche and Bogaert, 2019; esp. on the Corniche, Mouloudi, 2009 and 2015.

312 Cf. Serhir, 2017.

313 Cf. Beier, 2016: 22, and 2017: 28.

314 Cf. Wüst and Nicolai, 2022: 13.

to the multifaceted branding that goes along with its urban restructuring, is realised by a great diversity of actors and at different scales, and positions the city at several spatial and temporal interfaces.

In 2004, in the context of starting to liberate cities from slums, the government presented a comprehensive national programme that envisaged the construction of 15 "New Towns," which were reduced to four a few years later. The labels "green" and "sustainable" were attached to the first plans only afterwards and were widely considered a form of greenwashing. In contrast, the newer projects were designed with an ecological claim from the very beginning. The *ville nouvelle* Chrafate, still in its infancy on the outskirts of Tangier, was the first project to be promoted as a modern "Green City," but in the end, the communication was dominated by images of exclusivity and singularity.[315] One of the main characteristics of the New Towns Programme is the extensive use of large billboards for urban marketing and image promotion; gigantic numbers put these projects out of the ordinary. If we compare the promising images and slogans with the disillusioning reality on the ground, a vast enterprise of urban illusionism appears, which Jean-Marie Ballout calls "territorialisation through image."[316] For these projects, what counts is again not so much the materiality of the results as the performative effectiveness of the discourses that accompany them. In addition to these mass constructions, further large-scale settlement projects, most of them directly adjacent to existing urban structures, also claim ecological and social sustainability.[317] Among them, the *Ville Verte Mohammed VI de Benguerir* is promoted as a technology hub accompanying the conversion of a former mining area. As "Africa's first green city" with a polytechnic university at its heart, it is set to become a continental hub for environmentally relevant research and education. The project aims to contribute to the royal, national, and local image, as well as to improve the reputation of the responsible mining company, which is in the process of transforming its activities, even if it has not yet succeeded in overcoming social and territorial marginalisation.

Such intensive communication about "green" showcase projects and technologies first and foremost serves place branding, but also shines a favourable light on the current ruler. Morocco likes to present itself as a pioneer of sustainability in the Mediterranean region and the Arab world. Thus, the widely branded "sustainable cities" are in line with Morocco's general endeavours to institute green policies. The conception of its sustainable energy transition follows an imaginary of

315 Cf. Barthel, 2015a and 2015b; Ballout, 2015 and 2017; Sidi Boumedine and Signoles, 2017.

316 Ballout, 2017.

317 Cf. Barthel, 2015a; esp. on Benguerir, Harroud, 2020.

"green modernisation" that serves the ideological stabilisation of the regime as well as catering to activists' demands.[318] While cities in the Gulf States are primarily propagating a regional and global pioneering role in the race to be the greenest and most sustainable city, Morocco considers itself a role model of ecological projects and sustainable policies in North Africa and on the entire African continent, which also represents a possible export destination for projects, technologies, and expertise.[319] Specifically, the country brands itself as a green leader among African nations and the voice of Africa at international conferences. Mohammed VI personally is at the "green heart"[320] of these endeavours, and the Moroccan energy transition is presented as a strategic decision by the far-sighted monarch. The organisation of the COP22 2016 in Marrakech was a milestone in enhancing Morocco's national and the king's personal brands, which still contrast with green land grabbing and the violation of social rights in the name of sustainable development.[321]

Smaller cities in Morocco also increasingly endeavour to improve their images and attractiveness by employing branding strategies, often integrating national endeavours to develop tourism. Essaouira, for instance, already began to evolve as a flourishing town distinct among other Moroccan places a few decades ago.[322] A group of Moroccan actors have marketed the city as a cultural product to visitors and tourists, invested in the historic centre, and organised art events and renowned music festivals. Reputed as the "Wind City" and surfers' paradise, Essaouira builds on its image as a liveable and visitable place with a creative spirit and relaxing atmosphere. Chefchaouen, long considered the prototype of a marginalised small town cut off in the mountains, managed since the 2000s to turn its image as the "capital of kif" into the more positive brand "La Perle Bleue" (The Blue Pearl) of the North.[323] It capitalised on its local material and immaterial wealth to win as large an audience as possible. The logo adopted in 2013 was only the most visible aspect of this branding process. The Andalusian cultural and patrimonial heritage that make it "Granada's little sister" is at the centre stage of the strategy and includes the restoration of buildings according to an obligatory architectural charter. This strategy extends to preserving the natural environment and declaring itself an eco-city; to its listing as a UNESCO heritage together with three other cities for their Mediterranean diet; to efforts to create a local

318 Cf. Haddad et al., 2022.
319 Cf. Nicolai, 2022.
320 Nicolai, 2022: 731.
321 Cf. Bogaert, 2019.
322 Cf., e.g., Bauer, Escher, and Kniper, 2006.
323 Cf. Ghailane, 2022.

label of origin; and to organising traditional and modern music, song, poetry, and film festivals. Finally, the city is mediated by TV documentaries and as a stage for TV series and movies. This new image has been fabricated in joint local efforts, especially by actors from civil society associations and the municipal president, who managed to network with local, national, and international actors.

The "advanced regionalisation" tackled in the mid-2010s intended to give Moroccan regions more autonomy and competencies to strengthen economic development. One region after the other launched regional development programmes; for the more peripheral entities, specific public economic and social development agencies have been established. At the same time, they also entered "latent" interregional competition. However, as some solution-oriented publications state, accompanying promotion campaigns to communicate "differentiating advantages" are rather exceptional; they propose to use existing urban, regional, and national agencies to strengthen territorial marketing.[324]

10 "Dubai Elsewhere": Branding on MENA's Periphery and in Adjacent Regions

Dubai's and other Gulf cities' and nations' successes have induced stakeholders "elsewhere" to copy not only their economic and urban development models, but also their branding strategies – this also spread to MENA's immediate peripheries and adjacent regions of the Islamicate world like Africa, Central Asia, and the Indian subcontinent.[325] At the same time, neo-patrimonial authoritarian regimes in need of legitimacy and modelled on the Arab world exist in sub-Saharan Africa[326] or have established themselves in recent decades in Turkic-speaking countries,[327] which is why Pauline Jones Luong speaks of their political "Middle Easternization."[328]

South of the Sahara, Dubai's "glitz, glamour, and flashiness" have been an appealing vision, and its hyper-capitalistic urban development model has become a reference that serves as symbolic power.[329] Based on a few success stories, Africa started to gain a reputation as the new rising star of the 21st century, full of eco-

324 Cf., e.g., Echattabi and Khattab, 2021.
325 For "Dubaisation," "Dubaification," and "Gulfication," cf. above. Cf. also Haines, 2011.
326 Cf., e.g., Erdmann and Engel, 2007.
327 Cf., e.g., Lewis, 2012.
328 Jones Luong, 2003.
329 Cf. Stoll, 2010; Watson, 2014.

nomic promise that changed the long-prevailing image of a lost continent. From West to East Africa and south to Angola, large-scale luxurious and widely advertised urban greenfield and waterfront transformation projects have been conceived, often with the help of Gulf investors and sometimes backed by soaring income from oil and other resources. Among the urbanistic trends since the 2000s, "smart", "tech", "sustainable," and "green" city labels have also entered the rhetoric of African political and economic elites, together with a popular claim to development that immunises against criticism.[330] The development into "world-class" metropolises is presented as a necessary means to kick off national economies and used to rebrand countries with a modern and progressive image. However, this speculative urbanism has not always resulted in finishing the proposed projects or achieving promised aims, but instead contributed to the further social and spatial fragmentation of cities.

While separated by the vast desert, places at the sub-Saharan fringe have old historical and reinvigorated close transregional connections with North Africa. As we have seen, to promote its foreign policy ambitions and especially its economic trade and investment links, Morocco brands itself as an African nation with strong historical and cultural ties with areas south of the Sahara. In one of the following chapters, Ute Röschenthaler explains how difficult it is to control a product brand in the case of Chinese green tea in Mali, which initially arrived there in the 19th century via Morocco and still alludes to this provenance and related trade networks of that time. In this transition zone between North and sub-Saharan Africa on the periphery of the MENA region, Sudan is another country that has to struggle with a reputation for lasting dictatorship and war and with building a stable multiethnic and multireligious nation brand. In the 2000s, with the beginning oil production, authorities endeavoured to give its capital Khartoum a "brand"-new face as an African outpost of Gulf investment and urbanism.[331] Likewise, Mauritanian authorities had started to follow the Emirates' model and stage their capital to stand up to the perceived race for competitiveness. Hence, in Nouakchott, too, luxury ventures dominated over social housing projects. In both these metropolises, the urban megaprojects followed international planning principles and took inspiration from the postmodern and fascinating urbanism of the Gulf, but also tried to adapt to the local context, e.g. with architectural styles and project names that bear Arab cultural and historical references – not least to reaffirm the contested Arabness of their countries. However, the widely announced pharaonic undertakings mostly remained literally at the project stage.

330 Cf. also Côté-Roy and Moser, 2019.

331 Cf. for both Sudan and Mauritania, Choplin and Franck, 2014.

Further south, Eko Atlantic City in Lagos is an outstanding and widely promoted example of a Gulf-style urban megaproject and claims to be the largest undertaking of this kind in Africa.[332] On the Horn of Africa, Djibouti was regarded as one of the first African examples to follow Dubai's economic model of an interconnected port/free zone/airport hub, realised with capital and expertise from the Emirate. It benefited from co-branding as a recognised partner and participated in Dubai's reputation for quality management.[333] In neighbouring Ethiopia, Addis Ababa showed first symptoms of being infected by "Dubai fever" at the end of the 2000s. Developers, architects, and state authorities endeavoured to promote the city as the "next Dubai."[334] Major constructions started to transform the urban physiognomy and to pave the way for an investor-dominated city. As in the Gulf, economic megaprojects and inherent economic progress have been attributed to the national ruler. After his sudden death, Ethiopia's President and Prime Minister (r. 1991–2012) Meles Zenawi was branded across the capital with images and posters as the architect of the country's vision for future economic and political progress.[335] This iconographic campaign used the Renaissance Dam on the Blue Nile River as the key visual symbol of the country's aspiration for regional exceptionalism and was declared Zenawi's boldest initiative.

When the Central Asian republics became independent after the fall of the Soviet Union, historical ties with the Middle East were quickly restored and rulers learnt rapidly from its autocratic regimes.[336] Namely, old and new capitals had to be transformed to meet the expectations for the domestic and international recognition of the newly installed presidents. A major example was the new capital of post-Soviet Kazakhstan, proclaimed in late 1997 and subsequently renamed Astana (intermittently Nur Sultan, after the then-president). Numerous authors have investigated the branding strategies behind the building of its impressive urbanscape and architecture. The city was praised the "City of the 21st century" whose architecture had overcome "Western thinking" and was compared to Dubai and planned capital cities in the world; in fact, it is reminiscent of the Gulf's many "instant city" projects.[337] The dominating large central axis climaxes in the presidential palace, which paraphrases a fictive national architectural tradition and recalls the Emiral Palace in Abu Dhabi, while at the other end, the national oil company's

332 Cf. Watson, 2014.

333 Cf. Chorin, 2010.

334 Cf. Stoll, 2010.

335 Cf. Izabela Orlowska's paper "Branding a Hero, Forging New Symbols: The Aftermath of Ethiopia after Meles Zenawi" at the *Deutsche Orientalistentag* 2017 in Jena.

336 Cf. again Jones Luong, 2003.

337 Cf. Brorman Jensen, 2008.

headquarters follows the style of Dubai's iconic Atlantis Hotel. As the new "court architect," Norman Foster was able to design several outstanding buildings, and President Nursultan Nazarbayev (r. 1991–2019) was glorified in the official media as the ultimate visionary of the new capital. Accordingly, urban planning, power symbolism, and the cult of personality have intrinsically interwoven. Iconic architecture serves primarily uncritical branding purposes that conceal tangible power interests and a project to shape a national identity at the domestic, regional, and global levels. New images of the country aim to counter existing ideas about post-Soviet bureaucracy, corruption, and oppression (as well as those conveyed by the ridiculing film with the fictitious reporter Borat). Besides extravagant urban development, sport, namely participation in international events, and higher education, such as the founding of "world-class" universities, have been central components used for national branding strategies that parallel Qatar's endeavours.[338]

In Aşgabat, Turkmenistan, another "presidential" capital, the head of state likewise presents himself as an urban architect and planner, glorified by numerous sculptural and architectural monuments, and legitimises his rule with identitarian buildings and a general urbanistic staging of power.[339] But even in much poorer Tajikistan, Dushanbe's cityscape is experiencing serious transformation, financed by foreign, including Gulf Arab investors.[340] The developing Gulf tourism and business, as well as representations of Dubai's success in the media, reinforce the Gulf-style branding. Closely related to the spectacular architecture and urban hyper-modernity, an Islamic lifestyle oriented towards a romanticised and hybrid Gulf-inspired Islamic image has become fashionable, and consumption brands with an imprint of piety have been increasingly considered to be of high quality and to bestow prestige.[341] "[T]he manufacturing of modern urban identities is in line with the launched urban renewal that promotes the 'Dubaisation' or 'Gulfication' (...) of Central Asian's urban centres and repositions the meta-narrative of Dushanbe's future as a modern, rising and Muslim city."[342]

Dubai-inspired branding has also extended to South Asia. During the 1970s oil boom, the UAE had become the central destination for labour migration from the South Indian state of Kerala; vice versa, remittances from the Gulf are an essential part of local income and have induced far-reaching socioeconomic reconfigura-

338 Cf. Fauve, 2015; Eggeling, 2020. Sim, 2012: 87, and Koch, 2018: 56–57, also mention the Borat case.
339 Cf. Fauve and Gintrac, 2009, on both Astana and Aşgabat. Cf. also Koch, 2018, on Astana and other Central and East Asian and Gulf capitals.
340 Cf. Stephan-Emmrich, 2017.
341 Cf. also Stephan-Emmrich and Mirzoev, 2016.
342 Stephan-Emmrich and Mirzoev, 2016: 17.

tions in the local "Gulf pockets."[343] Initially, investment focused on the construction of individual "Gulf houses," especially in rural areas; but already in the 1990s, it shifted to prestigious residential quarters, tourism resorts, and shopping centres. With that, futuristic Dubai-style megaprojects popped up in the large cities of Kerala just as in other Indian metropolises.[344] Advertisements in Gulf newspapers for ultramodern apartment complexes directly address the South Asian diaspora (Fig. 6a). In general, the opening of the Indian economy in the last three decades has been linked with extensive national and international product and tourism marketing.[345] At the same time, India's federal states have endeavoured to position themselves independently. Kerala, "God's own Country," in particular, has been regarded as a pioneer in Indian place branding.[346] In a photo essay, Sophie-Therese Trenka-Dalton demonstrates that images and titles of business and advertising signs in urban and rural areas of Kerala intensely refer to Dubai and other Gulf places.

Fig. 6: The Dubai brand beyond the MENA region
a) Advertisement in Omani newspapers for apartment blocks in Kerala; b) Dubai Takeaway, Manchester; c) Dubai Jeweller, Leipzig.
Sources: Oman Observer, 3 June 2010; Photos Steffen Wippel, 2009 and 2010.

Middle East-related branding has also appeared in Western Europe. As shown above, film festivals like the Berlinale use the Middle East to brand themselves. Dubai appears as a reference and marker in word or assimilated logos (*dhow, Burj Al Arab*) in daily and non-daily places of consumption (Fig. 6b and c). The decades-long presence of Muslim immigrants and refugees has left its mark on the

343 Cf. Venier, 2010. Cf. also several contributions in Reisz, 2010: esp. 476–483.
344 On the example of Delhi's satellite city Gurgaon, cf. Haines, 2011.
345 Cf., e.g., Kerrigan, Shivanandan, and Hede, 2012.
346 Cf., for instance, Vasuvedan, 2008.

urban landscape of European cities. Names alluding to iconic buildings, places, and personalities from the MENA region also serve to brandmark mosques in the European diaspora and demonstrate specific affiliations, as Helle Lykke Nielsen shows in her contribution to this volume.[347] Such Islamic place-making is also expressed, for instance, in cemeteries and burial grounds in Denmark.[348] Like such globalised brands as Coca Cola and Google, Arab-Muslim gravestones do not refer to the context in which they are placed, neither in text nor in form, and almost always look the same wherever they are placed. These decontextualised tombs function as a means of creating a transnational space in the diaspora, thus branding Islam in a non-Muslim context. This reflects a process in which Muslims are creating a space and a new, anchored identity for themselves in their countries of residence.

11 Outlook

This chapter has highlighted the varying intensity and scope of branding in various countries in the MENA region (and beyond) – or at least the varying degrees of coverage in academic publications, which certainly reflect the respective uses of branding. Application-oriented works have been largely omitted here; however, a growing body of academic literature, gradually extending from its initial focus on Dubai and then on Doha and other Gulf places to other parts of the region, can be observed in recent years, which deals with this field of research both empirically and theoretically/critically. There are even more articles and books available that have a different focus but consider product, personal, and above all place branding as an important aspect. But in the end, still, the geographic area targeted in this volume is by far underrepresented compared with the amount of specific scientific work on branding in other regions of the world, and many issues need to be studied from various angles and perspectives. Unlike political studies of conflicts and regimes, cultural issues, or urban development, a comprehensive publication on the diverse facets and regional manifestations of branding products, persons, and places is still missing. This volume aims to fill these important gaps.

The breadth of terminology in the existing literature varies from branding, marketing, promotion, advertising, and image building to public diplomacy. The purposes, media employed, responsible actors, and addressees are manifold; branding is often directed simultaneously to domestic audiences and external pub-

347 For a long version, cf. Lykke Nielsen, 2021.
348 Cf. Lykke Nielsen, 2018.

lics. Delimitations between place and personal branding, product and place branding, and several hierarchies of places repeatedly blur. Branding and the use of worlding strategies have generally intensified with increasing integration into globalisation, adoption of neoliberal agendas, and the attraction of postmodern experimentalism – often at the cost of growing socio-spatial discrepancies and favouring the stabilisation of authoritarian rulers. Imitation and emulation of established branding models play a crucial role, and geopolitical aspects and geoeconomic goals are central in the drafting of many branding strategies. Finally, there is no unique branding model, but producers, politicians, and PR managers are learning from each other and conceive their branding strategies, depending on given constraints and challenges. All of this is explored in greater depth in the following parts of this volume.

In her ground-breaking comparative study of Qatar and Kazakhstan, Kristin Anabel Eggeling, for instance, formulated a number of opportunities for further research, which this book has intended to tackle in great part.[349] What has been done is to extend the context of branding across objects, fields, and places to have a rich, theoretically informed empirical fund of insights for further comparison, finding similarities and divergences, and, especially, showing the phenomenon's complexity. In particular, a number of contributions address the questions by whom and to which ends branding is being exercised and practiced – particularly in cases where political, personal, and place brands overlap and interpenetrate or when the plurality of relevant actors and brand-makers is being considered. Moreover, a few chapters show the historical depth of branding endeavours. Others study the reception and perception of brands among different audiences, which is a more difficult task than to investigate its production; there are also examples of the ethnographic immersion and participant observation that Eggeling requests. Islam-, North Africa-, and Gulf-related product and place branding on the periphery have also been included in this volume. Furthermore, it includes branding of and by unconventional places such as mosques and shrines, slums, and camps. Finally, the book has been open to and, in fact, includes a variety of alternative theoretical and conceptual approaches to branding from a broad range of disciplines and subdisciplines, as well as from interdisciplinary standpoints. But first, the next introductory chapter presents the genesis and broader outline of the book and introduces its different parts and individual contributions.

349 Cf. Eggeling, 2020: 241–243.

Bibliography

Abdallah Ali. "Night-time Economy in Beirut: Modernization and Re-branding as a Recovery Mechanism for Tourism Development in Lebanon." In *The 2015 WEI International Academic Conference Proceedings Barcelona, Spain*, edited by The West East Institute: 7–23. 2015. http://www.westeastinstitute.com/wp-content/uploads/2015/02/Ali-Abdallah.pdf. Accessed 25 March 2015.

Abdalmajid, Jilan, and Ioanna Papasolomou. "Contemporary Nation Branding Under Complex Political Conditions: The Case of Palestine." In *Innovation and Capacity Building: Cross-disciplinary Management Theories for Practical Applications*, edited by Demetris Vrontis, Yaakov Weber, Alkis Thrassou, S. M. Riad Shams, and Evangelos Tsoukatos, 187–205. Cham: Palgrave Macmillan, 2018.

Abotera, Mohamad, and Safa Ashoub. "L'espace des panneaux publicitaires en Égypte: reproduire la nature et dominer les représentations." *Les Cahiers d'EMAM* 33 (2020). http://journals.openedition.org/emam/3201. Accessed 8 December 2020.

Abu Dhabi Media Office. "About ADMO." https://www.mediaoffice.abudhabi/en/abu-dhabi-media-office/. Accessed 10 February 2023.

Acuto, Michele. "High-rise Dubai Urban Entrepreneurialism and the Technology of Symbolic Power." *Cities* 27.4 (2010): 272–284.

Adanali, Yaşar Adnan. "The Reign of 'Madness' in Istanbul: Economies of Scale of Urban Transformation." *Trialog: A Journal for Planning and Building in the Third World* 108.1 (2011): 41–45.

Adham, Khaled. "Cairo's Urban Deja Vu: Globalization and Urban Fantasies." In *Planning Middle Eastern Cities: An Urban Kaleidoscope in a Globalizing World*, edited by Yasser Elsheshtawy, 134–168. Abingdon, New York: Routledge, 2004.

Adham, Khaled. "Rediscovering the Island: Doha's Urbanity from Pearls to Spectacle." In *The Evolving Arab City: Tradition, Modernity and Urban Development*, edited by Yasser Elsheshtawy, 218–257. Abingdon, New York: Routledge, 2011.

Adham, Khaled. "Modes of Urban Diffusion: Culture, Politics and the Impact of the Recent Urban Developments in the Arabian Gulf Cities on Cairo's Vision 2050." In *Under Construction: Logics of Urbanism in the Gulf Region*, edited by Steffen Wippel, Katrin Bromber, Christian Steiner, and Birgit Krawietz, 233–245. Farnham, Burlington: Ashgate, 2014.

Adham, Khaled. "Kairo: Kopie Dubais oder Keynesianismus auf Droge." *Inamo: Informationsprojekt Naher und Mittlerer Osten* 23.89 (2017): 19–23.

Aggarwal, Praveen, Kjell Knudsen, and Ahmed Maamoun. "Brands As Ideological Symbols: The Cola Wars." *Journal of Business Case Studies* 5.2 (2009): 27–34.

Al Amoudy, Saeed. "Makkah Al-Mukaaramah: A Second Tier City for Religious Tourism." In *City Imaging: Regeneration, Renewal and Decay*, edited by Tara Brabazon, 201–208. Dordrecht et al.: Springer, 2014.

Al Balushi, Maha, Irfan Butt, and Khadija Al Siyabi. "Review of Awareness and Views on Branding Oman as a Nation." *International Journal of Business Tourism and Applied Sciences* 5.1 (2013): 5–19. http://www.ijbts-journal.com/images/main_1366796758/0112-Maha.pdf. Accessed 23 January 2014.

ALECSO. "Capitals of Arab Culture." *Arab League Educational, Cultural and Scientific Organization*, 26 April 2019. Tunis. http://www.alecso.org/nsite/en/mn-culture-2/projects-and-programs/capitals-of-arab-culture. Accessed 2 September 2021.

Al-Ghazzi, Omar, and Marwan M. Kraidy. "Neo-Ottoman Cool 2: Turkish Nation Branding and Arabic-Language Transnational Broadcasting." *International Journal of Communication* 7 (2013): 2341–2360. https://ijoc.org/index.php/ijoc/article/download/1881/1006. Accessed 17 February 2022.

Ali, Asim, and Shatha Al-Aswad. "Persian Gulf-based SWFs and Financial Hubs in Bahrain, Dubai and Qatar: A Case of Competitive Branding." *World Economics* 13.3 (2012): 109–125.

Aljem, Sanae, and Cristiana Strava. "Casablanca's Megaprojects: Neoliberal Urban Planning and Socio-Spatial Transformations." *Trialog: A Journal for Planning and Building in a Global Context* 135.4 (2018) [2020]: 12–19.

Allouche, Yasmina. "Restrictions sur les produits turcs: Le Maroc a-t-il rejoint le boycott saoudien?" *Middle East Eye, édition française* 28 October 2020. https://www.middleeasteye.net/fr/decryptages/maroc-boycott-saoudien-turquie-arabie-relations-commerciales. Accessed 10 February 2022.

Alraouf, Ali A. "The Knowledge Urbanity in Qatar: An Alternative Dynamic." In *Knowledge-Based Urban Development in the Middle East*, edited by Ali A. Alraouf, 60–79. Hershey: IGI Global, 2018.

Alserhan, Baker Ahmad. "Islamic Branding: A Conceptualization of Related Terms." *Brand Management* 18.1 (2010a): 34–49.

Alserhan, Baker Ahmad. "On Islamic Branding: Brands as Good Deeds." *Journal of Islamic Marketing* 1.2 (2010b): 101–106.

Aly, Hend. "Royal Dream: City Branding and Saudi Arabia's NEOM." *Middle East–Topics & Arguments* 12.1 (2019): 99–109. https://archiv.ub.uni-marburg.de/ep/0003/article/view/7937/7873. Accessed 23 February 2023.

Alzadjali, Badar D. *Nation Brand in Oman: Studying Stakeholders Views On "Branding Oman".* Master's Thesis, Master of Science in Marketing Management, Faculty of Business and Law, De Montfort University, Leicester, 2010.

Amarouche, Maryame, and Koenraad Bogaert. "Reshaping Space and Time in Morocco: The Agencification of Urban Government and its Effects in the Bouregreg Valley (Rabat/Salé)." *Middle East–Topics & Arguments* 12.1 (2019): 44–54. https://archiv.ub.uni-marburg.de/ep/0003/2019/230/7934. Accessed 10 March 2022.

Amour, Philipp O. "Islamophobia and the Brand of Osama: What's in a Name? What's in an Image?" *Siyaset, Ekonomi ve Yönetim Araştırmaları Dergisi* 6.2 (2018): 63–74.

Andersson, Ida. "Placing Place Branding: An Analysis of an Emerging Research Field in Human Geography." *Geografisk Tidsskrift-Danish Journal of Geography* 114.2 (2014): 143–155.

Arlk, Elvan. "Bio Istanbul: A Speculative, Segregationist, and Sustainable Urbanism." *Jadaliyya* 16 February 2015. https://www.jadaliyya.com/Details/31785/Bio-Istanbul-A-Speculative,-Segregationist,-and-Sustainable-Urbanism. Accessed 2 August 2019.

Aronczyk, Melissa. *Branding the Nation: The Global Business of National Identity.* [Oxford]: Oxford Scholarship Online [Oxford University Press], 2013.

Assaf, Laure. "La Corniche d'Abu Dhabi: Espace public et intimités à ciel ouvert." *Arabian Humanities* 2 (2013). http://cy.revues.org/2625. Accessed 20 August 2014.

Avraham, Eli. "Destination Marketing and Image Repair during Tourism Crises: The Case of Egypt." *Journal of Hospitality and Tourism Management* 28 (2016): 41–48.

Bagaeen, Samer. "Brand Dubai: The Instant City; or the Instantly Recognizable City." *International Planning Studies* 12.2 (2007): 173–197.

Balakrishnan, Melodena Stephens. "Dubai – A Star in the East: A Case Study in Strategic Destination Branding." *Journal of Place Management and Development* 1.1 (2008): 62–91.

Ballout, Jean-Marie. "'Villes nouvelles' et urbanités émergentes dans les périphéries de Constantine et Marrakech." *L'Année du Maghreb* 12 (2015): 55–74.

Ballout, Jean-Marie. "Un bilan intermédiaire du Programme de villes nouvelles au Maroc." *Les Cahiers d'EMAM* 29 (2017). http://emam.revues.org/1316. Accessed 3 March 2017.

Bandopadhyaya, Suvojit. "Branding the Islamic State of Iraq and Syria." *Global Media and Communication* 15.3 (2019): 285–301.

Bani Hashim, Alamira Reem Al Ayedrous. "Branding the Brand New City: Abu Dhabi, Travelers Welcome." *Place Branding and Public Diplomacy* 8.1 (2012): 72–82.

Bank, André, Thomas Richter, and Anna Sunik. "Durable, Yet Different: Monarchies in the Arab Spring." *Journal of Arabian Studies: Arabia, the Gulf, and the Red Sea* 4.2 (2014): 163–179.

Barthel, Pierre-Arnaud. "Aménager la lagune de Tunis: Un modèle d'urbanisme et de développement durable?" *Autrepart* 39.3 (2006): 129–146.

Barthel, Pierre-Arnaud. "Global Waterfronts in the Maghreb: A Mere Replication of Dubai? Case Studies from Morocco and Tunisia." In *Under Construction: Logics of Urbanism in the Gulf Region*, edited by Steffen Wippel, Katrin Bromber, Christian Steiner, and Birgit Krawietz, 247–258. Farnham, Burlington: Ashgate, 2014.

Barthel, Pierre-Arnaud. "Le Maroc à l'heure de l'éco-urbanisme: Innovations et décalages sur le terrain des premiers projets urbains 'verts'." In *Le Maroc au présent: D'une époque à l'autre, une société en mutation*, edited by Baudouin Dupret, Zakaria Rhani, Assia Boutaleb, and Jean-Noël Ferrié. Casablanca: Centre Jacques-Berque, 2015a. http://books.openedition.org/cjb/1001. Accessed 9 May 2019.

Barthel, Pierre-Arnaud. "Exporting French-style 'Sustainable Cities' to Morocco." *Metropolitics*, 1 May 2015b. http://www.metropolitiques.eu/Exporting-French-stylesustainable.html. Accessed 7 May 2015.

Baş, Ahmet, and Marie Delaplace. "Bidding for Olympic and Paralympic Games, A Tool for Transportation Investments and Tourism? The Case of Istanbul." *Journal of Convention & Event Tourism* 24.2 (2023): 182–204.

Bauer, Susanne, Anton Escher, and Sebastian Knieper. "Essaouira, 'The Wind City' as a 'Cultural Product'." *Erdkunde* 60 (2006): 25–39.

Beck, Martin. *Kritik der Politischen Ökonomie Katars: Zur Debatte über soziale Menschenrechtsverletzungen im Vorfeld der Fußballweltmeisterschaft 2022.* La Marsa: Friedrich-Ebert-Stiftung, 2022.

Beier, Raffael. *Shifting Urban Policies in North Africa after the "Arab Spring": Urgent Reaction or Real Changes?* Berlin: Klaus Schwarz, 2016.

Beier, Raffael. "Tunis + Casablanca: 'Worlding' und Sozialverträglichkeit." *Inamo: Informationsprojekt Naher und Mittler Osten* 23.89 (2017): 24–28.

Beier, Raffael. "Worlding Cities in the Middle East and North Africa: Arguments for a Conceptual Turn." *Middle East-Topics & Arguments* 12.1 (2019): 28–34. https://archiv.ub.uni-marburg.de/ep/0003/2019/230/7828/. Accessed 22 November 2022.

Belguidoum, Saïd, and Olivier Pliez. "Pratiques transnationales dans un comptoir de 'la Route de la soie': Algériens et Égyptiens à Yiwu (Chine)." *Les Cahiers d'EMAM* 26 (2015). http://journals.openedition.org/emam/927. Accessed 3 May 2019.

Belkadi, Ezzohra. "Marketing territorial de Casablanca: Etude de l'image de marque." *International Journal of Innovation and Applied Studies* 13.3 (2015): 704–714. http://www.issr-journals.org/links/papers.php?journal=ijias&application=pdf&article=IJIAS-15-144-03. Accessed 13 January 2021.

Belkadi, Ezzohra. "The Adoption of Residents of The City Brand: A Case Study of Casablanca City." *Expert Journal of Marketing* 7.2 (2019): 112–119. http://marketing.expertjournals.com/ark:/16759/EJM_711belkadi112-119.pdf. Accessed 13 January 2021.

Berrada, Mehdi. "Consommation: Au Maroc, trois marques boycottées suite à un appel sur les réseaux sociaux." *Jeune Afrique* 26 April 2018. https://www.jeuneafrique.com/555554/economie/consommation-au-maroc-trois-marques-boycottees-suite-a-un-appel-sur-les-reseaux-sociaux/. Accessed 10 February 2022.

Bertelsmann Stiftung. *Bertelsmann Transformation Index 2020.* https://bti-project.org. Accessed 20 May 2020.

BIE. *Bureau International des Expositions.* Paris. https://www.bie-paris.org/site/en. Accessed 17 January 2022.

Blichfeldt Olsen, Andreas. "A Global Map of Qatar's Sponsorships in Sports." *Play the Game* 22 December 2022. https://www.playthegame.org/news/a-global-map-of-qatar-s-sponsorships-in-sports/. Accessed 17 February 2023.

Bloom Consulting. *Country Brand Ranking: 2019 2020 Trade Edition.* Madrid, 2019a. https://www.bloom-consulting.com/en/pdf/rankings/Bloom_Consulting_Country_Brand_Ranking_Trade.pdf Accessed 13 January 2022.

Bloom Consulting. *Country Brand Ranking: 2019 2020 Tourism Edition.* Madrid, 2019b. https://www.bloom-consulting.com/en/pdf/rankings/Bloom_Consulting_Country_Brand_Ranking_Tourism.pdf Accessed 13 January 2022.

Bogaert, Koenraad. "Imider vs. COP22: Understanding Climate Justice from Morocco's Peripheries." In *Cities*, edited by Mona Harb and Eric Verdeil, 30–33. Washington, DC: Tadween Publishing, 2019.

Boissière, Thierry, and Yoann Morvan, "Erbil: An Unfulfilled Dream of Urban Modernity." In *Cities*, edited by Mona Harb and Eric Verdeil, 14–18. Washington, DC: Tadween Publishing, 2019.

Bolleter, Julian. "Para-Scape: Landscape Architecture in Dubai." *Journal of Landscape Architecture* 4.1 (2009): 6–19.

Bonte, Marie. "'Gay Paradise – kind of': Les espaces de l'homosexualité masculine à Beyrouth. *EchoGéo* 25 (2013). http://echogeo.revues.org/13498. Accessed 10 October 2013.

Bonte, Marie. "'Eat, Drink and Be Merry for Tomorrow We Die': Alcohol Practices in Mar Mikhael, Beirut." In *Drinking Dilemmas: Space, Culture and Identity*, edited by Thomas Thurnell-Read, 81–98. Abingdon, New York: Routledge, 2016.

Bonte, Marie. "Ordinary Drinking? Place and Politics of Alcohol in Lebanon." In *Alcohol in the Maghreb and the Middle East since the Nineteenth Century: Disputes, Policies and Practices*, edited by Elife Biçer-Deveci and Philippe Bourmaud, 67–91. Cham: Palgrave Macmillan, 2021.

BrandFinance. *Brandirectory: The Largest Brand Value Database in the World.* London. https://brandirectory.com/. Accessed 6 January 2022.

Bromber, Katrin. "The Sporting Way: Sport as Branding Strategy in the Gulf States." In *Under Construction: Logics of Urbanism in the Gulf Region*, edited by Steffen Wippel, Katrin Bromber, Christian Steiner, and Birgit Krawietz, 119–130. Farnham, Burlington: Ashgate, 2014.

Bromber, Katrin, and Birgit Krawietz. "The United Arab Emirates, Qatar, and Bahrain as a Modern Sport Hub." In *Sport Across Asia: Politics, Cultures, and Identities*, edited by Katrin Bromber, Birgit Krawietz, and Joseph Maguire, 189–211. New York, London: Routledge, 2013.

Bromber, Katrin, Birgit Krawietz, Christian Steiner, and Steffen Wippel. "The Arab(ian) Gulf: Urban Development in the Making." In *Under Construction: Logics of Urbanism in the Gulf Region*, edited by Steffen Wippel, Katrin Bromber, Christian Steiner, and Birgit Krawietz, 1–14. Farnham, Burlington: Ashgate, 2014.

Brorman Jensen, Boris. *Dubai: Dynamics of Bingo Urbanism.* Copenhagen: Fonden til udgivelse af Arkitekturtidsskrift B, 2007.

Brorman Jensen, Boris. "Astana – Steppens Dubai." *Arkitekten* 15 (2008): 36–43.

Brorman Jensen, Boris. "Masdar City: A Critical Retrospection." In *Under Construction: Logics of Urbanism in the Gulf Region*, edited by Steffen Wippel, Katrin Bromber, Christian Steiner, and Birgit Krawietz, 45–54. Farnham, Burlington: Ashgate, 2014.

Brückerhoff, Björn. "Al-Qaida als globale Marke: Markenkommunikation des Terrorismus." *Die Gegenwart* 38 (2004). http://www.neuegegenwart.de/ausgabe38/terror.htm. Accessed 24 October 2022.

Bsheer, Rosie. "Choking Mecca in the Name of Beauty – and Development (Part 1)" and "(...) (Part 2)." *Jadaliyya*, 21 October and 19 November 2010. https://www.jadaliyya.com/Details/23545 and https://www.jadaliyya.com/Details/23578. Accessed 23 February 2023.

Buchakjian, Gregory. "Beirut by Night: A Century of Nightlife Photography." *Middle East Journal of Culture and Communication* 8 (2015) 256–281.

Burs, Gerhard Martin. *Mediale Präsentation in der Gegenwartsarchitektur: Das Beispiel der Vereinigten Arabischen Emirate.* Bielefeld: Transcript, 2016.

Cattedra, Raffaele. "Chapitre I: Les grands projets urbains à la conquête des périphéries." *Les Cahiers d'EMAM* 19 (2010): 58–72.

Çavdar, Ayşe. "Building, Marketing and Living in an Islamic Gated Community: Novel Configurations of Class and Religion in Istanbul." *International Journal of Urban and Regional Research* 40.3 (2016): 507–523.

Champigny, Zoé. "Les images de la (re)construction des villes du Kurdistan irakien. Créer et promouvoir le Kurdistan de demain: S'inscrire dans un système capitaliste." *Les Cahiers d'EMAM* 33 (2020). https://journals.openedition.org/emam/3246. Accessed 5 January 2021.

Choplin, Armelle, and Alice Franck. "Seeing Dubai in Khartoum and Nouakchott: "Gulfication" on the Margins of the Arab World." In *Under Construction: Logics of Urbanism in the Gulf Region*, edited by Steffen Wippel, Katrin Bromber, Christian Steiner, and Birgit Krawietz, 271–284. Farnham, Burlington: Ashgate, 2014.

Chorin, Ethan. *Articulating a "Dubai Model" of Development: The Case of Djibouti.* Dubai: Dubai School of Government, 2010.

Clarke, Colin P. "Expanding the ISIS Brand." *The National Interest* 17 February 2018. https://nationalinterest.org/feature/expanding-the-isis-brand-24550?n. Accessed 27 January 2023.

Cooke, Miriam. *Tribal Modern: Branding New Nations in the Arab Gulf.* Berkely, Los Angeles, London: University of California Press, 2014.

Coombe, William, and Jad Melki. "Global Media and Brand Dubai." *Place Branding and Public Diplomacy* 8.1 (2012): 58–71.

Coslett, Daniel E. "(Re)branding a (Post)colonial Streetscape: Tunis's Avenue Habib Bourguiba and the Road Ahead." *International Journal of Islamic Architecture* 6.1 (2017): 59–96.

Côté-Roy, Laurence, and Sarah Moser. "'Does Africa Not Deserve Shiny New Cities?' The Power of Seductive Rhetoric around New Cities in Africa." *Urban Studies* 56.12 (2019): 2391–2407.

Cravatts, Richard L. "The Brand Image of Nations: Israel." *American Thinker* 16 February 2007. https://www.americanthinker.com/articles/2007/02/the_brand_image_of_nations_isr.html. Accessed 19 January 2023.

Crilley, Rhys, and Ilan Manor. "Un-nation Branding: The Cities of Tel Aviv and Jerusalem in Israeli Soft Power." In *City Diplomacy: Current Trends and Future Prospects*, edited by Sohaela Amiri and Efe Sevin, 137–160. Cham: Palgrave Macmillan, 2020.

Cugurullo, Federico. "Exposing Smart Cities and Eco-cities: Frankenstein Urbanism and the Sustainability Challenges of the Experimental City." *Environment and Planning A: Economy and Space* 50.1 (2018): 73–92.

Cummings, Veronika, and Aurel von Richthofen. "Urban Sustainability as a Political Instrument in the Gulf Region Exemplified by Projects in Abu Dhabi." *Die Erde* 148.4 (2017): 253–267.

Dajani, Muna. "Danger, Turbines! A Jawlani Cry against Green Energy Colonialism in Occupied Syrian Golan Heights." *Jadaliyya* 22 April 2020. https://www.jadaliyya.com/Details/41010/Danger,-Turbines-A-Jawlani. Accessed 18 May 2021.

Dart, Jon. "'Brand Israel': Hasbara and Israeli Sport." *Sport in Society: Cultures, Commerce, Media, Politics* 19.10 (2016): 1402–1418.

De Jong, Martin, Thomas Hoppe, and Negar Noori. "City Branding, Sustainable Urban Development and the Rentier State: How do Qatar, Abu Dhabi and Dubai Present Themselves in the Age of Post Oil and Global Warming?" *Energies* 12.9, article #1657 (2019): 1–26.

de Losada, Agustí Fernández. *The Downside of the International Impact of City Branding.* Barcelona: Centro de Información y Documentación Internacionales en Barcelona, 2019. https://www.cidob.org/en/content/download/73958/2364662/version/6/file/594_OPINION_AGUSTI%20FERNANDEZ%20DE%20LOSADA_ANG.pdf. Accessed 25 July 2020.

Derichs, Claudia, and Thomas Demmelhuber. "Monarchies and Republics, State and Regime, Durability and Fragility in View of the Arab Spring." *Journal of Arabian Studies* 4.2 (2014): 180–194.

Dines, Nick. "Moroccan City Festivals, Cultural Diplomacy and Urban Political Agency." *International Journal of Politics, Culture, and Society* 34 (2021): 471–485.

Dinnie, Keith. *Nation Branding: Concepts, Issues, Practice.* Oxford, Burlington: Butterworth-Heinemann, 2008.

Dinnie, Keith, ed. *City Branding: Theory and Cases.* Basingstoke, New York: Palgrave Macmillan, 2011.

Divandari, Ali, Amir Ekhlassi, and Kamal Rahmani. "Devising a Branding Model for Multipurpose Mega-projects in Entertainment, Residential, Tourism, and Sport in Iran." *Journal of Vacation Marketing* 20.1 (2014): 73–91.

Doherty, Ronald J. "Introduction." *International Journal of Islamic Marketing and Branding* 1.1 (2015): 1–4.

Duaei, Kamaluddin. "Qom After Islamic Neo-Liberalism: A Narrative of the City in Limbo." *Middle East–Topics & Arguments* 12.1 (2019): 55–65. https://archiv.ub.uni-marburg.de/ep/0003/article/view/7932. Accessed 23 February 2023.

Dumortier, Brigitte. "Ras al-Khaïmah, l'essor récent d'une ville moyenne du Golfe." *Arabian Humanities* 2 (2013). http://cy.revues.org/2575. Accessed 21 August 2014.

Dumortier, Brigitte. "The Cultural Imperative: Saadiyat Cultural District in Abu Dhabi between Public Policy and Architectural Gesture." In *Under Construction: Logics of Urbanism in the Gulf Region*, edited by Steffen Wippel, Katrin Bromber, Christian Steiner, and Birgit Krawietz, 171–190. Farnham, Burlington: Ashgate, 2014.

East West Communications. *Branding Indexes.* Washington, DC, 2021. https://www.eastwestcoms.com/. Accessed 4 August 2021 (links to subpages with indexes expired).

Echattabi, Hicham, and Ahmed Khattab. "The Place Marketing Strategy in Moroccan Regions: Conditions of Applicability." *Journal of Economic and Social Thought* 8.2 (2021): 42–54.

Eggeling, Kristin Anabel. *Nation-branding in Practice: The Politics of Promoting Sports, Cities and Universities in Kazakhstan and Qatar.* Abingdon, New York: Routledge, 2020.

El Aouni, Fatimazohra, Rosalía Cascón-Pereira, and Ana B. Hernández-Lara. "Building the 'Morocco' Brand as a Tourist Destination: The Role of Emigrants and Institutional Websites." *Journal of Urban Regeneration and Renewal* 6.3 (2012): 252–263.

el-Gawhary, Karim. "Sex Tourism in Cairo." *Middle East Report* 196, 25.5 (1995): 26–27.

El Rhazi, Anass. "L'ONMT lance sa nouvelle campagne internationale 'Maroc, Terre de Lumière'." *Le Desk* 21 April 2022. https://ledesk.ma/encontinu/lonmt-lance-sa-nouvelle-campagne-internationale-maroc-terre-de-lumiere/. Accessed 24 April 2022.

Elsheshtawy, Yasser. *Dubai: Behind an Urban Spectacle.* Abingdon, New York: Routledge, 2010.

Elsheshtawy, Yasser. "A Mall in Morocco or Dubai in Africa." *Dubaization: Reflections on Middle Eastern Urbanism, Inspired by Dubai*, 16 February 2012. http://dubaization.com/post/27099232531/a-mall-in-morocco-or-dubai-in-africa. Accessed 14 February 2014.

Elsheshtawy, Yasser. *Sultans of Green: Arab Gulf Cities and the New Urban Agenda.* Dubaization: Reflections on Architecture & Urbanism, Inspired by Dubai, 10 August 2018. https://dubaization.com/post/176821563973/sultans-of-green-arab-gulf-cities-and-the-new. Accessed 1 August 2019.

Erdmann, Gero, and Ulf Engel. "Neopatrimonialism Reconsidered: Critical Review and Elaboration of an Elusive Concept." *Journal of Commonwealth and Comparative Politics* 45.1 (2007): 95–119.

Farag, Alshimaa Aboelmakarem. "The Story of NEOM City: Opportunities and Challenges." In *New Cities and Community Extensions in Egypt and the Middle East: Visions and Challenges*, edited by Sahar Attia, Zeinab Shafik, and Asmaa Ibrahim, 35–49. Cham: Springer, 2019.

Fauve, Adrien. "Global Astana: Nation Branding as a Legitimization Tool for Authoritarian Regimes." *Central Asian Survey* 34.1(2015): 110–124.

Fauve, Adrien, and Cécile Gintrac. "Production de l'espace urbain et mise en scène du pouvoir dans deux capitales 'présidentielles' d'Asie Centrale." *L'Espace Politique* 82 (2009). http://espacepolitique.revues.org/index1376.html. Accessed 5 November 2012.

Feighery, William G. "Tourism and Self-Orientalism in Oman: A Critical Discourse Analysis." *Critical Discourse Studies* 9.3 (2012): 269–284.

Fischer, Johan. "Branding Halal: A Photographic Essay on Global Muslim Markets." *Anthropology Today* 28.4 (2012): 18–21.

Florida, Richard, Charlotta Mellander, and Karen King. *The Global Creativity Index 2015.* Toronto: Martin Prosperity Institute, University of Toronto, 2015. https://ec.europa.eu/futurium/en/system/files/ged/31_-most_creative_countries_-_global_creativity_index_2015_-_canadian_mgt_school.pdf. Accessed 8 December 2022.

Frede, Britta. "In an Era of Terror Threats: Negotiating the Governance of a (Trans)Local Islamic Heritage in the Islamic Republic of Mauritania." In *Claiming and Making Muslim Worlds: Religion and Society in the Context of the Global*, edited by Jeanine Elif Dağyeli, Claudia Ghrawi, and Ulrike Freitag: 131–157. Berlin, Boston: De Gruyter, 2021.

Fruh, Kyle, Alfred Archer, and Jake Wojtowicz. "Sportswashing: Complicity and Corruption." *Sport, Ethics and Philosophy* 17.1 (2023): 101–118.

Fuhrmann, Malte. "Beer, the Drink of a Changing World: Beer Consumption and Production on the Shores of the Aegean in the 19th Century." *Turcica* 45 (2014), 79–123.

FutureBrand. *The FutureBrand Country Index 2020: A Unique Country Perception Study.* 2020. https://www.futurebrand.com/futurebrand-country-index-2020/download-fbci-2020. Accessed 13 January 2021 (limited access).

Gaillard, Mathilde. *Vers un nouveau modèle d'urbanisme au Maroc et en Tunisie: Quand les grands projets urbains envahissent les waterfronts – Une littoralisation de l'aménagement au Maghreb entre développement urbain et creusement des marginalités.* Projet de Fin d'Etude, Institut d'Urbanisme de Grenoble, Université Pierre Mendès-France, 2016. https://dumas.ccsd.cnrs.fr/dumas-01419409v1/file/Gaillard%20Mathilde.pdf. Accessed 23 August 2021.

Galtier, Mathieu. "Tunisie: Le retour de l'étrange mégaprojet Tunis Sports City." *Jeune Afrique* 11 March 2022. https://www.jeuneafrique.com/1326858/economie/tunisie-le-retour-de-letrange-megaprojet-tunis-sports-city/. Accessed 13 June 2022.

GaWC. "The World According to GaWC." Loughborough: Globalization and World Cities Research Network. https://www.lboro.ac.uk/microsites/geography/gawc/gawcworlds.html. Accessed 20 November 2022.

Geisler, Philip. "Challenging the Hagia Sophia: The Selimiye Mosque in Edirne as Ottoman Empire Branding." In *The Heritage of Edirne in Ottoman and Turkish Times: Continuities, Disruptions and Reconnections*, edited by Birgit Krawietz and Florian Riedler, 91–151. Berlin, Boston: Walter de Gruyter, 2020.

Ghailane, Khalid. "Du processus de production d'une nouvelle image de la ville de Chefchaouen (Rif occidental)." *Les Cahiers d'EMAM* 34 (2022): 171–200. http://journals.openedition.org/emam/4654. Accessed 30 January 2023.

Ghannam, Ouafaa, and Azzedine Ghoufrane. *Quels leviers pour édifier une stratégie de marque pour le Maroc?* Rabat: Institut Royal des Etudes Stratégiques, 2016. https://ires.ma/sites/default/files/docs_publications/RAPPORT-MARQUE-MAROC_0.pdf. Accessed 9 March 2023.

Ginesta, Xavier, and Jordi de San Eugenio. "The Use of Football as a Country Branding Strategy. Case Study: Qatar and the Catalan Sports Press." *Communication & Sport* 2.3 (2014): 225–241.

Govers, Robert. "Brand Dubai and its Competitors in the Middle East: An Image and Reputation Analysis." *Place Branding and Public Diplomacy* 8.1 (2012): 48–57.

Govers, Robert, and Frank Go. *Place Branding: Glocal, Virtual and Physical Identities, Constructed, Imagined and Experienced.* Basingstoke, New York: Palgrave Macmillan, 2009.

Gräf, Bettina. *Islamische Gelehrte als politische Akteure im globalen Kontext: Eine Fatwa von Yusuf Abdallah al-Qaradawi.* Berlin: Klaus Schwarz, 2003.

Gräf, Bettina. "Yūsuf al-Qaraḍāwī: State of Research." In *The Global Mufti: The Phenomenon of Yūsuf al-Qaraḍāwī*, edited by Bettina Gräf and Jacob Skovgaard-Petersen, 17–26. London: C. Hurst & Co., 2009.

Gundala, Raghava Rao, Arthur Lok Jack, and Hanin Khawaja. "Brand Management in Small and Medium Enterprise: Evidence from Dubai, UAE." *Global Journal of Business Research* 8.1 (2014): 27–38. https://ssrn.com/abstract=2323011. Accessed 24 April 2023.

Günel, Gökçe. *Spaceship in the Desert: Energy, Climate Change, and Urban Design in Abu Dhabi.* Durham, London: Duke University Press, 2019,

Gutberlet, Manuela. "Staging the Oriental Other: Imaginaries and Performances of German-speaking Cruise Tourists." *Tourist Studies* 19.1 (2019): 110–137.

Haddad, Christian, Cengiz Günay, Sherin Gharib, and Nadejda Komendantova. "Imagined Inclusions into a 'Green Modernisation': Local Politics and Global Visions of Morocco's Renewable Energy Transition." *Third World Quarterly* 43.2 (2022): 393–413.

Haines, Chad. "Cracks in the Façade: Landscapes of Hope and Desire in Dubai." In *Worlding Cities: Asian Experiments and the Art of Being Global*, edited by Ananya Roy and Aihwa Ong, 160–181. Malden, Oxford: Blackwell, 2011.

Harroud, Tarik. "'Sustainable' Entrepreneurial Urbanism in Morocco: What Change(s) for Mining Cities?" *Justice spatiale/Spatial Justice* 15 (2020). http://www.jssj.org/wp-content/uploads/2020/09/JSSJ-15-HARROUD-EN.pdf. Accessed 25 March 2021.

Hartal, Gilly, and Orna Sasson-Levy. "The Progressive Orient: Gay Tourism to Tel Aviv and Israeli Ethnicities." *Environment and Planning C: Politics and Space* 39.1 (2021): 11–29.

Hashim, Alamira Reem Bani, Irazábal, Clara, and Byrum, Greta. "The Scheherazade Syndrome: Fiction and Fact in Dubai's Quest to Become a Global City." *Architectural Theory Review* 15.2 (2010): 210–231.

Hayden, Craig, and Efe Sevin. "The Politics of Meaning and the City Brand: The Controversy over the Branding of Ankara." *Place Branding and Public Diplomacy* 8.2 (2012), 133–146.

Hazime, Hanan. "From City Branding to E-brands in Developing Countries: An Approach to Qatar and Abu Dhabi." *African Journal of Business Management* 5.12 (2011): 4731–4745.

Hindelang, Laura. *Iridescent Kuwait: Petro-Modernity and Urban Visual Culture since the Mid-Twentieth Century.* Berlin, Boston: Walter de Gruyter, 2022.

Hoffmann, Bruce. "Terrorismus als Markenzeichen." *Der Tagesspiegel* 13 September 2006.

Hofmann, Sabine. "Von der Idee zum Algorithmus. Entwicklung und Charakteristika des Transnationalen Innovationssystems Israels." In *Wissensökonomie und Digitalisierung: Geschichte und Perspektiven*, edited by Yaman Kouli, Peter Pawlowsky, and Markus Hertwig, 91–127. Wiesbaden: Springer VS, 2020.

Homes & Leisure. "Map Shows Every Country's Tourism Slogan." https://www.familybreakfinder.co.uk/holidays/map-every-countrys-tourism-slogan. Accessed 13 January 2022.

Hvidt, Martin. "Planning for Development in the GCC States: A Content Analysis of Current Development Plans." *Journal of Arabian Studies* 2.2 (2012): 189–207.

Ibahrine, Mohammad. "Nation Branding in the Gulf Countries." In *Intersections Between Public Diplomacy & International Development: Case Studies in Converging Fields*, edited by James Pamment, 103–123. Los Angeles: Figueroa Press, 2016.

Ibrahim, Rebwar, Sabah Mushatat, and Mohamed Gamal Abdelmonem. "Authenticity, Identity and Sustainability in Post-war Iraq: Reshaping the Urban Form of Erbil City." *Journal of Islamic Architecture* 3.2 (2014): 58–68.

ICESCO. "Capitals of Islamic Culture." *Islamic World Educational, Scientific and Cultural Organization.* Rabat. https://www.icesco.org/en/capitals-of-islamic-culture/. Accessed 2 September 2021.

Iğsız, Aslı. "Brand Turkey and the Gezi Protests: Authoritarianism, Law, and Neoliberalism (Part Two)." *Jadaliyya* 13 July 2013. https://www.jadaliyya.com/Details/29089. Accessed 5 March 2013.

Iğsız, Aslı. "From Alliance of Civilizations to Branding the Nation: Turkish Studies, Image Wars and Politics of Comparison in an Age of Neoliberalism." *Turkish Studies* 15.4 (2014): 689–704.

International Islamic Marketing Association. http://www.iimassociation.com/. Accessed 24 January 2023.

International Journal of Islamic Marketing and Branding. http://www.inderscience.com/jhome.php?jcode=ijimb. Accessed 24 January 2023.

Ipsos. "London Ranks as the Top 'City Brand': Sydney Emerges in Second Place, while Paris Declines from First in 2017 to Third in 2020." Press release. New York, 6 April 2020. https://www.ipsos.com/sites/default/files/ct/news/documents/2020–04/city-brands-2020-press-release_final-april-2020.pdf. Accessed 17 January 2022.

IRES. *La réputation du Maroc dans le monde: Country RepTrak® 2021.* Rabat: Institut Royal des Etudes Stratégiques, The RepTrak Company, 2021. https://www.ires.ma/images/PDFs_publications/REPUTATION_DU_MAROC_DANS_LE_MONDE_2021.pdf. Accessed 10 November 2021.

Iriqat, Dalal. "Palestinian Nation Branding via Public Diplomacy." *International Relations and Diplomacy* 7.5 (2019): 202–216.

Ishtiaq, Sheikh Muhammad, and Kamran Ahmed Siddiqui. "Branding by Islamic Banks in Pakistan: A Content Analysis of Visual Brand Elements." *Journal of Marketing Management and Consumer Behavior* 1.2 (2016): 33–44.

Jacobs, Jessica. "Re-branding the Levant: Contested Heritage and Colonial Modernities in Amman and Damascus." *Journal of Tourism and Cultural Change* 8.4 (2010): 316–326.

Jones Luong, Pauline. "The Middle Easternization of Central Asia." *Current History* 102.666 (2003): 333–340.

Kama, Amit, and Yael Ram. "'Hot Guys' in Tel Aviv: Pride Tourism in Israel." *Israel Studies Review* 35.1 (2020): 79–99.

Karl, Stefan. "Eine Airline-Werbung, die keine Airline-Werbung ist: The Soul of Arabia." Berlin: Shanghai Berlin | Neue Marken-Kommunikation, 8 November 2010. http://wir.shanghai-berlin.de/?p=345. Accessed 9 October 2012 (link expired).

Kechichian, Joseph A. *Oman and the World: The Emergence of an Independent Foreign Policy.* Santa Monica: Rand, 1995.

Kehrer, Michaela. "Transnationale Konsumgüterunternehmen in Ägypten: Lokale Kultur im globalen Marketing." In *Wirtschaft im Vorderen Orient: Interdisziplinäre Perspektiven*, edited by Steffen Wippel, 215–234. Berlin: Klaus Schwarz, 2005.

Kerrigan, Finola, Jyotsna Shivanandan, and Anne-Marie Hede. "Nation Branding: A Critical Appraisal of Incredible India." *Journal of Macromarketing* 32.3 (2012): 319–327.

King, John Mark. "Nation Branding: Coverage and Perceptions of Qatar in Major World Newspapers." In *Estableciendo puentes en una economía global, Vol. 1: Ponencias*, edited by Julio Pindado García and Gregory Payne, article #50 [no pages]. Salamanca: Escuela Superior de Gestión Comercial y Marketing, ESIC, 2008. https://dialnet.unirioja.es/descarga/articulo/2720192.pdf. Accessed 23 January 2014.

King, John Mark, and Mohamed Zayani. "Media, Branding and Controversy: Perceptions of Al Jazeera in Newspapers around the World." *Journal of Middle East Media* 4.1 (2008): 27–43.

Klinger, Thibaut. *L'Oman contemporain: Aménagement du territoire et identité nationale.* Berlin, Boston: Walter de Gruyter, 2022.

Klingmann, Anna. "Branding Saudi Arabia's Capital: How Riyadh Uses Urban Place Marketing, Mega-Events, and Urban Destinations as Tools to Brand the City in Line with Vision 2030." *International Journal of Ekistics and the New Habitat: The Problems and Science of Human Settlements* 81.2 (2021): 39–51.

Koch, Natalie. "'Building Glass Refrigerators in the Desert': Discourses of Urban Sustainability and Nation Building in Qatar." *Urban Geography* 35.8 (2014): 1118–1139.

Koch, Natalie. *The Geopolitics of Spectacle: Space, Synecdoche, and the New Capitals of Asia.* Ithaca, London: Cornell University Press, 2018.

Kokoschka, Alina. *Waren Welt Islam: Konsumkultur und Warenästhetik in Syrien 2000–2011.* Berlin: Kulturverlag Kadmos, 2019.

Krause, Rolf F. "Wem gehört der Golf?" *Petermanns Geographische Mitteilungen* 145.2 (2001): 14–17.

Krawietz, Birgit. "Falconry as a Cultural Icon of the Arab Gulf Region." In *Under Construction: Logics of Urbanism in the Gulf Region*, edited by Steffen Wippel, Katrin Bromber, Christian Steiner, and Birgit Krawietz, 131–146. Farnham, Burlington: Ashgate, 2014.

Krawietz Birgit. "Designing Edirne's Heritage Trail and Turkish Oil Wrestling." In *The Heritage of Edirne in Ottoman and Turkish Times: Continuities, Disruptions and Reconnections*, edited by Birgit Krawietz and Florian Riedler, 233–282. Berlin, Boston: Walter de Gruyter, 2020.

Krawietz, Birgit, and Florian Riedler. "Outlook." In *The Heritage of Edirne in Ottoman and Turkish Times: Continuities, Disruptions and Reconnections*, edited by Birgit Krawietz and Florian Riedler, 534–552. Berlin, Boston: Walter de Gruyter, 2020.

Krüger, Paul-Anton. "Kleine Fluchten: Im Norden von Teheran hat sich eine Kunstszene mit Galerien und Cafés entwickelt, die dem kosmopolitischen Leben der westlichen Metropolen näherkommt als jeder andere Ort im Gottesstaat Iran." *Süddeutsche Zeitung* 21 July 2017: 10.

Laura. "Tourism Slogans for Every Country in the World: From Catchy to Cringeworthy." *Find the Pearls Travel.* https://findthepearlstravel.com/country-tourism-slogans/. Accessed 12 January 2022.

Lebel, Julien. *Emirates Airline, Etihad Airways et Qatar Airways: Des compagnies aériennes d'envergure mondiale au service du rayonnement des émirats de Dubaï, d'Abou Dhabi et du Qatar.* Paris: Ifri, 2019. https://www.ifri.org/sites/default/files/atoms/files/lebel_compagnies_aeriennes_emirats_2019_1.pdf. Accessed 25 July 2019.

Le Matin. "S.M. le Roi annonce la candidature du Maroc, avec l'Espagne et le Portugal, pour abriter la Coupe du Monde 2030." 14 March 2023. https://lematin.ma/express/2023/mondial-2030-sm-roi-annonce-candidature-maroc-espagne-portugal/387681.html. Accessed 15 March 2023.

Lewis, David. "Understanding the Authoritarian State: Neopatrimonialism in Central Asia." *Brown Journal of World Affairs* 19.1 (2012): 115–126.

Lister, Charles. *Al-Qaeda versus ISIS: Competing Jihadist Brands in the Middle East.* Washington, DC: The Middle East Institute, 2017. https://www.mei.edu/sites/default/files/publications/PP3_Lister_CTQaeda_0.pdf. Accessed 27 January 2023.

Loewert, Patrick, and Christian Steiner. "The New Administrative Capital in Egypt: The Political Economy of the Production of Urban Spaces in Cairo." *Middle East–Topics & Arguments* 12.1 (2019): 66–75. https://archiv.ub.uni-marburg.de/ep/0003/article/view/7933. Accessed 23 February 2023.

Lucarelli, Andrea, and Per Olof Berg. "City Branding: A State-of-the-art Review of the Research Domain." *Journal of Place Management and Development* 4.1 (2011): 9–27.

Lykke Nielsen, Helle. *Branding islam: Om muslimsk place-making i Danmark.* Odense: Center for Mellemøststudier, Syddansk Universitet, 2018. https://portal.findresearcher.sdu.dk/files/141043987/Branding_islam_om_muslimsk_placemaking_i_Danmark_1806.pdf. Accessed 24 March 2023.

Lykke Nielsen, Helle. "What's in a name? Danske moskeer i et onomastisk perspektiv." *Tidsskrift for islamforskning* 15.1 (2021): 75–106.

Made in Morocco. "@madeinmorocco.org – Marke: Fotos." *Facebook* 7 October 2014. https://www.facebook.com/madeinmorocco.org/. Accessed 10 February 2022.

Made in Morocco. *Proudly Moroccan, Truly International.* https://www.madeinmorocco.org/. Accessed 10 February 2022.

Madichie, Nnamdi O., and Lynda Madichie, L. "City Brand Challenge 101: Sharjah in a Globalised UAE Context." *International Journal of Business and Globalisation* 11.1 (2013): 63–85.

Mahroum, Sami, and Yasser Alsaleh. *Place Branding and Place Surrogacy: The Making of the Masdar Cluster in Abu Dhabi.* Fontainebleau, Singapore, Abu Dhabi: INSEAD, 2012. https://papers.ssrn.com/sol3/papers.cfm?abstract_id=2188936. Accessed 23 January 2014.

Makdisi, Karim. “Doha as Host and Site for the UN Framework Convention on Climate Change Negotiations.” In *Qatar: Aspirations & Realities*, edited by the Heinrich Böll Stiftung, 5–10. Tunis, Beirut, Ramallah, 2012. https://www.boell.de/sites/default/files/perspectives_middle_east_issue_4_1.pdf. Accessed 16 January 2020.

Margraff, Jonas. “Städtebauliche Großprojekte, Heritage Marketing und urbane Transformation: Neoliberale Entwicklungsprozesse in Muscat und Manama.” In *Neoliberale Urbanisierung: Stadtentwicklungsprozesse in der arabischen Welt*, edited by Ala Al-Hamarneh, Jonas Margraff, and Nadine Scharfenort, 107–147. Bielefeld: Transcript, 2019.

Margraff, Jonas, and Nadine Scharfenort. “Neoliberalismus und urbane Regeneration in Muscat und Doha.” *Inamo: Informationsprojekt Naher und Mittler Osten* 23.89 (2017): 11–16.

Medway, Dominic, and Gary Warnaby. “What’s in a Name? Place Branding and Toponymic Commodification.” *Environment and Planning A* 46 (2014): 153–167.

Menara. “L’ONMT présente son nouveau dispositif de promotion de la destination Maroc.” 22 April 2021. https://www.menara.ma/fr/article/lonmt-presente-son-nouveau-dispositif-de-promotion-de-la-destination-maroc. Accessed 14 February 2022 (link expired).

Michael, Chris, and Ami Sedghi. “The World Cities with the Most Powerful Brands: Get the Data.” *The Guardian* 6 May 2014. https://www.theguardian.com/cities/datablog/2014/may/06/world-cities-most-powerful-brands-get-the-data. Accessed 14 January 2022.

Ministère de l’Artisanat, de l’Economie Sociale et Solidaire. *Stratégie Nationale de Labellisation dans le Secteur de l’Artisanat.* PowerPoint Presentation. Institut Royal des Etudes Stratégiques. 2015. https://www.ires.ma/images/pdfs/Forums/Rencontres/presentation_strategie_labellisation_ires.pdf. Accessed 21 October 2016.

Moghadam, Amin. “Kulturelle Bewegungen zwischen Teheran und Dubai: Die Herausbildung eines (trans-)regionalen künstlerischen Feldes.” In *Jenseits etablierter Meta-Geographien: Der Nahe Osten und Nordafrika in transregionaler Perspektive*, edited by Steffen Wippel and Andrea Fischer-Tahir, 269–282. Baden-Baden: Nomos, 2018.

Moghadam, Amin. “The Staging of Cultural Diversity in Dubai: The Case of Dubai Art Fair.” *Identities, Global Studies in Culture and Power* 28.6 (2021): 717–733.

Molho, Jérémie. “Putting the City on the World Art Map: Star Curators and Nation Branding.” *International Journal of Politics, Culture, and Society* 34 (2021): 455–470.

Moock, David. *Deutsche Firmen in Bahrain: Standortmarketing und Standortwahl.* Berlin: Klaus Schwarz, 2012.

Morocco Now. “Qu’est-ce que ‘Morocco NOW’, la nouvelle marque économique du Maroc?” *Le Figaro* 13 October 2021a. https://www.lefigaro.fr/services/qu-est-ce-que-morocco-now-la-nouvelle-marque-economique-du-maroc-20211013. Accessed 4 February 2022.

Morocco Now. “Morocco Now, the Future Proof Industrial Platform to Capture Opportunities.” *Facebook* 4 November 2021b. https://www.facebook.com/MoroccoNow.Official. Accessed 10 February 2022.

Mouloudi, Hicham. “L’aménagement de la Corniche de Rabat (Maroc) face au défi de l’environnement et du développement durable: Quand la société civile prend le devant de la scène publique.” *Les Cahiers d’EMAM* 17 (2009): 11–28.

Mouloudi, Hicham. *Les ambitions d’une capitale: Les projets d’aménagement des fronts d’eau de Rabat.* Rabat: Centre Jacques-Berque, 2015.

Moussawi, Ghassan. “Queering Beirut, the ‘Paris of the Middle East’: Fractal Orientalism and Essentialized Masculinities in Contemporary Gay Travelogues.” *Gender, Place & Culture* 20.7 (2013): 858–875.

Moussawi, Ghassan. “Queer Exceptionalism and Exclusion: Cosmopolitanism and Inequalities in ‘Gay-friendly’ Beirut.” *The Sociological Review* 66.1 (2018): 174–190.

Moussawi, Ghassan. “The Fraught Nature of Exceptional Gay Spaces.” *International Journal of Urban and Regional Research* [2019]. https://www.ijurr.org/spotlight-on/queering-urban-studies/the-fraught-nature-of-exceptional-gay-spaces/. Accessed 6 January 2022.

Musharbash, Yassin. “‘Es ist die beste Zeit, in Mossul zu leben’: Wie Bürger in der ehemaligen Hauptstadt des ‘Islamischen Staate’ um eine bessere Zukunft ringen.” *Die Zeit* 51, 9 December 2021.

Nastasi, Michele. “A Gulf of Images: Photography and the Circulation of Spectacular Architecture.” In *The New Arab Urban: Gulf Cities of Wealth, Ambition and Distress*, edited by Harvey Molotch and Davide Ponzini, 99–129. New York: New York University Press, 2019.

Nation Branding. “Siegel+Gale on Egypt’s New Tourism Logo.” 20 July 2011. https://nation-branding.info/2011/07/20/siegel-gale-egypt-new-tourism-logo/. Accessed 12 January 2022.

Nicolai, Katharina Elisabeth. “A Green Gambit: The Development of Environmental Foreign Policy in Morocco.” *The Journal of North African Studies* 27.4 (2022): 714–740.

Noori, Negar, and Martin De Jong. “Towards Credible City Branding Practices: How Do Iran’s Largest Cities Face Ecological Modernization?” *Sustainability* 10.5 (2018): article #1354, 1–16.

Nüsse, Andrea. “Aufbruch im Orient.” *Der Tagesspiegel* 27 January 2008: 5.

Nüsse, Andrea. “Türkei will jetzt Türkiye heißen: Von der zu großen Nähe zum Truthahn.” *Der Tagesspiegel* 1 June 2022. https://www.tagesspiegel.de/politik/tuerkei-will-jetzt-tuerkiye-heissen-von-der-zu-grossen-naehe-zum-truthahn/28392368.html. Accessed 2 June 2022.

Olwi, Alyaa. “The Use of Foreign Languages in Saudi Television Advertisements.” *British Journal of Middle Eastern Studies* (2022). https://doi.org/10.1080/13530194.2022.2132215 (Online first).

Öner, Aslı Ceylan, and Burkay Pasin. “Emerging Towers in Bayraklı: Sustainability as a Branding Strategy or a Tool for Local Development?” *Buildings* 5 (2015): 834–859.

ONMT (Office National Marocain du Tourisme). *Facebook* 21 April 2021. https://www.facebook.com/onmtcorporate/reviews/?ref=page_internal. Accessed 14 February 2022.

Ooi, Can-Seng. “Paradoxes of City Branding and Societal Changes.” In *City Branding: Theory and Cases*, edited by Keith Dinnie, 54–61. Basingstoke, New York: Palgrave Macmillan, 2011.

Oraman, Yasemin, Fuat Yılmaz, and Derya İlkay Abdikoğlu. “Wine Branding: Why is it Important for Boutique Wine Sector Growth in Turkey?” In *Proceedings of the Jubilee International Scientific Conference “Bulgaria of Regions” organized on the occasion of 25 anniversary of University of agribusiness and rural development*, 595–605. Plovdiv: Talent, 2017.

Pérez, Carlota. “Le Maroc se joint au boycott des produits turcs par l’Arabie Saoudite: Le 15 octobre, Rabat a imposé des restrictions aux chaînes de supermarchés turcs et a augmenté de 90 % les taxes sur les produits ottomans importés.” *Atalayar* 22 October 2020. https://atalayar.com/fr/content/le-maroc-se-joint-au-boycott-des-produits-turcs-par-larabie-saoudite. Accessed 10 February 2022.

Peterson, J.E. “Qatar and the World: Branding for a Micro-state.” *Middle East Journal* 60.4 (2006): 732–748.

Ponzini, Davide. “Mobilities of Urban Spectacle: Plans, Projects, and Investments in the Gulf and Beyond.” In *The New Arab Urban: Gulf Cities of Wealth, Ambition and Distress*, edited by Harvey Molotch and Davide Ponzini, 79–96. New York: New York University Press, 2019.

Popper, Nathaniel. “Israel Aims to Improve its Public Image.” *Forward* 14 October 2005. https://forward.com/news/2070/israel-aims-to-improve-its-public-image/. Accessed 19 January 2023.

Rajasekar, James, and Unnikammu Moideenkutty. "Oman Air: Challenges of Repositioning Through Business Level Strategy." *Asian Journal of Management Cases* 4.2 (2007): 117–141.

Ram, Uri. "'Don't drink stupid, drink committed.' Die Verwässerung des Engagements." *Forschungsjournal Neue Soziale Bewegungen* 18.4 (2005): 53–64.

Rasool, Mohammed. "'Crazy Love': Crisis-Hit Lebanon Unveils Controversial New Tourism Slogan." *Vice World News* 5 November 2021. https://www.vice.com/en/article/jgmqep/crazy-love-crisis-hit-lebanon-unveils-controversial-new-tourism-slogan. Accessed 4 March 2023.

Reichenbach, Anke, and Najla Ibrahim. "'Pulling At Our Heartstrings': Emirati-Themed Leisure Venues as Places of Belonging." *Urban Anthropology* 48.1/2 (2019): 129–181.

Reisz, Todd, ed. *Al Manakh 2: Gulf Cont'd.* Amsterdam: Stichting Archis, 2010.

Reisz, Todd. *Showpiece City: How Architecture Made Dubai.* Stanford: Stanford University Press, 2020.

Resonance. *World's Best City Brands 2017: A Global Ranking of Place Equity.* Vancouver, New York, 2017. https://www.mos.ru/upload/documents/files/9743/WorldsBestCityBrands.pdf. Accessed 4 August 2021.

Reuß, Anna. "Ein Schritt vor, zwei auf der Stelle: Beim Thema Golfstaaten denken viele an mangelnde Frauenrechte. Klischees und Vorurteile helfen jedoch nicht weiter." *Journal für Internationale Politik und Gesellschaft*, 16 December 2022. https://www.ipg-journal.de/regionen/naher-osten/artikel/ein-schritt-vor-zwei-auf-der-stelle-6390/. Accessed 16 December 2022.

Rietmann, Helena. *Ecological Modernization in the United Arab Emirates? The Case of Masdar Eco-City.* Berlin, Boston: Walter de Gruyter, 2021.

Ritchie, Jason. "Pinkwashing, Homonationalism, and Israel-Palestine: The Conceits of Queer Theory and the Politics of the Ordinary." *Antipode* 47.3 (2015): 616–634.

Rizzo, Agatino. "Sustainable Urban Development and Green Megaprojects in the Arab States of the Gulf Region: Limitations, Covert Aims, and Unintended Outcomes in Doha, Qatar." *International Planning Studies* 22.2 (2017): 85–98.

Roelcke, Annegret. "Constructing the 'Capital of Peace:' Changing Branding Strategies for Istanbul's Eyüp Quarter." *Middle East–Topics & Arguments* 12.1 (2019): 110–120. https://archiv.ub.uni-marburg.de/ep/0003/article/view/7931. Accessed 23 February 2023.

Rumelili, Bahar, and Rahime Suleymanoglu-Kurum. "Brand Turkey: Liminal Identity and its Limits." *Geopolitics* 22.3 (2017): 549–570.

Rutter, Richard, John Nadeau, Fiona Lettice, Ming Lim, and Suwaid al Shamaisi. "Place Branding of Seaports in the Middle East." *Place Branding and Public Diplomacy* 14.3 (2018): 197–212.

Salama, Ashraf M.A., and Florian Wiedmann. *Demystifying Doha: On Architecture and Urbanism in an Emerging City.* Farnham, Burlington: Ashgate, 2013.

Sama, Schluwa. "A Periphery Becomes a Center? Shopping Malls as Symbols of Modernity in Iraqi Kurdistan." *Middle East–Topics & Arguments* 5 (2015): 89–98. https://archiv.ub.uni-marburg.de/ep/0003/article/view/3642/3663. Accessed 28 January 2022.

Sangeeta, Peter, Victor Anandkumar, and Savita Peter. "Role of Shopping Festivals in Destination Branding: A Tale of Two Shopping Festivals in the United Arab Emirates." *Anatolia: An International Journal of Tourism and Hospitality Research* 24.2 (2013): 264–267.

Schaffrinna, Achim. "National Branding: Die Tourismuslogos der Länder." *Design Tagebuch.* https://www.designtagebuch.de/wiki/tourismus-logos/. Accessed 12 January 2022.

Scharfenort, Nadine. *Die Formel 1 als Symbol: Abu Dhabi im "Geschwindigkeitsrausch"?* GIGA Focus Nahost 11. Hamburg: German Institute of Global and Area Studies, 2010.

Scharfenort, Nadine. "Off and Running: Qatar Brands for FIFA World Cup, and Life Beyond." In *Under Construction: Logics of Urbanism in the Gulf Region*, edited by Steffen Wippel, Katrin Bromber, Christian Steiner, and Birgit Krawietz, 71–87. Farnham, Burlington: Ashgate, 2014.

Scheffler, Thomas. "'Fertile Crescent', 'Orient', 'Middle East': The Changing Mental Maps of Southwest Asia." *European Review of History* 10.2 (2003): 253–272.

Schmid, Heiko. "'Paris du Proche-Orient' ou 'Hongkong sur Méditerranée'? Bilan de la reconstruction dans le centre-ville de Beyrouth." *Observatoire de Recherche sur Beyrouth et la Reconstruction, Lettre d'information* 14 (2001): 13–16.

Schmid, Heiko. "Economy of Fascination: Dubai and Las Vegas as Examples of Themed Urban Landscape." *Erdkunde* 60 (2006): 346–360.

Schulman, Sarah. "Israel and 'Pinkwashing'." *The New York Times* 22 November 2011. https://www.nytimes.com/2011/11/23/opinion/pinkwashing-and-israels-use-of-gays-as-a-messaging-tool.html. Accessed 29 February 2012.

Sedra, Dounia, and Hicham El Bayed. "Branding the City: The Case of Casablanca-Morocco." *Place Branding and Public Diplomacy* 18 (2022): 181–189.

Seidman, Steven. "The Politics of Cosmopolitan Beirut: From the Stranger to the Other." *Theory, Culture & Society* 29.2 (2012): 3–36.

Semple, Laure. "Le mégaprojet du Dubai Water Canal: Fabrique d'une ville mondiale à travers la construction d'un réseau touristique." *Géoconfluences* 20 January 2017. https://geoconfluences.ens-lyon.fr/informations-scientifiques/dossiers-thematiques/de-villes-en-metropoles/corpus-documentaire/doubai-canal-ville-mondiale. Accessed 8 May 2022.

Serhir, Sonia. "Hay Ryad à Rabat: De la ville nouvelle au quartier?" *Les Cahiers d'EMAM* 29 (2017). http://emam.revues.org/1376. Accessed 3 March 2017.

Sheikh Moussa, Lynn. "Crazy Love: Lebanon's Tourism Ministry Piggybacks on Instability for New Campaign." *Beirut Today* 5 November 2021. https://beirut-today.com/2021/11/05/crazy-love-lebanons-tourism-ministry-piggybacks-on-instability-for-new-campaign/. Accessed 23 January 2023.

Shenker, Jack. "Egypt, Rebranded: Illusions of Prosperity and Liberty amid a Thwarted Revolution." *Cairo Review of Global Affairs* 24 (2017): 71–79. https://www.thecairoreview.com/wp-content/uploads/2017/01/cr24-shenker-1.pdf. Accessed 1 February 2022.

Shirazi, Faegheh. *Brand Islam: The Marketing and Commodification of Piety.* Austin: University of Texas Press, 2016.

Shoaib, Turki Mohammed. *Place Branding in a Globalizing Middle East: New Cities in Saudi Arabia.* PhD thesis, School of the Built Environment, Oxford Brookes University, 2017. https://radar.brookes.ac.uk/radar/file/88098f91-21f6-46a7-9b7a-a271a34f8cd5/1/TurkiShoaib_PhD_Thesis_2017_RADAR.pdf. Accessed 22 December 2020.

Shoaib, Turki, and Ramin Keivani. "Branding the New City: Exploring Place Branding in Saudi Arabia." *Journal of Place Management and Development* 8.3 (2015): 254–265.

Sidi Boumedine, Rachid, and Pierre Signoles. "Les villes nouvelles en Algérie: Une question apparemment réglée, mais une réalité complexe." *Les Cahiers d'EMAM* 29 (2017). http://journals.openedition.org/emam/1323. Accessed 30 September 2019.

Sim, Li-Chen "Re-branding Abu Dhabi: From Oil Giant to Energy Titan." *Place Branding and Public Diplomacy* 8.1 (2012): 83–98.

Skey, Michael. "Sportswashing: Media Headline or Analytic Concept?" *International Review for the Sociology of Sport* (2022). https://doi.org/10.1177/10126902221136086 (Online first).

Sons, Sebastian. *Katar.* Bonn: Bundeszentrale für politische Bildung, 2022. https://www.bpb.de/system/files/dokument_pdf/BPB_Info-aktuell-39-2022-Katar_barrierefrei.pdf. Accessed 11 November 2022.

Stadnicki, Roman. "Sissi-City, la 'nouvelle capitale' d'Egypte: Enquête sur une publicité bien gardée." *Revue du Crieur* 8.3 (2017): 62–89.

Steiner, Christian. *Tourismuskrisen und organisationales Lernen: Akteursstrategien in der Hotelwirtschaft der Arabischen Welt. Eine Pragmatische Geographie.* Bielefeld: Transcript, 2009.

Steiner, Christian. "From Heritage to Hyper-reality? Tourism Destination Development in the Middle East between Petra and the Palm." *Journal of Tourism and Cultural Change* 8.4 (2010): 240–253.

Steiner, Christian. "Iconic Spaces, Symbolic Capital and the Political Economy of Urban Development in the Arab Gulf." In *Under Construction: Logics of Urbanism in the Gulf Region*, edited by Steffen Wippel, Katrin Bromber, Christian Steiner, and Birgit Krawietz, 17–30. Farnham, Burlington: Ashgate, 2014.

Steiner, Christian. "Das Dubai-Modell: Stabilisierung durch Stadtentwicklung." *Inamo: Informationsprojekt Naher und Mittler Osten* 23.89 (2017): 6–10.

Steiner, Christian, and Steffen Wippel. "Urban Development in the Middle East and North Africa: Deconstructing Visions, Politics, and Identities." *Middle East–Topics & Arguments* 12.1 (2019): 5–16. https://archiv.ub.uni-marburg.de/ep/0003/article/view/8022. Accessed 22 November 2022.

Stephan-Emmrich, Manja. "'Duschanbe goes global': Golfisierung oder Islamisierung? *Inamo: Informationsprojekt Naher und Mittler Osten* 23.89 (2017): 43–46.

Stephan-Emmrich, Manja, and Abdullah Mirzoev. "The Manufacturing of Islamic Lifestyles in Tajikistan through the Prism of Dushanbe's Bazaars." *Central Asian Survey* 35.2 (2016): 346–362.

Stephenson, Marcus L. "Tourism, Development and 'Destination Dubai': Cultural Dilemmas and Future Challenges." *Current Issues in Tourism* 17.8 (2014): 723–738.

Stoll, Katrina. "Dubai Fever: The Dream of an Urban Model in Ethiopia." In *Cities of Change, Addis Ababa: Transformation Strategies for Urban Territories in the 21st Century*, edited by Marc Angélil and Dirk Hebel, 151–155. Basel, Boston, Berlin: Birkhäuser, 2010.

Strava, Cristiana. "A Tramway Called Atonement: Genealogies of Infrastructure and Emerging Political Imaginaries in Contemporary Casablanca." *Middle East–Topics & Arguments* 10.1 (2018): 22–29. https://archiv.ub.uni-marburg.de/ep/0003/article/view/7590. Accessed 10 March 2022.

Strohmaier, Alena. *Medienraum Diaspora: Verortungen zeitgenössischer iranischer Diasporafilme.* Wiesbaden: Springer VS, 2019.

Tagesschau. "Türkei will anders betitelt werden: Von 'Turkey' zu 'Türkiye'." 31 May 2022a. https://www.tagesschau.de/ausland/tuerkei-will-international-nicht-mehr-turkey-genannt-werden-101.html. Accessed 5 March 2023.

Tagesschau. "UN bestätigen Namensänderung: Turkey heißt jetzt Türkiye." 3 June 2022b. https://www.tagesschau.de/ausland/turkey-tuerkiye-101.html. Accessed 3 June 2022.

Tagesschau. "Asiatische Winterspiele 2029: Wettkämpfe mitten in Saudi-Arabiens Wüste." 4 October 2022c. https://www.tagesschau.de/sport/sportschau/asiatischewinterspiele-saudiarabien-101.html. Accessed 4 October 2022.

Tagesschau. "Einstimmige FIFA-Entscheidung: Saudi-Arabien richtet Klub-WM 2023 aus." 15 February 2023. https://www.tagesschau.de/sport/sportschau/klub-wm-saudi-arabien-101.html. Accessed 15 February 2023.

Taylor, Peter J. *World City Network: A Global Urban Analysis.* London, New York: Routledge, 2004.

Thornton, Gary. "Dubai Logo." *Inspirational Geek* 25 September 2015. https://inspirationalgeek.wordpress.com/2015/09/25/dubai-logo/. Accessed 10 January 2022.

UCLGA. *United Cities and Local Governments of Africa.* Rabat. https://www.uclga.org/. Accessed 23 January 2023.

Ullmann, Viktor. "Through the Lens of the Political: The Staging of Iranian Cinema at the Berlinale." Humboldt-Universität zu Berlin. *iaaw Newsletter* 6 (2020): 6–7. https://www.projekte.hu-berlin.de/de/newsletteriaaw/newsletter-6/iaaw_newsletter-6.pdf. Accessed 1 February 2022.

Ulrichsen, Kristian Coates. "Mohammed bin Salman's Regional Rebranding Campaign." *Policy Analysis.* Arab Center Washington DC, 16 December 2021. https://arabcenterdc.org/resource/mohammed-bin-salmans-regional-rebranding-campaign/. Accessed 21 December 2021.

Uncles, Mark, and Julia Saurazas. "Purchasing Local and International Brands: The Intention-Behaviour Link Among Arabs, Asians and Westerners in the U.A.E." In *ANZMAC 2000 Visionary Marketing for the 21st Century: Facing the Challenge, Proceedings of the Australian & New Zealand Marketing Academy Conference, 28th November–1st December 2000*, edited by Aron O'Cass, 1301–1305. Gold Coast: Griffith University, School of Marketing and Management, 2000. http://anzmac.org/conference/2000/CDsite/papers/tuv/Uncles1.pdf. Accessed 10 January 2014 (link expired).

Uysal, Ülke Evrim. "A Brief History of City Branding in Istanbul." In *Global Place Branding Campaigns across Cities, Regions, and Nations*, edited by Ahmet Bayraktar and Can Uslay: 117–131. Hershey, PA: IGI Global, 2017.

Vanolo, Alberto. *City Branding: The Ghostly Politics of Representation in Globalising Cities.* New York, Abingdon: Routledge, 2017.

Vasuvedan, Smitha. "The Role of Internal Stakeholders in Destination Branding: Observations from Kerala Tourism." *Place Branding and Public Diplomacy* 4.4 (2008): 331–335.

Venier, Philippe. "Les Gulf Pockets du Kerala: Des territoires marqués par l'émigration internationale." In *Circulation et Territoire dans le Monde Indien Contemporain*, edited by Véronique Dupont and Frédéric Landy, 241–266. Paris: EHESS, 2010.

Vignal, Leïla. "La 'nouvelle consommation' et les transformations des paysages urbains à la lumière de l'ouverture économique: L'exemple de Damas." *Revue des mondes musulmans et de la Méditerranée* 115–116 (2006). http://journals.openedition.org/remmm/3011. Accessed 8 March 2023.

Vignal, Leïla. "Dubai on Barada? The Making of 'Globalized Damascus' in Times of Urban Crisis." In *Under Construction: Logics of Urbanism in the Gulf Region*, edited by Steffen Wippel, Katrin Bromber, Christian Steiner, and Birgit Krawietz, 259–270. Farnham, Burlington: Ashgate, 2014.

Wagenhofer, Sophie. "Framing Jewish Identity in the Museum of Moroccan Judaism in Casablanca." In *Framing Jewish Culture: Boundaries and Representations*, edited by Simon J. Bronner, 293–311. Oxford, Portland, OR: The Littman Library of Jewish Civilization, 2014.

Wagenhofer, Sophie. "Branding the Moroccan Nation: From Post-Colonial Discourse to Global Participation." *H-Soz-Kult, Forum: Nation*, 15 September 2021. https://www.hsozkult.de/debate/id/diskussionen-5263. Accessed 11 February 2022.

Walter, Daniel. *"Calming Down" the Megalopolis: State-Sanctioned Murals and Tehran's Visual Cityscape.* MA thesis, Center for Middle Eastern Studies, Lund University, 2016.

Warshel, Yael. "So-called Firsts Scored by the Moroccan 'Muslim, Arab, African, post-colonial' and Amazigh Atlas Lions at the 2022 World Cup Football Games." *The Journal of North African Studies* 28.2 (2023): 219–229.

Watson, Vanessa. "African Urban Fantasies: Dreams or Nightmares?" *Environment & Urbanization* 26.1 (2014): 215–231.

Westwood, Sheena. “Branding a ‘New’ Destination: Abu Dhabi.” In *Destination Brands: Managing Place Reputation*, edited by Nigel Morgan, Annette Pritchard, and Roger Pride, 197–212. Oxford, Burlington: Butterworth-Heinemann, 3rd ed., 2011.

Wikimedia, 2010. *Location map for Middle East (Greater Middle East).* 28 October 2010. https://commons.wikimedia.org/wiki/File:Middle_East_location_map.svg. Accessed 4 January 2022.

Wikipedia. “Arab Capital of Culture.” https://en.wikipedia.org/wiki/Arab_Capital_of_Culture. Accessed 2 September 2021a.

Wikipedia. “Hauptstadt der Islamischen Kultur.” https://de.wikipedia.org/wiki/Hauptstadt_der_Islamischen_Kultur. Accessed 2 September 2021b.

Wikipedia. “European Capital of Culture.” https://en.wikipedia.org/wiki/European_Capital_of_Culture. Accessed 2 September 2021c.

Wikipedia. “List of Cities by International Visitors.” https://en.wikipedia.org/wiki/List_of_cities_by_international_visitors. Accessed 17 February 2022a.

Wikipedia. “World’s Fair.” https://en.wikipedia.org/wiki/World’s_fair. Accessed 17 January 2022b.

Wikipedia. “World Tourism Rankings.” https://en.wikipedia.org/wiki/World_Tourism_rankings. Accessed 17 February 2022c.

Wikipedia. “Asian Games.” https://en.wikipedia.org/wiki/Asian_Games. Accessed 15 February 2023a.

Wikipedia. “Bids for Olympic Games.” https://en.wikipedia.org/wiki/Bids_for_Olympic_Games. Accessed 20 January 2023b.

Wikipedia. “FIFA Club World Cup.” https://en.wikipedia.org/wiki/FIFA_Club_World_Cup. Accessed 20 January 2023c.

Wikipedia. “United Nations Climate Change conference.” https://en.wikipedia.org/wiki/United_Nations_Climate_Change_conference. Accessed 22 February 2023d.

Wilson, Nathaniel L. “Branding Terrorism.” *Fikra Forum.* Washington, DC: The Washington Institute for Near East Policy, 8 October 2014. https://www.washingtoninstitute.org/policy-analysis/branding-terrorism. Accessed 27 January 2023.

Windecker, Gidon, and Peter Sendrowicz. “Katar zwischen Marketing und Realpolitik: Smartes Geschäftsmodell für einen Mikrostaat?” *KAS Auslandsinformationen* 1 (2014): 86–106. http://www.kas.de/wf/doc/kas_36582-544-1-30.pdf. Accessed 21 January 2014.

Wippel, Steffen. *Islam als “Corporate Identity” von Wirtschafts- und Wohlfahrtseinrichtungen: Eine Fallstudie aus Ägypten.* Berlin: Das Arabische Buch, 1995.

Wippel, Steffen. *Wirtschaft, Politik und Raum: Territoriale und regionale Prozesse in der westlichen Sahara.* Berlin, Tübingen: Hans Schiler, 2012.

Wippel, Steffen. “Oman and the Indian Ocean Rim: Economic Integration Across Conventional Meta-Regions.” In *Regionalizing Oman: Political, Economic and Social Dynamics*, edited by Steffen Wippel, 159–183. Dordrecht, Heidelberg et al.: Springer, 2013.

Wippel, Steffen. “Port and Tourism Development in Oman: Between Economic Diversification and Global Branding.” In *Under Construction: Logics of Urbanism in the Gulf Region*, edited by Steffen Wippel, Katrin Bromber, Christian Steiner, and Birgit Krawietz, 101–118. Farnham, Burlington: Ashgate, 2014.

Wippel, Steffen. “Beyond the Gulf Metropolises: The Urban Transformation of Salalah in the Arising Post-Oil Era.” *Trialog: Zeitschrift für das Planen und Bauen im globalen Kontext* 114.3 (2013) [2015]: 36–41.

Wippel, Steffen. *The Reality and Hyperreality of Other Places: Integrated Tourism Complexes and Container Ports in Oman.* Berlin: Klaus Schwarz, 2016a.

Wippel, Steffen. "Salalah Globalized: Developing, Fragmenting, and Marketing a 'Secondary City' at Spatio-Temporal Interfaces." In *Gulf Cities as Interfaces*, edited by George Katodrytis and Sharmeen Syed, 69–105. Cambridge: Gulf Research Centre Cambridge, 2016b.

Wippel, Steffen. "Sindbad the Sailor Revived? Oman and its Indian Ocean Links." In *The Transnational Middle East: People, Places, Borders*, edited by Leïla Vignal, 122–147. Abingdon, New York: Routledge, 2017.

Wippel, Steffen. "Tanger (Marokko): Stadtumbau, neue Infrastrukturen und die Herausbildung transregionaler Verflechtungen." In *Jenseits etablierter Meta-Geographien: Der Nahe Osten und Nordafrika in transregionaler Perspektive*, edited by Steffen Wippel and Andrea Fischer Tahir, 283–302. Baden-Baden: Nomos, 2018.

Wippel, Steffen. "Edirne as a Secondary City: Global Reconfiguration of the Urban." In *The Heritage of Edirne in Ottoman and Turkish Times: Continuities, Disruptions and Reconnections*, edited by Birgit Krawietz and Florian Riedler, 484–533. Berlin, Boston: Walter de Gruyter, 2020.

Wippel, Steffen. "'Tanj'Afrique': Transregionale Verflechtungen einer boomenden Metropole." *Stichproben: Wiener Zeitschrift für kritische Afrikastudien* 21.40 (2021): 185–216.

Wippel, Steffen. "Neue Bahnen für den Nahen Osten und Nordafrika: Der rasche Aufschwung des schienengebundenen Nahverkehrs. " *Geographische Rundschau* 4 (2022): 44–49.

Wippel, Steffen. *Die Schokoläden von Dubai: Spezialisierung und Preziosisierung in einer erlebnisorientierten Shopping Mall.* 2024 (work in progress).

Wippel, Steffen, Katrin Bromber, Christian Steiner, and Birgit Krawietz, eds. *Under Construction: Logics of Urbanism in the Gulf Region.* Farnham, Burlington: Ashgate, 2014.

Wippel, Steffen, and Andrea Fischer-Tahir, eds. *Jenseits etablierter Meta-Geographien: Der Nahe Osten und Nordafrika in transregionaler Perspektive.* Baden-Baden: Nomos, 2018.

Wüst, Andreas, and Katharina Nicolai. "Cultural Diplomacy and the Reconfiguration of Soft Power: Evidence from Morocco." *Mediterranean Politics* (2022). https://doi.org/10.1080/13629395.2022.2033513 (Online First).

ZAD Group. "Country Case Insight – Egypt: Egypt – An Aspiring Modern State." In *Nation Branding: Concepts, Issues, Practice*, edited by Keith Dinnie, 37–41. Oxford, Burlington: Butterworth-Heinemann, 2008.

Zumbrägel, Tobias. *Sustaining Power after Oil: Environmental Politics and Legitimacy in Qatar, Saudi Arabia and Kuwait.* PhD thesis, Philosophische Fakultät, Friedrich-Alexander-Universität Erlangen-Nürnberg, 2020. https://opus4.kobv.de/opus4-fau/files/15971/DissertationTobiasZumbraegel.pdf. Accessed 30 April 2021.

Steffen Wippel

Studying Branding in the Middle East in Challenging Times: Outline of the Edited Volume

1 Focus of the Book: Common Topics and Crosscutting Themes

This edited volume investigates branding in the Middle East and North Africa (MENA), including some studies from adjacent regions and the wider Islamicate world. The book critically analyses processes of strategic communication and image building and covers three major objects of branding – consumer brands, place brands, and personal brands – as the regional unfoldings of a global phenomenon. However, the main focus is on place branding – probably due to my own research focus and knowledge of colleagues, but also to a certain preference or fashion in the current research landscape. Often following the example of Dubai, project sites, cities, and nations are trying to enhance their public reputation by means ranging from creating novel architecture and organising attention-drawing cultural and sport events to announcing strategic urban and national visions. "Green" and "sustainable" branding has been added to this in recent years. While branding in the Western world and many emerging economies has been meticulously analysed, comprehensive investigations are still missing for the MENA region, except for some Gulf countries. Some of the existing literature, for example on urban branding or Islamic branding, is again very technical and application-oriented. This was the motivation behind compiling this volume, which fills important gaps in the research on branding in this part of the world.

In addition to filling the numerous empirical gaps, the contributions to this volume simultaneously integrate the conceptual framework presented in one of the preceding introductory chapters. They contribute to spatially decentring the branding phenomenon beyond the global West and to temporally historicising it beyond the all-too-recent present. Hence, historical case studies supplement the focus on contemporary branding efforts. Isolated empirical studies for application-oriented purposes contrast with by far the majority of critical, theory-driven empirical case studies. However, the understanding and terminology of branding may well diverge between the individual authors. In particular, they look at the diversity of the actors involved in branding and marketing activities and their often conflicting interests, motives, and strategies. They investigate channels and forms

https://doi.org/10.1515/9783110741100-007

of branding, including the intended purposes, the contents of messages conveyed to a broad range of addressees (sometimes the famous "creative class"), and the (in)consistencies of communication measures. A major interest exists in the entanglements of different spatial and hierarchical scales, but also of different kinds of branded objects, which often cannot be clearly separated and which show phenomena of umbrella-branding and co-branding.

In the Middle East in particular, branding is also always a matter of countering negative associations with the region, which exist worldwide and often have to do with unrest, violence, and intolerance, and of generating new, more positive images by rebranding. At the same time, communication strategies are directed inward, at consumers who are willing to buy as well as at citizens in a nation-building process that is often still unfinished or in a city inhabited by a very heterogeneous population. Attention in this volume is therefore paid to temporal reconfigurations of certain images and to how objects of branding are positioned in time and space. Some authors point out that not only products, places, and persons are branded *in* the Middle East, but also that the region itself (and parts of it) are being branded, or references to the region serve to brand items elsewhere.

This book thereby regularly goes beyond simply presenting the ubiquitous logos and slogans, which continue to be central instruments of the widely employed branding strategies. Rather, the individual chapters also take into account the complexity of the tools used, ranging from widely visually reproduced individual architectures and entire cityscapes to other material artefacts, but also to natural products, the help of the personal reputations of producers and potentates, economic and urban development strategies and planning policies, the expressed visions behind them, and a variety of social, cultural, and political activities, and even the deliberate resort to experiential and (social) media reports. Sometimes, branding strategies that seem surprising for the region and are unusual in its study come up, such as those regarding the advertising of alcohol brands, a reputation as a gay destination, the branding of refugee camps, the use of slum eradication for urban branding purposes, or naming mosques in the European diaspora. Place branding, which is dominant in the studies collected here, thereby also reveals a multiplicity of places beyond cities and nations that are subject to branding, but often less noticed.

Processes of singularisation and qualification of the objects of branding, not only of consumer products, are described several times. Similarly, repeatedly addressed are the general conditions under which branding takes place and that have a strong impact on the MENA region – namely globalisation, neoliberalisation, and postmodernisation, as well as, in a regional perspective, increased endeavours for "worlding" and widespread lasting authoritarian rule, but also of a series of further political and economic crises, disruptions, and turmoil. Such ruptures and reconfigurations that have frequently happened on the local, regional, and global levels have shaken up established images of persons and places, but also enabled the repositioning of existing and the establishing of new brands. It is also recurrently shown how visions overtake reality, simulations precede or even replace actual realisations, and the unspoken and the concealed are basic for promotional representations that preferably turn to the embellished, cleansed, and smoothed.

These papers make it clear how greatly brands are socially – and especially politically – constructed, even if the relevant actors like to essentialise them again and again. In the MENA region, the race for attention and recognition, the struggle to advance in relevant rankings, and imitation and adoption effects are evident in the increasing global competition, but also in the regional context, especially in the repeatedly highlighted "Dubaisation" effect. Likewise, branding goes hand in hand with processes of fragmentation and persistent inequalities that are triggered by underlying developments and policies, but it often even directly promotes them itself. As will be shown in individual cases, the population can react to branding from above with strategies of appropriation and resistance, as well as with its own place-making strategies or at least critical brand reception. Especially in the authoritarian contexts of the Middle East and North Africa (as well as some neighbouring regions), branding is particularly successful, but also necessary to stabilise the power of the rulers in the face of lacking democratic legitimisation strategies and crumbling traditional social contracts. Political personal branding, often in unison with or derived from the branding of, for example, cities, therefore plays a significant role in the region. In contrast, participatory processes (that could also ensure that the population will consequently "live" a brand) are rare in these countries or remain opaque in the few cases in which they have been formally prompted.

Geopolitical aspects, interstate relations, and interurban competition are essential aspects of branding, especially in such a conflict-ridden region as the MENA. Despite the increasing importance of geo-economic considerations, e.g. relating to trade and tourism, hard, especially regional geopolitics continues to be of great significance in the mutual struggle for and defence against political influence. However, the comparative approach of the anthology also shows clear differences between the diverse parts of the MENA region in the intensity and characteristics of branding. The different contributions demonstrate how branding plays out in varying contexts in a region that is ultimately quite heterogeneous, e.g. in terms of the extent of neoliberalisation or authoritarianism. The triangle of the Gulf states, Turkey, and Morocco, which is represented here several times, is particularly active in the branding business, while it was more difficult to acquire contributions on other countries less well known for branding efforts.

Given the nature of the book – its conceptual input, the breadth of empirical, yet theoretically informed case studies, and the range of authors and disciplines included – it aims at an international public of researchers and students. It addresses scholars in area studies such as Islamic, Middle Eastern, and Gulf Studies and to a certain extent in broader Asian and African Studies. Other readers might be found in disciplines such as human geography, international relations and international economics, media and urban studies, and the broader field of social and cultural sciences who are interested in issues of branding, marketing, image- and identity-building, and public diplomacy in and across their disciplines.

2 Background: How this Book Came to be Made

In retrospect, "branding," by whatever name, has always been at least a subcutaneous and increasingly explicit aspect of the editor's own research. Starting with my PhD project in the early 1990s, which studied Islamic economic and social institutions in Egypt, I also investigated the development of their "Corporate Identity," which was the catchy conceptual term at that time.[1] Subsequently, processes of regional formation and transregional entanglement long dominated my research on MENA countries. Here, I have also repeatedly addressed branding issues, when governments, business associations, and the like use economic, trade, and transport links to brand their country in regional terms and vice versa. Finally, especially in urban studies, to which I have progressively turned since the late 2000s, attention to branding endeavours has acquired a central place on my research agenda. This first started with early-developed attention strategies of Arab Gulf cities and extended particularly to new and resurging port cities that try to place themselves favourably in cross-regional positions – which links to previous research themes of regionalisation, but from local perspectives. A major collaborative outcome was a conference and an edited volume on the Arab Gulf "under construction," which was developed together with a group of colleagues and already included elaborations on national and urban branding policies and emulation strategies "elsewhere." This research increasingly also encompassed other parts of the MENA region, in particular extensive work on past and ongoing urban reconfigurations, emerging transregional ties, and with that, the branding of Tangier, Morocco. However, until then, these issues had been treated only as sub-

1 For the publications mentioned in this paragraph, compare the references in the preceding chapter.

ordinate aspects of contemporary attention-oriented postmodern and neoliberal urban development, but had not been part of separate publications.

From this initial interest in branding trends in the Middle East, several project ideas matured, which finally, for various reasons, could not be realised in the envisaged formats. In one of these proposals, developed in the field of Islamic Studies, I cooperated with colleagues from the *Freie Universität Berlin*, who are now all present in this volume. Earlier, I had already organised a first panel on "Branding the Middle East" in 2017, at the 33rd German Congress of Oriental Studies *(Deutscher Orientalistentag*/DOT) at the University of Jena, Germany. The call for papers attracted so many proposals that, over one and a half days, we filled five sessions of presentations, which produced much insight into current developments and showed the potential for a larger publication. Due to other obligations and research foci, the idea to continue with it lay dormant since then. In the meantime, I had the opportunity, together with the geographer Christian Steiner from the Catholic University of Eichstätt, Bavaria, to be guest editors of a special issue on "Urban Development" of the academic online journal *Middle East–Topics & Arguments* published in 2019. In it, several authors, now contributors to this anthology, addressed branding issues, which again demonstrated their topicality.[2] Thus, it was not until late 2020 that I took up the idea for an edited volume again and asked the speakers and other colleagues who were working on related topics at the time about a joint publication. The response was overwhelming, and another call helped to fill some existing concept- and content-related gaps and to include further perspectives. The de Gruyter publishing house also rapidly welcomed the publication of the volume. In September 2022, parts of our joint research in progress were presented again by their authors at another *Orientalistentag*, the 34th DOT convened in Berlin, and at the 12th Nordic Society for Middle Eastern Studies Conference at the University of Iceland in Reykjavík, which demonstrated the variety and multifaceted nature of branding processes in the MENA region, as well as the multiple possible perspectives on them, and which helped to promote the upcoming publication.

The book does not propose a single perspective or have a "one-size-fits-all" approach, but has been open to a variety of empirical issues, academic disciplines, and theoretical concepts. The authors represent a wide range of disciplines: from architecture, urban planning, and urban studies to social and cultural anthropology, political and social sciences, and geography and history; they also include scholars from different fields of economics, from diverse area studies, namely Arab, Islamic, Middle East, and even North American Studies, as well as from

2 Cf. Steiner and Wippel, 2019.

disciplinary backgrounds like journalism, media and arts, religious studies, and philology. They are of Western, Arab, and Iranian origin and working in the Global North as well as in the Global South, at European and North American, Middle Eastern and North African research institutions and universities. This all allows for a variety of topics and perspectives. Often, the contributions of colleagues are based on their long-standing research work with a different focus, which, however, also considered branding aspects – sometimes implicitly rather than explicitly – and which have now been intentionally recalibrated to issues of branding. In many cases, the authors developed their own conceptual framing of their topic in preliminary sub-chapters, while others made in-text references to conceptual sources.

Such a volume and theme also lend themselves to numerous pictures. These serve not so much as pleasurable illustrations of extensive and otherwise uninterrupted text as they are usually closely linked to the respective text and its interpretations. Some of them are the authors' own photographic documentations of the branding activities. Although copyright issues make it increasingly difficult, even in the European publishing industry, to make use of illustrations from third parties, it was possible to create an illustration-rich volume with the friendly help and advice of the publisher.

All chapters were written in 2021 and 2022. Unfortunately, the precarities of academic life – this is true especially for German universities, but much more severe, given the general life situation, e.g. in Lebanon, under simultaneous conditions of Covid, political unrest, and economic crisis – did not allow all the scholars who were willing to contribute and had even already started to write, to complete their papers.

3 The Organisation of the Book: Multiple Perspectives on "Branding the Middle East"

All in all, the book now has about 35 longer and shorter chapters, including a few "snapshots," all organised in five parts. The parts of the book range from branding in the field of consumption, culture, and lifestyle to branding countries, cities, and other places.

In a short opener, "Branding a Seafaring Nation: The Sailing Ship Monument at on Al Wazarat Roundabout in Muscat, Oman," which precedes the actual texts, *Steffen Wippel* explains the volume's cover image of a ship monument displayed in the Omani capital, and embeds it in national and local branding efforts, namely the construction of continuities from past maritime traditions to contemporary transregional connections, especially within the wider Indian Ocean region.

3.1 Part I: Introduction

The introductory part written by *Steffen Wippel* is divided into a brief lead-in on "A Thoroughly Branded, but Little-Known Middle East" and three subsequent chapters. The first chapter, "Branding as a Global Phenomenon: From Theory to Practice and Vice Versa," explores general theoretical and conceptual approaches to branding, which serve as the broader framework for this book. It includes a passage through the global, mostly Western, history of branding, a clarification of terminology, and the global macro-contexts in which contemporary branding takes place. The second chapter, "Branding the Middle East: A Review of Regional Manifestations of a Global Phenomenon," presents a synthesis of existing literature. It gives an overview of empirical developments and their interpretations in the MENA region, from product and personal branding to a *tour d'horizon* of place branding, starting from its hotspot along the Arab side of the Gulf, through West Asia and the Maghreb, to the region's peripheries. This chapter, "Studying Branding in the Middle East in Challenging Times: Outline of the Edited Volume," provides the general aim, genesis, and structure of this volume and explains its various parts and the individual chapters that follow.

3.2 Part II: Consumption, Culture, and Lifestyle

The next part starts with branding in the field of consumption, culture, and lifestyle. Here, branding commodities plays a central role. First of all, this relates to beverages, from "national" milk products in Arab Gulf countries to tea in Mali, but also to advertising alcohol, such as a colonial drink in North Africa, wine in Morocco, and hard liquor in Lebanon, and their links to nationalism, history, and way of life. Islamic features, like branding Dubai the capital of the Islamic economy and the spiritual brand conveyed by a religious scholar, contrast with selling Beirut as a gay- and queer-friendly place, which nonetheless displays much Orientalism. Fakes that are not really fakes contribute to the Islamisation of fashion brands. And finally, with omnipresent billboards, signs, and logos, South Indian products and places, too, want to partake in Dubai's glamour and fame.

Dairy products seemed to gain a new political significance on the Arabian Peninsula in 2017, when Qatar was suddenly placed under an air, land, and sea embargo by its Gulf neighbours. While the country's entire food supply chain was affected, residents in Qatar were especially concerned with their access to milk products, because the embargo's two leaders, Saudi Arabia and the UAE, were their primary source. In the wake of the embargo, dairy acquired a new importance for how people understood Qatar's sovereignty. These events spurred the government to invest heavily in kickstarting domestic milk production by flying in thousands of milk cows to a dairy farm that came to be described as a nationalist champion for the country's food independence. The "cowlift" was a dramatic spectacle, but it is part of a broader trend of "milk nationalism" seen among the Arab Gulf monarchies. *Natalie Koch*'s chapter "Milk Nationalism: Branding Dairy and the State in the Arabian Peninsula" traces this longer history and asks why branding national dairy companies has been so important in Saudi Arabia, the UAE, Qatar, and Oman. As a study in political geography, she employs the lens of critical geopolitics to analyse the history and narrative construction of milk nationalism in these countries. As a kind of co-branding initiative, milk nationalism in the Gulf countries both draws upon and builds contemporary understandings of the state and sovereignty.

Foreign consumer goods have been promoted also *in* and *through* the Maghreb. Generally speaking, branding spells out, builds up, and enhances the properties of a product and is intrinsically connected with monetary, symbolic, social, and identity-related values, images, and assets. The time, creativity, and money invested in building up the brand are legally acknowledged by intellectual property law, which aims to reward owners for their efforts. A good example is Chinese green tea, which was introduced to the Sahel via Morocco in the 19th century and became a national drink in Mali in the 2000s. More than a hundred brands can be found in Bamako's largest marketplace. Many of them have Arabic names or hint at Islamic festivities and historical trading towns; their designs show Moroccan motifs or Tuareg drinking tea. In her chapter "Branding Chinese Green Tea in Mali," *Ute Röschenthaler* examines the example of the *Achoura* brand, which is the best-selling Chinese green tea in Mali, in adjacent countries, and in the Sahelian diasporas. Based on interviews with the major tea importers and on observations in African and Asian markets, she traces the creation and rise of the brand in 2013 and discusses its various challenges, including brand piracy, rumours, and health issues. The chapter argues that brand value is complicated to control and requires hard work, convincing strategies, and a portion of good luck to persist in a dynamic and competitive market.

In the colonial age, North Africa also served as an exotic background for branding a popular French alcoholic drink. Alcohol in general, and wine and absinthe in particular, were seen as representing both France's imperial power and the colonial Maghreb. Local Francophone newspapers were filled with adverts for different kinds of alcohol, and the coastal cities were decorated with the slogans of the most famous brands of the time. These adverts aimed at the minority settler society and European travellers in a predominantly abstinent Muslim context and often incorporated orientalist imagery related to nature, urban sceneries, and local people. Some showed idyllic depictions of the "benefits" of the French presence in the region, while others portrayed a life in the colonies that was indistinguishable from life in the *Métropole.* In her chapter titled "Selling Alcohol to the Muslims? Making Byrrh a Brand in the Colonial Maghreb," *Nina Studer* analyses the advertising campaigns of a particular southern French aperitif in the 20th-century Maghreb. Byrrh was a popular drink among Europeans – and some of the colonised Muslims – and presented itself as staunchly supportive of France's colonial mission. This chapter asks how Islam and the Maghreb were portrayed in these adverts and which views of colonialism were chosen to be depicted.

Alcohol drinking and marketing remains an issue also in contemporary MENA countries. Today, Morocco is a relatively important wine producing *and* consuming country and endeavours to reposition and enhance the quality and image of its product. Advertisements for locally produced wine, a controversial commodity in an Islamic environment, have gained new prominence, at least in local magazines written in French. As *Steffen Wippel* shows in his snapshot "Branding Wine in Morocco: New Efforts to Qualify a Contested Commodity," the adverts adapt to a global visual language to address the senses of both a young and a more settled local public and to singularise and qualify the newly created brands in the eyes of these potential consumers.

In a short chapter "From City to Society: Alcohol Advertising in Lebanon," *Marie Bonte* seeks to give insight into the promotion of alcohol in Lebanon, focusing on local and international brands. In this weakly regulated market, alcohol is not only featured as a model for social relationships, but is also used as a tool for urban and national branding. This branding helps to shape collective identities, celebrates an attachment to the territory, and endeavours to communicate Beirut's cosmopolitanism, as well as seeking to display a positive and "modern" image of the country. More recently, alcohol branding began to tackle wider social and political issues and to support civil society claims against strict rules for official marriage defined by religious (Islamic and Christian) law.

Along with beverages, fashion plays a central role in Middle Eastern product and lifestyle branding. In particular, Western, international brands are much requested, but often too expensive for large segments of the population. Hence, fake brands – using famous global logos on locally fabricated textiles of minor quality – are found in shops and markets across the region and are in principle subject to legal prosecution. At the same time, religiously conforming clothing has become widely demanded. Based on examples from the Levant, but also from Berlin's multicultural district of Neukölln, *Alina Kokoschka* shows that "fictitious fakes" have emerged that combine the reputation of international symbols with an equally reputed stylish Islamic fashion. In her essay "False Fakes, Fictitious Fashion, and the Liberation of Logos: On the Islamisation of International Brands," she explores the fake side of the Middle Eastern brand culture. However, the author's main interest is in reinterpretations of Western brands in the framework of Islamisation. This concerns commodities that carry a famous logo but differ significantly from items the brand is known for. These made-up commodities use the "fiction value," inseparable from contemporary branding strategies, to tell a new story – as fictitious fakes, they have begun to refashion Western fashion.

Not only have Western brands become objects of reference and imitation in the Middle East; conversely, Dubai and the Gulf have grown so attractive that products and places elsewhere, too, want to shine in their glow. In her photographic essay "Dubai Gold and Diamonds: Tracing Dubai's influence on the South Indian State of Kerala," which is part of a larger visual arts and documentary project, the artist *Sophie-Therese Trenka-Dalton* shows shop signs and street billboards in the cities of Kochi and Kozhikode and in the rural environment of the Malappuram district, whose motifs and texts refer to the Emirates and other Gulf states.[3] These references allude directly to affluence and modernity, and Dubai in particular developed into an original cultural motive. Much more than simply strategically branding products and firms, these advertisements tell us about individual desires and collective nostalgia among citizens and migrants from Kerala.

Concomitantly, Dubai has added more and more facets to its already multiplex brand. In his chapter "The Branding of Dubai as the Capital of the Islamic Economy," *Heiko Schuss* studies an initiative launched in 2013. Production of and trade in *ḥalāl* products and services has developed into an increasingly attractive and profitable global industry. The article investigates the implementation of Dubai's strategy to become the global centre of the Islamic economy and the synergies with and contradictions to other elements of its place branding. It shows that Dubai plays an important role, both in the wider sense of a Muslim world economy and in the narrow sense of an economy conforming to Islamic precepts. Nevertheless, there are competing *ḥalāl* hubs in the Gulf region and the wider Islamic world, and Dubai does not seriously attempt to transform its economy into a fully-fledged Islamic economy. *Ḥalāl* goods and services are only a part of its wider diversification strategy and are built on synergies with other existing sectors. The emirate's strategy is to offer both secular and Islamic goods and services for a diverse spectrum of cus-

---

3 The photographs belong to the broader "Kerala Trilogy" project, which along with the "Gulfi" also included the videos "Dubai Ports World Kochi" and "Coir Kerala" (on the processing of coconut fibre). This work is part of her long-term project "Dubayyland." Cf. Trenka-Dalton, 2022.

tomers, and it therefore plays on the vagueness of such designations as "Islamic" and "ḥalāl." In fact, within the development strategy and the place branding of Dubai, the Islamic economy strategy plays only a secondary role.

The entanglement of religion and politics is also in the focus of academic research, e.g. on Islam in Egypt. Lisa M. Franke seeks to nuance the concentration on pious activism and the idea that Islam dominates everyday life in this country. Her research on individual pieties, on being religious and *doing* being religious, opens up especially the worlds of individuals who are different in the sense that they seek inspiration from television preachers because, for various reasons, they have stopped going to their local mosques on Fridays. At the centre of the paper "Islamic Ideals, the Concept of Love, and Processes of Individualisation: Muṣṭafā Ḥusnī's Writings and his Spiritual Brand" is an individual, yet religiously toned lifestyle. Drawing on fieldwork with young Alexandrians, the article considers how their spirituality is influenced by the personal brand of an Islamic television guide, who includes everyday life experiences in his interpretation of religious sources. This development hints at tendencies away from mainstream Islam and asks about alternative versions of belief. The article analyses the preacher's self-marketing and his way of conveying religious, social, and sometimes even political information and tries to understand the relationship between public versions of Islam and processes of individualisation.

In contrast, in his chapter "Queer Brands, Branding Queerness: Fractal Orientalism and Selling Gay-Friendly Beirut," *Ghassan Moussawi* examines the ways the Euro-American press has branded contemporary Beirut as a gay-friendly city and destination for gay tourists, using his concept of "Fractal Orientalism." While many cities use gay-friendliness as a means to attract and mobilise the pink economy, what happens when imperial centres brand a city as gay-friendly? He asks how Beirut has become gay-friendly in these representations. For whom is it gay-friendly, what do such designations make possible, and what do they obscure? Finally, he investigates how such designations affect local queer communities. Drawing on his ethnography of queer formations in Beirut, he highlights the (un)intended social and political consequences of such designations and illustrates how they shrink the spaces for local queer communities, especially trans, genderqueer, and working-class queer people, and how this complicates LGBT asylum-seeking from Lebanon in Western countries.

3.3 Part III: State Branding

The third part on state branding starts from early modern Ottoman practices of imperial branding and leads to strategies of contemporary nation branding.

These include the search for a unifying national logo and for a green brand in the UAE and the link between branding and spatial planning in Oman, while Egyptian destination marketing oscillates between addressing a Western-oriented and a more conservative Arab public. Gulf states also used stamps to demonstrate national progress. Lastly, Gibraltar increasingly endeavours to imagine itself as an economic and cultural bridge between Europe and the Maghreb.

Branding has rarely been recognised as a relevant theme in architectural history. Therefore, *Philip Geisler* reminds us of Fredric Jameson's programmatic imperative "Always historicize!" His contribution "Sinan's Iconic Practices: Staging Early Modern Ottoman Architecture and Power" supplements the discussion of branding in the Middle East with a historical assessment in order to better problematise its global power in modern capitalism. As an example, it studies the work of the Ottoman Empire's famous 16th-century chief architect Sinan. Conceived in a context of early globalisation, cultural power struggles, and new media technologies, three of his outstanding creations in Edirne and Istanbul illuminate the ways an emancipated architect used imperial architecture as a strategy of communication and image construction. Sinan's perceptual strategies staged the iconic architect, developed recognisable architectural styles, constructed mental (hyper-) images, and conceptualised buildings through iconicity and urban design. This reveals how Ottoman iconic practices fully exploited the twofold quality of urban icons as physical objects bound to a place and as circulating images with supraregional availability. Illustrating the imperial legacies of capitalist branding, these cases suggest the importance of delving into the transregional and transdisciplinary history of strategic architectural communication before the age of (post)modern corporate design.

Turning to contemporary issues, the chapter "Branding the United Arab Emirates as Nation Building? Constructing Unity versus Acknowledging Diversity" discusses the 2019 project to create a nation-brand logo for the UAE in terms of its potential range of meanings. It takes an interdisciplinary approach between anthropology and contemporary history. The chapter is situated within the wider literature regarding nation branding and the construction of Emirati identity. Its authors, *Moritz A. Mihatsch* and *Richard Gauvain*, advance three main arguments. Firstly, the nation-brand project is clearly to be understood within the frame of nation building in a federation of seven distinct emirates. Secondly, the design and promotion of this project reinforce established political hierarchies and structures. Thirdly, the same project may be understood as one of multiple strategies by which the UAE government also embraces the seemingly contradictory dimensions of its local/traditional and global/modern cultural and political realities. The study is based on the analysis of official documents, promotional material from social media, media discourses, and interviews with participating artists, as well as a sample of regular Emiratis' reception of the project.

In the next chapter, *Thibaut Klinger* asks "Branding and Spatial Planning in Oman: A Neoliberal Turning Point in Politics?" As in other Gulf countries, branding belongs to Oman's national political strategy. Since his 1970 coup, Sultan Qaboos has tried to create an "imagined community" and a unified territory resistant to threats of secession and civil war; spatial planning has been at the core of this strategy. During the 1990s, globalisation spread at a faster tempo, and competition between countries, regions, and cities grew, so that they felt the need to promote export marketing and to define their brand. This was also the case with the Sultanate, especially when Qaboos emphasised the priority of economic diversification. Nation branding then means featuring competitive identity and storytelling. This shift has been accompanied by an evolution of governance in accordance with the neoliberal model. Corporate branding influences nation branding, while "visions" give a key role to the sovereign and his personal branding. These developments replace politically oriented planning with entrepreneurial management. In terms of action, the multiplication of "projects" aims to boost the territory while serving the interests of the economic elite that surrounds the monarch. This evolution privileges the country's iconic places at the risk of rifts between the different parts of the territory, contrary to what Qaboos sought at the beginning of his reign.

Then, *Karin Ahlberg* decidedly turns to destination marketing. The end product for sale in tourism is an experience, which is structured by each traveller's expectation. That expectation is formed by dreams and fantasies of the place, of enchantment, of leaving the mundane behind. Tourism marketing, therefore, is about selling a fantasy. Iconic Egyptian tourism images may appear banal or arbitrary, but in fact are the outcome of meticulous global research into customers' imaginaries. The chapter "Balancing Islam: Overlapping Images of Egypt as a Destination for International and Arab Tourists" builds on interviews with the campaign architects and tourism experts who were in charge of producing Egypt's official promotion in the late 2000s. It zooms in on two campaign ads released in 2009. Targeting the two main source markets, the Arab and the international market, their diverging symbolisms conjured up two starkly different destinations: one with bustling oriental street life, modern malls, and exotic nightlife, the other with serene landscapes of wonder and blue water. That references to Arab Muslim culture were centre stage in one campaign and omitted in the other was no coincidence, but shows how Egypt's tourism promotion is produced in close dialogue with larger political and cultural processes. Accordingly, the chapter sheds light on the uneasy relation between glossy tourism ads, darker geopolitical realities, and the role of the imagination in tourism.

Laura Hindelang's snapshot "Mobile Images: Stamps as Branding Tools in the Gulf States" discusses the relevance of these "business cards of states" (Walter Benjamin) as a means of political place branding. Gaining complete control over postal services was a crucial step towards political independence for the Gulf countries that were either Trucial States or British quasi-protectorates. With the takeover came the task of creating new stamp designs and developing a political iconography that could advertise the process of nation building. Stamps were especially powerful as mobile transmitters of images in the pre-electronic messages era and were spread by mail over the world. A close reading of a small selection of pictorial stamps issued by Kuwait and other Gulf states in the second half of the 20th century reveals the visual strategies employed and the motifs and iconographies used for self-promotion vis-à-vis both national and international audiences. The analysis shows that images of maps and national emblems, impressive buildings (preceding the more recent run for starchitecture), and petroleum infrastructure became seminal markers in their place-branding strategy to demonstrate the progress of formerly Bedouin societies.

More and more projects, and finally cities and states, are being branded as "green" and "sustainable." Accordingly, Dubai's government invests in diverse efforts to brand the emirate accordingly. This comes as an extension of its successful place branding as a business hub and a tourist destination and is part of its efforts to instigate a green shift as a strategic plan for future energy adaptation and to secure an international position. Methodologically, the chapter "Greening the Desert: Emirati Youth's Perceptions of Green Branding" is based on qualitative data from in-depth interviews with focus groups encompassing young Emirati women in higher education in Dubai and their written reflections. *Gergana Alzeer* and *Tilde Rosmer* apply the theoretical Brand Box Model with its two dimensions of functionality and representationality to guide their questions and analysis. The thematic analysis of the data collected focuses on experiences, perceptions, and emerging themes of green branding among these young women students. The authors find that the themes were clearly driven by their local culture, including the role of the Emirati leadership, heritage, and religion, as well as by the speedy modernisation of the UAE. This demonstrates that, in the local understanding, "green" does not always necessarily equal "sustainable," as it often focuses on greening the desert and the city as important aspects of the quality of life.

Several examples from Europe are also included in this volume. As *Dieter Haller* shows, against the background of the current Brexit, Gibraltar has rediscovered its strong human, cultural, and economic links with Tangier and Morocco on the opposite side of the Strait and has started to brand itself accordingly. The place's name (originally, in Arabic, *Ǧabal Ṭāriq*, the "Mountain of Tarik," after the commander who in 711 AD crossed the Strait and led the Muslim conquest of the Iberian Peninsula) already reflects its historical significance. The article "Branding Gibraltar: British, Mediterranean, European, or a Bridge between Two Worlds?" widens the scope of the economic concept of branding by embedding it in local and translocal politics and identity building. It explores different branding periods of the British overseas territory from the 1960s onwards and its shift from a local to a British and a European identity to a link between the continent and Northern Africa. Local politicians, entrepreneurs, and other decision makers have developed a number of cultural, infrastructural, and economic activities with Morocco, stressing common bonds and ties. As both sides of the Strait of Gibraltar have been densely interconnected in multiple ways for many centuries, the key question of this chapter is how Gibraltar makes use of which former links in its new strategy.

3.4 Part IV: City Branding

Part IV decidedly turns to city branding. Opposite Gibraltar, Tangier is similarly being placed at spatial, but also at cultural and temporal interfaces; its multi-scalar and multimedia branding of places has also become obvious in other case studies in this book. As in Cairo, urban branding relates mostly to brand-new developments and imagines and sells a prosperous future. Yet, "slum-free" urban action programmes are another means to brand cities (and the rulers behind), e.g. in Egypt and Morocco, while often passing over the local populations' interests. In contrast, in Gulf cities like Kuwait, urban advertising may outlast long-abandoned projects, whereas in a Turkish neighbourhood, local people attempt to adopt official branding narratives and enforce them against repression "from above." The brand development of the Iranian city of Qom, which reflects a turn towards an Islamically gilded capitalism, is closely related to its "Tehranisation." But first, a chapter will investigate local residents' brand perceptions of Casablanca, which presents itself as having the first comprehensive city-branding strategy in Africa.

In 2016, Casablanca was the first city in all Africa to initiate an urban branding strategy, aimed at enhancing its attractiveness for local people, investors, and tourists. According to the chapter "City Branding and Residents' Perception: The Case of Casablanca," this strategy accompanies an ambitious development plan that embraces economic, social, and environmental challenges that the metropolis is called upon to manage rapidly and innovatively. After five years of the strategy's deployment, the two authors, *Dounia Sedra* and *Hicham El Bayed*, restudy the perceptions that Casablanca residents have of their own city and also of the development of its place brand. In their analysis using an online image assessment, they recognise the degree of local citizens' involvement in the dynamics of place branding and allow them to express their views about the development plan's effects on their daily lives.

In his paper "The Multilevel Branding of Tangier at Temporal and Spatial Interfaces," *Steffen Wippel* points to the multi-scalar aspects of place making. He starts his analysis of the branding of the northern Moroccan metropolis from a comparative historical perspective: already in the first half of the 20th century, the city was strongly marketed to attract travellers and residents, but also economic and financial institutions. After a post-independence period of stagnation, it has experienced another rapid urban transformation in recent years. Its main goals are to become an international hub for trade, a major place for foreign investment, and a recognised tourism destination. The article is interested in how a wide range of actors at different national, local, and project levels contribute in multiple ways to the construction of brands for Tangier and specific places in it. Special attention is directed to how strategic communication positions the city in space and time, especially between different world regions, between several civilisational realms, and between a great past and a prosperous future. Methodologically, the study is based on repeated fieldwork in the city from 2013 onwards, including expert interviews and photo-geographic excursions, the thorough assessment of written documents in printed media or available in the Internet, and the analysis of illustrations and other images used in branding.

Beyond glittering images and iconic buildings, the label "slum-free" has become another synonym of urban modernity and progressive development, leading many local and central governments to reinforce policies against self-constructed housing. Since the turn of the millennium, UN-Habitat and the Cities Alliance have promoted the slogan "Cities without Slums" as a development objective. Soon, the "slum-free" brand reached North Africa, as well. Morocco initiated the "Villes Sans Bidonvilles" programme in 2004. King Mohammed VI has declared that informal settlements endanger the country's development plans and its global competitiveness. In 2015, Egyptian President El Sisi announced the objective of an "Egypt Without Slums" as part of a wider strategy to modernise the country through megaprojects and construction. In their comparative study "Constructing Legitimacy through Pro-poor Housing? Branding Cities in Egypt and Morocco as 'Slum-free'," *Raffael Beier* and *Hassan Elmouelhi* argue that this label enables governments to propagate quantitative development successes and to enhance national and international political legitimacy, while simultaneously fostering repressive and neoliberal urban planning agendas. Following this, they ask about the consequences of this branding strategy for the place in city life of those who dwell in informal settlements in Cairo and Casablanca.

Khaled Nezar Adham's essay "The Power of the Speculative Image: On Branding Desert Developments and Selling Cairo's Urban Future" addresses the question of how current branding and promotional methods and visualisation techniques used by real estate developers to promote their residential and commercial offerings are implicated in the political economy of the urbanisation process in today's Egypt. The essay builds on the premise that the planning, designing, and building of new cities and large-scale urban developments reflect the way we organise the relationship between our imagined urban future and our lived present. The article argues that the functional power of the various visual and experiential techniques lies in their ability to transform into "urban lifestyle script" materials that can be used to make the future a source of extractable revenue for the present. This concept refers to a set of expectations loosely shared by a globally oriented class of citizens about the quality of certain lifestyle forms in a prototypical global city. Based on this concept, the essay investigates the layouts of showrooms, architectural visualisations, and TV promotional materials produced for large-scale real estate in Cairo and aims to shed light on how they can become instrumental in constructing a memory of the future and transforming it into current wealth.

Planned to respond to the demands of post-oil economic diversification, Gulf cities are also the result of an image policy aimed at creating an urban spectacle of modernity. Current images of urban projects setting their sights on being avant-garde and out of proportion are heirs to a relatively old policy of creating showcase cities. Urban communication is conceded to single-niche private sector stakeholders, blurring the boundaries of governmental approaches and strategy. Worse still, systematic recourse to visual communication and the proliferation of urban advertisements has produced a series of counter-effects. The chapter "Branding Backlash: The Erring of Urban Advertising in Gulf Cities" first reveals the tensions generated by the advertisers' domination of the urban scene. Then it shows how urban images tend to become independent of the projects they support, thereby accentuating the process of virtualisation. Lastly, the chapter addresses the excesses of urban neoliberalism, including the symptomatic obsolete and misused billboards, particularly in Kuwait City, where the author *Roman Stadnicki* has carried out systematic surveys. This photo-rich essay is based on fieldwork and qualitative research conducted in the UAE, Qatar, and Kuwait from 2011 to 2019, during which urban imagery was understood as both a method and an object of research to address the political, economic, and social dynamics at work in the urban field.

Kamaluddin Duaei confirms the recent global trend of place (re-)branding as an opportunistic urban strategy, in which numerous cities across the West Asian and North African regions have undergone both physical and representational developments. Qom, widely if unofficially recognised as the religious capital of Iran, constitutes an authentic case of this fashion, too, exhibiting both similarities to other cases and its own unique features. The glimpse this short piece with the title "Qom to Tehran and Back, Express: Branding a 'Suburb'?" takes of the city intends to provide insight into how its urban reconfiguration has been influenced by its geographical adjacency to the national capital. While partially satisfying the desire for consumer amenities, the project of modernising the Islamic city in light of Tehran has fostered a new place that is not so much a neutralised Tehran or another case of Dubaisation, as an increasing "Tehranisation" of Qom.

As already demonstrated, conflicts around or fuelled by a brand often arise between state power and the local population. In "Who is Branding Beyoğlu? Commodification and Surveillance of Public Space in Istanbul," *Pekka Tuominen* studies an urban district that exemplifies a specific form of secular urbanity. Debates about different qualities of public space throughout its history have formed a distinct historical consciousness, mostly running parallel to but occasionally colliding with other senses of authenticity and modernity. In Beyoğlu, the celebrated sense of freedom of expression in public space coexists with powerful practices of surveillance and repression; the illustrious past of its secular modernity becomes entangled in unsparing commodification of its key symbols. At specific events, such as the yearly May Day demonstrations, its associated senses of inclusion and belonging are put into question, often in violent terms. Therefore, the distinct image of urbanity, exemplified by the egalitarianism of boulevards and public squares, has become a battlefield of historically rooted understandings of the desired characteristics of contemporary cities. The quarter's brand has been both contested and revitalised throughout its history, often with significant changes of emphasis. Its historical trajectory remains contested and invites citizens from different backgrounds to the quotidian work of constantly redefining their position through its urban transformation.

3.5 Part V: Place Branding

The final part of this book addresses the branding of further, uncommon and less studied, places. The brandings of the new town of NEOM in Saudi Arabia and of the Eyüpsultan neighbourhood in Istanbul both primarily serve the self-promotion of political leaders. More ephemeral sites, like refugee camps, also undergo branding processes, while mosque naming in Denmark relates to diverse national (geo)political backgrounds in the Middle East. In Istanbul, from past to present, tulips have been showcased ubiquitously as a symbol of Ottomanism. And conclusively demonstrating immaculateness, cleanliness, and purity, untainted by the downsides of daily life, can be a particular goal of branding, as is practiced in Dubai in its pursuit of maximum attractiveness.

First, *Hend Aly* investigates "Place Branding as a Political Act: Approaching Saudi Arabia's NEOM beyond its Shiny Façade." The megaproject beside the Red

Sea was first announced in 2017 by Saudi Crown Prince Mohammed bin Salman. As his "brainchild," NEOM (which is short for "new future") cannot be understood apart from his aspirations, and its place branding is used as a spatial realisation of self-branding and power reaffirmation. Hence, the chapter foregrounds place branding as a political act composed of processes, actors, and narratives, triggered by local and international dynamics, and entailing political and socioeconomic consequences. Importantly, by systematically applying this lens to NEOM's branding, the chapter propagates the value of broadly approaching place branding as a political act. The study is based on analysing the project's branding documents and platforms, including the launch event, its official website and YouTube channel, and statements by major stakeholders. It first engages with academic debates on branding the city in a neoliberal context. It then explores NEOM's branding processes, involved actors, and main branding narratives as constituent pillars of the political act of place branding. The last section gives two solid examples of how NEOM's branding narratives reflect the Crown Prince's power aspirations and realise his self-brand.

The snapshot "Two Politicians and a Shrine: Competing Personal Brands around Eyüpsultan in Istanbul" examines how rival Turkish politicians brand themselves by visiting a famous shrine attributed to a Companion of the Prophet in Istanbul. In doing so, it investigates the close interplay between personal branding and place branding. Taking its name from the shrine, the surrounding neighbourhood features prominently in contemporary Sunni Islamist and Ottoman revivalist narratives, such as those promoted by the ruling Justice and Development Party. Many who consider themselves secular regard President Erdoğan's often-performed public prayers there as an aggressive demonstration of the Islamisation of politics. By analysing Turkish news coverage and social media, *Annegret Roelcke* shows how Ekrem İmamoğlu, of the secularist Republican People's Party and Istanbul's mayor since 2019, has also branded himself by praying at the Eyüpsultan shrine. At the same time, he combines this with visits to other shrines in the neighbourhood that are connected to groups such as the Alevis, which allows him to position himself in opposition to the polarising Sunni Islamist discourse. By incorporating Eyüpsultan into the image of his own powerful brand, İmamoğlu also opens up the place's predominantly Islamist image to alternative claims.

Melissa Gatter, then, turns to two Syrian refugee camps in Jordan that are decorated with the colourful brandmarks of international nongovernmental and UN-related organisations, while emblems of Gulf countries are generously stamped on donated items. In contrast, enforced by the policing of space by aid organisations and Jordanian security, Syrian flags do not appear in either camp. Based on data collected during ethnographic fieldwork between 2016 and 2018, her chapter "Who

Labels the Camp? Claiming Ownership through Visibility in Jordan" examines how branding in both sites constitutes a regime of visibility that sustains corporate humanitarianism and donor politics and goes hand in hand with simultaneous depoliticisation and "NGOisation" trends. It argues that these symbols have marked the camps as belonging not to their residents, but instead to their humanitarian governors, who claim not only spatial ownership, but also credit for their presence in the world's largest refugee crisis. Camp residents form their own associations with the logos in their everyday spaces, but they also become extensions of these brands through strategic brand placement. However, this chapter argues, this visibility does not signify accountability to refugee beneficiaries. On the contrary, these brands work to deflect responsibility onto either the individual donor in the Global North or the host country.

In her chapter "Branding the Middle East in the Diaspora: Names of Mosques in Denmark," *Helle Lykke Nielsen* elucidates that mosques in Europe can be seen as sites of everyday geopolitics. By regarding toponyms as a discursive construction of narratives that are compressed and materialised into a short form, names of mosques have the potential to express a sense of belonging and thus to brand mosque affiliations with various states, ideologies, and actors *in* and *through* the Middle East. This onomastic analysis of mosque names takes Giraut and Houssay-Holzschuch's theoretical framework for naming as a starting point and combines it with the concept of scaling. Following a brief overview of the complex practices of naming mosques in Denmark and a few methodological reflections, two mosques in Copenhagen and Odense illustrate how the choice of names situates them in the geopolitical landscape. The chapter concludes that not only do the two mosques position themselves differently towards the Muslims and the Danish majority; they also use their names in ways that suggest that they want to minimise the risk of triggering discussions of geopolitical issues with the Danish majority. For the Muslims, one place-branding strategy indexes Islamic tradition to obtain religious fame, which eventually can be exchanged for political reputation; another highlights cultural prestige and political greatness that are used as a branding device for recognition and heritage.

Symbols used in place branding sometimes extend across several scales, from nations to cities and specific urban places, and cover widely separated times. In her contribution to this volume, "Showcasing Tulips in Istanbul," which is based on several field visits and close inspection of the secondary literature, newspaper articles, Turkish MA theses, and a number of visuals, *Birgit Krawietz* starts from the finding that the tulip is certainly one of the most famous cultural icons of Turkey; but as a highly "polyvalent symbol," it defies close confinement. Her text first takes stock of some prominent historical contexts going back to the Ottoman Empire, namely the "Tulip Age" of the 18th century, and discusses the religious underpinnings of its display. The first part of the chapter demonstrates the extreme variability of tulip messages and the religiously ambivalent profile of this flower. Today, the tulip has been integrated as a history-laden emblem into Turkey's contemporary nation branding and destination marketing. Even an ancient metropolis like Istanbul now feels compelled to reframe its old worthies and new assets in a thoroughly branded fashion. Consequently, in the second part of her article, the author highlights certain more recent representations of this flower and asks what kind of branding is taking place. She states that the tulip plays a major role in both these periods of enhanced global outreach, although they are separated by up to three centuries.

In the final chapter "Architecture and the Myth of Immaculate Form in Dubai," *Philip Geisler* examines some of the city's residential and multifunctional projects, their form, and urban materiality to conceive of the deeper aesthetic meaning of hypermodern spatial production. He suggests that the myth of the immaculate form is at the heart of Dubai's corporate architectural culture. Vis-à-vis the emirate's flawed socio-political realities, immaculateness epitomises the quintessential counter-narrative and operates as an aesthetic echo of its investor and tourism strategy. Immaculate form evolves out of Dubai's specific configuration of space that orchestrates architecture through geometric design principles, seamless and reflecting surfaces, and technologically controlled and isolated climatic totalities. As a consequence of these architectural aesthetics, urban megaprojects, master-planned neighbourhoods, and individual buildings foster the interiorisation of space in a place whose rapid modernisation project is staged as inherently protected from the contagion of surrounding systems and an overcome past. The paper argues that this projected spatial closure foregrounds an aesthetic and at the same time a socio-political purification that grows out of American and European post-war corporate modernism.

The book closes with a list of contributors. This separate list of biographical notes at the end of the volume reflects individual status and affiliation (often subject to rapid interim change in the contemporary academic system) at the time when the articles were written.

Bibliography

Steiner, Christian, and Steffen Wippel, eds. *Urban Development.* Thematic issue. *Middle East–Topics & Arguments* 12.1 (2019). https://archiv.ub.uni-marburg.de/ep/0003/issue/view/230. Accessed 22 November 2022.

Trenka-Dalton, Sophie-Therese. "Work." http://trenka-dalton.info/work/. Accessed 14 February 2022.

Part II: **Consumption, Culture and Lifestyle**

Natalie Koch

Milk Nationalism: Branding Dairy and the State in the Arabian Peninsula

1 Introduction

Dairy products seemed to gain a new political significance in the Arabian Peninsula in June 2017. Qatar was suddenly placed under an air, land, and sea embargo by its Gulf neighbours – locally referred to as a "blockade" – that temporarily disrupted the country's food supply chain. While all foodstuffs were affected, residents in Qatar were especially concerned with their access to dairy products. The Middle East's two major dairy companies – Almarai and Al Dahra – hail from Saudi Arabia and the UAE respectively. And the Saudi and Emirati governments were leading the blockade. In the wake of the 2017 embargo news, dairy acquired a new importance for how people understood Qatar's sovereignty and the wellbeing of the nation.

What followed was a unique expression of "milk nationalism" that spurred the development of a new Qatari dairy brand, Baladna. With Qatari government support, the company was able to import thousands of cows from abroad, as well as new high-tech milking machinery, to begin producing Qatar's own milk in short order. The embargo further entrenched the nationalist branding of Saudi and Emirati dairy companies Almarai and Al Dahra, which were already major agribusiness conglomerates with a deep geopolitical reach into food, agriculture, shipping, storage, and transportation sectors across the MENA region and beyond.[1] Watching the embargo unfold on the other end of the Arabian Peninsula, leaders in Oman understood that they, too, were susceptible to a crisis such as Qatar was experiencing, and they similarly applied anxious narratives about food sovereignty and milk nationalism in promoting their own dairy projects.

This chapter asks why branding national dairy companies has been so important in these four Gulf Arab states and why dairy is accorded special attention in the broader arena of food geopolitics in the region. I employ the lens of critical geopolitics to analyse the history and narrative construction of milk nationalism in Saudi Arabia, the UAE, Qatar, and Oman. Critical geopolitics is a leading framework in contemporary political geography that employs discourse analysis to interrogate geographic imaginaries, concepts, and practices. It recognises "the function-

1 Cf. Hanieh, 2018.

https://doi.org/10.1515/9783110741100-008

ing of geographical knowledge not as an innocent body of knowledge and learning but an ensemble of technologies of power concerned with the governmental production and management of territorial space."[2] In this case, I examine state and corporate histories and texts to explain how milk nationalism circulates as a branding discourse in the Gulf countries and how it both draws upon and builds contemporary understandings of the state and sovereignty.

2 Food Nationalism and State Branding

The territorial state – a political entity exercising sovereignty over a defined space – is one of the most important political geographic concepts defining our contemporary world.[3] The sheer diversity of practices that produce states can be overwhelming, but scholars who examine the "state effect" – as the practice-centred approach to theorising the state can be defined – consistently point to nationalism as an especially important discursive pillar of state-making.[4] Indeed, in most of the academic literature, the idea of branding a state is not referred to as "state branding" but "nation branding."[5] There has always been slippage between the concepts of "state" and "nation," but in nearly all case studies of nation branding, as well as in its casual usage, the speaker is discussing a branding project assigned to a territorial state.

Nationalism is key to processes of state-making because its core idea – that the "nation" is a discretely defined community – is typically territorialised. That is, the nation is typically imagined to have a particular homeland or a spatial extent where it must be able to exercise supreme control over politics, social life, ideas, material infrastructures, and people themselves. The territory to which a nation is imagined to "belong" is politicised in many ways, but it is most often understood to be a kind of lifeblood for the community. Without the land and the sustenance it offers, the people are imagined to be lost. Assigning territory this important place in the biological reproduction of the nation is an important part of many nationalisms. Biological themes are common to other elements of nationalist imagery specific to the human landscape, too, typically reflecting proscriptive thinking about how the community should reproduce itself through marriage, sex, birth and dying, combat and sacrifice, and most relevant for this chapter – access to food and life essentials.

2 Ó Tuathail, 1996: 7.
3 Cf. Kuus and Agnew, 2008; Moisio et al., 2020.
4 See Anderson, 1983; Billig, 1995; Mitchell, 1999; Painter, 2006; Paasi, 2020.
5 Cf. Aronczyk, 2013; Kaneva, 2012; Saunders, 2017; Volčič and Andrejevic, 2011.

"Food nationalism" refers to the wide range of nationalist storylines that are applied in some way to food. Scholars have examined food nationalism in a range of contexts, including by researching specific nationalist food brands, dishes that are said to be distinctive to the nation, national ways of relating to food in the home or community, broader issues of access to food and its production, and more.[6] Another important theme in understanding food nationalism pertains to the geopolitics of food, where nationalist discourses are expressed through the ideas of "food sovereignty" or "food security."[7] Food is an important issue everywhere in the world, but in the MENA region, many leaders assign food a special political significance because their national homelands are predominantly desert.[8] Limited access to water combined with arid soils make large-scale agricultural production a challenge for many countries in the Middle East – including the Arabian Peninsula.

Limited food access may be seen as a national challenge, but the opposite – bountiful food for the nation – can be seen as a key nationalist victory for any leader who can successfully demonstrate the ability to provide ample sustenance for the people. It is at this intersection of these ideas about food, the nation, and leadership that we can begin to see how food nationalism fits in the contemporary practices of branding the Gulf state. Food access was a major concern for Gulf leaders prior to the discovery of oil, after which it was easier to secure imports. The region's food situation changed quite dramatically between the 1930s and the 1970s, as many leaders in the Arabian Peninsula staked their legitimacy on their ability to secure food, typically through strategic alliances with outside powers like the United States and the British Empire.[9] New Gulf relations with these powers led to a number of local agricultural projects, which started to change their food landscapes. However, following the British withdrawal from the region, its reconfigured political geographies combined with the intensive globalisation of food supply chains means that large-scale food imports became the norm by the 1980s.

Yet the early experiments with local dairy farming in Saudi Arabia and the UAE seemed to have a special allure. Where other food ventures failed or lost funding, dairy held fast. Why? As this chapter details, different political contexts across the Arabian Peninsula shaped local relationships with dairy production and the eventual national branding of milk. These local histories are important, but they

6 Cf. Caldwell, 2002; DeSoucey, 2010; Goff, 2005; Ichijo and Ranta, 2016; Ichijo, Johannes and Ranta, 2019; Klumbytė, 2010.

7 Cf. Atkins and Bowler, 2001; Conversi, 2016; Hopma and Woods, 2014; Trauger, 2015.

8 Cf. Al-Ansari, 2018; Babar and Mirgani, 2014; ECSSR, 2013; Elmi, 2017; Harrigan, 2014; Joseph, 2018; Joseph and Howarth, 2015; Koch, 2021a, 2021b; Lippman, 2010; Monroe, 2020; Woertz, 2013, 2018.

9 See Bowen-Jones and Dutton, 1983; Jones, 2010; Koch, 2021a; Woertz, 2013.

should also be understood within a broader global history of equating milk with modernity – and its special power to promote national thriving, not just surviving.[10] Although the focus of this chapter is on cow's milk, some scholars have also examined these nationalist celebrations of milk with reference to the milk of horses, camels, or sheep.[11] Indeed, for many outside observers who know the significance of camels in Gulf society, it can seem surprising that cow milk should be the centre of Gulf milk nationalism. To understand this, we need to examine the history of how dairy production began and, with it, the dual branding of dairy and the state in the Arabian Peninsula.

3 Milk Nationalism in Four Gulf Countries

3.1 Saudi Arabia

The first efforts to develop commercial-scale dairy farming in the Arabian Peninsula can be traced to the agricultural developments in Saudi Arabia's Al Kharj district, just south of Riyadh, in the 1950s. Al Kharj was a region famous for its limestone sinkholes, which offered ready access to the area's underground aquifers. In 1942, the American geologist and Saudi royal advisor Karl S. Twitchell headed the United States' Agricultural Mission in Saudi Arabia – a trek across the country to survey its water and agricultural landscape. Twitchell had already spent time in the area and knew that the Saudi King Ibn Saud wanted American support to develop it as a large-scale farm. Aramco (the Arabian American Oil Company, which later became Saudi Aramco) had already been managing the Al Kharj farming operations, but Twitchell secured US government funding to send a team of Arizona farmers to take over operations in 1944. The team left in 1946 and the farm reverted to Aramco control.

The Arizona team, headed by David Rogers, made its mark in Al Kharj, especially by expanding the production of alfalfa, which was then heralded as an ideal feed for milk cows in Arizona. But the initial spark to develop a dairy farm in Al Kharj came only after Ibn Saud's son, then-Crown Prince Saud, visited Rogers on an agricultural tour in Arizona in 1947. Saud was completely enchanted by the Arizona cattle industry and the dairy farms he visited there. Not long afterward, he started pushing Aramco to build him his own "Grade A Dairy" at Al Kharj. The

10 See Atkins, 2010; Clay and Yurco, 2020; DuPuis, 2002; Sinno, 2020; Smith-Howard, 2014; Valenze, 2011; Wiley, 2011, 2014.

11 Cf. Alhadrami, 2002; Goff, 2005; McGuire, 2017.

company eventually acquiesced and put the Texas farmer Sam Logan in charge of the project. Logan imported the necessary equipment and a range of cattle breeds from the US, and the cows were fed with the region's now-plentiful alfalfa supply.[12]

The dairy was an instant success and Logan was soon at work building two more in the region – one for the Saudi Finance Minister, Sheikh Abdallah Sulaiman, who had been championing the Al Kharj initiatives since the 1930s, and one for Saud's son Prince Abdullah bin Saud. The early Al Kharj dairy farms not only showed that local dairy production was possible, but also that royal family members and well-connected elites could stand to reap significant profits by securing (variably configured) state subsidies for their agricultural projects – which included privileged access to land and water in exchange for milk. All of this was justified in the name of "food security," although the food and milk itself primarily went to feed the vast royal family networks in Riyadh. Nonetheless, as Sulaiman and other later agricultural elites learned at this time, the early scripts of milk nationalism served them well in securing state benefits, regardless of who was actually drinking that milk.

The royal Al Kharj farms were always described as being an exemplar that could be scaled up across the entire country, though its desert farming vision stayed relatively confined to the region until a new golden age of agricultural investments in Saudi Arabia began in the 1970s. Following the world food crisis of 1972–75 and the 1973 oil crisis, when US President Richard Nixon threatened to embargo Gulf food supplies, "food security" was suddenly charged with new political and nationalist significance in the Arabian Peninsula. Actors in different political and economic sectors used the food security narrative to pursue their interests, but it was especially powerful for large farmers seeking government subsidies in the wake of the dual 1970s crises. The scale of subsidies that Gulf governments accorded to food production exploded thereafter, especially in Saudi Arabia.[13]

Almarai, headquartered in Al Kharj and now the largest dairy company in the Middle East, was one of the early beneficiaries of these subsidies.Almarai was founded in 1977 by Prince Sultan bin Mohammed bin Saud Al-Kabeer (who remains with the company as the chairman of its board) with the support of two Irish brothers. Like many other food products, "milk has no single brand or logo to support its marketing. While there may be recognition of multinational corporate names such as Nestlé most fluid milk is consumed from local processors with

12 For a fuller account and reference to the archival records on these developments, see Koch, 2021a.

13 Cf. Bowen-Jones and Dutton, 1983; Elhadj, 2004; Gerlach, 2015; Nowshirvani, 1987; Lambert and Bin Hashim, 2017; Wallensteen, 1976; Woertz, 2013.

indigenous brands."[14] That said, Almarai has developed a strong association between its brand and milk products. In doing this branding work, the advertisements also brand the nation. Often this works through implicit references to nationalist themes, such as in Fig. 1, which emphasise, in one advert, milk's ability to strengthen the individual's body by transforming the cow product into human muscle and, in the other, to unite a wholesome family in Gulf national dress. Together these images are vague enough to apply to any Gulf context, but bolster the ideas of biological health that underpin all nationalist narratives in the region.

Fig. 1: Two Almarai advertisements: "Make yourself stronger" (left) and "The flavour of authenticity and quality" (right)
Sources: Boles, 2020; Almarai, 2018.

While consumers in Saudi Arabia and regionally largely imagine Almarai as a milk company, it has actually expanded into additional products like juice, baked goods, and infant formula, and it now manages a massive global logistics network for the distribution of food, grain, and more.[15] Almarai's spectacular growth is never recognised in the media or its own public relations as the result of equally spectacular governmental subsidies. Nor is it acknowledged that the state-controlled sovereign wealth fund, the Public Investment Fund (PIF), now owns significant shares in the company and exerts considerable influence on its direction. Rather, Almarai is celebrated as a company committed to Saudi national ideals, modernisation, and

14 Wiley, 2011: 12.

15 Cf. Fabbe et al., 2018; Hanieh, 2018: 127–128; Lambert and Bin Hashim, 2017.

its "painstaking dedication to quality."[16] This dynamic corporate configuration reflects a significant transformation of Saudi elites' effort to brand the state as a place burdened with food security concerns. This in turn consolidates the idea of a freestanding Saudi state acting to protect its sovereignty, but simultaneously justifies Almarai's spirited efforts to deepen their control of global agro-commodity circuits including agricultural inputs, storage, processing, trade, and distribution.

The food security discourse, Adam Hanieh explains, has thus "validated state-led support of the largest capital groups involved in agribusiness activities, helping gird their internationalisation through regional and international agro-circuits, and simultaneously reinforcing their control over domestic agricultural production and distribution."[17] These transnational flows of milk, food, and other agricultural goods all work to bolster the Saudi state, insofar as the "agro-circuits" Hanieh describes can become an important means of exerting influence beyond the state's borders – whether through the ownership of land and serving as an important employer and tax-generator in other countries, or by controlling huge shares of other countries' food markets. The seemingly wholesome milk nationalism celebrated by Almarai is in fact enlisted in a broader geopolitical field, whereby its deepening control of food supply chains extends well beyond Saudi borders. This was felt intensely in Qatar in 2017, as we will see later in the chapter.

3.2 The United Arab Emirates

The UAE's first experience with locally producing cow milk was also tied to a colonial model farm project – in this case the British Digdagga Agricultural Trials Station in the northern emirate of Ras al-Khaimah. Colonial administrators opened Digdagga in 1955, but it was not until 1969 that the farm manager Robert McKay first tried his luck with a milk cow experiment. That year he received a herd of 28 Friesian dairy cows from the United Kingdom, which would go on to produce approximately 170–265 litres of milk a day.[18] The fact that the cows not only survived the summer heat, but actually produced milk at all was deemed a feat. These were European-bred animals with different climate tolerance, but unlike the handful of Brahman cows imported from India that one might have previously seen in the Gulf, they were milk-producing specialists. The Digdagga staff provided extra water for the cows and, to cool them on demand, they developed an early

16 Rasooldeen, 2012. See also National Geographic, 2012.
17 Hanieh, 2018: 118.
18 Cf. MacLean, 2017: 97.

misting technology – something that would later become standard in Gulf dairy facilities. Digdagga-branded milk was soon stocked in the groceries stores across the UAE, and the cows were treated as celebrities.[19]

The cows provided a convenient nationalist story that they, like the Emirati people themselves, could not just survive but thrive in the Arabian desert's harsh climate. The British managers left Digdagga in early 1972, shortly after the UAE's independence, but the cows remained and the dairy operations were expanded. Though Digdagga now has over 1,200 Holstein Friesians producing milk, the brand remains quite small. Rather, this early experiment with dairy was more of a proof-of-concept for Al Dahra, which is today the most influential dairy company in the UAE. The company was founded only in 1995, but it controls a significant share of the Emirati milk market and exports regionally. Like Digdagga Dairy, Al Dahra's 3,200-cow herd in the UAE consists entirely of Holsteins.[20]

Unlike Digdagga's limited corporate profile, Al Dahra's trajectory has closely tracked with the Saudi Almarai model – meaning that milk and dairy farms are an important part of its brand image, but that it is really a much broader agro-commodity conglomerate. Like Almarai, it has a sprawling network of subsidiaries across the globe, reaching into virtually every part of the food supply chain. For example, in addition to a sprawling network of trade, processing, and logistics holdings, Al Dahra subsidiaries own over 160,000 hectares of farmland in many countries in Africa, North America, Asia, and Europe. Analogously to Almarai and Saudi Arabia, Al Dahra is firmly under the control of one the UAE's diverse sovereign wealth funds. In May 2020, Abu Dhabi Developmental Holding Company (ADQ) agreed to acquire a 50 per cent stake in Al Dahra.[21]

ADQ is a large holding company established in 2018 that is owned by the government of Abu Dhabi. Board Chairman is Sheikh Tahnoon Bin Zayed Al Nahyan, the country's current National Security Advisor and son of the UAE's "founding father" Sheikh Zayed bin Sultan Al Nahyan. ADQ's primary objective is to fulfil the Abu Dhabi development agenda, including "accelerating the transformation of the emirate into a globally competitive and knowledge-based economy."[22] Again like Almarai and the Saudi PIF, "food security" figures prominently in how ADQ narrates its investment in Al Dahra. When the 2020 deal was announced, its CEO explained: "Al Dahra will complement our existing efforts to extend ADQ's reach in food production and distribution. With our investment, Al Dahra will be well posi-

19 Cf. Zacharias, 2013. On the water demands made by Gulf dairies, see Shadbolt, 2013.

20 Cf. Al Dahra, 2021. According to the company's website, the bulk of its dairy is now produced in Serbia, where it has approximately 16,000 cows in seven different farms.

21 Cf. ADQ, 2021.

22 Khaleej Times, 2020.

tioned to further expand its reach and footprint while enabling Abu Dhabi to reach its goals of continuing to diversify its food sources and growing into a regional food hub."[23]

Here again, we see the nationalist idea of protecting the country's food supply, which is actually about a larger effort to become a global player in the "agro-circuits" that enable the UAE to exert influence beyond the state's borders. Through the fusion of Gulf state funding and corporate ownership structures, the early version of Holstein milk nationalism has been amplified into something much larger than milk. And yet, milk's wholesome image has facilitated government elites' branding of the Gulf state not as an actor seeking to expand its geopolitical influence overseas, but, in a simpler story, as a benevolent authority seeking to strengthen the national body and provide for its food needs. Together with the Saudi variant, Emirati milk nationalism was experienced in Qatar in 2017 not as a benevolent force, but as a particularly vengeful one.

3.3 Qatar

As noted at the outset of this chapter, Qatar was suddenly placed under an air, land, and sea embargo in June 2017.[24] When the news broke, residents rushed to Qatar's grocery stores to stock up on food. They were keenly aware that the country imported nearly all of its food, and especially from the UAE. In response, the Qatari government and its sovereign wealth fund's subsidiary Hassad Food worked around the clock with partners in Iran and Turkey, which were not participating in the embargo, to re-source products and establish new distribution and logistics networks.[25] Milk products were especially prominent in the social media and everyday conversations that rippled out from the panic-buying episode and even after the new supply chains were mostly normalised, milk was a flashpoint. The embargo was spearheaded by Saudi and Emirati leaders – those countries with the largest share of Qatar's dairy market.

23 Quoted in Khaleej Times, 2020.

24 A detailed discussion of the crisis is outside the scope of this paper, but relations among the Gulf states have been unsteady for years. The embargo of Qatar was initially justified after a hack of Qatari government sites planted content that Saudi and Emirati leaders found inflammatory, but the embargo leaders in those countries quickly expanded their complaints about Qatar's regional policies and actions. For a general introduction to the crisis, see Bianco and Stansfield, 2018; Miller, 2018.

25 Cf. Sergie and Wilkin, 2017. For Hassad Food's narration of this process, see HSSD, 2018.

Although grocery stores in the country had long stocked products from countries that were not participating in the embargo, consumers were annoyed with the quality and durability of the dairy products from other countries. During my fieldwork in Qatar in 2019, for example, many Doha residents told me that substitute Turkish milk products were frequently rotten or of poor quality. When I pointed out that Qatari supermarkets had always carried Turkish dairy products and there were never problems before, none of my interlocutors could explain what led to the quality problem. Whether exaggerated or not, these anecdotes built what had come to be a dominant version of Qatar's newly formed milk nationalism. In this narrative, the Turkish help in the wake of the embargo was a kind gesture, but not a sustainable solution to Qatar's food security issue. What the country needed was milk independence. And this was to come from one place: Baladna Farms.

Like Almarai in Saudi Arabia and Al Dahra in the UAE, Baladna is now imaged as *the* Qatari national milk brand. In the wake of the embargo, the country faced numerous food-related challenges that were arguably more significant than accessing milk. Yet milk was symbolically important and the dairy company was held up as the most prominent icon for the country's effort to retake its sovereignty by retaking its ability to provide its population with locally produced dairy.[26] Baladna, which means "our country" in Arabic, began in 2014 as a small sheep and goat farm. It was quickly transformed into a major dairy operation in 2017, when Qatar Airways flew in nearly 5,000 Holstein milk cows from Europe and North America.[27] The company quickly became a nationalist symbol of the Qatari "defensive" response to the Saudi and Emirati "offensive," in which those governments tried to use their monopoly of the Gulf dairy markets as a geopolitical weapon.

But as Baladna's operations chief John Dore defiantly quipped: "The people that have shot themselves in the foot are the Saudis. If the blockade was lifted, there is so much pro-Qatar sentiment and nationalist pride that the people will buy Qatar milk, not Saudi. (...) If we can make enough milk, the people in Qatar will buy it."[28] That is, if there was no milk nationalism in Qatar before the embargo began, there was an intense new form of it thereafter. Indeed, many Qatar residents I spoke with in 2019 – citizens and non-citizens alike – spoke of Baladna with deep reverence. For them, it was an exemplar of national perseverance and the government's ability to overcome the audacious challenges posed to their basic right to food.

---

26 Cf. Koch, 2021b.

27 Cf. The Economist, 2018; Sergie, 2017.

28 Quoted in Wintour, 2017.

This nationalist storyline is vividly illustrated at the farm itself, just north of Doha, which has been transformed into a kind of dairy theme park. Inside the main building, visitors can watch the cows being milked by machines and can learn the site's history through a brief introductory film. In it, dramatic news clips announce the embargo and then the bold narrator's voice tells the Baladna story, layered over images of the cows being imported and the farm being developed: "Our vision is to become a pillar of national self-sufficiency to support building an independent nation – a nation where its goodness comes from its own produce. For 'Made in Qatar' to be universally recognized for quality products."[29] The 4:45-minute video runs on loop in the visitor centre, echoing through the halls and lending a sombre sense of nationalist pride both in the milk being mechanically sucked from the cows in the adjacent milking gallery, and in the country of Qatar more broadly.

The story about how Baladna milk can promote positive associations with "Made in Qatar" is simultaneously one of branding the milk and the country. The milk and all other corporate materials carry a symbol that references the Qatari national flag with the slogan in English and Arabic, "Proudly made in Qatar" (Fig. 2). In this way, we see the corporate production of nationalism that is so common in the Gulf countries.[30] But the famous "cowlift" that enabled Baladna's rapid shift to commercial-scale dairy production was also an act of state-making that both drew upon and further entrenched state institutions in Qatar. It was only possible with strong government support, both directly and indirectly through the parastatal Qatar Airways and Hassad Food, the agriculture-focused subsidiary of the Qatar Investment Authority. The country's quick resolution of the supply chain problems was also heralded as a success of longer-term government planning that had begun with the introduction of the Qatar National Food Security Programme (QNFSP) in 2008.[31]

QNFSP is now defunct, but it was established after the global food crisis of around 2006–2008 as a taskforce under the Office of the Heir Apparent (then Sheikh Tamim bin Hamad Al Thani, the current Emir) with a goal of developing a more coherent governmental approach to (potential) supply disruptions. One of the QNFSP's objectives was to diversify Qatar's supply routes, which was reflected in the 2010 start of construction on a new deep-water port facility that allowed

29 English translations from Arabic were included as subtitles. A more detailed discussion of this video and the farm can be found in Koch, 2021b. The full video clip is available at the author's website with the password "national" at: http://nataliekoch.com/gndp/.

30 Cf. Koch, 2020.

31 Cf. Al-Ali, 2017; Al-Ansari, 2018; Lambert and Bin Hashim, 2017; Miniaoui, Irungu, and Kaitibie, 2018.

larger ships to dock, where previously the country depended on redistribution chains via the UAE's Jebel Ali port. The new Hamad port was also designed to accommodate livestock and bulk grain imports, as well as grain storage.[32] Opened in September 2017, just three months after the embargo began, it now can presumably host as many dairy cows as the country's new milk nationalism demands. The port can also send Qatari milk overseas – as it has been doing since 2019.[33]

Fig. 2: Baladna milk bottle with the "Proudly made in Qatar" logo on the bottom left
Photo: Natalie Koch, 2019.

3.4 Oman

The nationalist spectacle of Baladna also had an effect elsewhere in the region. In Oman in particular, many people watched with a degree of foreboding as Qatar's government and people navigated the challenges of the embargo. In fact, the Omani government had already begun planning for such an eventuality through its own National Food Security initiative, akin to the QNFSP. This included the development of Mazoon Dairy as the "flagship dairy company" of the initiative, with

32 Cf. Koch, 2020; Siegel, 2013; Smith, 2019.
33 Cf. Peninsula, 2019.

a stated objective of improving "self-sufficiency in dairy production in the Sultanate of Oman."[34] It was incorporated in January 2015, but construction of the facilities stalled – beginning only in October 2017, a few months after the embargo was imposed on Qatar. Starting with 3,400 Holstein milk cows and a goal to expand the herd to 25,000 by 2026, Mazoon's distribution finally began in October 2019.[35]

As in the other Gulf countries, Omani milk nationalism has been heavily supported by state funding and other supports. In the case of Mazoon, this has included not only a close relationship with the National Food Security initiative, but also backing from government pension and investment funds and the Oman Food Investment Company (OFIC) – a state-owned-enterprise designed to "promote Oman's food security."[36] OFIC also controls a second dairy operation, the Al Morooj Dairy Company, but this is essentially just a milk collection project – it involves collecting milk from small farmers in the Dhofar region to process and sell through a centralised facility.[37] Because it involves a full-fledged, commercial-scale dairy farm, Mazoon is the posterchild of the celebratory milk nationalism in Oman today. Mazoon's diffuse web of government support can also be seen in its strategic partnership with Sultan Qaboos University (a state-sponsored institution) to use its facilities for R&D, recipes, and packaging.[38] The terms of this partnership are somewhat unclear, but this is notable because the Sultan Qaboos University's College of Agriculture has long sold its own milk products on campus. As Fig. 3 illustrates, the packaging is very simple but prominently features an Omani national emblem.

The nationalist ideas of food sovereignty and food security figure prominently in the scripting of Oman's recent dairy projects, as does the idea that the national body can be strengthened by increasing its consumption of milk. But even more than in the other Gulf countries, nationalisation of the workforce, "Omanisation," is especially prominent in the celebration of Mazoon's contribution to the country's development. According to the company's website, "The project opens wide opportunities in the employment market for Oman. The Project is expected to reach around 90% Omanisation in 10 years. It would employ approximately 2300 staff in Year 10 and will also provide indirect employment through forwarding and backward linkage effects of the project."[39] In addition to its own rhetoric, Mazoon is held up in other media outlets as an exemplar of how large state invest-

34 Mazoon Dairy, 2021.
35 Cf. FPT, 2018.
36 FPT, 2018.
37 Cf. Oman Food, 2021.
38 Cf. FPT, 2018; Oman Food, 2021.
39 Mazoon Dairy, 2021.

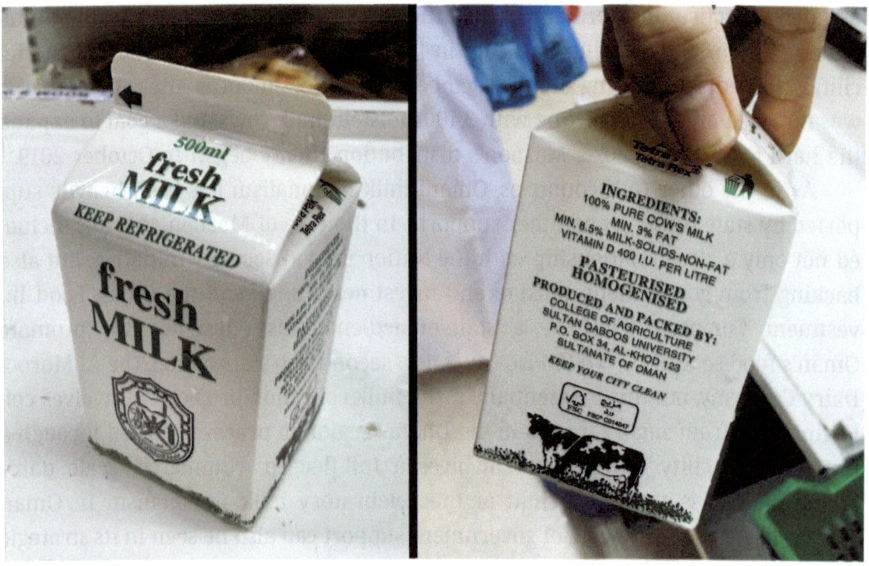

Fig. 3: Sultan Qaboos University's College of Agriculture-produced milk, with an Omani state seal as the logo
Photos: Natalie Koch, 2020.

ments in the corporate sector (here commercial agriculture) can create jobs for Omanis. The workforce nationalisation agenda is found across the Arabian Peninsula, but the Mazoon case is exemplary of the polysemic nature of milk nationalism – the national branding of dairy can be applied to any range of state agendas that legitimise its power. Domestic milk production thus helps to show that the Omani state is concerned about the welfare of its people on many levels, including their longer-term job prospects. That is, from the Omani perspective, branding the milk as a force for good is equally about branding the state as a force for good.

4 Conclusion

The irony of the 2017–2021 regional embargo of Qatar was that it created an opening for new regional competitors to Saudi and Emirati dairy companies, which had previously dominated Gulf markets in the last decade. It provoked a new expression of milk nationalism in Qatar, which seemed to politicise milk in a new way. Yet, milk was already immensely political in the Gulf region. And milk has a long history of being associated with ideals of modernity, national prosperity, and wellbeing around the world.[40] In this respect, the Arabian Peninsula is no exception to a much broader global pattern. Yet the milk nationalism in Saudi Arabia, the UAE, Qatar, and Oman has resulted in significant state support being directed to the dairy industries, in a way that stands apart from elsewhere in the world.

The heavy involvement of sovereign wealth funds in each country's leading dairy brands is indicative of the fuzzy relationship between state and non-state enterprises in the Gulf region. Their support for dairy has arisen from the funds' involvement in government-defined food security agendas, which reflects the fact that milk has become an important symbol in the effort to demonstrate concrete steps toward food independence. Of course, simply producing dairy locally does not free the Arabian Peninsula from its overwhelming dependence on food imports. But by branding the dairies as national, they can circulate as important icons that the governments can then use to brand the state. As a branding discourse, milk nationalism both draws upon and builds contemporary understandings of the state in the Gulf countries – as independent, benevolent, and wholesome. The credibility of this nationalist storyline, just like any branding effort, cannot be objectively assessed but rests with the eye (or tastebuds) of the beholder.

Bibliography

ADQ (Abu Dhabi Developmental Holding Company). "Who We Are." 2021. https://adq.ae/who-we-are. Accessed 8 August 2021.

Al-Ali, Mustafa Semsia. "Growing Food Pyramids in the Sand: How Sustainable Are Qatar's Self-Sufficiency and Foreign Agro-Investment Policies?" *Journal of Agriculture and Environment for International Development* 111.2 (2017): 409–424.

Al-Ansari, Tareq. "Food Security: The Case of Qatar." In *The Gulf Crisis: The View from Qatar*, edited by Rory Miller, 28–38. Doha: Hamad bin Khalifa University Press, 2018.

Al Dahra. "Dairy." https://www.aldahra.com/product-portfolio/dairy. Accessed 8 August 2021.

Alhadrami, G. A. "Animals That Produce Dairy Foods | Camel." In *Encyclopedia of Dairy Sciences*, edited by John Fuquay, 351–357. San Diego: Academic Press, 2nd ed., 2002.

Almarai. "Almarai-Laban-Website-Split Arabic." Riyadh, 2018. https://www.almarai.com/en/corporate/almarai-laban-website-split-arabic/. Accessed 8 August 2021 (link expired).

Anderson, Benedict. *Imagined Communities: Reflections on the Origin and Spread of Nationalism.* London: Verso, 1983.

Aronczyk, Melissa. *Branding the Nation: The Global Business of National Identity.* Oxford: Oxford University Press, 2013.

Atkins, Peter J., and Ian R. Bowler. *Food in Society: Economy, Culture, Geography.* London: Arnold, 2001.

40 Cf. DuPuis, 2002; Valenze, 2011; Wiley, 2011, 2014.

Atkins, Peter J. *Liquid Materialities: A History of Milk, Science, and the Law.* Burlington: Ashgate, 2010.

Babar, Zahra, and Suzi Mirgani. *Food Security in the Middle East.* Oxford: Oxford University Press, 2014.

Bianco, Cinzia, and Gareth Stansfield. "The Intra-GCC Crises: Mapping GCC Fragmentation after 2011." *International Affairs* 94.3 (2018): 613–635.

Billig, Michael. *Banal Nationalism.* Thousand Oaks: Sage, 1995.

Boles, Youssef. "Social Media Advertisement for Almarai Company." *Béhance* 7 August 2020. https://www.behance.net/gallery/102051609/Social-media-advertisement-for-Almarai-company?tracking_source=search_projects_recommended%7Calmarai. Accessed 8 August 2021 (link expired).

Bowen-Jones, Howard, and Roderick Dutton. *Agriculture in the Arabian Peninsula.* London: Economist Intelligence Unit, 1983.

Caldwell, Melissa L. "The Taste of Nationalism: Food Politics in Postsocialist Moscow." *Ethnos* 67.3 (2002): 295–319.

Clay, Nathan, and Kayla Yurco. "Political Ecology of Milk: Contested Futures of a Lively Food." *Geography Compass* 14.8 (2020). https://doi.org/10.1111/gec3.12497.

Conversi, Daniele. "Sovereignty in a Changing World: From Westphalia to Food Sovereignty." *Globalizations* 13.4 (2016): 484–498.

DeSoucey, Michaela. "Gastronationalism: Food Traditions and Authenticity Politics in the European Union." *American Sociological Review* 75.3 (2010): 432–455.

DuPuis, E. Melanie. *Nature's Perfect Food: How Milk Became America's Drink.* New York: New York University Press, 2002.

ECSSR. *Water and Food Security in the Arabian Gulf.* Abu Dhabi: Emirates Center for Strategic Studies and Research, 2013.

Elhadj, Elie. *Camels Don't Fly, Deserts Don't Bloom: An Assessment of Saudi Arabia's Experiment in Desert Agriculture.* Water Issues Study Group, Occasional Paper 48. London: School of Oriental and African Studies/King's College London, University of London, 2004. https://www.soas.ac.uk/water/publications/papers/file38391.pdf. Accessed 21 September 2021.

Elmi, Abdirashid A. "Food Security in the Arab Gulf Cooperation Council States." In *Sustainable Agriculture Reviews*, edited by Eric Lichtfouse, 89–114. Cham: Springer, 2017.

Fabbe, Kristin, Safwan Al-Amin, Esel Çekin, and Natalie Kindred. *Almarai Company: Milk and Modernization in the Kingdom of Saudi Arabia.* Cambridge: Harvard Business School, 2018.

FPT (Food Processing Technology). "Mazoon Dairy Company's Integrated Dairy Farm, Al Sunaynah, Oman." (Ca.) 2018. https://www.foodprocessing-technology.com/projects/mazoon-dairy-companys-integrated-dairy-farm-al-sunaynah/. Accessed 10 August 2021.

Gerlach, Christian. "Famine Responses in the World Food Crisis 1972–5 and the World Food Conference of 1974." *European Review of History* 22.6 (2015): 929–939.

Goff, Patricia M. "It's Got to Be Sheep's Milk or Nothing! Geography, Identity, and Economic Nationalism." In *Economic Nationalism in a Globalizing World*, edited by Eric Helleiner and Andreas Pickel, 183–201. Ithaca: Cornell University Press, 2005.

Hanieh, Adam. *Money, Markets, and Monarchies: The Gulf Cooperation Council and the Political Economy of the Contemporary Middle East.* New York: Cambridge University Press, 2018.

Harrigan, Jane. *The Political Economy of Arab Food Sovereignty.* Houndmills: Palgrave Macmillan, 2014.

Hopma, Justa, and Michael Woods. "Political Geographies of 'Food Security' and 'Food Sovereignty.'" *Geography Compass* 8.11 (2014): 773–784.

HSSD. “Hassad Contribution During Blockade.” *YouTube* 28 March 2018. https://www.youtube.com/watch?v=oTtbE8VjphE. Accessed 8 August 2021.

Ichijo, Atsuko, and Ronald Ranta. *Food, National Identity and Nationalism: From Everyday to Global Politics.* New York: Palgrave Macmillan, 2016.

Ichijo, Atsuko, Venetia Johannes, and Ronald Ranta. *The Emergence of National Food: The Dynamics of Food and Nationalism.* London: Bloomsbury Academic, 2019.

Jones, Toby Craig. *Desert Kingdom: How Oil and Water Forged Modern Saudi Arabia.* Cambridge: Harvard University Press, 2010.

Joseph, Sabrina. “Farming the Desert: Agriculture in the Oil Frontier, the Case of the United Arab Emirates, 1940s to 1990s.” *British Journal of Middle Eastern Studies* 45.5 (2018): 678–694.

Joseph, Sabrina, and Brigitte Howarth. “Fertile Sands: Colonial Politics and the Development of Land and Water Resources in the Trucial States, Mid- to Late 20th Century.” *The Arab World Geographer* 18.3 (2015): 139–168.

Kaneva, Nadia. *Branding Post-Communist Nations: Marketizing National Identities in the “New” Europe.* New York: Routledge, 2012.

Khaleej Times. “The Acquisition of the Stake in Abu Dhabi-Based Al Dahra is Subject to Certain Regulatory Approvals.” 14 May 2020. https://www.khaleejtimes.com/business/local/adq-to-acquire-50-percent-stake-in-al-dahra-holding-company. Accessed 8 August 2021.

Klumbytė, Neringa. “The Soviet Sausage Renaissance.” *American Anthropologist* 112.1 (2010): 22–37.

Koch, Natalie. “The Corporate Production of Nationalism.” *Antipode* 52.1 (2020): 185–205.

Koch, Natalie. “Desert Geopolitics: Arizona, Arabia, and an Arid-Lands Response to the Territorial Trap.” *Comparative Studies of South Asia, Africa and the Middle East* 41.1 (2021a): 88–105.

Koch, Natalie. “Food as a Weapon? The Geopolitics of Food and the Qatar-Gulf Rift.” *Security Dialogue* 52.2 (2021b): 118–134.

Kuus, Merje, and John Agnew. “Theorizing the State Geographically: Sovereignty, Subjectivity, Territoriality.” In *The Sage Handbook of Political Geography*, edited by Kevin R. Cox, Murray Low, and Jennifer Robinson, 95–106. Los Angeles: Sage, 2008.

Lambert, Laurent A., and Hisham Bin Hashim. “A Century of Saudi-Qatari Food Insecurity: Paradigmatic Shifts in the Geopolitics, Economics and Sustainability of Gulf States Animal Agriculture.” *The Arab World Geographer* 20.4 (2017): 261–281.

Lippman, Thomas W. “Saudi Arabia’s Quest for Food Security.” *Middle East Policy Council Journal* 17.1 (2010): 90–98.

MacLean, Matthew. *Spatial Transformations and the Emergence of “the National”: Infrastructures and the Formation of the United Arab Emirates, 1950–1980.* PhD thesis, Department of History, New York University, 2017.

Mazoon Dairy. “Company Profile.” 2021. https://www.mazoondairy.om/company-profile/. Accessed 8 August 2021.

McGuire, Gabriel. “Cultural Histories of Kumiss: Tuberculosis, Heritage and National Health in Post-Soviet Kazakhstan.” *Central Asian Survey* 36.4 (2017): 493–510.

Miller, Rory. *The Gulf Crisis: The View from Qatar.* Doha: Hamad bin Khalifa University Press, 2018.

Miniaoui, Hela, Patrick Irungu, and Simeon Kaitibie. *Contemporary Issues in Qatar’s Food Security.* MEI Insight 185. Singapore: Middle East Institute, National University of Singapore, 2018. https://mei.nus.edu.sg/publication/insight-185-contemporary-issues-in-qatars-food-security/. Accessed 10 August 2021.

Mitchell, Timothy. “Society, Economy, and the State Effect.” In *State/Culture: State-Formation after the Cultural Turn*, edited by George Steinmetz, 76–97. Ithaca: Cornell University Press, 1999.

Moisio, Sami, Natalie Koch, Andrew E. G. Jonas, Christopher Lizotte, and Juho Luukkonen. *Handbook on the Changing Geographies of the State: New Spaces of Geopolitics.* Northampton: Edward Elgar, 2020.

Monroe, Kristin V. "Geopolitics, Food Security, and Imaginings of the State in Qatar's Desert Landscape." *Culture, Agriculture, Food and Environment* 42.1 (2020): 25–35.

National Geographic. "Operation Almarai." *National Geographic TV Abu Dhabi* 17 September 2012. https://www.natgeotv.com/me/operation-almarai (available to stream online at https://www.dailymotion.com/video/x5lklrp). Accessed 8 August 2021.

Nowshirvani, Vahid. "The Yellow Brick Road: Self-Sufficiency or Self-Enrichment in Saudi Agriculture?" *MERIP Middle East Report* 145 (1987): 7–13.

Oman Food. *Oman Food Investment Holding Co.* https://omanfood.om/. Accessed 10 August 2021.

Ó Tuathail, Gearóid. *Critical Geopolitics: The Politics of Writing Global Space.* Minneapolis: University of Minnesota Press, 1996.

Paasi, Anssi. "Nation, Territory, Memory: Making State-Space Meaningful." In *A Research Agenda for Territory and Territoriality*, edited by David Storey, 61–82. Northampton: Edward Elgar, 2020.

Painter, Joe. "Prosaic Geographies of Stateness." *Political Geography* 25.7 (2006): 752–774.

Peninsula. "Qatari Dairy Exports First Batch of Products." 28 March 2019. https://www.thepeninsulaqatar.com/article/28/03/2019/Qatari-dairy-exports-first-batch-of-products. Accessed 6 June 2019.

Rasooldeen, Md. "Almarai's Pursuit of Quality Ensures Unique Success Story." *Arab News* 9 June 2012. www.arabnews.com/almarai%E2%80%99s-pursuit-quality-ensures-unique-success-story. Accessed 8 August 2021.

Saunders, Robert A. *Popular Geopolitics and Nation Branding in the Post-Soviet Realm.* New York: Routledge, 2017.

Sergie, Mohammed. "Qatar Crisis: First Batch of Dairy Cows Airlifted to Sidestep Saudi-Led Blockade." *The Independent* 12 July 2017. https://www.independent.co.uk/news/business/news/qatar-crisis-latest-news-cows-saudi--arabia-doha-milk-boycott-dairy-flown-in-airlift-boycott-a7836786.html. Accessed 6 June 2019.

Sergie, Mohammed, and Sam Wilkin. "Qatar Tries to Ease Food-Supply Fears as Crowds Throng Shops." *Bloomberg* 7 June 2017. https://www.bloomberg.com/news/articles/2017-06-06/qatar-tries-to-quell-food-supply-fears-after-crowds-throng-shops. Accessed 6 June 2019.

Shadbolt, Peter. "Milking the Desert: How Mega-Dairies Thrive in Saudi Sands." *CNN* 18 December 2013. https://www.cnn.com/2013/12/18/world/meast/milking-the-desert-saudi-dairy-farms/index.html. Accessed 8 August 2021.

Siegel, Benjamin R. *Hungry Nation: Food, Famine, and the Making of Modern India.* Cambridge: Cambridge University Press, 2018.

Sinno, Nadine. "Intifada Cows and Israeli National Security: Reanimating Civil Resistance in the Wanted 18." *Middle East Critique* 29.2 (2020): 199–217.

Smith-Howard, Kendra. *Pure and Modern Milk: An Environmental History since 1900.* Oxford: Oxford University Press, 2014.

Smith, Matt. "How is Qatar Coping with its Economic Embargo?" *BBC News* 10 January 2019. https://www.bbc.com/news/business-46795696. Accessed 6 June 2019.

The Economist. "Milk Sheikhs: Why Qatar is Raising Cows in the Desert." 19 May 2018. https://www.economist.com/middle-east-and-africa/2018/05/17/why-qatar-is-raising-cows-in-the-desert. Accessed 6 June 2019.

Trauger, Amy. *Food Sovereignty in International Context: Discourse, Politics and Practice of Place.* New York: Routledge, 2015.

Valenze, Deborah M. *Milk: A Local and Global History.* New Haven: Yale University Press, 2011.

Volčič, Zala, and Mark Andrejevic. "Nation Branding in the Era of Commercial Nationalism." *International Journal of Communication* 5 (2011): 598–618.

Wallensteen, Peter. "Scarce Goods as Political Weapons: The Case of Food." *Journal of Peace Research* 13.4 (1976): 277–298.

Wiley, Andrea S. "Milk for 'Growth': Global and Local Meanings of Milk Consumption in China, India, and the United States." *Food and Foodways* 19.1–2 (2011): 11–33.

Wiley, Andrea S. *Cultures of Milk: The Biology and Meaning of Dairy Products in the United States and India.* Cambridge: Harvard University Press, 2014.

Wintour, Patrick. "Land of Milk and Money: Qatar Looks to Farms to Beat the Gulf Boycott." *The Guardian* 20 October 2017. https://www.theguardian.com/world/2017/oct/20/land-of-milk-and-money-qatar-looks-to-farms-to-beat-the-gulf-boycott. Accessed 6 June 2019.

Woertz, Eckart. *Oil for Food: The Global Food Crisis and the Middle East.* Oxford: Oxford University Press, 2013.

Woertz, Eckart. "Geopolitics, Food and Agriculture." In *Crisis and Conflict in Agriculture*, edited by Rami Zurayk, Eckart Woertz, and Rachel Bahn, 28–39. Boston: CABI, 2018.

Zacharias, Anna. "Dubai Witnesses Birth of a Nation's Milk Supply." *The National* 1 September 2013. https://www.thenationalnews.com/uae/environment/dubai-witnesses-birth-of-a-nation-s-milk-supply-1.656821. Accessed 8 August 2021.

Ute Röschenthaler

Branding Chinese Green Tea in Mali

1 Introduction

Branding spells out, builds up and enhances the properties of a product, a place, or an individual. It is a complex notion that is intrinsically connected with values, images, and assets, be they monetary and/or symbolic, social, or identity-related. These values also imply notions of ownership, especially in the commodity world. Branding connects conceptual ideas with the product as its added value, which concomitantly renders the brand its owners' exclusive property. The time, creativity, and money that they invest in building up the brand are legally acknowledged by intellectual property law that aims at rewarding owners for their efforts.

In the market, the added brand value becomes visible in sales figures that can considerably exceed the material or use value of a product.[1] The green tea sector in Mali is a good example. More than a hundred green tea brands are to be found on the *Grand Marché*, Bamako's largest market place, which has an entire section exclusively for Chinese green tea. These brands represent various varieties and qualities of tea, yet even those of the same quality have amazingly different brand values. The value of a brand is difficult to pin down and control, as it comes and stays "by the grace of God," as the Malian tea importers would say. As quickly as it has arrived, it might also disappear again.

This chapter examines what is at stake with brand-named Chinese green tea in Mali using the example of the *Achoura* brand. *Thé Achoura* is currently the best-selling Chinese green tea in Mali, adjacent countries, and the Sahelian diasporas. Its name refers to the tenth day of the first month in the Muslim calendar and resonates well with Islam, the religious affiliation of the large majority of Malians.

Based on research on markets in Africa and Asia since 2005 and on interviews with the most successful Malian tea importers, this study follows the creation and rise of *Achoura*, as well as the various challenges, including brand piracy, rumours, health issues, and envy, that it had to face. The chapter begins by discussing brand value and embedding the creation of tea brands in the history of the arrival of Chinese green teas in Mali via Britain and Morocco in the early 19th century, the emergence of Malian tea brands in the 1990s, and its becoming a national drink in the 2000s. It then presents the importer of *Thé Achoura* and the creation of

1 See Nakassis, 2013: 114.

https://doi.org/10.1515/9783110741100-009

the brand in 2013, its success, and the challenges it had to face. Finally, the study discusses the package design and tea publicity that form part of the brand's regime of value.[2] The argument presented here is that brand value is complicated to manage and requires hard work, convincing brand strategies, and a portion of good luck to persist in a dynamic and competitive market.

2 Tea History and Brand Creation

When green tea arrived in northern Mali in the early 19th century, it was known as *ataya*, the Moroccan-Arabic term for tea. At that time, it was consumed only by Saharan traders and their guests in an impressive but exclusive ritual. Tea arrived on camel back across the Sahara, but little did people know that it had travelled across half the globe from China via Britain and Morocco to the Sahel towns. Only after independence in 1960, when the Malian president travelled to China and, with Chinese help, began to establish a small tea plantation in the country's south did the Malian majority become aware of its origin and became interested in its consumption. More tea was imported, and it was now available in several varieties indicated by numbers following the Chinese tea standards, of which a Chunmee with the number *quatre-mille-once* (4011) was the most desired. During that time, the state was the only legal importer of luxury products, including tea, sugar, milk, salt, tobacco, and canned tomatoes;[3] private importation of these items was prohibited, yet a few brand-name Chinese green teas also appeared in Mali, smuggled into the country.

The boom of the green tea brands began only following the 1991 economic reforms that permitted private traders to import it. At first, as before, tea was imported in large wooden boxes, but soon importers created small 25 g packages that contained the exact amount of tea that was required for one tea ritual. Over the course of the 1990s, printed plastic sachets that were meanwhile in use were placed in folding cartons emblazoned with images and brand names. In the late 1990s, the first Malian tea brands were registered with the *Centre Malien de Promotion de la Propriété Industrielle*, CEMAPI, the local office for trademark protection.

In the following years, growing numbers of traders – Malians and a few Chinese – imported increasing quantities of tea. Each importer created their own tea brand, as the packaging took place right in the tea factory in China. Most of them

2 See Appadurai, 1986.

3 See Takacs, 1991.

travelled themselves to China to select the tea and decide on a brand name and a package design that distinguished their tea brand from that of other importers. Importers now became owners of brands that were their exclusive intellectual property, an asset that they had to defend against competitors.

Consumers embraced the colourful packages, which lent more prestige than unbranded tea sold loosely. By selling the brand-name teas in sealed packages, however, the importers prevented consumers from gaining trust in them by inspecting the tea leaves and smelling their aroma before purchasing. Consumers had to invest a lot of trust in the importer and believe that the promise offered by the brand was reliable. They trusted their trader more than the package inscription and the related advertisement, if there was any.[4] Word of mouth by other consumers and the recommendations of traders were important for a brand's success, more than the appeal of the colourful package design and the brand name. Wholesalers could exert much influence in making a particular importer's tea brand sell. Thus, whilst some importers were able to sell several shipping containers of tea a month, with a purchasing value of about 100,000 EUR each, others took several months or more to sell a single container of tea.

Success in making a tea brand sell and thus in creating brand value depended on a combination of understanding the tea market, guaranteeing stable product quality, handling one's competitors wisely, conversing with other traders, investing in social projects, counterbalancing gossip and rumours, and managing an extensive distribution network.

Even though the quality that many tea packages contained was the same or better, they would not sell but remain unsold in the warehouses of the many less lucky importers. In contrast, popular teas were already sold before the container load from China had arrived in the importer's warehouse. If this was the case, it reflected the popularity of a brand, but that condition could also easily create a surfeit on the market and subsequently a supply crisis, when, for instance, the arrival of the tea was delayed because the Chinese supplier had problems delivering the ordered quantity and the importer had already used the money of the wholesalers to order more tea to be sure there was no gap in the supply chain. If the tea did not arrive or contained poor tea, the brand value could drastically decrease and/or the importer easily be financially ruined.

4 See Fanselow, 2009; Applbaum, 2005; Röschenthaler, 2022.

3 The Importer of *Thé Achoura*

During the 2010s, about a dozen tea importers became successful in selling tea in larger quantities, managed to control the tea market, and, through their steady supply, contributed to making it Mali's national drink. Together they own an estimated one-third of the tea brands on the Malian market. The many other brands are owned by occasional importers attempting to emulate the successes of the influential tea importers. The story of the most successful brand of tea – *Thé Achoura* – will now be briefly related.

Achoura was created in 2013. At the time, the owner, a young man in his early thirties, was very successfully selling the brand *Taoudeni* that he had created in 2009 under the auspices of his older cousin, after having collected some experience as a simple salesman and in the business of another tea importer. He first invested the profits from the sales of *Taoudeni* in purchasing larger quantities of tea, then in warehouses for storing it and in lorries for transporting the tea from the West African port where it arrived to the warehouses in landlocked Mali. In 2013, he had saved enough to be able to create his own company and register the brand in his own name. He travelled to China to select the variety of tea he wanted for *Achoura*, in a quality that was suitable for Malian consumers: not cheap, but also not too expensive. In no more than three years, in 2016, this importer had constructed a huge new office building and then began to diversify his products. He created employment in rearing chicken and cattle, then also sold *Achoura* milk, so that if a problem developed with importing tea from China or with an unmanageable surfeit of *Achoura* on the market, he would be able to continue trading these other products.

With his two successful tea brands, he demonstrated that it was possible to bring a tea onto the market and quickly sell it in large quantities. Whilst other importers had large billboards and commercials on radio and TV, he did not even invest much in advertising. He only had small posters that he distributed among customers (Fig. 1). Other tea brands contained the same good quality of tea, but did not easily sell, so that their owners could not recover their investments quickly enough to continue importing more tea.

During several three- to four-hour interviews, the owner of *Achoura* was very welcoming, telling me about his tea business in his small office near the *Grand Marché*. He was born in northern Mali, had studied accountancy in Algeria, then during his work for another tea importer had travelled to China to visit tea gardens and factories and to select good-quality tea, until he began to work with his cousin, who granted him initial capital and documents for importation. These experiences enabled him to successfully place his brands on the market.

Once a brand has arrived in the mind of the people, the money flows, as he put it: "It is like a money-producing machine (*c'est comme une machine qui produit de l'argent*)."[5]

Fig. 1: Entrance to the office of the owner of Thé Achoura
Photo: Ute Röschenthaler, Bamako, 2016.

Soon, he was selling *Taoudeni* and *Achoura* throughout Mali and in adjacent West African countries, including Guinea, Burkina Faso, Côte d'Ivoire, Senegal, Mauritania, and Niger, and also as far as Central Africa (Gabon, Congo-Brazzaville) and even East Africa (Mozambique). Additionally, other traders conveyed the popular teas also to other countries in which it was not worthwhile to sell an entire container each month. Altogether, according to his own calculation, the owner of *Achoura* sells a monthly average of 40 containers, which makes him the most successful Malian, if not African, tea importer. With his enterprise, he also created employment for young Malians, fostered development in the country, and was known for philanthropic donations. Online media reported that in 2017, he was involved as the patron of an event, organised by *Miroir Media*, a global communication agency, during which 12 local enterprises were nominated for excelling in creating innovation, employment, and development, in social responsibility, or in environmental respect. For his generosity, the owner of *Achoura* was also awarded

5 This information is based on various interviews with the importer in Bamako in 2013 and 2016.

a trophy.[6] Acknowledging his endeavours, one journalist wrote that this importer represented "the Malian dream. He started from nothing to now reign supreme in the tea market in Mali and in the international market. He employs hundreds of young Malians and invests heavily in social and cultural events, especially those involving youth."[7]

4 Challenges the *Achoura* Brand Had to Face

One of the challenges was to manage brand piracy. Every tea brand, once it became popular – i.e. when more than five containers per month of it were sold in Mali – has sooner or later fallen victim to brand piracy. Brand piracy was more easily discovered when importers employed representatives in their widely dispersed distribution networks in the country and abroad. These were aware of the quantity of tea that the importer distributed and thus able to identify surplus sales of counterfeited tea and infringed tea packages.

Achoura was pirated, too. In 2016, a trader in a rural market was observed selling infringed *Achoura* in packages that had the same design and colours as the original, but its brand name was instead *Amine*. The seller was forced to disclose from whom he had purchased the tea, and, confronted with a high fine to pay, the pirate admitted his fault and promised to stop selling pirated *Achoura*. His excuses were accepted, as Malians prefer to solve such issues among themselves in an amiable way. However, sometime later, he imported again a container of pirated *Achoura*. This time, he was sued and forced to pay the damages.[8] A similar case happened in 2016 in Bamako when a tea brand emblazoned with the design and colours of *Achoura* but with the name *Charifa* was found.[9] In mid-2019, *Achoura* was again pirated by a Guinean importer. Once he was informed about it, the owner of *Achoura* travelled to Conakry to get hold of the pirate. The tea, which did not even have any health certificate, was confiscated and the trader sued. If he was not stopped, consumers could be deceived by the similarity of the design, notice the low quality and refuse to buy *Achoura* again or, worse, make its owner responsible for their health problems. The owner of *Achoura* then informed the Chinese government, which closed the factory that produced the counterfeited tea.[10] In principle, customs officials and traders could, if in

6 See Sissoko, 2018.

7 See ndc-info, 2021.

8 For this published case, see OAPI, 2019.

9 Interview with the importer in Bamako in 2016.

10 See Traoré, 2019.

doubt, send the tracking number of the container load to China to inquire from which factory the tea was dispatched for verification, but they generally lacked the knowledge to differentiate between the various package designs. Consumers, too, often illiterate, did not read the brand name but asked for the package with that particular image.

Despite his generous and humble attitude, the owner of *Achoura* was also confronted with the envy of detractors. Someone had discovered packages of *Achoura* tea that contained toxic substances. The laboratory analysis of the *Institut national de recherche en santé publique* (INRSP) confirmed the suspicion in a report that was later published in social media and caused quite a stir. Images were posted that crossed out tea *Achoura* as poisonous. Some authorities even felt empowered to confiscate *Achoura* tea in various rural retail shops. The government became involved and eventually the knowledge spread that the shop from which the samples were taken had placed the tea on containers of pesticides, which contaminated the packages. Moreover, only these few packages of *Achoura* had been analysed from more than a hundred brands on the market. Behind the stir were individuals who intended to bring down the brand value and interrupt the importer's success.[11] The affair dragged on from October 2020 to February 2021 whilst the owner of *Achoura* defended himself against the ongoing social media reports and collected evidence of the background to the matter and commissioned tests from several independent laboratories, including in France, which clarified that the tea was non-toxic. On 4 March 2021, he organised a press conference and his lawyers announced the all-clear for the consumption of *Thé Achoura*. Only this one batch had been found which contained toxic substances.[12] During this complicated time, the owner of *Achoura* relied upon numerous friends in Bamako who continued to support the brand.

Rumours such as these are powerful and can easily destroy the brand value of a tea. Consumers can quickly decide not to purchase the brand again, as the toxic substances are not seen but perhaps tasted. From one day to another, a tea might become unsaleable, as has happened to other once-popular brands. Consumers were very sensitive to changes in taste and quality. It has often happened that a tea at first had good quality, and after some time either the supplier or the importer lowered the quality, and that meant the brand's end. This was especially the case when a tea had become popular and created a surfeit,[13] i. e. when the demand was greater than the supply that producers were able to deliver and subsequently

11 See Malikunafoni, 2021.

12 See Adohoun, 2021.

13 See also Nakassis, 2013.

reduced the quality to solve the problem. In such a context, traders would say: "He [the importer] pirated himself (*il s'est piraté soi-même*)."[14] Amazingly, however, the detractors of *Achoura* had been unable to reduce the brand's value. Its owner defended himself with good arguments in the social and national media and maintained the trust of the consumers. *Achoura* remains to this day (still in 2023) the most popular tea brand in Mali.[15]

5 Themes that Tea Brands Communicate

The survival of *Achoura* was above all due to the agency, trustworthiness, and philanthropic donations of its owner; these were the basis of its brand value. Notwithstanding, a closer look at the meanings that brand designs and names convey will be of interest to understand the working of tea brands. The design of *Achoura* takes a straightforward approach: it is held in red and yellow colours and depicts a Moroccan three-legged teapot next to a glass filled with tea above a sand dune below palm fronds (Fig. 1). The brand name *Achoura* resonates well with Muslim beliefs, as mentioned earlier.

Different from some other tea packages – especially those owned by Chinese importers, which often depict tea plantations, Chinese-style architecture, or landscapes – not much refers to *Achoura's* origin from China. The design rather alludes to the tea's 19th-century provenance via Morocco, similar to many other package designs that depict Tuareg drinking tea in front of tents or camel caravans winding across sand dunes or that have names that refer to trading towns prominent at that time.

Still other brand designs and names have nothing at all to do with the product tea that the packages contain. These are the event-related brands commemorating national and global events that are of concern to Malians, such as the Gaza conflict in the mid-2000s (*Thé Gaza Super*), the creation of the independent television station *Africable* in 2004 (*Thé Africable*), the election of Barack Obama as American

14 See Röschenthaler, 2022.

15 Compare this incident to another example from Mali, in which a cultural entrepreneur lost all his brand value when he was at the height of his career and ready to establish his own independent radio station but – after the 2012 coup – was not granted a licence by the new government. In no time, his large fan community dissolved, the annual concerts based on his radio show could no longer be organised, and he could no longer sell the DVDs of each event or the fabric printed with his image that he had created for his fans to wear at the event. Cf. Röschenthaler, 2016.

president in 2008 (*Thé Obama*), or the fiftieth anniversary of Mali's political independence from France in 2010 (*Thé Cinquantenaire*).[16]

Green tea advertising in the media and on billboards employs a different repertoire. The images displayed on billboards and in commercials focus mostly on the product itself and on individuals enjoying tea. When commissioned by Malians, these adverts do not refer to the Chinese origin of tea. A few have been observed that were commissioned by Chinese brand owners showing, for example, a Chinese woman pouring tea into a bowl, but such images do not resonate well with Malians' ideas of tea consumption. Malians consume green tea in an elaborate ritual that is performed in small groups of friends – never with Chinese people who do not drink the Malian brewed tea – and such scenes are shown in many variations in TV commercials. They present tea as a popular Malian drink, consumed by common Malians who generally associate tea with people from the northern part of the country. From there it arrived on camel back from Morocco across the Sahara. Unlike tea advertisement in Morocco, however, Malian publicity does not employ royal imagery. Traders from northern Mali are credited with having sound knowledge of good tea and being trustworthy tea sellers, whereas Chinese traders are stereotyped as selling cheap products. Selling cheap products has worked well for many commodities, but not for Chinese green tea, a sector that Malian importers were able to defend against their Chinese competitors.

6 Conclusion

The Malian green tea brands are a montage or bricolage of local, global, and regional elements that connect to the experience of local consumers but do not particularly acknowledge the Chinese origin of the product. All their design elements contribute to the value of the brand, but as the owner of *Achoura* ascertained: a tea package can have a beautiful design and a good-sounding name and there can be much advertisement for it in the media, but all these items are not what makes a tea sell. Word of mouth and the recommendation of the traders are decisive in convincing consumers of the good taste of a tea, together with the importer's trustworthiness and an efficient distribution network so that large – but not too large – quantities can be sold without creating a surfeit. All these issues form part of the brand value and need to be managed wisely, requiring what the owner of *Thé Achoura* termed the capacity of "mastering the work of tea."

16 See the tea packages at Röschenthaler, 2021.

Bibliography

Appadurai, Arjun. "Introduction: Commodities and the Politics of Value." In *The Social Life of Things*, edited by Arjun Appadurai, 3–63. Cambridge: Cambridge University Press, 1986.

Applbaum, Kalman. "The Anthropology of Markets." In *A Handbook of Economic Anthropology*, edited by James Carrier, 275–289. Cheltenham: Edward Elgar, 2005.

Adohoun, Cyril. "Mali: Thé Achoura: Aucun danger lié à sa consommation selon les analyses." *Maliactu* 9 April 2021. https://maliactu.net/mali-the-achoura-aucun-danger-lie-a-sa-consommation-selon-les-analyses/. Accessed 14 May 2021.

Fanselow, Frank. "The Bazaar Economy or How Bizarre is the Bazaar Really?" *Man* 25 (2009): 250–265.

Malikunafoni. "Affaire de thé Achoura: Quand le vice de forme se mélange au conflit d'intérêt." *Abamako* 7 March 2021. http://news.abamako.com/h/248585.html. Accessed 14 May 2021.

Nakassis, Constantine. "Brands and Their Surfeits." *Cultural Anthropology* 28.1 (2013): 111–126.

ndc-info. "The Achoura: A Big Cabal Denounced." *Nouvelles du Continent* 9 March 2021. https://ndc-info.com/societe/the-achoura-denonce. Accessed 14 May 2021.

OAPI (Commission Supérieure de Recours auprès de l'OAPI). *Session du 14 au 18 Octobre 2019: Décision no. 008/19/OAPI/CSR.* Yaoundé: Organisation Africaine de la Propriété Intellectuelle, 18 October 2019. http://www.oapi.int/Ressources/Recours2019/octobre_2019/008_19_OAPI_CSR.pdf. Accessed 12 January 2021.

Röschenthaler, Ute. "Aspiring to Be Praised with Many Names: A Media Entrepreneur in Mali." In *Cultural Entrepreneurship in Africa*, 224–244, edited by Ute Röschenthaler and Dorothea Schulz. London: Routledge, 2016.

Röschenthaler, Ute. *Virtual Green Tea Museum.* https://www.virtualgreenteamuseum.de. Accessed 6 September 2021.

Röschenthaler, Ute. *African Agency in China's Tea Trade: Commercial Networks, Brand Creation and Intellectual Property.* Leiden: Brill, 2022.

Sissoko, Mariam. "Promotion de l'excellence dans le secteur des affaires au Mali: L'Agence 'Miroir Media' prime les meilleures entreprises!" *Niarela* 2018. https://niarela.net/societe/promotion-de-lexcellence-dans-le-secteur-des-affaires-au-mali-lagence-miroir-media-prime-les-meilleures-entreprises. Accessed 14 May 2021 (link expired).

Takacs, Wendy E. *Domestic Purchase Requirements for Import Licence Allocations in Mali.* Policy, Research, and External Affairs Working Papers WPS 569. Washington, DC: World Bank, 1991.

Traoré, Moussa. "Contrefaçon du thé Achoura: Accusé, un Opérateur économique guinéen, comparaît ce lundi." *Mosaiqueguinée* 2019. https://mosaiqueguinee.com/contrefacon-du-the-achoura-accuse-un-operateur-economique-guineen-comparait-ce-lundi/. Accessed 14 May 2021.

Nina Salouâ Studer

Selling Alcohol to the Muslims? Making Byrrh a Brand in the Colonial Maghreb

1 Introduction

The French aperitif Byrrh, produced by *Maison J. & S. Violet Frères,*[1] was the most successful of the so-called quinquinas or wines made with quinine bark in France in the late 19th and early 20th century[2] and one of the most popular drinks among French settlers and travellers in the colonial Maghreb.[3] There is no secondary literature on Byrrh in the colonial Maghreb and very little is written about its general history.[4] In addition to the written source material – newspaper articles, travel accounts, and medical recommendations – this chapter will focus on the textual and visual representations of Byrrh in various adverts. This chapter will analyse advertising campaigns propagated by *Maison Violet Frères* between 1880 and 1940 published in francophone North African newspapers, as well as those advertisements that depicted the Maghreb or Maghrebis in France. After a general introduction to its history and its representation as a healthy, "hygienic" drink, this chapter will analyse the brand's references and use of the Maghreb in its advertisements. This chapter thus studies an early instance of branding in North Africa by asking the following questions: How did Byrrh's advertising campaigns develop in the colonial Maghreb? What role did Muslims play in adverts directed towards European settlers? How was the Maghreb portrayed in adverts aimed at consumers in France?

These questions focus on how Byrrh was advertised to the colonisers. French travellers, settlers, and soldiers in the colonial Maghreb knew that Muslims were not allowed to drink alcohol. French accounts usually depicted the consumption of alcohol in the Muslim world through the "one drop" rule: They believed that, according to Islam, one drop of alcohol turned a Muslim into an unbeliever. Yet,

1 In this chapter, the company will be referred to as *Maison Violet Frères.*

2 Cf. Nourrisson, 2013: 123.

3 Reports of European Byrrh consumption can be found in the travel literature on North Africa. See, for example, Eudel, 1909: 44.

4 The book by André Bainville is the most thorough study of the history of Byrrh to date. Cf. Bainville, 2000.

https://doi.org/10.1515/9783110741100-010

Byrrh was also happily consumed by some of the Muslim colonised, even though their Byrrh consumption was not discussed by the majority of French authors and not depicted in advertising campaigns.[5] There were, however, some rare adverts for Byrrh that included Arabic text. The daily newspaper *L'Écho d'Oran*, for example, published in October 1934 an advert for Byrrh that showed a bottle and the French slogan "Quinine stimulates and strengthens." Between the French text and the image of the bottle is a text in Arabic that says: "Drink Byrrh with quinine. Byrrh refreshes the spirit, Byrrh strengthens the body, Byrrh elevates the mind."[6] The conscious choice of publishing this advert with an accompanying text in Arabic seems to be part of an effort to make the drink accessible to the Algerian colonised. Overall, however, the Muslim colonised seem to have been excluded from *Maison Violet Frères*' intended customer base, as they were usually neither addressed nor depicted as customers in their advertising campaigns.

Generally speaking, the interconnections between Byrrh's advertising campaigns and the colonial Maghreb can be divided into three groups. The first consists of adverts aimed specifically at French settlers, focusing on their homesickness and their need to recreate France in the colonies. The second group are those adverts that clearly supported France's colonial mission in the Maghreb, be it through the unstated idea that France's presence enhanced the life of the colonised or through the glorification of the military aspect of French colonialism. The third group of adverts was not aimed at those living in the Maghreb, but at the French in the *Métropole*. These adverts played upon the *wanderlust* of French customers by incorporating stereotypes of North Africa as an Orient that was both exotic and, being within the French realm, safe.

2 Advertising the Healthfulness of Byrrh

In 1860, the brothers Simon and Pallade Violet founded a company, the *Maison Violet*, in the South of France to sell fabrics and wine. In 1873, they registered the brand "Byrrh," a wine with added quinine and a secret mix of ingredients.[7] The name was allegedly chosen randomly, based on labels on fabric samples. The Violets liked it because it sounded like the word for wine ("vi", pronounced "bi") in

5 On the anecdotal Byrrh consumption of Muslims, see Tharaud and Tharaud, 1930: 183.
6 L'Écho d'Oran 23,398, 12 October 1934: 11. All translations into English are by the author. When referencing a specific advert in a newspaper, the details are only in the footnotes. However, the names of the newspapers are listed in the bibliography under the heading "Consulted Newspapers." If Byrrh is mentioned in a newspaper article, the reference is included in the bibliography.
7 Cf. Battini, 2017: 66.

Catalan and also like "beer."[8] From the beginning, the Violets branded Byrrh as hygienic and invigorating.[9] This focus on health was not unique to Byrrh. Until the 1920s, most alcohol adverts portrayed specific drinks as health-fostering and quasi-medicinal.[10] Byrrh's most regularly recurring slogans were "hygienic tonic" and variations thereof,[11] and a glass of Byrrh before each meal[12] was often recommended as a hygienic option for consumers of all ages.[13]

The success of *Maison Violet Frères* was meteoric. Byrrh was soon a very popular aperitif in France. From the very beginning, the skilled and creative use of adverts was central to the success of Byrrh. *Maison Violet Frères* used all new forms of media: posters, wall paintings, adverts on kiosks and trams, postcards, and various little gifts.[14] According to the French historian Stéphane Le Bras, "[T]he first mass advertisements [in France] propagated fashionable aperitifs, chief among them Dubonnet and Byrrh,"[15] which led to a number of aperitif brands dominating urban advertising in France at the end of the 19th century.[16] The popularity of Byrrh continued to rise in the 20th century and decreased only after the Second World War. In 1961, Byrrh was sold to Dubonnet-Cinzano, which in turn was bought by Pernod-Ricard in 1976.

3 Fostering French Homesickness

In addition to this focus on health, *Maison Violet Frères* explicitly framed Byrrh as a drink for the French in the colonies, a drink through which French people could continue a life they were used to in the *Métropole*. Indeed, *Maison Violet Frères* framed Byrrh as a drink particularly well suited to life in the colonies. An advert in *La Dépêche Coloniale Illustrée*, which was published fortnightly, claimed in 1905, "[I]ts real febrifugal properties make it sought after in hot countries, where it becomes a drink of prime usefulness."[17] As its international success grew, *Maison*

---

8 Cf. Battini, 2017: 67.

9 See, for example, Touillier-Feyrabend, 2006: 57; La Revue Marocaine 4, 5 May 1913: 2.

10 Cf. Tsikounas, 2004: 99.

11 Cf. Victor, 1909: 11; Questions Diplomatiques et Coloniales 26,273, July 1908: 846.

12 Cf. Favre, 1889: 131.

13 Cf. Julia, 1908: 12; Victor, 1909: 11.

14 Cf. Nourrisson, 2013: 124; Howard, 2008: 433.

15 Le Bras, 2014.

16 The American historian H. Hazel Hahn, for example, stated in her 2009 book *Scenes of Parisian Modernity* that, in Paris, adverts for several brands – among them Byrrh – were "ubiquitous" from the 1890s onward. Hahn, 2009: 151. See also Howard, 2008: 430.

17 La Dépêche Coloniale Illustrée 14, 31 July 1905: 2.

Violet Frères established agencies in Paris, London, and Buenos Aires[18] and eventually employed agents for Algeria, Tunisia, and Morocco.[19] From the mid-1880s onward, simple adverts for Byrrh can be found in newspapers in Algeria.[20] *Maison Violet Frères* used the same advertising strategies that had been so successful in France. Posters and wall paintings advertised Byrrh in both cities and the countryside. The fortnightly Algerian newspaper *Annales Africaines* even complained about "hideous publicity" by *Maison Violet Frères* in the Algerian countryside in an article published in January 1931: "The French Touring Club Review produced in its January issue several photographs of the curious cliffs of Constantine, on which several huge billboards were displayed. All over Algeria, picturesque sites are damaged by advertising panels. The oases of the South have just recently been particularly infested by *Byrrh* and *Crédit Lyonnais*."[21] *Maison Violet Frères* also used exhibitions in the region to advertise Byrrh; their goal was to introduce the European population, as well as the colonised, to imported French products.[22]

In the images used in newspaper adverts aimed at French settlers, the Maghreb and Maghrebis played almost no role. The many Byrrh adverts in the francophone newspapers of the region showed French people drinking a French product, most of them in a setting that clearly belonged to the *Métropole*. In the mid-1930s, for example, there was a series of adverts in several North African newspapers, which showcased French modernity by reproducing images of how Byrrh was prepared in the South of France. These adverts showed both the idyllic nature of the French countryside that the grapes were grown in[23] and the innovation of the various production processes.[24] The workers[25] and consumers[26] in these adverts were clearly French. One of the final images of this series showed a blonde French woman with a glass of Byrrh with the description: "The pretty perfumed mouth, red from good health and always fresh thanks to BYRRH."[27] Another series of ad-

18 Cf. Gasnier, 2006: part 1, 81.

19 Before the establishment of agencies in North Africa, Byrrh had been sold by general traders. Cf. Le Petit Oranais 9,024, 23 March 1918: 2; L'Écho d'Alger (EA) 2,901, 4 March 1920: 3; Le Petit Marocain (PM) 5,787, 1 February 1936: 5.

20 Cf. Le Petit Colon Algérien 2,260, 21 September 1884: 4.

21 Anonymous (Annales Africaines), 15 January 1933.

22 Cf. Caquel, 2018: 169. Byrrh was, for example, mentioned among the French products exhibited at the Franco-Moroccan Exhibition in Casablanca in 1915 and the General Exposition of Oran in 1930. Cf. Périgny, 1915: 302–303; Anonymous (L'Afrique du Nord Illustrée), 19 April 1930: 11.

23 Cf. EA 9,852, 27 July 1937: 5; PM 6,938, 5 August 1937: 3.

24 Cf. PM 6,710, 6 October 1937: 4; EA 9,927, 10 October 1937: 5.

25 Cf. PM 6,981, 7 September 1937: 4.

26 Cf. EA 10,001, 23 December 1937: 5; PM 6,843, 25 December 1937: 4.

27 PM 6,835, 17 December 1937: 4.

verts placed in North African daily newspapers in the late 1930s showed various French individuals, in European clothes, smiling and describing how they preferred to drink their Byrrh.[28]

There were, however, exceptions to this pattern. Another series of adverts from the mid-1930s showed French people drinking Byrrh at home, in cafés and bars, or in the countryside. In one of them, palm trees and a cityscape with a North African cupola can be seen through the window of an urban home.[29] Another shows two French men sitting on a terrace, drinking Byrrh under a parasol with palm trees in the background. A presumably North African waiter brings them another bottle of Byrrh, while two Muslim men in traditional clothes walk along the terrace in the background.[30] This same series of adverts also mentioned in the accompanying text that Byrrh was now made from grapes from both the South of France and Algeria.[31]

Maison Violet Frères also embraced a "modern" French lifestyle in the colonies and sponsored a variety of social,[32] cultural,[33] and especially sports-related causes.[34] For *Maison Violet Frères*, such contributions had a long tradition, as they had, for example, financed the construction of a hospital in Thuir, the brothers' home city in the *Pyrénées-Orientales*. Byrrh also sponsored a trip of the adventurer Jean de Logivière and his sister – who remained unnamed in the various articles that recounted the journey – through Africa that started in 1935 and ended in Algeria in 1936 and that was framed as an expedition and a pioneering feat.[35] *Maison Violet Frères* saw the efforts of the de Logivières as a boost to French morale[36] and as another way of advertising.[37] The goal of *Maison Violet Frères* was clearly to in-

28 Cf. EA 10,331, 18 November 1938: 6; EA 10,347, 4 December 1938: 6.
29 Cf. EA 9,441, 10 June 1936: 8.
30 Cf. EA 9,584, 21 October 1936: 5.
31 Cf. EA 9,596, 12 November 1936: 7.
32 Cf. Anonymous (PM), 24 January 1939; Anonymous (PM), 14 July 1938.
33 In 1939, for example, they cosponsored a charity ball in Morocco. Cf. Anonymous (PM), 21 March 1939.
34 Anonymous (Echo des Sports du Département de Constantine), 17 October 1934; Anonymous (PM), 11 January 1936.
35 This journey was regularly commented on in North African newspapers and those dedicated to colonial matters. See, for example, Anonymous (La Gazette Coloniale & l'Empire Français), 7 May 1936: 2; Anonymous (Les Annales Coloniales), 30 May 1938.
36 Cf. Anonymous (Les Annales Coloniales), 12 June 1935.
37 The daily newspaper *Le Petit Marocain* openly called the journey of the de Logivières a "one-year propaganda and prospecting trip through Africa, in favour of a number of French products." Anonymous (PM), 18 June 1935.

spire both the colonial and the colonised elements in the countries the de Logivières travelled through to consume French products.

4 Byrrh and Colonialism

While undeniably an advertising campaign, this one-year trip by the de Logivière siblings was also seen as a means of propaganda for France itself. An article in *La Gazette Coloniale*, published in May 1936, for example, reported on the trip and then stated, “We would be neglecting our duty if we did not also congratulate Maison Byrrh, the famous aperitif, which, by equipping the truck, gave the valiant pioneers the means to carry out this fine work of colonial propaganda.”[38] This backing of the de Logivières' trip was, however, not the only way in which *Maison Violet Frères* supported French colonialism. In 1914, the *Imprimerie J. E. Goossens, Paris-Lille-Bruxelles* published a series of military postcards intended for use by French soldiers in the trenches.[39] Many depicted French soldiers successfully fighting the Germans in previous wars and were clearly meant to boost morale.[40] This same postcard series also showed French soldiers in conflict with North Africans during the different colonial wars. All of these postcards set in North Africa show the slogan “Byrrh, recommended tonic and hygienic wine.”[41]

Two of these postcards are marked as showing scenes set in Morocco. The first features armed French soldiers confronted with fleeing, largely unarmed Moroccans, running towards a walled Moroccan city in the background.[42] The other postcard shows a French soldier standing in front of a tent, talking to two sitting Moroccan men. In front of the Moroccan man is an elaborately decorated table, on which stands a bottle of Byrrh and two coffee cups. One of the Moroccan men and the French soldier each hold a glass of Byrrh. Another French soldier can be seen in the background with two horses. Above him is a French aeroplane, behind them a Moroccan walled city and palm trees (Fig. 1). This postcard shows the words “Infanterie” and “Au Maroc.” Two more postcards of this series are clearly set in the Maghreb, though no location is specified. One depicts several armed French soldiers in the distinct uniforms of the *Zouave* infantry regiments. In the

38 Anonymous (La Gazette Coloniale & l'Empire Français), 7 May 1936. *L'Afrique du Nord Illustrée* similarly stated in April 1936 that this effort had been “Good work also for the national propaganda in our colonies and in foreign territories.” Anonymous (L'Afrique du Nord Illustrée), 18 April 1936: 7.

39 Cf. Gasnier, 2006: part 1, 81–82.

40 Cf. Gasnier, 2006: part 1, 83.

41 Indeed, most of the postcards of this series have this slogan. Cf. Gasnier, 2006: part 3, 182–183.

42 Byrrh postcard. Infanterie de Marine. Combat au Maroc. 1914.

Fig. 1: Byrrh postcard. Infanterie. Au Maroc. Imprimerie J. E. Goossens, Paris-Lille-Bruxelles. 1914 Private collection of the author.

background one can see several Muslim men, firing rifles at them. Behind these Muslim men is a walled North African city. The inscription below the image says: "Zouaves" and "L'assaut" (Fig. 2). A fourth postcard shows a French *Zouave* regiment setting up camp in a North African countryside.[43]

The French historian Richard Gasnier suggested in his 2006 dissertation that the "enemy, German or Arab" was often intentionally placed in the background of these images "hardly visible and barely defending himself." These pictures instead depicted French "heroism, vigilance, and discipline,"[44] because they were intended to inspire Frenchmen at the front by reminding them of their past "victories." By showing colonial wars side by side with fights against the current enemy in the First World War, *Maison Violet Frères* implicitly showed support for France's colonial mission.[45]

43 Byrrh postcard. Zouave au campement. 1914.

44 Gasnier, 2006: part 3, 183.

45 Another postcard in this same series shows the colonised in a more positive way, as it depicts colonial troops landing in order to support France in the war against the Germans. Byrrh advert. Débarquement des Troupes Coloniales. 1914.

Fig. 2: Byrrh postcard. Zouaves. L'assaut. Imprimerie J. E. Goossens, Paris-Lille-Bruxelles. 1914 Private collection of the author.

5 Exoticism as a Brand

Finally, there were Byrrh adverts aimed at French consumers in France that used "exotic" Muslim imagery and Orientalist fantasies. This should, however, be seen in the wider context of Byrrh adverts being set against all kinds of historical and geographical backgrounds. *Maison Violet Frères* liked to portray Byrrh as a global drink, and in their various different advertising campaigns almost everyone, from Noah and his sons[46] to polar bears[47] and Santa Claus,[48] was depicted as enjoying Byrrh. The notable exception was people from France's various colonies. France's colonised were usually shown as serving and observing in these adverts, and only very rarely as consumers.[49]

Some adverts used North Africa as a setting without incorporating North Africans. In 1930, for example, the artist René Vincent created an advert for Byrrh showing a European woman sitting on a camel with a glass of Byrrh in her

46 Advert for Byrrh. Georges Léonnec, 1935.
47 Advert for Byrrh. B. de. Beaupre. Postcard, 1906.
48 Advert for Byrrh. Georges Léonnec, 1931.
49 There were, however, some exceptions: compare Fig. 1.

hand. She looks down at a European man, who holds up another glass of Byrrh on a tray. In the background are palm trees and a North African city with a minaret.[50] The Maghreb is depicted as an exotic holiday destination whose enjoyment can be enhanced by Byrrh.

In 1931, the French artist Georges Léonnec created a poster, showing a Maghrebi man in traditional clothes smiling at a European woman while he serves her a glass of Byrrh (Fig. 3). The woman, in European clothes, sits on North African carpets and pillows under a palm tree, a parasol and some roses by her side. According to the French historian Pascal Blanchard, this poster was first shown at the *Exposition coloniale internationale* in the Bois de Vincennes, Paris, between May and November 1931,[51] and should consequently be seen in the specific context of France triumphantly representing its colonial successes. Underneath the picture it says: "Byrrh... with water, Madame, kif kif [i.e. it is the same as] the oasis in the desert."[52] While the encounter is completely innocent, there are traces of an adventure incorporated in the imagery chosen to represent Byrrh.

Fig. 3: Advert for Byrrh. Georges Léonnec, 1931
Private collection of the author.

50 Advert for Byrrh. René Vincent, 1930.

51 Cf. Blanchard, 2011: 295. The advert was also published in a May issue of the weekly newspaper *L'Illustration* in 1931 that featured an article on the exposition.

52 Advert for Byrrh. Georges Léonnec, 1931.

6 Conclusions

This chapter on the colonial history of Byrrh adverts analysed aspects of branding in, with, and from the Maghreb. In their advertising campaigns in and about the Maghreb, *Maison Violet Frères* combined the idea of Byrrh being especially healthy in the colonies, with French settlers longing for life in the *Métropole*, and staunch support for France's colonial mission with titillating exoticism. *Maison Violet Frères* branded Byrrh as French and also as actively pro-French. They also depicted Byrrh as a means of support for French settlers in the colonial Maghreb, whom adverts showed as leading respectable, healthy, and modern lives in the colonies, indistinguishable from life in the *Métropole*. These adverts – aimed at a minority settler society in a predominantly Muslim context – incorporated North African architecture and scenery, but showed Muslims in subservient roles and as non-consumers. Byrrh clearly supported French soldiers in World War I by reminding them with a series of postcards of past victories against the present enemy and against the colonial Other. Finally, Byrrh spoke to the French in the *Métropole* who wanted to travel and see the world, by presenting North Africa in adverts as "the Orient," but safely under French control.

Bibliography

Anonymous. "L'Exposition Générale d'Oran." *L'Afrique du Nord Illustrée* 19 April 1930: 9–12.

Anonymous. "Sus aux enlaidisseurs." *Annales Africaines* 15 January 1933: 29.

Anonymous. "XIe Grand Prix Cycliste de la Ville de Bône." *Echo des Sports du Département de Constantine* 89, 17 October 1934: 6.

Anonymous. "Vers l'Afrique française pendant un an..." *Les Annales Coloniales* 66, 12 June 1935: 2.

Anonymous. "Un car publicitaire Byrrh va parcourir pendant un an 25.000 kilomètres de routes africaines." *Le Petit Marocain* (PM) 5,680, 18 June 1935: 2.

Anonymous. "Grande réunion gymnique et cycliste." *Le Petit Marocain* 5,766, 11 January 1936: 8.

Anonymous. "De la première à la plus récente tournée." *L'Afrique du Nord Illustrée* 781, 18 April 1936: 6–7.

Anonymous. "Raid automobile colonial." *La Gazette Coloniale & l'Empire Français* 248, 7 May 1936: 2.

Anonymous. "Retour de mission en Afrique." *Les Annales Coloniales* 22, 30 May 1938: 5.

Anonymous. "XVIIème Grand Concours de boules du 'Petit Marocain.'" *Le Petit Marocain* 6,874, 14 July 1938: 8.

Anonymous. "Œuvre de Noël des enfants pauvres." *Le Petit Marocain* 5,966, 24 January 1939: 5.

Anonymous. "L'œuvre privée d'assistance sociale 'Le Vestiaire.'" *Le Petit Marocain* 5,721, 21 March 1939: 5.

Bainville, André. *Byrrh: Petite Histoire d'une Grande Marque.* Saint-Rémy-de-Provence: Équinoxe, 2000.

Battini, Jacques. "Les vins médicinaux." *Histoire des Sciences Médicales* 51.1 (2017): 61–70.

Blanchard, Pascal. "Le Maghreb et l'Orient en France: Un siècle de présence dans les expositions et les exhibitions (1849–1937)." In *Zoos humains et exhibitions coloniales: 150 ans d'inventions de l'Autre*, edited by Pascal Blanchard, Nicolas Bancel, Gilles Boëtsch, and Sandrine Lemaire, 285–297. Paris: La Découverte, 2011.

Caquel, Marie. *Transferts culturels et gastronomie: Les relations entre la France et le Maroc de la fin du XIXe siècle jusqu'à nos jours.* PhD thesis, University of Lorraine, Faculty of History, 2018.

Eudel, Paul. *Hivernage en Algérie.* Paris: Evreux, 1909.

Favre, Joseph. *Dictionnaire universel de cuisine et d'hygiène alimentaire.* Vol. 1. Paris: Librairie-Imprimerie des halles et de la bourse de commerce, 1889.

Gasnier, Richard. *Les affiches publicitaires d'alcool: Images et société (1880–1920).* PhD thesis, University Lumière Lyon 2, Faculty of Geography, History, Art History and Tourism, 2006.

Hahn, H. Hazel. *Scenes of Parisian Modernity: Culture and Consumption in the Nineteenth Century.* Basingstoke: Palgrave Macmillan, 2009.

Howard, Sarah. "The Advertising Industry and Alcohol in Interwar France." *The Historical Journal* 51.2 (2008): 421–455.

Julia, Alfred. *Monographie de la ville de Perpignan: Avec un historique de ses vieux monuments.* Perpignan: Imprimerie A. Julia, 1908.

Le Bras, Stéphane. "Vin, littérature de guerre et construction identitaire: Le cas des soldats languedociens pendant la Grande Guerre." *Cahiers du Centre d'histoire* 39–40 (2014). https://journals.openedition.org/siecles/2806. Accessed 24 February 2021.

Nourrisson, Didier. *Crus et cuites: Histoire du buveur.* Paris: Perrin, 2013.

Périgny, Maurice de. "L'exposition franco-marocaine de Casablanca." *Bulletin de la Société de Géographie Commerciale de Paris* 37 (1915): 284–304.

Tharaud, Jérôme, and Jean Tharaud. "Fez ou les bourgeois de l'Islam: IV: Histoire d'Azouaou." *Revue des Deux Mondes* 56.1 (1 March 1930): 170–199.

Touillier-Feyrabend, Henriette. "Le dit sous interdits: L'expression publicitaire et la loi." *Ethnologie Française* 36.1 (2006): 55–63.

Tsikounas, Myriam. "Quand l'alcool fait sa pub: Les publicités en faveur de l'alcool dans la presse française, de la loi Roussel à la loi Évin (1873–1998)." *Le Temps des Médias* 1.2 (2004): 99–114.

Victor, Sébastian. *Traité pratique de la préparation des vins de luxe: Vins de liqueur, vins secs et doux, vins mousseux, vins toniques et apéritifs, vins d'imitation, mistelles, analyse des moûts et des vins.* Paris: Masson et Cie, 1909.

Newspapers Consulted for Adverts

La Dépêche Coloniale Illustrée
La Revue Marocaine
L'Écho d'Alger (EA)
L'Écho d'Oran
Le Petit Colon Algérien
Le Petit Marocain (PM)
Le Petit Oranais
L'Illustration
Questions Diplomatiques et Coloniales

Steffen Wippel

Branding Wine in Morocco: New Efforts to Qualify a Contested Commodity

When I started conducting research on Morocco in the late 1990s, I rarely stumbled across public promotion of wine in the media, and sales outlets in big cities were mostly dark, hidden shops in the city centre or grille-sequestered sections in a corner of the upcoming hypermarkets. The production and consumption of wine – or more generally speaking, of alcohol – are delicate issues in the Middle East and North Africa. While the worldwide expansion and transformation of the wine industry under conditions of globalisation has attracted much academic attention, relatively little has in fact been written on wine growing and production in majoritarian Muslim MENA countries in modern times, except for more historical and religious treatises.[1]

In the Arab world, wine production and exportation considerably declined after the end of colonialism and especially after a certain "re-Islamisation" since the 1970s that tabooed (public) wine consumption even among the more Westernised, well-off strata of the national population. Consequently, alcohol sales were mostly restricted to specially controlled and secured outlets with limited access for Muslims. Wine cultivation also has very often been reduced or almost abandoned, as in the case of Algeria, especially after the ravages of the civil war in the 1990s. Only Lebanese wine still seems to enjoy a certain transregional reputation (with wine from Israel being a special case in the regional context), but in several places winemakers have now started to struggle for better qualities against all odds.

Morocco has long been a major cultivator and producer of wine, one of the most important in the Arab world. But with independence in the late 1950s and the subsequent "Morocconisation" of the economy, many winegrowers, mostly of French origin, left and with them went a large amount of expertise. Winemaking was concentrated in the hands of a few state companies and turned into mass production of limited quality.[2] Branding wine was very present during colonial times, with adverts in many newspapers and journals (at least those in French or other foreign languages or in media abroad), and even in the 1960s and 1970s, adverts for

1 This edited volume includes two other chapters on the branding of alcoholic beverages, one in colonial North Africa and the other in contemporary Lebanon. Cf. Studer and Bonte, in this volume.

2 For the modern history of winegrowing, see El Fasskaoui, 2012.

https://doi.org/10.1515/9783110741100-011

alcoholic drinks could still be found in some intellectual papers.[3] While from a current observer's perspective, these adverts can be considered rather conventional and old-fashioned, this was in line with the wine branding of that time in Europe.

I was astonished when I returned to Morocco in 2013 after an interim of several years doing research in Arab Gulf countries (where access to alcohol was even more limited) to find a relatively conspicuous number of eye-catching, glossy advertisements for wine in some – again mostly Francophone – newspapers and magazines.[4] At the same time, local friends told me that winegrowing had changed over recent years, with more individual, both national and foreign winegrowers emerging again and a growing effort to produce wines of enhanced (and sometimes organic) quality to fulfil the expectations of advanced wine drinkers. The potential of wine tourism in Morocco seems also to have attracted a certain, even if still limited attention.[5] Doing most of my field research in the formerly international and again rapidly globalising northern Moroccan city of Tangier,[6] I was also overwhelmed by a rather ostentatious and widespread presence of shops selling wine – nearly a dozen to be discovered rapidly over a few days in the central parts of the city – whose displays were easily detectible from outside. Nevertheless, I also discovered a concomitant debate in social media on the growing marketing of wine, some asking whether this is licit in a Muslim country, while others countered that "we grow wine, export wine and drink wine" and why not advertise it publicly then – a debate that remains to be further explored. In contrast, the Islamist-led government has increased alcohol taxes again in recent years, yet seemingly without any great effect on consumption. In the course of that, also a certain number of articles has been published for interested connoisseurs on the "new" Moroccan wine and on winegrowers modernising, as well as on the fact that little wine is being exported,[7] but that it is mostly consumed inside the country, which quantitatively could not be done by foreign tourists alone.[8]

---

3 Cf., for instance, adverts "Ambassadeur N° 1 du Terroir Marocain" for *Gris de Boulaouane*, in *Le Monde Diplomatique* March 1970, Supplément "Le Maroc dans la voie du développement et du progrès": 36 and "Le whisky de l'année" for *Vat 69*, in *Lamalif* 30 (May-June 1969): 43.

4 This short piece relies on a few side observations and therefore remains preliminary. Thanks to Birgit Krawietz, FU Berlin, and Christian Steiner, KU Eichstätt, for their helpful hints and critical comments.

5 Cf. Kagermeier, El Fasskaoui and Harms, 2013.

6 Cf., e.g., my chapter in this volume.

7 In fact, the volume of Moroccan wine exports had, with ups and downs, declined considerably from the early 1960s (about 200 million liters per year) to reach its nadir in the mid-1980s (less than 10 million liters), where it has remained since then. However, in value, exports slightly grew again, from less than four to roughly 10 million USD. Cf. UN Comtrade, 2019.

8 On drinking habits, cf. Bonte, 2011; Chaudat, 2020.

Worldwide, over recent decades, branding wine – including winegrowing places and producers – has become a major issue, discussed in professional fora, public media, and academic publications.[9] It is considered of utmost importance in the wine selling process and integrates an era in which an economy (and for some, even an entire society) of singularities has started to dominate.[10] Singularisation of products involves continuous processes of (re-)valorisation and (re-)qualification along the whole value chain to make these wares outstanding, distinguished, and incommensurable. Product branding is an essential part of these processes directed at wholesalers, as well as at final consumers. Regularly, wine, especially of superior quality, is mentioned as a characteristic product for singularisation. It is peculiarly suited to this due to the diversity of grapes and origins, since it symbolises a certain prestige referring to luxury and lifestyle, and because it represents upscale markets where simple price equilibrium between supply and demand is less important than on standard markets for mass products.[11] It becomes clear that wine quality is based not only on intrinsic characteristics that can be improved by enhanced oenological cultivation and processing techniques, but also on its evaluation, comparison, and propagation by many mediating instances and personalities communicating with the target audience across the various hubs of production networks. Conveying narrative, aesthetics, design, and ethical qualities plays a particular role.

As for branding wine in Morocco, adverts there have adapted to a global language of singularising individual brands and presenting them in a hypermodern style far away from the exoticising image setting, more Oriental than Mediterranean, that was common in colonial times and mostly showed palms, casbahs, silhouettes of a medina, including mosques, archways, veiled women, and men on camels and in front of desert dunes.[12] Instead, they follow a global pattern of advertising a relaxing and passionate atmosphere, pointing to the excellence of the high-class product and its cajoling aromas and using a pure, reduced design in labelling and presenting the bottles. To give but a few examples:

- *Le Clos des Vignes*, produced by the private *Celliers de Meknès*, promises "an explosion of aromas," symbolised by a bottle leaping skyward like a rocket surrounded by swirling individual grapes, all held in pure white and red violet colours (Fig. 1a). This bubbling advert confers an image of a leisure drink

9 See, e.g., Beverland, 2006; Harvey, White, and Frost, 2014.

10 Compare Karpik, 2010; Reckwitz, 2017; Callon, Méadel, and Rabeharisoa, 2002.

11 Cf. the studies by Rainer, Kister, and Steiner, 2019; Pütz, Rainer, and Steiner, 2020.

12 Today, the exoticising *Touareg* brand is an exception to the rule, especially as this ethnic group is not really present in Morocco and lives far away from the winegrowing regions in the North.

rather than a premium one and seems to address mainly younger, pleasure-seeking consumers.

- A silhouette of a female face against backlight dominates the *Eclipse* advert. Especially the chin evokes the lunar crescent corresponding to the small logo at the upper margin. On a black background, the white script, logo, and facial outline contrast with the image on the lower right edge of four small, soberly designed bottles of white, rosé, and red wine produced by *Les deux domaines.* This more sensual advertisement asks the connoisseur to merely "close your eyes, let the aromas mount, and live a pure moment of exception." (Fig. 1b)
- A more settled, academic public appears to be in the focus of the new *CB Signature* brand produced by Thalvin. With the ambiguous slogan "Excellence has its Signature," black handwriting written with a pen whose shadow takes the form of a bottle; a filled and labelled black glass bottle on a white ground, the golden nib of the pen, and the lettering on the wine bottle label lend it a touch of luxury (Fig. 1c). The term "signature" plays on its polysemy that also points to meanings such as (the guarantee of) authenticity, character, recognisability, and hallmark.

Fig. 1: Wine adverts in Moroccan newspapers
Sources: Adverts (a) "Le Clos des Vignes." TelQuel 640, 24–30 October 2014: 19; (b) "Eclipse." Les Documents de L'Economiste 9, November 2013; (c) "Thalvin CB." TelQuel 591, 25–31 October 2013.

Hence, while being an age-old wine-growing region,[13] Morocco only recently has turned part of its wine production to better intrinsic qualities and can be considered one of the providers of "new world wines" in a globalised wine industry. To enhance the extrinsically ascribed qualities of its products, wine branding, too, has experienced a new topicality in Morocco. Mostly very different from earlier Orientalising trends, it has adapted to global standards to singularise the new brands and varieties, emphasising their emotional and atmospheric dimensions. To create authenticity, it relies on "style consistency," rather than too much on "heritage."[14] But since large-scale advertisements in public street space and value creation through elegantly designed shop atmospheres do not appear to be permissible, wine branding is still largely limited to a certain range of printed media, apart from virtual space. It thus first endeavours to give Moroccan brand wines more visibility in the local market. It turns to a mostly national cosmopolitan public that continues or rediscovers the pleasures of wine consumption at steep prices, despite tightening societal debates on the admissibility of wine drinking and the upstream stages of growing, producing, and selling wine.

Bibliography

Beverland, Michael. "The 'Real Thing': Branding Authenticity in the Luxury Wine Trade." *Journal of Business Research* 59 (2006): 251–258.

Bonte, Marie. "Ethiques et pratiques éthyliques en milieu urbain marocain." *Confluences Méditerranée* 78.3 (2011): 145–156.

Callon, Michel, Cécile Méadel, and Vololona Rabeharisoa. "The Economy of Qualities." *Economy and Society* 31.2 (2002): 194–217.

Chaudat, Philippe. "Les usages de l'alcool à Meknès (Maroc): Entre interdits, censure et autocensure." *L'Année du Maghreb* 22 (2020): 263–274.

El Fasskaoui, Brahim. "La vitiviniculture marocaine: héritage colonial et situation actuelle." In *L'héritage colonial du Maroc: Actes du 8e colloque maroco-allemand, Bayreuth 2011*, edited by Herbert Popp, and Mohamed Aït Hamza, 117–126. Bayreuth: Naturwissenschaftliche Gesellschaft Bayreuth, 2012.

Kagermeier, Andreas, Brahim El Fasskaoui, and Tim Harms. "Wine Tourism in Morocco? Tentative Approaches, Challenges and Perspectives." In *Wine and Tourism: A Value-added Partnership for Promoting Regional Economic Cycles*, edited by Lena-Marie Lun, Axel Dreyer, Harald Pechlaner, and Günter Schamel, 115-130. Bolzano: Europäische Akademie, 2013.

Karpik, Lucien. *Valuing the Unique: The Economics of Singularities.* Princeton: University Press, 2010.

13 The main winegrowing areas in Morocco are the moderately temperate Saïss plain around Meknès, the Oriental region, and the Rabat hinterland.

14 Compare Beverland, 2006.

Pütz, Robert, Gerhard Rainer, and Christian Steiner. “Vom Lagenwein zum off-shore brand: Qualifizierung und Raumproduktion in globalen Produktionsnetzwerken.” In *Waren–Wissen–Raum: Interdependenz von Produktion, Markt und Konsum in Lebensmittelwarenketten*, edited by Nina Baur, Julia Fülling, Linda Hering, and Elmar Kulke, 217–257. Wiesbaden: Springer VS, 2020.

Rainer, Gerhard, Jutta Kister, and Christian Steiner. “Qualifizierungsstrategien in regionalen Restrukturierungsprozessen: Die Neuerfindung Südtirols in einem globalisierten Weinmarkt.” *Geographische Zeitschrift* 107.2 (2019): 130–156.

Reckwitz, Andreas. *Die Gesellschaft der Singularitäten: Zum Strukturwandel der Moderne.* Berlin: Suhrkamp, 2017.

UN Comtrade. *Database.* https://comtrade.un.org/data. Accessed 18 July 2019.

Printed Newspapers and Magazines Consulted for Adverts

Lamalif
Le Monde Diplomatique
Les Documents de L’Economiste
TelQuel

Marie Bonte

From City to Society: Alcohol Advertising in Lebanon

1 Enhancing the City

"Beirut is getting on the international map when it comes to alcohol." According to this bar manager, who gave me an interview in 2015,[1] the capital city of Lebanon does drink, and the country is part of globalised trade networks of alcoholic beverages. Although a part of the population disapproves of it because of religious or moral standards, alcohol trade and consumption are legal in Lebanon. Alcohol can be produced locally, like arak, wine, some beers – and recently also some spirits – or imported and then will be taxed at a low rate. Alcohol is also widely (though not uniformly) available and visible: in bars, clubs, and restaurants, and also in advertising. Brands or alcohol suppliers take advantage of weak regulation on the location of billboards and alcohol advertising. For instance, they are not required to advise moderate drinking. However, in Lebanon, as anywhere else, alcohol advertising cannot be compared to ads for other consumer goods. The message is often distanced from the substance itself, thus avoiding the issue of its toxicity, to underline its positive meanings: pleasure, fun, and conviviality. The difference between various alcohol products is therefore based on their marketing and the narratives connected to their brands.[2] These are meant to create an attachment to the brand, but in Beirut, it is the attachment to the city, or more precisely to a certain version of it, that is used as a leitmotiv.

The Absolut Beirut advertising illustrates this (Fig. 1). The poster, created in 2005, is another variation of the "Absolut Metropolis" campaign. In this campaign, the famous Swedish vodka brand combines its name and the shape of its bottle with a wide range of urban settings, to catch the spirit of different cities: a Parisian metro entrance, the Brooklyn Bridge, etc. Here, the bottle appears between dancing bodies. Instead of monuments or architectural features, this advertisement shows a select club with white benches, golden heels, shiny legs, light dresses, and fancy pants. It draws on the most valuable thing Beirut has to offer: its nightlife. If the picture defeats Orientalist assumptions, it simultaneously fosters narratives about the city's exceptionality, which itself is a source of inspiration for the

1 Interview conducted in March 2015 in Beirut.
2 Cf. Chrzan, 2013.

https://doi.org/10.1515/9783110741100-012

Fig. 1: The Absolut Beirut advertising
Source: Absolut, 2013.

advertising creation. This cliché therefore associates Beirut with its nightclubs. Alcohol is not only featured as a model for social relationship, success, and lifestyle, but also emerges as a tool for branding the city. Built on exchanges, circulations, diversity, and individual freedoms, the picture claims that Beirut is different from other cities in the Middle East. Just look at its nights: the luxury, the glitz, and the glamour are co-extensive with the liquor referred to – and with the drinkers, who are also the Lebanese party people.

The myth of the "city that never sleeps" is taken up by the whisky brand Ballantine's, which in 2015 released the "Beirut edition" bottle.[3] The promotional text emphasises the city's contradictions (between tradition and modernity, between old and new), sophistication, and diversity, which reflect the complexity of the whisky blend's flavours. On the bottle, it is once again Beirut in its most attractive expression: an aerial view, by night. The coastline is clearly recognisable, while the scars seem to have disappeared in the darkness. The city is thus sublimated, but from the top. Conversely, the bottle "Li Beirut"[4] of Three Brothers gin, released in 2021, focuses on a small part of town, the northern hillside of Achrafieh (Fig. 2). The area can be identified by its staircases and colourful buildings, some of which still preserve the neo-Levantine style. This panorama is more authentic

3 Cf. Ballantine's LB, 2021.

4 "Li Beirut" translates to "to Beirut" and works as a tribute to the city, as well as referring to Fairuz's famous song released in 1984.

and intimate and also refers to a different type of nightlife that moves away from the select clubs to more "friendly" and down-to-earth bars and pubs. The latter are found extensively in the neighbourhood.

Fig. 2: The "Li Beirut" Bottle of the Three Brothers gin brand
Source: Maalouf, 2021. Courtesy of the designer.

2 From City to National Branding

In Lebanon, partly due to the small size of the country, alcohol advertising can easily be national in scope. Ads refer to cultural, historical, or social elements of unity, such as the celebration of independence, Mother's Day, or the Lebanese army. In her work on Turkey, Sylvie Gangloff shows how, in the social spheres that drink alcohol (upper and urban classes, intellectuals, often on the left of the political spectrum), people associate it with a particular nationalism, which promotes domestic production (*Rakı*, Turkish beer, and wine) and a modern, open, and cosmopolitan image of Turkey.[5] Partly shaped by advertising, representations of alcohol in Lebanon also contribute to spreading a positive and "modern" image of the country by expressing differentiation from neighbouring countries or challenging the idea of a constantly war-torn state. In this regard, the evocation of

5 Cf. Gangloff, 2015 and 2021.

so-called Lebanese resilience to conflicts and instability has been at the core of the various advertising campaigns carried out for the Johnnie Walker brand, which belongs to the global alcohol producer giant Diageo.

The campaign started in 2006, in the aftermath of the July War, when the Leo Burnett Company designed and displayed a huge poster on the northern highway that exits Beirut.[6] On this billboard, the war is represented by its material consequences: a bridge is damaged. The famous shape of the walking man is accompanied by the usual message, "keep walking." However, this is not an ordinary advertisement of a spirit brand. It shows the need for the people to move forward despite the losses and destruction caused by the conflict. And it is precisely the consumption of alcohol – and more broadly, celebration and parties – that best ensures this continuity. Finally, drinking whisky becomes more or less a patriotic act, because it is raised to a stance: not being disturbed by foreign aggression. In a way, the self-branding processes usually at work in alcohol adverts are shifting. This whisky is no longer a question of being friendly or having taste, but rather of agreeing with a specific meaning that is attributed to a population and a territory. In this poster, Johnnie Walker made alcohol a tool for national branding that emphasises resilience. During an interview, a member of the Leo Burnett Company explained how these whisky campaigns are addressed not only to drinkers, but to all Lebanese people: "We had a succession of campaigns that made the brand, and brought the Lebanese and the brand closer: they believe in their resilience and their capacity to progress in this country (...). So we told a story (...)."[7]

3 Tackling Social and Political Issues

Alcohol advertising is not only used as a tool for national branding, it can also be involved in the demands of civil society, as shown by the "Absolut Civil Love" campaign run by the Swedish brand (Fig. 3). Initiated in 2018, this campaign addresses a civic issue and directly tackles the Lebanese law that prohibits interfaith marriages.[8] This campaign started with statements on billboards, social media, and radios. The message "We declare civil love" was intended to support ethnically and religiously mixed unions, as well as same-sex couples. Several billboards combined the iconic shape of the vodka bottle with the caption. Using the lexicon of love and

---

6 Cf. Pfanner, 2006, including a picture of the billboard.

7 Interview conducted in April 2018 in Beirut. Translation by the author.

8 In Lebanon, the only legal form of marriage is religious. However, civil marriages (between different communities or not) that have been held abroad are officially accepted.

tolerance, the brand went along with the claims of civil society. The brand then created the Civil Love Boat, able to navigate off the coast and the territorial waters, where national Lebanese legislation no longer applies. After the first interdenominational wedding was celebrated, a video[9] displayed the couple's union and the party on the boat. One could see guests drinking the world-renowned vodka, commonly available in Beirut's nightlife venues. The comments accompanying the clip explained how civil marriage could eradicate the legacies of the Lebanese Civil War (1975–1990) and that clashes between religious communities should be replaced by unions. By doing this, the campaign was able to provide an alternative for couples to marrying abroad by giving them the opportunity to marry each other close to their home country.

Fig. 3: Absolut Civil Love
Source: Alghossein and Francis, 2018b.

This unusual marketing may be viewed as intrusive, considering the political and social issues relating to civil marriage in Lebanon. But this campaign and the others show that in Lebanon, alcohol ads are not made only to expand market share or convert abstinent people. They rather enhance the reputation of a (partly) disapproved product by highlighting its pacifying and hedonistic virtues, relying on attachment to Beirut or the whole country. They tell stories, and restyle clichés.

9 Cf. Alghossein and Francis, 2018a.

Bibliography

Absolut. "Absolut Beirut." http://absolutads.com/gallery/reklama.php?id=1157&lang=en. Accessed 9 September 2021.

Alghossein, Mo, and Jimmy Francis. "Absolut Civil Love." *YouTube* 11 October 2018(a). https://www.youtube.com/watch?v=rpPvHsYw-gw. Accessed 9 September 2021.

Alghossein, Mo, and Jimmy Francis. "Absolut – Civil Love." https://www.civillove.com. Accessed 22 November 2018(b) (link expired).

Ballantine's LB. "Beirut Edition." https://stage-www.ballantines.com/en-LB/products/ballantines-beirut-edition. Accessed 9 September 2021.

Chrzan, Janet. *Alcohol: Social Drinking in Cultural Context.* New York: Routledge, 2013.

Gangloff, Sylvie. *Boire en Turquie: Pratiques et représentations de l'alcool.* Paris: Editions de la Maison des Sciences de l'Homme, 2015.

Gangloff, Sylvie. "Drinking in Turkey: From Social Coexistence to Ideological Confrontation." In *Alcohol in the Maghreb and the Middle East since the Nineteenth Century: Disputes, Policies and Practices*, edited by Philippe Bourmaud and Elife Biçer-Deveci, 135–159. Oxford: Palgrave Macmillan, 2021.

Maalouf, Tony. "Beirut." *Instagram* 13 November 2021. https://www.instagram.com/p/CWNZspPM1 L1/. Accessed 12 December 2021.

Pfanner, Eric. A Brash Message to a Wounded Country. *The New York Times* 4 September 2006. https://www.nytimes.com/2006/09/04/business/media/04walker.html. Limited access. Accessed 21 January 2022.

Alina Kokoschka

False Fakes, Fictitious Fashion, and the Liberation of Logos: On the Islamisation of International Brands

1 Framework

Counterfeit products – imitations of existing branded commodities – are being distributed on a new level globally.[1] The Middle East is one of the hotspots for counterfeit items, especially in the field of fashion. The aim of this article is to shed light on a special phenomenon amongst fake products: commodities that carry a widely known brand logo but do not aim to imitate the original. This does not involve badly made copies but rather made-up branded commodities: "fictitious fakes." How are we to read these goods, which do not alter the logos on them to avoid legal penalty, but switch the underlying material, the commodity itself?

The topic of counterfeiting is usually examined from a legal point of view, or indeed from an ethical angle that already implies looking at – and judging – matters from the brand holder's perspective.[2] This essay does not engage with this kind of reasoning, as it contributes little to our understanding of the life that brands and their logos lead in a local context. My approach here is phenomenological at the outset and committed to aesthetic questions in the analysis. Since literature on contemporary aesthetic phenomena in Muslim cultures and societies is scarce, literature from the field of commodity aesthetics, established by the German philosopher Wolfgang Fritz Haug, has proven more than helpful.[3] The descriptive and analytic account presented here is based on empirical material – objects, photos, and video documentation of commercial settings, shop windows, advertisements, and commodities in use, enriched by structured interviews – that was gathered in multiple research situations between 2005 and 2017 across the Middle East. I focus particularly on Syria and Lebanon, as I am most familiar

1 See Davidson, Nepomuceno, and Laroche, 2017: 479.

2 For example, Davidson, Nepomuceno, and Laroche, 2017; Beebe, Haochen, and Madhavi, 2015; Chaudhry and Zimmerman, 2009. This focus is challenged by ethnographic work on the topic. Magdalena Craciun, 2008: 8 cites a Turkish *imitasyoncu* (the one whose work it is to imitate): "Isn't it a crime to sell what cost you 2 euros for 40 euros? Or is it a crime to sell it for 3 euros?"

3 Cf. Kokoschka, 2019: 78–102.

https://doi.org/10.1515/9783110741100-013

with their commodity world.[4] Observations from German cities with a strong Arab community, rooted mainly in those two countries, enrich the material beyond research trip opportunities. Space considerations preclude a comparative overview, as does my aim of highlighting the bigger picture of a phenomenon that is generally neglected.

2 Apparently Legal Apparel

No matter whether the outlet is a proper shop, an official market, or an illegal street stand, fake branded goods are on sale throughout the Middle East. But the starting point of this article is not the manifold imitations of high-priced commodities that want to prove their originality by using a visible logo. I set out to draw attention to a very special phenomenon that appears in the brandscape of Muslim cultures and societies within the framework of Islamisation: "fictitious fakes." These are fashion items that are branded with a known logo, accurately reproduced, but applied to a material that does not belong to the repertoire of the brand cited. This is in contrast to fakes that show a slightly altered known logo applied to an item that the brand does produce, with the intention to look as much like the original as possible (Fig. 1). So, to explore the phenomenon of fictitious fakes, first a word is necessary on brands in the region, their "normal" imitations, and the logic of logos.

After long decades of restrictions in and boycotts on Syria, some international brands became available in the course of economic openings (*infitāḥ*), especially after 2001. As a result of legal amendments relating to foreign investments and imports, they found their place within a vibrant brandscape consisting of local Syrian, Arab, and Chinese branded products. Along with the new brands came new aesthetics in fashion and shopping environments.[5] Still, the range of original international brands on display in Syria remained limited. While in the first decade of Bashar al-Assad's reign (2001–2011) the selection was restricted to a few

4 For Syria, I will need to report in the past tense since with the beginning of the uprising and subsequent war in 2011, my research there was put on hold. I do not have enough information about the extent to which certain segments of the market are still operating despite the ongoing war. Moreover, the ever-increasing social inequality in the country has most likely changed the brands' significance. Personal reports suggest that there is growing conspicuous consumption amongst the few rich.

5 On local Syrian brands and the variety of shopping environments, see Kokoschka, 2019: ch. 5. Leïla Vignal, 2006 was among the first to analyse the new patterns of consumption after the economic opening.

Fig. 1: "Elvis" Jeans as an imitation of Levi's Jeans, Beirut
Photo: Alina Kokoschka, 2017.

landmark brands that were meant to signal the openness of the new Syria under Hafiz al-Assad's son, few to no limitations in brand availability can be noted for Lebanon. Shopping areas like the rebuilt downtown area of Beirut and the numerous malls that attract tourists from across the Muslim world are accompanied by large-scale advertising with enormous visibility in public space. However, Syrians could also be considered familiar with the brands not available in their own country. Satellite TV has contributed to widespread brand knowledge, as have easy travelling conditions between Syria and Lebanon and the many Syrians living in Europe and North America.[6]

Despite the extreme differences between officially socialist Syria and purely capitalist Lebanon, both countries share an exclusive scene for fake branded goods. These fakes, which are by no means considered "shameful,"[7] are sold not only out of car boots or under the counter, but also in stores along main shopping

6 On logo recognition in the Middle East, see Graf, 2013.

7 Davidson, Nepomuceno, and Laroche, 2017, use shame as an important category in the analysis of fake consumption.

streets such as the famous Hamra in Beirut, where "real" brand stores can also be found. On the one hand, this indicates ignorance of international trade-related property rights agreements; on the other, it demonstrates people's appreciation of branded commodities despite their lack of authenticity. Notwithstanding their seemingly lower value in practices of social distinction, fake branded commodities function as objects that open *a*, if not *the* world, and indeed, one without nation-state borders, travel restrictions, or visa requirements.

In the Middle Eastern countries I have done research on so far, the phenomenon of fake branded commodities emerges particularly in the world of fashion.[8] This is also the case in Syria and Lebanon. Some pieces in the field of clothing and accessories are copied more often than others. These are items that frequently have big logos as a design element, namely sweatshirts, T-shirts, trousers, bags, and shoes. It is these items that also emerge as fictitious fakes.

3 Logo Inflation

In order to understand fake culture in the Middle East, we must first acknowledge that logos and the brands they represent are not treated mainly as originals that need to be protected in order to preserve their value – neither legally and politically, nor by broad sections of consumer society. Brand awareness is strong, and the attitude towards brands is enthusiastic, yet the logic of value stability or even increase based on limited supply does not work. Usually, brands function in the same way as currencies: the fewer the items, the more valuable they are; duplication leads to devaluation. This is not the case in the Middle East.

The reasons for this cannot be discussed in detail here; they still await an analysis as deep as Byung-Chul Han's philosophical analysis of Chinese copying practices.[9] The Berlin based South Korean philosopher sheds light on Western societies' and China's extreme differences in the understanding of the original work of art and then arrives at an explanation for different modes of copying in China. One of them is *shanzai*, which denotes fakes that become "new originals." If we look at these new originals, or the "fictitious fakes" in the Middle East, one factor might be the minor role played by authorship in "Islamic Art." The notion of authorship – and with it the Western idea of an original that must not be copied unless the copy is identical *and* marked as a copy – is not well established outside Western

8 In my estimation, it is a matter of the means of production. In the region, manufacturing textiles has a tradition and, especially in Syria, industrial structures were available. This is not the case with other brand sectors like electronics.

9 Cf. Han, 2017.

art history. Second, we need to acknowledge that logo and commodity are often treated separately. Independent of the commodity itself, logos are transferable to other visual and material contexts. There, they might even appear in a mixture with other symbols or logos. As they are even on sale as badges, they can be easily applied to any new background.

It is important to notice that this phenomenon of giving logos new contexts differs from the trend that was prevalent in Western countries in the 1990s, which involved editing logos and using them on no-name T-shirts and sweatshirts. This decade's notorious brand obsession allied itself with new digital resources for image and graphic editing. Thus, "Adidas" became "Adihash", while "Ford" became a swear word. This was meant to express criticism of capitalism and consumerism and found its accompanying treatise in Naomi Klein's *No Logo.*[10] In the case under discussion here, possible criticism does not target capitalist society. Instead, it pursues a do-it-yourself market opening – one that enables the inclusion of Muslims milieus and ideas of lifestyle that were not represented before.[11]

4 The Value of Fiction or Fictitious Fakes in an Islamic Context

Brands have developed increasingly dense and polished narratives to sharpen their identity. The media theorist and art historian Wolfgang Ullrich draws a parallel between the type of fiction that novels or films use and fiction that is narrated around certain brands and their commodities.[12] This brand fiction comes with a range of emotional promises that mirror consumers' hopes and aspirations. Ullrich has been criticised for his prognosis that one day the fictional aspect of commodities might be valued as highly as that of literature and the like. Yet, his term "fiction value" has proven useful. It describes the narratives that are constructed by brands as a value in addition to the commodity's "use value."[13] Ullrich states

10 Cf. Klein, 1999.

11 Nevertheless, in Lebanon a small urban milieu engages politically with brands and their political impact on the region, as can be seen in graffiti in Beirut. In a rare case, a Western logo, the Nike "swoosh," even took on a second life as a logo for a Muslim organisation propagating a Muslim lifestyle based on the practice of quantifiable good deeds (*ḥasanāt*). The group's name "Ghaier" (change) was sprayed on Beirut walls around 2012, see Kokoschka, 2019: 173–175. Ghaier's website is no longer available.

12 Cf. Ullrich, 2011: 114–116.

13 This can be defined as a good's usefulness in satisfying individual or societal requirement, want, or need.

that commodities attain fictional value only in affluent societies. Once we look at the examples below, it becomes clear that commodities can also be accorded a fictional value in societies that are anything but affluent. The only difference is that it is the consumers and local producers that come up with the fiction, not the original brand.

While fake fashion's attempts to create perfect reproductions is known to consumers across the globe, it is less widely acknowledged that the logos of international brands find a new story to be told about them in local settings. Here, two instances will be discussed. First, the combination of logos with symbols from a context that is alien to the brand. Second, the application of the logo to an unknown material. In both examples, "symbolically dense" brands[14] play a major role.

4.1 French Crescent? The Case of Coco Chanel

The French *haute couture* brand Coco Chanel uses its two identical initials as the basis of its logo. The letters are intertwined, one "C" mirroring and facing the other. Among logos that have developed a life of their own in the Middle East, this is one of the most popular. As a "liberated logo" – one that has been detached from its initial (material) context and developed its own "biography" – it appears in new symbolic surroundings.[15]

In contrast to the Nike logo, which has become a political symbol in different contexts and has thus been sprayed on walls along with political claims, the double C does not leave the realm of fashion accessories. Still, it appears in surprising places. Sometimes it is used as a decorative element on its own, blown up to many times its usual size and embellished with gold and glitter. This is based on the contemporary fashion of Islamic symbols that are on sale for home decoration. And indeed, Chanel and the *Qur'ān* or the name of the Prophet are on sale as decorative items in the same shops, in the same manner, from Beirut and Istanbul to Berlin (Fig. 2 and 3). This makes an interesting yet initially puzzling find. However, the CC's more frequent use as one element in an agglomeration of symbols explains how it has been able to develop an independent standing in the realm of contemporary Islamic symbols.

14 Kravets and Örge, 2010: 205.

15 Igor Kopytoff's assertion of a "biography of things" can be fruitfully expanded to logos, cf. Kopytoff, 1986.

Fig. 2 (left): Illuminated Qur'an, Berlin, Sonnenallee
Fig. 3 (right): Illuminated Chanel Logo, Berlin, Sonnenallee
Photos: Alina Kokoschka, 2021.

The Chanel double-C is frequently combined with a central Islamic symbol: the crescent (*al-hilāl*). The crescent embellishes minarets across the world and is therefore one of the most distinctive signs of Islam.[16] The sickle moon defines many aspects of Muslim life, such as the beginning and end of the fasting month of *Ramaḍān*. Since the 12th century AD, it has also been in use as a symbol on jewellery.[17] A necklace that combines the crescent and the Chanel C is thus not an unpredictable new context for the Chanel logo, since the C picks up on the crescent's semi-circular curve. What makes the two symbols enrich each other then? Most obviously it is the very similar shape of the crescent that makes it attractive. Then, mirroring similar to the one seen in the logo is a Sufi practice and can be found in calligraphy as well as in Sufi jewellery,[18] though it is usually letters that are mirrored, not image symbols like the crescent. Last, if we follow art historian Jale Nejdet Erzen's words that in Sufi Islam "it is through symbols that one

16 Cf. Kadoi, 2014.
17 Cf. Schacht and Ettinghausen, 2012.
18 On the relation between mirrored calligraphies and mathematics, see Beinhauer-Köhler, 2011: 40.

is awakened; it is through symbols that one is transformed; and it is through symbols that one is expressive,"[19] then wearing a *haute couture* logo can be considered not only a means of religious expression through a publicly visible symbol, but even a spiritual tool.

The example shows how international brand logos interact with Islamic symbols. The new alignment produces two changes. First, the logo becomes Islamically modified. A new, religious dimension of meaning is added to the brand narrative. At least in the context of Muslim cultures and societies, this increases the brand's fictional value. What cannot be estimated at this point is the extent to which the Islamically modified fictional value implies a loss of value in local Christian contexts, for example. Second, the Islamic symbol of the crescent is slightly modified. Usually, it makes an appearance on its own. Here, in terms of its aesthetic treatment, the image symbol of the crescent moves closer to mirrored Sufi letter symbols. The religiously marked crescent and the Latin C converge.

4.2 Islamic Garments Meet French *Haute Couture*

Many countries in the Middle East have developed a designer scene that focuses on Islamic fashion or produces garments that meet the demands of Muslim wearers. With respect to the potential for social distinction, these brands have long achieved value equal to that of international brands.[20] In pre-war Syria, no such scene had emerged. Non-branded yet fashionable Islamic attire and scarfs were on sale in great variety, but none of them came with an original brand logo.[21] Then, all of a sudden, shop windows were hung with *ʿabāyas* that seemed to be designed by French *haute couture* companies (Fig. 4).[22] Huge glittery Pierre Cardin and Christian Dior logos made women look modest and yet cosmopolitan, well versed in high fashion. Price, finish, and design made it clear that these items could not have been original brand items. Still, they were bought and worn – the logo read as a material quotation from the "text" of international *haute cou-*

---

19 Cf. Erzen, 2007: 71.

20 Like "Aker" or "Hermine" in Turkish *tesettür* fashion. In view of "infidel brands," the local brands' distinctive value might even be higher; compare Izberk-Bilgin, 2012: 685.

21 A case in point here is the Syrian company *Shukr*, whose target group was unambiguously Muslim. The items were distinguished, though, by their renunciation of any form of embellishment, including logos.

22 An *ʿabāʾa* (colloquial Arabic *ʿabāya*) is a wide, ankle-length women's gown, usually black. It has found its way into Syrian Islamic fashion from the Gulf region.

ture. In Lebanon, similar logos were on sale separately and allowed for a do-it-yourself fictitious fake (Fig. 5).

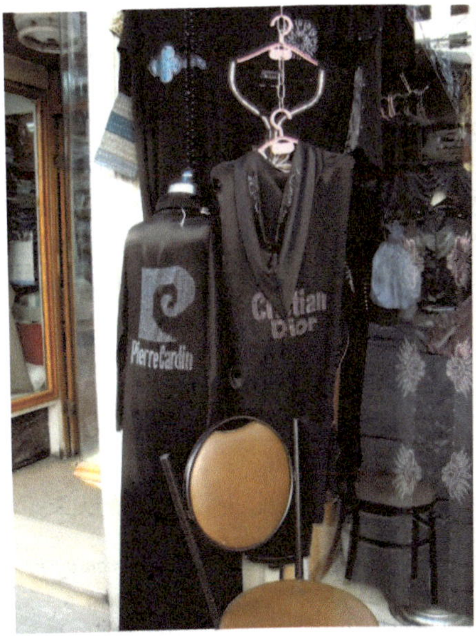

Fig. 4 (left): Abayas branded with Dior and Cardin logos, Damascus
Fig. 5 (right): Coco Chanel logo on sale, Beirut
Photos: Alina Kokoschka, 2009 and 2017.

In the case of *ʿabāya* and headscarf, it is not an Islamic symbol that adds an Islamic touch to the brand. It is the material item the logo is applied to. The fictitious *haute couture* fashion opens up the possibility that great designers will one day design Islamic fashion and that Islamic garments can become part of a Muslim cosmopolitan lifestyle in Syria or Lebanon. And that is a characteristic of fiction: it has the power to construct desired ideals and possibilities, sometimes even utopias.

5 Have "Faith in Fakes"

In contemporary utopias, "the present is now seen not as a reality that has to be destroyed and replaced by a totally different society, but as a time-space from which we need to depart."[23] Fictitious fakes offer a possibility for that departure

23 Vieira, 2010: 22.

– regardless of whether people have "faith in fakes"[24] and their transformative power or if these slightly anarchic items subtly alter images of Islam by reason of their sheer existence. Just like original branded items, they are a tool for shaping utopias from what there is. In Syria and Lebanon, they play an important part in the overall narrative of a better, more prosperous Muslim society to come – contrasting with lasting harsh political and economic realities. With these made-up brand items, the market is opened up to local consumers' own authority. It is receptive to the inclusion of affluence and beauty as portrayed in the media and exemplified by the upper-class areas of Syria and Lebanon. The fictional value of these seemingly false fakes is that of an Islamic lifestyle that has it all, even French *haute couture* and possible appearances on the catwalk. Fiction allows for the playful. It does not have to be real.

Bibliography

Beinhauer-Köhler, Bärbel. *Gelenkte Blicke: Visuelle Kulturen im Islam.* Zurich: Theologischer Verlag, 2011.

Chaudhry, Peggy, and Alan Zimmerman. *The Economics of Counterfeit Trade: Governments, Consumers, Pirates and Intellectual Property Rights.* Berlin: Springer, 2009.

Craciun, Magdalena. "Researching Fakes: Practising Anthropology Out of the Corner of One's Eye." In *Anthropology Matters* 10 (2008): 1–11. https://www.anthropologymatters.com/index.php/anth_matters/article/download/32/56?inline=1 Accessed 27 October 2021.

Davidson, Alexander, Marcelo Vinhal Nepomuceno, and Michel Laroche. "Shame on You: When Materialism Leads to Purchase Intentions Toward Counterfeit Products." *Journal of Business Ethics* 155.2 (2017): 479–494.

Erzen, Jale Nejdet. "Aesthetics: An Alternative Way to Knowledge." *The Journal of Aesthetics and Art Criticism* 65.1 (2007): 69–75.

Eco, Umberto. *Faith in Fakes: Travels in Hyperreality.* London: Vintage, 1995.

Graf, Andreas. *Transkulturelle Bildkommunikation: Die Wahrnehmung westlicher Firmenlogos im Nahen Osten.* Marburg: Tectum, 2013.

Han, Byung-Chul. *Shanzhai: Deconstruction in Chinese.* London: The MIT Press, 2017.

Izberk-Bilgin, Elif. "Infidel Brands: Unveiling Alternative Meanings of Global Brands at the Nexus of Globalization, Consumer Culture, and Islamism." *Journal of Consumer Research* 39 (2012): 663–687.

Kadoi, Yuka, "Crescent (Symbol of Islam)." In *Encyclopaedia of Islam: THREE (Online)*, edited by Kate Fleet, Gudrun Krämer, Denis Matringe, John Nawas, and Everett Rowson. Leiden: Brill, 3rd ed., 2014. doi:10.1163/1573-3912_ei3_COM_25588.

Klein, Naomi. *No Logo: Taking Aim at the Brand Bullies.* Toronto: Knopf, 1999.

24 I borrow Eco's title from 1995.

Kokoschka, Alina. *Waren Welt Islam: Konsumkultur und Warenästhetik in Syrien 2001–2011.* Berlin: Kadmos, 2019.

Kopytoff, Igor. "The Cultural Biography of Things." In *The Social Life of Things: Commodities in Cultural Perspective*, edited by Arjun Appadurai, 64–94. New York: Cambridge University Press, 1986.

Kravets, Olga and Örsan Örge. "Iconic Brands: A Socio-Material Story." *Journal of Material Culture* 15 (2010): 205–232.

Schacht, J., and R. Ettinghausen. "Hilāl", In *Encyclopaedia of Islam: Second Edition*, edited by P. Bearman, T. Bianquis, C.E. Bosworth, E. van Donzel, and W.P. Heinrichs. Leiden: Brill, 2012. doi:10.1163/1573-3912_islam_COM_0286.

Sun, Haochen, Barton Beebe, and Madhavi Sunder (eds.). *The Luxury Economy and Intellectual Property: Critical Reflections.* New York: Oxford University Press, 2015.

Ullrich, Wolfgang. "Philosophen haben die Welt immer nur verschieden interpretiert – verändern Produktdesigner sie auch?" In *Warenästhetik: Neue Perspektiven auf Konsum, Kultur und Kunst*, edited by Heinz Drügh, Christian Metz, and Björn Weyand, 111–118. Berlin: Suhrkamp, 2011.

Viera, Fátima. "The Concept of Utopia." In *The Cambridge Companion to Utopian Literature*, edited by Gregory Claeys, 3–27. Cambridge: Cambridge University Press, 2010.

Vignal, Leïla. "La 'nouvelle consommation' et les transformations des paysages urbains à la lumière de l'ouverture économique: L'exemple de Damas." *Revue du Monde Musulman et de la Méditerranée* 115–116 (2006): 21–41.

Sophie-Therese Trenka-Dalton

Dubai Gold and Diamonds: Tracing Dubai's Influence on the South Indian State of Kerala

With the Arabian Peninsula's oil boom, the United Arab Emirates became a key destination for labour migration from the South Indian state of Kerala from the 1970s onwards. Today, Keralites are one of the largest groups of expats living and working in the Emirates. This decades-long exchange shapes both the individual biographies and the economic structure of Kerala. Every family has members who have worked in the Gulf States. In return, the remittances form a substantial part of Kerala's gross national product. The income is invested primarily in the private living standard of families: houses, education, and dowries in the form of gold. The COVID-19 pandemic has severely decimated job opportunities on the Arabian Peninsula and it remains to be seen how this will affect Kerala's economy.

The selected photo series is based on the video work *Dubai Gold and Diamonds* (2018), which was shot in the cities of Kochi and Kozhikode and throughout Malappuram district. The photos show business and advertising signs in urban and rural surroundings with images and titles referring to the Emirates and other Gulf states. Travel agencies advertise with images of iconic buildings such as the *Burj Al Arab* (Fig. 4), and shops are named after UAE cities like the restaurant Sharjah Palace or the car repair shop Abu Dhabi Motors. The jewellery chain store Dubai Gold and Diamonds, which the project takes its title from, has several branches in Malappuram district (Fig. 2 and 3). Some of the Indian shops directly copy the name and font of Emirati companies. For example, the Emirates Residency guesthouse in Kochi uses the typography of the airline Emirates (Fig. 1). References to the Gulf states often appear in connection with Western consumer electronics (Fig. 6). These were unavailable in India during the 1980s and '90s and were accordingly sought-after gifts expected from Gulf returnees. Today this still echoes in giving electronics markets in Kerala names like Gulf Bazar or Dubai Souk.

In the Indian context, Kerala is extraordinarily multireligious with large Christian and Muslim communities. Although members of all religions leave for work in the Gulf states equally, direct references in public space are visible especially in the predominantly Muslim Malappuram district. Gulf returnees establish small shops with reminiscent names or businesses designed for Non-Resident Keralites (NRKs) who visit home and bring, for example, new eating habits with them, which are catered to in restaurants like Arabian Hut (Fig. 5). The association of prosperity and modernity with the Gulf states is immediately visible in the numerous busi-

https://doi.org/10.1515/9783110741100-014

ness and advertising signs. Traveling to Dubai in particular has become a cultural motif in its own right (Fig. 4 and 8). All in all, this Kerala-specific phenomenon is not primarily the result of strategic business branding; instead, the self-made character and intricacy of the image and word combinations tell of individual longings and collective nostalgia through the medium of idealising advertisement.

The artistic research and video project *Dubai Gold and Diamonds* was realised in 2017 and 2018 with the support of the Goethe Institute/Max Mueller Bhavan Bangalore and the Kochi Biennale Foundation.

Dubai Bazar
Abu Dhabi Motors
Sharjah Food Palace
Al Ain Optics
Emirates Residency
UAE Exchange
Shawarma Expres
Dubai Diagnostic Center
Oodh Zone
Dubai Gold and Diamonds
Cafe Sahara
Dates City
Dubai Fashion World
Gulf Hotel
Gulfgate Hairfixing
Dubai Gold Souk
Hotel Arabian Hut
Hotel Gulf Hut
Grand Arabian Family Restaurant
Saudi Bakery
Hotel Babul Yemen
National Gulf Hyper Market
Gulf Bazar

Fig. 1: Emirates Residency Guesthouse, Kochi

Fig. 2: Dubai Gold and Diamonds
Jewellery store sign, Chemmad, Malappuram district

Fig. 3: Dubai Gold and Diamonds
Jewellery store billboard, Malappuram district

Fig. 4: Airline Travels
Travel agency advertisement, Othukkungal, Malappuram district

Fig. 5: Hotel Arabian Hut
Restaurant, Kakkanchery, Malappuram district

Fig. 6: Dubai Mobile
Store sign, Kottakkal, Malappuram district

Fig. 7: Hello Dubaikkaran
Movie billboard, Kochi

Fig. 8: Nahana Pardhas
Clothing store advertisement, Chemmad, Malappuram district

All photos: Sophie-Therese Trenka-Dalton, 2017.

Heiko Schuss

The Branding of Dubai as the Capital of the Islamic Economy

1 Introduction

In 2013, Dubai launched an initiative to forward its position as the Capital of the Islamic economy. This chapter will study this initiative by analysing publications of the Dubai Islamic Economy Development Centre (DIEDC) and secondary literature. As "place brands consist of connected chains of associations that build a joint network,"[1] the main questions of this chapter are which synergies and contradictions exist between this Islamic economy strategy and other elements of Dubai's place branding and how the endeavour to brand Dubai as a hub of the Islamic economy fits into its general economic development strategy. Furthermore, how does the claim to be the global centre of the Islamic economy relate to reality? To answer this question, the position of Dubai and the United Arab Emirates (UAE) within the global Islamic economy will be evaluated.

2 The Global Islamic Economy and the Global *Ḥalāl* Economy

What does "Islamic economy" mean in the context of Dubai's initiative of 2013? The term itself is ambiguous, and perhaps it was chosen exactly because of its ambiguity. The *State of the Global Islamic Economy Reports*, which are supported by the DIEDC,[2] makes it clear that it is not about a change to the economic system propagated by Islamic economists. Rather it is about the spread of *ḥalāl* products and services. So why is the slogan "Capital of the Islamic Economy" and not "Capital of the *Ḥalāl* Economy"? Besides the emphasis on the *ḥalāl* economy, these reports refer to the current and future market potential of the Muslim world population. Is the global Islamic economy, in this understanding, then defined by the economic transactions of Muslims, irrespective of whether these transactions are *ḥalāl* or not? That would contradict the aims of a *ḥalāl* economy. Or does the use of the term "Islamic economy" imply that Muslims around the world should prefer

1 Zenker and Braun, 2017: 273.
2 For the most recent issue used, see DinarStandard, 2020.

https://doi.org/10.1515/9783110741100-015

ḥalāl goods and services despite the potential of alienating Muslims with a secular lifestyle?

The dichotomy of *ḥalāl* and *ḥarām* is important for those Muslims who embrace their religion by stressing orthopraxy. Goods and actions can be divided into those that are allowed (*ḥalāl*) and those that are forbidden (*ḥarām*).[3] To define these categories, believers refer to common knowledge, their religious traditions and, in more difficult cases, the opinions of Islamic law scholars. More and more *ḥalāl* products and services are defined by numerous competing *ḥalāl* certification organisations, which obviously also influences the economic sphere. While the *ḥalāl* economy started with the *ḥalāl* food industry, this endeavour has broadened to many other sectors, like *ḥalāl* pharmaceuticals, cosmetics, fashion, travel, recreation, media, etc. Related to the religious interdiction of interest or usury (*ribā*), the initiatives of Islamic finance have a similar intention and are therefore subsumed in this text under the category of *ḥalāl* or Islamic economy.

It is hard to estimate the actual size and potential of the *ḥalāl* economy. Available data are provided by organisations involved in advertising the *ḥalāl* economy, among them the DIEDC. According to the *State of the Global Islamic Economy Report 2020/21*, the estimated consumer spending of Muslims worldwide in the aforementioned sectors (excluding Islamic finance) in 2019 was about 2.02 trillion USD.[4] The report then estimates that Islamic finance assets reached 2.88 trillion USD. Such statements have to be taken with a grain of salt. Obviously, these numbers do not tell us how much of this potential volume is *ḥalāl* or has a *ḥalāl* certificate of some kind. While in the food sector, the vast majority of products can be assumed to be *ḥalāl*, in other sectors, this cannot be taken for granted. Nor can it be assumed that every Muslim is interested in consuming a more comprehensive range of *ḥalāl* products and services. Thus, just summing up the consumption of Muslims in certain sectors is a way to overestimate the economic potential of the *ḥalāl* economy and make investments there look more attractive.

3 Beyond this, a more detailed distinction between *wāǧib* (mandatory), *mandūb*/*mustaḥabb* (recommended), *ǧā'iz* (allowed), *makrūh* (reprehensible), and *ḥarām* (forbidden) is used in Islamic law. But the categories of *mandūb*/*mustaḥabb* and *makrūh* have no worldly legal consequences. See Rohe, 2005: 103.

4 See DinarStandard, 2020: 5.

3 Dubai's Development Strategy and Place Branding

In order to put Dubai's Islamic Economy initiative into perspective, it is necessary to look at its general development strategy and place branding. Oil revenues provided Dubai with the capital to develop its infrastructure and economy. As its oil reserves were limited, Dubai's rulers understood well the need to diversify its economy. They built their strategy on the city's geographic location, which is favourable for transport and logistics services, and its merchant tradition. In the transport sector, Dubai built Port Rashid and Jebel Ali, which is among the biggest container ports in the world. Dubai is now a hub for transporting passengers and goods for the Gulf region and, more generally, between the global East and West. Another part of the strategy was to make Dubai a centre of tourism. As the emirate's natural resources and historical heritage sites are more limited than in other locations in the Middle East, the tourism strategy is to provide exceptional shopping and leisure experiences. All the facilities that offer this experience – luxury hotels, some of the world's largest shopping malls, etc. – had to be built from scratch, and favourable regulations had to be implemented to allure international luxury brands to come to Dubai.

The development of the infrastructure and the transport and tourism sectors goes hand in hand with high investments in the construction sector. As owning real estate in Dubai became more attractive, construction projects were launched to change Dubai's waterfront. All these economic activities needed supporting services, especially from the financial sector. Accordingly, transforming Dubai into a financial centre was another essential part of the development strategy. Since its beginning, Islamic finance was an important, but not dominating part of Dubai's financial sector, as the first private Islamic commercial bank in the world, Dubai Islamic Bank, was already founded in 1975.[5]

Dubai's development strategy and its place branding experienced modifications due to the global financial crisis around 2008/09. Investing in Dubai's construction projects and real estate had developed into a bubble economy that burst during the crisis. It became clear that the development strategy was too concentrated on the construction sector and that systemic risks had been neglected. As a result, Dubai was forced to seek a bailout from its more conservative neighbour

5 See Hafeez et al., 2016: 390–397; Govers and Go, 2009: 85–92; Stephens Balakrishnan, 2008: 70–76; Kahf, 2005: 21.

Abu Dhabi.[6] In response to these challenges, Dubai is trying to diversify its economy further by supporting new sectoral clusters, like healthcare, higher education, and media, in order to make its success sustainable. Among these efforts is the initiative, launched in 2013, to strengthen the Emirate's role in the Islamic economy. For the various new industries, Dubai created a lot of small enclaved spaces often designated "free zones." It has been successful in attracting a broad spectrum of investors, yet the results are often mediocre, for example regarding the quality of the numerous private academic institutions.[7]

The place branding that accompanies the development of Dubai's economy presents the city as a place of dreams, concentrating on the aspects of global leadership, excellence, luxury, fascination, and security. This branding is established via mega-projects and spectacular events that attract global attention. It intends to address people from all over the world, so openness to diverse cultures is an important element, too. Products from Western and Islamic brands are offered to consumers from different countries and lifestyles.[8] At the same time, efforts are made to connect this image with the Emirate's historical heritage and traditions.[9] The Dubai Plan 2021 formulates inclusive economic and social goals like becoming "A Pivotal Hub in the Global Economy," "A City of Happy, Creative & Empowered People," "An Inclusive & Cohesive Society," and "A Smart & Sustainable City."[10] All these goals aim to enhance attractiveness for people of different cultures. They are not in contradiction to the goal of becoming a centre of the Islamic economy, but nor do they convey a specific Islamic or Arab character.

4 Dubai's Initiative to Become a Leading Hub of the Islamic Economy

After the global financial crisis, Dubai's leadership started the initiative "to transform Dubai into the capital of Islamic economy."[11] To this purpose, the Dubai Islamic Economy Development Centre was founded in 2013, which envisioned making Dubai a "[g]lobal hub of Islamic economy promoting standards & driving

6 See Smith, 2014: 294–295.

7 See De Jong, Hoppe, and Noori, 2019: 21–22.

8 See El-Bassiouny, 2017: 583–584; Govers and Go, 2009: 88.

9 See Govers and Go, 2009: 103.

10 Quotes are from Government of Dubai, The Executive Council, 2014. See also De Jong, Hoppe, and Noori, 2019: 9–10.

11 DIEDC, n.d.: 3.

growth and innovation across all sectors."[12] The aim is to achieve top rankings in all categories of the Islamic economy, "to promote Dubai /UAE as the prime destination and global reference for international halal companies," to "[m]ake Dubai the global reference point for Islamic economy standards," and to "[p]osition Dubai as a pioneer of the Islamic digital economy."[13] A consistent theme in the formulation of these aims is the ambition to become the leader in the Islamic economy. Another prominent topic is the emphasis on innovation, combined with ethics to serve humanity. Furthermore, this initiative seeks to combine a global outlook with Dubai's cultural identity, e.g. by "establishing of world-class Islamic cultural attractions and art & design events."[14]

A characteristic of this initiative is its comprehensiveness in addressing the different potential sectors of the *ḥalāl* economy and multiple dimensions of its development, for example research, standardisation, production, fairs, and marketing. Connected with this programme, a number of Dubai-based organisations have been founded, like the Islamic Economic Fiqh Forum, the International Halal Accreditation Forum, the Emirates International Accreditation Centre, the Dubai Center for Islamic Banking and Finance, the Global Islamic Economy Summit, the Islamic Economy Award, and the Incubator for Digital Islamic SMEs. These organisations and their activities helped address the various aims of the strategy and keep Dubai's Islamic economy initiative present in the media. In 2017, a revised Islamic Economy Strategy was developed that identified three core sectors: Islamic finance, *ḥalāl* products, and Islamic lifestyle. The last category is possibly the most innovative one, because it contains not only *ḥalāl* fashion and tourism, but also culture and art.[15] The strategy also puts stress on background factors that are seen as enabling pillars, namely the development of Islamic Knowledge, Islamic Standards, and the Islamic Digital Economy.[16]

In order to evaluate the significance of this initiative within the general place branding of Dubai, it is useful to have a look at some other key strategy documents, like the Dubai Plan 2021, which was launched in 2014, and the Dubai Industrial Strategy 2030, which followed in 2016. The Dubai Plan 2021 outlines six strategic fields, namely Economy, Society, People, Experience, Government, and Place. Within the topic of the economy, there are three main aims, "sustainable growth," to become "one of the world's leading business centers," and to be "the most business friendly city and a preferred investment destination." The second aim is further

12 DIEDC, n.d.: 8.
13 DIEDC, n.d.: 15, 19, 20.
14 DIEDC, n.d.: 2, 17.
15 See DIEDC, n.d.: 3, 5.
16 See DIEDC, n.d.: 10.

explained as being "[c]onsistently ranked as one of the top 5 global centers for trade, logistics, tourism and finance as well as internationally recognized as the leading financial and trading center at the heart of the Islamic economy."[17] Among nine key economic performance indicators used to follow up the strategy's success, just one refers to the goals of the Islamic economy, namely the Composite Indicator for Islamic Economy.[18] Among the six strategic objectives in the vision statement of the Dubai Industrial Strategy 2030, one is "Adopting of Islamic Standards" and to "[b]ecome a center for the global Islamic products market."[19] This plan targets six industrial subsectors, namely aerospace, maritime, pharmaceuticals and medical equipment, aluminium and fabricated metals, fast-moving consumable goods, and machinery and equipment. The Islamic economy and *ḥalāl* industries are explicitly mentioned under the heading of fast-moving consumable goods.[20] These key documents show that the Islamic economy initiative is integrated with Dubai's general place-branding strategy, but at a secondary level and certainly not as a dominant theme. This approach might already raise some doubts about the seriousness of the claim to become the centre of the Islamic economy.

5 Assessment of Dubai's Islamic Economy Initiative

To assess the success of the Islamic economy initiative, Dubai's position in the Islamic and the *ḥalāl* economy will be analysed. As it is difficult to separate the numbers for Dubai from the rest of the country, data for the entire UAE will be used as a proxy to evaluate the success of Dubai's strategy. According to the Global Islamic Economy Indicator regularly published by *The State of the Global Islamic Economy Report*, in 2020/21, the UAE ranks third after Malaysia and Saudi Arabia. With respect to the different sectors, the UAE takes first place in the sectors of Modest Fashion and Media & Recreation, second in Muslim-Friendly Travel and Pharma & Cosmetics, and third in *Ḥalāl* Food and Islamic Finance.[21] These results are based not only on what Muslims spend in these sectors, but also include scores in governance, awareness, and social considerations. This approach is supposed to measure the "current health and development of the overall Islamic economy

17 Government of Dubai, The Executive Council, 2014: 17–18.

18 See Government of Dubai, The Executive Council, 2014: 18.

19 See Government of Dubai, The Executive Council, n.d.: 7.

20 See Government of Dubai, The Executive Council, n.d.: 8–9.

21 See DinarStandard, 2020: 15.

ecosystem."[22] The surprisingly high ranking of the UAE also benefits the country's corresponding branding and marketing efforts.

In absolute numbers, according to the same report, the UAE is neither among the five biggest *ḥalāl* food consumer markets (these are Indonesia, Bangladesh, Egypt, Nigeria, and Pakistan), nor among the five largest *ḥalāl* food exporters to the Organisation of Islamic Cooperation (OIC) countries.[23] Nevertheless, *ḥalāl* standards play an important role in the food sector of the UAE, as the inhabitants have very high meat consumption, and around 80 % of the country's food is imported.[24] The UAE, therefore, has a strong interest in developing and communicating *ḥalāl* standards to meet the needs of its population.[25] Furthermore, the country plays an important role in the processing and re-exporting of *ḥalāl* food products.[26]

Islamic Banking in the UAE grew in absolute and relative terms between 2013 and 2020. The share of the UAE in global Islamic banking assets increased from 7 % to 9.2 %, and the share of Islamic banking within the UAE in 2020 was 19 %. It seems nevertheless exaggerated to call the UAE or Dubai the hub of Islamic finance in the Gulf region. With 28.5 % and 22.1 % respectively, Saudi Arabia and Iran have much higher shares of global Islamic banking assets. Islamic banking has reached a market share of 100 % in Iran, 68 % in Saudi Arabia, 42 % in Kuwait, and 27.7 % in Qatar. In Bahrain, Islamic banking has a lower share of 15.3 %, but it is considered an important centre of innovation for Islamic finance.[27] The UAE has a strong position in the Islamic bond (*sukuk*) market. Its share of global *sukuk* issuances increased from 6 % in 2013 to 8.1 % in 2020, and it is also an important place for trading *sukuk*. However, in 2020, the shares of *sukuk* issuances of Malaysia (29.5 %), Saudi Arabia (18.2 %), Indonesia (11.8 %), Turkey (8.7 %), and Kuwait (8.3 %) were still higher.[28]

The UAE is considered strongest in the sector of Muslim-friendly travel, as it ranks second among the top Muslim travel destination countries, measured in the number of estimated inbound Muslim travellers, and second among the top outbound Muslim travel countries, measured in travel spending. In cosmetics and modest fashion, the UAE ranks second and fourth, respectively, among countries exporting such kinds of goods to other OIC countries. On the other hand, in

---

22 Thomson Reuters, 2016: 8.
23 See DinarStandard, 2020: 40–41.
24 See Randeree, 2019: 1161.
25 According to the 2005 census, 76 % of the total population of the UAE, including non-citizens, were Muslims. See United States Department of State, Office of International Religious Freedom, 2020: 3.
26 See Stanley, 2018.
27 See IFSB, 2014: 11, 15, and 2021: 6, 8, 9, 12.
28 See IFSB, 2014: 23, and 2021: 21.

pharmaceuticals and the media and recreation sector, the UAE does not reach a rank among the top five countries.[29] These numbers convey a more differentiated picture of Dubai's place in the global Islamic economy than the Global Islamic Economy Indicator does.

Besides these indicators, it is useful to look at Dubai's contributions to developing international standards for *ḥalāl* products and services. In an initiative of the DIEDC and the Emirate's Authority for Standardisation and Metrology, ten organisations from different countries and regions – Australia, the Gulf Cooperation Council, Egypt, New Zealand, Pakistan, Saudi Arabia, Spain, the UAE, the UK, and the USA – founded the International Halal Accreditation Forum, which is headquartered in Dubai.[30] It is interesting that Malaysia, a global leader in the development of *ḥalāl* standards and therefore a competitor in this field, is missing from the list. Furthermore, in 2019, a unified pan-Arab framework for the mutual recognition of *ḥalāl* certificates was announced in the UAE.[31]

While its claim to be the world capital of the Islamic economy might be unsubstantiated, it can be concluded that Dubai occupies a strong position in the Islamic economy and has also made progress in several of its fields since launching the Islamic economy initiative. Despite this success, a major change in the organisational structure of this initiative has taken place: with Law No. 7 of 2021, the Ruler of Dubai dissolved the DIEDC and transferred its duties and functions to the Department of Economic Development (DED).[32] In the media, this step was not widely discussed, and increasing the efficiency of government institutions was given as a reason for this restructuring.[33] In 2016, the DED had founded the Global Islamic Business Excellence Center, which established the Global Islamic Business Award. Nevertheless, the Islamic economy does not occupy a prominent place within the strategy of the DED. The six strategic pillars of the DED are economic growth, economic competitiveness, business community happiness, economic foresight and planning, advancing the DED, and financial sustainability. Just two of 24 subgoals refer to the Islamic economy, namely to boost *ḥalāl* trade and empower the Islamic economy. It remains to be seen which further activities the DED will develop in this field after taking over the duties and functions of the DIEDC.[34]

---

29 See DinarStandard, 2020: passim.

30 See Zawya, 2016.

31 See PR Newswire US, 2019.

32 See Government of Dubai, The Supreme Legislation Committee, 2021.

33 See Arabian Business, 2021.

34 See Government of Dubai, Department of Economic Development, 2022a and 2022b; The Global Islamic Business Excellence Center, n.d.

6 Conclusion

All the indicators discussed above show that Dubai plays an important role in the Islamic economy, both in the broader sense of a Muslim world economy and in the narrow sense of a *ḥalāl* economy conforming to Islamic precepts. Dubai's Islamic economy initiative fits well into its diversification strategy and is built on synergies with other existing sectors. The infrastructure established and the experience gained in the transport, trade, retail, tourism, finance, and construction sectors can be used to offer *ḥalāl* goods and services efficiently and successfully. Moreover, Dubai and the UAE are experienced in using the concepts of *ḥalāl* goods and services and can capitalise on their expertise to make the regulations of the *ḥalāl* economy more consistent and compatible with the rest of the Islamic world.

Nevertheless, it would be exaggerated to call Dubai the global capital of the Islamic economy, as there are other competing *ḥalāl* hubs in the Gulf region and the wider Islamic world. Dubai also does not seriously attempt to transform its economy into a fully-fledged Islamic economy. *Ḥalāl* goods and services are only a part of its wider diversification strategy. The strategy of Dubai is to offer both secular and Islamic goods and services for a diverse spectrum of customers. So, first of all, Dubai's branding activities emphasise cultural tolerance and openness to the world. The branding of Dubai as the capital of the Islamic economy intentionally uses the ambiguity of the term "Islamic economy," which ranges between addressing customers from the Muslim world irrespective of their religiousness, on the one hand, and the promotion of *ḥalāl* products and practices in all fields of life, on the other. This ambiguous use reduces the dissonance with other elements of its place branding. It aims to attract those Muslim consumers looking for *ḥalāl* goods and services without alienating Western or secular Muslim customers. Accordingly, in other strategy papers of the Emirate, the Islamic economy plays only a secondary role. The dissolution of the DIEDC might even signal that the Islamic economy is losing importance within Dubai's overall branding strategy.

The branding and image of Dubai fit a specific interpretation of Islam that has no problem with consumerism, luxury, etc., as long as the minimum legal criteria for *ḥalāl* goods, services, and contracts are met. It also works well in and does not challenge the secular frame of a capitalistic world economy. However, its emphasis on luxury is questionable for those who stress the value of moderation within Islam.[35] The blend of Western and Islamic brands might not be acceptable for Mus-

35 See El-Bassiouny, 2017: 584. Social problems, like the equality gap in citizens' and labour rights and in remuneration between nationals and immigrants, who make up more than 80 % of Dubai's

lims with a more puritan worldview. But the ability of Dubai to attract the rich and prosperous of the Muslim world to its shopping malls shows that this compromise between secular and Islamic values is successful in economic terms.

Bibliography

Arabian Business. "Dubai Ruler Issues Laws to Restructure Some Gov't Entities: Sheikh Mohammed Says New Legislations Aims to Raise the Efficiency of Government Institutions." 4 May 2021. https://www.arabianbusiness.com/politics-economics/463047-dubai-ruler-announces-restructuring-of-some-govt-entities. Accessed 9 January 2022.

De Jong, Martin, Thomas Hoppe, and Negar Noori. "City Branding, Sustainable Urban Development and the Rentier State: How Do Qatar, Abu Dhabi and Dubai Present Themselves in the Age of Post Oil and Global Warming?" *Energies* 12.1657 (2019). doi:10.3390/en12091657.

DinarStandard. *State of the Global Islamic Economy Report 2020/21: Thriving in Uncertainty.* Produced with the support of the Dubai Islamic Economy Development Center. 2020. https://cdn.salaamgateway.com/reports/pdf/456642acf95a783db590e5b104cae94046047101.pdf. Accessed 10 October 2021.

DIEDC. *Dubai the Capital of the Islamic Economy.* Dubai Islamic Economy Development Centre, n.d. https://ded.ae/DED_Files/StudiesAndResearch/DIEDC-English-Overview_1521109783.pdf. Accessed 2 January 2022.

El-Bassiouny, Noha M. "The Trojan Horse of Affluence and Halal in the Arabian Gulf." *Journal of Islamic Marketing* 8.4 (2017): 578–594.

Government of Dubai, Department of Economic Development. "Dubai Economy & Tourism: Our Strategy." https://ded.ae/page/en/our_strategy. Accessed 9 January 2022a.

Government of Dubai, Department of Economic Development. "Dubai Economy & Tourism: The Global Islamic Business Excellence Center." https://ded.ae/page/en/excellence_center. Accessed 9 January 2022b.

Government of Dubai, The Executive Council. *Dubai Plan 2021.* Dubai, 2014. https://www.dubaiplan2021.ae/c/document_library/get_file?uuid=14167c30-550d-546c-5b72-587a3d1e5c7a&groupId=1028358. Accessed 2 January 2022.

Government of Dubai, The Executive Council. *Dubai Plan 2021: Dubai Industrial Strategy 2030.* Dubai, n.d. https://www.dubaiplan2021.ae/c/document_library/get_file?uuid=49c80717-efb5-6fec-8bc9-b79041534b71&groupId=1028358. Accessed 2 January 2022.

Government of Dubai, The Supreme Legislation Committee. *Law No. (7) of 2021 Dissolving the Dubai Islamic Economy Development Centre.* Dubai, 27 April 2021. https://dlp.dubai.gov.ae/Legislation%20Reference/2021/Law%20No.%207%20of%202021%20Dissolving%20the%20Dubai%20Islamic%20Economy%20Development%20Centre.html. Accessed 9 January 2022.

Govers, Robert, and Frank Go. *Place Branding: Glocal, Virtual and Physical Identities, Constructed, Imagined and Experienced.* New York: Palgrave Macmillan, 2009.

population, and especially the exploitative labour conditions for the majority of low-paid immigrant workers, also contradict the professed Islamic values, see Smith, 2014: 293–294.

Hafeez, Khalid, Pantea Foroudi, Keith Dinnie, Bang Nguyen, and Sanjai K. Parahoo. "The Role of Place Branding and Image in the Development of Sectoral Clusters: The Case of Dubai." *Journal of Brand Management* 23.4 (2016): 383–402.

IFSB. *Islamic Financial Services Industry Stability Report 2014.* Kuala Lumpur: Islamic Financial Services Board, 2014. https://www.ifsb.org/download.php?id=4416&lang=English&pg=/sec03.php. Accessed 31 October 2021.

IFSB. *Islamic Financial Services Industry Stability Report 2020.* Kuala Lumpur: Islamic Financial Services Board, 2020. https://www.ifsb.org/download.php?id=5724&lang=English&pg=/sec03.php. Accessed 31 October 2021.

IFSB. *Islamic Financial Services Industry Stability Report 2021.* Kuala Lumpur: Islamic Financial Services Board, 2021. https://www.ifsb.org/download.php?id=6106&lang=English&pg=/sec03.php. Accessed 31 October 2021.

Kahf, Monzer. "Islamic Banks: The Rise of a New Power Alliance of Wealth and Shari'a Scholarship." In *The Politics of Islamic Finance*, edited by Clement Moore Henry and Rodney Wilson, 17–36. Reprint. Karachi: Oxford University Press, 2005.

PR Newswire US. "Arab Countries Agree on New Framework for Halal Certificates Mutual Recognition." 18 February 2019. https://www.prnewswire.com/il/news-releases/arab-countries-agree-on-new-framework-for-halal-certificates-mutual-recognition-820818096.html. Accessed 31 October 2021.

Randeree, Kasim. "Challenges in Halal Food Ecosystems: The Case of the United Arab Emirates." *British Food Journal* 121.5 (2019): 1154–1167.

Rohe, Mathias. "Islamisches Wirtschaften aus rechtlicher Sicht." In *Globalisierung und Ethik: Ludwig-Erhard-Ringvorlesung an der Friedrich-Alexander-Universität Erlangen-Nürnberg*, edited by Harald Herrmann and Kai-Ingo Voigt, 103–125. Heidelberg: Physica-Verlag, 2005.

Smith, Richard G. "Dubai in Extremis." *Theory, Culture & Society* 31.7/8 (2014): 291–296. Accessed 31 October 2021.

Stanley, Iona. "UAE Strengthens its Position in Global Halal Market." *Gulf News* 18 February 2018. https://gulfnews.com/going-out/uae-strengthens-its-position-in-global-halal-market-1.2175122. Accessed 31 October 2021.

Stephens Balakrishnan, Melodena. "Dubai – A Star in the East: A Case Study in Strategic Destination Branding." *Journal of Place Management and Development* 1.1 (2008): 62–91.

Thomson Reuters. *State of the Global Islamic Economy Report 2016/17.* In collaboration with DinarStandard. 2016. https://ded.ae/DED_Files/SGIE-Report_f1_DIGITAL_1477897639.pdf. Accessed 16 January 2022.

United States Department of State, Office of International Religious Freedom. *United Arab Emirates 2020 International Religious Freedom Report.* 12 May 2021. https://www.state.gov/wp-content/uploads/2021/05/240282-UNITED-ARAB-EMIRATES-2020-INTERNATIONAL-RELIGIOUS-FREEDOM-REPORT.pdf. Accessed 1 January 2022.

Zawya. "10 Countries Sign Memorandum of Understanding to Establish International Halal Accreditation Forum in Dubai." 9 May 2016. https://www.zawya.com/mena/en/press-releases/story/10_Countries_Sign_Memorandum_of_Understanding_to_Establish_International_Halal_Accreditation_Forum_in_Dubai-ZAWYA20160509104824/. Accessed 16 January 2022.

Zenker, Sebastian, and Erik Braun. "Questioning a 'One Size Fits All' City Brand: Developing a Branded House Strategy for Place Brand Management." *Journal of Place Management and Development*, 10.3 (2017): 270–287.

Lisa Maria Franke

Islamic Ideals, the Concept of Love, and Processes of Individualisation: *Muṣṭafā Ḥusnī*'s Writings and his Spiritual Brand

1 Introduction

This article deals with the televised religious guide Muṣṭafā Ḥusnī. His teachings, oral and written, are part of the analysis, in addition to his self-marketing as a spiritual brand. Ḥusnī is one of several Islamic guides in Egypt; however, he focuses not only on religious education, but also on education and advice in everyday life practices. While he is very present on television and has an active social media profile, he also publishes books and other written material. In his writings, he highlights the importance of balancing one's life and one's beliefs. His self-marketing is one of the keys to his success and the reason his many adherents follow him.

Since the "Egyptian Revolution" of 2011, understandings of Islam have undergone substantial changes in the country. The ousting of President Hosni Mubarak was followed by the election of the Muslim Brotherhood's Mohammed Morsi, whose presidency has greatly affected the way Islam is perceived. Restrictions imposed during Morsi's rule in the name of religion, such as the closure of cinemas, disappointed many Egyptians who had been supportive of the regime's "Islamisation project."[1] In the direct aftermath of the revolution, public debates over religiosity ensued, and an unprecedented momentum of political and religious plurality translated into a wide array of movements and political factions in the public sphere.[2] This in turn was reflected in a dynamic of re-positioning and questioning of political and religious authorities. For many individuals, this also included reconsidering their religious identities. As Khaled Fahmy states in his reflection on the downfall of the Muslim Brotherhood in 2013: "Egyptian society finds itself, confronting and raising (…) very, very deep questions (…). [W]hat to do with Islam? What is the proper position of (…) Islam (…)?"[3] While this holds true for the broader political debate, in this article, I examine how these questions have specifically impacted the positioning of public religious figures like Muṣṭafā Ḥusnī. I also ask how his personal brand and the impulse for change effectively set in motion a

1 Cf. Haenni, 2016; El Esrawi, 2019; Brown, 2015.
2 Cf. Haenni, 2016.
3 Fahmy, 2013.

https://doi.org/10.1515/9783110741100-016

process of individualisation, of which many Egyptians with whom I spoke felt in need. And more generally: what mechanisms and strategies does the branding of religious influencers employ to deal with these social dynamics and requests for alternative religious guidance?

The change in leadership from Mohammed Morsi to President Abdel-Fatah al-Sisi in 2013 was characterised by the imposition of greater restrictions than before the "Revolution" in an attempt to limit the impact of the Muslim Brotherhood. In particular, public religious spaces such as mosques were regulated.[4] Based on my research in post-revolutionary Egypt, I noticed that many people were finding new or rather different ways of doing being Muslim.[5] Because some of these people were interested in or impacted by influencers such as Muṣṭafā Ḥusnī, my initial, heuristic questions asked explicitly about the influence of public religious figures and the power of personal brands on individual's negotiating of their intimate religiosities: What role do public religious figures[6] play in these processes and how do they create and design their brand accordingly? What is the specificity of Muṣṭafā Ḥusnī and how can the attraction of his brand be assessed? What is the content of his spiritual message and why do many believers follow his guidance?

The turmoil of the revolution and its aftermath have been meticulously described and analysed by various scholars.[7] Mona Abaza in particular highlighted how, since the revolution, young individuals searching for identities are torn between agency and passivity.[8] She identifies insecurities, generational differences, and misunderstandings in terms of values and appreciation amid dystopian environments. This article relates to the existing academic scholarship and deals with searches for identity among young Egyptians, but goes a step further by adding to the analysis the dimension of the public religious figure Muṣṭafā Ḥusnī and his brand.

From 2016–2019, I lived in Alexandria to carry out ethnographic research for the ERC project "Private Pieties. Mundane Islam and New Forms of Muslim Religiosity: Impact on Contemporary Social and Political Dynamics," at the University of Göttingen. During this fieldwork, the appeal and phenomenon that Muṣṭafā Ḥusnī and others like him had for my interlocuters caught my attention. Thus, the following analysis and findings are based on the interviews I conducted as part of that project. This research on individual pieties, being religious, and

4 Cf. Bano and Benadi, 2018.
5 Cf. Franke, 2021b.
6 See Brown, 2015.
7 Cf. Saad, 2012; Fahmy, Boutaleb, and El Chazli, 2019; Schielke, 2015; Abaza, 2012, 2014.
8 Cf. Abaza, 2020.

doing being religious, provided me with insights into the worlds of individual believers and their sources of spirituality. The brand of Muṣṭafā Ḥusnī must be especially highlighted in this respect, because many of my interlocutors referred to him and his programs as a source of spiritual inspiration and guidance. In addition to Muṣṭafā Ḥusnī and his brand, I examined those voices that hint at tendencies away from mainstream Islam and express alternative options and different versions of belief.[9]

My primary sources consist of qualitative individual interviews and group discussions, participative observation, and written, audio, and visual sources of Muṣṭafā Ḥusnī in Arabic (leaflets, "grey literature," websites, books, TV and radio programs, and social media). I also consulted the *Qur'ān* and *Ḥadīṯ* to follow up on the respective religious references made by Ḥusnī and my interlocutors. I conducted interviews with Muslim Egyptians who consider themselves to be "different" in terms of religiosity and social expectations. All their names have been anonymised, and personal details have been changed. I spoke with both men and women aged between 15 and 75, some of whom participated in the 25 January revolution.[10] All are Alexandrians from middle-class milieus with high school or university degrees. Alexandria formed the centre for my research; having grown up in Alexandria myself, I relied on and was grateful for my social network there. In addition, Alexandria is a vibrant city with diverse and heterogeneous religious milieus, such as Sunni, Coptic, Sufi, and Salafi communities.

2 Definition of the Notion "Brand"

The notion of *brand* has undergone substantial changes in the past decades. Globalisation, modernity, and processes of individualisation visible in the wider region of the Near and Middle East have led to alternative concepts and understandings of the term, in the sense that a focus on the social dimension of the brand is becoming increasingly important. Many theoretical approaches have been developed around the idea that brands resemble an interplay between the consumer and the product. More precisely, from a perspective within the discipline of management, the brand amplifies the product's value for the consumer to identify it as a positive and thus valuable item.[11] According to Kevin Lane Keller, who further develops the idea of the brand as identificatory in the "product-consumer-

9 Cf. Winegar, 2014.
10 Cf. Mehrez, 2012.
11 See Maehle, Otnes, and Supphellen, 2011.

brand" relationship further, the brand is the purposefully developed and constructed (by interested parties) heart of an item, which can be a service or a product. Thus, the brand is the encompassing characteristic of the product that indicates its quality. The purchaser, the consumer, and ultimately the user are given an image that guarantees its value at the same time as it serves as a symbol and a narrative of the product.[12] The intention is to incorporate the product in the feelings and minds of the consumers and to give it a unique standing in worldwide competition. Recognition, association, identification, and emotional commitment are deliberate outcomes, as much as loyalty and memorability.[13] This development that takes into account emotions and puts the consumer at centre stage has outgrown previous approaches focusing on the functional and/or ethical aspects and profits of the notion of the brand.[14] With the new attention to the clients and their identities, brands aim to add to and influence these identities in order to foster an engaged consumer-brand-product relationship. From a business perspective, globalisation and international rivalry thus demand such poly-dimensional approaches that adhere to social, emotional, and spiritual, i.e. religious needs, as well as mere functional levels.[15]

> The functional dimension reflects the perception of benefits of the product or service associated with the brand. The social dimension considers the identification role of the brand in terms of creating connections with a group and supporting consumers' identities. The mental dimension reveals the ability to support the individual mentally, which is becoming an inspiration for achievement in consumers' lives. Finally, the spiritual dimension reflects the perception of the social responsibility of the brand (...).[16]

Gad calls the perception of the multidimensional framework of branding "Brand Mind Space" to support the idea that "unless you keep on stretching your brand it will implode and eventually vanish in people's minds."[17] The case of Muṣṭafā Ḥusnī shows that the notion of the brand has transformed from the product brand to a personal brand that is designed around the public personality, the message, and the performance of Muṣṭafā Ḥusnī himself. The personal brand, then, focuses on the individuals, their spiritual development, and their well-being by offering transparent and trustworthy services and religious content. At the same time, while it seems clear that the brand of Muṣṭafā Ḥusnī is a personal brand, it is dif-

12 Cf. Keller, 2003.
13 Cf. Paswan, Spears, and Ganesh, 2007; Darrat, 2011.
14 Cf. Ind, 2003.
15 Cf. Ind, 2003.
16 Mourad and El-Karanshawy, 2013: 151.
17 Gad, 2003: 187. Cf. also Mourad and El Karanshawy, 2013.

ficult to clearly specify what or who is being branded. The relationship between the person, namely Muṣṭafā Ḥusnī, and the religion, i.e. Islam, meanders in the public presentation and re-presentation of Muṣṭafā Ḥusnī. This fluidity is typical of the personal spiritual brand in which the person himself embodies and conveys the religious message by means of his own self. Thus, the personal brand of Muṣṭafā Ḥusnī necessarily consists of the religious message that he conveys, of himself as model believer, and of the products and interactions that he creates to communicate with his audience. His brand can be interpreted as serving individuals and the majority by encouraging them to stay on the religious path or to start being religious and consequently to live a religious life conforming to the Islamic principles that Ḥusnī preaches, explains, and invites his audience to include in its everyday routines. According to his writings, he aims at making Islam visible and interesting, especially to a modern, young, middle-class generation of Egyptians. The intention is to increase their spirituality and to harmonise society by focussing on concepts of love and religiosity in interpersonal relationships, with the idea of encouraging individuals, communities, and societies to engage in peaceful and appreciative social interaction.[18]

3 Who is Muṣṭafā Ḥusnī?

Muṣṭafā Ḥusnī was born in Egypt on 28 August 1978. He is a graduate of Ain Shams University in Cairo and obtained his BA degree in Business in 2000.[19] After changing from being a businessman to becoming a preacher of Islam, he took courses at the Institute of Training Preachers to receive a certificate that enables him to legally teach the guiding of Islam to a larger public. The institute is part of the Egyptian Ministry of Awqaf and an official training institution for religious content that teaches Sunni Islam.

Ḥusnī regularly holds sessions and call-in shows on various Egyptian television channels, among them the global satellite channels *Iqra'* and *On E.* He not only presents these programs as preacher, but is also their producer. His weekly program on *Iqra'* is broadcast every Friday. Apart from programs on television, Ḥusnī is also present on radio; for example, his *'Aiš al-laḥẓa* (Live the moment) is aired on *Nujuum FM.* During the month of Ramadan, Ḥusnī has special programs on television and on radio.

18 See Ḥusnī, 2020.
19 Cf. Wikipedia, 2021.

In addition to his media presence on more than 13 television and radio programs, Ḥusnī also preaches and lectures at different mosques in Cairo, such as the Yusuf Al-Sahabi Mosque in Hejaz Square in Heliopolis and the El-Hosary Mosque in 6th of October City. His Wednesday weekly lessons take place after *ṣalāt al-maġrib* (sunset prayer) in summer and after *ʿišāʾ* (evening) prayer in winter. The lectures are taught under the title *al-Ḥadīṯ al-Qudsī* and focus on conveying religious content alongside everyday life advice.[20] At the Bilal Mosque in Moqattam, he delivers the Friday prayer (*khuṭba*) twice a month.

In addition to preaching in mosques, Muṣṭafā Ḥusnī is a writer and the author of numerous books. Some of the titles, style, and content are transcribed from his lectures or broadcast programs, while others are new and independent manuscripts. A common characteristic of all his books is that the name of the author is highlighted in large letters on the cover, along with his picture. The book titles range from *Al-kanz al mafqūd* (The Hidden/Lost Treasure), *Risāla min Allāh* (A Message from God) and *Qiṣṣat ḥubb* (Love Story) to *Siḥr al-dunyā* (The Magic/Enchantment of the World). The titles hint at the content and the entanglement of religious with worldly tasks.

As has been shown, Ḥusnī is a public person, a writer, and a religious guide. However, his activities are not limited to established broadcast media and written sources; he also engages with online social media.[21] Here, his activities are broad and encompass networks such as Facebook, Twitter, TikTok, Instagram, and SoundCloud. With almost 57 million followers on these platforms and 4.67 million on YouTube, his social media presence is noteworthy. As of early 2021, his YouTube video lectures have received more than 287 million views.[22]

While his media presence is steadily growing with a rising numbers of clicks, listeners, and viewers, especially on social media, Ḥusnī has also faced problems and complaints from his opponents. In June 2020, for example, a complaint submitted by an Egyptian lawyer to the Public Prosecutor and the State Security Prosecution charged him with being a supporter of the Muslim Brotherhood. The legal complaint stated that Ḥusnī was opposed to the current political leadership by supporting the Muslim Brotherhood. This accusation was based on a tweet in which Ḥusnī wrote in Egyptian Arabic: "In times of (mental) chaos, mingle only with your close loved ones. And do not mingle with the (mental) groups because they may lead you to wrong and prevent you from taking the right path. Don't be influ-

20 These are the sayings directly attributed to the prophet Muḥammad and thus represent a special category of *Ḥadīṯ*.

21 Cf. Hirschkind, 2012; Kazi, 2016.

22 See The Muslim 500, 2021.

enced by the majority."[23] However, he did not face any charges or consequences following the complaint.

Regardless of this incident, Muṣṭafā Ḥusnī is a popular religious guide who enjoys a large audience not only in Egypt, but globally. His lectures and preaching are well-received and often cited in everyday conversations, as I noticed during my field research. In addition, Ḥusnī participates in social activities and hosts various charity events, for example as the Director of the Ammar al Ard Charity Foundation for Human Development. He also offers special services to his community, such as selling *Qur'ān* recitations as an app for smartphones. To reach his audience directly and to interact with the participants, he regularly invited individuals, both adults and children, to various competitions, ranging from preaching to *Qur'ān* recitation.[24] These competitions are publicly visible and encourage the active participation of his followers. Other public events such as public performances and rallies are also part of Ḥusnī's agenda and transform his virtual character into a real one, available and visible beyond the screen.

It is striking that Muṣṭafā Ḥusnī is a religious teleguide who combines global religious trends with local social transformations. These local social transformations are closely linked to global processes of individualisation and an increasing use and consumption of social media. Throughout the past decade, "imagined communities" – to borrow the term from Benedict Anderson – have been transferred from public or private spaces to virtual spaces in the digital realm.[25] According to Mohamed Ismail, "Hosni's discourse represents a glocal form of Islam that takes into consideration globalization and the reconciliation of dissonant hybrid identities by neglecting the traditional Islamic meta-narratives concentrating on the mini-narratives that achieve salvation and self-help."[26] Muṣṭafā Ḥusnī has transformed himself into his own brand that displays various layers, such as religious, social, and individual dimensions. While he does not sell his private life, political opinions, or a specified religious direction, he propagates a lived religion and religious vitality to be practiced by individuals. He calls for individuals to be agents in their intimate ability to create and modify religion. Ḥusnī claims that the definition of religion is not only in the hands of the authorities – although he is not explicitly against them – and that disenchantment with public religion can be met only by making religion enchanting in the intimate space of the individual.[27]

23 Wikipedia, 2021. Translated from Arabic by the author.
24 Cf. Ismail, 2020.
25 Cf. Anderson, 2006.
26 Ismail, 2020: 146.
27 See Weber, 2004.

Employing the figure of himself by embodying worldliness is visible in his appearance. In public, he wears a shirt sometimes combined with a jacket, dark trousers, and a wristwatch.[28] His short beard is trimmed, and he usually smiles, looking directly into the camera. He looks neat, fresh, healthy, and happy. This appearance, which incorporates an idealised version of himself as an open-minded, (enchanted) modern Muslim, is a crucial element of his brand image. In line with conveying a flexible and modern religious message, he gives access to Islam through various media, thus making religion available to everyone at any time. According to Ḥusnī, accessibility is key if religion is to be part of everyone's everyday life.

However, while I listened to many supportive opinions, not everyone I talked to during my field research was fond of his programs or his public figure. Amira for example, a 49-year-old mother of two, unemployed, living in a middle-class quarter of Alexandria said:

> Muṣṭafā Ḥusnī is very popular among so many people. Everyone likes him. They like how he speaks, the topics he discusses, that he only talks about life and Islam and not about politics. I don't like him. I think he is fake. To me, what he says doesn't feel real or authentic. And this sleek appearance, always happy, and although he tries to be on the same level as us, I have the feeling that he thinks he is better than us. And I don't like that. We should listen to God and to our hearts and not some self-made sheikh who is not qualified to teach us how to be religious. This is my opinion. What I can see is the big business that he created around his figure, that he is a businessman selling his soul for his own profit. How can this be religiously accepted?[29]

From the perspective of consumption in the context of religious information and material, Ḥusnī tries to combine selling his personal brand with selling Islam. To be precise, this selling of Islam is actually selling certain aspects of Islam. These aspects suit the multifaceted religious identities of his audience, which is heterogeneous and diverse in terms of age, profession, relation to God (i.e. Islam), experience in practicing religion, gender, marriage status, and place of residence.

---

28 Cf. Ḥusnī, 2020.

29 Interview conducted by the author, Alexandria, 23 May 2021. All quotes from interviews have been translated by the author.

4 Branding Strategies Beyond Religious Normativity

Interestingly, academics in the Global North often call Muṣṭafā Ḥusnī and other religious guides televangelists or television preachers – terms that I do not favour in the context of Islam, since they come from Christian backgrounds.[30] From an emic perspective, these guides are sheikhs or *šuyūḫ* (plural; *šaiḫ* singular); for pragmatic translation reasons I will use the term religious guide, religious teleguide, or religious influencer alongside the Arabic term *šaiḫ*.

The branding strategies of these religious teleguides go well beyond the religious content that they aim to convey. According to Yasmin Moll: "At the same time, the success of the televangelists' own shows increasingly relies on their ability to navigate between, and capitalize on, different genres and forms of media that go beyond any conventional boundaries of the 'religious' or even the specifically 'Islamic.'"[31] Here, Moll gives the example of how popular music is employed in the trailers and opening sequences of the television shows of Ḥusnī and others, which gives the impression that they are mimicking music videos. Muṣṭafā Ḥusnī's show *Al-kanz al mafqūd* (The Hidden/Lost Treasure) for example, features the well-known voice of popular Egyptian singer Mohamed Fouad.[32] Regarding this branding strategy, it is noteworthy that the worldly song vocalised by Mohamed Fouad is not perceived as contradicting the religious teachings of Muṣṭafā Ḥusnī. On the contrary, in combination, the song and the lecture are perceived as mutually affecting each other and thereby intensifying the message.[33]

And this is exactly what Muṣṭafā Ḥusnī aims at, namely, to establish a brand of his own that triggers a natural emotion among his followers in the sense that religion, i.e. Islam, exists on the same level as everyday life expectations and requirements.[34] The brand here is not a fixed entity but oscillates between the person and the religion. It is thus not surprising that worldly music is played in the opening sequences, as part of the branding intention. During my fieldwork in Alexandria, I encountered a life-work-religion balance approach among many believing Muslims who are searching for an ecological "green" version of Islam that is compatible with their own well-being, a phenomenon that I called "*organic* Islam."[35]

---

30 Cf. Moll, 2010b.
31 Moll, 2010a.
32 See Moll, 2010a.
33 See Moll, 2010a.
34 Cf. Kreil, 2006; Lewis, 2010.
35 Cf. Franke, 2021a.

The brand of Muṣṭafā Ḥusnī follows a similar path. Focusing on the spirituality and not the normative aspect of Islam, this brand is built around the voices and needs of its followers, who are, as stated above, often young and educated and who belong to middle-class milieus.[36] These voices can be followed on social media, where they express their needs and mostly ask for inspiration and guidance and how Islam can be maintained and practiced, as well as about the meaning of life.[37] Thus, innovation and being aware of trends and future developments are key aspects of the image Muṣṭafā Ḥusnī wants to convey.[38] Through interaction with his followers, he is able to perceive their needs and requests and to respond to them by answering with an entangled personal and religious brand that they can identify with.[39] The relation between him and his public has become a natural and dynamic process of mutual inspiration. The transformative power of this brand in the sense of transforming one's self by becoming more religious was noteworthy during many of the interviews I conducted in Egypt. These interlocutors for instance referred to Ḥusnī as an example of how Islam should be discussed, taught, and portrayed in public. As fellow Egyptians, they were proud of this brand from a nationalist perspective and added that more religious guides should follow his example. As Dalia, one of my interlocutors, stated, the importance lies in the combination of the content and the wrapping of the message:

> Muṣṭafā Ḥusnī is not a *šaiḫ* like the others that we know. He is dressed normally, and he speaks our language [i. e. Egyptian Arabic], he talks about everyday life, issues that concern us as teenagers, young adults, and family members. It is a lot about relationships with others. And it is also about how we can remain spiritual in an Islamic sense in our hectic lives that are dominated by work, family, and commuting. His unique ability is to remain calm and not shout during his shows, to use examples from his own environment, to take us seriously and not treat us like little stupid children. We feel understood and valued even in our imperfections and failures. And he also conveys the message of the holy *Qur'ān* in an understandable way; it is not just about citing and referencing; he gives illustrative examples and how the times of our prophet Muḥammad, *peace be upon him*, can be understood and incorporated in our everyday lives today. It is not that I am a regular follower, but I understand how he reaches out to us and how this makes a difference for many of us who are struggling with Islam. Not because they doubt, but because our lives have become so busy, and we often do not make enough time for our belief. Muṣṭafā Ḥusnī helps us to be practicing Muslims no matter how crazy our schedules have become.[40]

36 Cf. Echchaibi, 2011.
37 Ryder, Ian 2003: 352.
38 See Wise, 2003; Winegar, 2008.
39 Cf. Ryder, Ian 2003.
40 Interview conducted by the author, Alexandria, 18 June 2021.

In her account, Dalia hinted at a request that many of my interlocutors had – a balanced life in line with Islamic norms that still leaves enough scope for personal interpretation and creativity: a life-religion balance that is similar to the work-life-balance approach mentioned above.[41]

5 Emotions, Love, Compassion: Spiritual and Religious Content

My analysis and assessment of the content of Muṣṭafā Ḥusnī's material in his sermons, shows, social media, and books is in line with most of my interlocutors' impressions, who stated, for example, that they noticed "a focus on relationships," as Dalia put it. More generally, a focus on emotions, especially on love and compassion, can be identified. Muṣṭafā Ḥusnī takes the individual into consideration and highlights that, as a single person, one should aim at "higher" results in social relationships.[42] He advises his followers to maintain a religious mindset by practicing religion on a daily basis – he refers here to regular praying and reading the *Qur'ān*, in particular. According to Ḥusnī, Islam and society in Egypt can flourish and grow only if social relationships are prioritised in terms of emotions, love, care, and compassion. Moreover, Ḥusnī considers it necessary for religiosity to be fostered and included in even the busiest everyday life. Ḥusnī therefore does not present Islam as a religion that is normative and punishing; rather he points to the spirituality of Islam and its compatibility with personal interests, development, and success. His main message is to see and read beyond the written word. This approach will reveal the true message and enlighten everyone's spirituality and relationship with God. By using illustrative examples from his own life, he evokes proximity with his audience. To these everyday life examples, he regularly adds examples from the *Qur'ān* and *Ḥadīṯ*, first by recitation and then by explanation.[43]

Another aim of Ḥusnī is to bring the written sources (especially the *Qur'ān* and *Ḥadīṯ*) closer to people and to make the texts clearer for the masses. These sources need interpretation, since neither their content nor their language is self-explanatory. Thus, by repeating the message in Egyptian Arabic and fleshing it out with examples from everyday life, the audience can get closer and closer

41 See Franke, 2021a.
42 Cf. Ismail, 2020.
43 See Moll, 2012.

to God.[44] Ḥusnī encourages his followers to engage with the written sources, even if they are not fully understood, since through repetition and recitation an enhanced religious mindset will be achieved, in the sense of being closer to God, and thus being connected more deeply to one's religious self. Rituals such as praying and fasting, as well as kind and loving behaviour towards others, are equally important.[45] The key to a successful, prosperous, and satisfying life, then, is not necessarily fully understanding Islam as religion per se, but having a strong faith and spirituality by practicing religion in terms of rituals. The improvement of the individual and intimate self is at centre stage in these programs, as in Ḥusnī's book *Fann al-ḥayāh* (The Art of Life).

Salvation and afterlife are not necessarily key concepts that he focusses on. However, some of his shows are called *Allāh* (God), *'Alā bāb al-janna* (At the Door to Paradise) and *'Alā ṭarīq Allāh* (Road to Allah) and clearly focus on how his followers can collect *ḥasanāt*[46] in order to be ready for paradise.[47]

6 Concluding Remarks

As has been demonstrated, brands, especially personal brands in the realm of spirituality, are designed with a focus on enhancing the consumer's religiosity as in being religious and *doing* being religious. The mindsets and emotional desires of individuals are put at centre stage. Individual needs, comfort, and a sense of well-being are projected onto the brand. These intimate conditions are expected to bring a return on the customers' investment of time and money, with an added value at the personal level of satisfaction. In this sense, the individual becomes emotionally more satisfied by consuming the brand's product. According to many of my interlocutors, personal spiritual brands are often accused of influencing or manipulating their audience. Thus, the notion of trust comes into play as an important factor for the persistence of the brand, something that Muṣṭafā Ḥusnī focuses on by excluding political issues from his lectures. By incorporating his religious messages in everyday life processes, he also employs mechanisms and practices of transparency and integrity to give credibility, authenticity, and profoundness to his own brand. The focus of the present example, then, is on relationships in terms of social links between the brand and the consumer, i. e. the social

44 Cf. Ismail, 2020.

45 Cf. Franke, 2021a.

46 *Ḥasanāt* is the Arabic term for deeds, good deeds, and points that count toward being granted permission to enter paradise.

47 Cf. Saleh, 2012; Schulz, 2006; Mittermaier, 2019.

spirit. Consequently, for my interlocutors, trust and transparency are the most important reasons for them to "follow" the personal brand of Muṣṭafā Ḥusnī and to listen to his religious guidance, while at the same time maintaining and fostering their individuality. In this sense, engaged "following" does not mean uniformity, but rather defined individuality by decidedly listening, reading, or watching certain parts or episodes of Ḥusnī's programmes and selecting the religious content of his personal brand. Consumers judge spiritual brands based on these categories, which in turn leads to controlling strategies by the actors behind the brands to assess and continuously improve their offers, namely in terms of performance; this can then lead to the co-creation of brands by their consumers. For this, Ḥusnī's engagement and direct interaction with his followers on social media, and his responding to their demands, serves as a strong example. His personal spiritual brand leads in the domain of religious guidance in Egypt and beyond and uses various channels in print and online media to reach its customers. As a brand, Muṣṭafā Ḥusnī focusses on the individuals as consumers of his services, thus aiming at enhancing and fostering their spiritual mindset and religious practices.

Bibliography

Abaza, Mona. "The Revolution's Barometer." *Jadaliyya* 12 June 2012. http://www.jadaliyya.com/pages/index/5978/the-revolutions-barometer. Accessed 10 September 2020.

Abaza, Mona. "Post January Revolution Cairo: Urban Wars and the Reshaping of Public Space." *Theory, Culture & Society* 31.7–8 (2014): 163–183.

Abaza, Mona. *Cairo Collages: Everyday Life Practices after the Event.* Manchester: Manchester University Press, 2020.

Anderson, Benedict. *Imagined Communities: Reflections on the Origin and Spread of Nationalism.* London: Verso, 2006.

Bano, Masooda, and Hanane Benadi. "Regulating Religious Authority for Political Gains: Al-Sisi's Manipulation of al-Azhar in Egypt." *Third World Quarterly* 39 (2018): 1604–1621.

Brown, Jonathan A. C. "Is Islam Easy to Understand or Not? Salafis, the Democratization of Interpretation and the Need for the Ulema." *Journal of Islamic Studies* 26.2 (2015): 117–144.

Darrat, Mahmoud A. "A Conceptual Investigation Into the Effects of Cultural Animosity on Middle Eastern Consumers' Purchase Intentions." *Journal of Islamic Marketing* 2.1 (2011): 5–13.

Echchaibi, Nabil. "From Audio Tapes to Video Blogs: The Delocalisation of Authority in Islam." *Nations and Nationalism* 17.1 (2011): 25–44.

El Esrawi, Mouataz. *Explaining the Downfall of Egyptian President Mohamed Morsi.* PhD thesis, Lebanese American University, Beirut, 2019.

Fahmy, Khaled, Assia Boutaleb, and Youssef El Chazli. "From the Archive to the Revolution and Back: Another History of the Egyptian State." *Critique Internationale* 84.3 (2019): 127–144.

Fahmy, Khaled. "How The Muslim Brotherhood Fell from Power." 17 September 2013. https://khaledfahmy.org/en/2013/09/17/how-the-muslim-brotherhood-fell-from-power/. Accessed 3 February 2021.

Franke, Lisa. "Individuality Beyond the Beaten Track: Self-Pietization, Qur'ān Circles and Organic Islam in Contemporary Alexandria." In *Negotiating the Religious in Contemporary Everyday Life in the "Islamic World"*, edited by Roman Loimeier, 39–67. Göttingen: Göttingen University Press, 2021a.

Franke, Lisa. "Muslimness on Demand: Critical Voices of Islam in Egypt." *Religions* 12.3 (2021b). https://doi.org/10.3390/rel12030152.

Gad, Thomas. "Leadership Branding." In *Beyond Branding: How the New Values of Transparency and Integrity are Changing the World of Brands*, edited by Nicholas Ind, 183–198. London: Kogan Page, 2003.

Haenni, Patrick. "The Reasons for the Muslim Brotherhood's Failure in Power." In *Egypt's Revolutions: Politics, Religion, and Social Movements*, edited by Bernard Rougier and Stéphane Lacroix, 19–39. New York: Palgrave Macmillan, 2016.

Hirschkind, Charles. "Experiments in Devotion Online: The YouTube Khuṭba." *International Journal of Middle East Studies* 44.1 (2012): 5–21.

Ḥusnī, Muṣṭafā. *Siḥr al-dunyā* (The Magic/Enchantment of the World). Cairo: Dār Nahḍat Miṣr lil-Našr, 2020.

Ind, Nicholas (ed.). *Beyond Branding: How the New Values of Transparency and Integrity are Changing the World of Brands.* London: Kogan Page, 2003.

Ismail, Mohamed Hossam. "Postmodern Analysis of New Preachers of Islam in Egypt: A Cultural Study of Mustafa Hosni's Digital Media Platforms." *Media Watch* 11.1 (2020): 145–163.

Kazi, Taha. "The Changing Dynamics of Religious Authority on Pakistani Religious Television." *Culture and Religion* 17.4 (2016): 468–485.

Keller, Kevin Lane. *Strategic Brand Management: Building, Measuring and Managing Brand Equity.* Upper Saddle River, NJ: Prentice-Hall, 2nd ed., 2003.

Kreil, Aymon. *La piété et la foi: La zebîba, marque de prière, et les signes d'engagement religieux masculins au Caire.* PhD thesis, Université de Neuchâtel, 2006.

Lewis, Reina. "Marketing Muslim Lifestyle: A New Media Genre." *Journal of Middle East Women's Studies* 6.3 (2010): 58–90.

Maehle, Natalia, Cele C. Otnes, and Magne Supphellen. "Consumers' Perceptions of the Dimensions of Brand Personality." *Journal of Consumer Behavior* 10.5 (2011): 290–303.

Mehrez, Samia, ed. *Translating Egypt's Revolution: The Language of Tahrir.* Oxford: Oxford University Press, 2012.

Mittermaier, Amira. *Giving to God: Islamic Charity in Revolutionary Times.* Berkeley: University of California Press, 2019.

Moll, Yasmin. "Islamic Satellite Channels and the Ethics of Entertainment in Egypt." *Arab Reform Bulletin* 21 April 2010a. Carnegie Endowment for International Peace. https://carnegieendowment.org/sada/40646. Accessed 13 March 2021.

Moll, Yasmin. "Islamic Televangelism: Religion, Media and Visuality in Contemporary Egypt." *Arab Media & Society* 10 (2010b): 1–27.

Moll, Yasmin. "Storytelling, Sincerity, and Islamic Televangelism in Egypt." In *Global and Local Televangelism*, edited by Pradip Ninan Thomas and Philip Lee, 21–44. London: Palgrave Macmillan, 2012.

Mourad, Maha, and Hatem El Karanshawy. “Branding Islamic Studies: Exploratory Study in the Middle East.” *Journal of Islamic Marketing* 4.2 (2013): 150–162.

Paswan, Audhesh K., Nancy Spears, and Gopala Ganesh. “The Effects of Obtaining One’s Preferred Service Brand on Consumer Satisfaction and Brand Loyalty.” *Journal of Services Marketing* 21.2 (2007): 75–87.

Ryder, Ian. “Anthropology and the Brand.” In *Beyond Branding: How the New Values of Transparency and Integrity are Changing the World of Brands*, edited by Nicholas Ind, 139–160. London: Kogan Page, 2003.

Saad, Reem. “The Egyptian Revolution: A Triumph of Poetry.” *American Ethnologist* 39 (2012): 63–66.

Saleh, Ibrahim. “Islamic Televangelism: The Salafi Window to Their Paradise.” In *Global and Local Televangelism*, edited by Pradip Ninan Thomas and Philip Lee, 64–83. London: Palgrave Macmillan, 2012.

Schielke, Samuli. *Egypt in the Future Tense: Hope, Frustration, and Ambivalence before and after 2011.* Bloomington: Indiana University Press, 2015.

Schulz, Dorothea E. “Promises of (Im)Mediate Salvation: Islam, Broadcast Media, and the Remaking of Religious Experience in Mali.” *American Ethnologist* 33.2 (2006): 210–229.

The Muslim 500. “Sheikh Mustafa Hosny: Televangelist.” *The Muslim 500: The World’s Most Influential Muslims 2022*, 95. Dabuq: The Royal Islamic Strategic Studies Centre, 2021. https://bit.ly/3piKfaH. Accessed 15 March 2021.

Weber, Max. *Politics as a Vocation.* Indianapolis: Hackett, 2004.

Wikipedia. “Muṣṭafā Ḥusnī”. https://ar.wikipedia.org/wiki/مصطفى_حسني. Accessed 15 March 2021.

Winegar, Jessica. “Purposeful Art Between Television Preachers and the State.” *ISIM review* 22.1 (2008): 28–29.

Winegar, Jessica. “Civilizing Muslim Youth: Egyptian State Culture Programmes and Islamic Television Preachers.” *Journal of the Royal Anthropological Institute* 20.3 (2014): 445–465.

Wise, Lindsay Rebecca. *Words from the Heart: New Forms of Islamic Preaching in Egypt.* PhD thesis, University of Oxford, 2003.

Ghassan Moussawi

Queer Brands, Branding Queerness: Fractal Orientalism and Selling Gay-Friendly Beirut

1 The Making of Gay-Friendly Beirut

What makes a city, region, and/or country gay- or queer-friendly, and who determines what areas and spaces are deemed as such? How do designations of gay-friendliness circulate, and what are their consequences for places and the people who live and reside there? When it comes to South West Asia and North Africa (SWANA), more specifically the Arab World, the relationship to gay-friendliness is paradoxical. That is, on the one hand, people associate SWANA and the Arab World as regions that are homophobic and, thus, labelled backward in comparison with their Euro-American counterparts. On the other hand, there is a proliferation of Euro-American journalistic accounts, travelogues, and gay tour guides about gay life in the Arab World, claiming that while the Arab World is homophobic, there are *some* places in the region that are *actually* gay-friendly – albeit in a way that is different from dominant understandings of LGBTQ life and gay-friendliness.

Taken together, these approaches have been used by Euro-American journalistic accounts to highlight Beirut as a gay-friendly destination in a "homophobic region." To make the case that Beirut is gay-friendly, such travelogues and journalistic accounts simultaneously compare it with and distance it from Euro-American cities and cities in the Arab World. For example, they claim that while some aspects of gay life in Beirut might resemble those of a major European or American city, it will never be *as* open. However, given that it is part of the Arab World, Beirut becomes the best-case scenario for gay life in the region. Therefore, by distancing it from other Arab cities, which are seen as more homogeneous, these travelogues leave Beirut seeming cosmopolitan and somewhat similar, but not identical to European and US cities. Thus, Beirut seems exceptional only because it is part of the Arab World. Arriving at such assertions and to make gay life in Beirut intelligible to Western audiences, these accounts rely on Euro-American "metrics" of gay-friendliness like the presence of gay neighbourhoods, visible LGBTQ communities and LGBTQ organising, thriving gay nightlife, and legal protections to "measure" the extent to which Beirut is or can be gay-friendly. While these accounts speak of gay lives in the Arab World, they do not engage with the extensive scholarly literatures on non-normative gender and sexualities in the Arab

https://doi.org/10.1515/9783110741100-017

World, both historical and contemporary, which document the lives of LGBTQ individuals and communities from multiple perspectives.[1]

The Orientalist positions mentioned above, such as using dominant metrics of gay-friendliness to locate gay life in the Arab World or claiming that the Arab World is a homogenous homophobic region, are vexing. These designations position places on a spectrum from gay-friendliness to homophobia that lead some spaces to be seen as progressive and forward-looking versus others that are traditional, homophobic, and "stuck in time," without mentioning the histories and presents of colonialism that have shaped and reshaped gender and sexual cultures in those places.[2] Historically, Euro-American Orientalist travelogues have written about same-sex desires and practices in the Arab World documenting homosexual practices as being predominant and normalised aspects of the fabric of Arab societies, thereby marking the Arab and Muslim World as spaces of degeneracy and sexual licentiousness in comparison with centres of empire, mostly Europe.[3] However, more contemporary non-scholarly iterations about gay life in the Arab World focus on and highlight the homophobic nature of the region by citing the continuous existence of colonial anti-sodomy laws and the lack of legal protections for sexual and gender minorities. This shift from representing the Arab and Muslim World as degenerate regions where people practice homosexuality to contemporary representations of these spaces as homophobic due to the lack of legal and social protections for LGBTQ people shows how metrics for sexual openness are arbitrary, change over time, and how dominant brandings of places as gay-friendly become a sign of progressiveness.

In this piece, I reflect on the case of Beirut, which has become branded as an exceptional gay-friendly city in the Arab World, from the year 2005 onwards. From pre-civil war designations of Beirut as the Paris or the Switzerland of the Middle East, to contemporary iterations of Beirut as the Provincetown, Christopher Street, or San Francisco of the region, Euro-American spaces become the optic by which Beirut can be understood as gay-friendly, but only to a certain extent.[4] In the following, I first ask what it means to determine a space as gay-friendly and whom are they deemed to be gay-friendly for? Second, I unpack the ways that cities

1 See El-Rouayheb, 2005; Khalaf and Gagnon, 2006; Makarem, 2011; Merabet, 2014; Naber and Zaatari, 2014; Moussawi, 2015, 2020; Chamas, 2021.

2 See Rao, 2020.

3 See Puar, 2002; Patil, 2018; Moussawi, 2020.

4 Provincetown is a coastal city on Cape Cod peninsula, Massachusetts, known as a gay-friendly destination in the US, whereas Christopher Street is a major street in the West Village in New York City, where, provoked by police brutality and violence against gay and trans people, the 1969 Stonewall riots took place.

and countries become branded as gay-friendly, either by internal or external ascriptions. Doing so, I illustrate how Beirut has become branded as a gay-friendly destination through a process I call "fractal Orientalism." Third, I pay particular attention to the structural and political consequences that such designations create and set in place. Drawing on my ethnography of queer formations and everyday violence in Beirut, I show how these brandings affect local LGBTQ and queer communities, arguing that they produce shrinking LGBTQ spaces for local queer people – particularly trans, genderqueer, working-class people, and racially minoritised refugees. In addition, given my experience as an "expert witness" for gay asylum seekers from the Middle East, I demonstrate how these representations have made it much harder for LGBTQ people to seek asylum if they reside in Lebanon. While one can focus on regions, countries, cities, or spaces within cities, in this piece I move between multiple scales of analysis to capture the complex processes involved in such brandings and the (un)intended consequences they have on local queer communities.

2 Branding Gay-Friendliness

Since the mid-1990s, gay-friendly designations have become central in coding places as progressive and/or backward and traditional. Often, spaces in the Global South are seen as inherently homophobic and as places where gay people cannot live and thrive. When some places are "found" to be gay-friendly, they are regarded with surprise and seen as exceptional, given the geographic location they are placed in. One cannot think of brands without highlighting processes of packaging and commodifying spaces and people as available for consumption to those with economic or other forms of privilege, such as national, racial, gender, or class privilege. That is, brands are central to the workings of neoliberalism and transnational racial capitalism that attempt to "sell" commodities. Applied to gay-friendliness, such brands promise potential tourists (and some residents) experiences of sexual freedom and liberation, even if fleeting.

When people think of gay tourism, they don't often think of the Arab World as a destination, though historically, North Africa and the Levant have been described as places for homosexual self-exploration for European white men and travellers.[5] Travel and encounters with people in "foreign" places have a history of racialising populations and places through the relational uses of gender and sexual normativity. For example, metropoles and centres of empire have historically used first-per-

5 See Boone, 1995, 2014; Moussawi, 2013.

son written accounts and encounters, such as travelogues, to document gender and sexual non-normativities in the Global South to relationally define and uphold *their own* proper and normative gender and sexual cultures.[6] Thus, to speak about gay-friendliness and gay-friendly designations, one needs to pay attention to colonialism and empire, not as merely historical events, but also – to borrow Patrick Wolfe's conceptualisation of settler colonialism – as structures that endure.[7] Though Lebanon "allegedly" gained independence from the French in 1945, centres of empire still determine the extent to which the country and its capital city are or have the potential to be gay-friendly.

While some states are currently making various efforts to brand their country, nation, and/or cities as gay-friendly to attract the "pink dollar," the case of Beirut is different, as it is a city that has become branded as gay-friendly through mostly external factors, such as Euro-American press and other outlets mentioned above. Some countries use gay-friendliness and gay rights as a sign of progressiveness to distract from violent state-led practices against other minorities, a process that has become known as "pinkwashing."[8] While gay-friendly brands are used as a means to attract and mobilise the pink economy, what happens when centres of empire brand a city as gay-friendly?

3 Fractal Orientalism

My book *Disruptive Situations* addresses the ways Beirut has become gay-friendly and how such discourses are circulated at multiple levels: global, regional, and local, using what I call fractal Orientalism or "Orientalism within the Middle East." Since the Syrian troops' withdrawal from Lebanon in 2015, Beirut has been hailed as the new gay-friendly destination in the region. The discourses that circulated around this new branding of Beirut came from Euro-American travelogues, journalistic accounts, and gay travel guides, such as *Spartacus International* – the most widely sold gay tour guide. Besides the examples given above, Beirut has also been dubbed, e.g., the "Amsterdam," "French Riviera," and "sin city" of the Middle East.[9] Based on first-person narratives by white gay cisgender men in Beirut, these travelogues circulate narratives about these travellers' experiences of the city's gay life – though never through the lens of those who reside there. In these travelogues, locals are painted as non-agentic; rather, they become racialised subjects who would do

6 See Patil, 2018.

7 See Wolfe, 2006.

8 For more on pinkwashing and Israel, see Schulman, 2011.

9 Quotes from Moussawi, 2020: 29.

anything to cater to white gay tourists. For example, some journalists, travelogues, and gay guides report that even Lebanese and Arab heterosexual men engage in same-sex acts with white Euro-American tourists. They "explain that this sexual 'fluidity' (read as confusion) is due to the lack of a clearly defined and developed gay identity" and as an inherent attraction to and desire for whiteness (though not explicitly spelled out as such).[10]

To understand how cities become externally branded as gay-friendly, I argue that we must use multi-scalar analysis that attends to the changing nature of relational understanding of the "other." As Edward Said argues, discourses circulate and recirculate through citational practices.[11] These travelogues cite each other as examples of "truth" or evidence of gay life in Beirut. To gauge gay life in cities, people usually look for the presence of laws that protect sexual and gender minorities and the presence of gay-friendly establishments, gaybourhoods, and activist spaces. Building on postcolonial and transnational feminisms, I suggest that these contemporary neoliberal representations of Beirut use and rely on what I call fractal Orientalism, which "uses relational distinctions to produce Lebanon as exceptional and gay friendly – that is, 'modern,' but *only* within the context of the Arab World."[12] Taken from mathematics, physics, and geometry, fractals are geometric shapes that repeat themselves infinitely across multiple scales.[13] They are found in nature, for example in snowflakes, tree branches, and lightning, yet they "hide in plain sight."[14]

Scale and fractals become important heuristics to unpack how Beirut becomes branded as gay-friendly in these travelogues. Rather than take for granted that Orientalism produces a single binary of East/West, I zoom in and out to capture the multiple scales by which fractal Orientalism simultaneously works, using the same distinctions (i. e. on each level), such as progressive/traditional or gay-friendly/homophobic. At the global level, the West is seen as more gay-friendly than the Arab World. At the regional level, Lebanon is seen as more open than its Arab counterparts. Furthermore, the same binary is used at the national level, where Beirut becomes the only gay-friendly city in the midst of "the homophobic" rural areas and cities in Lebanon. Finally, this extends to neighbourhoods within Beirut, where Christian quarters are described as freer and more open than their Muslim counterparts. As a theoretical lens, fractal Orientalism "is an imperial structure or imposition that functions transnationally, regionally, at the level of the nation and the

10 Moussawi, 2020: 45.

11 See Said, 1978.

12 Moussawi, 2020: 8.

13 For more, see Moussawi, 2020.

14 For more on fractals, see Rose, 2012.

city; hence, it provides us with a multi-scalar spatial model that uncovers how distinctions are made, circulated, and remade."[15] Therefore, it is based on processes of othering that are constantly shifting. While these fractal Orientalist accounts rely on the co-existence of difference – primarily through the narrative of Beirut as a city that encompasses 18 different religious sects, where no one sect is a majority – it is done by means of a neoliberal practice that aims to celebrate and sell Beirut as a cosmopolitan city, unlike its Arab counterparts. Celebrating Beirut's diversity and difference without attention to structural inequalities erases the experiences of the majority who are actively marginalised and dispossessed by the state. In addition, such celebrations of difference rely on flattened understandings of diversity and culture.

While this branding of Beirut as gay-friendly is not an internal ascription, some segments of Beiruti society reproduce these narratives, defending their experience of Beirut as a gay-friendly city. However, this is done only by those who are structurally privileged, whether through gender, class, citizenship, and racial privileges. Those who do argue that Beirut is, indeed, exceptional, including local gay tourist organisations, refer to victories in gay rights by citing the Lebanese Medical Professional Association's outlawing of the French anal examinations or the fact that the anti-sodomy law hasn't been applied lately. However, this is not the case, since the anti-sodomy French penal code continues to target those who already occupy marginalised positions in society.[16] That is, these marginalised communities are legally persecuted for their practices, while others from upper social strata and white gay tourists are not.

4 External Branding and its Structural and Political Consequences

As demonstrated throughout this reflection, focusing on the gay-friendly nature of Beirut obscures structural inequalities, people's relation to power, and the state-led violence against those who are already marginalised. By branding Beirut as a gay-friendly destination and city, these travelogues, guides, and journalistic accounts assume and create a homogenous LGBTQ population in Lebanon, without attending to the pluralities and inequalities that constitute these communities. While painting Beirut as gay-friendly, these representations focus only on cis-white gay

15 Moussawi, 2020: 7–8.
16 See Makarem, 2011.

men's experiences and their encounters with other cisgender men. Thus, they completely erase the experiences of trans, genderqueer persons, and women.

Not everyone has access to experience Beirut as gay-friendly, particularly those who are already structurally marginalised by Lebanese society and the state, such as queer refugees, trans, non-binary, and gender non-normative persons and working-class people, to name a few. In these accounts, one of the first consequences is that Beirut becomes branded as gay-friendly by erasing the inherent structural inequalities within Lebanese and Beiruti societies. Beirut becomes gay-friendly for upwardly mobile, white, able-bodied men who have the privileges of transnational mobility. That is not to say that gay-friendly cities in the Global North are all-inclusive, given that gay-friendly destinations still discriminate against certain populations, whether in the United States or Europe. For example, gay-friendly spaces are still racialised, classed, laud gender normativity, and are ableist.[17]

Second, when these first-person narratives circulated in global journalistic outlets, such as the *New York Times* and gay travel guides like *Spartacus International*, they outed a number of gay establishments and spaces, giving them an international reputation for being gay-friendly. Gay establishments that were featured in the accounts gained international visibility and became even more inaccessible to Lebanese LGBTQ populations, by becoming more expensive – since they can now rely on the transnational pink dollar. In addition, such bars and informal cruising areas became well-known in the city and thus suffered from more scrutiny and surveillance. This created shrinking spaces and even more limited access for segments of Lebanese LGBTQ communities.

Third, and one of the most devastating consequences, is that this branding has made and continues to make it much harder for those who are seeking asylum outside of Lebanon for fear of persecution for being gay, lesbian, trans, and/or HIV-positive. Black and Brown LGBTQ asylum seekers are seen and treated with suspicion by Western European and North American nation-states, through racialised processes and the assumptions that they are trying to "trick" the asylum and immigration systems. Thus, they have to endure not just the precarious lives they are living, but the burden of proof to show that they are *actually* lesbian, gay, and/or trans – as understood by dominant framings of gayness and trans-ness. That is, they must *illustrate* that they are actually queer, and their proofs must be intelligible, believed, and accepted by immigration official and courts.

In my experience as an "expert witness" for LGBTQ asylum seekers from Lebanon, Western European and US immigration laws and courts have made it much

17 See El-Tayeb, 2011; Haritaworn, 2015.

harder, if not impossible, for Lebanese LGBTQ individuals to gain asylum. Courts draw on the representations of Beirut as gay-friendly and open, thus creating a greater "burden of proof" for those seeking asylum from Lebanon than for refugees from other Arab or Muslim countries. This not only impacts Lebanese people, but also Syrian and Palestinian refugees who try to seek asylum outside of Lebanon based on their gender and sexuality. Thus, in my own work, I have to provide much more context to show how Beirut is gay-friendly *only* for those who already occupy privileged positions in society. Many have been denied asylum because Beirut has been branded a gay-friendly destination. While branding cities as gay-friendly might attract more economic prosperity through gay tourism, it does have a number of consequences that further the marginalisation and dispossession of those who do not enjoy class, racial, and gender- and sexual-normative privileges. As long as we use dominant Euro-American metrics of gay-friendliness to arbitrarily "assess" other places – like visibility, pride parades, openly gay establishments, and rainbow flags – we will continue to reproduce Orientalist narratives of the Middle East and Arab World, without any attention to nuance and the complexities of LGBTQ lives.

Bibliography

Boone, Joseph. "Vacation Cruises: Or the Homoerotics of Orientalism." *Publications of the Modern Language Association* 110.1 (1995): 89–107.

Boone, Joseph. *The Homoerotics of Orientalism.* New York City: Columbia University Press, 2014.

Chamas, Sophie. "Lil Watan: Queer Patriotism in Chauvinistic Lebanon." *Sexualities* (2021): 1–22.

El-Rouayheb, Khaled. *Before Homosexuality in the Arabic Islamic World 1500–1800.* Chicago: University of Chicago Press, 2009.

El-Tayeb, Fatima. *European Others: Queering Ethnicity in Postnational Europe.* Minneapolis: University of Minnesota Press, 2011.

Haritaworn, Jin. *Queer Lovers and Hateful Others: Regenerating Violent Times and Places.* Chicago: Pluto Press, 2015.

Khalaf, Samir, and John Gagnon, eds. *Sexuality in the Arab World.* London: Saqi Books, 2006.

Makarem, Ghassan. "The Story of Helem." *Journal of Middle East Women's Studies* 7.3 (2011): 98–112.

Merabet, Sofian. *Queer Beirut.* Austin: University of Texas Press, 2014.

Moussawi, Ghassan. "Queering Beirut, the Paris of the Middle East: Fractal Orientalism and Essentialized Masculinities in Gay Travelogues." *Gender, Place and Culture: A Journal of Feminist Geography* 20.7 (2013): 858–875.

Moussawi, Ghassan. 2015. "(Un)Critically Queer Organizing: Towards a More Complex Analysis of LGBTQ Organizing in Lebanon." *Sexualities* 5.6 (2015): 593–617.

Moussawi, Ghassan. *Disruptive Situations: Fractal Orientalism and Queer Strategies of Beirut.* Philadelphia: Temple University Press, 2020.

Naber, Nadine, and Zeina Zaatari. "Reframing the War on Terror: Feminist and Lesbian, Gay, Bisexual, Transgender, and Queer (LGBTQ) Activism in the Context of the 2006 Israeli Invasion of Lebanon." *Cultural Dynamics* 26.1 (2014): 91–111.

Patil, Vrushali. "The Heterosexual Matrix as Imperial Effect." *Sociological Theory* 36.1 (2018): 1–26.

Puar, Jasbir K. "Circuits of Queer Mobility: Tourism, Travel and Globalization." *GLQ: A Journal of Lesbian and Gay Studies* 8.1–2 (2002) :101–138.

Rao, Rahul. *Out of Time: The Queer Politics of Postcoloniality.* New York: Oxford University Press, 2020.

Rose, Michael. "Explainer: What Are Fractals?" *The Conversation* 11 December 2012. https://theconversation.com/explainer-what-are-fractals-10865. Accessed 20 March 2022.

Said, Edward. *Orientalism.* New York: Vintage, 1978.

Schulman, Sarah. "Israel and 'Pinkwashing.'" *New York Times* 22 November 2011. http://www.nytimes.com/2011/11/23/opinion/pinkwashing-and-israels-use-of-gays-as-a-messaging-tool.html. Accessed 10 March 2022.

Wolfe, Patrick. "Settler Colonialism and the Elimination of the Native." *Journal of Genocide Research* 8.4 (2006): 387–409.

Part III: **State Branding**

Philip Geisler

Sinan's Iconic Practices: Staging Early Modern Ottoman Architecture and Power

1 Introduction: "Always Historicize" Architectural Branding

"Always historicize!"[1] is the programmatic imperative that Marxist literary theorist Fredric Jameson sees as the intellectual operation essential to a critical understanding of the structural nature of culture and the interpretive categories that conceive of it. Jameson proposes that the creation of literary works has always been inextricably linked to political contexts. He takes this as a cue to shift analytical interest away from purely aesthetic readings and to foreground the centrality of political interpretations of culture. This frames creative works and subjects of the past in terms of their emergence through historical constrictions, unconscious ideologies, and structural causalities.[2]

Based in this epistemological framework, this chapter is concerned with the question of how architectural history can contribute to the historicisation of branding in the Middle East. Jameson's remarks invite wider historical problematisation in assessing the more recent strategy of branding in architecture, which I understand in a broad way as the strategic conveying of constructed identity through architecture by businesses, cities, nations, and other entities, driven by a capitalist economic logic.[3] I will use "strategy" as the central concept to trace a history of perceptual tactics that eventually became condensed in branding.[4]

My aim is to evaluate the extent to which interpretive approaches to the past centred on the concepts of politics and power can inform a critical understanding of regional contributions to the global history of branding and the strategic uses of architecture in more recent times. More specifically, and rather than suggesting a linear genealogy or a generalised trans-historical reading, I wish to highlight a specific moment in the architectural history of the Ottoman Empire. I argue that in the 16th century, Ottoman frameworks of building practice merged individual

1 Jameson, 1982: 9.

2 See Jameson, 1982: 56.

3 This follows the definition of Klingmann, 2007.

4 On the theme of strategy and the communicative status of architecture, see Gutzmer, 2015: 15–18.

https://doi.org/10.1515/9783110741100-018

and institutional factors in the production of architecture formative for the architectural strategy of branding.

To avoid conflating imperial with later architectural production strategies under the regimes of capitalist consumption and consumerist profit gains, I suggest employing the concept of "iconic practices" for the context of the 16th century. This frames historical architecture in terms of the merging of the materiality of buildings, the locality of their experience, and the intangibility of globally circulating mental and visual images.[5] Iconic buildings are not simply outstanding, tall, or spectacular landmarks, but exemplify the social production of architecture as part of institutionally authorised meaning making.[6] Through their iconicity, buildings partake in consolidating and producing hegemonic power hierarchies. The question of how their iconic status is constructed and conveyed includes their association with image flows, veneration, myth making, and their visual and textual representation. Iconic practices produce architecture that conveys controlled stories, associations, and imaginaries, which in turn condense reality and images. The concept emphasises human creative practices and material environments that strategically represent the cultural convictions of larger power systems.[7]

In the first part of this contribution, I review various threads found in recent literature to provide an overview of the architectural, intellectual, theoretical, and historical prerequisites of branding as a global strategy. My intervention questions the paradigm of Westernisation in cultural interpretations of the era of capitalist globalisation and takes up earlier suggestions to historicise perceptual strategies of urban icons through diachronic, global, and multidisciplinary approaches.[8] By focusing on iconic architectural practices in the early modern Ottoman Empire – as one strain among many in the region – I advance an understanding of regional and imperial contributions to this architectural strategy, beyond its unfolding in Europe and North America.

The subsequent parts examine how Ottoman architecture and urban design of the 1570s and 1580s in Edirne and Istanbul reflect strategic iconicity and image construction. I will connect a summary of my own previous research on the Selimiye Mosque in Edirne (completed in 1574), designed by the Ottoman chief architect Sinan (died in 1588), with considerations on the architect's tomb (completed in

5 See Ethington and Schwartz, 2006: 11–12; Kress, Schalenberg, and Schürmann, 2011: 11.

6 See Sklair, 2017: 17, 41–49.

7 See Sklair, 2017: 24.

8 See Kress, Schalenberg, and Schürmann, 2011: 11–14. They reference Ethington and Schwartz, 2006, who highlight that comparative research should aim at greater historicisation of urban icons across the world and who focus on medialisation strategies, controlled uses and perception, and the appropriation of buildings.

1587) located at the northern corner of the Süleymaniye complex in Istanbul, on the one hand, and the city's district and urban mega project of Yenibahçe (built around Sinan's mosque in the 1570s–1580s), on the other. The remarkable simultaneous occurrence of an iconic architect persona, media innovations, and advances in architectural culture based in imperial wealth informs us about early uses of architecture as a strategic and communicative rather than expressive sign.[9] With its reading of iconic practices, this chapter illustrates the multilevel entanglements of image construction that merge a personal image, architecture, and urban as well as imperial identities in the early modern Middle East.

2 Transregional and Transdisciplinary Histories

Numerous publications assess architectural branding in Europe and North America and sometimes in South East and East Asia in the 20th and the 21st centuries. For the Middle East, we gain an understanding of architectural branding in studies that address contemporary architecture, urban form, and place identity. These comprise investigations of the relationship of signature architecture and the positioning of cities on the global economic stage, as well as studies that theorise architectural branding in the Middle East as part of the more global evolution of branding, which frame buildings and architectural representation through systemic critiques of mental capitalism and economies of attention and experience.[10] Most of these publications foreground Western-centric historical narratives.

Studying the structural unfolding of branding as a perceptual strategy of persuasion before the 20th century has rarely been a part of historical examinations.[11] This lacuna seems to be especially relevant for discussions of Middle Eastern architecture as such, which I wish to differentiate from the many existing contributions on urban space and place making. This is despite the circumstance that the architectural practice of branding today shapes design practice, concepts of monumentality, cultural narratives, and urban form across the globe as an essential tool that

9 See Eco, 1977: 45–49. Eco's notion was previously raised in Vonseelen, 2012: 89.

10 I refrain from listing publications on these broader topics here. On large-scale urban planning and the iconicity of master plans, see Salewski, 2011. For a global study of city branding, see Dinnie, 2011. On architecture and its relation to the economy of attention and mass media, see Franck, 2005: 173–217. For a reading through the framework of the experience economy, see Klingmann, 2007. Cf. also Kress, Schalenberg, and Schürmann, 2011; Kamleithner and Meyer, 2011.

11 It has been researched mainly in management-related fields and the sociology of organisations. Critical assessments in the humanities and in architectural history are rare, see Vonseelen, 2012: 12–14.

controls mental images, human perception, and physical movement in built environments.[12] Narrowly connected to Western contributions, modern marketing, and translocal "place-wars,"[13] branding, as an expression of the power of global capital and commodification, has rarely been recognised as a relevant theme in the field of architectural history.

With this remark, I refer to a lack of deeper historical studies revealing the historicity of the perceptual and aesthetic concepts used in architectural identity strategies of the industrial and post-industrial capitalist eras. My approach to historicising the perceptual strategies of branding mirrors the need for a transregional and transdisciplinary project that discerns regional historical legacies enabling modern and post-modern global architectural strategies of communication. Some scholars have begun to consider such historical and theoretical underpinnings of branding, reaching back to European intellectual history and architectural theory.

Gerhard Burs has explained that after the invention of perspectival representation, early modern architectural drawings gained a strong similarity to natural perception and incorporated the visualisation of entire environments, including landscapes and depicted humans.[14] In the 18th century, drawings became more autonomous as they shifted to represent subjective experiences and atmospheres of built structures. He frames this history of architectural drawings in Europe as a central precondition for today's virtual architectural realities and their perceptual effects.

The connection between identity, experience, and projected image in the making of places evolved out of modern European philosophy and psychology, as Robert Govers and Frank Go have highlighted.[15] They discuss changing debates on the relation between material objects, their perception, and ideas in the works of René Descartes, John Locke, and Pierre Bayle, whom they see as founders of the concepts of image linked to identity and perceptual illusion. Their consideration of the works of Immanuel Kant, Clemens Brentano, and Martin Heidegger on subjective experience is interwoven with remarks on the importance of modern cognitive psychology for branding strategies.

Tanja Vonseelen has focused on the communicative function of architecture discussed in early modern Italian and French concepts of architectural theory, rhetoric, and representation found in the works of Leon Battista Alberti and Sebas-

12 See Govers and Go, 2009: 2–9.

13 Short, 2014: 238.

14 See Burs, 2016: 51–160.

15 See Govers and Go, 2009: 23–33.

tiano Serlio.[16] In her view, this genealogy continued in the 17th- and 18th-century French movement of *architecture parlante*, promoting architectural form as a direct signifier of the function and character of a building. The fantastic architectural drawings of Étienne-Louis Boullée and Claude-Nicolas Ledoux capitalised on the iconic, emotional, and immersive effects of architecture on the human senses.

In her study of iconic architecture, Leslie Sklair has referenced Reinhard Bentmann and Michael Müller's work on the emerging countryside villas in 16th-century Italy. Through the aesthetics and artistic quality delivered by Palladio as an iconic architect, this building type, in their view, rationalised the emerging class order of the region's new nobility of urban landowners who dominated a rural working class, consolidating power hierarchies in a context of early capitalism and idealised agriculture.[17] She also contextualises major mosques of the Islamic world through their iconic functions within distinct hegemonic systems.[18] In delineating Islamic design traditions incorporated in contemporary iconic structures in Malaysia, Morocco, and Sudan, Sklair proposes that iconic architecture merges local and global components and mobilises regional historical legacies beyond mere formal images of history. She emphasises that "historically, in most societies, religious authorities dominated the first era of what we now see as architectural icons, [while] states and empires dominated the second era (...)."[19] Building on this idea, the next section illustrates how early modern iconic building practices in Ottoman architectural culture represent another formative strain within this transregional history of architectural branding.

3 Iconic Practices in 16th-Century Ottoman Architecture

Sinan's 16th-century building projects were situated in an environment that structurally resonates with the era of capitalist globalisation. His architecture responded to a context of early globalisation, marked by religious, political, and cultural power struggles across the Mediterranean and wider European and Asian geogra-

16 See Vonseelen, 2012: 51–85 and 12–13, note 4, on the genealogy of the scholarly discussion of corporate architecture since the 1980s. Müller-Rees, 2008 examines the corporate architecture of Cartier and the power of the brand in exclusive fashion.

17 See Sklair, 2017: 11–14, 161–162.

18 Others who highlight such historical lineages of architectural communication and identity expression are Vonseelen, 2012: 17, 30; Kress, Schalenberg, and Schürmann, 2011: 8; Kamleithner and Meyer, 2011: 23.

19 Sklair, 2017: 4.

phies.[20] The dynamics of global mobility and connection enabled the cultural exchange of knowledge and trade, leading to a vast wealth of resources, stability, and efficient bureaucracy that became available for Ottoman building projects.[21] Accompanied by newly emerging media technologies, these developments resulted in a unique concurrence of factors guiding the use of architecture as an iconic strategy channelled through Sinan's personal agenda.

3.1 Sinan's Tomb, Istanbul (1587)

In his work for various sultans, lasting approximately half a century, Sinan oversaw the completion of over 300 structures, including imperial mosques and mosque complexes, schools, hospitals, mausoleums, palaces and mansions, bridges, bathhouses, and aqueducts. His unique status as an iconic and emancipated architect is manifested in the structure and urban prominence of his tomb (Fig. 1). Sinan carefully constructed his own image through this site, his endowment deed, and autobiographies.[22] As Gülru Necipoğlu has noted, the collective aspect of his works, "created with the mediation of the corps of royal architects (...), came to be almost completely overshadowed by the unabashed self-aggrandizement through which Sinan successfully controlled the shaping of memory over the generations."[23]

The tomb is located at a triangular plaza north of Sinan's Süleymaniye complex (inaugurated in 1557). It was built adjacent to his main residence in Istanbul. The burial site inside the walled city indicates Sinan's close relationships with the sultan and the ruling circles, who allowed him to place his tomb in an exceptionally iconic urban environment. The v-shaped wall encloses a raised prayer platform. Sinan's sarcophagus is placed on top with a headstone sculpture of a coiled turban roofed by a baldachin. A domed octagonal water dispenser on a platform is placed at the enclosure's apex.

The epitaph points to the strategic fashioning of Sinan's status as an iconic architect, which is achieved through this structure. As it refers to the Süleymaniye as "a sign of the highest paradise,"[24] its inscription above a grilled window directly connects the work of the buried man, whose presence is visually affirmed in his monumentalised sarcophagus, with the adjacent architecture that is staged as a

20 See Subrahmanyam, 1997; Fletcher, 1995.

21 See Geisler, 2020: 132, 141.

22 See Doğan, 2012: 27–29; Ateş, 1990; Yerasimos, 1990: 242.

23 See Necipoğlu, 2005: 152.

24 Necipoğlu, 2005: 147.

testament to Sinan's achievements as an iconic example. The inscription also states that Sinan built more than 400 small mosques (*masjids*) and Friday mosques in 80 locations.

Fig. 1: Sinan's tomb with water dispenser, Istanbul, 1587
Photo: Vince Millett. "Tomb of Mimar Sinan." *Flickr* 2 March 2008. https://www.flickr.com/photos/brokendrumphotography/2335348484/in/photostream/. Accessed 13 August 2021. Courtesy of the photographer.

Mentioning Sinan's water channels and bridges as equal to the Milky Way, the epitaph insinuates the religious and mythological connotations of water. By charging the tomb architecture and its direct environment in such ways, the epitaph monumentalises the small-scale structure while aggrandising the image of its designer. His genius is honoured and proven by the sound, scent, and touch of flowing water brought to a hilltop platform in the city. The symbolism of the rule over nature through engineering knowledge is complemented by the topos of benediction associated with water and, as Jale Nejdet Erzen has pointed out, by honouring the non-visual qualities of the city.[25]

Necipoğlu emphasises that the water dispenser was not part of Sinan's own *waqf* (charitable endowment), but was financed by Sultan Süleyman's endow-

25 See Erzen, 2004: 169.

ment.[26] Sinan had earlier sent a petition to the Sultan reporting that many individuals living around the area of the mosque had requested the construction of a water dispenser at this "place of passage at the intersection of three streets distant from the [neighbourhood's] fountain."[27] His emphasis on the transitory qualities of this intersection highlights his strategic choice of location. Legally a part of Süleyman's *waqf*, the water dispenser was added to the corner of Sinan's tomb enclosure in 1587 shortly before the latter's death. Following this visual configuration, though, it has commonly been read as Sinan's own charity for the city.[28] Orchestrating his own commemoration, Sinan "blur[red] the boundaries of the sultan's and the chief architect's waqfs"[29] and merged two projected personal images – Süleyman's and his own – in one public hyper-image at a prime urban location marked by large numbers of daily passers-by.

At this newly established urban destination of monumental architecture, the tomb's layout plan is designed in the form of an open pair of compasses, the technical drawing instrument with two joined arms used by architects, as Oktay Aslanapa first noted.[30] If this angled compass were to draw a full semicircle, it would outline an ideal panoramic 3D-axial view onto the Süleymaniye's northernmost corner with the whole compound opening up towards the south. By designing his tomb architecture as a direct figurative symbol, Sinan expresses his profession's corporate identity and connects his own image with the Süleymaniye complex in ways that visibly render the chief architect the mastermind of this sultanic endowment as a virtuosic ruler over urban topography, design, and views. As Necipoğlu comments, the tomb "inscribed the chief architect's signature on his architectural masterpiece."[31]

3.2 Yenibahçe, an Urban Mega Project in Istanbul (1570s–1580s)

The small-scale structure of his tomb illustrates that Sinan has to be seen as both an architect and an urban designer. His consciousness for self-fashioning resonated not only with his tomb, but also with some other architectural and infrastructural projects of his that directly benefitted neighbourhoods in which other royal

26 See Necipoğlu, 2005: 151.
27 Aygen Bilge, cited in translation in Necipoğlu, 2005: 151.
28 See Necipoğlu, 2005: 151.
29 Necipoğlu, 2005: 151.
30 See Aslanapa, 1986: 205.
31 Necipoğlu, 2005: 151.

architects resided. As the master plan community of Yenibahçe shows, the objective of expressing the image and corporate identity of the imperial architects went beyond individual buildings and encompassed entire districts. After Sinan had endowed a *masjid* (Fig. 2), fountain, and elementary school in this new quarter, it was branded *Mimar Sinan Mahallesi.*[32]

Fig. 2: Sinan's mosque, Yenibahçe/Fatih, Istanbul, reconstruction from 1976 with 16th-century minaret and foundations
Photo: Beyza Uzun, 2021. Courtesy of the photographer.

Such iconic practices were not concealed, as Sinan's endowment deed refers to this area as "the quarter associated with himself."[33] The very scope of this endowment resonates with later urban master plan projects and included shops, three residential houses, an elementary school, a small mosque with seven adjacent residences, as well as seven residences with shops, all designed by Sinan.[34] Mathematical trea-

32 Based on historical maps, Doğan, 2012 discusses the history of this quarter around Sinan's *masjid* up until its renaming as *Akşemseddin Mahallesi* in 2008.
33 Necipoğlu, 2005: 149.
34 See Necipoğlu, 2005: 149.

tises with great value for the practice of architecture were kept in the area's *masjid* that was located close to Sinan's first residence, named *Şehnameci Evi*, and Sinan's *Sarugez* bathhouse.[35] With its name, its administration as an urban ensemble, and as a centre of architectural knowledge and the architectural class, this quarter acquired a carefully projected image expressive of the collective identity of the imperial corps of architects, with Sinan as its representative icon. After various earthquakes and the great fires of 1782 and 1918, none of Sinan's original buildings remain except his *masjid's* minaret and foundations.[36]

3.3 The Selimiye Mosque, Edirne (1568–1574)

As Howard Crane points out, the evolution of Ottoman architecture in the 16th century made structures "tangible symbols – icons – expressive of the values, authority, power, and legitimacy embodied in the person of the prince and his state."[37] The discernable style of architecture developed by Sinan connected building aesthetics, regional traditions, and the consolidation of imperial rule across the Ottoman Empire. The Selimiye Mosque (Fig. 3), a multi-use complex originally including a courtyard, a roofed market, three schools, and gardens, exemplifies this function of architecture as urban icons in the context of strategic communication and power.[38]

In an earlier article, I have discussed that the iconic practices shaping the complex concern the recognisable use of an overall architectural form referencing and challenging the Hagia Sophia in Istanbul as an icon of Ottoman triumph and the inheritance of imperial, hegemonic power. With its four minarets positioned around the central dome, the Selimiye forms a "unique urban imprint"[39] of Selim II. In his urban intervention in Edirne, Sinan subjugated older structures and redefined the urban scheme. Here, Sinan used architectural design and narratives to achieve urban domination and mark political hegemony. The strategy of urban and mental domination originates in the mosque's internal integration and rational building concept. As all elements serve the visual elevation of the cen-

35 See Doğan, 2012: 24.

36 The *masjid* was still open and intact in 1840 and presumably destroyed by the great Fatih fire in 1918. It was reconstructed in 1976 according to a sketch by Cornelius Gustav Gurlitt; see Doğan, 2012: 20–21.

37 Crane, 1991: 173.

38 Here and in the following paragraphs, see Geisler, 2020: 122–131.

39 Geisler, 2020: 133.

tral dome, Sinan oriented his building towards the architectural element that was most important in global comparisons of cultural achievements at this time.

Beyond design and urban staging, the early modern production of mental images through literary narratives reflects a strategic process of iconisation that canonises structures and anchors them in collective consciousness. After the completion of the Selimiye, Islamic religious legends about the Hagia Sophia were rewritten to initiate an image transfer from the former Byzantine cathedral to the newly erected sultanic mosque. This creation of architectural narratives reached its height in the 16th to 18th centuries.[40] They entangled religious buildings in the region in teleological narratives of Islamic triumph over Christianity, relating some to prophecies pronounced by the Prophet Muhammad.[41] These narratives became central tools in the achievement of immaculate images of power, glossing over contradictions and ruptures in the architectural visualisation of triumph.

Sinan's image construction through iconic architectural design led European travellers to create textual and visual representations of the Selimiye. Before the construction of the Selimiye, Edirne had assumed a place in Ottoman collective memory as the empire's second capital. The new mosque complex created an early modern fame beyond its borders, drawing travellers and diplomats to the city and redefining its visual and mental images within and beyond the Ottoman Empire. Topographical engravings and architectural drawings of Edirne circulated in Western Europe in travelogues, like Johann Christoph Wagner's 1684 account.[42] The Austrian envoy's secretary, Johann Andreas Christoph Kempelen, related that the Selimiye surpassed prominent buildings in 18th-century Europe and in Antiquity.[43] In 1717, Lady Mary Wortley Montague commented on the mosque's ingenious urban dominance and described it as the noblest building she had ever seen.[44] Some travellers restated and thus legitimised the architectural legends.

These accounts displayed the successful implementation of projected architectural form and narrative. They affirmed the mental images and hegemony of Ottoman cultural achievement through the iconic status of architecture. Essential in this iconic design process was Sinan's ability to exploit topography as a stage for architectural domination. As a landmark, the Selimiye shifted Edirne's urban identity by visibly connecting it to sultanic power and placed Edirne on the map. This productively entangled architectural dominance and political hegemony as the

40 See Morkoç, 2010; Watenpaugh, 2004.

41 See Yerasimos, 1990: 128–143; Necipoğlu, 1992: 200.

42 See Geisler, 2020: 132, 144, note 160.

43 See Kreiser, 1982: 124–127; Geisler, 2020: 133.

44 See Halsband, 1965: 358.

Fig. 3: Selimiye Mosque, Edirne, 1564
Photo: Khirashima. "Selimiye Mosque." *Wikimedia Commons* 13 November 2019. Creative Commons BY-SA 4.0, https://creativecommons.org/licenses/by-sa/4.0. https://commons.wikimedia.org/wiki/File:Ist-Ath_-_99_cropped.jpg. Accessed 4 October 2021.

more insidious and subtle form of power that is reproducible at the level of culture and its shifting signs.

4 The Imperial Legacies of Starchitecture, Joint Ventures, and Signature Buildings

The iconic practices pursued through Sinan's tomb, Yenibahçe, and the Selimiye put a unique and identifiable stamp on their urban environments. The spectacular contrasts, historical references, and formal uniqueness of individual structures effectuated the dissemination of architectural representations and narratives. This allowed for the global construction of cultural topoi of immaculacy and magnificence. The triangulation of an emancipated architect, architectural and urban form, and mental image construction formed a wider set of perceptual strategies, which the following section identifies as imperial legacies of architectural branding.

4.1 Staging the Iconic Architect

Sinan creatively orchestrated his own "brand stretching" through his projects. His endowments anticipate the modern architectural practices of creating social foundations, architectural fellowship programs, and student collectives elevated through their status as disciples that became key elements in producing the iconic status of architects in the first half of the 20th century. Through (auto-)biographical accounts like his *Tezkiretü'l-Bünyan* (*The Record of Construction*), Sinan used media to frame architecture in textual narratives.[45] In his tomb, he carved his personal image in stone. It reveals his strategic use of façades as autonomous elements that serve image construction. Similarly, the Selimiye's design gave canonical form to a monumental Ottoman mosque complex and simultaneously specified Sinan's image as an architect who was able to reach his explicitly stipulated goal of surpassing the Hagia Sophia through visual strategies.[46]

As an emancipated architect, Sinan successfully realised his own agenda within the Ottoman bureaucratic system. His buildings not only consolidated Ottoman power, they also displayed the oeuvre of a famous architect persona and Ottoman official. This unique historical circumstance led to various instances of image transfer between the architect, his commissioners, his own buildings, and earlier structures, as well as the symbiosis of the architect's image with his built legacy.

45 See Çelebi, 2002. For an English translation, see Saatçi and Sözen, 1989. Cf. also Crane, Akın, and Necipoğlu, 2006.
46 See Geisler, 2020: 111–112.

Today, this symbiosis of starchitect images and their oeuvres is an essential element of the transnational capitalist icon project.[47] Sinan staged himself as an iconic architect through such perceptual strategies. His undated endowment deed documents that he performed the cultural practice of funding the construction of schools and other socially beneficial structures and of ensuring his commemoration through prayers after his passing.[48] By designing a whole district for the architectural class that was soon named for him, he effected his own framing as a shortcut for the profession of architecture and for Ottoman cultural achievements in general.

4.2 Recognisability, Repetition, and Symbolic Form

A second perceptual strategy was the creation of coherent and "catchy" design features. Sinan condensed cultural coherence within the imperial boundaries by connecting regionalised styles with an overall structural and aesthetic scheme. By relating the Selimiye to the Süleymaniye and engaging in long-distance stylistic dialogues with structures in Bursa and other towns, he forged the recognisability of Ottoman architecture through the handling of building materials, decoration, layout plans, and especially elevation plans. As iconic design features were repeated throughout the empire, buildings became poignant signs that catered to the consistent visualisation of Ottoman and Sunni identity.

Through centralised and controlled architectural production, 16th-century Ottoman architecture reached a high degree of regional coherence that frames imperial iconic practices as a precursor of modern visual identity construction. Sinan's tomb, capped by the large turban headstone, supplements this by using blatantly obvious metaphors, both written and sculptural. The tomb's layout plan in the form of an architect's compass blurs the boundary between architecture and sculpture because an overarching symbolic form dominates the architectural elements.[49]

47 See Sklair, 2017: 62–69.

48 See Doğan, 2012: 27–28; Ateş, 1990.

49 On this phenomenon in 20th-century corporate architecture, see Vonseelen, 2012: 20.

4.3 Mental Image Construction

A third perceptual strategy of branding that can be historicised through Ottoman iconic building practices is the construction and communication of mental images, including the creation of superimposed hyper-images. In the Selimiye, Sinan synthesised various architectural elements – spolia, overall form, standardised minarets, building materials – that function as interacting signifiers and that trigger mental images. The signifiers of size and height played an additional part in referencing territorial expanse, triumphant conquests, economic wealth, and cultural inheritance. The incorporation and reform of Byzantine building styles in the Selimiye and the production and dissemination of myths about the building illustrate how Sinan used historical references to elevate buildings. As the Selimiye's form epitomises the Ottomans' status as the heir of the Byzantine Empire, its architectural image and mobilisation of historical forms legitimises the inheritance of power. In its relation to the Hagia Sophia, the Selimiye exemplifies the strategy of image transfer enabled by architectural form and textual practices. The effects of this mental image construction played out already in the building process. Framed as especially innovative, qualitative, and spectacular, the Selimiye's construction was closely followed in Europe.[50]

The connections between Sinan's tomb and the Süleymaniye, both in terms of their endowment deeds and their spatial organisation, show that Sinan orchestrated image construction as a major objective of *waqfs* with great virtuosity. The organisation of visual axes and flows of passers-by elevated his own autonomous image. Here, Sinan forged another powerful joint venture of images by entangling his burial site with Sultan Süleyman's imperial mosque. The essential objective of such strategies of image construction and multidirectional mental referencing in Ottoman architecture was the domination of urban space and its mental readings.[51]

4.4 Iconicity, Experience, and the Aura of Buildings

The disseminated visual representations of Ottoman architecture transformed dynamics in the relationship between the localisation and the aura of buildings. They helped establish the global iconic status of structures by integrating political and

50 See Geisler, 2020: 118.

51 On the role of domination as a goal in contemporary architectural branding, see Short, 2014: 246.

social acceptance as well as wide cultural validation.[52] The more effectively a building's iconicity was planned and orchestrated, the more poignant were the visual and textual representations of structures as dominating forms in urban skylines.[53] The effectiveness of the iconisation of architecture was propelled by recent technological innovations in printing and improved travel infrastructures. These advanced early modern strategies of exploiting buildings to serve the communication of power. As buildings became famous to those who were able to access their visual representations, they became known before an actual encounter.

More important than detailed architectural descriptions were travellers' affective reactions to buildings like the Selimiye, which they described in superlative terms. Before the mass reproduction of architectural images, such circulating representations and texts were formative for an architectural practice conscious of spectacular form as a condition for global prominence. The monumentality of the Selimiye was reinforced through such visual and textual politics that complemented and predetermined the experience of the direct encounter. An additional element that served the creation of monumentality and sustained the iconicity of architecture was the incorporation of the mental connotations of sites generated by their previous uses. To stage his tomb, Sinan mobilised the iconic environment of the Süleymaniye. Before Sinan's interventions in Yenibahçe, the area had been known as a noble and extravagant neighbourhood.[54] In Edirne, the Selimiye was built on royal grounds where the city's Old Palace had once stood.[55]

4.5 Architecture as Urban Design and Prime Location

Sinan organised Ottoman urbanity through large-scale building projects with multi-use components. As a marked district of the corporate identity of architects, Yenibahçe exemplified an urban design thinking that is prevalent also in Sinan's tomb and the Selimiye. The mosque even gained the status of a signature building functioning as a unique urban logo visible from a distance as a marked sign in the urban skyline. As Sklair notes, the urban silhouette as a visual site psychologises architecture by framing the city as a reference of belonging, identity, and pride in the eyes of its inhabitants.[56] This sustains the construction of urban images

52 See Kress, Schalenberg, and Schürmann, 2011: 8.
53 On the general concept of iconicity, see Jencks, 2005.
54 See Doğan, 2012: 23.
55 On the role of historic environments as part of branding in more recent times, see Glöckler, 1995: 99.
56 See Sklair, 2017: 157.

and the formation of a city's identity as it relates to a specific sultan or urban function.[57]

By conceiving the Selimiye, Yenibahçe, and his tomb through urban design, which accentuates notions of multifunctionalism and structural relations to adjacent buildings and areas, Sinan created prime urban locations. The tomb-fountain and the mosque complex with market, courtyard, and gardens generated multi-use spaces that unfolded urban experiences oscillating between the elevated space of religion, culture, and power, on the one hand, and everyday mass uses and popular readings, on the other. By involving spectators and visitors, all three cases gained their status as prime urban locations through their beneficial contributions to everyday social life. Their experiential immediacy, paired with architectural quality, display of building technology, vast scale, and urban integration, served to distinguish these urban sites and generate attention.

5 Conclusion

The exercise of Ottoman iconic practices in architecture included perceptual strategies of staging the iconic architect, developing recognisable and repeated architectural styles, constructing mental images, and conceptualising buildings through iconicity and urban design. What is notable about this historical moment and place is the conjunction of perceptual approaches under an iconic architect, who used architectural communication to mobilise controlled visual rhetoric and identity construction. Besides aspiring to perceptual domination and reproducing political hegemony, Ottoman iconic practices fully developed the twofold quality of urban icons as physical objects bound to a place and as circulating images.[58] As Ottoman chief architect, Sinan exploited this dual character of iconic architecture by designing accessible, inviting, and at the same time highly hegemonic spaces.[59] His buildings functioned both as icons in their built environments and as visual pictograms shortcutting larger cultural and political convictions.[60] Particularly, these tangible monuments and urban configurations instigated intangible feelings of the dignity of larger ideas of power, as well as Ottoman and Sunni worldviews, directed towards affective levels of perception. This exploitation of accessible-inaccessible and open-controlled dualisms of iconic architecture continues

57 See Eldem, Goffman, and Masters, 1999; Geisler, 2020; Watenpaugh, 2004.

58 On the twofold character of urban icons in the 20th century, see Ethington and Schwartz, 2006.

59 See Geisler, 2020: 123.

60 A phenomenon of urban icons first remarked upon by Kamleithner and Meyer, 2011: 23.

up to the present, marking its discursive framing between the professional sphere and the popular realm with mass appeal.

Hence, before the context of capitalist globalisation, iconic practices in architecture established constitutive perceptual features and architectural knowledge of branding as a strategy of communication. In both temporal contexts, architecture is mobilised as part of mass communication to control perception and movement, persuade recipients, and subtly influence readings and convictions. Assessing Sinan's tomb, the Selimiye, and Yenibahçe in terms of strategy, communication, and power illustrates how the perceptual components assembled in 20th-century marketing strategies can be traced historically and regionally. This highlights that capitalist profiling strategies did not evolve ahistorically. In a certain sense, the concept of branding is itself an act of branding in that it conceals the historical legacies that were reassembled in a new mix of strategies under capitalist regimes. Historicising the practice and tools of branding in a diachronic, transregional manner problematises how capitalist interest incorporated imperial legacies for profit making.

Such diachronic, global, and multidisciplinary approaches to architecture generate a broader picture of how a global architectural history of branding can be written. By integrating regional and wider historical studies into the project of mapping this history, our understanding of a globally omnipresent architectural phenomenon advances beyond Western-centric narratives of intellectual history and architectural theory. The architectural cultures, literary works, visual aesthetics, and philosophical approaches found in the early modern Middle East provincialise European historiographies of corporate architecture and foreground the global formation of its perceptual strategies. By focusing on the iconic practices in the Ottoman Empire, this contribution has assessed one historical context among many to show how regions outside of Europe have participated in the cultural production of architectural strategies that have been globalised under transnational capitalism. Although modernism and postmodern marketing have caused substantial ruptures in architectural cultures, a nuanced transregional and diachronic historicisation of architectural branding illuminates the continuing influence of imperial strategies in architecture.

Bibliography

Aslanapa, Oktay. *Osmanlı devri mimarîsi: Orhan Gazi'den başlayarak sonuna kadar padişahlara göre gelişmesi (Architecture of the Ottoman Period: Its Development under the Sultans Beginning with Orhan Gazi and until the End).* Istanbul: İnkılâp Kitabevi, 1986.

Ateş, İbrahim. *Mimar Sinan vakfı (The Pious Foundation of Mimar Sinan).* Istanbul: Türk Dünyası Araştırmaları Vakfı, 1990.

Burs, Gerhard Martin. *Mediale Präsentation in der Gegenwartsarchitektur: Das Beispiel der Vereinigten Arabischen Emirate.* Bielefeld: Transcript, 2016.

Çelebi, Sâî Mustafa. *Yapılar kitabı: Tezkiretü'l-Bünyan ve Tezkiretü'l-Ebniye (Mimar Sinan'ın anıları) (The Book of Buildings: Tezkiretü'l-Bünya and Tezkiretü'l-Ebniye (Memoirs of Mimar Sinan)).* Edited by Hayati Develi, Samih Rifat, and Doğan Kuban. Istanbul: Koçbank, 2002.

Crane, Howard. "The Ottoman Sultan's Mosques: Icons of Imperial Legitimacy." In *The Ottoman City and its Parts: Urban Structure and Social Order,* edited by Irene A. Bierman, Rif'at A. Abou-El-Haj, and Donald Preziosi, 173–243. New Rochelle: Aristide D. Caratzas, 1991.

Crane, Howard, Esra Akın, and Gülru Necipoğlu. *Sinan's Autobiographies: Five Sixteenth-Century Texts.* Leiden, Boston: Brill, 2006.

Dinnie, Keith, ed. *City Branding: Theory and Cases.* Basingstoke, New York: Palgrave MacMillan, 2011.

Doğan, Sema. "'Bu fakir'ül hakir'in mescidi': Mimar Sinan Mescidi ('The Mosque of this Humble One': The Mosque of Mimar Sinan)". *Restorasyon ve Konservasyon Çalışmaları Dergisi* 8 (2012): 20–29.

Eco, Umberto. *Zeichen: Einführung in einen Begriff und seine Geschichte.* Frankfurt am Main: Suhrkamp, 1977.

Eldem, Edhem, Daniel Goffman, and Bruce Masters. "Conclusion: Contexts and Characteristics." In *The Ottoman City between East and West: Aleppo, Izmir, and Istanbul,* edited by Edhem Eldem, Daniel Goffman, and Bruce Masters, 207–214. Cambridge, UK: Cambridge University Press, 1999.

Erzen, Jale Nejdet. *Sinan: Ottoman Architect. An Aesthetic Analysis.* Ankara: Middle East Technical University, 2004.

Ethington, Philip J., and Vanessa R. Schwartz, eds. Special Issue *"Urban Icons". Urban History* 33.1 (2006).

Fletcher, Joseph F. "Integrative History: Parallels and Interconnections in the Early Modern Period 1500–1800." In *Studies on Chinese and Islamic Central Asia: Collected Articles of Joseph Fletcher,* edited by Beatrice Manz, 1–35. Aldershot: Variorum, 1995.

Franck, Georg. *Mentaler Kapitalismus: Eine politische Ökonomie des Geistes.* Munich: Hanser, 2005.

Geisler, Philip. "Challenging the Hagia Sophia: The Selimiye Mosque in Edirne as Ottoman Empire Branding." In *The Heritage of Edirne in Ottoman and Turkish Times: Continuities, Disruptions and Reconnections,* edited by Birgit Krawietz and Florian Riedler, 91–151. Berlin, Boston: De Gruyter, 2020.

Glöckler, Thomas. *Strategische Erfolgspotentiale durch Corporate Identity: Aufbau und Nutzung.* Wiesbaden: Deutscher Universitätsverlag, 1995.

Govers, Robert, and Frank Go. *Place Branding: Glocal, Virtual and Physical Identities, Constructed, Imagined and Experienced.* Basingstoke, New York: Palgrave MacMillan, 2009.

Gutzmer, Alexander. *Architektur und Kommunikation: Zur Medialität gebauter Wirklichkeit.* Bielefeld: Transcript, 2015.

Halsband, Robert, ed. *The Complete Letters of Lady Mary Wortley Montagu, Vol. 1: 1708–1720*. Oxford: Oxford University Press, 1965.

Jameson, Fredric. *The Political Unconscious: Narrative as a Socially Symbolic Act*. Ithaca: Cornell University Press, 1982.

Jencks, Charles. *The Iconic Building: The Power of Enigma*. London: Frances Lincoln, 2005.

Kamleithner, Christa, and Roland Meyer. "Urban Icons: Architektur und globale Bildzirkulation." *Informationen zur Modernen Stadtgeschichte* 2 (2011): 17–31.

Klingmann, Anna. *Brandscapes: Architecture in the Experience Economy*. Cambridge, MA: The MIT Press, 2007.

Kreiser, Klaus. "Zwei unbekannte Beschreibungen des Serails von Edirne aus den Jahren 1740/41." *Osmanlı Araştırmaları* 3 (1982): 119–142.

Kress, Celina, Marc Schalenberg, and Sandra Schürmann. "Spektakel, Allheilmittel, Forschungsfeld: Perspektiven auf 'Urban Icons.'" *Informationen zur Modernen Stadtgeschichte* 2 (2011): 7–16.

Morkoç, Selen B. *A Study of Ottoman Narratives on Architecture: Text, Context and Hermeneutics*. Bethesda, Dublin, Palo Alto: Academia Press, 2010.

Müller-Rees, Vanessa. *Haute Architecture: Eine Untersuchung der Baustrategie der Marke Cartier und der Corporate Architecture von Luxusmodemarken seit 1990*. Munich: Deutscher Kunstverlag, 2008.

Necipoğlu, Gülru. "The Life of an Imperial Monument: Hagia Sophia after Byzantium." In *Hagia Sophia from the Age of Justinian to the Present*, edited by Robert Mark and Ahmet Ş. Çakmak, 195–225. Cambridge, UK, New York, Oakleigh: Cambridge University Press, 1992.

Necipoğlu, Gülru. *The Age of Sinan: Architectural Culture in the Ottoman Empire*. London: Reaktion Books, 2005.

Saatçi, Suphi, and Metin Sözen, eds. *Mimar Sinan and Tezkiret-ül Bünyan*. Istanbul: MTV Film Television Video Sanayi ve Tic, 1989.

Salewski, Christian. "Ikonischer Städtebau: Entwicklung und Folgen großmaßstäblichen symbolischen Entwerfens im globalen Kontext." *Informationen zur Modernen Stadtgeschichte* 2 (2011): 83–94.

Short, John Rennie. *Urban Theory: A Critical Assessment*. London: Palgrave MacMillan, 2nd ed., 2014.

Sklair, Leslie. *The Icon Project: Architecture, Cities, and Capitalist Globalization*. New York: Oxford University Press, 2017.

Subrahmanyam, Sanjay. "Connected Histories: Notes Towards a Reconfiguration of Early Modern Eurasia." *Modern Asian Studies* 31.3 (1997): 735–762.

Vonseelen, Tanja. *Von Erdbeeren und Wolkenkratzern: Corporate Architecture. Begründung, Geschichte und Ausprägung einer architektonischen Imagestrategie*. Oberhausen: Athena, 2012.

Watenpaugh, Heghnar Zeitlian. *The Image of an Ottoman City: Imperial Architecture and Urban Experience in Aleppo in the 16th and 17th Centuries*. Leiden, Boston: Brill, 2004.

Yerasimos, Stéphane. *Légendes d'empire: La fondation de Constantinople et de Sainte-Sophie dans les traditions turques*. Paris, Istanbul: Maisonneuve, Institut Français d'Études Anatoliennes d'Istanbul, 1990.

Moritz A. Mihatsch and Richard Gauvain

Branding the United Arab Emirates as Nation Building? Constructing Unity versus Acknowledging Diversity

1 Introduction

In 2019, for the second time, the United Arab Emirates (UAE) started a project to create a logo to represent the identity of the UAE in the form of a "nation brand."[1] Nation branding as a concept emerged in the late 1990s as a product of the neoliberal shift towards a global competition of places and in extension of place branding. The field is characterised by a number of dominant practical and marketing discourses. Keith Dinnie, who wrote the first textbook on nation branding, described the "key objectives" of nation branding as centring "upon the stimulation of inward investment, the promotion of a country's branded exports and the attraction of tourists."[2] Dinnie does not anticipate the effects of nation branding on the nation – the nation brand is merely meant to communicate to the outside world. Indeed, Browning and de Oliveira spy a "dissonance" between nation branding and nation-building.[3] The same relationship is at the centre of a more critical body of literature, which sees "nation branding as a compendium of discourses and practices aimed at reconstituting nationhood through marketing and branding paradigms."[4] In this understanding, nation branding is viewed as a form of commercial, neoliberal nationalism.[5] Particularly in places where the nation may be perceived as "under construction" – due, for instance, to a recent declaration of independence and/or conflict – nation branding projects can intersect with nation-building, such as in South Africa[6] or Suriname.[7]

Only a handful of articles have tackled nation branding in the Middle East. Those that do tend to carry a practical and marketing focus. For instance, Zeined-

1 The previous project was completed in 2012, but the logo was rarely used thereafter. Cf. Hughes, 2012; Essaidi, 2012.
2 Dinnie, 2007: 31.
3 Cf. Browning and Oliveira, 2017: 492.
4 Kaneva, 2011: 118.
5 Cf. Volčič and Andrejevic, 2011: 614.
6 Cf. Cornelissen, 2017: 525.
7 Cf. Hoefte and Veenendaal, 2019: 173.

https://doi.org/10.1515/9783110741100-019

dine compares nation branding in the UAE and Qatar.[8] Notably though, the article treats Dubai and Abu Dhabi individually, rather than as components of the UAE. The most comprehensive discussion of nation branding in the Middle East is Miriam Cooke's book *Tribal Modern: Branding New Nations in the Arab Gulf.* Cooke observes: "Cultural uniqueness is being fabricated out of whole cloth to distinguish new countries from each other but also from their past. The challenge is to mesh individual memories of belonging to an unbounded territory with official histories of borders and flags."[9] Additionally, multiple MA theses explore the topic. For example, Moshashai explored the UAE's Vision 2021 as a tool to further the UAE's nation brand, concluding: "The goal behind Vision 2021 is therefore to project a certain image to the world, one which is characterized by tolerance, high-modernism and dynamism."[10]

To date, scholars have primarily focused on the practical and marketing aspects of nation branding in Middle Eastern contexts (the UAE included). This chapter, by contrast, argues that, as a project, nation branding in the UAE must be understood through the lens of nation-building. Accordingly, the project is situated within the wider literature on the construction of Emirati identity. This chapter advances the following arguments: first, the design and promotion of the UAE's nation branding project reflects and reinforces established political hierarchies and structures. Simultaneously, it is one of multiple strategies by which the UAE government seeks to embrace the seemingly contradictory dimensions of the local/traditional versus the global/modern. Many Emiratis are in agreement both with the UAE's established hierarchies and structures and with the government's efforts to reconcile the dualisms. Incorporated into the nation brand project is a comparatively fresh appreciation of the role of visual arts in promoting national solidarity. However, not all Emiratis perceive the nation branding process – or the winning logo – in a positive light; and a minority questions its relevance to their own cultural and political identity.

The chapter relies on material published by the UAE government, a variety of interviews, and the UAE's media discourse on the subject. Due to restrictions imposed by Covid-19, it was not possible to conduct interviews in person. Instead, all research took place virtually, through interviews on Skype and other media. Moritz Mihatsch spoke to three artists – Aysha al-Hemrani, Azza al-Qubaisi, and Abdulqader al-Rais – involved directly in the nation brand project. To gain an understanding of how ordinary Emiratis view the project, Richard Gauvain conducted

8 Cf. Zeineddine, 2017.

9 Cooke, 2014: 170.

10 Moshashai, 2018: 77.

one-on-one interviews with twenty-five former students from the American Universities in Dubai and Ras al-Khaimah, where he worked from 2009 to 2017. The interviews consisted of ten pre-prepared questions and were semi-structured. Interviewees were aged 25–42; just over 40 % were female. A key correspondent agreed to distribute anonymous online surveys at her place of employment, in Dubai's Expo 2020 project. 31 colleagues completed the survey, which consisted of the same ten questions adapted slightly to fit the new format. Overall, the sample size of interviewees is small; hence, findings must be treated as suggestive.[11]

The chapter continues by reflecting on the unique history of the UAE as a political unit and exploring key trends in the literature on the construction of Emirati identity. The next section describes the stages of the nation brand project. The fieldwork findings are then introduced and discussed in light of the literature's key trends.

2 Nation-Building and National Identity in the UAE

The history of the UAE as a nation-state begins in December 1971, when six of the seven "sheikhdoms" – Abu Dhabi, Dubai, Sharjah, Ajman, Umm al-Quwayn, and Fujairah – formally proclaimed the UAE as an independent state with its own constitution. The seventh sheikhdom or emirate, Ras al-Khaimah, delayed slightly to secure better terms, before joining the federation in February 1972.

Reflecting on the UAE's short but complex history, scholars have drawn attention to the internecine rivalries that characterised tribal life in the seven pre-federation sheikhdoms of "The Trucial States", a place where, historically, coups had frequently occurred and that was now united only inasmuch as its separate leaders had agreed to a truce with Britain. At first the new federal state remained a fragile compromise, and particularly the nature of the political alliance between Abu Dhabi and Dubai, both of which maintained their own air forces until the end of the 1990s, was unclear. While some scholars continue to remark on the potential for friction between the different emirates, a consensus has emerged that, despite (or more accurately because of) the inequalities between the different emirates, political stability – as well as major economic and technological advance – has been mostly achieved.

11 For overall readability and brevity, quotes from the interviews and questionnaires are given without further referencing.

The country's leadership offers its own official, necessarily sanitised, version of the UAE's history.[12] Not surprisingly, this version glosses over tribal divisions and leadership squabbles, attributing the modern economic success to the wisdom and charisma of the federation's first leaders. Two men stand out: the "Father of the Nation", Sheikh Zayed Al Nahyan (1918–2004) of Abu Dhabi, and Sheikh Rashid Sa'id Al Maktoum (1912–1990) of Dubai. The official history reports how these two men met to agree upon an "Initial Accord" – to conduct "foreign affairs, defence, security and social services and to adopt a joint immigration policy." In only a short space of time, they won over the remainder of the leaders and their peoples to the concept of a federation of monarchies. In addition to paying tribute to leadership, the UAE's official history notes key factors embedded in the fabric of the land and people: the enduring importance of the area as a trading centre and the richness (and harshness) of the geographical environment. Before oil, there was the pearl trade, bringing wealth as pearls were exported across the globe. The rapid expansion of the UAE's economy, the result of the discovery and production of oil in the early 1960s, fits neatly within this narrative. The official version of the UAE's history invariably concludes by celebrating the fact that all Emiratis now enjoy free education, healthcare, and social support from the federal government. This achievement – and others, such as "the remarkable advancement of Emirati women in every aspect of life" – stand as a testament to the proud successes of the UAE as a nation-state. The same accounts also celebrate the development of a concrete "Emirati national identity" alongside and – in this narrative at least – superior to traditional allegiances to tribe: the UAE "is the only federal state in the Arab world that has not only survived but succeeded in creating a distinctive national identity with the passage of time."

The emergence of this concrete national identity – rooted in (what is presented as) a single, shared history – can at least partially be explained as necessary due to the political transformation of the UAE from a confederation into a more centralised entity. Especially today, with sovereignty invariably legitimised through the nation, pooling sovereignty necessitates a different imagined community as a legitimating basis. There was another component here, however. The death in 2004 of the UAE's founder Zayed Al Nahyan – whose charismatic personality had long served as a central unifying symbol – galvanised the UAE's authorities into launching any number of nation-building projects so as strengthen Emirati ties to the nation.

Parallel to and intersecting with discussions of Emirati history, we find a flourishing ethnographic debate on the construction of Emirati national identities.

12 For the quotes in this paragraph, see UAE Ministry of Presidential Affairs, 2018.

Three trends within this literature are identified here. The first explores the country's burgeoning heritage industry. In this approach, an Emirati identity is formed by and with primary reference to its political elites. Ordinary activities – such as traditional gatherings and practices – are invested with multiple meanings, which are purposefully framed in relation to the nation and its hierarchies. Sulayman Khalaf adopts this perspective, for instance, when he explains the popular sport of camel racing as "a newly invented tradition" – one that was consciously created by the UAE's heritage department to promote a pastime sufficiently "authentic," as a strategy to assuage rising anxieties among the local population regarding the UAE's changing economic and technological landscape, as well as its worries over the massive influx of immigrant workers.[13] In the face of such changes, Khalaf argues that the UAE's heritage industry itself was created with the aim of "manipulating cultural symbols" to bolster the state's narrative on Emirati identity.

The second trend within the literature on Emirati national identity explores the juxtaposition of global and local dimensions. Martin Ledstrup argues that, while such tensions between global and local (and modernity and tradition) are found in many societies, there is something uniquely Emirati about the choices taken by young locals to maintain the balance between these opposing conceptual categories.[14] When going to bars, for instance, Ledstrup's respondents make sure not to wear their traditional robes to avoid these being polluted by either the settings or the alcohol. Ledstrup notes that, while the same individuals enjoy going to bars and drinking, they understand such pleasures to be inherently non-Emirati, "global," and, therefore, as not to be mingled with pure symbols of local tradition. Conversely, Ledstrup's Emirati respondents embrace "car culture" – a quintessentially global phenomenon – by decking out their imported cars in the colours of the flag and with images of Sheikh Zayed in the run-up to National Day. In the former example, Ledstrup's respondents attribute danger to the global and seek to preserve the purity of the local; in the latter example, his respondents seek to localise – and thereby to appropriate – the global. For Ledstrup, Emiratiness is best understood in terms of the choices whether to conform, transgress, or appropriate perceptions of national identity in relation to the global/local.

In contrast to the aforementioned authors, a third trend explores what it means to identify as an Emirati while simultaneously cherishing allegiances to one's specific emirate and/or tribe. As tribal loyalty has historically led to political tensions, this is potentially a sensitive subject. Jane Bristol-Rhys, however, has discussed competing historical narratives among Emiratis. She identifies five such

13 Cf. Khalaf, 2000.
14 Cf. Ledstrup, 2019.

narratives, each of which explains the formation of the federation in different terms by favouring a particular sheikh and his people (although Sheikhs Zayed and Rashid – not necessarily in this order – are always treated as the most significant). As Bristol-Rhys observes, the role of the British in these contrasting narratives – as villains or friends – also differs. Among Bristol-Rhys' narratives, the final one belongs to the younger generation: "[I]t is a narrative of unqualified success, no doubts, no misgivings and the promise of a brighter future." There is no need to speak of pre-Federation history at all: "In the same way that the times of pre-Islamic *jahiliyya* is ignored, young Emiratis avoid talking about their pre-oil past."[15]

3 The Nation Brand Project

On 2 November 2019, one day before Flag Day, the UAE announced a project to create a national logo. Sheikh Mohamed Al Maktoum wrote on Twitter: "Today, we launch a new national project to share the UAE's story with the world. The UAE's nation brand project will reflect our unique values."[16] The launch video firmly embedded the project in classical nation branding projects, comparing it to logos used for tourism promotion and public diplomacy from Singapore to Egypt. Sheikh Mohamed bin Zayed Al Nahyan (known as MBZ), Crown Prince of Abu Dhabi, who co-hosted the project, stated: "We are at the heart of the global economic, social, and cultural movement. We must have new tools that (...) reflect our civilisational and human values."[17] While official early announcements framed the logo as primarily addressed to the outside world, the project's social media channels posted mostly in Arabic,[18] demonstrating that the brand-making process was intended primarily for a local audience.

This was not the first initiative that aimed to strengthen a collective UAE national identity. The same aim permeated the language of the UAE Vision 2021, originally formulated in 2010, which is organised under the headings "United in Prosperity," "United in Knowledge," "United in Destiny," and "United in Responsibility."[19] The vision specifically mentioned a shift of national identification from the individual emirates to the UAE: "The Federation will continue to rise in the national consciousness to represent the defining point of allegiance for all Emiratis."[20] Since 2013, the annu-

15 Bristol-Rhys, 2009: 116.
16 Al Maktoum, tweet 2 November 2019, 11:00 AM.
17 Al Nahyan, tweet 2 November 2019, 10:04 AM. Translation by the authors.
18 Cf. The United Arab Emirates Nation Brand, 2021; UAE Nation Brand, 2021a and 2021c.
19 UAE Ministry of Cabinet Affairs, 2010.
20 UAE Ministry of Cabinet Affairs, 2010.

al Flag Day similarly celebrates a united nation. Other events, such as the Expo Dubai 2020, as well as the "Year of 50" on the occasion of the fiftieth anniversary of UAE independence, also strengthen the narrative of national unity. Kristian Alexander and Leonardo Mazzucco described the Expo as "nation-building through spectacle."[21] Love for the leadership is, of course, woven into the same narrative. Flag Day marks the day when the presidency passed from the UAE's founder Zayed Al Nahyan to his son Khalifa. The official "pillars" of the Year of 50 include "contemplat[ing] the values and achievements of (...) the UAE's Founding Fathers" and "inspiring youth to have their vision about the next 50 years."[22] The new nation brand logo has been linked directly to this anniversary, as it will represent the UAE in the coming fifty years.[23] Additionally, various heritage sites and exhibitions convey the same message. For instance, before stepping up to the viewing platform, visitors to Dubai's *Burj Khalifa* encounter an exhibit commemorating the UAE's founders. Interestingly, this exhibition includes noteworthy non-Emiratis, such as the captain of the highest crane used to build the tower.

For the nation brand project, a group of artists and creatives was assembled and presented to the public as the "Inspiring 49." The executive councils of the seven emirates each selected seven representatives. The Inspiring 49 included 24 women and 25 men. It represented different generations: the youngest participant was the author Dubai Abulhoul, born in 1996; the most senior artists – whom Aysha al-Hemrani, one of the 49, called "the first generation of UAE artists" – were Abdulqader al-Rais and Obaid Suroor. Al-Rais was already twenty and had started his artistic career when the UAE were founded in 1971. Suroor studied Fine Arts in Cairo and graduated in 1979. Interestingly, none of the artists were paid. Azza al-Qubaisi – a sculptor and jeweller and one of the seven team leaders – said that she participated because she wanted to be "part of our national identity giving" and that "it was a great honour" and "an opportunity to be part of something that will be historical."

The Inspiring 49 participated in a two-day workshop from 18 to 19 November 2019 at the Dubai Design District. In the workshop, the artists were divided into seven groups, each including one member from each of the seven emirates. The first day featured a series of opening remarks and training presentations – al-Qubaisi described it as "a crash course" aiming "to put us in the right direction, and to motivate and inspire us." Members of the groups began to work together in small exercises. The second day was more focused. By its end, the groups had all pro-

21 Alexander and Mazzucco, 2021.

22 UAE Telecommunication Regulatory Authority, 2021.

23 See Al Maktoum, tweet 17 December 2019, 12:56 PM.

duced two to three different proposals – in varying degrees of completion – for the UAE's nation brand. Each proposal was attached to a story that explained the logic of the design and its symbolism. Recalling the different concepts, al-Qubaisi observed, "We all had overlaps because we all have similar backgrounds and feelings towards our country."

The creative step complete, a third party – unidentified in the official narrative and unknown to our interviewees – condensed the different concepts into three polished nation brand proposals. Al-Hemrani said that one of the three final options "derived from our idea," even if it was "quite different"; and for the logo, which was selected for the nation brand in the end, he remarked, "I actually know the exact group that presented that." Al-Qubaisi however argued that the winning logo was derived from proposals by two teams. She further pointed out that for the narratives explaining the symbolism of the three final options "99 % were taken from [the explanations attached to the draft logos by] the different teams." However, the details of this were never made public. Al-Hemrani said: "They don't announce it like this, like: this group won." Instead, the logos are presented as the product of all 49 artists. Both the fact that the third party remains unnamed and the fact that no specific groups were highlighted as winners demonstrate the importance of portraying Inspiring 49 as *collective authors* of the nation brand. The tactic of representing the Inspiring 49 themselves by a logo – four green and red geometric shapes, forming an abstract "49"[24] – reflects the same aim. Ultimately, all aspects of the creative process must be viewed within the mechanics and as integral part of the state-led nation branding exercise.

The three proposed logos (cf. Fig. 1) were called "7 Lines," "The Palm," and "Emirates in Calligraphy." Each logo was introduced to the public with a short explanation of its symbolism.[25] The calligraphic logo reflects "authenticity and originality," with the "rolling curves of the font captur[ing] the flow of ocean waves merging with the sand dunes of UAE's golden desert." "The smooth and harmonious movement of the letters symbolises the constant human and social progress." The palm tree was presented as "forming an indispensable part of its [the UAE's] history and distinctive identity as an unconditional giver." The plant's ability to survive adverse natural conditions is meant to reflect "the willpower of the leaders and people of UAE." Finally, the 7 Lines are meant to represent the seven emirates and their seven leaders who "united their people's aspirations under one flag." The lines collectively shape the map of the UAE and the colours of the design

24 The logo is shown, for example, in one of the announcement videos on the UAE Nation Brand YouTube channel, UAE Nation Brand, 2019: Min. 0:44.

25 These narratives were broadly publicised. All quotes in this paragraph are taken from the official press release: Aamir, 2019.

Fig. 1: The three prosed logos in the UAE nation brand project
Sources: UAE Nation Brand, 2021b; The National, 2019.

refer to the colours of the flag. "The lines, vibrant in colour, reflect the UAE's ongoing journey of development driven by a wave of progress, innovation, excellence, and boundless aspirations."

With the three logos ready, an online vote took place from 17 to 31 December. The vote was open internationally to Emiratis and non-Emiratis. Al Maktoum explained the decision to open the vote to the whole world: "Everyone contributed to our country's success story, and we invite everyone to be part of choosing the best logo that represents our story. (...) People's participation from all over the world reflects the values of openness and inclusivity we adopt in the Emirates."[26] The UAE authorities promised that, for each vote submitted in the two weeks, they would plant a tree, thus linking the project to battling climate change. The vote attracted 10.6 million votes from 185 countries. Only 15 % of the votes came from the UAE, which still topped the list of countries by number of votes, followed by India, the US, Egypt, and Saudi Arabia. Al-Qubaisi said that "as a campaign it went really well, a lot of the people I know, my friends, my family totally engaged with it at a very personal level."

The "7 Lines" logo was officially announced as the winner on 8 January 2020. The logo is used together with the slogan "Impossible is Possible," referencing a quote from Al Maktoum: "The word 'impossible' is not in leaders' dictionaries. No matter how big the challenges, strong faith, determination and resolve will overcome them."[27] Since then, the logo has been broadly used by authorities, for example on stamps, and by various UAE-based companies, like on a credit card

26 Salim, 2019.
27 UAE Ministry of Cabinet Affairs, 2010.

Fig. 2: Instagram post celebrating the successful Mars mission, showing the nation brand logo superimposed on the red planet
Source: nationbranduae, 2021.

by Emirates Islamic. Most remarkable were a marketing campaign for domestic tourism, which also was the first federal tourism campaign, and the use of the logo on the Emirati Mars probe (Fig. 2). Sarah al-Amiri, Minister of State for Advanced Sciences, stated: “By attaching the UAE Nation Brand to the Hope Probe, we are showing that the essence of our identity, principles, objectives and actions are not bound by earthly limitations.” And referencing the brand’s slogan, she continued: “We have built a nation that does not think there is such a thing as ‘impossible.’”[28]

28 Khaleej Times, 19 January 2020.

4 Field Research and Analysis

4.1 Hierarchy, Heritage, and Art

Discussing the newly invented tradition of camel racing, Khalaf treats the construction of national identity as a top-down initiative, intended to bolster solidarity as well as established political hierarchies – what Prasenjit Duara would call "regimes of authenticity."[29] Khalaf's approach fits neatly in the present context: the nation brand project clearly upholds key governmental messages.

The most important of these messages is that the UAE has been and will continue to be unified through inspired political leadership and intra-emirate collaboration. In this regard, it is noteworthy that, in the promotional material and social media videos, the statements of Al Maktoum and MBZ were highlighted throughout, while the artists who belonged to the Inspiring 49 were represented mostly collectively by a logo. Recollections by the artists themselves indicate that their sense of personal reward for this project lay, to use al-Qubaisi's words, in contributing to "our national identity giving," rather than in receiving money or prestige. For the Inspiring 49, much of the project's significance was tied to the *process* by which the nation brand logo was designed (rather than to the result). Reflecting on his experiences as part of the project, al-Rais describes this process as manifesting the inherently unified and unifying nature of the UAE, not only between individuals from different emirates, but also between different genders and generations. Al-Rais attributes such harmony to the influence of the UAE's leadership.

Collating information from our interviews and the survey, we find an understanding among our respondents that the nation brand project should be perceived as an exercise both in building national solidarity and in promoting loyalty to leadership. The fact that virtually everyone interviewed had encountered the project speaks for the effectiveness of the government's promotion. However, several of the individual respondents also noted that the winning nation brand logo, while intended to be special, is one of several such logos: "There are many logos; the Expo itself has its own logo, which I personally prefer." Interestingly, only 13% of the survey respondents and two of the individual respondents explained the main motivation behind the project as "promoting tourism and business." By contrast, 55% of the survey's respondents – many of whom have advanced degrees in the field of business – attributed the main motivation to a desire "to build a culturally united people (…) to promote the UAE's leadership and unity," while a fur-

29 Cf. Duara, 2004: 29–34.

ther 29 % believed that it was mainly "to promote a forward-looking attitude." Over all, most interviewees did not interpret the significance of the nation brand project primarily in business terms.

The above confirms Khalaf's analysis of UAE identity construction as an inherently political and hierarchising project. The UAE's nation brand, however, does introduce a distinctive element to this type of argument. While exploring the heritage industry's re-imagining of traditions, Khalaf acknowledges the role of creativity in the construction of identity. But he rarely integrates the contributions/roles of art or artists, as distinct from historical heritage-based re-imaginings. When our respondents in Dubai and Ras al-Khaimah were asked whether they saw an intrinsic connection between national identity and the art world, very few answered in the affirmative. Although an appreciation of art was not seen as something that was antithetical to Emirati identity (several respondents mentioned Abu Dhabi's new Louvre Museum and other museums as culturally significant destinations), in our discussions, it was never volunteered as a distinctively Emirati quality.

It is interesting, then, that the artists involved explicitly perceive this situation to be changing. As al-Hemrani observed, while the first generation of Emirati artists were not traditionally taught art in school curricula and they do not feature in the official history summarised above, the UAE government has begun to recognise the "huge impact – economically as well – of artists and the creative community." Al-Hemrani's observation is supported by the speech given by the designer of the UAE's flag, Abdullah Mohammed al-Maeena, on the first day of the nation brand workshop, in which he remarked that "the history of the Emirates is made by the creative sons and daughters of the nation."[30] In this new narrative, the Inspiring 49 are not simply creating a logo; they, and by extension the UAE's creative community as a whole, are contributing to building and are themselves an expression of Emirati identity.

This new aspect of identity construction shares many of the hierarchising attributes identified by Khalaf. While the artists took part in what seems to have been a generous and collegial sharing of ideas, the group leaders were nevertheless the oldest individuals from each emirate (although not all were male). Even in the context of art, seniority commands the greatest respect. An anecdote from al-Rais eloquently makes this point. The logo was officially announced at an event that brought together the Inspiring 49 and various members of the UAE leadership. When the group photograph was taken, al-Rais recalls how, usually at such events, "the sheikhs should be in the front and the artists in the back [... yet, this time],

30 UAE Nation Brand Twitter, tweet 18 November 2019, 6:13 PM.

Sheikh Abdullah bin Zayed, the foreign minister, took my hand and made me [stand] in his place [in front] and [went] to stand in the back of me." In a richly symbolic act, al-Rais' lifetime of work as an artist was honoured, as he himself arrives at a sufficiently venerable age to enter the pantheon of Emirati leaders.

4.2 Between Local and Global

Ledstrup explores the construction of identity in relation to people's choices of how to negotiate the seemingly contradictory, yet overlapping spheres of the local and global in everyday life. The nation brand project, its logo (and responses to it) provide a rich opportunity to consider this dualism in the UAE. The government's own narrative, in line with its own official history, is that – thanks to wise leadership – Emirati culture manages to incorporate and embrace both local and global dimensions. This is done intentionally: the government opened the voting process on the UAE nation brand logo to a truly international audience; at the same time, however, it has chosen only Emirati artists to contribute to the project and promoted it in Arabic on its social media channels.

The apparent tension between a cosmopolitan, inclusive Emiratiness and a more atavistic, essentialist view, has long been part of the UAE's nation-building efforts. For example, the Vision 2021 stated the goal: "Emiratis' solid national character will be upheld as a main source of inspiration for the protection and preservation of national identity. *In the face of increasing multiculturalism*, this is a crucial matter of national pride and social stability."[31] Moshashai thus observed diplomatically that the Vision 2021 promoted "cosmopolitanism whilst keeping a certain distrust of multiculturalism."[32] However, these boundary lines may be fading. As mentioned above, the exhibit at *Burj Khalifa* highlights also the contributions of non-Emiratis. Reflecting this development, Alexander and Mazzucco argued, "The language of tolerance is deeply embedded within the UAE official state narrative."[33] In line with this, al-Hemrani argued, "I don't think the UAE is only consisting of Emirati citizens. Yes, we do have benefits and privileges as citizens, but at the same time we have people who are second- and third-generation expats who are living here." The fact that the government set out intentionally to use the nation brand (among other strategies) as a means to communicate its cosmopolitan outlook was both recognised and appreciated by the majority of our re-

31 UAE Ministry of Cabinet Affairs, 2010. Added emphasis.

32 Moshashai, 2018: 66.

33 Alexander and Mazzucco, 2021.

spondents. At the same time, this construction of a more globalised identity, tolerant of differences, is not uncontested among Emiratis, as Alexander and Mazzucco pointed out.[34]

Navigating this intersection of the local and the global has brought with it certain challenges for the artists. The question of how to visually express the quintessential nature of the UAE without preferring a particular emirate and without slipping into irrelevance by choosing an image that might be interpreted as insufficiently Emirati occupied their minds during the artists' workshop in Dubai. Al-Rais neatly summarises this dilemma when critiquing the proposed palm tree logo: "The problem with the palm tree is that it is not only present in the Emirates, but in all countries in the Gulf, in all Arab countries. (…) Even in America. It is not special." To overcome this challenge, al-Hemrani observes, "We all worked really hard on trying to identify what makes us Emirati."

The eventual winner of the competition was received favourably not only by the artists, but also by most of our respondents. This leaves us with the question whether the logo was primarily intended for a local or a global audience or a mixture of both. For al-Hemrani, the aim of the nation brand logo was primarily to unite the global (i.e. non-Emiratis) and locals who live inside the UAE: "We needed something that presents us in the UAE" "to expats and locals." Making no distinction at all between expatriates and locals in the UAE, al-Qubaisi, by contrast, explained the motivation for designing the logo as "50/50" – "internationally and locally." Overall, our interview and questionnaire respondents agree with this view. Interestingly, however, al-Rais noted that the chosen logo might indeed resonate more effectively with an audience in the UAE, on the grounds that foreigners might not recognise its map outline. Discussions of the concepts of global versus local often segue into related discussions of the modern (and globalised) versus the traditional. Al-Hemrani's observation that the chosen logo "is maybe a bit too modern" is, therefore, noteworthy. The same reservation – that the seven lines seem too modern, too abstract, not sufficiently and concretely Emirati – was politely expressed in several of the interviews. On such occasions, however, this reservation was usually accompanied by an acknowledgement that it would have been hard to find a better compromise.

Al-Hemrani's observation reminds us of Ledstrup's argument: contemporary Emiratiness is uniquely linked to discussions of – and choices pertaining to – the global/modern and the local/traditional. In the present discussion, it is worth mentioning that, among our respondents, there were instances of resistance to aspects of the government's strategy to fuse the local/traditional and the global/mod-

34 Alexander and Mazzucco, 2021.

ern. On a handful of occasions, discussion of the nation brand project with respondents in both Dubai and Ras al-Khaimah spurred less familiar responses regarding the political direction in which the UAE is now heading. The UAE's decision in August 2020 to normalise political relations with Israel may not be expected to arise from a discussion on nation branding. However, when asked what aspects of globalisation they found most problematic, one respondent based in Dubai expressed discomfort at precisely this development. While careful not to criticise the decision made by the UAE's leadership, the conversation moved from a reflection on the UAE's economic progress and of how the nation brand reflects a creative, business-minded approach to an admission that this has forced compromises with which they are less than comfortable. Another respondent, in Ras al-Khaimah, remarked tersely that the sole reason that the UAE had "forsaken its brothers and sisters in the Arab world" was "to improve its nation brand."

4.3 Local Identities

Unlike Khalaf and Ledstrup, Bristol-Rhys explores the construction of an Emirati identity in terms of competing narratives. Not surprisingly, given the nature of this project – to present a unified nation, bolster a sense of national identity, and endorse political and cultural hierarchies – neither the artists nor most of the respondents were interested in discussing the nation-state project in terms of tribal difference. This is not to say that the artists were not keenly aware of local differences. As al-Hemrani succinctly stated, "The UAE is not very big, [but] it is totally different when you go to different emirates." Reflecting this duality of unity and separateness, the workshop of the Inspiring 49 was characterised by a particular Emirati version of identity politics: each emirate was represented equally and each emirate selected its own creatives, and at the workshop each team consisted of members from all emirates. In the end, as individual artistic contributions were not recognised, an appearance of unity was generated. Indeed, the final nation brand acknowledges the separateness of the emirates while emphasising the unity of the whole, by featuring seven parallel stripes, which together form one shape, but neither meet nor overlap.

As Bristol-Rhys and others have shown, tribal and inter-emirate differences persist beneath the seemingly harmonious veneer of the modern UAE. It is not our intention to dwell on these differences here. In the context of the nation brand project itself, they deserve brief mention. Conversations with two respondents from tribes traditionally based in Ras al-Khaimah explicitly acknowledged that the nation brand project was of "no interest" and "something quite alien" to them. A single respondent, in Dubai, was even bolder: "and what about the *'aja-*

mis [Persians] and the Shi'is, and the *bidun* [stateless people living in the emirates], what has this got to do with any of them?"

Such ideas *do* persist, even among some members of the younger generation. However, as Bristol-Rhys would predict, the overwhelming majority of our respondents (all aged in their twenties to forties) expressed little interest in the divisions that preceded the foundation of the state and the discovery of oil. In their view, the unified nation that Vision 2021, for example, aims to will into existence – by continuously repeating the mantra of unity – appears to have become a reality. This also is apparent in a statement by al-Qubaisi describing the differences between emirates: "The culture and tradition aspects differ slightly, the accent of the spoken Arabic also differs from one emirate to the other, in the past it used to be from one tribe to the other, [... also] our food and spices and how we cook and how we engage [differ between emirates]." However, this no longer sounds like competing sub-state nationalisms, but rather like forms of local patriotism, which one would find in regions and cities throughout the world. As new generations of Emiratis have grown up after the unification of the UAE, past differences have become less important; after all, as Ernest Renan argued in 1882, "Forgetting (...) is a crucial factor in the creation of a nation."[35]

5 Conclusion

This chapter has demonstrated how the UAE nation brand project should also be understood as an internally directed project of nation-building. This overlap of nation branding and nation-building is not entirely new for the UAE; it also characterised the earlier Vision 2021 project. Responding to three trends in the literature on the construction of Emirati national identity, this chapter has explored ways in which certain processes of and discourses about Emirati national identity were privileged (or ignored), both in the processes by which the nation brand logo was created and in the responses of Emiratis to these processes (and its result).

In the present context, nation branding – and the winning logo – supports the (ongoing) creation of a "regime of authenticity." In so doing, it legitimises the political strategies of the leadership. Regimes of authenticity are invariably exposed to tensions between tradition and modernity, the national and the global, and authenticity and capitalism.[36] Constructing itself as a trading community with cosmopolitan interactions reaching back centuries (while, in reality, consisting of a rela-

35 Renan, 1990: 11.
36 Duara already observes this about nationalism more broadly; cf. Duara, 2004: 29–34.

tively recent (con)federal state) may be seen as particularly affected by these strains between the local/tribal, the national/federal, and the global. The present research demonstrates how the nation brand project crystalises and amplifies the official narrative, while adding to it an aesthetic dimension. While deeply entrenched differences persist and not all political decisions are popular, it also suggests that most Emiratis are persuaded by the government discourse on the nation.

Bibliography

Aamir, Moh[ame]d, and Nour Salman. "Voting Starts to Select New Logo to Represent the UAE to World." *Emirates News Agency* 1 December 2019. https://www.wam.ae/en/details/1395302810921. Accessed 1 July 2021.

Al Maktoum, Sheikh Mohammed bin Rashid. *Twitter Account.* https://twitter.com/HHShkMohd. Accessed 1 July 2021.

Al Nahyan, Mohamed bin Zayed. *Twitter Account.* https://twitter.com/MohamedBinZayed. Accessed 1 July 2021.

Alexander, Kristian, and Leonardo Jacopo Maria Mazzucco. "Beyond the Bedouin Path: The Evolution of Emirati National Identity." *Middle East Institute* (blog) 1 December 2021. Washington, DC. https://www.mei.edu/publications/beyond-bedouin-path-evolution-emirati-national-identity. Accessed 24 December 2021.

Bristol-Rhys, Jane. "Emirati Historical Narratives." *History and Anthropology* 20.2 (2009): 107–121.

Browning, Christopher S., and Antonio Ferraz de Oliveira. "Introduction: Nation Branding and Competitive Identity in World Politics." *Geopolitics* 22.3 (2017): 481–501.

Cooke, Miriam. *Tribal Modern: Branding New Nations in the Arab Gulf.* Berkeley: University of California Press, 2014.

Cornelissen, Scarlett. "National Meaning-Making in Complex Societies: Political Legitimation and Branding Dynamics in Post-Apartheid South Africa." *Geopolitics* 22.3 (2017): 525–548.

Dinnie, Keith. *Nation Branding: Concepts, Issues, Practice.* Burlington: Elsevier, 2007.

Duara, Prasenjit. *Sovereignty and Authenticity: Manchukuo and the East Asian Modern.* Lanham: Rowman & Littlefield, 2004.

Essaidi, Zara. "Choose the New UAE Logo." *Design Home* (2012). http://www.designhome.ae/choose-the-new-uae-logo/. Accessed 1 July 2021.

Hoefte, Rosemarijn, and Wouter Veenendaal. "The Challenges of Nation-Building and Nation Branding in Multi-Ethnic Suriname." *Nationalism and Ethnic Politics* 25.2 (2019): 173–190.

Hughes, Michael. "UAE Nation Brand: How Much Public Involvement is too Much?" *Truly Deeply* (2012). https://www.trulydeeply.com.au/2012/07/uae-nation-brand-how-much-public-involvement-is-too-much/. Accessed 1 July 2021 (link expired).

Kaneva, Nadia. "Nation Branding: Toward an Agenda for Critical Research." *International Journal of Communication* 5 (2011): 117–141.

Khalaf, Sulayman. "Poetics and Politics of Newly Invented Traditions in the Gulf: Camel Racing in the United Arab Emirates." *Ethnology* 39.3 (2000): 243–261.

Khaleej Times. "How UAE Leaders Reacted to Brand Logo Selection." 8 January 2020. https://www.khaleejtimes.com/news/general/how-uae-leaders-reacted-to-brand-logo-selection. Accessed 1 July 2021.

Khaleej Times. “UAE Nation Brand Logo to Hitch a Ride on Mars Hope Probe.” 19 January 2020. https://www.khaleejtimes.com/government/uae-nation-brand-logo-to-hitch-a-ride-on-mars-hope-probe. Accessed 25 July 2023.

Ledstrup, Martin. *Nationalism and Nationhood in the United Arab Emirates.* Cham: Springer International Publishing, 2019.

Moshashai, Daniel. “National Visions as Instruments of Soft-Power in the Gulf Region: The Case of the UAE and Its ‘Vision 2021.’” Master’s thesis, Master of Advanced International Affairs, Johns Hopkins, School of Advanced International Studies, Bologna, 2018.

nationbranduae. “Tammat al-muhima bi-najāḥ: Wuṣūl misbār al-amal ilā al-mirrīkh yaʿkis ṣūrat al-imārāt al-ḥaqīqiyya lil-ʿālam wa-masīrat khamsīn ʿāman min al-ṭumūḥ wal-iṣrār wal-najāḥ.” [Mission Accomplished: The Arrival of the Hope Probe to Mars Reflects the True Image of the Emirates to the World and the Fifty-year March of Ambition, Determination, and Success.] *Instagram* 10 February 2021. https://www.instagram.com/p/CLHiwOeH2Tk/. Accessed 1 July 2021.

Renan, Ernest. “What Is a Nation?” In *Nation and Narration*, edited by Homi K. Bhabha, 8–22. London: Routledge, 1990.

Salim, Sahim. “Have your Say in Conveying UAE’s Story to the World.” *Khaleej Times* 18 December 2019. https://www.khaleejtimes.com/news/general/have-your-say-in-conveying-uaes-story-to-the-world-. Accessed 1 July 2021.

The National. “1.5 million Votes Cast in Search for UAE Brand Logo: One of Three Logos Will Be Chosen to Represent the Emirates to the Rest of the World.” 21 December 2019. https://www.thenationalnews.com/uae/1-5-million-votes-cast-in-search-for-uae-brand-logo-1.954497. Accessed 1 July 2021.

The United Arab Emirates Nation Brand. *Facebook.* https://www.facebook.com/NationbrandUAE. Accessed 1 July 2021.

UAE Ministry of Cabinet Affairs. *UAE Vision 2021.* 2010. https://www.vision2021.ae/docs/default-source/default-document-library/uae_vision-arabic.pdf. Accessed 1 July 2021.

UAE Ministry of Presidential Affairs. “The Formation of the Federation.” *Our Archives* (2018). https://www.na.ae/en/archives/historicalperiods/union.aspx. Accessed 1 July 2021.

UAE Nation Brand. “Iṭlāq mubādara al-hawiyya al-iʿlāmiyya lil-imārāt” [Launching the Nation Brand Initiative of the Emirates]. *YouTube* 3 November 2019. https://youtu.be/6vPRuSpCB7w. Accessed 1 July 2021.

UAE Nation Brand. *Instagram.* https://www.instagram.com/nationbranduae/. Accessed 1 July 2021a.

UAE Nation Brand. “Media Kit.” https://www.nationbrand.ae/en/mediakit. Accessed 1 July 2021b.

UAE Nation Brand. *Twitter Account.* https://twitter.com/theemirates. Accessed 1 July 2021c.

UAE Telecommunication Regulatory Authority. *Year of the 50th.* 2021. https://u.ae/en/about-the-uae/the-uae-government/year-of-the-50th. Accessed 1 July 2021.

Volčič, Zala, and Mark Andrejevic. “Nation Branding in the Era of Commercial Nationalism.” *International Journal of Communication* 5 (2011): 598–618.

Zeineddine, Cornelia. “Nation Branding in the Middle East: United Arab Emirates (UAE) vs. Qatar.” *Proceedings of the International Conference on Business Excellence* 11.1 (2017): 588–596.

Thibaut Klinger

Branding and Spatial Planning in Oman: A Neoliberal Turning Point in Politics?

1 Branding Oman as a Way to Deal with Globalisation

As he rose to power in 1970, Sultan Qaboos bin Said Al Said[1] had to unify the Omani territory and people, to create an "imagined community" in the sense of Benedict Anderson, and especially to defeat threats of secession and civil war. Spatial planning was the core of his strategy: it was the main topic of his speeches, in which he championed modernising Oman and integrating it into globalisation. During the 1990s, the pace of globalisation increased: countries, regions, and cities were competing more intensely for international funds, inward investment, technology, and skills transfer, and so they felt the need to define their "brand," that is "the unique, multidimensional blend of elements that provide the nation with culturally grounded differentiation and relevance for all of its target audiences."[2] However, the central issues are: What are the effects of branding on Omani governance, does it tend to replace spatial planning, and, if so, to what extent?

In the 1990s, globalisation led countries, regions, and cities to compete to receive foreign direct investment or to benefit from technology transfers. According to Edward Luttwak, this competition is like "economic warfare."[3] Simon Anholt, considered the father of nation branding due to a seminal article from 1996 and one of the most active consultants for governments and local authorities, points out that "today, the world is one market. The rapid advance of globalisation means that every city and every region must compete with every other for its share of the world's consumers, tourists, investors, students, entrepreneurs, international sporting and cultural events, and for the attention and respect of the international media, of other governments, and the people of other countries."[4] According to Renaud Vuignier, this statement at the beginning of Anholt's book *Competitive Identity* exemplifies the degree to which the normative points of view of branding consultants dominate studies about branding without a real em-

1 Sultan Qaboos died in January 2020.

2 Dinnie, 2016: 5.

3 Luttwak 1990: 17–23.

4 Anholt, 2007: 1.

https://doi.org/10.1515/9783110741100-020

pirical basis.[5] Nevertheless, Anholt's book seems to be instructive for the case of Oman and shows how part of the policy implemented by Qaboos since 1970 and the country's new orientation since the 1990s (economic diversification and participating in globalisation) join themes of branding, even if it started before the notion was really formalised and used. Furthermore, the criticisms addressed to branding also highlight the difficulties of Omani governance and the questions its new orientation raises.

1.1 The Branding Turn in the Middle East and North Africa and in Oman

The Middle East and North Africa (MENA) testifies to a great vitality of branding, particularly in the cities of the Gulf since Kuwait played a pioneering role from the 1950s onwards.[6] Omani branding began with the *Ithraa* ("enrichment" in Arabic) agency, created in 1996, with the mission "to promote the business benefits of Oman to a global audience, strengthening the image and profile of the Sultanate as an investment and business destination, and building a strong economy."[7] It designed a first logo for Oman, representing a *khandjar*, the emblematic dagger of the Sultanate (Fig. 1).

Fig. 1 First logo for Oman
Source: Ithraa, 2021.

In 2008, the Minister of Heritage Faysal bin Ali Al Said commissioned the Brand Oman Management Unit (BOMU) to design a new "Brand Oman" brand. It combines the calligraphy of the name "Oman" with the colourful evocation of characteristic elements of Oman (Fig. 2)[8] and is usually accompanied by the slogan "Beauty has an address."[9] Far from the urban exuberance of Dubai, the chosen image is

5 See Vuignier, 2018: 3 and 97.

6 On the pioneering role of Kuwait, cf. Al-Nakib 2016.

7 Ithraa, 2021.

8 On the logo, cf. Ithraa, 2016.

9 For example, on the homepage of the Omani Ministry of Tourism https://omantourism.gov.om/. Accessed 11 April 2021.

therefore that of nature and heritage in the face of architectural modernity and of beauty in the face of the willingly kitschy extravagance of the neighbouring emirate.

Fig. 2: The new "Brand Oman" logo launched in 2008
From left to right, the logo represents "embroidery," "mountains," "turtle," and "dhow."
Source: Ithraa, 2016: 9–10.

Clearly, the 2008 turning point was directly inspired by Simon Anholt; the minister declared in an interview at that time that "the only sort of government that can afford to ignore the impact of its national reputation is one which has no interest in participating in the global community, and no desire for its economy, its culture, or its citizens to benefit from the rich influences and opportunities that the rest of the world offers them."[10] He took his inspiration word for word from Simon Anholt's comments published a few months earlier on his site and repeated in several of his articles.[11] This statement seems to illustrate the shift from marketing to branding noted by Vuignier: whereas marketing is based on functional and rational elements, place branding seeks to arouse emotional, mental, and psychological associations with the target territory through the image that is given. It can be noted that there is a back and forth: nation branding can be reinforced by a campaign to promote national products of the "made in" or "country-of-origin effect" type.[12] The "Made in Germany" of the late 19th century is one of the oldest examples of this type of promotion. Today, it is a question of supporting exports by marketing them with a logo that reinforces national branding and often evokes a de-

10 Radboy et al., 2010.
11 See, for example, Anholt, 2009.
12 See Dinnie, 2016: 100–103.

cisive and visually remarkable cultural element. This is also the case with the logo for Omani products, which was defined in 2008: the "swirling" calligraphy of Oman evokes a kind of QR-code (Fig. 3). It is

> a nation initiative to develop a nation initiative to develop, promote and support Omani products and services for a brighter, better future for everyone in Oman. The pride of Oman is at the very heart of this brand. The concept of the brandmark identity is inspired by the positive evocations of sustainable growth, regeneration and recycling, internal energy, purity, equality, and order. These evocations and emotions are encapsulated in an iconic graphic form which reads the word Omani in Arabic. It is represented by a carefully and mathematically drawn dynamic form that symbolises the central role that Omani products and services will take in the development and advancement of Oman for its national and economic growth.[13]

Fig. 3: The "Origin Oman" logo for Omani products 2008
Source: Oman Chamber of Commerce and Industry, 2011.

The dithyrambic presentation of the logo also illustrates the frequent confusion, noted by Vuignier, between the territorial brand tool and the general approach to improving the attractiveness of a territory, which is aggravated by the fact that "determining the real role played by the brand tool in the attractiveness of a territory is complex."[14] This is the case externally, as evidenced by the *Omani Products Catalogue*, published by the Oman Chamber of Commerce and Industry (OCCI) in 2011. It lists Omani companies and highlights the "swirling" logo

13 Origin Oman, 2008: 2.

14 Vuignier, 2018: 23. All quotes from Vuignier were translated by the author.

"Made in Oman." Its foreword confirms the mix between marketing and branding, between territory and products: "The slogan, 'Omani Products: Made in Oman, made for the World' is gaining popularity with concerned marketing efforts (...). *The Omani Products Catalogue* is a supportive attempt and a primary step in the Government's efforts in boosting the popularity and acceptance of Omani products to a larger global audience;" and further on, "[this catalogue] is also a humble effort of OCCI in promoting Oman's business worldwide."[15]

On the domestic front, hopes are also high. According to the territorial brand's user guide, the Omani products logo "symbolises" the role of the secondary and tertiary sectors in the Omani economy, as part of the strategy to diversify the contributors to the gross domestic product to reduce dependence on hydrocarbons. Is there hope that the logo will play an active role in this strategy, and, if so, to what extent? Thus, on the institutional website, the "Origin Oman" campaign, to which the logo belongs, is aimed at consumers on Omani soil, Omani or expatriate, who are invited to play an active role in the country's economic policy by letting themselves be guided by this brand: "In brief, Origin Oman offers every Oman-based resident an opportunity to help promote the sultanate's products and services, and by doing so, help create employment opportunities, stimulate the national economy and reduce carbon emissions."[16]

1.2 How Effective is Branding Oman?

It could be noted that the branding may differ, depending on whether it concerns tourism or industry. The comments accompanying the promotional activities show that the branding of the industry and the tourism sectors is well designed for the same target. Highlighting the beauty of Oman's nature and the richness of its heritage serves to promote Omani products, but also to justify the choice of a selective tourism, presumed to be more respectful of these riches. The real effectiveness of these actions deserves an in-depth study. In any case, Vuignier notes that branding can participate in "a narrative or storytelling" and, thus, "it can through this phenomenon of overall effect make the attractive territory even more attractive: the relevant factors for the company can be transformed from (potentially) attractive into actually attractive."[17] Such a "narrative" seeks to highlight the territory's identity in order to make it an asset in the globalisation process: this approach is not

15 Oman Chamber of Commerce and Industry, 2011: 9 and 11.

16 Origin Oman, 2021.

17 Vuignier, 2018: 160.

only outward-looking, as it can likewise be an opportunity to raise awareness internally, particularly in order to enhance its value and attractiveness. This is what Simon Anholt underlines in his analysis of "Competitive Identity" (CI), which he proposes as the indispensable form of branding today: "I would claim that the first and most important component of any national CI strategy is creating a spirit of benign nationalism amongst the populace, notwithstanding its cultural, social, ethnic, linguistic, economic, political, territorial and historical divisions."[18] The promotion of Omani products with the "Origin Oman" logo fits perfectly into this perspective if we are to believe the commentary provided on the institutional home page: "The campaign's principal objective is to engender national pride and encourage consumers and companies to choose locally made products and services bearing the Origin Oman logo."[19] Whether in Anholt's words or on the Brand Oman website, it is striking to rediscover terms abundantly present in Qaboos' speeches: beyond pride[20] in Omani national heritage and civilisation, these speeches exhort readers to consolidate national identity beyond old divisions. From this point of view, there is a nice continuity between the first quarter century of Qaboos' reign and the following decades with a change of target: after having sought to forge a united country, the discourse on national identity is now being addressed to the outside world to "sell" Oman, in a branding approach.

Alongside this continuity, there are several indications of at least a strong turning point. A 2013 study conducted by two members of Sultan Qaboos University and a marketing consultant on Brand Oman interviewed 300 "randomly selected" Omanis, of whom 241 responded fully to a questionnaire.[21] 71% were convinced that Oman is "a country of rich culture and heritage," and 54% answered that "tourists picture Oman as a country with rich culture and heritage." To this is added the conviction that "cultural tourism" is the right path for the country to take and that this then benefits the image of exported products, such as the Wave brand of the Oman Ceramics Company for bathroom accessories or the famous *Amouage* perfumes: half of the respondents admit to being insufficiently trained in branding, but that they are convinced of the need for it and to use it for economic promotion. In contrast, we note that 80% do not know about the BOMU organisation, which manages the brand, which is perhaps not the most embarrassing thing, but more than half are not convinced by the chosen logo, which is said to poorly express the Omani identity. Beyond its limitations, the study un-

18 Anholt, 2007: 16.

19 Origin Oman, 2021.

20 An easy scan of the Sultan's speeches in their English versions shows that the word "pride" is used at least once in every speech.

21 See Balushi, Butt, and Al-Siyabi, 2013.

derlines that, if the population can adhere to the idea of enhancing the country's characteristics, a logo is not enough to create an effective national narrative, and Anholt's quoted words do not say otherwise: Competitive Identity is not just about a logo and a slogan.

2 Toward a New Neoliberal Governance?

2.1 Place Branding, Corporate Branding, and Personal Branding

Simon Anholt's theorisation and Renaud Vuignier's analysis of branding emphasise that branding is not only a communication action, but also implies the transformation of the territory and the mobilisation of the population. In other words, it is a matter of governance and raises institutional questions. Vuignier points out that "place branding" normally involves several political levels, local authorities, and a certain amount of consultation with the population. Yet, in the case of Oman, it is limited to consultation at the level of governorates and to workshops at a technical level. The very top-down Omani framework is more in line with "corporate branding" and the promotion of products.[22]

The Omani slogan "Beauty has an address" emphasises the desire to preserve an environment whose beauty is a prominent feature of the country's image. "Landscape is one of the great equalisers of nation branding":[23] landscapes such as the desert dunes of the East (or Wahiba Sands), the jagged lines of the coasts of Musandam (an Omani exclave separated from the rest of the Sultanate by the United Arab Emirates (UAE)), and high-altitude terraces of the Jebel Akhdar, and the verdant nature of Dhofar are all assets for the image of the Sultanate, as other landscapes are for so many emerging countries. Even then, they can only really attract if there is development and promotion, as is the case for Dhofar (the southernmost governorate, close to the Yemen border). As it is the only Omani region to receive the summer monsoon and thus offer lush green landscapes in the summer, it now hosts a "Khareef Festival"[24] from 21 June to 9 September. The strong growth in this festival's attendance, which has doubled in ten years, is a challenge for the development of the territory: the governorate has had to in-

---

22 See Vuignier, 2018: 44–45.

23 Dinnie, 2016: 69.

24 *Kharīf* classically refers to autumn but, in Oman, to the summer monsoon season, which affects parts of Dhofar and South Yemen.

crease its hotel capacities, occasionally supplemented by army tents at the time of the greatest influx, and to adapt its road network, while an extension of the airport of Salalah was inaugurated in 2016 to enable it to receive international flights, notably from Europe. All this is supposed to support the development of Duqm, a former small fishing settlement, now a new economic special zone with an oil refinery and an industrial port: about halfway between Muscat and Salalah, Duqm is also expected to serve as a stopover point for Omanis and citizens from other Gulf Cooperation Council (GCC) countries on their way to Dhofar.

A place of beauty, Oman also aims to be a safe place, which is not the dominant image of the Middle East. According to the World Economic Forum's 2019 ranking, it is the third-safest tourist destination in the world, behind Finland and Iceland, making it the safest in the MENA, ahead of the UAE (ranked seventh).[25] This ranking is part of the more general Travel & Tourism Competitiveness Index presented by the World Economic Forum, which places Oman in 58th position in overall tourism competitiveness, behind the UAE (33rd) and Qatar (51st), but ahead of Saudi Arabia (69th). In two years, Oman has moved up eight places and not only has the highest regional increase in "human resources and labour market," but also in terms of international openness, a sustainable environment, and infrastructure in general.[26] This image of Oman seems to be in line with the comment of the report's editors that "the surest way for a country to benefit from its tourist industry, (...) is to invest in infrastructure which keeps the needs of the local population as well as visitors in mind."[27]

According to the World Economic Forum, "safety & security" are not limited to security from crime, represented by Royal Oman Police stations, whose number and size strike the visitor.[28] It includes a broader conception of security to which the allegedly peaceful character of the population contributes: this results from the widespread "culture of diplomacy" in the Sultanate, as analysed by Jeremy Jones and Nicholas Ridout. For them, there is "a culture in which a great deal of care and thought is devoted to managing social relations through the avoidance of conflict and the pursuit of shared interests through dialogue and collective decision-making."[29] This culture is said to have its roots in the national conception of religion and, at the household level, in the *majlis* (a kind of lounge to receive

---

25 Cf. World Economic Forum, 2019: 71.

26 See Oman Observer, 2019. In 2020, Oman was ranked the fifth-safest country in the world, cf. Oman Observer, 2020.

27 Bruce-Lockhart, 2019.

28 See World Economic Forum, 2019: 92.

29 Jones and Ridout, 2012: 39–40.

guests), which embodies the Omani “ideology of politeness,”[30] and at the level of the *ḥāra*, the former neighbourhood that was marked by tribal sociability and community-based water management of the *aflāj*, irrigation canals for palm groves.

Security and peace are also the result of Qaboos’ spatial planning policy, which had to assert itself in a country marked by historically on-going tribal struggles and power rivalries between the Sultan of Muscat and the Imam based in the inland residence of Nizwa. Today, the challenge is to offer peace and security to tourists and foreign investors. In the past and nowadays, it is about governance that gives extraordinary weight to the ruler and the elite around him through the “Visions” or *ru’yāt*, which are adopted in the various Gulf States and in Oman in particular, with Vision 2020, launched in 1995, and Vision 2040, adopted in 2020. These documents fully participate in a personal branding that makes the wisdom of the sovereign an element of the country’s identity, but also an argument to reassure investors and attract them to the country: accordingly, the expression “the wise guidance of His Majesty Sultan Qaboos” is omnipresent in official documents. In the document synthesising Vision 2040, edited in September 2019 and completed after Qaboos death, it appears at the top of the pillars on which Oman must rely for its future.[31] On this point, as is often the case, Oman fits into a regional whole – but with nuances. As for its neighbours, these “visions” “imply a quasi-transcendental or, at least, instinctual core that is difficult to contest (…) [and they] become ‘nationalised’, monopolised and functionalised to legitimise the dominant role of the ruler.”[32] From this point of view, there is indeed a modification of governance because, traditionally, the tribal chief did not have to have a particular vision, but deep experience that allowed him to arbitrate within an equilibrium that did not change much. The image of the sovereign and his vision go beyond the cult of personality and act as branding to attract tourists and investors and assure the population that the ruler is adapting the country to globalisation.

2.2 Entrepreneurialism and “Agencification”

According to Simon Anholt, creating a national Competitive Identity implies involving the population, and Oman seems to show a real effort to do so.[33] The preparation of the Vision 2040 document led to the creation in 2016 of the National

30 This concept is borrowed from Barth, 1983: 98.
31 See Ministry of National Economy, 2019: 13.
32 Bromber et al., 2014: 7.
33 Cf. Anholt, 2007: 16.

Program for Bracing the Economic Diversity, also known as *Tanfeedh*, a transcription of the word “implementation” in Arabic. The aim is to “implement” the objectives of the ninth Omani Five-Year Plan 2016–2020 by drawing inspiration from the Economic Transformation Program realised by the Performance Management & Delivery Unit (PERMANDU) in Malaysia. *Tanfeedh* organised a series of labs and workshops over six weeks, culminating in a project presented at open days in the different governorates and on social networks. As Qaboos states in the preface to the *Tanfeedh Handbook*, there is a growing awareness that “it is necessary that all Omanis have to cooperate.”[34] On the one hand, this statement seems to correspond to neoliberal policies whose “new forms of governance are often legitimized on the basis of their superior ability to offer a more inclusive, non-hierarchical, and participatory approach to planning,”[35] in apparent contrast to the former centralist and top-down spatial planning. On the other hand, should the *Tanfeedh* experience be seen as an Omani version of public debate or a screen hiding the “‘coalitions’ of public and semipublic actors” behind “only a highly formalized form of public participation that maintains key power in the hands of the existing elite structure and even prevents newly emerging elites (…) to enter the established networks of governance and dominant elite coalitions”?[36]

The shifting to corporate governance is also marked by “agencification,” which seems to particularly affect the tourism sector, as has been studied in the example of Morocco.[37] In the Sultanate, it is exemplified by the Oman Tourism Development Company (OMRAN), established in 2005 as a tourism developer for small to medium developments.[38] In 2014, OMRAN became responsible for large developments, including mixed-use real estate projects, and for all tourism infrastructure development from the Ministry of Tourism and now for the implementation of the National Tourism Strategy (NTS).[39] According to its official website, OMRAN is now the “executive arm of the Sultanate” in the field of tourism: one may wonder whether this does not strip the state, here the Ministry of Tourism, for the benefit of an agency. The state structure is being duplicated or bypassed, as what characterises the neoliberal “New Urban Policy” is “the subordination of formal government structures to new institutions and agencies, often paralleled by a significant redistribution of policymaking powers, competencies, and responsibilities.”[40] In

34 Tanfeedh, 2017: 7.

35 Swyngedouw, Moulaert, and Rodriguez, 2002: 579.

36 Swyngedouw, Moulaert, and Rodriguez, 2002: 571.

37 On “agencification,” cf. Amarouche and Bogaert, 2019.

38 Omran is the English transcription of the Arabic *‘umrān*, meaning “civilisation.”

39 See Omran, 2014: 15 and 2021a.

40 Swyngedouw, Moulaert, and Rodriguez, 2002: 561.

the same way, OMRAN's Board of Directors includes four ministers – the Minister of Commerce and Industry, the Minister responsible for Financial Affairs, the Minister of Tourism, and the Minister of Housing – and appears to form a second government responsible for strategic sectors of economic development: the slogan "Growth through tourism" on the institutional brochure summarises this strategic character.

3 The Shift from Planning to Branding

3.1 From Planning to Projects

Martin Hvidt points out the many obstacles to making the "visions" a reality: lack of reliable statistics, weak administrative management, and, conversely, the weight of the state in relation to the private sector.[41] The lack of co-ordination and the constant change of competence areas and names of the responsible institutions already limited the implementation of state planning from 1970 to the 1990s. The study of urban planning even leads Khalfan Al-Shueili to wonder whether planning is not limited to labelling what already exists without giving coherence to development.[42] The progressive replacement of planning by urban entrepreneurialism[43] and the new importance of branding raises the question of the effects of the new governance generated on the conception of the territory. For David Harvey,

> entrepreneurialism focuses much more closely on the political economy of place rather than of territory. By the latter, I mean the kinds of economic projects (housing, education, etc.) that are designed primarily to improve conditions of living or working within a particular jurisdiction. The construction of place (a new civic centre, an industrial park) or the enhancement of conditions within a place (intervention, for example, in local labour markets by re-training schemes or downward pressure on local wages), on the other hand, can have impacts either smaller or greater than the specific territory within which such projects happen to be located.[44]

Thus, while the distribution of land for the construction of individual houses is blocked in the Muscat Capital Area, development is taking place around large proj-

41 See Hvidt, 2019: 4.
42 See Shueili, 2015: 245–264.
43 On this notion, see Harvey, 1989: 4.
44 Harvey, 1989: 7.

ects led by OMRAN. Opened in 2016 a ten-minute drive from Muscat International Airport, the new Oman Convention and Exhibition Centre (OCEC) is supposed to boost the growth of tourism in the meetings, incentives, conferences, and exhibitions (MICE) sector. The presentation booklet describes it as "an integral part of a Madinat Al Irfan Urban Centre" and in harmony with the wadi it overlooks.[45] In fact, it lies to the east of a 4 x 2.5-kilometre area, while the Integrated Tourism Complex (ITC) Muscat Hills occupies the other end. The future Madinat al-Irfan city is located between the OCEC and the ITC. It is supposed to be "a new urban centre within Muscat" and "a model for urban development."[46] This sounds like a failure of urban policy by the relevant ministries and its replacement by integrated projects that exemplify an "urban development (...) led by more or less vague master plans for individual projects and construction zones, which generate a random and fragmented development of urban spaces."[47] Certainly, the construction of such places is presented as a means of offering benefits to the population. According to its corporate brochure, managing such places enables OMRAN to assert: "we are proud to have achieved significant socio-economic benefits for Oman."[48]

3.2 Iconic Places and the Heterogenisation of Space

By analysing the production of "social space," Henri Lefebvre notes, "such a space contains things yet it is not itself a thing or material 'object' (...) it has a content (...) any space implies, contains and dissimulates social relationships."[49] If any territory wishes to launch a branding process, its promotion must take into account its particular balance between nature and culture, which according to Lefebvre characterises space, and must show or hide the relationships that make it a social space. This point is related to the problem of maps, whose ambiguity in what they do or do not show is highlighted by Lefebvre:

> to compare different maps of a region or country (...) is to be struck by the remarkable diversity among them. Some, such as maps that show 'beauty spots' and historical sites and monuments to the accompaniment of an appropriate rhetoric, aim to mystify in fairly obvious way. This kind of map designates places where a ravenous consumption picks over the last remnants of nature and of the past in search of whatever nourishment may be obtained from

45 On this project, see Omran, 2020b.
46 Omran, 2021b.
47 Bromber et al., 2014: 8.
48 Omran, 2020a: 4.
49 Lefebvre, 1991: 82–83.

> the *signs* of anything historical or original. If the maps and guides are to be believed, a veritable feast of authenticity awaits the tourist.[50]

This ambiguity is present in the map in OMRAN's institutional brochure.[51] Black squares with numbers on the map and in the legend refer to the governorates in which OMRAN-managed establishments, hotels, or tourist sites are present. The country appears only as a plain grey background. From a graphic and aesthetic point of view, this representation is perfectly defensible, highlighting the sites at first glance, in coherence with the title "OMRAN's portfolio," which plays a bit on the word, referring both to a series of images and to a set of documents, even property titles. Such a representation accentuates the idea of branding based on a few specific images of the country, which appears like a blank slate onto which a few hotspots are placed. It is reminiscent of the "non-places" of which Marc Augé speaks, "a space which cannot be defined as relational, or historical, or concerned with identity."[52] "In the non-places of supermodernity, there is always a specific place (...) for 'curiosities' presented as such,"[53] in this case, sea turtles, an Omani woman busy with a craft activity, a resort with an unobstructed view... Perhaps we should not over-interpret what is merely an institutional communication brochure, obeying a graphic fashion? But perhaps it also reflects another approach to the territory? This assumption is also plausible, insofar as this brochure presents OMRAN's activity as having the ambition to play a real role as a lever for the country's economy: "With our aim to fulfil Oman's vision 2040, tourism development is the key pillar of our growth program. As we celebrate our 15th anniversary, we are proud to have achieved significant socio-economic benefits for Oman by improving the capacity, expanding the scope and nurturing the potential of its rapidly growing tourism sector"[54] – yet, such a development strategy concentrates on a few premium tourism hotspots, but largely neglects the rest of the country.

It is not certain then that branding leads to "interaction between local, regional, national and global levels," according to the "concept of nested scales."[55] In a highly centralised country marked by top-down governance, the risk is great that these iconic places remain "non-places" without any real driving effect for the territory. It should be noted, however, that the theme of decentralisation is pre-

50 Lefebvre, 1991: 84.
51 See Omran, 2020a, map off-text.
52 Augé, 1997: 77–78.
53 Augé, 1997: 138–139.
54 Omran, 2020a: 4.
55 Vuignier, 2018: 166–167.

sent in many documents, such as Vision 2020,[56] which refers to the delegation of competences to the regions' administrations and directorates to produce more flexibility in order to improve the level of execution and to reduce administrative centralisation. Adopted in 1996, this document found some realisation with the establishment of the governorates or *muḥāfaẓāt* in 2011, which are involved in the development of the regional and the national development strategies. Adopted in 2019, Vision 2040 aims at continuing decentralisation to be achieved by 2022, as an element of sustainable development. However, in fact, this term does not refer to a transfer of competences to elected local authorities, or even to local state services. It refers to the establishment of "local management and leadership" that will be "capable of planning and decision-making" within the framework of national directorates, with a view to local development, creating jobs, and promoting innovation.[57]

In any case, the NTS launched by the Omani government in 2016 with a view to 2040 to boost the tourism sector and to increase its contribution to GDP to 6 % is clearly based on this type of design: "the creation of unique tourism clusters that utilise the natural and cultural resources available to them will be key to the implementation of the NTS."[58] The leverage or driving role that such "clusters" must play is underlined by the multiplication of expressions evoking maps: for OMRAN's CEO, James Wilson, it is a question of integrating the Sultanate into the globalisation of tourism, and a facility such as the new OCEC in Muscat "has truly put Oman on the map," while, conversely, the due increase in hotel offerings must be translated into a "reshaping of the map" by decreasing the national share of Muscat from 53 % to 31 % and increasing that of Dhofar from 12.6 % to 23.8 %.[59] 14 tourism clusters are integrated in a double approach: the first sets three levels of experience, namely "luxury," "premium," and "medium"; the second groups "experiences" into nine "business models" around the themes of incense, Omani breakfast, nature, clothes, family rest, etc.[60]

Both approaches, highlighting iconic places and reshaping the tourism sector with clusters, reflect a branding process aimed at making the country's tourism offer more visible and at making it a lever for economic growth. The NTS aims, firstly, to attract a greater number of annual tourists, increasing them from 3.2 million in 2017 to 11.7 million in 2040, and secondly, to attract them all year round, rather than solely in the current tourist season, from autumn to spring: "the ulti-

56 Compare Oman Government, 1996: chapter 2.6.1.1.b.4.
57 See Ministry of National Economy, 2020: 36–37.
58 OBG, 2017: 216.
59 Cf. OBG, 2017: 220.
60 Interview with Carlton Seymour, advisor for the Oman Tourism Strategy, 27 April 2016.

mate goal is to transform Oman from a seasonal, high-end destination to one that appeals to a variety of travellers throughout the year," according to Maitha Al Mahruqi, Undersecretary of the Ministry of Tourism.[61] This reorientation involves the multiplication of events in order to maintain a tourist flow, the major example of which is the aforementioned Khareef Festival. Other festivals have also grown: the "Muscat Festival," with "traditional" shows, funfair, and fireworks,[62] and the "Muscat International Book Fair," which now benefits from the recently opened OCEC. These examples testify to an undeniable effort to develop tourism, by foreigners and also by the Omanis themselves. This is the Omani translation of "festivalisation" as a central mean for "promoting the city through periodic international events."[63]

The Khareef Festival illustrates the ambiguous effects of an approach strongly linked to branding in contrast to the spatial planning traditionally implemented by the State. The advertising clip for the 2017 edition presented on Omani television shows the logo common to the different editions of the festival on the left. On it, the representation of coconut palms highlights the green nature of Dhofar during the monsoon season, while the silhouettes of a couple with two children illustrate the family character of this form of tourism. On the right, the clip shows a traditional Gulf coffee pot, or *dalla*, formed by the calligraphic Arabic slogan *'Umān al-rakhā' wal-namā'* ("Oman, prosperity, and growth"): it combines the supposedly traditional conviviality with consumption that should boost the economy. This image is based on family visits to "glamorous" natural sites around waterfalls, as in Ayn Athum or Wadi Darbat, or geysers produced by the sea unleashed by the monsoon in Mughsail, or entertainment parks like Nawai Dhofar Amusement Park & Arcade or Atina Land, the latter being managed by the Omani group Seerabeec, which specialises in organising shows such as at the Muscat Festival. There are also public promenades and a municipal complex including a "Heritage Village," the Al Murooj theatre,[64] and the Salalah Water Theme Park, which is under construction. Leisure facilities cluster along Atina Road in the Salalah plain. The economic growth linked to the festival can also be seen in the investments since the 2010s at the beginning of this road in the hospitality industry and retail sector, which involve the economic elite of Oman and other GCC countries. There is the Hamdan Plaza Hotel, renovated in 2012, which belongs to the al-

61 Cf. OBG, 2017: 213.

62 See Chakraborty, 2021. Holidify is a start-up in the New Delhi suburb of Nodia, whose website provides tourist information. This article shows that the festival is well known among Indian tourists.

63 Hall, 2004: 257.

64 Its name *al-murūj*, meaning "meadows," recalls the agricultural past of the Salalah plain.

Ghafri group, the largest in Dhofar. On the opposite side, a Lulu Hypermarket, the ninth Omani shop of the Emirates-based group founded by Indian billionaire Yusuff Ali M.A., was opened in 2011. The flagship facility of the place is the Salalah Gardens Mall, opened in November 2013 (Fig. 4). It was carried out by the Kuwaiti group United Real Estate Company (URC), a real estate branch of the Kuwait Projects Company group (KIPCO) that also operates the Salalah Gardens Hotel. The complex joins establishments operated by KIPCO in Kuwait, Lebanon, Egypt, and Morocco.

Fig. 4: Salalah Gardens Mall
Photo: Thibaut Klinger, 2015.

4 Conclusion

Different aspects of branding have imposed themselves in Oman: corporate branding, place branding, and personal branding: the sultanate is thus following MENA's branding turn. On the one hand, since the 1990s, this process is part of neoliberal governance, as in Europe and North America. Agencification displaces part of the power of the administrative apparatus put in place from 1970 onwards, and the political discourse on identity tends to fade behind an agenda marked by entrepreneurship. Spatial planning by a proactive state has been gradually abandoned in favour of governance through projects and iconic places, as can be seen in the extension of the Muscat Capital Area to the west, near Muscat International Airport, and in Dhofar, in connection with the Salalah Khareef Festival. In both cases, the policy serves the interests of the sultan and Omani, Indian, and GCC countries' economic elite, some of whose families have dominated the country since the 19th century. On the other hand, there is a risk that the divide between the beneficiaries of this new policy and the rest of the population, between the iconic, intensely branded places and the less promising areas, will fuel frustration and resentment: this is a major challenge for the new sultan, Haitham bin Tariq, who acceded to the throne after al-Qaboos' death in early 2020. He is one of the first Omani royals to present himself as a businessman, especially by sharing stakes in the Blue City project, a mega tourism-devoted new city south of Sohar. Therefore, he will probably continue the transformation analysed in this study.

Bibliography

Al-Nakib, Farah. *Kuwait Transformed: A History of Oil and Urban Life.* Stanford: Stanford University Press, 2016.

Al-Shueili, Khalfan Said Mubarak. *Towards a Sustainable Urban Future in Oman: Problem & Analysis (Muscat as a Case Study).* PhD thesis, Glasgow School of Art, 2015.

Amarouche, Maryame, and Koenraad Bogaert. "Reshaping space and time in Morocco: The agencification of urban government and its effects in the Bouregreg Valley (Rabat/Salé)." *Middle East – Topics & Arguments* 12.1 (2019): 44–54. https://archiv.ub.uni-marburg.de/ep/0003/article/view/7934. Accessed 8 May 2021.

Anholt, Simon. "Why Nation Branding does not exist." Copenhagen: Bjerg Kommunikation, 16 January 2009. https://kommunikationsmaaling.dk/artikel/why-nation-branding-does-not-exist/. Accessed 13 April 2020.

Anholt, Simon. *Competitive Identity: The New Brand Management for Nations, Cities and Regions.* Basingstoke: Palgrave Macmillan, 2007.

Augé, Marc. *Non-places: Introduction to an Anthropology of Supermodernity.* London, New York: Verso, 2nd ed., 1997.

Balushi, Al-Maha, Irfan Butt, and Khadija Al-Siyabi. "Review of Awareness and Views on Branding Oman as a Nation." *International Journal of Business and Economics* 5.1 (2013): 7–20. http://www.ijbts-journal.com/images/main_1366796758/0112-Maha.pdf. Accessed 5 May 2021.

Barth, Fredrik. *Sohar: Culture and Society in an Omani Town.* Baltimore: The Johns Hopkins University Press, 1983.

Bromber, Katrin. "The Sporting Way: Sport as Branding Strategy in the Gulf States." In *Under Construction: Logics of Urbanism in the Gulf Region*, edited by Steffen Wippel, Katrin Bromber, Christian Steiner, and Birgit Krawietz, 119–130. Farnham, Burlington: Ashgate, 2014.

Bromber, Katrin, Birgit Krawietz, Christian Steiner, and Steffen Wippel. "The Arab(ian) Gulf: Urban Development in the Making." In *Under Construction: Logics of Urbanism in the Gulf Region*, edited by Steffen Wippel, Katrin Bromber, Christian Steiner, and Birgit Krawietz, 1–14. Farnham, Burlington: Ashgate, 2014.

Bruce-Lockhart, Anna. "These are the Top Countries for Travel and Tourism in 2019." World Economic Forum, 4 September 2019. https://www.weforum.org/agenda/2019/09/most-travel-tourism-competitive-countries-2019/. Accessed 12 April 2021.

Chakraborty, Anuradha. "Muscat Festival 2021: Experience the Omani Cultural Fiesta!" Holidify, 2021. https://www.holidify.com/pages/muscat-festival-2430.html. Accessed 4 June 2021.

Dinnie, Keith. *Nation Branding: Concepts, Issues, Practice.* London, New York: Routledge, 2nd ed., 2016.

Hall, Peter. "Creativity, Culture, Knowledge and the City." *Built Environment* 30.3 (2004): 256–258.

Harvey, David. "From Managerialism to Entrepreneurialism: The Transformation in Urban Governance in Late Capitalism." *Geografiska Annaler B Human Geography* 71.1 (1989): 3–17.

Hvidt, Martin. "Development Plans and Visions in the Arab Gulf Countries: What is the Likelihood that they will be implemented?" *News Analysis.* Syddansk Universitet, Center for Mellemøststudier, January 2019. https://static.sdu.dk/Flexpaper/aspnet/pdf/Hvidt%20article%20January%202019.pdf. Accessed 8 May 2021.

Ithraa. *Brand Oman: Brandmark Application Guidelines.* Muscat, 2016. https://ithraa.om/Portals/0/IthraaPDF/BrandOman/Brand%20Oman_brandmark%20application%20guides_2016eng.pdf?csrt=2141699112875170 62. Accessed 12 May 2021.

Ithraa. "About Ithraa." 2021. https://ithraa.om/About-Ithraa. Accessed 10 June 2021.

Jones, Jeremy, and Nicholas Ridout. *Oman, Culture and Diplomacy.* Edinburgh: Edinburgh University Press, 2012.

Lefebvre, Henri. *The Production of Space.* Oxford, Cambridge: Blackwell, 1991.

Luttwak, Edward N. "From Geopolitics to Geo-economics: Logic of Conflict, Grammar of Commerce." *The National Interest* 20 (1990): 17–23.

Ministry of National Economy. *Oman Vision 2040: Vision Document.* Muscat, 2019. https://www.2040.om/Oman2040-En.pdf. Accessed 13 April 2021.

OBG. *The Report: Oman 2017.* London: Oxford Business Group, 2017.

Oman Chamber of Commerce and Industry. *Omani Products Catalogue: Made in the Sultanate of Oman... Made for the World.* Muscat, 2011.

Oman Government. *Oman Vision 2020.* Muscat, 1996.

Oman Observer. "Sultanate Scores High in Global Tourism Ranking." Muscat, 7 September 2019. https://www.omanobserver.om/article/25190/Main/sultanate-scores-high-in-global-tourism-ranking. Accessed 4 June 2021.

Oman Observer. "Oman Ranked Fifth Safest Country in the World." Muscat, 9 July 2020. https://www.omanobserver.om/sultanate-scores-high-in-global-tourism-ranking/. Accessed 11 April 2021.

Omran. *Operating Review 2014.* Muscat, 2014. https://issuu.com/eomran/docs/operatingreview2014_eng. Accessed 8 May 2021.

Omran. "Publications." Muscat, 2020a. https://omran.om/publications/. Accessed 5 May 2021.

Omran. "Oman Convention & Exhibition Centre: Where the World Meets." Muscat, 2020b. https://www.omran.om/wp-content/uploads/2020/03/OCEC_2020-brochure-.pdf. Accessed 8 May 2021.

Omran. "Growth Through Tourism." Muscat, 2021a. https://omran.om/omran/about-omran1/. Accessed 4 June 2021.

Omran. "Madinat Al Irfan." Muscat, 2021b. https://www.omran.om/madinat-al-irfan/. Accessed 8 May 2021.

Origin Oman. *Origin Oman Identity Usage Guidelines.* Muscat, 2008. https://www.originoman.om/media/2046/OriginOmanGuidelines.pdf. Accessed 13 May 2021.
Origin Oman. "About Origin Oman." https://www.originoman.om/about-origin-oman.aspx. Accessed 4 June 2021.
Radboy, Babak, Sophia Al-Maria, Shumon Basar, Tiffany Malakooti, Andy Pressman, Michael C. Vazquez, Parag Khanna, and Nelson Harst. "This Brand is Your Brand: Evaluating a Selection of Exemplary Nation Brands." *Bidoun* 21 (2010). https://www.bidoun.org/articles/this-brand-is-your-brand. Accessed 4 June 2021.
Swyngedouw, Erik, Frank Moulaert, and Arantxa Rodriguez. "Neoliberal Urbanization in Europe: Large-Scale Urban Development Projects and the New Urban Policy." *Antipode* 34.3 (2002): 547–582.
Tanfeedh. *Tanfeedh Handbook.* Muscat, 2017.
Vuignier, Renaud. *Attractivité des territoires et place branding: Etude exploratoire de la sensibilité des décideurs d'entreprise à la marque territoriale.* PhD thesis, Université de Lausanne, 2018.
World Economic Forum. *The Travel & Tourism Competitiveness Report 2019: Travel and Tourism at a Tipping Point.* Geneva, 2019.

Karin Ahlberg

Egypt With or Without Islam: The Work Behind Glossy Tourism Advertisements

1 Introduction

In 2009, the Egyptian Tourism Authority (ETA) released two campaign videos. But except for the slogan "Egypt – where it all begins," the ads had little in common. One showcased empty landscapes, sun-kissed ancient monuments, and blue water, emphasising relaxation and awe. The other video highlighted busy street culture and vibrant street life spiced up with oriental pop music and *Arabian Nights* aesthetics. It was easy to get the impression that two different destinations were put on display. This split-destination image was, however, far from a mistake, but the outcome of an ambitious production process.

Starting from this observation, this chapter explores the processes, decisions, and local contexts underpinning the production of Egypt's official marketing material in the 2000s. Scholarship on tourist advertisements in the Middle East has emphasised the uneasy relationship between marketing content and orientalist stereotypes and has explored the mismatch between representation and reality.[1] My research demonstrates that highly romantic and orientalist tourist ads emerge not out of ignorance, but as a result of informed decisions. To understand *how* and *why* particular enticing images reoccur, we need to ask: whom are the ads meant to entice, and how do marketing professionals know their customers? What is the complex history behind the ads' affective affordances that explains why the two video ads turned out so differently?

Egypt is one of Africa's most important tourist destinations, and the sector is a key source of income for the state and a tenth of the population. Despite being a major industry in the country, tourism is associated with tensions in the predominantly Muslim society. The core of the dilemma is that the key *attraction* among Arab tourists – Islam and Muslim culture – is simultaneously the key *deterrent* among tourists unfamiliar with Islam. Using the two campaign ads as a departure point, this chapter investigates how marketing professionals and tourism experts have navigated this complex tourism landscape and diverging understandings of Islam and Muslim culture when designing promotions.

1 Cf. Al-Mahadin and Burns, 2006; Bryce, 2007; Henderson, 2008; El Jalil, 2009.

https://doi.org/10.1515/9783110741100-021

The text is divided into three sections. Section one takes the two video ads as a starting point for exploring the work that goes into producing Egypt's tourism campaigns. It analyses a particular logic of destination marketing that, in addition to the ordinary marketing of a product (in this case the destination), must co-produce that very end product in dialogue with the potential consumer. The next section outlines Egypt's major tourist groups and their tourism practices, to contextualise why it made sense to brand Egypt as two different destinations. To provide deeper insight into this design choice, the last section turns to some of the political challenges associated with tourism in Egypt, and how these issues are addressed in the campaigns through silences and absences.

This piece draws on long-term doctoral fieldwork in Egypt in 2011–2013, with cultural mediators who convey the image of Egypt to the outside world through journalism, tourism promotion, or personal interactions. I build on interviews and conversations with a dozen tourism bureaucrats, experts, and marketing professionals involved in the production of the official tourism promotion of Egypt in the 1990s and 2000s.[2] In addition, I have conducted analyses of official tourist marketing material and numerous reports about tourist flows and statistics.

2 Two Destinations

In 2009, Egypt's new slogan "Egypt – where it all begins," was about to be launched. It was the result of a collaboration between the ETA and two international marketing bureaus, J. Walter Thompson (JWT) and MindShare. As part of the launch, a range of still- and moving-image marketing material had been produced. Two colourful one-minute video ads, both ending with the new slogan either in English or Arabic, were soon circulated widely through international channels. Apart from a shared format and slogan, however, the videos' imagery has little in common. For someone unfamiliar with both Arabic and English language, it could have come as a surprise that they were the outcome of the same production process and campaign team. They had been produced for Egypt's two main source markets,

2 Throughout the 2000s, the Egyptian tourism industry experienced massive growth beyond expectations and goals, turning it into a main pillar of the economy. The 2011 popular uprisings put an end to this era. Tourism flows plummeted and the industry entered a deep crisis from which it has still to recover. Since then, the politics of revolution, novel representations of Egyptians in news media coverage, and domestic violence have influenced most marketing efforts. This article is interested in understanding promotional activities under less exceptional conditions, because it allows for an analysis of more general rationales and patterns.

which the profession refers to as the "Arab market" and the "international market."

Fig. 1: Screenshots from the international version of "Egypt – where it all begins"
Source: Experience Egypt, 2010a.

The "international" campaign (see Fig. 1) displays a mother and daughter on a white horse in awe at the sight of the pyramids in a vast desert landscape. A solitary tourist walks around the impressive columns in the Karnak Temple complex. Scenes of magnificent monuments and empty landscapes in the golden hour are interspersed with images of beaches and turquoise water presented in a calm tonality. Traditional oriental music and atmospheric flute tones create the effect of mystery and serenity. In interviews, I learned that the concept of "storytelling" underpinned the ads: as a tourist, "you always leave Egypt with a story."[3] The campaign furthered this concept by mixing the landscape views with close-ups of faces expressing amazement or fun. Emphasising the individual experience, the protagonists in the videos take photos and selfies. In the next scene, the same photos are displayed as memories in albums, underscoring the idea of leaving Egypt with a story.[4]

3 Interview with El Hout, 2012.

4 This ad displays a few scenes from busy Cairo traffic, the historic bazar, and a rooftop bar, which marks a break with previous international campaigns' systematic omission of local culture.

In the second video (Fig. 2), which targets the "Arab market," adventure and mystery is the central theme. A smartly dressed male tourist arrives in a luxury hotel with his family. Scenes of busy street life, oriental restaurants, and nightlife pass by to the beat of oriental pop music. Soon, the protagonists are surrounded by jumping servers and female dancers, colourfully dressed as *Arabian Nights* figures in Aladdin-style costumes. Rich colours convey animated street life, energy, and mystery. Like the other campaign, the scenes are filmed from the point of view of the tourist, sometimes a bit shaky, as though to highlight the individual experience. The idea of storytelling comes across more easily in the Arabic slogan, *maṣr bidāyit al-ḥikāya*, literally: "Egypt – the beginning of the story."

Fig. 2: Screenshots from the Arab version of "Egypt – where it all begins"
Source: Experience Egypt, 2010b.

Far from representing ordinary life in Egypt, the two campaigns show how selective and romantic marketing materials seamlessly conjure up two destinations imbued with different affordances and expectations. To this end, different orientalised versions of Egypt are employed: the Western gaze of an unpopulated Pharaonic Egypt in the tranquil desert, and the exoticising and eroticising oriental gaze of Egypt used in the Arab ad.[5] What a content analysis misses is that these imageries were actively chosen and calibrated to appeal to the different target groups. While campaign designers were conversant with the complex history and meaning of the tropes employed in the campaigns, they explained that the ob-

5 Much has been said about the legacy and power of these stereotypes, beginning with Said, 1978.

jective of the campaigns was to sell Egyptian tourist products to non-Egyptian travellers, not to portray contemporary Egypt. From that professional perspective, it was irrelevant if their campaigns corresponded to life in the country or to how Egyptians, including themselves, felt about the material.[6]

This disregard for "accurate representation" might appear crude, but it stems from a particular logic of consumption inherent in modern tourism, which puts images and marketing at the centre of the business. Promotion of a destination must do several things at once. It needs to convince a potential consumer to buy a trip, but it also needs to plant the idea of what the product actually is because the tourist product – a trip – is not solely made up of tangible elements, such as hotels, weather, and interactions with locals. At its core, tourism is also about experience, and experience is structured by broader imaginaries of the place as well as the tourists' individual fantasies and expectations.[7] This latter aspect also explains why the marketing professionals I interviewed described their job not as branding, but as promotion. If destination *branding* aims at indexing one coherent and recognisable idea or image of a place, destination *marketing* alludes to multiple but still legible imaginaries and travel possibilities to resonate with as many tourists as possible. From this view, Egypt's image could be branded in terms of the quality of the product, but the job of marketing material was to animate and activate potential customers' dream factories and to speak to their "tourism imaginaries."[8]

This image-centric logic is reflected in the extensive investments in the marketing of Egypt in the 2000s. Funded by public and private actors, the marketing effort was structured by time-limited contracts between the ETA and the marketing agency that offered the best creative concepts. Worth 40–60 million USD in the 2000s, it was the largest contract awarded at the time by a public institution in Egypt to a market agency. Hence, the competition was fierce. The practice of contracting agencies was initiated in 1993 after a series of terror attacks against tourists were framed as an "image problem" that needed to be restored by improved and systematised marketing.[9] Since then, global marketing agencies and the ETA

6 Several marketing experts wanted to insert images from the Revolution in the campaigns after the 2011 uprisings, but these attempts were abandoned because tourists associated them with danger and insecurity, not joy and excitement; cf. interviews with Altaranissi, 2012, and Loesch, 2012. Cf. also Ahlberg, 2017: ch. 3.

7 Cf. Mitchell, 2002: 199–200; Jenkins, 2003; West, 2016. This logic explains why tourism marketing and destination branding and promotion are huge industries; cf. Aronczyk, 2013; Kant, 2009.

8 Tourism imaginaries is a concept explored in depth by Salazar, 2012. Cf. also interviews with El Ezaby, 2013, and El Hout, 2012.

9 Cf. interview with Omar, 2012; Wahab, 1996.

have produced promotional strategies and content based on sophisticated knowledge of the market and the target groups. Insights into the target groups' imaginaries of Egypt and travel incentives are produced through the agencies' global networks and multifocal research. This combines detailed digital surveillance of individual travellers' opinions and focus group dialogue with big data analysis of larger travel patterns and research on the newest travelling trends. Another focus is Egypt's appearance in new media and public debates, which marketing agencies track closely in order to understand the larger political picture in different markets.[10] The advertisement materials, such as the videos analysed here, constitute the tip of the iceberg in the agencies' quest to know, meet, or possibly alter a potential traveller's attitudes. So, who travels to Egypt and with what expectations?

3 Knowing Your Markets

Egypt is one of the oldest tourist destinations. In fact, *tour-ism* as a concept and practice first emerged in Egypt in the mid-19th century as part of Thomas Cook's package tours to the country and the Holy Land.[11] The ancient heritage was for generations the backbone of the industry – "Everyone wants to see the pyramids before they die"[12] – but today, there are many types of tourism on offer: heritage, beach, urban, medical, religious, spiritual, diving, golf, marriage celebration, "summering" (see below), backpacking, the Arabic language, and more. Overriding this multitude, however, is the categorisation of the ten to fifteen million annual visitors as "Arab visitors" or "international tourists." Reflected in the video ads above, this division is understood as apolitical and simply the reality of the business.[13] What insights into these two groups' desires and travel habits motivate the promotion of Egypt as two separate destinations?

Inter-Arab travel in the shape of trade or for religious pilgrimage and education has long been a defining feature in the Muslim world. With the expansion of modern tourism, new groups of Arab visitors travelled to Egypt for summer vacation and urban enjoyment. Since the founding of the Ministry of Tourism in 1966 and the establishment of official tourism statistics, Arab visitors have consistently constituted at least a third of incoming tourists. The wealthier countries in the Gulf

10 This is something that all interviewees spoke about.

11 Cf. Hunter, 2004.

12 Interview with Dera, 2012; cf. Wynnes-Huges, 2013.

13 The two groups' different interests and practices are the topic of Wynn's monograph, 2007, in which she also accounts for the broader contexts behind these differences, such as historical narratives, global power relations, and cultural exchanges.

have since been attractive incoming markets. These visitors typically go to Cairo, Alexandria, or adjacent coastal resorts for relaxation and urban life in a place "almost like home."[14] Engaging in the practice of summering (*istiyāf*), they return as summer guests or owners of second homes. On average, they spend more nights in Egypt than "international" tourists do.[15] "Sightseeing" is an alien concept to this tourist group, which wants to experience vibrant street life and local culture. These tourist practices explain why ordinary Egyptians often do not see Arab guests as "tourists," a label they reserve for Western travellers. An Arab guest is called a "visitor" (*zayir*) or just a "Gulfie" (*khalīgī*).

Islam is a key factor in why Gulf tourists prefer Egypt to other destinations. For Muslim tourists adhering to conservative practices of Islam, it can be challenging to travel to non-Muslim countries where it can be difficult to adhere to prayer times, locate the correct prayer direction, or find *ḥalāl* food. Diverging views on dress codes, moral behaviour, and gender mixing further complicate the experiences of these travellers.[16] These hazards are assumed to disappear in a Muslim destination. The food will automatically be *ḥalāl*, prayer places will be easy to find, and the local population is assumed to share the same primary Muslim values.[17] But this type of "Islamness" is only half of the reason why Egypt is an attractive destination to Gulf Arabs in particular. Many of these visitors prefer Egypt because it has more *liberal* religious attitudes and legislation than their home countries.[18] As reflected in the video ad, Arab tourists dream of travelling to Egypt to enjoy gender-mixed places, nightlife, cinemas, and even belly dancing.

The other main source market is "international tourists" – basically non-Arab tourists – who make up the other two thirds of incoming travellers. Driven by the fascination with ancient Egyptian culture, a primary interest among this group is Pharaonic sightseeing along the Nile. A recurring detail in tourism ads, but also in museum exhibitions, popular culture, and school textbooks depicting ancient Egyptian monuments, is the absence of ordinary people. This has created an impression of a civilisation without inhabitants.[19] Since the time of Thomas Cook, travellers' imaginaries of empty ancient landscapes have served to separate heritage tourists from ordinary life. Indeed, most international travellers lack knowledge of and interest in Cairo's rich Islamic heritage and contemporary culture. Cutting out these aspects, pre-packaged sightseeing tours shuttle tourists directly from

14 This is something all interviewed experts touched upon.

15 Cf. Cole and Altorki, 1998, for an account of tourism development along the north coast.

16 Cf. Jafari and Scott, 2014; Battour and Ismail, 2016.

17 Cf. Interview with Loesch, 2012.

18 This was something all experts touched upon; cf. Wynn, 2009, and Steiner, 2010.

19 Cf. Gregory, 1998; MacDonald and Rice, 2003.

their hotels to famous ancient sites and then back to their hotels. To achieve the empty-landscape effect and deliver the expected experience of Pharaonic Egypt, heritage sites have been encircled with fences and local villages have been demolished.[20] That the international video ad has placed the protagonists alone in the famous sites flirts with this fantasy.

But heritage tourism is no longer the core activity for international tourists visiting Egypt. From the 1990s onwards, the development of beach resorts along the Red Sea coasts massively boosted tourist flows.[21] In 2010, 70 per cent of international visitors were sun-and-sea tourists.[22] Beach tourists share their quest for pleasure and relaxation with Arab visitors, and their lack of interest in local culture with heritage tourists. But while the latter group travels to Egypt to experience its *unique* heritage, for beach tourists, geographical location matters less. Beach destinations do not compete through difference, but sameness – offering the generic concept of "sun and sea" – making price and accessibility the competitive factors.[23] This logic is evident in the Red Sea resorts. Far away from the populous Nile, these "offshore places" sell "a glamorous image in conformity with transnational archetypes (architecture, leisure, consumption and lifestyle)."[24] In the absence of local history or organic culture, many resorts have been designed from scratch to correspond to tourist dreams of a holiday paradise. This fantasy is strikingly detached both from Egyptian local culture and from ancient heritage sites.[25]

While the markedly diverging tourist interests highlight several market segments, cultural and linguistic proximity to Egypt acts as the decisive factor for the two-market separation: Arab tourists want to experience local culture and exciting nightlife in a Muslim setting envisioned as almost-home. International tourists, on the other hand, have little interest in contemporary life, but come either for pharaohs or for faraway beaches. As discussed in the previous section, marketing materials are not produced with the intention to correspond to ordinary life in Egypt, but this overview of tourist habits and expectations reveals that the ads do correspond to a reality of sorts, since each campaign reflects and draws on the

20 Mitchell, 2002: 197–200, highlights how Luxor heritage sites were designed to minimise "unregulated contact with the tourists and increase their physical separation from the local community" following complaints from tourists. On the physical separation and enclave tourism in the region, cf. Meskell, 2005, and Hazbun, 2008.

21 Cf. Richter and Steiner, 2008; Vignal, 2010.

22 Cf. interviews with Dera, 2012, and El Ezaby, 2013.

23 Cf. interview with Omar, 2012.

24 Vignal, 2010: 70.

25 Cf. Daher, 2006; Hazbun, 2008.

dreams and preferences of the different market segments. To ensure that marketing material does its job, it is tested on focus groups and adjusted in accordance with the feedback received. In the campaign targeting the international market, the imagery had to be centred on the iconic Pharaonic symbols and empty beaches, so as not to confuse the target group, which normally displays "a limited understanding of what Egypt is."[26] My interviewees also explained that eroticised or exotified stereotypes are consciously inserted in the ads to entice consumers, but the Arab ad frames the evocative female dancers as a natural part of the scenery, not as objects of male entertainment as they are commonly known.

Ironically, while the production of the campaigns builds on meticulous research into customers' fantasies of the destination, these imaginaries in themselves are far from being fact-checked or challenged. Instead, they are returned to the customers reproduced and repackaged more attractively – the mystery of ancient monuments, desert landscapes, bustling street life, and entertainment.[27] But as we have seen, this image-centric logic of tourism – this almost closed loop – is not only found at a representational or hermeneutic level;[28] it is engraved in tourism sites and reflected in design of landscape. The tourist experience – framed by imaginations, marketing images, and the product as presented and imagined – unfolds in places that ultimately carry other histories and stories that not only fall outside the tourist fantasy, but also threaten to quell it. This leads us to a third aspect of tourist marketing: the art of dealing with negative associations.

4 Outside the Frame

On the ground and in marketing material, the Arab and the international markets appear as two separate routes whose roads rarely cross. Yet, in one sense, the two markets are intricately entangled. What constitutes the main selling point in the Arab market – Islam and Muslim culture – is not only *ignored* by international tourists, but even acts as a prime *deterrent*.[29] This tension is less prominent in the imagery of the campaigns, but it becomes discernible when the focus turns to what

26 Interview with Loesch, 2012.

27 Mazzarella, 2017: 108–109, argues that personalised ads based on our digital personas have given rise to a fantasy of "perfect addressability" because our digital footprints reveal who we are and what we want before we know it ourselves. In a similar way, tourist ads deliver the dream that you have not yet dreamed.

28 Cf. Jenkins, 2003; Caton and Santos, 2008.

29 Cf. Al-Hamarneh and Steiner, 2004; Hazbun, 2006.

has been left outside the frame and to the strategies and sensibilities that marketing professionals employ to navigate this dilemma.

International tourists' limited interest in Islam in contemporary Egyptian culture is grounded in a complex history of imbalanced relationships. The obsession with antiquities and the tendency to erase local people, ancient or contemporary, from representations to site design means that visitors' limited knowledge is rarely expanded. The legacies of orientalism and foreign domination have heightened the barriers of enclavism. In the tourism industry, international tourists are known for possessing a general fear of Muslim or Arab "others" generated by parameters such as political unrest, violent news images, prejudices about Islamic precepts, and widespread ideas about the oppression of women in Islam.[30] The generalised nature of this fear has meant that a crisis anywhere in the Middle East will push tourist flows down in the whole region, as evinced by the 1991 Gulf War in Iraq, which sent Egypt's tourist flows to rock bottom.[31] In the 1990s, the association between Islam and violence directed at tourists added a new layer to this fear. In Egypt, Islamist extremists started to target heritage tourists as part of a guerrilla war against the Egyptian state.[32] Hundreds of terror attacks were carried out in the Nile Valley. As mentioned, the tourist industry treated the violence primarily as an image problem. But this would change with the attack at the Hatshepsut Temple in Luxor in 1997, in which 58 tourists and four Egyptians where killed.

At the time of this horrific attack, the Red Sea resorts were about to be launched. To avoid any association with the violent scenes from the Nile Valley, the ETA decided to uncouple the resorts from the mainland completely. In the following years, the "Red Sea Riviera" was promoted as a generic beach destination, "where the sun shines 365 days a year." Not only were Islamic and Muslim symbols left out of the marketing campaigns. Typical Egyptian imagery – such as the ancient heritage and deserts – was also erased. With time, as tourism started to recover, ancient symbols were slowly reinserted into the tourist imagery. But even at the time of research, marketing professionals consciously excluded symbols of Islam in promotions targeting international markets.[33] To avoid triggering fear and anxiety, ordinary scenes of life in Egypt (women in veils, praying people) were left out of the picture.[34] The only Egyptians entering the tourist frames at

30 Cf. Ahlberg, 2017: ch 3; Wynn, 2006; Steiner, 2010.

31 Cf. interview with El Ezaby, 2013; Wahab, 1996; Morakabati, 2013; Ahlberg, 2017.

32 These attacks in turn were legitimated by the belief that foreign tourists were immoral *kuffār* (unbelievers); cf. Aziz, 1995.

33 Cf. interview with Dera, 2012.

34 Cf. interviews with Omar, 2012, and El Ezaby, 2013. Cf. also Wynne-Hughes, 2012.

that time were stereotypical tourist figures, such as camel drivers, *felucca* (a traditional sailing boat) sailors, or welcoming servants.

As we have seen above, however, Islamic symbols and Muslim culture constitute the core message to the Arab market. This emphasis, like the omission of Islamic imageries in international promotions, can be historicised in light of global events. Directly after 9/11, global tourism pundits predicted a major crisis in tourism, particularly in the Middle East. Instead, intraregional tourism boosted travel statistics as Arabs increasingly chose Muslim-friendly destinations. In the wake of the 9/11 attacks and the war on terror, Arab travellers faced tedious security clearances, a surge in Islamophobia, and even hostility in European and North American destinations.[35]

Egyptian marketing actors were quick to mobilise these sentiments of stigmatisation and hostility directed towards Muslims and Arabs in the West. With the slogan *nawwartu maṣr*, a common welcome phrase roughly translated as "you brightened up Egypt," campaigns in the 2000s emphasised shared cultural and religious values. At the time, Muslims reported having to hide or tone down their Muslim identities in the West. In contrast, Egyptian tourism ads openly celebrated Islamic symbols and culture. Friendly and smiling Egyptians in the ads not only underscored that Arabs were welcomed and cherished, but also employed orientalist themes to gesture towards the long history of affinities centred on Islamic culture. In the same period as campaigns to international tourists made efforts to avoid relating Egypt to Islam, then, the very same Western sentiment – Islamophobia – explains why Muslim imagery and references came to dominate campaigns directed to Arab markets.

5 Concluding Remarks: Content and Context

This chapter started with the question why Egypt was promoted as two different tourist destinations in the course of the 2000s. The analysis that moved from content to markets to context underlines how Egypt's marketing strategies are skilfully tailored and calibrated in relation to different market segments, diverging tourism fantasies, and other competing imaginaries of the place. One insight is that marketers seek to animate travellers' fantasies by employing positively connoted symbols, at the same time as they try to avoid activating politically charged and scary associations of the same place. Any decision to insert or cut out certain symbols, in our case representations of locals or Islamically connoted signs, is in-

35 Cf. Al-Hamarneh and Steiner, 2004; Hazbun, 2006.

formed by sophisticated research and subsequent testing of the campaign in focus groups. This means that the exotic stereotypes and simplistic representations found in glossy marketing material are a reflection not of campaign designers' ignorance, but of their professionalism and knowledge of the target groups' desires.

Hence, a focus on the voices of the campaign architects illustrates how productive analysing tourism advertisements beyond questions of marketing content and promotional strategies can be. In the context of the Middle East and Egypt, promotional material provides a mirror to the dilemmas of running tourism in a Muslim Arab country and highlights tourism's deep entanglement with global politics. In the 2000s, terror attacks on tourists, outspoken Islamophobia, and wars put a mark on the region. These wider geopolitical trends exacerbated a lasting tension in the Egyptian tourist industry, where the main attraction for potential Arab visitors – Islam and Muslim culture – became a major deterrent in the international incoming market. This tension explains why marketing actors promoted Egypt as two separate destinations at that time, as illustrated by the two video ads analysed above.

This chapter has made a case that marketing and promotion must be understood within the context of the larger tourism industry. The main issue lies far beyond the promotional material itself, the campaign architects and marketing professionals who are well aware of the material's shortcomings or limitations, and, for that matter, those who buy a trip after encountering a campaign ad. The core of the issue lies in the "reality of the tourist business." Like many countries in the Global South, Egypt's economic reliance on tourism is significant and the ambition to deliver desirable tourism products correspondently high. This explains why potential customers' imaginaries are subject to careful and minute research by marketing agencies. It is here that the irony of tourism marketing appears. The aim of their research is not to further common knowledge, but to conjure up travel dreams of the destination and then provide the corresponding tourist products to ensure that the actual trips meet the expectations that the customers (do not yet know they) have. As tourism is one of the world's biggest businesses and image producers, the world as the tourist sees it continues to be (re)produced.

But imaginaries are unstable. The 2011 uprising inserted novel representations of Egyptians into global imaginaries. Young, educated Cairenes frequently figured in news media talking about democracy and rights, a stark contrast to the camel drivers, waiters in oriental dress, and exotic dancers in tourism promotion. As a response, the 2011 campaign "We are Egypt" turned "ordinary" Egyptians into the campaign's main protagonists. In place of tourists, these Egyptians, who, in fact, represented the upper-middle-class elite, were enjoying their country and inviting foreign guests to do the same. Since then, tourism-marketing campaigns have allowed less-polished versions of the nation to be part of advertisement messages. This shift is not unique to Egypt. Due to the growing influence of social media, the claustrophobic frames imposed by established media infrastructures – news media, tourism marketing, and political branding – are losing their representational dominance. The new folksy marketing trend indexes a growing desire among travellers to experience destinations not only as exotic, sanitised, and "other," but also as places inhabited by local people, who, like tourists, lead ordinary lives and dream of the good life.

Bibliography

Ahlberg, Karin. *They Are Destroying the Image of Egypt: Tourism, Statecraft and Infrastructures of Image Making, 1990–2013.* PhD thesis, University of London, School of Oriental and African Studies, 2017.

Al-Hamarneh, Ala, and Christian Steiner. "Islamic Tourism: Rethinking the Strategies of Tourism Development in the Arab World after September 11, 2001." *Comparative Studies of South Asia, Africa and the Middle East* 24.1 (2004): 175–186.

Al-Mahadin, Saba, and Peter Burns. "Visitors, Visions and Veils: The Portrayal of the Arab World in Tourism Advertising." In *Tourism in the Middle East*, edited by Rami F. Daher, 137–160. Clevedon: Channel View Publications, 2006.

Amar, Paul. *The Security Archipelago.* Durham: Duke University Press, 2013.

Aronczyk, Melissa. *Branding the Nation: The Global Business of National Identity.* Oxford: Oxford University Press, 2013.

Aziz, Heba. "Understanding Attacks on Tourists in Egypt." *Tourism Management* 16.2 (1995): 91–95.

Battour, Mohamed, and Moh[ame]d Nazari Ismail Ismail. "Halal Tourism: Concepts, Practises, Challenges and Future." *Tourism Management Perspectives* 19 (2016): 150–154.

Bryce, Derek. "Repackaging Orientalism: Discourses on Egypt and Turkey in British Outbound Tourism." *Tourist Studies* 7.2 (2007): 165–191.

Caton, Kellee, and Carla Almeida Santos. "Closing the Hermeneutic Circle? Photographic Encounters With the Other." *Annals of Tourism Research* 35.1 (2008): 7–26.

Cole, Donald. P., and Soraya Altorki. *Bedouin, Settlers, and Holiday-Makers: Egypt's Changing Northwest Coast.* Cairo: American University in Cairo Press, 1998.

Daher, Rami F. *Tourism in the Middle East: Continuity, Change and Transformation.* Toronto: Channel View Publications, 2006.

El Jalil, Sabreen. "Images of Egypt in United Kingdom Tour Operators' Brochures." *Tourismos: An International Multidisciplinary Journal of Tourism* 5.2 (2009): 179–191.

Experience Egypt. "Egypt Where It All Begins (Official)." *YouTube* 25 May 2010a. https://www.youtube.com/watch?v=wcPYLL1B1uQ&ab_channel=ExperienceEgypt. Accessed 14 October 2022.

Experience Egypt. "Spirit of Egypt." *YouTube* 28 May 2010b. https://www.youtube.com/watch?v=alcAnzykWdU. Accessed 14 October 2022.

Gregory, Derek. "Scripting Egypt: Orientalism and the Cultures of Travel." In *Writes of Passage: Reading Travel Writing*, edited by James S. Duncan and Derek Gregory, 114–150. New York: Routledge, 1998.

Hazbun, Waleed. "Explaining the Arab Middle East Tourism Paradox." *The Arab World Geographer* 9.3 (2006): 201–214.
Hazbun, Waleed. *Beaches, Ruins, Resorts: The Politics of Tourism in the Arab World.* Minneapolis: University of Minnesota Press, 2008.
Henderson, Joan. C. "Representations of Islam in Official Tourism Promotion." *Tourism Culture & Communication* 8.3 (2008): 135–145.
Hunter, F. Robert. "Tourism and Empire: The Thomas Cook & Son Enterprise on the Nile, 1868–1914." *Middle Eastern Studies* 40.5 (2004): 28–54.
Jafari, Jafar, and Noel Scott. "Muslim World and Its Tourisms." *Annals of Tourism Research* 44 (2014), 1–19.
Jenkins, Olivia. "Photography and Travel Brochures: The Circle of Representation." *Tourism Geographies* 5.3 (2003): 305–328.
Kant, Amitabh. *Branding India: An Incredible Story.* New York: HarperCollins, 2009.
MacDonald, Sally, and Michael Rice, eds. *Consuming Ancient Egypt: Encounters with Ancient Egypt.* London: University College of London, 2003.
Mazzarella, William. *The Mana of Mass Society.* Chicago: University of Chicago Press, 2017.
Meskell, Lynn. "Sites of Violence: Terrorism, Tourism, and Heritage in the Archaeological Present." In *Embedding Ethics: Shifting Boundaries of the Anthropological Profession*, edited by Lynn Meskell and Peter Pels, 123–146. New York: Berg, 2005.
Mitchell, Timothy. *Rule of Experts: Egypt, Techno-Politics, Modernity.* Berkeley: University of California Press, 2002.
Morakabati, Yeganeh. "Tourism in the Middle East: Conflicts, Crises and Economic Diversification, Some Critical Issues." *International Journal of Tourism Research* 15.4 (2013): 375–387.
Richter, Thomas, and Christian Steiner. "Politics, Economics and Tourism Development in Egypt." *Third World Quarterly* 29.5 (2008): 939–959.
Said, Edward. *Orientalism.* New York: Vintage Books, 1978.
Salazar, Noel B. "Tourism Imaginaries: A Conceptual Approach." *Annals of Tourism research* 39.2 (2012): 863–882.
Steiner, Christian. "Impacts of September 11th: A Two-Sided Neighbourhood-Effect?" In *Tourism in the Muslim World: Bridging Tourism Theory and Practice, Vol. 2*, edited by Noel Scott and Jafar Jafari, 181–205. Bingley: Emerald Group Publishing, 2010.
Vignal, Leïla. "The New Territories of Tourism in Egypt: A Local–Global Frontier?" *Cybergeo: European Journal of Geography* 509 (2010). http://cybergeo.revues.org/23324. Accessed 22 December 2016.
Wahab, Saleh. "Tourism and Terrorism: Synthesis of the Problem with Emphasis on Egypt." In *Tourism, Crime and International Security Issues*, edited by Abraham Pizam and Yoel Mansfeld, 175–186. Hoboken: John Wiley & Sons, 1996
West, Paige. *Dispossession and the Environment.* Columbia: Columbia University Press, 2016.
Wynn, Lisa L. *Pyramids & Nightclubs.* Austin: University of Texas Press, 2007.
Wynne-Hughes, Eliza. "Who Would Go to Egypt? How Tourism Accounts for 'Terrorism'." *Review of International Studies* 38.3 (2012): 615–640.

Cited Interviews

Altaranissi, Ayman. Director General, Egyptian Tourism Federation (ETF). Cairo, 9 June 2012.
Dera, Hazim. Chairman and CEO, Look. Cairo, 10 December 2012.
El Ezaby, Amr. Advisor, Ministry of Tourism; Former Chairman, Egyptian Tourism Authority (ETA). Cairo, 20 February 2013.
El Hout, Shaimaa. Project Director, J. Walter Thompson (JWT Cairo branch). Cairo, June 2012.
Loesch, Victoria. Client Leadership Director, Mindshare. Cairo, 14 March 2012.
Omar, Rajia. Managing Director, Doyle Dane Bernbach (DDB Cairo branch). Cairo, 2 July 2012.

Laura Hindelang

Mobile Images: Stamps as Branding Tools in the Gulf States

1 Postage Stamps in the MENA Region: Typology, Function, and History

Postage stamps belong to the realm of political symbols. National postal administrations are responsible for designing and issuing stamps. The stamp's face usually displays the name of the state and/or the ruler's portrait. Despite their small size, stamps offer ample space for purposefully selected imagery that generally relates to the place of issue. Based on an art historical analysis of stamps issued by the Gulf states during the second half of the 20th century, I discuss postage stamps' potential for place branding from a historical perspective.

Given the proliferation of postal communication in the 20th century, stamps have long been familiar objects of everyday use and part of the widespread visual culture of the MENA region. Firmly glued to a postcard, an envelope, or a parcel, stamps circulate widely not only in geographical, but also in social and cultural terms. Especially because of their quotidian visual presence, stamps are able to "touch the everyday lives (and reflect the attitudes) of both governments and ordinary citizens more readily than grand political rhetoric or state ceremonial" and can become significant political symbols.[1] Designs can include ornamentation or graphics in combination with abstract, numerical, or pictorial images. Stamps are, in effect, artistic "miniature prints with a very wide circulation."[2] The textual information on stamps, including the monetary value, is an integral part of stamp design, and a special typography is often used. In the case of a non-Roman script like Arabic, the textual information is usually accompanied by the same word(s) in Roman letters, thus effectively displaying the state name twice, making the place branding even more powerful on a visual level.

So far, Middle Eastern postage stamps have not yet been considered tools of branding. Only a handful of scholars have discussed the stamps of modern Arab countries, and these have focused mainly on semiotics, scientific history, propaganda, and identity construction, usually overlooking questions of aesthetics and po-

1 Jeffery, 2006: 46.
2 Gabriel, 2009: 190 (the author's translation).

https://doi.org/10.1515/9783110741100-022

litical place branding.[3] This is surprising, given that stamps have long been recognised for their advertising and communicative function towards other states and people as "business cards of states."[4]

For the Gulf states, which were either Trucial States or British quasi-protectorates up until their independence in the 1960s and 1970s, gaining full responsibility over their postal services was a crucial step in their nation-building process. With it came the task of creating new stamp designs and developing a political iconography that could advertise these states internally and externally. Compared with the previously used, overprinted British and British-Indian stamps, it was a milestone to issue stamp series with, for example, Kuwaiti motifs, the name of the state of Kuwait, Arabic writing, and a national currency. Having analysed a multitude of postage stamps issued since the 1950s, I find the popularity of certain recurring groups of motifs that can be considered highly effective for (political) place branding quite striking.[5]

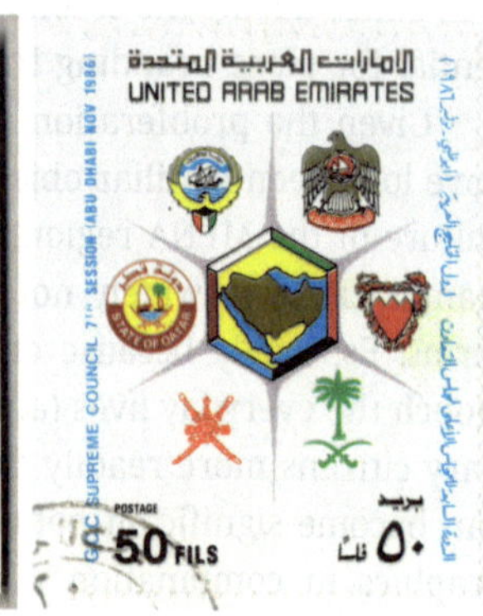

Fig. 1 (left): First flight cover of Swissair's route Kuwait – Zurich, issued 5 April 1976
Fig. 2 (right): 50 fils stamp, United Arab Emirates, GCC Supreme Council 7th session (Abu Dhabi, November 1986)
All stamps and images are from the author's collection.

3 See Hazard, 1960; Sivan, 1987; Badry and Niehoff, 1988; Reid, 1993; Kadoi, 2009.

4 Benjamin, 2009: 186. Benjamin was a passionate philatelist.

5 However, the Gulf states have also issued stamp sets with motifs that have nothing to do with the region, such as tropical birds, US space missions, and European composers. This shows the deliberate outward orientation of the stamps, but the choice of unrelated motifs in combination with what could be called "kitsch" pictorial stamp designs undermined the value of Gulf stamps in the 1970s and 1980s amongst collectors.

2 Map(ping) and Emblems: Stamps as a Reflection of Political Geographies

A stamp's basic function is to act as a receipt for the amount that the sender paid to the issuing body to transport a letter or package. Stamp cancellations on international envelopes and parcels document the interactions of different postal administrations, border regimes, and individual senders and receivers. A fascinating special case is the pre-printed envelopes with pictorial stamps that were occasionally issued to celebrate the opening of a new air route, for example the route Kuwait – Athens – Zurich, which was first flown on 5 April 1976 by Swissair (Fig. 1). The envelope displays one stamp with the official portrait of Kuwait's then-ruler and another medically themed stamp. It is imprinted with a drawing of Kuwait's Sief Palace, the seat of the ruler and the government, which underlines the political nature of this seemingly commercial enterprise. This visual display highlights the dependence of the modern postal services not only on air transportation, but equally on diplomatic relationships, relationships that became mapped through postal networks. Similarly, stamps have often promoted political rule over a clearly delineated geographic area through motifs of maps and national emblems. A good example of this is the relatively large stamp that commemorated the seventh session of the GCC Supreme Council held in Abu Dhabi in November 1986. The stamp motif is in fact the GCC logo, which consists of the mapped territory of all member states in a hexagon that is surrounded by the states' national emblems (Fig. 2). Such instances show that stamps are not only receipts, but can also be tools for political (place) branding

3 Architecture: Stamps Showcasing Cityscapes

The stamp culture of the MENA region has a long tradition of showcasing sites like dams and factories or standardised housing schemes as part of "Development Weeks" (Iraq, 1958) or of socialist planning agendas (UAR, 1961). In the Gulf, a strong tendency has developed to single out specific buildings and present each on an individual stamp that is often published at the same time as the inauguration or anniversary of the building. Such stamps form a travel guide of architectural sights that shows what is officially recognised as part of the urban landscape or architectural heritage of the issuing city-state. Over the years, the state of Kuwait has for instance selected the Al-Sabah Hospital (1967), the Telecommunications Centre (1972), the Kuwait Fund for Arab Economic Development (1974), and the iconic Kuwait Towers (1977), but also the Kuwait Hilton Hotel (1969) (Fig. 3).

Fig. 3: 20 fils stamp, Kuwait, Kuwait Fund for Arab Economic Development (established 31 December 1961), issued 1974

I read this as the philatelic prologue of today's branding strategy: Dubai and Qatar making international headlines by commissioning iconic buildings by starchitects like Jean Nouvel and Zaha Hadid.[6] Prior to the Internet, stamps long served as a mobile miniature travel guide that made the addressee a visitor to the Gulf's iconic cityscape through images.

4 Oil Derricks and Pipelines: Stamps Declaring the Gulf States "Petro-nations"

Over the decades, something like a "petro-philately," the philatelic study of oil-related stamps, developed among stamp collectors. In a 1988 article in the oil company magazine Saudi Aramco World, collector Raymond Schuessler explained that petro-philately included not only motifs related to the modern petroleum industry and petroleum-based products, but also those related to pre-modern uses of oil for shipbuilding, religious practices, and medicine. Throughout the 1950s and 1960s, petroleum, especially in the form of large-scale oil infrastructures like derricks, tanks, and pipelines, emerged as a frequent motif of postage stamps in the MENA region and elsewhere. It is noteworthy that the Gulf states also issued oil-related stamps to mark grand national festivities, such as the stamp showing a refinery in the Qatari set celebrating the ninth anniversary of independence in 1980 (Fig. 4) and a Kuwaiti stamp issued on the 17th anniversary of Kuwait's National Day in 1978 displaying a fictive skyline that merges iconic high rises such as the Kuwait Towers with the silhouette of an oil derrick (Fig. 5). The circulation of

6 For more details, see Hindelang, 2022a.

such petro-philatelic images reinforced the reputation that the Gulf states were "petro-nations."

Fig. 4 (left): 10 dirham stamp, Qatar, 9th anniversary of independence (3 September 1980), showing a petroleum refinery, Qatar's flag, and the vignette portrait of Sheikh Khalifa Bin Hamad Al Thani
Fig. 5 (right): 80 fils stamp, Kuwait, 17th anniversary of the National Day (26 February 1978), including the vignette portrait of Sheikh Jaber Al Ahmad Al Sabah

In conclusion, it is worthwhile to take into consideration the Gulf's often-overlooked 20th-century urban visual culture when discussing the contemporary phenomenon of place branding and political image building.[7] Postage stamps yield especially rich findings, as they are by definition a very visual, condensed, strategic, political, and mobile medium that has played a significant role in the way the Gulf states have presented themselves to the world.

Bibliography

Badry, Roswitha, and Johannes Niehoff. *Die ideologische Botschaft von Briefmarken: Dargestellt am Beispiel Libyens und des Iran.* Tübingen: Niehoff, 1988.

Benjamin, Walter. "Briefmarken-Handlungen." In *Walter Benjamin. Werke und Nachlaß, Kritische Gesamtausgabe: Einbahnstraße (1928)*, vol. 8, edited by Detlev Schöttker and Steffen Haug, 182–190. Frankfurt am Main: Suhrkamp, 2009.

Gabriel, Gottfried. "Ästhetik und Politische Ikonographie der Briefmarke." *Zeitschrift für Ästhetik und Allgemeine Kunstwissenschaft* 54.2 (2009): 183–201.

Hazard, Harry W. "Islamic Philately as an Ancillary Discipline." In *The World of Islam: Studies in Honour of Philip K. Hitti*, edited by James Kritzeck and Richard B. Winder, 199–232. London: Macmillan, repr. ed., 1960.

Hindelang, Laura. *Iridescent Kuwait: Petro-Modernity and Urban Visual Culture since the Mid-Twentieth Century.* Berlin: De Gruyter, 2022a.

7 See Hindelang, 2022b.

Hindelang, Laura. "Kuwait is the Past, Dubai is the Present: A Comparative Historiography of Spectacular Urbanism and Architectural Promotion in the Gulf." In *The History of Material Cultures and Visual Arts in Islamic Lands*, edited by Nourane Ben Azzouna, Sabiha Göloglu, and Markus Ritter, 209–222. Wiesbaden: Reichert, 2022b.

Jeffery, Keith. "Crown, Communication and the Colonial Post: Stamps, the Monarchy and the British Empire." *The Journal of Imperial and Commonwealth History* 34.1 (2006): 45–70.

Kadoi, Yuka. "Postage Stamps in Islamic Art." *Groove Art Online* 2 July 2009. doi.org/10.1093/gao/9781884446054.article.T2082293.

Reid, Donald M. "The Postage Stamp: A Window on Saddam Hussein's Iraq." *Middle East Journal* 47.1 (1993): 77–89.

Schuessler, Raymond. "Petrophilately." *Saudi Aramco World* 39.1 (1988). https://archive.aramcoworld.com/issue/198801/petrophilately.htm. Accessed 23 December 2021.

Sivan, Emmanuel. "The Arab Nation-State: In Search of a Usable Past." *Middle East Review* 19.3 (1987): 21–30.

Gergana Alzeer and Tilde Rosmer

Greening the Desert: Emirati Youth's Perceptions of Green Branding

1 Introduction

The United Arab Emirates (UAE) is becoming a successful example of governmental strategy of place branding in the Gulf and in the Middle East in general. Some claim that the UAE is the Middle East's most valuable brand, based largely on the country's strategic geographical location and function as a transit hub between global regions.[1] The branding efforts of the government include investments in modern infrastructure (including state-of-the-art ports; airports, airlines, office towers, and museums); hosting world events (including sports competitions and cultural and political meetings); and facilitating tourism, shopping, and entertainment.[2]

Of the seven United Emirates, Dubai has been described as the star of branding, with its international reputation as a travel hub, business centre, and tourist destination.[3] Dubai is therefore perceived as a model to be imitated by other Arab cities and nations.[4] Dubai has until recently been associated with business and the "world's tallest" skyscraper and "largest" shopping mall, as well as indoor skiing and hotel beaches. However, since Sheikh Mohammed bin Rashid Al Maktoum assumed rule in 2006, green branding has been added to the promotion of this city-emirate, aiming to enhance its attractiveness as a tourist destination and as one of the best places to live and to make investments.

As professors at a federal university in Dubai, we were intrigued by comments made by women students in discussions of the green shift in Dubai. It became clear to us that this group of Emirati youth had an understanding of "greening" that differed from that expressed by their country's leadership in strategies and policies, and we therefore set out to investigate their awareness of and reactions to the government's green branding efforts. In the current literature on branding, there is a lack of research on consumers' (citizens' or tourists') perceptions of green branding,[5] and there are no studies at all of this from the Gulf region. More-

1 See Zeineddine, 2017.
2 See De Jong, Hoppe, and Noori, 2019.
3 See Govers, 2012.
4 See De Jong, Hoppe and Noori, 2019; Zeineddine, 2017; Freire, 2012.
5 See Chan and Marafa, 2016.

https://doi.org/10.1515/9783110741100-023

over, in the growing literature on the branding of Dubai, there is no mention or reference to green branding; the research conducted focuses on its reputation as a smart city, a shopping city, or a city of wonders with man-made islands and the world's tallest building. This research fills both of these gaps by analysing Emirati youth's awareness and perception of the green branding of Dubai. Moreover, this research adds a non-Western case to the analysis of the understanding of "greening" that introduces a different perspective on greening that focuses on *making* green rather than *preserving* green.

2 Green City Branding

Branding is a marketing strategy that creates an image of the brand in the consumer's mind.[6] Place branding has become one of the most powerful marketing tools for cities, regions, and nations.[7] City branding aims to establish cities as key global players, empowering them economically and politically.[8] Until now, much of the available research focuses on how cities have established a brand associated with the desired image of the city. "City images (...) represent a total set of place impressions or perceptions based on attributes, functional expectations and symbolic meanings."[9] These images are communicated to consumers with the goal of projecting "a positive, unique and desirable identity."[10]

Green branding has emerged as part of city (and nation) branding: "Green identity branding provides cities with an opportunity to market their strengths and distinct qualities both within and across national boundaries."[11] However, green branding is substantially less researched than city branding,[12] which has generated a huge amount of literature, and there is not even a consensus among scholars on a definition of green branding.[13]

Green branding involves positioning products or places, as in our case, in accordance with their environmental credentials, where environmental values con-

6 See Kotler and Keller, 2015.

7 See Caldwell and Freire, 2004; Wang, 2019; DeJong, Hoppe, and Noori, 2019.

8 See Freire, 2012; DeJong, Hoppe, and Noori, 2019.

9 Chan and Marafa, 2016: 291.

10 Chan and Marafa, 2016: 291.

11 Wang, 2019: 377.

12 See Chan and Marafa, 2016.

13 See Boisen, Terlouw, and van Gorp, 2011; Ashworth and Kavaratzis, 2009; Moilanen and Rainisto, 2009; Anholt, 2007.

stitute the brand's true essence.[14] Usually this involves promoting places based on their natural attractions, as well as their commitment to, action for, and support for environmental values.[15] To make the city more attractive to consumers, urban spaces are made physically green,[16] hence green branding coincides with the global green shift and resultant increased societal demands for and awareness of environmental protection and sustainability.[17] Research has shown that increasingly more people feel unable to admire or respect countries or governments that pollute the planet.[18] Therefore, especially small countries aspiring for global recognition adopt green branding strategies as a way of establishing themselves as green leaders in the global market.[19] This reasoning applies directly to Dubai (and the UAE).

3 Context: The Green Branding of Dubai

The concept of "greening the desert" is not new in the UAE and was a pillar of Sheikh Zayed bin Sultan Al Nahyan's modernisation approach from the 1970s onwards. Sheikh Zayed was the first President of the UAE Federation and is credited with unifying the Emirates. Planting trees and other concrete greening measures have been part of Emirati nationalism since the establishment of the federation and as such constitute part of the legitimisation of power for the ruling sheikhs and the political system of paternalism.[20] Sheikh Zayed is portrayed as the leader who loved nature and who devoted himself to greening the desert.[21] Since the 1970s, the government and other organisations have planted millions of trees, for example in Sheikh Mohammed's recent one million trees initiative[22] before the 2020 World Expo in Dubai, which had sustainability as one of its three major themes.[23] In addition, all over the Emirates, grass and flowers have been planted to beautify their urban areas.

---

14 See Insch, 2011.
15 See The Place Brand Observer, 2021.
16 See Chan and Marafa, 2016.
17 See The Place Brand Observer, 2021.
18 See Anholt, 2010: 70.
19 See Morgan, Pritchard, and Pride, 2011.
20 See Ouis, 2002.
21 See Ouis, 2002: 338.
22 See Land Life, 2016.
23 The Expo was deferred to 2021/22 due to the Covid 19 pandemic.

The UAE is trying to turn "green" for a combination of reasons: environmental concern over the harmful effects of climate change in the region;[24] the negative portrayal of the country in the international community as a result of high per capita emissions in a global comparison;[25] a need to achieve greater economic diversification and move away from its rentier economy that is based on unsustainable resources;[26] and the realisation that the region is rich in renewable solar energy resources and has large uninhabited areas available for solar plantations.[27]

To illustrate how Dubai is becoming a regional trendsetter in green branding, in December 2014, the Dubai Plan 2021 was launched, aiming to brand the city as "sustainable," as a "city that uses its resources sustainably over the long-term and in line with international best practice levels in terms of consumption, efficiency, and management, and in its dependence on renewable energy sources."[28] Sheikh Mohammed has declared two goals for Dubai for 2050: to have the lowest carbon footprint per capita globally (contrasted with Dubai having the highest prior to 2006)[29], and to generate 75 per cent of Dubai's power from clean energy.[30]

To realise these goals, Sheikh Mohammed launched the Dubai Clean Energy Strategy in 2015: "The strategy (also) aims to make Dubai a global centre of clean energy and green economy."[31] An important component of these goals is the investment in the Mohammed bin Rashid al Maktoum Solar Park, described as "the largest single-site solar park in the world."[32] In 2021, the Green Hydro Project at the solar plantation was inaugurated and described as a "First-of-its-kind project in the MENA region."[33] Additionally, in March 2021, Sheikh Mohammed launched the Dubai 2040 Urban Master Plan that includes significant areas dedicated to green recreational spaces and public parks and states that 60 per cent of the emirate will be nature reserves and "rural natural areas."[34]

With its investments in renewable energy sources, Dubai is branding itself as leading in clean energy development by showing that there is the political will to realise a green shift, which makes it attractive for foreign investments in renewable energy specifically, as well as investment generally in a city that is perceived

24 See Günel, 2016.
25 See Zeineddine, 2017.
26 See Ferroukhi et al., 2017.
27 See Ferroukhi et al., 2017.
28 The Executive Council of Dubai, 2021: para. 3.
29 See Kunzig, 2017.
30 See DEWA, 2020.
31 U.AE, 2021: para. 1.
32 U.AE, 2020: para. 1.
33 DEWA, 2021: para. 1.
34 Godinho, 2021.

as modern, forward-thinking, and able to develop both technology and practices for a green shift.

4 Branding Theories and Methodological Approach

Scholars have developed several theories and models to study and discuss branding, especially within the field of business and marketing. These models include the "Brand Box Model";[35] the "Nation Brand Hexagon"; the "City Brand Hexagon";[36] "The European City Brand Barometer";[37] and the "Green Brand Hexagon."[38] Our main theoretical framework is based on the Brand Box Model that emphasises the consumers' perception of branding, rather than manufacturers' perception. This focus perfectly fits our study of Emirati women's perceptions of green branding in Dubai, since, as mentioned in the introduction, the present chapter focuses on the receivers' side of green branding, which is rather underexplored in branding studies, as most of them analyse the senders' side or the message itself. Previous research on branding has established that branding is characterised by a functional (technical and utilitarian) dimension and a personal (emotional and symbolic) dimension,[39] both of which contributed to the Brand Box Model theory. Accordingly, in this model, the two dimensions that influence a brand's strength with consumers are its functionality and its representationality.[40]

The functional dimension is primarily associated with the perception of the utilitarian aspect of the brand,[41] which captures the "consumer's concern for the performance capabilities of the product."[42] This dimension usually helps consumers with rapid decision-making about the brand's primary utilitarian aspects, such as its speed, quality, taste, and so on. In terms of green branding, this dimension usually appeals to the rational mind of the consumers by stressing the product's environmental benefits.[43]

35 See Chernatony and McWilliam, 1989.
36 See Anholt, 2006.
37 See Hildreth, 2006.
38 See Chan and Marafa, 2016.
39 Compare Hartman, Ibáñez, and Sainz, 2005; Lannon and Cooper, 1983; Munson and Spivey, 1981; Gardner and Levy, 1955.
40 See Chernatony and McWilliam, 1989.
41 See Chernatony and McWilliam, 1989.
42 Chernatony and McWilliam, 1989: 164.
43 See Hartmann, Ibáñez, and Sainz, 2005.

The representational or emotional dimension links to aspects of consumers' self-expression and other emotional needs, as the brand helps them express something about themselves, such as their values, beliefs, status, preferences, and so on.[44] Thus, there is "a set of consistent beliefs and meanings held by their purchasers and users which are associated with the product and service, but which exist over and above its obvious physical functioning."[45] In terms of green branding, the emotional dimension stresses benefits related to people's emotional needs, such as a sense of satisfaction from contributing to the improvement or protection of the environment or from exhibiting one's environmental consciousness.[46] It is important to note that all brands include a combination of both dimensions, with various degrees of functionality or representationality.[47]

In order to apply the Brand Box Model with its two dimensions to green branding, we built our approach on Cladwell and Feire's initial adaption of this model in their study of consumers' choices of destinations related to the branding of cities, regions, and countries.[48] In our research on Emirati women students' perceptions of green branding, the *functionality dimension* links to the *perceived* benefits and/or disadvantages of green branding in Dubai; and the *representationality dimension* links to their awareness and association(s) of greening, its meaning(s) and value(s) to them, and how green branding relates to their identity, culture, and traditional values.

We have also used elements from Simon Anholt's Nation Brand Hexagon that he adapted to city branding in the form of the City Brand Hexagon, constituting an index that allows global ranking of city brands of major global cities along six dimensions.[49] This model has been further adapted by many scholars, including Chan and Marafa,[50] who modified it to investigate consumers' perceptions of green branding in Hong Kong by creating the Green Brand Hexagon, which expands Anholt's "place" dimension to include ecological and environmental qualities. The Green Brand Hexagon helped us crystallise our focus group and interview questions, while also explaining some of the findings in relation to one or more of the hexagon's six dimensions (namely, green status, green space, green potential, green pulse, green citizenship, and green prerequisites).

44 See Hartmann, Ibáñez, and Sainz, 2005.
45 Chernatony and McWilliam, 1989: 165.
46 See Hartmann, Ibáñez, and Sainz, 2005.
47 See Cladwell and Freire, 2004; Chernatony and McWilliam, 1989.
48 See Cladwell and Feire 2004.
49 See Papp-Váry, 2011.
50 See Chan and Marafa, 2016.

Methodologically, to investigate the perceptions held by Emirati women students on green branding, we applied a constructivist paradigm using an exploratory approach. Since perceptions are linked to human experience that is constructed in myriad ways, including daily activities and socio-cultural values, this study requires a contextualised analysis.[51] Our participants, aged 19–23, were chosen using an incidental and convenient sampling method from students at the federal university where we work. Our study applied multiple levels of data gathering, including two focus groups each involving a group discussion among seven people, as well as 12 in-depth interviews with individual group participants. Following the focus groups, we asked the participants to write their reflections on greening and green branding based on their participation in the focus group. The focus groups were conducted in December 2020 and April 2021, and each lasted 120 minutes. The first group focused on environment and sustainability with green branding as one component, while the second focused entirely on green branding.

5 Discussion and Analysis: Emerging Themes

"Innovative," "entrepreneurship," "creativity hub with focus on the future: we are tomorrow," "diversified place, anyone is welcome," "anything is possible," and "Oasis, like a metropolis, in the middle of the desert": these are some of the expressions participants used to describe the brand, their city Dubai. It became very evident that the green branding of the city seemed to be last on their list. According to them, it is not as obvious as other aspects of the city branding that Dubai is well known for, such as its luxurious and elite lifestyle and its pioneer projects that attract tourists from all over the world (e. g. *Burj Khalifa*, the man-made islands, etc.). While the participants could easily speak of Dubai as a role model in branding, they struggled to think of examples of the "green branding" of the city. This confirms the impression of both Ouis[52] and Luomi that there is "… no profound environmental awareness among most UAE citizens"[53] and that green branding takes a secondary role in the UAE. To explore this point, the following analysis is organised in accordance with the themes that emerged when the participants expressed their perceptions and understanding of green branding. These themes are closely related in focus and content, and they thus naturally sometimes overlap.

51 See Scott, 1991.
52 See Ouis, 2002.
53 Luomi, 2012: 342.

5.1 Heritage and Modernity

As mentioned above, one of the focus group participants described Dubai as an "oasis." An oasis is "a fertile or green area in an arid region (such as a desert)" and "something that provides refuge, relief, or pleasant contrast."[54] The description of Dubai as a city oasis/haven captures visions of and realities created by the leaders that connect the past and the future. As such, this description relates to the natural environment of this desert country with its natural oases, as well as to the modernisation process it has gone through since the 1970s, a process that included greening as an important component. The positive notion of greening and living in an oasis correlates with the "green space" dimension of the Green Brand Model and the "place" dimension of the City Brand Hexagon models that link to the physical environment around us. Our study shows how participants express their level of understanding of the green branding of Dubai, based on their perceptions of and satisfaction with the city's material green physical spaces, which allows them to enjoy living in this place.

The "oasis" reference also relates directly to the idea of paradise that was part of Sheikh Zayed's greening-the-desert approach, in which he was bringing modernity to his nation not just by building schools, hospitals, and infrastructure, but also by planting trees and greenery using modern systems of irrigation.[55] The new city's parks provided shaded spaces for people to meet, play, and relax, inspired by the parks in European cities. Likewise, there is the religious aspect related to the green oasis/paradise vision – the colour of Islam is green, as are the images and ideas of paradise. Relating the development and greening of the Emirates to Islam simultaneously justifies and promotes green as both culture and modernisation – greening connects tradition with the future.

When asked how green branding relates to the local culture, several participants spoke about religion. The main focus was on the notion that, according to Islam, it is not permissible to waste resources. They provided examples, such as sharing leftovers from Ramadan *ifṭār* meals, not wasting water when performing ablution, and other instances. This led to a discussion about the differences between the older generations and their own, wherein the participants stated that, for older generations, not wasting (anything) came naturally, since they had less when growing up and did not take anything for granted, compared with their own generation. They then went on to discuss the idea or understanding of waste, and said that whilst their grandparents do not waste water or other natural

54 Merriam-Webster, 2021.

55 See Ouis, 2002; Al Fahim, 1995.

resources, they were not concerned about recycling plastic or other material waste. The participants interpreted this as a sign that the older generation did not fully understand the implications of plastic and other waste and recycling, since they lacked education about pollution, climate change, and renewable versus non-renewable resources.

From the field work, and as supported by the above discussion, two main emerging culturally and contextually based forces seemed to highly influence the participants' approach to and understanding of green branding. The first is their leaders as role models. In the close-knit Emirati society, tribal organisation that constitutes the basis of the political system offers the members a strong sense of security and belonging to a collective.[56] The leaders are highly respected, loved, and imitated as role models by their citizens, thus playing a major role in influencing their practices and decisions. In university classes, our Emirati women students often referred to the greening initiatives of their beloved leader Sheikh Zayed and how he engaged in planting trees and greening the desert, which became to be considered a national duty of each citizen and a symbol of their love for their country and its nature. They discussed how they had all participated in tree planting and cleaning-up events while in school, and they remembered that every year the government gave each family a tree to plant. One participant mentioned the connection between this heritage and preservation of nature with the recent attention paid to the indigenous *ghaf* tree that was declared the national tree in 2008.[57] In the last decade, there have been many campaigns to plant this and other local trees and plant species, instead of planting imported species that demand more water and can harm the local fauna.

Many participants mentioned how effective it is when a leader shares on social media his experiences of harmful effects on the environment. One example is when a sheikh posted photos of animals that had died from consuming plastic that campers left behind in the desert: "This was a wakeup call for me," one participant exclaimed. This example also connects to the second force influencing the participants' appreciation of green branding – namely the role of social media. The power of social media and its influence on youth has been discussed by many scholars.[58] Studies focused on the impact of social media on the Emirati youth describe the positive effects, such as providing information, expanding their networks, and exposing them to realities they would not have heard of outside of social media.[59] Many participants referred to social media with examples of how it

56 See Pinto, 2012; Heard-Bey, 2011.
57 See Connect with Nature, 2021.
58 See Omar and Dequan, 2020.
59 See Gjylbegaj and Abdi, 2019; Gjylbegaj and Jararaa, 2018.

informs their decisions and enhances their environmental awareness. This force becomes even more effective when used by their leaders.

Furthermore, the "metropolis" reference in connection with the branding of Dubai implies associations with high-rise buildings and six-lane highways, but it also directly relates to the modernisation process of the country and how greening was and is an integral and important component of this process, both in terms of the leaders' visions and city's actual development. Dubai's metropolis is the outcome of taking control of the natural habitat by making the harsh desert liveable and enjoyable for inhabitants, and the greening of this habitat is a visible side of this progress. Hence, in this context, greening is making and changing nature, not preserving it as in the Western perspective. This relates directly to the response by another participant who associated branding Dubai with the history of the development of the city and its "fast change(s)." She illustrated her comment with the speedy and continuous construction of buildings and infrastructure in Dubai. Indeed, since the 1970s, "New Dubai" has been built along a main road connecting Dubai and Abu Dhabi: "New Dubai consists to a large extent of lucrative cities within the city – from mega-projects providing particular services (...) to mixed-use developments for living, shopping, dining, and entertainment."[60]

The participant's reference to fast changes connects the past, present, and future and relates to the local cultural and economic context of Dubai as an "oilasis" where oil revenues are used to invest in business and tourism for a near future without oil, by transforming the city into a business and tourist "paradise."[61] The construction of this human environment from the empty sand dunes is a perfect example of a city built from *tabula rasa* – a place that was in an "empty state" before human involvement, a city built from scratch and branded as a new urban destination with labels chosen by the leadership.[62] "We are tomorrow," a participant commented, further adding her perception of the image of the city as new with endless potential and the ability to defy its ecological environment. Here again, we see the connotation of greening as making rather than preserving, which is unlike the Western perspective. This student shared her perception of a city where human imagination is the limit, resonating with another observer's description of Dubai's recent development as "a story of an ecological transformation that has accompanied its global image."[63] Other participants described Dubai using adjectives such as "luxurious," "futuristic," "innovative," and "a city that never sleeps," again confirming the perception of Dubai as a new, modern, futur-

60 Reichenbach, 2015: 128.

61 See Choudhary and Paul, 2018.

62 See Kanna, 2007: 24.

63 Choudhary and Paul, 2018: 4.

istic city. Thus, we can see here how consumers' perceptions reflect Dubai's already existing and evolving branding.

5.2 Awareness

The participants also exhibited awareness of the abstract concept of green branding that they associated with the "shift towards sustainability," "being eco-friendly," and "going green." One example provided was how certain fashion companies have "a green line" based on sustainably sourced material and/or production that is branded as environmentally friendly. The participants' perceived benefits of green city branding can be explained with the functional dimension of the brand.[64] This is clearly associated with the perceived utilitarian benefits and functions,[65] which will increase the consumers' level of satisfaction and positive attitude towards their city.[66] However, it became obvious that the participants' level of awareness of green branding in Dubai was mainly associated with concrete tangible green initiatives that they could see, experience, and benefit from in their daily lives as citizens. Thus, their lived experiences are associated with the lived space that, according to Lefebvre, involves the use of our hands, bodies, and senses interacting with the material world around us.[67] These concrete examples that the participants spoke of as contributing to the green branding of their city included: the Emirati Sustainability Pavilion at the Expo site that opened for visitors in 2021; the metro project that offers a green transportation option, despite the dominant car culture of the city (discussed in more detail below); the use of vending machines to return plastic bottles for money; the use of recycling bins; and the subsidised installation of solar panels on houses owned by locals. Interestingly, they never referred to Mohammed bin Rashid al Maktoum's Solar Park, or any of the aforementioned initiatives or projects.

While the participants lacked knowledge of the major projects, policies, and initiatives of Dubai's leadership in green branding and sustainability, they individually spoke of the need for more marketing and reinforcement of green policies to reach grass-roots society. They wanted the government to enforce stricter measures on the local population, including themselves, whom they described as too "indifferent" and "lazy" to go (more) green and to become (more) environmentally responsible: as one of the participants remarked, "Let us admit it, we are lazy..."

64 See again Chernatony and McWilliam, 1989.
65 See again Hartmann, Ibáñez, and Sainz, 2005.
66 See again Chan and Marafa, 2016.
67 See Lefebvre, 1991.

As for the generational gap, the participants discussed the need for more environmental awareness campaigns to reach the elderly population, as they feel that education has helped them become more aware than their parents and grandparents. While the elderly constantly remind the younger generation not to throw out food or wastewater, the youth expressed frustration that the older generations pollute and harm the environment due to their lack of awareness and knowledge. The participants used the example of plastic bags or plastic bottles: "My mom just hates using reusable bags, she says it is too much hassle, she says they are not handy or convenient, and she forgets to take them to the store." This expressed frustration indicates the participants' level of awareness of causes of climate change and pollution and thus an openness towards green branding, as well as how this needs to be modified to reach the different generations of the Emirati population.

5.3 Green Desert and Consumerism: A Paradox

From the perspective of climate change and the environment, two main paradoxes regarding greening as part of the modernisation and development of this country became evident in these students' understanding of greening. First, the funding for the physical greening of this place comes from oil revenues, which in turn contribute negatively to climate change. Second, the Emirati positive view of consumerism is not compatible with the common view of a green shift that advocates recycling and moderation; in the UAE, consumerism and sustainability are promoted side by side.[68]

The UAE's experience is unique, as its green shift is initiated by the government in a top-down approach, which is not comparable to the combined process of pressures from bottom-up activism in combination with top-down policies seen in most Western nations. To illustrate, the participants are aware that the process of desalination needed to realise the greening project is harmful to the environment. Nevertheless, they still had positive feelings and thoughts about greening this arid land, as they are "following the footsteps of their ruler," which is a common statement. They are also aware of the costs of their convenient and luxurious lifestyle, but they cannot envision Emirati society changing its consumerist habits in favour of a more sustainable way of life.

They all acknowledged the benefits of and need for the green branding of the city, stating how this will position Dubai globally as a sustainable place, thus add-

68 See Ouis, 2002.

ing more dimensions to its brand and status. Such perceived benefit embodies the "Green status" dimension of the Green Brand Hexagon, representing the global status and reputation of the city in relation to green resources. The participants also acknowledged that green branding can contribute to the economy and bring more tourists, but did not reflect on how this presumably would lead to further strain on the already depleted water resources and add to carbon emissions.

Most importantly to our participants, further greening will improve the quality of living in the city for them and their children, who will grow up in a greener environment. One aspect that contributes to the emotional dimension of green branding includes "nature-related benefits" that involve affinity with nature and the positive feelings related to and associated with being in direct contact with nature.[69] The fact that this green nature is not the natural local nature and has to be created was not perceived as a problem in this logic. When we asked the participants to describe "nature" in one or a few words, most responded by describing scenes from green nature in Europe and North America. Only a very few immediately thought of the sea and the desert.

Another participant spoke of how the electric Tesla car became popular locally not because of its environmental qualities, but mainly because of its expensive price and luxurious style. This was supported by other participants. For example, one stated: "They drive Tesla and throw garbage from the window." Such statements emphasise the need for more educational campaigns and the need to enforce more regulations to increase awareness of a green shift in order for such values to become innate and fully accepted by the city's consumers.

To our participants, lush green areas brand the city as green and improve the city's image, although they themselves admit that greenness is not native to their desert habitat. They acknowledge the environmental paradox of needing more water to create a greener environment in a place that lacks water resources and is dependent on a desalination process that contributes to pollution and climate change. Yet, to them, greening is positive and desirable as per their culture and religion. These findings make it evident how the Emirati idea of greening is different from the environmental perspectives in the West.

Several participants generally see that the green branding of their city has a very positive environmental impact beyond the city and the country. They suggested that by better marketing and emphasising the green branding of Dubai, which is already an established role-model city regionally, might encourage other cities to follow, and thus will spread the green shift. One of the participants suggested that to achieve a greener branding of Dubai, it should come somehow embedded within

69 See Hartmann, Ibáñez, and Sainz, 2005: 21.

the city's trendy and established brands: "Maybe Burj Khalifa could be known as the tallest building running on sustainable energy."

6 Conclusion

Emirati young women's understanding of Dubai's green branding is highly intertwined with religious values, cultural practices, and tribal hierarchies, all of which in various ways inform their level of awareness and care. Hence, the representationality dimension of their perceptions relates to their heritage and as such connects the past with the future. The functionality dimension of their perception is directly based on their actual experiences in this modern young city with its fast-paced changes, never-ending construction, consumerism, and comfortable lifestyle, all which are generally not understood as compatible with environmental values and a green shift. For many of the participants, greening is very often intertwined with modernity and advancement, meaning that greening means modernity through the ability to desalinate water and to populate and green the desert, thereby improving the status of the city, as well as their lives. Green branding to them literally means the visible and concrete oasis in the middle of the desert; one that is not only green, but also modern, advanced, happy, luxurious, and innovative. Seemingly, this understanding reflects their sense of national identity and pride in their country's achievements and modernisation, which began with their founding father, Sheikh Zayed.

Bibliography

Al Fahim, Mohammed A. J. *From Rags to Riches, A Story of Abu Dhabi.* Abu Dhabi: Makarem, 1995.

Anholt, Simon. "The Anholt-GMI City Brands Index: How the World Sees the World's Cities." *Place Branding and Public Diplomacy* 2.1 (2006): 18–31.

Anholt, Simon. *Competitive Identity: The New Brand Management for Nations, Cities and Regions.* New York: Palgrave Macmillan, 2007.

Anholt, Simon. "Towards 'Governmental Social Responsibility.'" *Place Branding and Public Diplomacy* 6.2 (2010): 69–75.

Ashworth, Gregory, and Mihalis Kavaratzis. "Beyond the Logo: Brand Management for Cities." *Journal of Brand Management* 16.8 (2009): 520–531.

Boisen, Martin, Kees Terlouw, and Bouke van Gorp. "The Selective Nature of Place Branding and the Layering of Spatial Identities." *Journal of Place Management and Development* 4.2 (2011): 135–147.

Braun, Virginia, and Victoria Clarke. "Using Thematic Analysis in Psychology." *Qualitative Research in Psychology* 3.2 (2006): 77–101.

Caldwell, Niall, and Joao R. Freire. "The Difference Between Branding a Country, a Region, a City: Applying the Brand Box Model." *Journal of Brand Management* 12.1 (2004): 50–61.
Chan, Chung-Shing, and Lawal M. Marafa. "The Green Branding of Hong Kong: Visitors' and Residents' Perceptions." *Journal of Place Management and Development* 9.3 (2016): 289–312.
Choudhary, Bikramaditya K., and Nian Paul. "Transforming Dubai: Oasis to Tourist's Paradise." *Contemporary Review of the Middle East* 5.4 (2018): 349–364.
Connect with Nature. "Ghaf Tree". https://connectwithnature.ae/knowledge-hub/ghaf-tree. Accessed 10 May 2021.
De Chernatony, Leslie, and Gil McWilliam. "The Strategic Implications of Clarifying How Marketers Interpret 'Brands.'" *Journal of Marketing Management* 5.2 (1989): 153–171.
De Jong, Martin, Thomas Hoppe, and Negar Noori. "City Branding, Sustainable Urban Development and the Rentier State: How Do Qatar, Abu Dhabi and Dubai Present Themselves in the Age of Post Oil and Global Warming?" *Energies* 12.9 (2019): 1–26.
DEWA (Dubai Electricity and Water Authority). "Renewable Energy Shaping the Future of Sustainability." Updated 5 January 2020. https://www.dewa.gov.ae/en/about-us/media-publications/latest-news/2020/01/renewable-energy-shaping-the-future-of-sustainability. Accessed 27 April 2020.
DEWA. "Under the Patronage and Presence of Ahmed bin Saeed Al Maktoum Dubai Inaugurates Green Hydrogen Project at Mohammed bin Rashid Al Maktoum Solar Park." Updated 20 May 2021. https://www.dewa.gov.ae/en/about-us/media-publications/latest-news/2021/05/green-hydrogen-project. Accessed 16 June 2021.
Ferroukhi, Rabia, Noor Ghazal-Aswad, Stella Androulaki, Diala Hawila, and Toufic Mezher. "Renewable Energy in the GCC: Status and Challenges." *International Journal of Energy Sector Management* 7.1 (2013): 84–112.
Freire, Joao R. "Special Section: Place Branding in the Middle East." *Place Branding and Public Diplomacy* 8.1 (2012): 46–47.
Gardner, Burleigh B., and Sidney J. Levy. "The Product and the Brand." *Harvard Business Review* (1955): 33–39. https://static.squarespace.com/static/52f06caee4b0c058f6084354/t/539070a1e4b0b4380bb48719/1401974945820/Levy_ProductandBrand.pdf. Accessed 8 January 2021.
Gjylbegaj, Viola, and Hussein M. Abdi. "The Effects of Social Media on Family Communication in the UAE." *Media Watch* 10.2 (2019): 387–397. https://doi.org/10.15655/mw/2019/v10i2/49632.
Gjylbegaj, Viola, and Osama Jararaa. "The Effects of Social Media on Youth's Interpersonal Communication in UAE." *International E-Journal of Advances in Social Sciences* 4.10 (2018): 23–29. https://doi.org/10.18769/ijasos.415493.
Godinho, Varun. "Sheikh Mohammed Launches Mega Dubai 2040 Urban Development Plan." *Gulf Business* 14 March 2021. https://gulfbusiness.com/sheikh-mohammed-launches-mega-dubai-2040-urban-development-plan/. Accessed 19 April 2021.
Govers, Robert. "Brand Dubai and its Competitors in the Middle East: An Image and Reputation Analysis." *Place Branding and Public Diplomacy* 8.1 (2012): 48–57.
Günel, Gökçe. "The Infinity of Water: Climate Change Adaptation in the Arabian Peninsula." *Public Culture* 28.2 (2016): 291–315.
Hartmann, Patrick, Vanessa A. Ibáñez, and F. J. F. Sainz. "Green Branding Effects on Attitude: Functional Versus Emotional Positioning Strategies." *Marketing Intelligence and Planning* 23.1 (2005): 9–29.
Heard-Bey, Frauke. *From Trucial States to United Arab Emirates.* Dubai: Motivate, 2013.

Hildreth, Jeremy. "An Introduction to Robust National Branding (Including a Case Study in Poland)." Paper presented at the Country Branding – International Identity and Image Conference. Budapest: DEMOS Hungary Foundation, 28 November 2006.

Insch, Andrea. "Conceptualisation and Anatomy of Green Destination Brands." *International Journal of Culture, Tourism and Hospitality* 5.3 (2011): 282–290.

Kanna, Ahmed. "Dubai in a Jagged World." *Middle East Report* 243 (2007): 22–29.

Kotler, Philip, and Kevin L. Keller. *Marketing Management.* Upper Saddle River: Pearson Prentice Hall, 2015.

Kunzig, Robert. "The World's most Improbable Green City." *National Geographic* 4 April 2017. https://www.nationalgeographic.com/environment/article/dubai-ecological-footprint-sustainable-urban-city. Accessed 15 March 2020.

Land Life. "One Million Trees: A 2020 Vision for the United Arab Emirates." 1 (2016): 18. http://magazine.landlifecompany.com/one-million-trees#:~:text=The%20UAE%20has%20a%20long,World%20Expo%202020%20in%20Dubai. Accessed 15 January 2021 (limited access).

Lannon, Judie, and Peter Cooper. "Humanistic Advertising: A Holistic Cultural Perspective." *International Journal of Advertising* 2.3 (1983): 195–213.

Luomi, Mari. *The Gulf Monarchies and Climate Change: Abu Dhabi and Qatar in an Era of Natural Unsustainability.* London: Hurst, 2012.

Merriam-Webster. "Oasis." *Merriam-Webster.com Dictionary.* https://www.merriam-webster.com/dictionary/oasis. Accessed 15 May 2021.

Moilanen, Teemu, and Seppo Rainisto. *How to Brand Nations, Cities and Destinations: A Planning Book for Place Branding.* New York: Palgrave Macmillan, 2009.

Morgan, Nigel, Annette Pritchard, and Roger Pride. "Tourism Places, Brands, and Reputation Management." In *Destination Brands: Managing Place Reputation*, edited by Nigel Morgan, Annette Pritchard, and Roger Pride, 3–20. Oxford: Butterworth-Heinemann, 3rd ed., 2011.

Munson, J. Michael, and W. Austin Spivey. "Product and Brand User Stereotypes Among Social Classes." In *Advances in Consumer Research*, edited by K. Ann Arbor Monroe, 696–701. Michigan: Association for Consumer Research. 1981. https://www.acrwebsite.org/volumes/9273/volumes/v08/NA-08. Accessed 8 January 2021.

Omar, Bahiyah, and Wang Dequan. "Watch, Share or Create: The Influence of Personality Traits and User Motivation on TikTok Mobile Video Usage." *International Journal of Interactive Mobile Technologies* 14.4 (2020): 121–137. doi: 10.3991/ijim.v14i04.12429.

Ouis, Pernilla. "'Greening the Emirates': The Modern Construction of Nature in the United Arab Emirates." *Cultural Geographies* 9.3 (2002): 334–347.

Papp-Váry, Árpád. "The Anholt-GMI City Brand Hexagon and the Saffron European City Brand Barometer: A Comparative Study." *Regional and Business Studies* 3.1 (2011): 555–562. https://journal.ke.hu/index.php/rbs/article/view/510. Accessed 10 January 2021.

Pinto, Vânia C. *Nation-Building, State and the Gender Framing of Women's Rights in the United Arab Emirates.* London: Ithaca Press, 2012.

Reichenbach, Anke. "Gazes That Matter: Young Emirati Women's Spatial Practices in Dubai." *Urban Anthropology* 44.1/2 (2015): 113–195. http://www.jstor.org/stable/24643138. Accessed 22 March 2021.

Scott, Joan W. "The Evidence of Experience." *Critical Enquiry* 17.4 (1991): 773–797. http://www.jstor.org/stable/1343743. Accessed December 9, 2020.

The Executive Council of Dubai. "The Place." https://www.dubaiplan2021.ae/dubai-plan-2021/. Accessed 16 June 2021.

The Place Brand Observer. "Green Brands and Sustainability Branding: Definition, Concepts, Theory." https://placebrandobserver.com/theory/green-brands-sustainability-branding/. Accessed 24 February 2021.

U.AE (The United Arab Emirates' Government Portal). "Mohammed bin Rashid Al Maktoum Solar Park." Updated 5 August 2020. https://u.ae/en/information-and-services/environment-and-energy/water-and-energy/types-of-energy-sources/solar-energy/mohammed-bin-rashid-al-maktoum-solar-park. Accessed 10 April 2021.

U.AE. "Dubai Clean Energy Strategy." Updated 15 June 2023. https://u.ae/en/about-the-uae/strategies-initiatives-and-awards/strategies-plans-and-visions/environment-and-energy/dubai-clean-energy-strategy. Accessed 15 June 2023.

Wang, Hui-Ju. "Green City Branding: Perceptions of Multiple Stakeholders." *Journal of Product and Brand Management* 28.3 (2019): 376–390.

Zeineddine, Cornelia. "Employing Nation Branding in the Middle East: United Arab Emirates (UAE) and Qatar." *Management and Marketing: Challenges for the Knowledge Society* 12.2 (2017): 208–221. doi: 10.1515/mmcks-2017–0013.

Dieter Haller

Branding Gibraltar: British, Mediterranean, European, or a Bridge between Two Worlds?

1 Introduction

This article examines the current branding of the British Overseas Territory of Gibraltar as a link between two worlds: Europe/the United Kingdom and Morocco.[1] Various political and civil society actors in the territory are involved in this process, which emerged in the run-up to Brexit and unfolded widely through its implementation. These local processes are embedded in wider geostrategic interests.

At present, we associate the concept of branding primarily with an economic strategy of emphasising the characteristics of a product or – in our case – a place, in order to assign a unique value, a unique selling proposition, in the consumer world. Many anthropological studies have used the example of European regions to work out how, in the course of European unification, special products of a region, especially food, are marketed as "authentic."[2] As a rule, these strategies have been interpreted primarily against the background of economic positioning within the European or global market in order to respond to the needs of customers who are seeking more authenticity.

The special contribution of anthropology to the study of branding places and regions is its emphasis on another dimension that goes beyond mere marketing strategies: the creation of cultural stereotypes and identities.[3] From this point of view, branding should not be understood exclusively in terms of external presentation; it also has an effect on the inner workings of a community.[4] Accordingly, the political-historical context, which often plays a decisive role in the branding of places or regions, remains underexposed in the primarily economic view of branding,

1 Thanks to Steffen Wippel, Dunja Moeller, Stefanie Hof, and Seda Sönmeztürk for helpful feedback and bringing this article into a readable English version. It is based on intensive anthropological fieldwork in Tangier and Gibraltar on cross-border, "transboughaz" (*Boughaz* = strait) relations in the context of the Brexit (2019/20) and on previous field research in Seville (1985/86), Gibraltar (1995/96), and Tangier (since 2013). Various publications on the subject bear witness to this research, including Haller 2000a–b, 2001a–b, 2016, and 2021.

2 Cf. Pratt, 2007; Leitch, 2003; Cavanaugh, 2007; Welz, 2016.

3 E.g. Anholt 2008, 2011; Fırat, Dholakia, and Venkatesh, 1995.

4 See Barr, 2012.

https://doi.org/10.1515/9783110741100-024

as it is able to strengthen cultural, social, and political ties internally and at the same time marks demarcations externally. This double effect was elaborated in detail by anthropologists, historians, and other social scientists, particularly in the 1980s, using the example of nation-state formation,[5] national myths,[6] ethnicity,[7] and borders,[8] and was incorporated – albeit inadequately – into branding research.[9]

This article takes a look at the example of the branding of the Gibraltarian community, which since the middle of the 20th century has been trying to reposition itself in the power triangle between the United Kingdom, Spain, and Morocco, primarily politically and only secondarily economically. A special role in the current branding of Gibraltar is played by the dense and partly centuries-old relations with the Moroccan cities of Tangier and Tetuan. These relations weakened since the integration of Tangier and the Spanish Protectorate into an independent Morocco in 1956: geopolitically, Morocco and Gibraltar oriented themselves toward different directions: the Arab world vs. the UK and the EU.

The first part of this article examines the preconditions that underlie Gibraltar's current branding. The next part traces Gibraltar's attempts to situate itself as British and, in a further step, as Mediterranean. This part of the text refers to the years between about 1960 and 2015. The third part focuses on the confusion that profoundly affected Gibraltar's self-placement and self-marketing. Due to the decision of the mother country to leave the EU with Brexit, the almost exclusively EU-friendly Gibraltar constituent territory was forced to re-locate itself on all levels – especially politically, economically, and culturally. This re-location revitalised old connections with Tangier and Tetuan and activated new ties to Morocco that emphasised mutual economic benefits and cultural commonalities. The text explores these processes in part four. However, the re-location resulted not only from local or regional initiatives. Therefore, part five elaborates how geopolitical interests have been instrumental in branding Gibraltar as a bridge between North and South.

5 See Hobsbawm and Ranger, 1983; Anderson, 1983; Hobsbawm, 1990.

6 Cf. Smith, 1984, 1993; Haller, 2007.

7 Cf. Barth, 1969.

8 Cf. Haller, 2000b and 2001b.

9 An exception is Olin, 2002: 246.

2 Historical Basis

For three centuries, the British Garrison or Crown Colony of Gibraltar maintained close economic, political, demographic, and cultural links with the Moroccan city of Tangier and other places in the Moroccan North. At times, these links were so dense and diverse that one can confidently speak of Tangier and Gibraltar as a single polity.[10] The tourism industry even marketed the two cities as a joint destination already in the early 20th century (Fig. 1–3). But these close ties became unravelled from the middle of the 20th century due to three political events.

Fig. 1 (left): Poster Bland Line Gibraltar–Morocco 1934
Fig. 2 (middle): Gibraltar Airways, Summer Timetable 21 April 1952
Fig. 3 (right): Target Guide Tangier Morocco Gibraltar. Edmonds Guide, 1968
Sources: Chipulina, 2015; Airline Timetable Images, 2022; Photo Dieter Haller, 2020.

On the one hand, Tangier and the Spanish North of Morocco were integrated into the new and formally independent Kingdom of Morocco in 1956. As a result, the North was reorganised not only politically but also economically in relation to the centres that now shaped the country's fate: Rabat and Casablanca. Tangier lost its position as a world trading and financial centre and thus its attractiveness for international banking, also for trade with Gibraltar. With the emigration of Moroccan Jews, Hindu merchant communities, the Hispanic population, and the

10 Compare Haller, 2021.

British upper class from Tangier and the North of the country, the ties between Morocco and Gibraltar also loosened.

Second, Spain implemented restrictions against Gibraltar from 1965 onwards, culminating in the closure of the border between Spain and the colony in 1969. Gibraltar was now deprived of two hinterlands and found itself in a territorially isolated situation: the established networks to Tangier and Tetuan hardly existed any more, and the Spanish workers from the *Campo de Gibraltar* in the province of Cádiz could now no longer work in the colony. The 10,000 or so Spaniards who worked in the dockyards, shops, restaurants, and households were replaced by Moroccan workers, the majority of whom no longer came from the North of Morocco, but from its southern regions. While in Gibraltar these Moroccans were regarded as strangers who hardly affected the ties to the neighbouring country, Gibraltarians increasingly oriented themselves toward the mother country: whereas young Gibraltarians had previously often studied in Spain and, like their parents, spoke Yanito – a mixed Hispanic-British language – now several years of study in Britain itself were specifically and generously encouraged. This and the development of satellite technology, which now made it possible to receive English television in Gibraltar, deeply anglicised the local population.

Third, Gibraltar joined the European Economic Community as part of the United Kingdom in 1973, while its Spanish neighbour was not yet part of the Community.

3 Branding Gibraltar as British and/or Mediterranean

During these years, Gibraltarians oriented themselves primarily towards the mother country and secondarily to Europe. The tourism industry marketed the small commonwealth as “Britain in the Sun” (Fig. 4). However, during their stay in Britain, most Gibraltarians experienced being perceived there not as true Britons, but as semi-exotic colony dwellers. Subsequently, nationalist currents arose again and again in Gibraltar, trying to establish a new identity: British like the Scots or Welsh, but not like the English; Mediterranean like the Portuguese, Genoese, and Catalans, but not like the Spanish.

I have described this process of branding as “British but different” several times.[11] It is reflected in the permanent exhibition of the Gibraltar Museum (now: National Museum of Gibraltar), where the specific ethnic mixture is praised

11 See, e.g., Haller, 2000b.

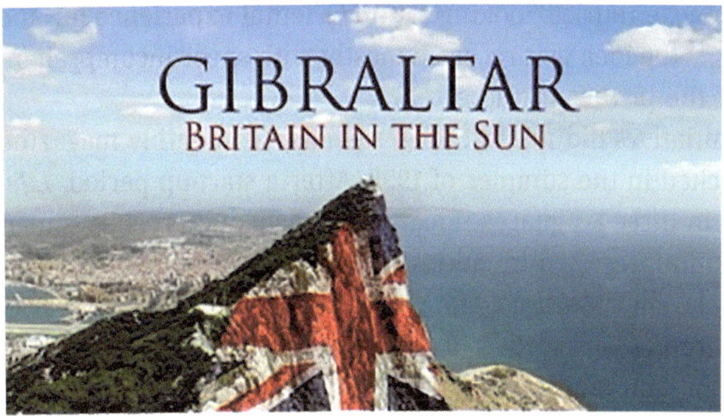

Fig. 4: Titlecard "Gibraltar: Britain in the Sun" of the documentary on Channel 5 (2013–present) Source: Wikipedia, 2021. Fair use.

and highlighted. Other components of the Gibraltarian mixture were not mentioned: the highly significant Jewish Sephardic community, the Hindu Sindhis – and the Moroccan Muslims.

Focussing on the latter, Gibraltar has not always cherished its Moroccans, as it does today in 2021, in the community's self-presentation as an open, multicultural city.[12] Only about 20 years ago, many wanted to get rid of the Muslim Moroccans. In January 1998, for example, the local government announced that it would provide financial aid to encourage the voluntary return of 700 long-term unemployed Moroccans. On the other hand, various political and cultural initiatives tried to strengthen *transboughaz* bonds. For example, the Independent Liberal Forum (ILF) fought for the rights of Moroccan workers from the early 2000s onwards. The ILF aimed "to increase human and social rights for all Gibraltar residents despite the apparent unpopularity of such an attitude in certain quarters on the Rock."[13] The Saudi King Fahd Foundation financed the construction of a mosque on the southern tip of the peninsula, which was already planned in the 1970s and completed during my fieldwork in the year 1996/97. But the mosque was not originally designed to meet the religious needs of the local Moroccan population. One of its spokespersons explained to me in 1996 that the Saudi builders had objected to "these underdeveloped hillbillies" even entering the mosque. Many Gibraltarians mistrustfully interpreted the construction as the Saudi claim to symbolically regain *Al-Andalus*, the historically Muslim-ruled Iberian Peninsula. I discussed the idea of constructing a small medina around the mosque that could at-

12 Cf. GSLP, 2019: 38.
13 The Gibraltar Chronicle, 2002.

tract (mostly elderly) European tourists looking for an Oriental experience but too fearful to cross the Straits;[14] the idea was received mostly with sheer incomprehension: Morocco was out of the picture in these years.

Most of these local initiatives did not last long, such as the monthly magazine *Lifestyle*, which was launched in the summer of 1996. After a start-up period, *Lifestyle* was to be published in three languages (English, Spanish, and French), aimed at an intellectual readership interested in culture, and was distributed through a network in Gibraltar, Spain, and Morocco. Other actors, for example Jon Searle, editor of *The Gibraltar Chronicle*, succeeded in founding a long-lasting association of Gibraltarian, Andalusian, and Moroccan journalists.

Whereas these developments became relevant mainly for the local community itself, Gibraltar's branding towards the outside did not stress any cultural specificity. Measures such as the EU cross-border programme Interreg II UK/Morocco/Gibraltar, which aimed to promote cooperation between the two territories, were largely unknown in the 1990s – even among local politicians. A first follow-up programme, Interreg III Gibraltar (UK)/Morocco, ran from 2000 to 2006,[15] but no successive programmes have been launched. In the heyday of neoliberalism and globalisation, Gibraltar marketed itself economically as a tax haven and financial centre for global clients, whether in Russia, the Middle East, or elsewhere.

The motherland, responsible for Gibraltar in immigration matters, exercised its function as guardian of the EU's external border. This concerns any immigration to Gibraltar via the maritime border with Morocco, which became more impermeable not only because of tighter migration control, but also because of the restriction of official transport links between Morocco and Gibraltar. Thus, at the beginning of the 1990s, for reasons of cost and independently of the process of European unification, the regular ferry service between Tangier and Gibraltar was discontinued. After that, travellers from Gibraltar to Morocco had to take either a direct flight across the Straits from Gibraltar Airport or ferries from the Spanish ports of Algeciras and Tarifa.

However, ferry and flight schedules between Gibraltar and Tangier repeatedly changed. On 23 November 1988, flights were suspended after a tragic accident in Tangier.[16] In June 1997, the private airline Rock Air flew to Tangier four times a day on a 20-minute flight. Apparently, however, this connection was also soon discontinued.[17] After some 20 years, regular flights between Tangier and Gibraltar

14 Cf. Haller 2021: 25–28.

15 European Commission, 2021.

16 Cf. Toler, 2013.

17 Cf. N.N., 2015.

have been operating again since 29 March 2015, twice a week with *Royal Air Maroc.*[18] In 2019, an additional helicopter service was established linking Gibraltar with Tangier and Tetuan, and an irregular ferry operates between Gibraltar and Tangier. Several economic initiatives were successful as well. Most important is certainly the supply of food, raw materials, and other materials, for example through the Gibmaroc Group. In December 2016, the Minister of Economy, the Minister of Tourism, and a representative of the Gibraltar Tourist Board toured Morocco to promote Gibraltar as a tourism destination.[19]

4 Branding Gibraltar as a Partner to Morocco

I have spent many years researching the border regions around the Strait of Gibraltar. For a long time, it seemed as if the situation had frozen: Spain and Gibraltar within the EU (but Gibraltar outside the Schengen Agreement) versus Morocco, which is outside the EU (linked by an association agreement, but not allowing the free movement of people). Now, with the referendum on the UK's exit from the EU, conditions have changed: however, until the actual exit date on 31 January 2020, it remained uncertain whether and when the UK and thus Gibraltar would leave and what this would mean for the relations between Spain, Gibraltar, and Morocco.

In this context, the growing integration of the Moroccan community into the social and political fabric of Gibraltar is crucial. In Gibraltar, the previous rejection of local Moroccans has changed over the years. In 2013, for example, Maroua Kharbouch became the first Gibraltarian with Moroccan roots to be elected Miss Gibraltar. In his 2019 Gibraltar National Day address, Chief Minister Fabian Picardo explicitly pointed out that most Moroccans who came to Gibraltar 50 years ago have since become British: they had helped to build modern Gibraltar and now the populace faces new challenges together.

Brexit is a traumatic experience for both Gibraltar, where the vote to remain in the EU was almost unanimous, and the Spanish hinterland, but it is less divisive for families and friends than in the motherland. Yet, the Gibraltarian government prepared itself early on for all possible twists and turns of a Brexit, as best it could. In this context, ties with Morocco and a change in Gibraltar's image as a steppingstone from North to South and vice versa gained unprecedented importance. For the first time, the governing parties' election 2020 manifesto mentioned "further

18 Gibraltar International Airport, 2015.
19 Cf. The Maghreb Times, 2016.

commercial ties between Gibraltar and Morocco."[20] The descendants of the Moroccan migrant workers of the 1960s and 1970s living in Gibraltar are now valued as an enrichment and part of the national identity. According to the manifesto, Arabic is to be offered as a school subject,[21] and a daily flight to Casablanca or Tangier[22] and forms of cultural exchange with Morocco[23] are to be established.

Gibraltar is thus increasingly oriented towards new and unproblematic existing business connections. High hopes are pinned on the British-Moroccan Free Trade Agreement of Autumn 2019. It is seen as particularly helpful for Gibraltar's economy. However, during a radio interview, the British Ambassador in Rabat warned Morocco against establishing too close ties with Gibraltar: "If we talk about Gibraltar and try to forge links between Gibraltar and Morocco, you Moroccans will have problems with the Spaniards."[24] As expected, the Gibraltar government rejected this statement. In April 2020, the newspaper *Panorama* referred to the increased economic cooperation between Gibraltar and Morocco, which is embedded in the British strategy regarding the exploitation of oil resources between Morocco and the Canary Islands.[25]

Fig. 5: Logo of the Strait of Gibraltar Association
Source: Strait of Gibraltar Association, 2019.

The election manifesto also explicitly welcomes and supports the opening of an office of the Gibraltar and Morocco Business Association (GMBA), which is supported by the Strait of Gibraltar Association (SGA) (Fig. 5). Christopher Bourne, director of the Gibraltar Business Centre, said:

> (...) we can obviously start doing more trade through Morocco, they have one of the biggest ports in the Mediterranean, so they have a lot of trade that comes through the Mediterranean and out to the rest of the world, and they come past Gibraltar, so it comes through and some of them use the Moroccan port, they've got a free port there. I would think that if we actually did start looking to Morocco; then we would actually be able to trade more easily with the rest

20 GSLP, 2019: 38.
21 Cf. GSLP, 2019: 94.
22 Cf. GSLP, 2019: 119.
23 Cf. GSLP, 2019: 134.
24 Quoted by The Gibraltar Chronicle, 2019.
25 Cf. Garcia 2020.

> of the world, it would just be a question of getting things as they are parked there and then bringing them over to Gibraltar.[26]

The GMBA was founded on 23 March 2019, because it was expected that Gibraltar's supplies would again have to be secured via Morocco and that workers would also have to be recruited from Morocco if Spain closed the land border again after a Brexit. On 8 August 2019, the online newspaper *noticiasgibraltar* published that the SGA president, Clive Reed, other members of the association, and Deputy Prime Minister Joseph García want to open up new foreign markets in the context of the Brexit.[27]

One day later, the English-language newspaper of Andalusia, *Sur*, reported that the GMBA would open an office in Tangier to boost economic and cultural exchange between the two regions.[28] The newspaper twice pointed out that this activity is not related to Brexit, but to the Gibraltarian government's general search for new economic ties. *Sur* referred to a press statement that assumed Spain would not close the border as it did in Franco's time. Both sides – Gibraltar and Spain – would only lose from a border closure, because Gibraltar imports goods and raw materials from Spain for about 1.5 million EUR a year and 15,329 residents of Spain work in Gibraltar.

It is explicitly stated several times that the GMBA is a private sector initiative. This is because Gibraltar is not allowed to launch foreign policy initiatives, which are still the responsibility of the motherland. But the head of the GMBA is a long-time activist of the ruling Labour Party (GSLP). The opening of the GMBA office in Tangier, scheduled for October 2019, had to be postponed due to elections in Gibraltar. However, the GMBA was already active in Tangier at this time. When I visited Tangier in February 2020, no official opening had taken place yet. Signs of both organisations, the GMBA and the SGA, are emblazoned on the entrance door to the building, and the Gibraltarian flag is displayed on a side window, where it is somewhat difficult to see from the street. In general, the *Tanjawis* know very little about Gibraltar, some even think it is an island. Therefore, for the time being, it is important for the GMBA and the SGA to hold events in Tangier to raise interest in the other side.

In Gibraltar itself, the GMBA promotes local initiatives that strengthen ties with Morocco, such as distributing Moroccan argan products in Gibraltar. In March 2021, collaboration with the coordinator of The Duke of Edinburgh's Inter-

26 Sputnik, 2019.

27 Cf. Noticiasgibraltar, 2019.

28 Cf. Bartlett, 2019.

national Award, Gibraltarian Saad Benyakoub, was announced.[29] In the same month, *Gibraltar Business Magazine* recognised the activities of the GMBA. Also in March, the Director of the GMBA received the Mayors Awards 2021 for his efforts to bring Gibraltarians back from Morocco during the pandemic.

The home of a Gibraltarian couple in the Kasbah, *Dar Henpris,* has become a focal point for Gibraltarians in Tangier and a meeting place for them and *Tanjawis.* The owners are active in the SGA and have an impact on various cultural fields. For example, 22 tablet computers were given to children of single Moroccan women during the pandemic. Joint projects between the two countries were agreed with a Moroccan arbitrator from the Chess Association. Since Autumn 2020, the SGA has also been hosting cultural events on Moroccan-Gibraltarian themes and streaming them online. For example, the sixth event on 23 March 2021 was watched live by 5,000 viewers from California to Dakar, from the Straits and Qatar to the Philippines.[30]

Other cultural events take place in Gibraltar independently of the SGA, such as a Tangier & Gibraltar Art Exhibition in December 2019 at John Mackintosh Hall, supported by the Gibraltarian Minister of Culture, John Cortes, among other people (Fig. 6). Cortes opened the exhibition pronouncing: "The exchange will marry both communities and integrate through culture the understanding of one another. I am very confident this exchange will be (...) the gateway for future cultural exchanges with other (...) neighbouring towns."[31]

Communication between the two cities via digital media is another binding force. Several online platforms take Tangier or Gibraltar as their theme; I myself started the Facebook group *TanGib* in the spring of 2019.[32] In addition, I posted a video on YouTube in October 2019 on the topic of "Tangier in Gibraltar, Gibraltar in Tangier."[33] Additional informal or private activities such as "Moroccan Night" by the Waterfront pub are organised, as well. There are also sporting links between the two cities, especially boat rallies.

29 Cf. Gibraltar Morocco Business Exchange, 2020.
30 Cf. Sacramento, 2021.
31 YGTV, 2019.
32 Cf. TanGib, 2018.
33 Cf. Haller, 2019.

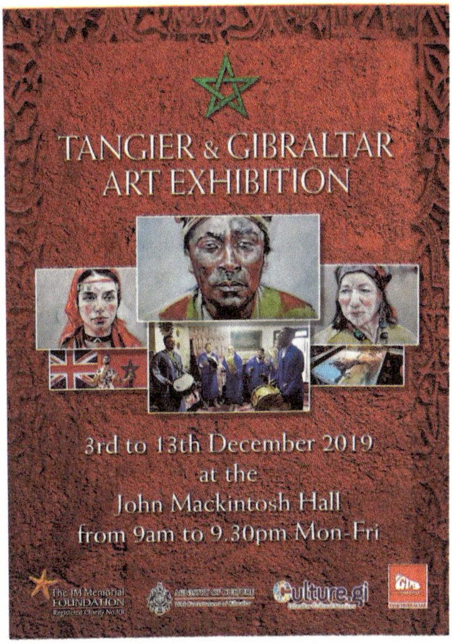

Fig. 6: Poster of the Tangier & Gibraltar Art Exhibition 2019
Source: Gibraltar Cultural Services, 2019.

5 Branding Gibraltar as a Bridge to and for Morocco and Africa

If Gibraltar's branding strategy as a stepping-stone between North and South was based on local initiatives alone, a partnership would not be sustainable, as Morocco's interest in the Overseas Territory would first have to be aroused. As Anholt remarked, "It's very hard for a country to persuade people in other parts of the world to go beyond these simple images and start to understand the rich complexity that lies behind them."[34] However, the current branding of Gibraltar as a link between the United Kingdom and/or Europe and North Africa not only seeks to ensure the survival of the community after Brexit, it also fits perfectly into larger geopolitical interests.

The three-year process from the Brexit referendum to leaving the EU on 1 January 2021 initially led to widespread shock in Gibraltar. This gave way to agony, as every sign in British politics that Brexit might be avoided was too often dashed in these three years. Locals preferred to stop talking about the issue altogether and ignore it. In public space, neither graffiti nor posters nor bumper stickers ex-

34 Anholt, 2011: 293.

pressed any opinion on the subject. For Brexit not only ran counter to the political and economic interests of the Gibraltarians, it also showed them their powerlessness: there was no possibility at all to influence the politics of the mother country. Thus, two options opened up: either to surrender to one's fate or to try to take it into one's own hands and develop one's own initiatives. Among the latter are the alignment with neighbouring Morocco and Chief Minister Picardo's push to join the Schengen area. Both initiatives were astonishingly courageous and testified to a new self-confidence, since Gibraltar has not yet had any competence to shape its external relations, which are still in the hands of the mother country.

One day before Brexit, it was agreed that Gibraltar would join the Schengen area as a non-EU territory. This decision not only has consequences for the inhabitants of the region (such as freedom of movement for Gibraltarians within the EU, especially to Spain), it also opens up the possibility for the United Kingdom to gain special access to the EU via Gibraltar – whose great importance was already evident on 9 January 2021, when Prime Minister Boris Johnson advocated the construction of a tunnel between Gibraltar and Northern Morocco.[35] Such projects – whether tunnels under the Strait or bridges across it – have been planned again and again in the past, mostly failing due to the geological difficulties of the complicated tectonic conditions.[36] However, earlier projects focused on the construction of a fixed link between Morocco and Spain. Johnson's proposal presents Gibraltar itself as a site for the first time. The realisation of this project "would secure and strengthen Great Britain's influence on the EU's North Africa policy."[37]

The idea of a tunnel fits in with Britain's increased engagement with Morocco and the Strait. In the first trade dialogue between Morocco and Britain in June 2020, Morocco offered itself to the British as a gateway to Africa, and former British minister Conor Burns already announced "the triangulation of Morocco, Africa and Britain."[38] Britons are particularly present in two zones designated for large tourism projects in northern Morocco, Marina Smir near Tetuan and Marchica near Melilla. The forecasts for a cable connection for renewable energies are also ambitious. An electrical cable to Gibraltar is to be laid to benefit from Morocco's renewable energy development. In return, Gibraltar plans to share its experience in the financial sector with the Alawite kingdom. Military cooperation between Gibraltar and Morocco is also to be strengthened. All this is perceived with concern in Spain. For, in addition, cooperation in agriculture is also to be

35 Cf. Urteaga, 2021.
36 Cf. Wippel, 2000.
37 Urteaga, 2021.
38 Moreno, 2020b.

expanded, which would hit farmers in the Spanish province of Huelva particularly hard: "Here we pay salaries and social security, a worker costs more than 60 euros, in Morocco 12 euros. How are we supposed to compete with that?" says the farmer Antonio Luis Martín. In addition to this, the UK sees Morocco as a stepping-stone to the West African markets.[39]

Britain's increased engagement in the region should also be understood in the context of geostrategic developments. Through its closest ally, the US has Gibraltar as an ideal base for further engagement in the Mediterranean, the Middle East, and North Africa. In the last weeks before his departure from office, President Trump recognised Western Sahara, whose status under international law has not yet been clarified, as part of the Moroccan state.

In return, Morocco officially recognised Israel, and embassies were opened. Although both countries have had close unofficial relations since the founding of the State of Israel, for example in the field of intelligence, "official" recognition has not yet been granted – probably in view of Morocco's role within the Arab world. Since the 1950s, the Alawite kings have always recognised themselves as patrons of Moroccan Jews, even though most of the latter now live in Latin America, France, and Israel. The Moroccan offer to the Sephardic-Moroccan Jewish communities of Ceuta and Melilla not only to invest more in northern Morocco but also to resettle "in the motherland" is to be understood against this background.[40] The offer was also made to the Jews of Gibraltar.[41] All these communities have close historical, economic, and family ties to northern Morocco. If they were to relocate to Morocco on a larger scale, this would mean a double weakening of Spain and its exclaves of Ceuta and Melilla, to which Morocco has always laid claim.

Morocco's traditional ties to the North (EU) and the East (Arab world) are now being followed by a strengthening of ties to the West (the US and UK, Latin America) after Morocco's foreign and economic orientation to the South (sub-Saharan Africa), especially in the 2010s. A British Gibraltar as an immediate neighbour is therefore of particular importance for Morocco's Atlantic orientation. As long as these interests of the UK, Morocco, and the US remain aligned, the branding of Gibraltar as a bridge between worlds will be credibly underpinned and maintained – even if the bridge is a tunnel.

39 Moreno, 2020b.
40 Moreno, 2020a.
41 Cf. Yaabouk, 2020.

Bibliography

Airline Timetable Images. "GB Airways – Gibair – Gibraltar Airways – Bland Line." Last updated 12 January 2022. https://www.timetableimages.com/ttimages/gt.htm. Accessed 20 January 2022.

Anderson, Benedict. *Imagined Communities: Reflections on the Origin and Spread of Nationalism.* London: Verso, 1983.

Anholt, Simon. "Place Branding: Is it Marketing, or Isn't it?" *Place Branding and Public Diplomacy* 4.1 (2008): 1–6.

Anholt, Simon. "Beyond the Nation Brand: The Role of Image and Identity in International Relations." In *Brands and Branding Geographies*, edited by Andy Pike, 289–305. Cheltenham, Northampton: Edward Elgar, 2013.

Barr, Michael. "Nation Branding as Nation Building: China's Image Campaign." *East Asia* 29.1 (2012): 81–94.

Barth, Fredrik. *Ethnic Groups and Boundaries: The Social Organization of Cultural Difference.* London, Oslo: Allen and Unwin, 1969.

Bartlett, Debbie. "As Brexit Looms, Gibraltar Welcomes the Idea of a Tangier Trade Office." *Sur* 9 August 2019. http://www.surinenglish.com/gibraltar/201908/09/brexit-looms-gibraltar-welcomes-20190809110344-v.html. Accessed 11 November 2020.

Cavanaugh, Jillian R. "Making Salami, Producing Bergamo: The Transformation of Value." *Ethnos* 72.2 (2007): 149–172.

Chipulina, Neville. "The People of Gibraltar: 1810 – The Bland Line – A Reputable Tavern Owner." 2015. https://gibraltar-intro.blogspot.com/2015/02/1810-bland-line-reputable-tavern-owner.html. Accessed 19 January 2022.

European Commission. *INTERREG III A: Gibraltar (United Kingdom) and Morocco.* https://ec.europa.eu/regional_policy/de/atlas/programmes/2000-2006/european/interreg-iii-a-gibraltar-united-kingdom-and-morocco. Accessed 20 July 2021 (link expired).

Fırat, A. Fuat, Nikhilesh Dholakia, and Alladi Venkatesh. "Marketing in a Postmodern World." *European Journal of Marketing* 29.1 (1995): 40–56.

Garcia, Joe. "Britain and Morocco to Strengthen Relations." *Panorama Online* 14 April 2020. http://www.gibraltarpanorama.gi/170128. Accessed 11 November 2020.

GibHeli. *Gibraltar Helicopter Tour "Africa"*. https://www.gibheli.com/. Accessed 20 July 2021.

Gibraltar Cultural Services. *Facebook*, 30 October 2019. https://www.facebook.com/culture.gi/photos/gibraltar-cultural-services-and-the-jm-memorial-foundation-are-pleased-to-announ/1199038873630541/. Accessed 24 November 2021.

Gibraltar International Airport. "Royal Air Maroc's Inaugural Gibraltar-Tangier-Casablanca Flight on Sunday." 2015. https://www.gibraltarairport.gi/content/royal-air-marocs-inaugural-gibraltar-tangier-casablanca-flight-sunday. Accessed 20 July 2021.

Gibraltar Morocco Business Exchange. 2020. https://www.facebook.com/GibMaroc/?ref=page_internal. Accessed 20 July 2021.

GSLP (Gibraltar Socialist Labour Party). *GSLP Liberals Manifesto 2019: … Aspire to the Best Gibraltar.* Gibraltar, 2019. https://www.gslp.gi/wp-content/uploads/2019/10/GSLP-Liberals-Manifesto-2019.pdf. Accessed 20 August 2021.

Haller, Dieter. *Gelebte Grenze Gibraltar: Transnationalismus, Lokalität und Identität in kulturanthropologischer Perspektive.* Wiesbaden: Deutscher Universitätsverlag, 2000a.

Haller, Dieter. “Romancing Patios: Die Aneignung der Stadt im Rahmen der ethnischen und nationalen Neubestimmung in Gibraltar.” In *Kulturwissenschaftliche Sichtweisen auf die Stadt*, edited by Waltraud Kokot, Thomas Hengartner, and Kathrin Wildner, 225–251. Berlin: Dietrich Reimer, 2000b.

Haller, Dieter. “Transcending Locality: The Diaspora Network of Sephardic Jews in the Western Mediterranean.” *Anthropological Journal on European Cultures* 9.1 (2001a): 3–31.

Haller, Dieter. “Das Lob der Mischung, Reinheit als Gefahr: Nationalismus und Ethnizität in Gibraltar.” *Zeitschrift für Ethnologie* 126.1 (2001b): 27–61.

Haller, Dieter. *Lone Star Texas: Ethnographische Notizen aus einem unbekannten Land.* Bielefeld: Transcript, 2007.

Haller, Dieter. *Tanger: Der Hafen, die Geister, die Lust.* Bielefeld: Transcript, 2016.

Haller, Dieter. “Tanger in Gibraltar, Gibraltar in Tanger.” *YouTube* 17 October 2019. https://www.youtube.com/watch?v=obZ8vTuK9tU. Accessed 20 July 2021.

Haller, Dieter. *Tangier/Gibraltar – A Tale of One City: An Ethnography.* Bielefeld: Transcript, 2021.

Hobsbawm, Eric. *Nations and Nationalism since the 1780s: Programme, Myth, Reality.* Cambridge: Cambridge University Press, 1990.

Hobsbawm, Eric, and Terence Ranger. *The Invention of Tradition.* Cambridge, New York: Cambridge University Press, 1983.

Leitch, Alison. “Slow Food and the Politics of Pork Fat: Italian Food and European Identity.” *Ethnos* 68.4 (2003): 437–462.

Moreno, Sonia. “Marruecos invita a los judíos a irse de Ceuta y Melilla para invertir al otro lado de la frontera.” *El Español* 18 June 2020a. https://www.elespanol.com/espana/politica/20200618/marruecos-invita-judios-ceuta-melilla-invertir-frontera/498451541_0.html. Accessed 11 November 2020.

Moreno, Sonia. “Marruecos ofrece a EEUU una base para cerrar Rota: Mohamed VI da facilidades a los americanos.” El Español 5 July 2020b. https://www.elespanol.com/espana/20200705/marruecos-eeuu-rota-mohamed-vi-facilidades-americanos/502700238_0.html

N.N., David. “World’s Shortest Intercontinental Flight Returns: Gibraltar-Tangier.” *UKpoints* 29 March 2015. http://www.ukpoints.com/2015/03/29/worlds-shortest-intercontinental-flight-returns-gibraltar-tangier/. Accessed 20 July 2021.

Noticiasgibraltar. “Gibraltar estudia abrir una oficina comercial en Tánger.” 8 August 2019. https://noticiasgibraltar.es/gibraltar/noticias/gibraltar-estudia-abrir-una-oficina-comercial-tanger. Accessed 11 November 2020.

Olins, Wally. “Branding the Nation: The Historical Context.” *Brand Management* 9.4–5 (2002): 241–248.

Pratt, Jeff. “Food Values: The Local and the Authentic.” *Critique of Anthropology* 27.3 (2007): 285–300.

Reyes, Brian. “Poll Suggests Gibraltarias Shrug off Brexit and Global Warming Fears.” *The Gibraltar Chronicle* 2 March 2020. https://www.chronicle.gi/poll-suggests-gibraltarians-shrug-off-brexit-and-global-warming-fears/. Accessed 22 July 2021.

Sacramento, Henry. Interview with Dieter Haller. 6th Cultural Event. *Facebook* 23 February 2021. https://www.facebook.com/groups/164010250597929/permalink/1407561679576107. Accessed 22 July 2021.

Smith, Anthony D. “National Identity and Myths of Ethnic Descent.” In *Research in Social Movements, Conflicts and Change: A Research Annual, Vol. 7*, edited by Louis Kriesberg, 95–130. Bingley, London: Emerald Publishing Limited 1984.

Smith, Anthony D. "The Ethnic Sources of Nationalism." *Survival* 35.1 (1993): 48–62.

Sputniknews. "Gibraltar Could Bolster Trade with Morocco to Offset Brexit Damage – Local Businessman." 17 October 2019. https://sputnikglobe.com/20191017/gibraltar-could-bolster-trade-with-morocco-to-offset-brexit-damage–local-businessman-1077075622.html. Accessed 30 June 2023.

Strait of Gibraltar Association. *Facebook*, 24 April 2019. https://www.facebook.com/GibraltarAssociation/photos/a.2517801951603355/2518061791577371. Accessed 24 November 2021.

TanGib. Facebook group. 2018. https://www.facebook.com/groups/1791743197593467. Accessed 22 July 2021.

The Gibraltar Chronicle. "MWA Complain about Hydrofoil." 20 August 2002.

The Gibraltar Chronicle. "Govt Complains to UK over 'Unacceptable' Comments by UK Ambassador to Morocco." 4 December 2019. https://www.chronicle.gi/govt-complains-to-uk-over-unacceptable-comments-by-uk-ambassador-to-morocco/. Accessed 22 July 2021.

The Gibraltar Independent Online. "Who is at Fault for Decrepit State of Gibraltar Private Rented Housing?" 2019. http://gibraltarindependent.com/who-is-at-fault-for-decrepit-state-of-gibraltar-private-rented--housing/. Accessed 30 April 2021 (link expired).

The Maghreb Times. "Gibraltar puts focus on Morocco." 5 December 2016. https://themaghrebtimes.com/gibraltar-puts-focus-on-morocco/. Accessed 11 November 2020.

Toler, Michael. "When Tangier & Gibraltar Were 'Tan-Gib.'" *Tangier American Legation* 13 August 2013. https://legation.ipower.com/blog/?p=113. Accessed 11 November 2020.

Urteaga, Diego. "Reino Unido estudia construir un túnel que una Gibraltar y Tánger." *Atalayar Online* 9 January 2021. https://www.atalayar.com/articulo/politica/reino-unido-estudia-construir-tunel-que-gibraltar-tanger/20210109163741149272.html. Accessed 30 June 2023.

Welz, Gisela. "Taste the Mediterranean: Food, Culture and Heritagisation." In *Mediterranean Research in the 21st Century*, edited by Mihran Dabag, Dieter Haller, Nikolas Jaspert, and Achim Lichtenberger, 407–427. Paderborn: Ferdinand Schönigh, 2016.

Wikipedia. "Gibraltar: Britain in the Sun." https://en.wikipedia.org/wiki/Gibraltar:_Britain_in_the_Sun. Accessed 25 November 2021.

Wippel, Steffen. "Die 'feste Verbindung' mit Europa: Infrastrukturprojekte über die Straße von Gibraltar und ihre symbolische Bedeutung für die regionalen Zugehörigkeiten Marokkos." *Asien Afrika Lateinamerika* 28.6 (2000): 631–676.

Yaabouk, Mohammed. "Les Juifs de Ceuta, Melilla et Gibraltar, futur investisseurs à Fnideq et Nador?" *Yabiladi* 16 June 2020. https://www.yabiladi.com/articles/details/95127/juifs-ceuta-melilla-gibraltar-futurs.html. Accessed 11 November 2020.

YGTV. "Gibraltar and Tangier Cultural Exchange." *Your Gibraltar TV* 26 November 2019. https://www.yourgibraltartv.com/society/20377-gibraltar-and-tangier-cultural-exchange. Accessed 11 November 2020.

Part IV: **City Branding**

Dounia Sedra and Hicham El Bayed

City Branding and Residents' Perception: The Case of Casablanca

1 Introduction

In 2015, Casablanca was the first city in Morocco and across Africa to adopt a place-branding strategy, which aimed to reconcile it with its residents and to increase its national and international attractiveness. The first image assessment used for the development of this strategy had identified several problems the city had been suffering from (infrastructure and public services out of step with the needs of inhabitants, pollution, insecurity, etc.). This diagnosis laid the foundations for an urban development plan spanning the period 2015–2020[1] and for an intense communication strategy, both of which aimed to ultimately improve the living conditions of residents and to positively affect the image they have of their city. Two major pillars were concerned with the improvement of residential attractiveness: namely, the development of new urban centres with a better offer of public services; and reinforcement of mobility by offering new sustainable and affordable transportation modes.

The development plan is almost finished now, and a large number of its programmed projects have been carried out. The objective of the present research is to have the residents, in another image assessment, judge the efforts undertaken locally during the last five years to improve their living conditions and express their opinions about the city brand. Thus, the research question is: what image do the inhabitants of Casablanca have of their city and its place-branding strategy?

2 Discovering the "White City" Casablanca

Casablanca is one of the oldest cities in North Africa. It was built on a prehistoric city called Anfa, which goes back thousands of years[2] and long succeeded in drawing the attention of historians, who were particularly impressed by its wealth and beauty. For instance, in the 16th century, the traveller Leo Africanus pointed out

1 Cf. Casablanca Events et Animation, 2017.

2 Cf. Raynal and Mohib, 2017.

https://doi.org/10.1515/9783110741100-025

that Anfa was a very large, beautifully built town that once enjoyed fertile lands and gardens.[3]

Historically, the reign of the Alaouite Sultan Sidi Mohammed Ben Abdallah (ruling 1757–1790) paved the way to the first city's development, endowing it with a large mosque and religious centres, which enabled it to take the name of *Ad-dār al-bayḍā'* ("The White House"). Its hispanised name *Casa Blanca* did not spread until 1781 with the installation of Spanish trading posts and the massive arrival of European traders. The establishment of the French protectorate in 1912 played a crucial role in the urban and economic development of the city. These different cultural influences are clearly reflected in its architecture. Hence, the city enjoys an exceptional heritage, expressed in its different aesthetic styles, which allowed it to join the tentative list of UNESCO world heritage in 2013.[4]

Economically, the port of Casablanca played a tremendous role in shaping the fate of the city, making it the country's largest metropolis, as well as its economic centre and financial capital. This dynamic was particularly enhanced in the aftermath of Morocco's independence, positioning it as the first catalyst of the Moroccan economy. Sectorally, Casablanca is known as the first national industrial hub, concentrating nearly a quarter of all this sector's activity. It greatly participates in Morocco's integration in several global value chains, notably in the aeronautics, automotive, and pharmaceutical industries. Casablanca is above all establishing itself as a regional centre for banking and insurance industries. It is also home to the Casablanca Stock Exchange, one of the most active Arab stock exchanges, along with Casablanca Finance City, which is recognised as the top financial centre in Africa and the fourth-most important in the entire MENA Region.[5] It enjoys a considerable position in the offshoring and outsourcing sector through the largest centre dedicated to these activities in all North Africa, namely Casanearshore Park.

Moreover, Casablanca is the leading national destination for business, medical, shopping, and cruise tourism. This positioning is reinforced by the presence of prestigious national and international tourist brands that invest in the areas of accommodation and catering. Its prestigious art deco architecture, its various monuments, and its diverse shopping facilities reinforce its attractiveness for domestic and foreign visitors.

The city is currently establishing itself as a regional hub for African investment, a dynamic driven mainly by its local companies operating in several strategic sectors. Casablanca's regional integration has made it the second largest "for-

---

3 Cf. Pierre, 2003.
4 Cf. UNESCO World Heritage Centre, 2013.
5 Cf. Wardle and Mainelli, 2021.

eign direct investment issuer" and the fourth most sought-after "destination for African investments" on the continent."[6] Casablanca is also the most populous city in Morocco and the Maghreb, with approximatively four million inhabitants. These powerful dynamics and growing population entail economic, environmental, and social issues that local management is called upon to meet and that challenge the city's attractiveness both residentially and economically.

3 Casablanca's City Branding: The First African Experience

The genesis of Casablanca's branding strategy dates back to 2013 and especially to a royal speech by King Mohammed VI in which he noted the necessity to change the management paradigms of the metropolis in order to raise it to the rank of an international city.[7] This speech was a prelude to launching the Casablanca Strategic Development Plan and its city-branding strategy.

To fulfil these directives, a participatory approach was adopted particularly with the different stakeholders, which led to pinpointing the perceived identity of the city, its image, and the major challenges that it has to face. For this, an identity profiling was established whose ultimate objective was to define the identity traits that make the city specific to its population and visitors. This work led to the identification of six major traits:[8]

- "Casa, citizen of the world": A metropolis anchored in Africa and connected to the rest of the world. A land of fruitful encounters, exchanges and diversity;
- "Casa, the effervescent": Encouraging, motivating, dynamic… Casablanca is a young city in constant motion;
- "Casa, between tradition and modernity": A modern city that is attached to the ancestral culture of the country thanks to its own urban culture, architecture, and artistic production;
- "Casa, city of opportunities": Given its role as economic engine, Casablanca is a city of growth, opportunities, and investments;
- "Casa, a laboratory city": Casablanca has often been a pioneer by hosting pilot experiences. It is a city that inspires and unlocks energies, where dreams of success come true;

---

6 Cf. IHS and UN-Habitat United, 2018.

7 See MAP, 2013.

8 Cf. Casablanca Events & Animation, 2016.

– "Casa, welcoming and warm": Land of welcome, tolerance, and exchange, whose identity consists of cultures and encounters over time.

The initial image assessment allowed the identification of the main attributes and problems associated with the city (cf. Table 1).[9]

Table 1: Positive and negative aspects of Casablanca
Source: Mellouk, 2014.

Positive aspects	Negative aspects
– An engine of economic and social development – A financial and technological hub – A major place for industry and real estate in Africa – A "business friendly" metropolis – A competitive place for investments and wealth creation – A cosmopolitan city by its culture, heritage, and architecture	– Inadequate infrastructure and transport, causing important urban imbalances – Pockets of unhealthiness in the heart and the periphery of the city, in contrast to the modernity envisaged for the city – A living environment penalised by degraded air quality – Public services need to be improved, especially those related to the provision of care – Industrial sectors that do not generate much added value – University-research-business links need to be strengthened

Based on these two diagnoses, in 2015 the public authorities officially launched a dedicated development plan, aimed at capitalising on the city's assets around four major hubs:[10]

– a living environment hub that aims to considerably improve the quality of life in the metropolis by diversifying housing and health offers;
– a platform hub that aims to facilitate mobility for inhabitants and visitors with new infrastructures, while improving the quality of the various road and rail equipment;
– an economic excellence hub that aims to consolidate Casablanca's position as the country's economic lever by raising it onto the podium of well-known African economic centres;
– an animation hub that aims to transform Casablanca into a real centre of attraction with sporting, cultural, recreational, and social offers.

9 Cf. Sedra and El Bayed, 2022.
10 Cf. Commission Régionale de l'Amélioration de l'Environnement des Affaires Casablanca-Settat, 2017.

Fig. 1: The WeCasablanca logo
Source: Casablanca Events & Animation, 2016: 11.

This ambitious plan has been accompanied since October 2016 by a city-branding strategy, the first of its kind in all Africa. The brand name "WeCasablanca" and its designed logo (cf. Fig. 1) were developed in several languages, with the objective of highlighting the multicultural and cosmopolitan character of the metropolis:

> **The identity of WeCasablanca**
> A metropolis with its own identity, with many facets, forged throughout its history by Moroccans from all over the country, as well as by the various foreign communities that meet there.
> These encounters gave birth to a very particular energy, creating value and collective momentum! Casablanca, a place with a positive identity that the locals translate as follows: all different and proud to be together.[11]

4 Branding Casablanca: Discovering the Residents' Perceptions

As presented in the previous sections, since 2016 the city of Casablanca has adopted a place-branding strategy to enhance its attractiveness for its residents, tourists, and investors. During the first months following its launch, the brand sparked a great deal of controversy on social networks and was not unanimously accepted by the people of Casablanca. This is the context of this study: its objective is to assess the image of Casablanca in the eyes of the inhabitants and that image's congruence with the managers' choice of positioning for the WeCasablanca brand. The

11 Casablanca Events & Animation, 2016. Translated from French by the authors.

study also aims to evaluate the degree to which residents have adopted the brand after five years of its deployment.

4.1 Methodology and Objectives

We opted for a non-probability sampling method for which the choice of individuals is not random but reasoned. In this case, the "technique of quotas" was used to define the sample characteristics in relation to those of the entire population. The final sample focused on 385 people, who best fit the characteristics of the population of the city in terms of gender representation and school level. The questionnaire was administered online and shared mainly in social networks during the two months of July and August 2020. We have repeatedly opted for open questions, given that the research deals with the dimensions of image, perception, and representations.

The research was carried out with the objective of confirming or invalidating two major hypotheses:

- H1: The image conveyed through the city's branding strategy is consistent with the perception of target audiences.
- H2: The residents are aware of the role that can be played by the brand, in terms of image and attractiveness.

The questions were designed around two categories of objectives (cf. Table 2):

Table 2: Objectives of the research
Source: Own compilation.

Objectives relating to the image of Casablanca	Objectives relating to the WeCasablanca brand
- Discover the image of the city in the eyes of its inhabitants - Measure the evocative power of the city vis-a-vis of the population - Discover the major assets/problems of the city, experienced day by day by its inhabitants - Compare this perception with the managers' choice of positioning of the brand	- Measure brand awareness - Check the credibility of the positioning of the brand - Check the degree of understanding of the "place brand" concept - Measure the degree to which the population has adopted the brand - Discover the power of the name "WeCasablanca"

4.2 Discovering the Image of the City of Casablanca

Regarding its "evocative richness", the city arouses various feelings among its inhabitants, which we classified into positive and negative aspects in their order of importance.

Table 3: Positive and negative evocations of Casablanca

Positive evocations	Negative evocations
	Stress
Big	Traffic jam
Alive	Disorder
Economy	Hell
Love	Polluted
My city	Dirty
Dynamic	Noisy
Energetic	Insecurity
Beautiful	Overcrowded
Diverse	Chaos
Metropolis	Contradictory
	Catastrophic

The analysis of the city's assets revealed three categories expressed by the interviewees: the most important category, economic potential (particularly diversity, economy and business opportunities), followed by the categories of multiculturality, and finally openness, geographical position and dynamism.

The diagnosis reveals also four categories of problems, namely traffic and congestion, followed by insecurity, delinquency, and criminality. The third-most-cited problem is pollution, which is closely linked to traffic, and finally a series of problems with almost the same importance, namely overpopulation, dirtiness, lack of civility and anarchy.

The valence of the associations related to the positioning and values of the city has revealed that the strongest positive ones are, in order: multiculturalism, energy, and openness. These values are perfectly in line with the positioning chosen for the brand. Weaker associations include the aspects of creativity, humanism, and the welcoming nature of the city.

The exploration of the imaginary and symbolism linked to the city allow to associate it with four colours, namely the grey, white, black and blue. Generally, these colours match those chosen for the visual identity of the brand, which are white, black and blue.

The majority of respondents believes that the city of Casablanca has changed over the past five years. The changes felt most strongly are in infrastructure and transport, but these remain insufficient in comparison with what the population expects. The respondents also see that the city is sorely lacking in green spaces, which have been replaced by a grey urbanisation.

4.3 Discovering the Image of the Brand WeCasablanca

Out of the 385 responses, the analysis shows that more than 65 % of the interviewees know the brand, especially through social networks and street display. This rate constitutes generally a good level of awareness. Paradoxically, most of those people say they do not follow the brand, especially in terms of publications, events and actions.

In relation to the expected ripple effects of the brand, more than 40 % of interviewees are convinced that the improvement in attractiveness will be limited, while 21 % claim that they are totally unaware of the objectives behind its implementation.

In a question relating to the evocative power of the brand and its name, 60 % of the interviewees are convinced that the brand is a bearer of hope and constitutes a basis around which efforts must be united to make the city move forward. The evoked words recall feelings of belonging and pride and also of solidarity/unity for the development of Casablanca. The remaining 40 % of those interviewed believe that the name means nothing and that efforts should be directed towards improving infrastructure and the means of transport. They claim that the place brand is not a priority and its funds should be allocated otherwise.

5 Concluding Discussion of the Field Study

Comparing the basic hypotheses designed for this research with the study's results, we come to the following conclusions.

For the first hypothesis (H1), generally, the study confirmed the positioning chosen for the place brand "WeCasablanca" around three components: openness, multiculturalism, and the energy emerging from the meeting of worlds. These elements perfectly join the city's positive aspects revealed by the 2015 identity/image diagnoses. However, in the minds of the inhabitants, the place has problems and negative associations, such as traffic jams, lack of security, delinquency, crime, and pollution. These perceptions remain unchanged since the first image assessment carried out in 2015.

The development strategy designed for Casablanca over the 2015–2021 period remains very ambitious and embraces several facets of the aforementioned problems. For the city's development plan to be successful, the inhabitants must first feel its results and see its impacts in their daily lives. Therefore, the managers of WeCasablanca must capitalise on this plan and its projects to reconcile the residents with their city. The brand should be called upon to closely follow the shaping of the Casablanca product and to present it to residents with the aim of changing perceptions and seeking mobilisation.

For the second hypothesis (H2), based on the conclusions of this study, we found that 60 % of interviewees are convinced that the brand carries hope and constitutes a basis around which efforts should be united to make the city move forward. However, the remaining 40 % say the branding will do nothing for the city, or they simply ignore the goals behind its implementation. To this end, the brand's managers are called upon to make more efforts to clarify its objectives and also to win the sympathy of the residents by:

- massively communicating about the projects carried out by the city that will likely change the daily life of the residents;
- simplifying the discourse used to reach all sections of the population;
- focusing on the strategy of "ambassadors" because of the proximity of these people to the target audiences. This will not only foster better appropriation of the brand, but also fuel reflections and strategies to improve its sustainability.

Thus, throughout this paper, we have tried to approach the residents of Casablanca's perceptions of their city and its branding strategy. Our analysis allowed us to note a sort of disinterest in the city's brand and its emanations and the persistence of certain negative associations with the city.

In our opinion, it would be interesting to conduct similar studies, but carried out by the city's managers on a larger scale. These investigations will make it possible to gradually adapt the development plan and the branding strategy to the growing needs of the population. This proximity would also make it possible to forge closer ties with the inhabitants and to involve them actively in the management of the city. Finally, in our opinion, residents' involvement is the cornerstone towards the success of the place brand "WeCasablanca," since they are the real ambassadors of the city and also the first ones to live and experience the territory on a daily basis.

Bibliography

Casablanca Events & Animation. *WeCasablanca: Nouvelle marque territoriale de la métropole.* Conférence de presse, Casablanca, 24 octobre 2016. http://www.wecasablanca.com/sites/default/files/EXEDPCASAEVENTVFBD.pdf. Accessed 25 August 2021.

Casablanca Events et Animation. "Etat d'avancement du Plan de Développement du Grand Casablanca 2015–2020." Extrait du Discours de Monsieur le Wali de la Région Casablanca-Settat, Université Hassan II – FSJES d'Ain Chock, 18 April 2017. https://www.wecasablanca.com/actualites/etat-davancement-du-plan-de-developpement-du-grand-casablanca-2015-2020. Accessed 2 September 2021.

Commission Régionale de l'Amélioration de l'Environnement des Affaires Casablanca-Settat. *Plan du Développement du Grand Casablanca 2015–2020.* Presentation 23 May 2017. hhttps://unhabitat.org/sites/default/files/download-manager-files/The%20State%20of%20African%20Cities.pdf. Accessed 15 August 2021.

IHS, and UN-Habitat. *The State of African Cities: The Geography of African Investment.* Erasmus University Rotterdam, and United Nations Human Settlements Program, 2018. https://unhabitat.org/sites/default/files/download-manager-files/The%20State%20of%20African%20Cities.pdf. Accessed 3 September 2021.

MAP. "Full Text of HM the King's Speech at Opening of First Session of Third Legislative Year of Ninth Legislature." *Agence Marocaine de Presse* 12 October 2013. http://www.mapnews.ma/en/activites-royales/full-text-hm-kings-speech-opening-first-session-third-legislative-year-ninth. Accessed 20 August 2021.

Mellouk, Mostapha. *Tous pour Casablanca Ville-Monde.* Paper presented at the Casa-Forum at the Green Growth Academy. Casablanca: Confédération Générale des Entreprises du Maroc, and Centre Marocain de Production propre, 2014. https://cgem.ma/upload/666425009.pdf. Accessed 15 August 2021.

Pierre, Jean-Luc. "Sur les traces de Léon l'Africain, aux origines de Casablanca." In *Le Bulletin de Liaison des Professeurs d'Histoire-Géographie de l'académie de Reims* 29–30 (2003). http://www.cndp.fr/crdp-reims/ressources/brochures/blphg/bul2930/pierre.htm. Accessed 25 August 2021.

Raynal, Jean Paul, and Abderrahim Mohib. "Casablanca des origines." In *Préhistoire de Casablanca: La Grotte des Rhinocéros*, edited by Institut National des Sciences de l'Archéologie et du Patrimoine, 11–33. Rabat: Ministère de la Culture, 2017.

Sedra, Dounia, and Hicham El Bayed. "Branding the City: The Case of Casablanca-Morocco." *Place Branding and Public Diplomacy* 18 (2022): 181–189.

UNESCO World Heritage Centre. "Casablanca, Ville du XXème siècle, carrefour d'influences." United Nations Educational, Scientific and Cultural Organisation 27 November 2013. https://whc.unesco.org/fr/listesindicatives/5848/. Accessed 24 September 2021.

Wardle, Mike, and Michael Mainelli. *The Global Financial Centres Index 30.* Long Finance, and Financial Centre Futures, 2021. https://longfinance.net/media/documents/GFCI_30_Report_2021.09.24_v1.0.pdf. Accessed 30 September 2021.

Steffen Wippel

The Multilevel Branding of Tangier at Spatial and Temporal Interfaces

1 Introduction

Endeavours to establish cities as brands have become a worldwide phenomenon. In the Middle East and Africa, too, cities have started to actively position themselves as attractive tourism destinations and investment sites and are trying to enhance their distinctiveness and recognisability. Gulf cities have become the most prominent – and often emulated – examples. Less attention has been given, for instance, to North African places.

Accordingly, this chapter starts from the assumption that systematic approaches to branding cities are still limited, notably for cities of the "Global South." Before I present my case study, I will begin with a few conceptual ideas. In particular, I will point to the multi-scalar aspects of place making and to the positioning of places at spatial, cultural, and temporal interfaces. In the empirical part, I will analyse the branding of Tangier, Morocco, from a comparative historical perspective. Already in the first half of the 20th century, the city attracted travellers and residents, but also economic and financial institutions. After a post-independence period of stagnation that I will skip here, in recent years, Tangier has experienced another rapid urban transformation. The main goals are to become an international hub for trade, a major place for foreign investment, and a recognised tourism destination. In terms of the conceptual reflections the article has a major interest in the multiple contributions from several actors on different national, local, and project scales to building brands for Tangier and particular places in it. It will critically investigate the tools and channels, forms, and contents of their attention strategies and their endeavours to create positively perceived images. Special attention will be directed to how strategic communication positions the city in space and time and at specific interfaces, e.g., between different world regions and between a great past and a prosperous future. A short summary concludes this chapter.

The following study is a side result from my research in recent years that analyses the urban transformations of Tangier and its emerging transnational and transregional ties.[1] Methodologically, it is based on repeated fieldwork in the

1 This article is based on a paper for the panel "Branding the Middle East" at the 33rd *Deutsche*

https://doi.org/10.1515/9783110741100-026

city from 2013 on, including expert interviews and photo-geographic excursions, the thorough assessment of written documents in printed media and available in the Internet (like leaflets, brochures, reports, advertisements, webpages), and the analysis of illustrations and other images used in branding.

2 The Rapid Spread of Contemporary Urban Branding

While in recent decades the importance of place branding has tremendously increased, the phenomenon is not totally new. In particular, there is long international experience with cultivating images and "selling" tourism destinations.[2] Yet, with the perception of increased globalisation pressure and interurban competition, the branding and marketing of places has become an increasingly important component in the geo-economically oriented neoliberal strategies and the postmodern restructuring of cities and, in parallel, has attracted increasing academic interest from empirical as well as theoretical perspectives.[3] Often, then, "branding" is understood as a comprehensive approach: as a form of strategic communication, it intends to generate beneficial perceptions and advantageous images of its object in a broad and heterogeneous public by extensively using historical, geographic, and sociocultural motifs. Besides its external function, namely to create a politically and economically exploitable image and to attain good standing, branding is also directed towards an internal audience to foster identification with given constituencies and social cohesiveness. It goes beyond the narrower "marketing" of nations, regions, cities, and project sites, which presents a geographically defined entity as a desirable product to a specific, directly targeted clientele. However, in concrete cases, practices and publications do not clearly differentiate between the two processes, which both serve image formation, identity creation, and the

---

Orientalistentag and 24th Congress of the German Middle East Studies Association in Jena on 19 September 2017. Hence, most of the empirical work was done in 2017: since then, several links referring to quotes have expired; other sources have been updated or verified using the Internet archive Wayback Machine, https://web.archive.org. I thank Birgit Krawietz, Freie Universität Berlin, and Christian Steiner, Katholische Universität Eichstätt, for critical comments on a previous version of this chapter. However, responsibility for the result is exclusively mine.

2 Compare, e.g., Ward, 1998.

3 Cf., for example, from Anholt, 2007, to Vanolo, 2017; for a review of literature on place and city branding, Gertner, 2011; Lucarelli and Berg, 2011; Vuignier, 2017. More detailed references are given in the introduction to this edited volume.

stimulation of attention.[4] As it is difficult to define a clear dividing line, in the following I will not consistently distinguish between the two terms, either.

Most of what has been written on place branding is rather descriptive and application-oriented research, transferring principles of brand development from products and firms to space-related entities. Usually, authors then develop comprehensive communication strategies with a broad spectrum of instruments and methods to promote places successfully. In general, they advocate a consistent package of communication measures with which all relevant actors have to abide in order to create as uniform an image as possible. Mostly, they stipulate a single responsible institution for branding, normally on the respective system level, e.g. in the case of city branding, on the level of the municipality.

In parallel, there is an increasing number of critical studies of branding processes in the social sciences and humanities. Accordingly, contemporary branding exemplarily reflects the eclectic, media- and experience-oriented character of postmodernity.[5] Urban research, in particular, considers the current staging and marketing of cities under postmodern conditions and tries to understand the production of cities as appealing places with a promising future.[6] Authors like Edward Soja point to the need to position cities in emerging inter-city networks and, in particular, emphasise the importance of simulation in and of contemporary cities. As cities and large urban development projects are increasingly shaped by mottos and themes, urbanism and urban marketing are increasingly engaged in creating "hyperreal" worlds.[7]

Critical approaches to the neoliberalisation of cities, too, underline the need felt by responsible actors to favourably position cities in tightened interurban competition by means of marketing and branding.[8] In the "entrepreneurial city,"[9] urban politics mutates, first, into location policy to strengthen competitiveness and integrate the city into global flows of commodities and capital; soft locational factors thereby achieve a particular significance in increasing attractiveness for demanding investors, a highly qualified workforce, affluent citizens, and free-spending tourists. Besides easily recognisable logos and slogans, "festivalisation"

4 In particular, in French, branding activities have often been labelled "marketing territorial." For the terminological shift and conceptual differentiation, cf. also Kavaratzis, 2004.

5 Cf. Fırat, Dholakia, and Venkatesh, 1995.

6 Cf. Soja, 2000, esp. ch. 7 and 11; Dear and Flusty, 1998.

7 For the Middle East, cf. also Steiner, 2010.

8 For the neoliberal transformation of cities, see, e.g., Brenner and Theodore, 2002; Heeg and Rosol, 2007; for the Arab world, Al-Hamarneh, Margraff, and Scharfenort, 2019.

9 Cf. Hall and Hubbard, 1998.

through widely discernible cultural, sports, and other big events[10] and the use of landmark architecture and prestige megaprojects are central components to make these places widely known and to produce symbolic capital.[11] Especially in many cities at water edges, extensive revitalisation programmes have transformed deteriorated former docklands into luxurious waterfronts for consumption and leisure purposes, after port activities have been more and more relocated out of inner cities.[12]

And finally, authors dealing with global and globalising cities also emphasise processes of integration into global urban networks,[13] which also seems to require urban authorities to position their strongholds prominently and clearly demarcate them from potential competitors. As this is not an exclusive prerogative of Northern cities, the term "worlding" has been coined for places in the Global South, which likewise want to position themselves highly in the flow of global attention, including with demonstrative branding strategies.[14] Authoritarian regimes, in particular, such as prevail in the Middle East and North Africa (MENA), are successful in implementing a quick, often admired urban restructuring at the expense of civic participation and objection rights.[15] Branding thereby also reflects existing power structures and proceeds selectively by excluding annoying aspects from spatial, temporal, social, and cultural attributions to places.

As endeavours to establish cities as brands have become a worldwide phenomenon, not only "global cities," but also "secondary cities" strive for far-reaching appeal.[16] In the MENA region, the most outstanding example of a strong city brand is doubtless Dubai. In the last decade, it has become a general role model for urban and economic development, but also for widely radiating attention strategies that many places in the Gulf region and beyond have endeavoured to copy.[17] Yet, Govers and Go still stated in 2009 that the emirate had only lately started to develop a passably coherent branding strategy.[18] In contrast, in the mid-2010s, Moroccan publications, for instance, still mostly focused rather abstractly on components

10 Cf. Häußermann and Siebel, 1993.
11 Cf. also Swyngedouw, Moulaert, and Rodriguez, 2002; Klingmann, 2007.
12 Cf., for instance, Hoyle, 2000; Prelorenzo, 2010.
13 Cf. Sassen, 2001; Taylor, 2004; for the construction and performance of world-cityness, cf. Doel and Hubbard, 2002.
14 Cf. Roy and Ong, 2011; for MENA cities, Beier, 2019.
15 Cf. Bromber et al., 2014.
16 Cf. Wippel, 2021b.
17 On Dubai in the global attention economy, cf. already Schmid, 2009; as an urban role model, Wippel et al., 2014.
18 Cf. Govers and Go, 2009: esp. 73–108.

of branding strategies and to-do lists to be adopted, with little empirical analysis, including for Tangier.[19]

3 Branding as a Multi-scalar Endeavour

A first assumption of my article is that a multitude of actors are undertaking urban branding and marketing on differing spatial scales and, hence, conveying a multi-faceted, often heterogeneous, and sometimes inconsistent image of the city to the addressed public. For this, wider conceptual references can be made, first, to the "geographies of scale." Numerous authors explicitly point to the different scalar levels on which social processes and space formation take place.[20] Especially in the context of current globalisation, a continuous rescaling occurs, i.e. repeated shifts between existing levels of agency and organisation.[21] Correspondingly, the responsibilities of certain institutions and the effects of political interventions and individual or collective identities, for instance, regularly jump across different spatial scales. In the 1990s, the multi-scalar dimensions of globalisation and the close entanglement of different spatial scales, notably the intertwining of the global and the local, have been conceptualised as "glocalisation."[22]

But in fact, beyond the continuous jumping within a nested hierarchy of clearly delineated scales, we can observe a progressive mutual blurring and interpenetrating of scales, which are ever more difficult to analytically distinguish from each other. Hence, relating to the subnational and especially the local, Saskia Sassen points to their constitution on multiple scales, while contemporary urban reconfigurations deploy at various levels.[23] In particular, global cities establish direct links to international urban networks by leaping across established national state hierarchies. Scale jumping and blurring also occur, e.g., when global and regional events have immediately repercussions on local development and vice versa. This conforms with Neil Brenner's understanding of cities as places in continuous re-territorialisation and as interfaces between multiple, overlapping, and shifting spatial scales.[24] Agency has become more and more multi-scalar, too, encompassing interventions by local, national, and transnational stakeholders on the urban level.

19 See, e.g., Laghzaoui and Abakouy, 2014; Marso, 2016.
20 See, e.g., Swyngedouw, 1997; Berndt, 1999; van Schendel, 2002.
21 Cf. also Brenner, 1999.
22 Cf. Robertson, 1995; see also Scholz, 2004: 221–258.
23 Cf. Sassen, 2003.
24 Cf., e.g., Brenner, 1997.

Neoliberal development in particular has induced significant changes in urban governance. While the neoliberal agenda has been implemented on the national scale, concomitantly the importance of the local level has grown, as responsibilities and competencies have been increasingly downscaled. In the course of the opening, deregulation, and privatisation of economic life, but also the commodification of other political, social, and cultural domains, the number of relevant actors who actively participate in urban politics and in planning and implementing large urban projects has multiplied. State authorities continue to be important players enforcing neoliberal policies and attracting global investors. Notably in the context of authoritarian regimes, large urban projects are being presented as auspicious "visions" of a caring ruler.[25] But urban development and the provision of public services have regularly been assigned to special agencies acting according to private sector principles, public-private partnerships, and a growing number of private investors, increasingly from abroad. Accordingly, it suggests itself that these manifold actors from different, difficult to define scales also intervene in city branding to promote their interests and positions, using manifold tools and media.

4 Branding Practices as Place Making at the Interface

Primarily, the study centres on the critical analysis of strategically communicated texts and images. The central question relates to the characteristics that are being emphasised to make Tangier and projects established there appear attractive and successful. Taking up Brenner's statement on cities as interfaces, another conceptual point I want to make is the idea of the integrating "interface," at which cities, in their branding, are being placed in spatial, temporal, and cultural terms. Application-oriented works often prefer a clearly referenced and easily recognisable positioning of places. In contrast, my central, second thesis is that, in order to (re)present the manifold facets of a city, to convey a positive image to the largest possible audience, and to accommodate the multitude of stakeholders in the process, branding often not only contrasts a city and its urban projects with competing places, but also situates them between different spaces, times, cultures, and life worlds and at connecting transitions and interstices. At the same time, this may also reflect diverse geostrategic orientations, especially of national political actors.

25 For the Gulf region, cf. Bromber et al., 2014: 7–8; Hvidt, 2019.

Approximately in the 1980s, the term "interface" was introduced in geography from the natural sciences. In the framework of economic geography and urban research, cities were conceptualised, on the one hand, as passages between the local and the global and especially as indispensable transnational brokers and nodal points between economic networks.[26] On the other hand, the city has been conceived as a platform, filter, and modulator of and between a multitude of cultural spheres and symbolic worlds, especially in the age of digital communication media.[27] In a wider understanding, notably French geographers have conceptualised interfaces as spheres of contact and exchange between regions, networks, and systems, which often articulate in hubs such as cities or specific infrastructures.[28] In contrast to rather territorially defined concepts of clear, distinct borders and spatial discontinuities, relational aspects of connection, mixture, blending, and transition have been particularly emphasised. That underlines also the positively connoted compatibility of diversity, concomitant qualities such as innovation and complexity, and the processual character of space and place production at such interfaces. While these sources still strongly conceive interfaces in physical terms (e.g., human–environment, culture–nature, urban–rural, land–sea[29]), here they are understood in the sense of a discursive positioning, as happens in the context of branding.

Hence, this chapter first goes into the question of which belongings, connections, and intersections those actors responsible for marketing and branding underline, contrast, and combine to achieve the most positive associations. The chapter's first interest is in the multiple geographical positioning of places in diverse larger regional settings or at the intersection of several world regions. This includes allusions to historical and (re)emerging inter- and transregional contacts and intermediary positions, as well as specific types of landscapes or climatic zones that are presumed to be attractive. With regard to the temporal positioning of cities, this article investigates references to their past, present, and future and as contact points between these temporal layers. Among them are allusions to con-

26 Cf. Hsu, 2005. Cf. also Baumann, Dietze, and Maruschke, 2017 on places like trade and port cities as intermediary "Portals of Globalization"; for Gulf cities as interfaces, Katodrytis and Syed, 2013. Interestingly, a quick look at explanations in Wikipedia suggests that in English "interface" is still much more closely linked to computer science, while the German "Schnittstelle" also refers to organisational aspects, and especially in French, geographical dimensions, as discussed in the following, have deserved a separate entry; cf. Wikipédia, 2021.

27 Cf. Georgiou, 2008; De Waal, 2013.

28 Cf. Groupe de recherches "Interfaces," 2008; Lampin-Maillet et al., 2010.

29 Particularly on the local level, this may also refer to the port-city interface, with regard to urban port and waterfront development; cf. Hoyle, 2000.

tinuing lines of tradition and historically formative experiences, which point to an envisaged desirable and successful future. Likewise, invented traditions and architectural styles with multiple spatiotemporal references have to be included. Finally, this article inspects Tangier's sociocultural positionings and especially its association with specific lifestyles and civilisational worlds. Such cultural assignments are often being spatialised and defined in terms of exclusive civilisational areas, but can also be multiple and overlapping. The contrasting or interlocking of rational economic and emotional life world dimensions is an important aspect in urban marketing.[30]

5 Branding Tangier in the "International Period" (1920s–'50s)

Tangier had long been a trade centre connecting trans-Saharan and trans-Mediterranean networks, and so it looks back on a long cosmopolitan past.[31] Between the 15th and 17th centuries, it experienced European – Portuguese, Spanish, and British – rule. In the 19th century, it had become the diplomatic capital of the Cherifian Empire, where foreign legations were established, which brought many sectors of the communal administration under their control. Around 1900, a new city began to develop outside the old walls and along the waterfront, where a modern harbour was set up and hotels and other leisure facilities were built. While in 1912 the French and Spanish protectorates were established over the rest of Morocco, Tangier in 1923 formally came under multinational administration that lasted until its reintegration into the Moroccan nation-state in 1956. At that time, it was an important port city, an attractive tourist destination, a haven for capital and refugees, and a favoured place for artists and outcasts.

During the "international period" from the 1920s to the '50s, Tangier's marketing concentrated on transport and tourism. In this liberal age, the urban and economic development of the city was mostly left to local and international private actors. Hence, it was notably the local tourism association that promoted Tangier with booklets, brochures, and posters, often with Orientalist motives, displaying the medina and casbah with arches, minarets, and traditional boats, or men and women in traditional costumes (Fig. 1a). Yet, for some years in the late 1930s, it regularly published an illustrated magazine called *Tanger-Riviera* that brought news

30 Cf. Mattissek, 2010.

31 For Tangier's past urban development, cf. Stuart, 1955; Ceballos López, 2009; Tafersiti Zarouila, 2012; for its port and waterfront, cf. also Wippel, 2022.

Fig. 1: Marketing Tangier in the International Era
a) Poster from Syndicat d'Initiative et de Tourisme de Tanger, by Jacques Majorelle, 1924; b) Cover of Tanger-Riviera magazine No. 1, 30 September 1937; c) Luggage sticker, Hotel El Minzah, Tangier [mostly dated 1950s].
Sources: Qatar National Library, 2022 (no known copyright); photo Steffen Wippel, 2017 (at Biblioteca Juan Goytisolo, Instituto Cervantes de Tánger); CER.ES, 2022.

of beach life, sports, and tourism in the city and displayed more modern illustrations including bathing costumes and cocktails (Fig. 1b). This was paralleled by the marketing of Tangier done by hotels and shipping, airline, and railway companies, whose poster motives, luggage tags, and small travel guides also showed a predilection for exotic palm- and mosque-decorated environments (Fig. 1c). Hence, "othering" in an exoticised, historicised African realm dominated, while a few media already placed Tangier at the cultural, temporal, and geographical interface with "modern" leisure habits that had developed along the European coasts of the Mediterranean.

Illustrated but at the same time text-loaded information-rich brochures, adverts in newspapers and magazines, and diligently designed posters habitually exhibited inside offices or hotel halls were the preferred modes of presentation and communication. Text was often multilingual, written in French, English, and sometimes Spanish, less in Arabic and other languages. Already during the international era, maps were used to promote Tangier as a place at a maritime crossroads where many shipping lines called and on the main rail route from Europe, notably France, to North Africa (Fig. 2). Accordingly, the small travel guide that the Rotterdam shipping company published in the 1950s stated: "Tanger, l'ancienne 'Tingis' des Romains, occupe une position géographique privilégiée. Grâce à sa situation favorable, face à l'Europe, et grâce aussi à la circonstance qu'elle est sur la

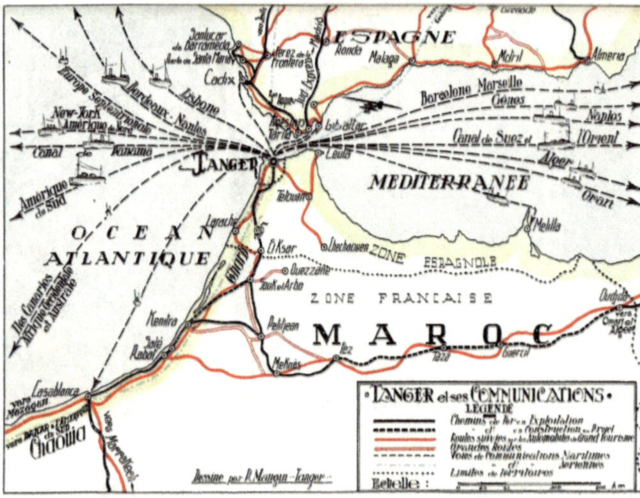

Fig. 2: Tangier's cartographic positioning at the intersection of sea-lanes and railroads
Source: Propaganda and Tourism Section of the Tangier Zone, 1929: 32 (picture retrieved from Robertson, 2006).

route des grandes lignes de navigation, elle est d'une importance qui va grandissant chaque jour."[32]

6 Multi-actor and Multi-scalar Branding of Tangier's Contemporary Transformations

After independence, Tangier was neglected, stagnated, and lost much of its economic prosperity, like the Kingdom's entire North. Only since the late 1990s has new attention been directed to its comeback. In particular, several megaprojects have been implemented, which are effectively transforming the urban landscape and the surrounding agglomeration.[33]

The first and most outstanding megaproject is the *Tanger Méditerranée* complex. New port facilities have been established outside the city, at the Strait of Gibraltar. Its core consists of the huge container port that opened in 2008 and mainly serves transhipment. The complex also includes the Great Industrial Plat-

32 Rotterdam Lloyd, n.d.

33 For Tangier's contemporary urban development, cf. in the following Tafersiti Zarouila, 2012; Haller, 2016; Haller, Wippel, and Reifeld, 2016; Wippel, 2019.

form encompassing several logistic and free zones, the Renault plant with an Automotive City, and additional industrial estates scattered across the Tangier Peninsula. *Tanger Ville* is the second large urban project; it is about to reconvert the old inner-city port area into a luxurious consumption- and leisure-oriented waterfront and to connect it to the revamped Corniche along the adjacent Tangier Bay.[34] *Tanger City Centre*, a huge international business complex and "Western-style" shopping mall, is developing a hitherto unused central terrain into a new urban pole.

To supplement these high-end structures, the *Tanger Métropole* programme envisions a large set of measures to develop infrastructural, social, and cultural amenities, including in the more peripheral and neglected quarters. And finally, in 2017, the agreement was signed to develop the *Cité Mohammed VI TangerTech*, a technopole and residential "New Town." Moreover, important transport infrastructure has been established, like motor- and expressways, a high-speed railway line to Casablanca, an expanded airport, and in the distant future, perhaps an underwater tunnel to Spain. Also, alongside other new towns for the working population, numerous gated communities, integrated tourism resorts, and first-class hotels have been designed for a well-off national and international clientele, mainly along the coast.

In the race for a good position among cities in the wider region, Tangier already registers some important advancement, which has been extensively recapitulated in national and local media and has created a good basis for successful branding. Notably, its container port rapidly advanced to rank 25 worldwide in terms of annual throughput in 2020 and is now the first port in Africa and the Mediterranean. TangerMed is one of the few key transhipment hubs of Mærsk, the biggest container shipping company worldwide, and the major hub for the Euro-African services of CMA CGM, offering the third-largest global transport capacity. As per the maritime "connectivity index," it has pushed the entire country from place 78 in 2004 to around 16–20 in recent years.[35] In 2012/13, the Financial Times group nominated the Tanger Free Zone as the best port free zone worldwide and in the following years repeatedly the most competitive free zone of Africa.[36] Within Morocco, Tangier has become the third-most populated city and the second industrial pole. In 2015, the Word Bank presented Tangier as one of six "model cities" in the Global South for its outstanding economic development and competitiveness.[37]

---

34 For port and waterfront development, cf. also Ducruet, Mohamed-Chérif, and Cherfaoui, 2011; Benabad, 2012; Wippel, 2022.

35 UNCTAD, 2021.

36 Cf. fDi Intelligence, 2020 (and earlier issues).

37 Cf. The World Bank, 2015.

According to the waterfront development agency, “Tanger a toujours été une ‘petite ville monde,’”[38] but it is surrounded by several ascending “world cities” in the North and the South, but itself has not yet been included even in the most comprehensive global city rankings.[39] In Morocco, only Casablanca has advanced to the category of an important world city that is considered instrumental in linking the country to the world economy. While the Kingdom’s economic capital with the affirmative slogan “WeCasablanca” claims to have set up the first comprehensive city branding strategy in Africa in 2016,[40] it was not yet included in the 2018 City Brand Index of 56 evaluated cities worldwide.[41] The Country Brand Index, at least, gives all of Morocco a mediocre 64th place worldwide.[42] But, with its economic boom and infrastructural and urban developments, Tangier has also experienced multifarious endeavours for branding in the last two decades again.

Today, public entities endeavour to make Tangier a “showcase city”[43] and are increasingly marketing the territory by presenting its advantages in TV spots and at international exhibitions and fairs. However, there is not a single entity responsible for Tangier’s urban branding; many actors and institutions from different sectors and with specific interests participate in constructing the image of the city. Compared with the colonial age, the number of actors intervening has even multiplied, and, in particular, the city’s promotion is being done on manifold scales.[44] First, several externally oriented public authorities on the national level market Tangier, e.g., as a tourist destination and investment site. Besides the national real estate developers, this is notably the case with the Ministry of Tourism and its affiliates, such as the National Tourism Office: in the mid-2010s, they promoted Tangier as a part of *Cap Nord*, one of the eight focus regions for tourism development in the national Vision 2020, and emphasised cultural, city, business, and conference tourism complemented by beach tourism on the nearby shores and ecological and hiking tourism in the hinterland.

Within the city, no central agency or PR city manager has unfolded discernible branding activities up to now. Tourism marketing, in principle, should be expected to be the task of the delegation of the Tourism Ministry, but the poorly equipped

38 SAPT, 2017.
39 Cf. GaWC, 2020.
40 WeCasablanca, 2021. Cf. also Dounia Sedra’s article in this edited volume.
41 Valet, 2018.
42 FutureBrand, 2020.
43 Chattou, 2011.
44 For the multiplicity of actors and the multi-scalarity of interventions in Tangier’s economic and urban development, cf. Wippel, 2019 and 2021a.

local tourism office does not display much information – a small brochure and, if you are lucky, a small city map. In contrast, in the mid-2010s, the regional tourism council, representing local tourism operators, started to develop a website covering the whole north-western region and accessible to the public and to publish documents addressing professionals in the sector.[45] Only very recently has a hop-on hop-off sightseeing bus been installed whose operator also gives tourist-oriented information on its Internet page.

Besides, parastatal special agencies, installed by the central state and public institutions in the course of the "agencification" of Moroccan urban policies,[46] promote their local projects internationally and are looking for clients and investors abroad. They have been assigned substantial power and great, private sector-like freedom of action in planning, implementing, and operating megaprojects. This is the case of the state-owned TangerMed Special Agency (TMSA), the holding responsible for the entire TangerMed platform, and its affiliates managing the numerous sub-projects. To attract terminal operators, shipping lines, and industrial companies, they vaunt the advantages of (being present in) Tangier, the favourable conditions for implementation, and the extraordinary geographic location accommodating the firms' interests to serve plenty of markets. At the same time, the transnational firms established there, like the two container terminal operators, Mærsk's APM Terminals and the Eurogate consortium, praise the port's equipment, too, which favours their businesses. The public *Société d'Aménagement pour la Reconversion de la Zone Portuaire de Tanger* (SAPT), which surveys the transformation of the inner-city waterfront, is perhaps the most active agency in co-constructing the city's new image. Together with the national port agency, it has founded the joint venture Tanja Marina Bay International to manage and develop the diverse port and marina activities, while Eagle Hills, a branch of Emaar from Dubai, has been commissioned to construct and market the new commercial, residential, and tourism real estate in the former harbour area.

Such international investment, real estate, and construction companies engaged in the upcoming tourism resorts and residential communities also contribute to conveying an attractive image of the city. However, following the economic, financial, and in part political crises in their home countries, such as Spain and the Gulf sheikhdoms, numerous widely announced projects had to be put on hold since the late 2000s or changed ownership and design, tarnishing to some extent the discourse on the city's bright future and imminent boom.

45 See, e.g., Regional Council of Tourism Tangier-Tetouan-Al Hoceima, 2016.

46 Cf. Amarouche and Bogaert, 2019.

7 Multi-Media Branding of Tangier

Today, the branding of Tangier makes intense use of a broad range of media including virtual communication tools. Brochures are still on display in agency and firm offices and in showrooms, but are also available in web-compatible format. The degree to which detailed information on websites is provided, however, varies considerably from one project and one institution to the other.[47] Depending on the addressees, texts are sometimes offered in even more languages today, sporadically including Chinese and Japanese.

In addition, outdoor advertising, 3D models, and virtual simulations play a pre-eminent role. Along the main traffic arteries, huge billboards present new real estate projects and waterfront developments for sale and often still under construction; on fences, posters advertising new buildings mask construction sites (Fig. 3a). Material models demonstrating the future designs of residential, office, and tourism complexes are exhibited in showrooms, like for the new Tanja Marina Bay and the Tanger City Centre (Fig. 3c). Images and films presented in the Internet show animated landscapes, multiple perspectives, and two- and three-dimensional indoor tracking shots; maps situate Tangier and project sites in narrower and wider geographical contexts. While the city is still "under construction," these media already present its future appearance to a broad public (Fig. 3b). All in all, substantial written information seems to play a lesser role than pictorial impressions and qualitatively enhanced graphic material. Even more, instead of formal, detailed, and technical development plans, urban "visions" presented by the king and communicated by public media, including illustrations of the monarch gazing at large site models and inaugurating new developments (Fig. 3d), confer projects a quasi-transcendental aura and makes them difficult to contest.[48]

A great variety of logos – from abstract arches and palms in tourism to maritime motifs alluding to sails in the marina project and geometrical patterns representing globality, connectivity, and diversity for port bodies, shopping malls, and the Expo 2012 (cf. below) – give visual expression to projects, sites, firms, and institutions in the city; slogans also help to merchandise them. Nevertheless, a central single logo or slogan advertising the city is missing – neither the regional nor the national tourism and investment agencies present such a wordmark. In contrast, "big names" among corporate investors, real estate developers, and planning offices symbolise international expertise and underline Tangier's global ambitions.

47 The use of social media has also increased, but often seems to use the same text modules and is left to a separate investigation.

48 Similarly for Gulf cities, compare Bromber et al., 2014.

Fig. 3: Billboards, models, and simulations
a) Billboard advertising the Tanja Marina project; b) Pictorial simulation of the new marina; c) 3D showroom model of Tanger City Centre; d) Mohammed VI visiting the TangerTech model.
Sources: Photo Steffen Wippel, 2015; Tanja Marina Bay, 2017; Photo Steffen Wippel, 2013; Tanger Experience, 2017.

This namely concerns Gulf investors in the tourism and residential sectors like *Qatari Diar*, the Bahraini Gulf Finance House, and Dubai's Emaar, as well as worldwide leading specialists in the field of transport and logistics, such as Mærsk, CMA CGM, Eurogate, and DHL, and global leaders in industrial production, from Renault-Nissan to Siemens, Decathlon, and Danone.[49]

Material objects also have an important role in making Tangier known and attractive to the outside world. This includes iconic urban megaprojects, new architectural landmarks, and renowned names involved in their construction, which are widely promoted, communicated, and, it is hoped, perceived (Fig. 4). The TangerMed Business Centre was designed by Jean Nouvel, winner of the 2008 Pritzker Prize, while "starchitects" like Rem Koolhaas, Zaha Hadid, and Ricardo Bofill participated in the urbanistic competition for the complex and the reconstruction of the inner-city waterfront. Tourism resorts and gated communities have been constructed in modern "Mediterranean," popular "Hispano-colonial," and allegedly

49 For this, see, e.g., the companies' "wall of fame" on websites and in brochures and reports, such as TMSA, 2021: 98–99, 112–113.

traditional “Andalusian” décor.[50] Close to the Tanger City Centre, the new TGV station inaugurated in 2018 is another remarkable building in steel and glass that adds to the adjacent main station in Neo-Moresque style opened in 2003. This also includes visions of future museums and the 540-metre Al Noor Tower temporarily announced by the Saudi Bin Laden group. The also unrealised Bab al Maghreb Tower was reminiscent of the Atlantis Hotel in Dubai, while people on the street even regard the new purified, concrete-covered corniche with its geometrically decorated towers and lampposts as representing some sort of “Dubai style.” Giant gantry cranes at the TangerMed container port have become repeatedly pictured iconic symbols for Tangier’s role as a transport hub; while repainted dockside cranes in the old port area are reminiscent of its historical trade legacy.

Fig. 4: Urbanistic landmarks
The new corniche at the eastern bay; painted dockside cranes at the old inner-city port; Tanja Marina Bay; the new railway stations from 2003 and 2018.
Photos: Steffen Wippel, 2017, 2018, 2018, 2020.

50 This contrasts with Daus’ observation that the “postmodern” holiday villages at nearby Tamouda Bay built in the 1980s copied Bauhaus-like occidental styles; cf. Daus, 2000: 311.

Finally, big events are also extensively used to brand Tangier especially as a place for culture. The city intensely participates in the festival fever that has broken out across Morocco, in particular in the fields of literature, film, and music. Among the most prominent, often annual events, we find the *Festival de Jazz* (TANJAzz), the Tangier International Film Festival, the *Festival de Cine Africano* (together with Tarifa, Spain), and the *Salon International de Tanger des Livres et des Arts*. In contrast, Tangier's internationally promoted application for the world exhibition Expo 2012 under the motto "Routes du monde, Rencontre des cultures. Pour un monde plus uni,"[51] which aimed at highlighting the city's global entanglements and for which extensive new construction was planned for the eastern side of the bay, failed in the last round against its South Korean competitor.

8 Locating Tangier at Spatial and Temporal Interfaces

Concerning the contents of statements disseminated in the context of urban marketing and branding, it is not too surprising that branding activities first endeavour to create a pleasant atmosphere, an ambiance of ease and beauty, and an impression of modernity and progressivity. Contemporary buzzwords often relate to global neoliberal and ecological canons. Catchwords such as "clusters," "ecosystems," "smart" and "green" cities, or "technopoles" and "science parks," as well as hints at construction and management according to "global standards" and to internationally established high quality are abundant. Projects are repeatedly "greenwashed": this is true, for example, of the New Town of Chrafate, which is advertised as a "green city,"[52] of the "zero emission" Renault factory,[53] and of the envisaged TangerTech City, which has been declared "environment-friendly";[54] environmental auditing has become a standard for establishing projects in the local free zones.

51 Association Tanger 2012, n.d.: 3.

52 Chabâa, 2013.

53 Renault Group, 2021.

54 TelQuel, 2017.

Box 1: Locating Tangier at interfaces between continents or seas

Tangier proudly overlooks the sea, In that particular point of the meeting of the Mediterranean and the Atlantic. It is located at the crossroads between the north and the south.[55]

Une position géostratégique
Porte ouverte sur l'Afrique, tournée vers l'Europe, la ville du Détroit possède une position géographique unique, trait d'union entre l'Europe et le reste du Maroc, entre l'Atlantique et la Méditerranée. De par cette position exceptionnelle, Tanger a toujours été favorable aux échanges et aux investissements.[56]

Extrait du discours de Sa Majesté le Roi Mohammed VI (Février 2003)
Nous procédons au lancement d'un des plus grands projets économiques dans l'histoire de notre pays. (...) Le Maroc consolide ainsi son ancrage dans l'espace euro-méditerranéen et dans son environnement maghrébin et arabe. Il valorise sa vocation de pôle d'échanges entre l'Europe et l'Afrique, la Méditerranée et l'Atlantique, (...).[57]

Thanks to its full integration with Tanger Med Port, the gateway to Europe, Mediterranean and Africa, TMZ [Tanger Med Zones] offers a compelling value proposition meeting the genuine needs of international investors and centered around. (...) TMZ is a fast growing hub on the Mediterranean at the doorstep of Europe for industrial, services and commercial activities.[58]

Remarkably, urban branding takes place between times and regions, repeatedly emphasising the unique economically and culturally important location of Tangier and of institutions and places in the urban agglomeration. Many texts, but also maps and illustrations, place the city geostrategically at accentuated regional interfaces. Space and location are not considered as constructed by human effort, but become naturalised. Geographically, Tangier is assigned an exposed location at the northernmost point of Morocco and Africa. Situated at the North-South interface, i.e. the continental transition where Europe and Africa meet, and, at the same time, at the maritime East-West passage from the Mediterranean to the Atlantic, it is considered a bridge and gateway (cf. exemplary quotes in Box 1).[59] This is particularly true of the new port, which is located at one of the busiest maritime lanes in the world and, hence, allows for establishing and linking multiple regional and transregional connections. Accordingly, the TangerMed Platform is presented as a node "at the heart of global trade" (Fig. 5). At the same time, the peninsula is regarded as a transit point for passenger traffic, freight carriage, and energy trans-

55 Regional Council of Tourism Tangier-Tetouan-Al Hoceima, 2016: 14.
56 Ibn Batouta Mall, 2017.
57 TMSA, 2021: 4.
58 Tanger Med Zones, 2017.
59 In the following boxes, headlines appear in italics and, in the original, are not always immediately followed by the rest of the quote. Separations of paragraphs are ignored; linguistic imperfections in English and French are retained without being specially marked.

port. For firms, the city's attractive location and manifold links are said to accommodate their interest in simultaneously serving national, regional North African, European, sub-Saharan, and world markets.

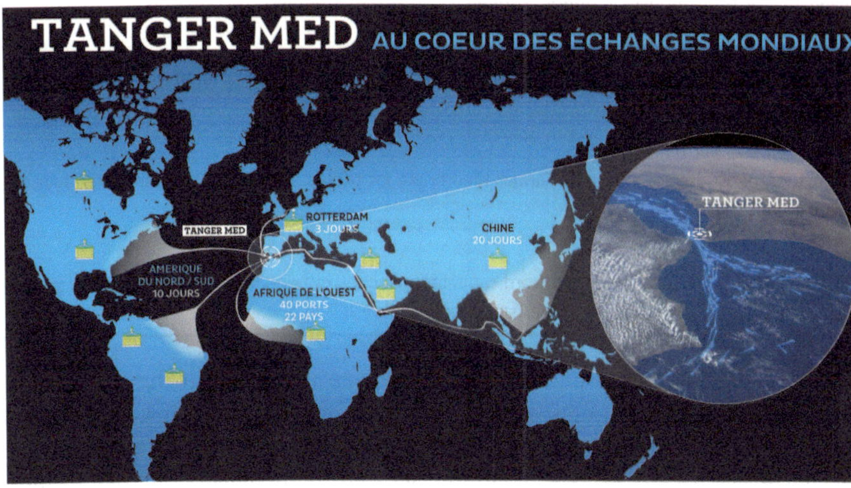

Fig. 5: Tangier's cartographic positioning in international trade
Source: Tanger Med, 2021.

In particular, the port helps to restore the city's and the kingdom's African connections, thereby supporting national regional and economic policies.[60] This reconnection is also true of land transport, since the last section of the so-called Tangier-Dakar Highway was completed more than a decade ago and terrestrial shipping has started from the logistical hub at TangerMed to West Africa. From the colonial "gate to Morocco" – first for diplomats and later for foreign residents and tourists – the city developed into Morocco's "gate to Europe" with increasing labour migration, and nowadays has become the "gate to Africa," according to manifold statements (Box 2). This African dimension has been repeatedly underlined, from the urban development plan of the late 1990s to statements of national ministries and state-owned agencies and releases by terminal operators and freight companies – including the possible wordplay between "port" and "porte" (gate) in French.

60 Compare Mareï and Wippel, 2020.

Box 2: Considering Tangier a "Gate to Africa"

La position géostratégique

Etant en constante relation avec, d'une part l'Europe, et les grandes routes maritimes d'autre part, [la région Tanger-Tétouan] est considérée comme 'la porte de l'Afrique[']. [61]

Africa's gateway to the world

(...) the EUROGATE Tanger container terminal is Africa's gateway to the world and a bridge between continents. [62]

La plateforme TIMAR Tanger Med

La situation géostratégique du port Tanger Med ouvre les portes de l'Afrique du Nord et de l'Afrique subsaharienne, (...). [63]

Positionnement du territoire

Porte de l'Afrique, la destination Cap Nord capitalisera sur ses histoires multiples, sa situation géographique de carrefour et son dynamisme économique. [64]

The sea-land interface is another transition zone appearing in the branding of Tangier (Box 3): it is not only served by various infrastructural installations, but is also a central element of on-going waterfront transformation. In its history, Tangier had long turned its back on the sea; despite its maritime legacy, no port existed; ships had to anchor off the coast and goods had to be transloaded on barges. A "real" port with moles and basins did not develop until the 20th century; but as access was limited to workers and passengers, it still sealed the sea off from the city. Today, most major projects, including tourism developments, are located along the entire peninsula's shores, where "sand and sea" or "ocean and mountains" meet. In particular, the reconversion of the old inner-city port promises "Uniting the port with the city" and "Bringing the sea to the city." [65]

61 CRI, 2010: 10.
62 Eurogate Tanger, 2021.
63 Timar Afrique, 2016.
64 Secrétariat d'Etat chargé du Tourisme, 2017.
65 Tanja Marina Bay, 2021.

Box 3: Communicating the city's sea-land interface

Le bien-être entre terre et mer[66]

Entre mer et montagne, les villes de Tanger et de Tétouan déploient un immense terrain de jeu riche en possibilités, des lieux inédits pour les baroudeurs![67]

Al Houara
At the Gates of Europe and Africa, where the Mediterranean meets the Atlantic, lies an elegant destination where sand and sea meet the verdant forest.[68]

Tangier's geographic location is equated with its location in a cultural transition zone (Box 4). Interpenetrating Islamic, European, overarching "Andalusian," and African influences and the passage and settling of many peoples are being highlighted and are said to have given the city its particular cosmopolitan and culturally rich character. This is closely linked with temporal interfaces: accordingly, Tangier has experienced a series of foreign presences and benefited from all of them. Its geostrategic position is presented as a historical constant. Mainly the multinational image of the city from colonial times is cultivated, including the presence of important – in general, mostly Western – artists from the late 19th century to the "Beat Generation" of the 1960s. This includes often referenced painters like Eugène Delacroix, Henri Matisse, and Francis Bacon, writers such as Paul and Jane Bowles, William Burroughs, Allen Ginsberg, and Tennessee Williams, and musicians from the Beatles to the Rolling Stones and Jimmy Hendrix, as well as other jet setters like Barbara Hutton and Yves Saint-Laurent. The king's candidature address for the Expo 2012 exemplarily sums up both, the linking of different world regions and of experiences from the past and progress in a near future: for him, Tangier represents a platform of convergence between continents and civilisations, a junction point par excellence between Africa, Europe, and the Arab world, including the American continents; its centuries-old strategic position and international diplomatic experience, together with its considerable current transformation, will propel it to a place among the primary economic poles of the Mediterranean South by 2015.[69]

66 Tanja Marina Bay International, 2016: 8.
67 ONMT, 2021.
68 Qatari Diar, 2017.
69 Cf. Association Tanger 2012, n.d.: 5.

Box 4: Branding Tangier's cultural and temporal interfaces

Une diversité culturelle
(...), la région Tanger-Tétouan jouit d'une culture millénaire. La population est caractérisée par son ouverture, et son multilinguisme, fruit d'un brassage de populations et d'origines diversifiées Avec la succession des Phéniciens, Romains, Carthaginois, byzantins, Vandales et Arabes, la population de la Région a acquis l'art de la tolérance.[70]

Tanger, ville mythique du bassin méditerranéen, traversée de vies millénaires, alimente l'imaginaire mondial avec son histoire antique, médiévale et moderne. Porte naturelle et stratégique, à la croisée de l'Europe, de l'Afrique et du Maroc, Tanger cosmopolite et éternellement mystérieuse se nourrit de ses échanges avec le monde. (...) Ville internationale avant l'heure, elle a tous les atouts pour retrouver, à l'ère de la globalisation, le statut qu'elle a acquis il y a un siècle.[71]

Une ville entre deux mondes
Tanger est une ville bouillonnante : le passé et le présent s'y mêlent avec harmonie. (...) Tanger est une croisée où convergent les influences. (...) Aux frontières de l'Europe et de l'Afrique, Tanger est une ville cosmopolite, où passé et présent coexistent.[72]

Tangier... the crossroad
As waters of the Mediterranean and the Atlantic intertwined at the foot of Tangier, it also combines the European, Arab and African cultures. A blend that surprises its visitors.[73]

The city's glorious past serves to overcome the negative reputation it had since its reintegration into the Kingdom and notably in the 1980s, when it was better known for drug trafficking, prostitution, and crime than for its historical and cultural richness.[74] It is becoming directly linked with its present transformation and expansion and its bright future as a major port city, tourist destination, and investment site and possesses a beneficial legacy in the current age of globalisation. Yet, the reference to older commercial activities and local personalities is much less explicit than to its cosmopolitan cultural heritage. In particular, one of Tangier's most famous sons has long been widely ignored in urban branding: the scholar, traveller, and explorer Ibn Battuta, who perambulated through Africa and Asia in the 14th century, could represent past and current worldwide connections and address several regional publics. Only the airport, a new peripheral settlement, and a small shopping mall are named after him; his pretended tomb in the medina is difficult to find. This contrasts with the highly commercialised, hy-

70 CRI, 2010: 11.

71 Tanja Marina Bay International, 2016: 4–5.

72 ONMT, 2017.

73 Regional Council of Tourism Tangier-Tetouan-Al Hoceima, 2016: 16.

74 Especially until 2010, guidebooks also contributed to the image of Tangier as a hetero- and homosexual heterotopia and a subversive, dangerous, and declining place; cf. Sanoussi, 2017.

perreal Ibn Battuta Mall in Dubai, representing the booming city's multifarious geographical ties.[75] Only recently, a young NGO started to organise a series of international events to commemorate Ibn Battuta's heritage, foster mutual cultural understanding, and put him on Tangier's map again. Finally, in 2022, the Ibn Battouta Memorial Exhibition, in one of the casbah's fortified towers restored by the SAPT, opened its doors to pay tribute to this legendary character.

9 By Way of Conclusion

This case study helps to fill a gap related to the branding of cities in the Global South and of secondary cities in particular; it largely fits and confirms the conceptual framework developed above. Corresponding to my first theory-based assumption, this overview of the branding of Tangier demonstrates that there is no comprehensive, consistent overall strategy for communicating a positive image of the city to the wider national and international public. Instead, many individual and collective, public and private, local, national, and transnational actors contribute to the (more or less strategic) construction of the booming city's image, mostly pursuing individual interests and addressing specific clienteles. Endeavours "from above" that brand Tangier among other places in Morocco, as well as branding "from below," which situates individual large and small projects in the local context and also co-brand the city, supplement still timid citywide efforts; nevertheless, they show many common features and direct the city's communicated image in similar directions. Moreover, branding is a multimodal endeavour: manifold material and virtual means are used to create such an urban brand.

In line with my second thesis, a central feature of branding Tangier is its positioning at manifold crossroads and interfaces of overlapping and interlinked geographical belonging and connectedness, especially between different (naturalised and essentialised) world regions such as "Europe" and "Africa." This emphasises Tangier's – and incidentally Morocco's – aspirations to be acknowledged as a global and transregional hub in transport, trade, and tourism, while several time horizons serve to link a glorified cosmopolitan past, a successful present, and an even brighter future. Problems, such as the progressing socio-spatial fragmentation of the city, transregional flows of drugs and migrants through the city, and underlying dependencies and imbalances that also appear at different levels are obviously eliminated from this strategic communication. To conclude, the city's branding perfectly aligns with the neoliberalisation, globalisation, and postmodernisation

75 Cf. Steiner, 2014.

of a secondary city that struggles for a favourable positioning in competitive inter-city and inter-port networks; but like urban development itself, branding happens in a rather fragmented way. Yet, even if Tangier might present an outstanding exemplary case, I suppose that we may find such multi-scale involvement and multi-regional positioning not only there, but also in many places, particularly in cities in the Global South.

Bibliography

Al-Hamarneh, Ala, Jonas Margraff, and Nadine Scharfenort, eds. *Neoliberale Urbanisierung: Stadtentwicklungsprozesse in der arabischen Welt.* Bielefeld: Transcript, 2019.

Amarouche, Maryame, and Koenraad Bogaert. "Reshaping Space and Time in Morocco: The Agencification of Urban Government and its Effects in the Bouregreg Valley (Rabat/Salé)." *Middle East – Topics and Arguments* 12.1 (2019): 44–54, 2019. https://archiv.ub.uni-marburg.de/ep/0003/article/view/7934. Accessed 20 August 2021.

Anholt, Simon. *Competitive Identity: The New Brand Management for Nations, Cities and Regions.* New York: Palgrave Macmillan, 2007.

Association Tanger 2012. *Tanger Expo 2012: Résumé exécutif.* Tanger, n.d. http://www.expo2012.ma/upload/telechargement/Resume%20executif.pdf. Accessed 29 November 2007 (link expired).

Baumann, Claudia, Antje Dietze, and Megan Maruschke. "Portals of Globalization: An Introduction." *Comparativ, Zeitschrift für Globalgeschichte und vergleichende Gesellschaftsforschung* 27.3/4 (2017): 7–20.

Beier, Raffael. "Worlding Cities in the Middle East and North Africa: Arguments for a Conceptual Turn." *Middle East–Topics & Arguments* 12.1 (2019): 28–34. https://archiv.ub.uni-marburg.de/ep/0003/2019/230/7828. Accessed 20 August 2021.

Benabad, Driss. "Projet de reconversion de la zone portuaire de Tanger Ville." *Portus* 24 (2012): 58–63.

Berndt, Christian. "Institutionen, Regulation und Geographie." *Erdkunde* 53.3 (1999): 302–316.

Brenner, Neil. "Globalisierung und Reterritorialisierung: Städte, Staaten und die Politik der räumlichen Redimensionierung im heutigen Europa." *WeltTrends* 17 (1997): 7–30.

Brenner, Neil. "Beyond State-centrism? Space, Territoriality, and Geographical Scale in Globalization Studies." *Theory and Society* 28.1 (1999): 39–78.

Brenner, Neil, and Nik Theodore. "Cities and the Geographies of 'Actually Existing Neoliberalism'." *Antipode* 34.3 (2002): 349–379.

Bromber, Katrin, Birgit Krawietz, Christian Steiner, and Steffen Wippel. "The Arab(ian) Gulf: Urban Development in the Making." In *Under Construction: Logics of Urbanism in the Gulf Region*, edited by Steffen Wippel, Katrin Bromber, Christian Steiner, and Birgit Krawietz, 1–14. Farnham, Burlington: Ashgate, 2014.

Ceballos López, Leopoldo. *Historia de Tanger: Memoria de la ciudad internacional.* Córdoba: Almuzara, 2009.

CER.ES. "Hotel El Minzah, Tanger." Etiqueta de hotel. Museo del Traje, Centro de Investigación del Patrimonio Etnológico. Ministerio de Cultura y Deporte, Red Digital de Colecciones de Museos de España. http://ceres.mcu.es. Accessed 9 May 2022.

Chabâa, Nadia. "Chrafate 'Green City.'" *AM/Architecture du Maroc* 57 (2013): 62–64.

Chattou, Zoubir. “Tanger à la croisée de nouvelles recompositions territoriales et de mobilités transnationales.” *Méditerranée* 116 (2011): 133–138. http://mediterranee.revues.org/5447. Accessed 3 November 2016.

CRI (Centre Régional d’Investissement Tanger–Tétouan). *Guide de l’Investisseur.* Tangier, 2010.

Daus, Ronald. *Strandkultur statt Stadtkultur: Die Metropolen des Mittelmeers zu Beginn des 21. Jahrhunderts.* Berlin: Babylon, 2000.

Dear, Michael, and Steven Flusty. “Postmodern Urbanism.” *Annals of the Association of American Geographers* 88.1 (1998): 50–72.

De Waal, Martijn. *The City as Interface: How New Media Are Changing the City.* Rotterdam: Nai010, 2013.

Doel, Marcus, and Phil Hubbard. “Taking World Cities Literally: Marketing the City in a Global Space of Flows.” *City* 6.3. (2002): 351–368.

Ducruet, César, Fatima Zohra Mohamed-Chérif, and Najib Cherfaoui. “Maghreb Port Cities in Transition: The Case of Tangier.” *Portus Plus* 1.1 (2011): 60–67.

Eurogate Tanger. “About Us.” http://www.eurogate-tanger.com/About-us/EUROGATE-Tanger. Accessed 2 August 2021.

fDi Intelligence. *Global Free Zones of the Year 2020: Recognising the World’s Best Free Zones for fDi.* Special Report, October/November 2020. https://www.fdiintelligence.com/content/download/78973/2597778/file/fDi%20Global%20Free%20Zones%20of%20the%20Year%202020.pdf. Accessed 16 October 2020.

Fırat, A. Fuat, Nikhilesh Dholakia, and Alladi Venkatesh. “Marketing in a Postmodern World.” *European Journal of Marketing* 29.1 (1995): 40–56.

FutureBrand. *FutureBrand Country Index 2020.* https://www.futurebrand.com/uploads/FBCi-2020-Assets/FutureBrand-Country-Index-2020.pdf. Accessed 4 August 2021.

GaWC (Globalization and World Cities Research Network). “The World According to GaWC.” https://www.lboro.ac.uk/gawc/gawcworlds.html/. Accessed 30 September 2020.

Georgiou, Myria. “Urban Encounters: Juxtapositions of Difference and the Communicative Interface of Global Cities.” *International Communication Gazette* 70.3–4 (2008): 223–235.

Gertner, David. “Unfolding and Configuring Two Decades of Research and Publications on Place Marketing and Place Branding.” *Place Branding and Public Diplomacy* 7.2 (2011): 91–106.

Govers, Robert, and Frank Go. *Place Branding: Glocal, Virtual and Physical Identities, Constructed, Imagined and Experienced.* Basingstoke, New York: Palgrave MacMillan, 2009.

Groupe de recherches “Interfaces”. “L’interface: Contribution à l’analyse de l’espace géographique.” *L’Espace géographique* 37.3 (2008): 193–207.

Hall, Tim, and Phil Hubbard, eds. *The Entrepreneurial City: Geographies of Politics, Regime and Representation.* Chichester et al.: John Wiley & Sons, 1998.

Haller, Dieter. *Tanger: Der Hafen, die Geister, die Lust. Eine Ethnographie.* Bielefeld: Transcript, 2016.

Haller, Dieter, Steffen Wippel, and Helmut Reifeld, eds. *Focus sur Tanger: Là où l’Afrique et l’Europe se rencontrent.* Rabat: Konrad-Adenauer-Stiftung, 2016.

Häußermann, Hartmut, and Walter Siebel, eds. *Festivalisierung der Stadtpolitik: Stadtentwicklung durch große Projekte.* Opladen: Westdeutscher Verlag, 1993.

Heeg, Susanne, and Marit Rosol. “Neoliberale Stadtpolitik im globalen Kontext: Ein Überblick.” *PROKLA: Zeitschrift für kritische Sozialwissenschaft* 149, 37.4 (2007): 491–509.

Hoyle, Brian. “Global and Local Change on the Port-City Waterfront.” *Geographical Review* 90.3 (2000): 395–417.

Hsu, Jinn-yuh. "A Site of Transnationalism in the 'Ungrounded Empire': Taipei as an Interface City in the Cross-border Business Networks." *Geoforum* 36.5 (2005): 654–666.

Hvidt, Martin. *Development Plans and Visions in the Arab Gulf Countries: What Is the Likelihood that they Will Be Implemented?* News Analysis. Odense: Center for Mellemøststudier, Syddansk Universitet, 2019. https://static.sdu.dk/Flexpaper/aspnet/pdf/Hvidt%20article%20January%202019.pdf. Accessed 11 March 2019.

Ibn Batouta Mall. "Tanger Ville." http://ibn-batouta.ma/centre/pourquoi-nous-choisir/tanger-ville/. Accessed 5 September 2017 (link expired).

Katodrytis, George, and Sharmeen Syed, eds. *Gulf Cities as Interfaces.* Cambridge, UK: Gulf Research Centre Cambridge, 2016.

Kavaratzis, Michalis. "From City Marketing to City Branding: Towards a Theoretical Framework for Developing City Brands." *Place Branding* 1.1 (2004): 58–73.

Klingmann, Anna. *Brandscapes: Architecture in the Experience Economy.* Cambridge, MA: MIT, 2007.

Laghzaoui, Fadoua, and Mostafa Abakouy. "Marketing territorial de Tanger entre gestation d'hier, manifestations d'aujourd'hui et mutations de demain." *Revista de Estudios Fronterizos del Estrecho de Gibraltar* 1 (2014): 1–29.

Lampin-Maillet, Corinne, Sandra Pérez, Jean-Paul Ferrier, and Paul Allard, eds. *Géographie des interfaces: Une nouvelle vision des territoires.* Versailles: Quæ, 2010.

Lucarelli, Andreas, and Per Olof Berg. "City Branding: A State-of-the-art Review of the Research Domain." *Journal of Place Management and Development* 4.1 (2011): 9–27.

Mareï, Nora, and Steffen Wippel. "Une perspective urbaine de la régionalisation du monde: Tanger, métropole (eur)africaine." *Belgeo: Revue belge de géographie* 4 (2020). http://journals.openedition.org/belgeo/43518. Accessed 9 November 2020.

Marso, Saida. "La marque 'ville', facteur d'attractivité territoriale: Cas de la marque ville 'Tanger'." *Revue Marocaine de recherche en management et marketing* 14 (2016): 235–243.

Mattissek, Annika. Stadtmarketing in der neoliberalen Stadt: Potentiale von Gouvernementalitäts- und Diskursanalyse für die Untersuchung aktueller Prozesse der Stadtentwicklung. In *Diskursanalyse meets Gouvernementalitätsforschung: Perspektiven auf das Verhältnis von Subjekt, Sprache, Macht und Wissen*, edited by J. Angermüller and S. van Dyk, 129–154. Frankfurt am Main, New York: Campus, 2010.

ONMT (Office National Marocain du Tourisme). "Une ville entre deux mondes." http://www.visitmorocco.com/fr/une-ville-entre-deux-mondes. Accessed 5 September 2017 (link expired).

ONMT. "Nature à Tétouan." https://www.visitmorocco.com/fr/voyage/tetouan/nature. Accessed 2 August 2021.

Prelorenzo, Claude. "Le retour de la ville portuaire." *Cahiers de la Méditerranée* 80 (2010): 157–167.

Propaganda and Tourism Section of the Tangier Zone. *Tangier: Winter Resort, Summer Resort.* Paris: Horizons de France, 1929.

Qatari Diar. "Al Houara." http://www.qataridiar.com/English/OurProjects/Pages/Al-Houara-.aspx. Accessed 5 September 2017.

Qatar National Library. "Syndicat d'Initiative et de Tourisme de Tanger: Tanger. Son site son climate." Vintage Travel Posters Collection. https://ediscovery.qnl.qa/islandora/object/QNL:00047762. Accessed 9 May 2022.

Regional Council of Tourism Tangier-Tetouan-Al Hoceima. *Professional Manual of Tourism: Edition 2016.* Tangier, 2016.

Renault Group. "Tangier Plant." https://www.renaultgroup.com/en/our-company/locations/tangier-plant/. Accessed 2 August 2021.

Robertson, George F. "Ephemeral Encounters Enduring Narratives: Visitor Voices of Tangier." *Space and Place* [blog]. 2006. http:/interactive-worlds.blogspot.com/2006/12. Accessed 16 April 2019.

Robertson, Roland. "Glocalization: Time-space and Homogeneity-heterogeneity." In *Global Modernities*, edited by Mike Featherstone, Scott Lash, and Roland Robertson, 25–44. London, Thousand Oaks, New Delhi: Sage, 1995.

Rotterdam Lloyd. *Tanger.* Rotterdam, n.d. [ca. 1950s].

Roy, Ananya, and Aihwa Ong, eds. *Worlding Cities. Asian Experiments and the Art of Being Global.* Chichester, Malden: Wiley-Blackwell, 2011.

Sanoussi, Anas. "Mises en désir de Tanger dans les guides touristiques imprimés: Formes latentes et transgressives." *Via: Tourism Review* 11–12 (2017). http://journals.opemnedition.org/viatoruism/1688. Accessed 14 June 2018.

SAPT (Société d'Aménagement pour la Reconversion de la Zone Portuaire de Tanger). "Le projet." http://www.sapt.ma/index.php/fr/le-projet/projet. Accessed 5 September 2017 (link expired).

Sassen, Saskia. *The Global City: New York, London, Tokyo.* Princeton, London: Princeton University Press, 2nd ed., 2001.

Sassen, Saskia. "Globalization or Denationalization?" *Review of International Political Economy* 10.1 (2003): 1–22.

Schmid, Heiko. *Economy of Fascination: Dubai and Las Vegas as Themed Urban Landscapes.* Berlin: Gebrüder Borntraeger, 2009.

Scholz, Fred. *Geographische Entwicklungsforschung: Methoden und Theorien.* Berlin, Stuttgart: Gebrüder Borntraeger, 2004.

Secrétariat d'Etat chargé du Tourisme. "Cap Nord." http://www.tourisme.gov.ma/fr/territoires-touristiques/cap-nord. Accessed 10 September 2017 (link expired).

Soja, Edward W. *Postmetropolis: Critical Studies of Cities and Regions.* Oxford, Malden: Blackwell, 2000.

Steiner, Christian. "From Heritage to Hyper-Reality? Tourism Destination Development in the Middle East between Petra and the Palm." *Journal of Tourism and Cultural Change* 8.4 (2010): 240–253.

Steiner, Christian. "Iconic Spaces, Symbolic Capital and the Political Economy of Urban Development in the Arab Gulf." In *Under Construction: Logics of Urbanism in the Gulf Region*, edited by Steffen Wippel, Katrin Bromber, Christian Steiner, and Birgit Krawietz, 17–30. Farnham, Burlington: Ashgate, 2014.

Stuart, Graham H. *The International City of Tangier.* Stanford: Stanford University Press, 2nd ed., 1955.

Swyngedouw, Erik. "Excluding the Other: The Production of Scale and Scaled Politics." In *Geographies of Economies*, edited by Roger Lee and Jane Williams, 167–176. London et al.: Arnold, 1997.

Swyngedouw Erik, Frank Moulaert, and Arantxa Rodriguez. "Neoliberal Urbanization in Europe: Large-scale Urban Development Projects and the New Urban Policy." *Antipode* 34.3 (2002): 542–577.

Tafersiti Zarouila, Rachid. *Tanger: Réalités d'un Mythe. Le mythe résiste.* Tangier: Zarouila, 2012.

Tanger Experience. "Les chinois investissent Tanger avec la 'Cité Mohammed VI Tanger Tech'." 21 March 2017. http://www.tanger-experience.com/societe/economie-actualites/les-chinois-investissent-tanger-avec-la-cite-mohammed-vi-tanger-tech/. Accessed 22 March 2017.

Tanger Med. "A propos de Tanger Med." https://www.tangermed.ma/. Accessed 2 August 2021.

Tanger Med Zones. "Message from the CEO." http://www.tangermedzones.com/en/message-from-general. Accessed 5 September 2017 (link expired).

Tanja Marina Bay. "Tanja Marina Bay." http://www.tanjamarinabay.ma/. Accessed 5 September 2017.

Tanja Marina Bay. “Port Reconstruction: Objectives.” http://www.tanjamarinabay.ma/en/la-reconversion/. Accessed 2 August 2021.

Tanja Marina Bay International. *Tanja Marina Bay, vivez l’expérience d’une marina urbaine au cœur de la baie de Tanger.* Tangier, [2016].

Taylor, Peter J. *World City Network: A Global Urban Analysis.* London, New York: Routledge, 2004.

TelQuel. “Un milliard de dollars pour la future ‘Cité Mohammed VI Tanger Tech’.” 20 March 2017. http://telquel.ma/2017/03/20/un-milliard-de-dollars-pour-la-cite-mohammed-vi-tanger-tech_1540033. Accessed 20 July 2017.

The World Bank. *Competitive Cities Knowledge Base: Appendices to Six Case Studies of Economically Successful Cities.* Document 101714, 2015. https://openknowledge.worldbank.org/bitstream/handle/10986/23573/AppendixesCompetitive0ci0ly0successful0cities.pdf?sequence=4&isAllowed=y. Accessed 3 February 2016.

Timar Afrique. *Plus de 35 ans de solutions innovantes.* Casablanca: Groupe Timar, 2016. http://www.timar-group.com/medias/images/Presentation_TIMAR_2016.pdf. Accessed 26 October 2016.

TMSA (Tanger Med Special Agency). *Tanger Med: Rapport Annuel 2020.* [2021]. https://www.tangermed.ma/wp-content/uploads/2021/04/Rapport_Annuel_Tangermed_VF-2020-WEB.pdf. Accessed 5 August 2021.

UNCTAD (United Nations Conference on Trade and Development). “Liner Shipping Connectivity Index, Quarterly: Q 1 2006–Q 2 2021.” UNCTADStat. http://unctadstat.unctad.org/wds/TableViewer/tableView.aspx?ReportId=92. Accessed 30 August 2021.

Valet, Vicky. “The World’s Most Reputable Cities 2018.” *Forbes* 23 August 2018. https://www.forbes.com/sites/vickyvalet/2018/08/23/the-worlds-most-reputable-cities-2018/?sh=1e11195c7b4d. Accessed 4 August 2021.

Vanolo, Alberto. *City Branding: The Ghostly Politics of Representation in Globalising Cities.* New York, Abingdon: Routledge, 2017.

van Schendel, Willem. “Geographies of Knowing, Geographies of Ignorance: Jumping Scale in Southeast Asia.” *Environment and Planning D: Society and Space* 20.6 (2002): 647–668.

Vuignier, Renaud. “Place Branding & Place Marketing 1976–2016: A Multidisciplinary Literature Review.” *International Review on Public and Nonprofit Marketing* 14.4 (2017): 447–473.

Ward, Stephen V. *Selling Places: The Marketing and Promotion of Towns and Cities 1850–2000.* London: E & FN Spon, 1998.

WeCasablanca. “Marque.” https://wecasablanca.com/en/we/. Accessed 30 July 2021.

Wikipédia. “Interface (géographie).” https://fr.wikipedia.org/wiki/Interface_(géographie). Accessed 26 July 2021.

Wippel, Steffen. “Stadtentwicklung in Tanger (Marokko): Rekonfigurationen des Urbanen im neoliberalen Kontext.” In *Neoliberale Urbanisierung: Stadtentwicklungsprozesse in der arabischen Welt*, edited by Ala Al-Hamarneh, Jonas Margraff, and Nadine Scharfenort, 33–74. Bielefeld: Transcript, 2019.

Wippel, Steffen. “Tangier’s Current Re-Configurations from a Multi-Scale Spatial Perspective: Emerging Transregional Ties and Local Repercussions.” In *Re-Configurations: Contextualising Transformation Processes and Lasting Crises in the Middle East and North Africa*, edited by Rachid Ouaissa, Friederike Pannewick, and Alena Strohmaier, 83–103. Wiesbaden: Springer VS, 2021a.

Wippel, Steffen. “The Globalisation of ‘Secondary Cities’ in the Middle East and North Africa: Conceptual Considerations and Empirical Findings.” *Hespèris-Tamuda* 56.4 (2021b): 47–95.

Wippel, Steffen. "Entre commerces & transports et loisirs & plaisirs: Reconfigurations et mondialisations du front de mer tangérois." *Cahiers d'EMAM* 34 (2022). https://journals.openedition.org/emam/4850. Accessed 16 May 2023.

Wippel, Steffen, Katrin Bromber, Christian Steiner, and Birgit Krawietz, eds. *Under Construction: Logics of Urbanism in the Gulf Region.* Farnham, Burlington: Ashgate, 2014.

Raffael Beier and Hassan Elmouelhi

Constructing Legitimacy through Pro-poor Housing? Branding Cities in Egypt and Morocco as "Slum-free"

1 Introduction

City branding has become an important component of neoliberal urban planning, spurred by the increasing popularity of entrepreneurial urbanism and growing international competition among cities to attract business, investors, and tourists.[1] Although the theoretical reasoning behind it derives mainly from experiences in Western contexts, where urban neoliberalism has resulted from growing private sector influence in response to dwindling public resources and a retreat of the state, city branding is also occurring in parts of North Africa, where strong states continue to shape urban planning agendas.[2] Here, neoliberal logics seem to be strongly interwoven with the central state's interest in the (re)development of its largest metropolitan areas, which Bogaert refers to as "neoliberal authoritarianism" in the case of Morocco.[3] Similarly, in Egypt, the growing influence of (foreign) private capital in planning and construction is entangled with the central state defending and enhancing its own leading role in strategic urban planning.[4] The crucial interdependence of neoliberal urban planning and the interests of a strong central state are most visible in urban megaprojects – Cairo's former vision Cairo2050 and the New Administrative Capital in Egypt[5] and CasablancaMarina, TangerMed, and the Bouregreg waterfront in Rabat/Salé in Morocco come to mind.[6] While their image aspirations follow neoliberal reasoning, their description as "presidential" or "royal" projects underlines the crucial political significance and leading role of the central state in city planning.[7] In their reach beyond city and national borders, such megaprojects serve two strategic purposes: to attract global attention and capital and to project images of modernity, progress, and po-

1 See Anttiroiko, 2015.
2 See Barthel, 2010; Steiner and Wippel, 2019.
3 See Bogaert, 2018.
4 See Barthel, 2010; Elmouelhi, 2019.
5 See Elmouelhi, 2019.
6 See Barthel and Planel, 2010; Mouloudi, 2010.
7 See Barthel, 2010.

https://doi.org/10.1515/9783110741100-027

litical stability to the outside world *and* its citizens in a bid to rectify reputations damaged by years of political turmoil.[8] By these means, urban megaprojects have become flagships for branding cities, nations, and ruling regimes.[9]

Branding strategies are not limited to megaprojects, however. Academically less well known is a related type of city branding directed at those parts of the urban society that state authorities perceive as a potential threat to new image constructions. This mostly means "slums" – *bidonvilles* in Morocco and *ashwa'eyat* in Egypt – that have suffered from negative stereotyping associating them with poverty, chaos, crime, and a lack of state control.[10] Constructed as *the* symbol of "underdeveloped" megacities,[11] the so-called slum has disturbed efforts by the ruling elite to project images of modernity, progress, and a powerful and caring state. In response, the "slum-free" brand has emerged in the context of the Millennium Development Goals (MDGs), supplementing classical forms of city branding strategies centring on megaprojects.[12] Achieving "slum-free" nations aims to show both external (i. e. tourists and investors) and internal stakeholders (i. e. marginalised populations) the government's dedication to "development" and a "pro-poor" attitude of the president or king.

This chapter sheds light on the histories, discourses, and consequences of the act and concept of branding cities as "slum-free" in Morocco and Egypt by regarding Morocco's *Villes Sans Bidonvilles* (Cities Without Slums) programme and the Egyptian government's goal of making the country "slum-free," initially by 2018.[13] Adopting a comparative approach, we aim to highlight an often-overlooked aspect of city branding, namely its effects on a local population rhetorically appropriated by state-led image building. Does city branding overlook its people or is it likely to drive improvement through socially sustainable housing solutions? Following these aims and questions, the chapter starts with a grounded literature discussion that reflects on the emergence of "slum-free" branding practices at the global level, as well as in Egypt and Morocco. Then, it reflects on slum dwellers' attitudes towards and perspectives on policies associated with "slum-free" branding, taking a comparative look at such policies' potential consequences for affected groups. It does so by building on previously published material gained through our

8 See Beier, 2019a.

9 See Steiner and Wippel, 2019.

10 See Bayat and Denis, 2000; Beier, 2020; Gilbert, 2007.

11 See Roy, 2011.

12 See Huchzermeyer, 2011.

13 After several extensions, the Egyptian Informal Settlements Development Fund announced in mid-2021 that the goal to make the country "slum-free" should be achieved by the end of 2021.

own, separate empirical field research in Casablanca and Cairo,[14] as well as the supervised work of students.[15] The chapter concludes with a comparative analysis of commonalities, but also differences between practices of "slum-free" branding in Egypt and Morocco.

2 Discourses, Interests, and Meanings Behind the "Slum-free" Brand

2.1 The Invention of the "Slum-free" Brand

The "slum-free" brand has its origins in international politics, dating back to the late 1990s when the United Nations Human Settlements Programme (UN-Habitat) and the World Bank jointly founded Cities Alliance to fight urban poverty and support liberal urban planning. The initiative was kick-started with the publication of the action plan "Cities Alliance for Cities Without Slums," which aimed to "improve the lives of 100 million slum dwellers by 2020."[16] In 2000, the UN repeated this objective in Millennium Development Goal 7.11, which initially quoted the initiative's bold slogan "Cities Without Slums." This reference was discarded some years later, but MDG 7.11 made the notion of "developed" cities as slum-free the norm.[17] Beyond the MDGs and its replacement by the more progressive Sustainable Development Goals (SDGs), the slogan continues to inform international policies and attitudes toward slums and is still part of the official logo of Cities Alliance.

Both the MDG 7.11 and Cities Alliance faced substantial criticism for bringing back the term "slum" with all its negative connotations.[18] Roy remarked that the slum has been made the "most common itinerary through which the Third World city (i.e. the megacity) is recognized."[19] In other words, MDG 7.11 with its focus on slums framed them as the ultimate expression of urban poverty and so-called underdevelopment.[20] Following this, Huchzermeyer criticises the normative slogan "Cities Without Slums" for offering governments a welcome opportuni-

14 See Beier, 2019b; Elmouelhi, 2014.
15 See Reda Ali, 2019.
16 Cities Alliance, 1999: 1.
17 See Huchzermeyer, 2011: 2.
18 See Gilbert, 2007.
19 Roy, 2011: 225.
20 See also Beier, 2020; Bhan, 2009.

ty to justify slum eradication policies with MDGs' call for development.[21] For example, in South Africa, "[f]raming 'slum' (...) clearance as a 'development' obligation under the Millennium Declaration (...) seemed convenient, particularly when the world was anxiously watching a country live up to the (...) requirements to host a soccer World Cup."[22] Although in their key publications[23] Cities Alliance and UN-Habitat have promoted participatory slum upgrading as "best practice," the less carefully formulated slogan has driven policies that tackle some of the symptoms rather than the causes of urban poverty, including by demolishing slums.[24] The quantitative methodology regarding the proportion of the urban population living in slums, informal settlements, or inadequate housing that is used to determine progress toward MDG 7.11 and its successor, SDG 11.1, has created a bad incentive for the large-scale demolition of slums.[25]

Most relevant to the remainder of this chapter is the crucial link of the "Cities Without Slums" slogan to neoliberal urbanism. Huchzermeyer writes that the international best practice of in-situ slum upgrading sits uncomfortably with international organisations promoting urban competitiveness and private engagement in city planning.[26] In contrast, some states may see slum eradication and resettlement as a welcome way to realise ambitious plans for urban redevelopment and "worlding."[27] This may include clearing centrally located land that is informally inhabited, displacing politically undesired population groups to urban margins and demolishing so-called urban eyesores to promote image- and profit-driven "urban fantasies."[28] The slogan "Cities Without Slums" has thus led to the resurgence of a developmentalist modernism fuelled by the neoliberal dogma of urban competitiveness and characterised by large-scale, often privately financed interventions prompting displacement and a growing number of evictions.[29] On the one hand, states have used the term "slum-free" to promote their visions of development and of a glass-and-steel modernity, which marks a visible counterpoint to the image of the congested and backward megacity in which the slum is central.[30] On the other hand, the slogan inspired a renaissance of large-scale housing and

---

21 See Huchzermeyer, 2011.
22 Huchzermeyer, 2011: 34–35.
23 See Cities Alliance, 1999; UN-Habitat, 2003.
24 See Bhan, 2009; Huchzermeyer, 2011.
25 See Beier, 2020.
26 See Huchzermeyer, 2011: 33.
27 Cf. Beier, 2019a.
28 Cf. Bhan, 2009; Watson, 2014.
29 See Brickell, Fernández Arrigoitia, and Vasudevan, 2017.
30 See Roy, 2011.

resettlement projects – some with explicit reference to the MDGs and “Cities Without Slums” – that move away from politically undesired in-situ upgrading policies.[31] Despite the tendency of these programmes to foster segregation, displacement, and marginalisation, politically, they mark and promote *visible* and measurable governmental engagement in the field of housing, as well as care for the poor, which may enhance the legitimacy of the ruling regime, as we will further outline below.

2.2 Moroccan Perspectives

In Morocco, the national *Villes Sans Bidonvilles* programme (VSBP) literally refers to the “Cities Without Slums” slogan. Established in 2004 and justified as a direct response to MDG 7.11, the aim of this housing and resettlement programme is to eradicate all *bidonvilles* in the country and to resettle its inhabitants mostly to apartment housing in new satellite neighbourhoods at the urban margins (cf. Fig. 1).[32] The Moroccan government evaluates the VSBP in a strictly quantitative way by regarding the number of cities that can officially be declared “slum-free” (in 2021, the official count was 59 out of 85 target cities).[33] Thus, VSBP’s primary objective is the physical and visible elimination of *bidonvilles.*[34]

Yet, the VSBP is framed as a social policy fostering inclusion in urban areas and has helped augment the image of King Mohammed VI as “the king of poor”[35] – a visible move away from that of his precursor, his less popular, strictly authoritarian father King Hassan II, who died in 1999.[36] In addition, in 2003, suicide attacks conducted by a number of Casablanca’s *bidonville* dwellers in the city centre, which some perceive as having directly influenced the development of the VSBP, seemed to provide proof that *bidonvilles* are breeding grounds of religious extremism, which (again) made their eradication a political urgency.[37] The offer of new and better housing to *bidonville* dwellers can thus be read in a sociopolitical way as a neo-patriarchal strategy to enhance the monarch’s own legitimacy. Hence, the call to make Morocco “slum-free” became part of the pro-poor branding strategy of the new royal regime, a “social” policy, and a powerful coun-

31 See Buckley, Kallergis, and Wainer, 2016.
32 See MHPV, 2012: 14.
33 See MHPV, 2021.
34 See Harroud, 2019: 16.
35 See Navez-Bouchanine, 2012: 171 and 216.
36 See Bogaert, 2018: 166.
37 See Navez-Bouchanine, 2012: 171.

Fig. 1: The construction of a new town on the urban margins of Salé, Morocco, for residents resettled from *bidonvilles*
Photo: Raffael Beier, 2021.

ter-narrative to the growing extremist influence on the urban peripheries following years of repression under King Hassan II. In his first *Discours du Trône* after the 2003 suicide attacks, King Mohammed VI underlined the precarious housing situation under which *bidonville* dwellers suffer and that "bear[s] the risk of becoming uncontrollable [so] that our cities would transform into places of exclusion, ostracism, [and] hate."[38]

Yet, the desire to make cities "slum-free" does more than brand the regime as pro-poor – it also serves a more economic purpose to showcase Morocco's development "progress" and "modernisation" to external and internal stakeholders. For example, in December 2012, one year after the start of the Arab Spring in Tunisia, the international marketing company Globus Vision described Morocco in a multiple-page supplement to the *Financial Times Germany* as an "impressive," economically strong provider of stability in a region in turmoil. The advertisement includ-

38 Quoted in MHPV, 2013: 75.

ed one short contribution titled "Morocco does away with its slums."[39] Thus, the declaration of 59 Moroccan cities as "slum-free" works to promote to potential investors the "success" of development agendas and efforts to eliminate signs of "backwardness" and "poverty." Focusing on a *bidonville* close to the airport of Casablanca, Arandel and Wetterberg note that the decision to demolish the houses and relocate the neighbourhood instead of upgrading existing structures was justified by the wish "to project an image of prosperity and modernity to visitors"[40] who arrive at the international airport.

The branding of cities in Morocco as "slum-free" is part of globally oriented city rebranding strategies. Under King Mohammed VI, Morocco has invested heavily in big urban projects aiming to create "world-class" cities following international role models.[41] Megaprojects such as CasablancaMarina and Casablanca Finance City aim to upgrade the image of Morocco's economic capital, transforming it with glass and steel into a modern, international financial hub attracting foreign direct investment and international business. Following Bogaert, these projects not only embody a national vision of urban modernity, but also simultaneously discredit slums as signs of backwardness, disturbing an image of "progress."[42] Indeed, in 2001, King Mohammed VI voiced his concerns about the growth of "insalubrious housing":

> This development (…) threatens our undertaken development efforts to ensure that our cities can attract productive investments. This is particularly relevant for the tourist sector, which is especially important to us. Architectural and urban beauty enhances the chance of attracting investment in this sector.[43]

In this sense, the "slum-free" brand becomes a tool used to turn neighbourhoods that supposedly embody poverty invisible[44] and to project images of urban modernity and national development to external stakeholders.

39 Globus Vision, 2012: 4, the authors' own translation.
40 Arandel and Wetterberg, 2013: 143.
41 See Barthel and Planel, 2010; Bogaert, 2018: 78–80; Mouloudi, 2010.
42 See Bogaert, 2018: 2.
43 Quoted in MHPV, 2013: 49.
44 See Harroud, 2019: 16.

2.3 Egyptian Perspectives

In Egypt, the "Egypt without Slums" plan (in Arabic *Miṣr bidūn 'aswā'iyyāt*) was announced during the first period of El Sisi's presidency in 2014, marking a new resoluteness and momentum in dealing with "the challenge of slums." In a related political speech, El Sisi referred to Egypt as a great country that should strive to become modern and progressive by providing all Egyptians the possibility to live a decent life: "It is impossible to allow such *ashwa'eyat* again!"[45] Following Sharp, "Egypt Without Slums" resembles a new war on urban informality that echoes former militarised approaches to slums dating back to the Siege of Imbaba in the 1990s.[46] However, unlike direct militarised confrontation, interventions today increasingly use the media to frame informality as a threat, on the one hand, and the government's efforts as proof of its care for its people and a desire for progress, on the other. Together with the construction of new cities and a new administrative capital, "Egypt Without Slums" forms part of "The New Republic" brand that aims to illuminate national power.

In June 2021, to celebrate seven years of El Sisi's presidency, a number of short national television advertisements included a new phrase – #thenewrepublic – that was to be used to brand efforts by the Egyptian government to renew its cities, including through slum relocation projects. "The Egyptians have succeeded in developing 298 *ashwa'eyat* unsafe areas in different governorates (...). 177,500 families have received new apartments in safe and healthy areas," one such advertisement proclaimed. Likewise, this on-going media campaign helps show the regime's care for the poor. For example, a documentary published by the Moral Affairs Department of the military in February 2021[47] compares the "miserable" conditions of the slum areas where 18,000 former *ashwa'eyat* families lived with their new housing environment in Cairo's new showcase resettlement site Al Asmarat (Fig. 2). The short documentary quotes several residents expressing their gratitude to the government for giving them the opportunity to improve their quality of life and for its care for the future of their children, moving them away from the suffering in *ashwa'eyat.* Such media discourses not only help to cast "Egypt Without Slums" as a pro-poor brand, but also foster the stigmatisation of informal areas. At the same

45 All quotes in this and the next paragraph are from the official Egyptian TV channels during the July 2021 celebration of the 1952 revolution and translated by the authors.

46 In 1992, the militant Islamist group *Al-Gama'a al-Islamiyya* announced the establishment of an independent Islamic state in the working-class district of Imbaba. The Egyptian state responded by putting the area under siege, mobilising a huge number of troops. See Bayat and Denis, 2000; Sharp, 2022.

47 See dmc, 2021.

time, resettlement sites such as Al Asmarat are closely supervised and controlled by urban management units often run by civil servants with a military background. On the one hand, such management units work to brand the resettlement site as "modern," because of their similarity to those of upper-class private compounds. On the other hand, they can be seen as a way of ensuring close control of residents who the state has historically perceived as a potential threat.

Since the Siege of Imbaba, the Egyptian state has considered urban informality an urgent security issue requiring immediate intervention.[48] At the national level, the Egyptian state created the Informal Settlements Development Fund (ISDF) through a presidential decree in 2008 in reaction to a rockslide in Cairo's Doueka area in Manshiet Naser. Shortly after its inception in 2009, the ISDF classified informal areas as either "unsafe" or "unplanned."[49] Unsafe areas, representing only one per cent of the total urban area in Egypt,[50] mainly require the relocation of dwellers to resettlement sites due to the supposed hazardous conditions of the sites. ISDF press releases, supported by a number of interviews with experts who are close to the process of decision-making, reveal that efforts since 2014 have focussed mainly on the demolition of unsafe areas and the relocation of their residents to new housing. The most recent ISDF progress report states that 41 unsafe areas remain all over Egypt and require the relocation of its inhabitants and the construction of 50,778 housing units before the end of 2021. The Egyptian government used this quantitative approach to show through the media the decrease in the number of unsafe areas. The ISDF provides each governorate with a list of target areas containing some basic information, including a map, the number of residents, and their assigned priority. In 2016, the ISDF allocated more funding for the construction of new housing units than in previous years (around 39 billion EGP, or approx. 2 billion EUR).[51] The governors have striven to facilitate relocation as fast as possible so that they could proudly declare "their" governorate slum-free. During the celebrations of National Day in the Port Said Governorate in December 2018, Port Said was proclaimed the first slum-free governorate.

Recent government action has revealed renewed political will to tackle unplanned areas, which is occurring at a fast pace and before introducing new laws or clear decision-making and implementation procedures. In closed workshops with selected practitioners in 2020, the ISDF presented its updated categorisation of unplanned areas together with the General Organization for Physical Planning (GOPP) and UN-Habitat Egypt. They now include centres of capital cities

48 See Sims, 2010.

49 See Khalifa, 2015.

50 See Hanafi, 2021.

51 See Hanafi, 2021.

Fig. 2: Aerial view of the Al Asmarat housing project showing the football field, church, service shops, and apartment buildings
Photo: Reham Reda Ali, 2019. Courtesy of the photographer.

of governorates as well as heritage areas. However, by August 2021, the prime minister had not approved or published these new categories. Despite this lack of institutionalisation of the new approaches, they are already being propagated through media channels. Ezbet El Haggana, an unplanned area in the east of Cairo, is a good example of how decisions are taken following presidential announcements and political propaganda. In May 2020, national television channels highlighted the president's visit to the area, accompanied by high government officials. During the orchestrated discussion, leading politicians highlighted the crucial need to improve the lives of the residents, emphasising the strong concern and clear will of the president in this regard.

3 Slum Dwellers’ Perspectives of Cities Becoming “Slum-free”

3.1 Stigmatisation in Egypt and Morocco

In Morocco, most slum dwellers have welcomed the royal initiative to resettle them in so-called *maisons en dur* (solidly built houses); some communities even took to the streets to demand quicker intervention by the state. While major opposition to the royal VSBP is relatively rare, resistance has centred rather on the means of implementation by criticising the unequal and corrupt allocation of property titles, insufficient investment in resettlement sites, and forced evictions.[52] The tendency to approve the housing programme is certainly driven by precarious living conditions in *bidonvilles* and a popular belief in the benevolence of the king. Yet, much of its support relates to the stigmatisation of *bidonvilles* (and stigmatising assumptions about their living conditions) as embodied by calls for “Cities Without Slums.”[53] For instance, in Casablanca’s largest *bidonville* Er-Rhamna, a young male resident declared:

> People in Er-Rhamna are divided in their opinions of resettlement. Many want to stay, but the majority want to leave. Many do not see the problems they will face. They would even accept it if they had to move to the moon. Discrimination is a huge problem. From birth, people here get told that they are second-class people.[54]

Thus, experiences of place-based discrimination (on the job market, in schools, with state representatives, etc.) drive people’s desire to move out of their stigmatised neighbourhoods[55] and at the same time create glorified projections of life after resettlement.[56]

The stigmatisation of *bidonvilles* in Morocco is not a new phenomenon, but the 2003 suicide attacks that triggered the VSBP intensified existing negative stereotypes.[57] In daily interactions with classmates or taxi drivers, many residents have avoided mentioning where they live out of shame and fear of direct stigma-

52 See Navez-Bouchanine, 2012.
53 See Beier, 2019b: 289–291.
54 Interview by Raffael Beier, 14 March 2017.
55 See Beier, 2019b: 172–173.
56 Cf. Zaki, 2007.
57 See Navez-Bouchanine, 2012: 212; Beier, 2020.

tisation.[58] Furthermore, the VSBP cemented the conviction that *bidonvilles* should not be part of cities, marking its residents even more as undesired urban dwellers. Thus, the "slum-free" brand has both enhanced residents' readiness to accept resettlement and their "displaceability"[59] following a further weakening of their urban citizenship status.

In Egypt, case studies in Cairo have shown similar stigmatisation of *ashwa'eyat* dwellers.[60] *Ashwa'eyat* residents experience place-based discrimination especially when dealing with the formal system – when being stopped at police checkpoints, when applying for jobs, or even when asking a girl living in a formal area for her hand in marriage. This also applies to residents of unplanned, well-established *ashwa'eyat*, even if their living conditions are better and their economic and social standards are higher than those living in "unsafe areas." Following the revolutionary protests in 2011, for example, residents of Ezbet Elhaggana wanted to rename their place of residency "Al Amal" (The Hope) to get rid of the stigma attached to their neighbourhood.[61] Recently, President El Sisi endorsed the renaming to show his commitment to tackling "unplanned areas." Furthermore, our previous fieldwork in Cairo showed that many *ashwa'eyat* residents, especially the youth, name another nearby formal area as their place of living. Several interviewed *ashwa'eyat* residents mentioned that after moving to the area, they preferred not to change their address on their national ID to avoid being harassed by police officers if they were asked to show it.[62] Arguably, many people hope to escape the stigma through resettlement. However, Al Asmarat residents are obliged to change the address stated on their national ID following their relocation. As all Al Asmarat residents have been relocated from *ashwa'eyat* areas, this makes them identifiable as former slum dwellers.[63]

3.2 Perspectives of Resettlement: Between Hope and Uncertainty

As argued above, in Morocco, experiences of territorial stigmatisation and discrimination have influenced a tendency among *bidonville* residents to welcome the royal VSBP. Some have interpreted it as the late recognition of their legitimate

58 See Beier, 2020.
59 See Yiftachel, 2020.
60 See Bayat and Denis, 2000; Elmouelhi, 2014; Reda Ali, 2019.
61 See Elmouelhi, 2013.
62 See Elmouelhi, 2014.
63 See Reda Ali, 2019

urban citizenship after years of empty promises, social marginalisation, and political repression.[64] Thus, a general expectation of upward social mobility is palpable, notwithstanding diverse individual attitudes towards resettlement. The prospect of a gain in status is strongly tied to the aesthetics of the new *maisons en dur*, which seem to conform more to an ordinary and socially respected way of inhabiting the city and which signify freedom from the stigma of *bidonvilles*.[65] From the perspective of the residents, resettlement presents a unique opportunity to renegotiate their place in society (expressed by a significant investment in the interior of the new apartments) and to move up the social ladder. Related hopes range from better protection from the elements and improved services and infrastructure to the diminishing presence of social problems such as youth delinquency, unemployment, and drug abuse. Thus, the macro-political agenda of achieving "slum-free" cities translates on the ground into a claim for recognised urban citizenship and improved living conditions.

Yet, there are also considerable uncertainties in the process of resettlement that have historically sparked opposition from *bidonville* residents. Most significant is the question of affordability, which may explain much of the failure of past attempts to relocate *bidonville* dwellers. In the context of Casablanca, the creation of a new financing scheme based on small-scale third-party funding has made it possible for many inhabitants to become owners of a new apartment at almost no cost.[66] Here, two families relocated from the *bidonville* are allocated one plot in the new town and instead of constructing the four-storey house themselves, they ask a third party to build the house and to provide temporary accommodation during the construction period. In return, the third party becomes the owner of the two lower floors, while the other two households each own one of the two topmost floors. Due to improved affordability, this "third-party scheme" has strengthened residents' approval of resettlement. However, the scheme has created new forms of uncertainty and risk, often caused by a sudden retreat by the third party, for example due to financial difficulties. Residents have had to cope with prolonged stays in temporary accommodation, incomplete and inadequate constructions, and additional administrative charges imposed on them.

In Egypt, resettlement was unquestionably the government's preferred policy in dealing with *ashwa'eyat* until 2010, although international development stakeholders saw it as a form of forced eviction.[67] After the 2011 Egyptian Revolution, the state for a number of years preferred not to resort to evictions from unsafe

64 See Navez-Bouchanine and Dansereau, 2002.
65 See Beier, 2021.
66 For more details, see Beier, 2021.
67 See Amnesty International, 2011.

areas. At present, resettlement to new housing is propagated by the media as one of the political achievements of the Egyptian state. The new housing projects in various cities have uniform unit designs and building prototypes financed through a special fund called *Tahya Masr* (Long Live Egypt) that is supported by a number of Egyptian businessmen and corporations.

Thus, resettlement as a concept carries contradictory meanings – it has been met with resistance, especially in the years directly following the 2011 revolution, while also embodying hope for a better life as marketed in national media. Certainly, for many groups of residents in unsafe areas, resettlement supports their hopes and aspirations for better living conditions and a better future for their children. However, resettlement creates several fears, including residents' uncertainty whether they are eligible to receive an apartment – this is due to possible corruption and their mistrust of public authorities. Furthermore, resettlement may also disadvantageously affect their means of generating an income, their daily routine, and their social life. These are discussed in detail in the following section.

4 Consequences of "Slum-free" Branding: New Everyday Realities Following Displacement and Resettlement

Large-scale housing programmes providing supposedly better housing to people living in informal areas may be politically framed as pro-poor policies. But despite potential gains in shelter quality, housing programmes that leave little choice to its "beneficiaries" inevitably create adverse effects often related to reduced accessibility and the changing character of neighbourhood relations.[68] This section describes the major challenges posed to resettled residents in Casablanca and Cairo by housing programmes associated with branding cities as "slum-free."

4.1 Access to the City and Urban Job Markets

In both cities, residents are usually resettled further away from the city centre and their previous place of residence, apart from a few exceptions such as Douar Skouila in Casablanca and El Max in Alexandria. Such constrained moves to peripheral sites have had a negative impact on resettled residents' ability to access

68 See Beier et al., 2022; Buckley, Kallergis and Wainer, 2016; Koenig, 2018.

central urban functions, including higher education institutions and employment opportunities. Common political assumptions about the continuation of employment and urban livelihoods as relatively straightforward following resettlement can be refuted.[69] Resettled former residents of Casablanca's *bidonville* Karyan Central, for example, experienced difficulties in continuing their previous jobs because even unreliable transport in the form of informal bus services and shared taxis is expensive.[70] Consequently, many factory workers who had been earning a minimum wage and who could previously walk to their workplace felt compelled to quit their jobs after relocation. And even though many residents resettled to Nouvelle Lahraouiyine found alternative employment, jobs closer to the resettlement site are scarce and more challenging to find. In addition, shop owners and market traders in Nouvelle Lahraouiyine suffer from a much smaller client base than in their previous location close to Karyan Central, which was famous for its central market.[71] Finally, in Nouvelle Lahraouiyine, the share of youth enrolled in higher education is significantly smaller than those living in more centrally located *bidonvilles*. The reasons, again, are unsafe and expensive means of transportation and an average increase in households' fixed expenditure.[72]

These observations are echoed in Cairo, where Abouelmagd showed that inhabitants of Ezbet Haridy, an informal area in Abbassiya near the centre of Cairo, had less financial security after resettlement: "Their economic status deteriorated due to loss of jobs, labour market, services around their old slum and loss of their financial assets that they left as animals and furniture."[73] In the case of Al Asmarat, the government tried to choose a site closer to the city to avoid the disadvantages of relocation to the city's periphery. However, despite the relative proximity of Asmarat to the city centre, transportation costs to access the closest shopping centres and places of work are still a financial burden. Some of the residents considered Al Asmarat a prime location due to its proximity to the upmarket Al Asmarat Heights gated community, but still expressed their dissatisfaction with the cost of and time taken to make daily trips after relocation.[74] Moreover, informal income generation in public spaces or on the ground floor of apartment buildings is banned under the regulations of the Al Asmarat housing management unit, which considers them "uncivilised" practices, even when this is the only source of income for certain families. Such bans thus further limit resettled people's oppor-

69 See Koenig, 2018.
70 Similar observations for the case of Rabat/Salé were made by Harroud, 2019.
71 See Beier, 2019b: 239–251.
72 See Beier, 2019b: 265–267.
73 See Abouelmagd, 2014.
74 See Reda Ali, 2019.

tunities for income generation in comparison with their previous places of residency. In addition, resettlement projects oblige residents to pay a monthly maintenance fee (approx. 300–400 EGP, or around 15–20 EUR), creating an additional financial burden that makes living at the resettlement sites less affordable.

4.2 Neighbourhood Relations

A second major challenge for relocated residents besides reduced access to urban economic opportunities is changes in social relations after relocation. In both countries, housing programmes contributing to the objective of "slum-free" cities focus on constructing standardised multi-storey apartment blocks in dormitory settlements that emerge from planners' drawing boards. These new built environments lead to new patterns of social interaction and the loss of the earlier, more consolidated and socially dense neighbourhoods often consisting of incrementally improved self-built houses. Several scholars have found Morocco's resettlement contributing to an erosion of previous social networks that were characterised by strong social ties and solidarity within multiple small neighbourhood pockets in *bidonvilles.*[75] A quantitative comparison of relationships among neighbours in Nouvelle Lahraouiyine and the inhabitants of Casablanca's *bidonville* Er-Rhamna, for example, showed that the former have significantly less trust in their neighbours, communicate less frequently with each of them, and help them less regularly. This was confirmed by statements by resettled residents who described their longing for their former social life in *bidonvilles.*[76]

In Egypt, President El Sisi praised the provision of finished and furnished apartments to relocated residents in Al Asmarat, as well as the construction of communal spaces and sports facilities, calling it a model that should be implemented across the country. However, the relocation process ignored the social relations entrenched over years of residing in *ashwa'eyat.* Relocated families were haphazardly assigned houses with no consideration of existing social ties among former neighbours and their desire to retain them.

In both countries, residents from the same former neighbourhood pocket have now been resettled in different locations, which has forced them to adapt to new spatial realities *and* new neighbours. In addition, under Morocco's third-party funding scheme, all resettled people moved to the upper floors of apartment buildings, which reduced access to public life on the streets compared with the denser

75 See Harroud, 2019; Zaki, 2007.
76 See Beier, 2019b: 233–235.

informal settlements, where social relations were fostered in shared (semi-)public spaces. Street life has been further compromised by regulations restricting informal street trade and markets, as mentioned above. Furthermore, the resettlement sites hardly allow for resident-led construction and maintenance of either infrastructure or housing – a fundamental domain of mutual help in *bidonvilles* and *ashwa'eyat*. Finally, we should note that the dissolution of previously existing social structures need not be viewed in a negative light – some resettled residents in Morocco, for example, have also appreciated a more anonymous social life. However, the social reconfigurations resulting from resettlement certainly pose a significant challenge to residents, affecting their feelings of well-being, belonging, and safety after resettlement.

5 Discussion of Findings and Conclusion

In Egypt and Morocco, the objective of "slum-free" cities that forms a central part of national branding strategies has triggered nationwide programmes that support the construction of low-income housing to provide shelter for residents resettled from so-called slums. A closer look at flagship projects like Al Asmarat in Cairo and Nouvelle Lahraouiyine in Casablanca reveals that slums are considered a challenge that can easily be addressed by accelerated housing construction. Such product-oriented approaches tend to ignore well-known adverse effects of relocation projects, such as negative financial impacts on resettled families, increased distance from economic opportunities, on-going stigmatisation, and weakened social cohesion as a result of the violent severing of strong social ties that marked life in so-called slums. Providing fully furnished flats in "orderly," organised settlements, such as Al Asmarat, seems preferred to continued access to the labour market and the protection of social networks.

Yet, despite their questionable effects, resettlement and housing projects have the power to be publicly marketed as positive political actions. They are not only about constructing houses for the poor, but also about enhancing political legitimacy. Like other urban megaprojects, resettlement projects support the construction sector and are used to showcase developmental progress and modernity; state-controlled television channels are primarily used for this purpose. These efforts also serve to attract the interest of potential and existing external stakeholders and investors. At the same time, advertising these projects serves to show that the state actively pursues inclusivity and social justice agendas and, hence, tries to balance the opposite impressions of a state mainly committed to exclusive megaprojects such as CasablancaMarina or Egypt's New Administrative Capital. We argue that slogans such as "Egypt Without Slums" and "Cities Without Slums" are part of wider branding strategies that seek to enhance the legitimacy of regimes under political pressure by promoting images of benevolent and pro-poor rulers concerned with the progressive development of "their" countries. The slogans aim to underline a certain political potency of authoritarian regimes, with striking similarities between a kingdom such as Morocco and a republic such as Egypt, in seeking rapid improvements in the quality of urban life, especially for underprivileged, vulnerable population groups. Thus, low-income housing and resettlement projects are alluring options for such regimes, especially in volatile political contexts in which regimes fear renewed political unrest and a loss of legitimacy.

Bibliography

Abouelmagd, Shaimaa. *The Rehabilitation of Inner City Slums in Cairo – A Livelihood Perspective: The Case Study of Ezbet-Haridy, Cairo – Egypt.* Paper presented at the Contemporary Urban Issues Conference, Informality: Rethinking the Urban. Istanbul: 13–15 November 2014.

Amnesty International. *"We are not Dirt:" Forced Evictions in Egypt's Informal Settlements.* London: Amnesty International, 2011.

Anttiroiko, Ari-Veikko. "City Branding as a Response to Global Intercity Competition." *Growth and Change* 46.2 (2015): 233–252.

Arandel, Christian, and Anna Wetterberg. "Between 'Authoritarian' and 'Empowered' Slum Relocation: Social Mediation in the Case of Ennakhil, Morocco." *Cities* 30 (2013): 140–148.

Barthel, Pierre-Arnaud. "Arab Mega-Projects: Between the Dubai Effect, Global Crisis, Social Mobilization and a Sustainable Shift." *Built Environment* 36.2 (2010): 132–145.

Barthel, Pierre-Arnaud, and Sabine Planel. "Tanger-Med and Casa-Marina, Prestige Projects in Morocco: New Capitalist Frameworks and Local Context." *Built Environment* 36.2 (2010): 176–191.

Bayat, Asef, and Eric Denis. "Who Is Afraid of *Ashwaiyyat?* Urban Change and Politics in Egypt." *Environment & Urbanization* 12.2 (2000): 185–199.

Beier, Raffael. "Worlding Cities in the Middle East and North Africa: Arguments for a Conceptual Turn." *Middle East–Topics & Arguments* 12.1 (2019a): 28–34. https://doi.org/10.17192/meta.2019.12.7828.

Beier, Raffael. *From the City to the Desert: Analysing Shantytown Resettlement in Casablanca, Morocco, from Residents' Perspectives.* Berlin: Logos Verlag, 2019b.

Beier, Raffael. "Ganz gewöhnliche Viertel: Stigma und Realitäten in Casablancas Slum Er-Rhamna." *sub\urban. zeitschrift für kritische stadtforschung* 8.3 (2020): 73–96.

Beier, Raffael. "From Visible Informality to Splintered Informalities: Reflections on the Production of 'Formality' in a Moroccan Housing Programme." *International Journal of Urban and Regional Research* 45.6 (2021): 930–947.

Beier, Raffael, Amanine Spire, Marie Bridonneau, and Corentin Chanet. "Introduction: Positioning 'Urban Resettlement' in the Global Urban South." In *Urban Resettlement in the Global South. Lived Experiences of Housing and Infrastructure between Displacement and Relocation*, edited by Raffael Beier, Amandine Spire, and Marie Bridonneau, 1–21. Abingdon, New York: Routledge, 2022.

Bhan, Gautam. "'This Is No Longer the City I Once Knew': Evictions, the Urban Poor and the Right to the City in Millennial Delhi." *Environment and Urbanisation* 21.1 (2009): 127–147.

Bogaert, Koenraad. *Globalized Authoritarianism: Megaprojects, Slums, and Class Relations in Urban Morocco.* Minneapolis: University of Minnesota Press, 2018.

Brickell, Katherine, Melissa Fernández Arrigoitia, and Alexander Vasudevan, eds. *Geographies of Forced Eviction: Dispossession, Violence, Resistance.* London: Palgrave MacMillan, 2017.

Buckley, Robert M., Achilles Kallergis, and Laura Wainer. "Addressing the Housing Challenge: Avoiding the Ozymandias Syndrome." *Environment and Urbanization* 28.1 (2016): 119–138.

Cities Alliance. *Cities Alliance for Cities Without Slums: Action Plan for Moving Slum Upgrading to Scale.* Washington: Cities Alliance & World Bank, 1999.

Elmouelhi, Hassan. "Revolution, Political Transformation and Urban Space in 'Ezbet El-Haggana.'" Cairobserver 18 January 2013. https://cairobserver.com/post/40833532410/revolution-political-transformation-and-urban. Accessed 10 June 2021.

Elmouelhi, Hassan. *Culture and Informal Urban Development: The Case of Cairo Informal Settlements.* Berlin: Dr. Köster, 2014.

Elmouelhi, Hassan. "New Administrative Capital in Cairo: Power, Urban Development vs. Social Injustice – an Egyptian Model of Neoliberalism." In *Neoliberale Urbanisierung: Stadtentwicklungsprozesse in der arabischen Welt*, edited by Ala Al-Hamarneh, Jonas Margraff, and Nadine Scharfenort, 215–254. Bielefeld: Transcript, 2019.

dmc. "Man aḥyāhā—min kābūs ilā ḥaqīqa rā'i'a.. sukkān ḥayy al-Asmarāt yu'abbirūn 'an sa'ādatihim bi-intiqālihim li-madīnatihim al-ǧadīda [Whoever Made it Alive – From a Nightmare to a Wonderful Truth: Residents of Al Asmarat Area Express Their Happiness about Moving to Their New City]." *YouTube* 11 February 2021. https://www.youtube.com/watch?v=zSd9aS_9acU. Accessed 29 November 2021.

Gilbert, Alan. "The Return of the Slum: Does Language Matter?" *International Journal of Urban and Regional Research* 31.4 (2007): 697–713.

Globus Vision. "Marokko schafft Armenviertel ab." Special supplement. *Financial Times Deutschland* 5 December 2012: 4. http://www.theworldfolio.com/files/old/1354707855.pdf. Accessed 27 October 2021.

Hanafi, Ihab. "Masr Gamila." TV program. *Channel 2* 7 July 2021. https://www.youtube.com/watch?v=ocM6pT5UDQI. Accessed 28 July 2021.

Harroud, Tarik. "D'une marginalité à l'autre: Droit à la ville et pratiques de réadaptation des 'bidonvillois' dans les nouvelles marges urbaines de Rabat." *Annales de géographie* 729–730 (2019): 14–37.

Huchzermeyer, Marie. *Cities With "Slums:" From Informal Settlement Eradication to a Right to the City in Africa.* Cape Town: University of Cape Town Press, 2011.

Khalifa, Marwa. "Evolution of Informal Settlements Upgrading Strategies in Egypt: From Negligence to Participatory Development." *Ain Shams Engineering Journal* 6.4 (2015), 1151–1159.

Koenig, Dolores. "Problems Endure Despite Policies: Urban Livelihoods After Forced Displacement." In *Challenging the Prevailing Paradigm of Displacement and Resettlement: Risks, Impoverishment, Legacies, Solutions,* edited by Michael M. Cernea and Julie K. Maldonado, 75–94. Abingdon, New York: Routledge, 2018.

MHPV (Ministère de l'Habitat, de l'Urbanisme et de la Politique de la Ville). *National Report: Curbing Shanty-Towns: The Moroccan Experience.* Rabat, 2012.

MHPV (Ministère de l'Habitat, de l'Urbanisme et de la Politique de la Ville). *Discours et Interviews de Sa Majesté le Roi Mohammed VI: "Habitat, Urbanisme et Politique de la Ville."* Service de la Gestion des Archives et de la Documentation, 2013. https://aua.ma/wp-content/uploads/2018/02/Royaume-du-Maroc.pdf. Accessed 21 June 2021.

MHPV (Ministère de l'Aménagement du Territoire National, de l'Urbanisme, de l'Habitat et de la Politique de la Ville). "Le programme national 'villes sans bidonvilles' (VSB)." http://www.mhpv.gov.ma/?page_id=956. Accessed 21 June 2021.

Mouloudi, Hicham. "Reaction 'From Below' to Big Urban Projects: The Case of Rabat." *Built Environment* 36.2 (2010): 230–244.

Navez-Bouchanine, Françoise. "Les nouvelles voies de la négociation dans les politiques de résorption des bidonvilles au Maroc: Entre recasement et accompagnement social." In *Effets sociaux des politiques urbaines. L'entre-deux des politiques institutionnelles et des dynamiques sociales: Algérie, Maroc, Liban, Mauritanie*, edited by Françoise Navez-Bouchanine and Agnès Deboulet, 166–218. Paris: Karthala, 2012.

Navez-Bouchanine, Françoise, and Francine Dansereau. "Les stratégies résidentielles dans la ville fragmentée: Le cas de la ville marocaine." In *Gestion du développement urbain et stratégies résidentielles des habitants*, edited by Francine Dansereau and Françoise Navez-Bouchanine, 19–65. Paris: l'Harmattan, 2002.

Reda Ali, Reham. *State-led Slum Relocation and Destination Satisfaction: Assessing the Quality of Housing Alternatives for the Poor – A Case Study of El-Asmarat Project, Egypt.* Master's thesis, Technical University of Berlin, 2019.

Roy, Ananya. *"Slumdog Cities: Rethinking Subaltern Urbanism." International Journal of Urban and Regional Research* 35.2 (2011): 223–238.

Sharp, Deen. "Haphazard Urbanisation: Urban Informality, Politics and Power in Egypt." *Urban Studies* 59.4 (2022): 734–749.

Sims, David. *Understanding Cairo: The Logic of a City Out of Control.* Cairo: American University in Cairo Press, 2010.

Steiner, Christian, and Steffen Wippel. "Urban Development in the Middle East and North Africa: Deconstructing Visions, Politics, and Identities." *Middle East–Topics & Arguments* 12.1 (2019): 5–16. https://doi.org/10.17192/meta.2019.12.8022.

United Nations Human Settlements Programme (UN Habitat). *The Challenge of Slums: Global Report on Human Settlements 2003.* London and Sterling: Earthscan, 2003.

Watson, Vanessa. "Seeing from the South: Refocusing Urban Planning on the Globe's Central Urban Issues." *Urban Studies* 46.11 (2014): 2259–2275.

Yiftachel, Orel. "From Displacement to Displaceability: A Southeastern Perspective on the New Metropolis." *City* 24.1–2 (2020): 151–165.

Zaki, Lamia. "Après le bidonville: Les relogés de Lahjajma (Casablanca): Entre déni et nostalgie." In *L'enseignement supérieur dans la mondialisation libérale*, edited by Sylvie Mazzella, 277–294. Tunis: IRMC, 2007.

Khaled Adham

The Power of the Speculative Image: On Branding Desert Developments and Selling Cairo's Urban Future

1 Introduction

In his book *Egypt's Desert Dreams*, the planner and economist David Sims provides an overview of the role of desert developments for successive governments in Egypt in creating the possibilities of future wealth by speculatively building real estate and by land sales.[1] One of the striking features in all the new desert cities, observes Sims, is the presence of "superblock" concessions, sold by the government to real estate developers, which always abut other large areas designated for individual land plots and for social housing estates. In recent times, these superblocks have dominated newer desert developments, particularly in the eastern and western desert expansions of metropolitan Cairo. In the New Administrative Capital, which is currently under construction, the government is taking a step further: the new city is entirely planned for and built by large-scale public and private property developers; its striking feature is the urban typology of a low-density, gated residential community.

The past four decades witnessed not only the transformation of desert lands through major urban projects, but also the steady rise of a real estate market, with successive governments progressively portraying large-scale property developers as the driving force of urban development and economic progress. True, urban observers in Egypt already began noticing these desert expansions and transformations in the late 1970s. From the turn of the 21st century onward, however, academic writing on these desert developments started to view urban production in Egypt as part of a wider state neoliberal economic shift, which they contend began in the early 1990s.[2] It is important to emphasise that these claims have always been empirically buttressed by referring particularly to these desert developments and more specifically to the gated residential communities as spectacularising Egypt's neoliberalisation.[3]

1 See Sims, 2015.
2 See Singerman and Ammar, 2006.
3 See, for one example, Denis, 2006.

https://doi.org/10.1515/9783110741100-028

Building on these researches, I want to further investigate the relationship between the developers' branding techniques and the economy associated with the realisation of their real estate offerings. Specifically, I will focus on showing how the use of promotional methods and visualisation techniques by large-scale real estate developers working on desert developments is intertwined with the political economy of the urbanisation process of today's Cairo. To do so, I build on the premise that the planning, designing, and building of new cities and large-scale urban developments reflect the way we organise the relationship between our imagined urban future and our lived present. I will argue that the functional power of the various visual and experiential techniques used to sell housing units lies in their ability to insinuate themselves into our memories as "urban lifestyle script" materials – an analytical concept that refers to a set of loosely shared expectations of a globally oriented class of citizens about the quality of certain lifestyle forms in a prototypical global city – that can be used to turn the future into extractable revenue for the present. To present my argument, the following discussions are divided into three main sections. In the first section, I present a very brief history of the recent re-emergence of large-scale desert property developers. I say "re-emergence," because conquering the desert through large-scale urban housing development is not without precedent in the city's modern history. This developmental logic goes back to the turn of the 20th century, to the establishment of the suburb Heliopolis by a private, foreign property developer.[4] What distinguishes the current round, however, I argue, is not only the current scale of these desert expansions, but also the active involvement of the state in the process, particularly in discovering the economic value of desert lands and in gradually adopting branding and promotional methods of new cities similar to those of private developers. In the second section, I show the functional aspect of the promotional methods used in selling the future developments and how they help construct a particular memory of that future in order to sell it. To do so, I discuss three cases from these large-scale developments. In the final section, I show how this memory constructed through promotional materials is linked to the functioning of the new economy, which is increasingly geared towards extracting revenue from the future through speculation.

4 See Adham, 2004.

2 The Developer and the Entrepreneurial Government: a Brief History

Urban planning is self-evidently an interdisciplinary field oriented towards the future. By definition, planning is a process of making choices among the options concerning the future that are available today, and then securing their implementation. As a temporal bridge between the future and the present, the planning and building of new cities and large-scale land developments reflect the way we organise and structure the relationship between our imagined urban future and our lived present. No doubt, architects and planners have always used models and perspective drawings as representational tools to show their clients how their buildings and residential developments would look after completion. It was only in the past two decades, however, that large-scale property developers and the government used such visualisations more frequently to brand and sell their housing and commercial space offerings. Before this date, the representational mode of planning new cities was limited to technical reports and land use drawings and analyses that only planners and specialised professionals could critically read, visualise, and comprehend. Today, the visualisations of the future of all so-called fourth-generation desert cities appear more like collections of eye-catching images and computer-generated videos of architectural and urban solutions similar to the ones private real estate developers produce to market and sell their luxurious residential units and commercial spaces in large-scale developments to those eager to invest. This state entrepreneurial spirit, particularly with regard to desert developments, has a history.

A plausible date to locate the origin of the government's discovery of the economic value of desert land is the 1979 inauguration of a subsidiary of the Ministry of Housing and Reconstruction, namely, the New Urban Communities Authority (NUCA). From its inception, the state land-managing organisation was assigned the developmental mission of planning and managing the economic use of the desert lands for a better redistribution of the population out of the congested Nile Valley, as well as to maximise the economic returns from these developments, mainly through land sales.[5] One of its early development ventures, however, was to build a luxury summer resort on the North Coast in the early 1980s. From the start, therefore, NUCA was a "planner and regulator on the one hand, and a developer and investor on the other."[6] It is a fact, however, that during this initial stage, new des-

5 See Adly, 2020.
6 Adly, 2020: 169.

ert lands were developed mainly to receive working and professional classes through the construction of state-subsidised housing blocks and to welcome citizen-investors through the allocation of individual residential plots.[7]

Towards the mid-1990s, another change within the government took place. Characterised by the implementation of a "much more state capitalist mode of development, large private real-estate developers became the main agents of progress."[8] Massive amounts of serviced desert lands were sold to private developers at negotiated below-market prices. NUCA also established partnerships with private developers to build residential compounds.[9] This period witnessed the emergence of gated residential compounds in the Al-Shaykh Zayed, New Cairo, and Al-Shorouq desert cities. Interestingly, at the time, these new cities had few public housing projects remaining in them that were from older developmental schemes. Al-Shaykh Zayed City, for example, was originally planned as a mixed-income city; it transformed as NUCA discovered the profit-making potential of land sales to developers. Thus we find luxury housing accommodating 71 % of the city's residents, while low-income housing accounts for only 15 %.[10] Today, NUCA still continues to establish partnerships with private developers in large-scale urban projects, such as Noor Capital Gardens in East Cairo, a 32 billion USD mega-development that will house a population of over 600,000 when completed in 2026. Once more, ultra-realistic videos and computer-generated images of the city are being used in the initial launch of the project in early June 2021.[11]

In 2004, desert land management took a more market-oriented turn. Aiming for increasing state revenues from land sales and reduced speculation, NUCA introduced a new pricing mechanism based on selling land plots in public auctions, which in fact raised land prices to new heights.[12] Thus we find these new desert settlements around Cairo increasingly catering to a new class of well-to-do Egyptians. Moreover, this housing category witnessed an increase in partnerships between NUCA and private developers to produce more high-end desert settlements. Significantly, in this historical stage of development, the former government acted like a private developer and, for the first time, used similar visualisation and branding techniques at the level of urban planning when it released the "Cairo Vision 2050" in 2009. This was a government-sponsored planning document that com-

7 See Sims, 2015: 128.
8 Sims, 2015: 128.
9 See Sims, 2015: 129.
10 See Keeton and Provoost, 2019.
11 See Abo Almajd, 2021.
12 See Adly, 2020.

prised various large-scale projects and was replete with computer-generated images and collages of a retrofitted city that viewers could barely recognise.[13]

After the 2011 January revolution, NUCA's model of planner-regulator-developer was pushed even further. NUCA has also decided to emulate high-end developers and establish its own version to capture some of the speculative value of land generated by selling housing units. First, in 2015, the government decided to develop the New Administrative Capital through an Egyptian joint stock company in partnership between the armed forces and NUCA. The promotion of the city from its announcement till today is heavily dependent on computer-generated images and 3D videos of places to come. I shall return to discuss and analyse an example from this project shortly. Moreover, in 2017, in partnership with another state entity, the Housing and Development Bank (HDB), NUCA launched a new high-end public property developer company, City Edge Development, a top-level Egyptian developer of suburban residential communities.[14] The flagship of the new company is the Gate Towers in New Alamain, one of the so-called fourth-generation cities, on the North Coast, where the prices of housing units were taken to new heights. Once again, ultra-realistic images of places to come were the main advertising materials used to promote the future coastal city. In the New Administrative Capital, City Edge Development is also involved in several large-scale real estate projects. Its prime development is the New Garden City, a 400-hectare development that harks back to a turn of the 20th-century development in Cairo, Garden City, and that is advertised with promotional images and videos as a themed revival of downtown Cairo's French-style buildings.

I would like to conclude this brief historical review with two comments: firstly, we can speculate several practical and economic reasons for the government's tendency to increasingly rely on large-scale developers to build the various desert projects, particularly given the recent pronounced political will, and to push to finish these projects in a very short span of time. For example, it is simpler and faster to sell fewer large tracts for developers than to sell many smaller, individual plots. In a similar vein, it is speedier and more efficient to complete large housing projects with a few developers, who are always keen to rapidly finish their projects and realise their profit, than to work with thousands of individual owners, who may not complete their buildings for years. From a design point of view, developers are presumably considered more reliable in guaranteeing a better overall uniform design quality and architectural character of their final residential products, as they typically hire renowned large-scale architectural firms. Finally, from an

13 See Adham, 2014; Cairo from Below, 2017.

14 See City Edge Development, 2021.

economic efficiency point of view, it is more profitable for the government to reduce the cost of supplying the infrastructure by transferring this responsibility to developers, who provide all electric, sewer, water, and rain drainage networks within their designated large land division. Secondly, the increasing reliance on visualisations and other sophisticated marketing and branding techniques intertwines with the rise of large-scale, private and public property developers. So, I would now like to move to and discuss in greater depth the developer's marketing and branding methods.

3 Constructing a Memory of the Future

In this section, I will argue that ultra-realistic, photo-like architectural videos and other visual representations used to brand coming projects evoke in us the sense that we can hold the future in our heads and construct memories of it as a yearned-for anthology of lifestyle snapshots. The power of these visualisations and experiential techniques, therefore, lies in their capacity to construct and inscribe in our memories a new, make-believe world that is graspable, credible, and desirable, which in turn can be sold in the present. Nowhere are these various architectural visualisations and publicity techniques better put to use to promote and raise the expectation of a future-to-come, to intertwine the present and the future, and to interlock dreams and finance than in the showrooms, TV commercials, and street billboards of large-scale real estate projects.

3.1 Showrooms, TV Commercials, and Street Billboards

Situated on the Moqattam Hills plateau overlooking Cairo, Emaar's showroom in Egypt is the gateway to its flagship project "Uptown Cairo."[15] Uptown Cairo comprises residential quarters, a Business Park, a commercial centre, and entertainment and sports facilities with a presumed total cost of two billion USD when completed. I will argue that the planned showroom is segmented into three distinct phases with clear objectives: establishing trust in the makers, constructing a memory of the future offerings, and introducing the financial method to acquire that future.[16] In the first phase, the visitor establishes trust and confidence in Emaar's ability to deliver: the visitor reaches the exceptionally large and elegant showroom

15 Emaar is a large-scale Dubai-based international real estate developer.
16 See Adham and Fahmy, 2010.

building via an avenue flanked with palm trees and sun-drenched billboards showing images of happy families and places to come. The showroom's large entrance lobby is full of eye-catching architectural renderings and photographs complementing a curated collection of mundane items that could likely fill the visitor's home – collectables and cultural artefacts that reflect his or her sense of luxury living. If the visitor did not know Emaar, now he or she knows the brand – it is the firm behind the world's tallest building, Burj Khalifa in Dubai, among other projects – and the visitor should trust it.

Fig. 1: Emaar's showrooms unmistakably feel like spaces in a museum
Photo: Todd Reisz, 2009. Courtesy of the photographer.

With confidence and trust established, the visitor moves to the second phase of the visit, the main showroom hall, via a magically lit tunnel, which accentuates the feeling that one is moving into another world, another Cairo. The renderings, physical models, and other representations of Emaar's projects in Egypt are located in the various showroom halls, which unmistakably feel like spaces in a museum. In addition to relying on a mix of photographs and architectural visualisations and models, Uptown Cairo's amenities and lifestyles are also represented by glass display cases filled with luxury items from famous consumer brands (see Fig. 1 and 2).

Emaar's vitrines preserve lifestyle like a museum and mix them with the architectural visualisations to evoke in the visitor's mind a dream world of luxury. The tour is additionally supplemented with mockup apartments and furnished model villas to further engrave the lavish lifestyle experience in the visitors' minds. Large photorealistic images of the landscape are set carefully behind the windows so visitors see how their future views from their future houses would look like.

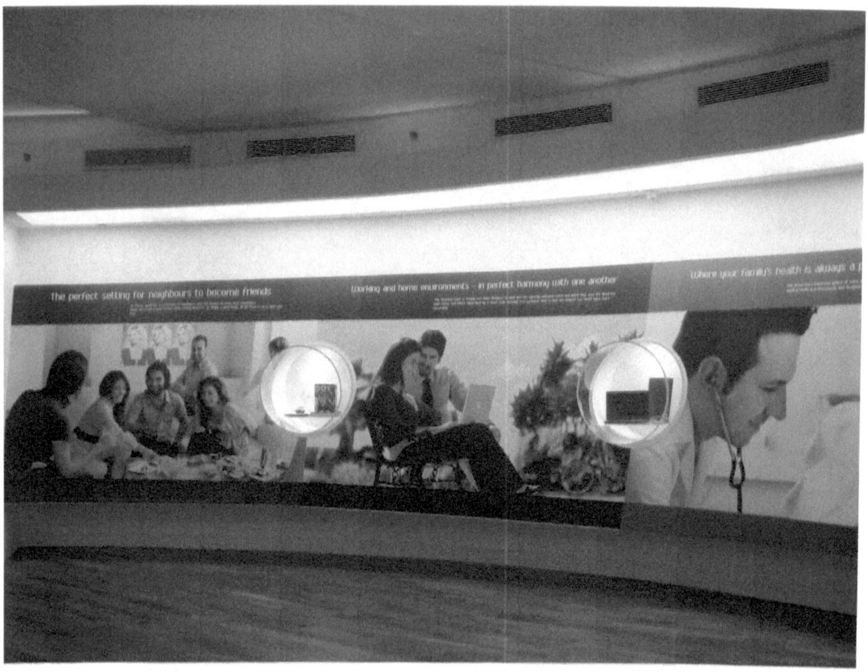

Fig. 2: Various visualisations intend to evoke in the visitor's mind a future world of luxury
Photo: Khaled Adham, 2009.

The tour ends with the third phase, in which visitors are introduced to various financing schemes to purchase a piece of this dream world. The whole visit experience proposes to potential buyers and investors that they can transform their lifestyles by investing in this exclusive, fancied future. In this context, the various visualisations and mockups function as tools aiding potential buyers to live the future, establish the conviction of its durability, and create memories of it. Undoubtedly the potential buyers who fall under the spell of these luxurious real estate projects belong to a small housing market segment that can afford the high price tag.

Constructing a memory of the urban future is not limited to visual techniques targeting a limited segment of high-end showrooms visitors. Other innovative marketing methods have also been employed for a much wider audience. Aiming to become a complete gated private city, the branding of the large desert development of "Madinaty," Arabic for "My City," is a case in point. Located along the Cairo-Suez highway, north of the New Administrative City, the 3,200-hectare development aims to house around 600,000 residents when completed. An American international architectural firm has designed it as several sub-compounds, each with its own basic facilities and services. The developer of the city is the Talaat Mostafa Group, one of the largest real estate conglomerates in Egypt, known for developing mixed-use real estate and hospitality projects across the country with a total land bank development of over 50 square kilometres.[17] Construction of the city began in 2006 with intermittent halts over the subsequent ten years because of the political unrest after the 2011 revolution and other legal challenges. Like Emaar's Uptown, Madinaty also has created its own on-site showroom. During the first years of branding the mega-project, the slogan used to induce potential buyers to establish trust and confidence in the developer was "From the Makers of Al-Rehab," referencing the company's earlier successful mixed-use development project in New Cairo.

Brochures, physical models, and furnished mockup houses and apartments were initially the main advertising tools. In 2019, with large sections of the sub-compounds and central facilities completed, the company introduced to Egypt a new branding approach: commercial songs made for the city development by superstar singers. First, the Syrian singer Asala introduced the brand to the viewers with her song "Madinaty."[18] The three-minute commercial song tells the story of a couple from the time they met through their wedding night to their establishing a family and having their first child. In this context, the various cinematic imageries and spectacles from the completed sections of the city are meticulously intertwined with the lyrics, the melody, and Asala's resonant voice to engrave in the memory of viewers that the future is already "here," thus establishing confidence in its durability and creating memories of the city. Building on the success of Asala's commercial song, two years later, a second TV commercial song for the city was released, "Life as it should be," by the Lebanese superstar singer, Ragheb 'Alama.[19] In this song, viewers learn about the various lifestyle aspects of the "happy residents" of Madinaty from 'Alama who, presumably for the purpose of the video, ap-

17 See the company's webpage, Talaat Mostafa Group, 2021.

18 See the YouTube commercial song, Asala, 2019.

19 See the YouTube commercial song, 'Alama, 2021.

Fig. 3: Noor City advertisement “the first residential city with the future’s technology”
Photo: Khaled Adham, 2021.

pears as one of its residents. Using music and songs in advertising is not new. Music serves the function of making any commodity, including the property offerings of Madinaty, more memorable to viewers as the melody, lyrics, and associated images, places, and lifestyles of the development linger in their minds.[20]

Building on its successful previous projects, and in partnership with NUCA, the Talaat Mostafa Group is currently introducing another mega desert project, namely, “Noor City.” Branded as a smart, eco-friendly city, the new 2,000-hectare development promises to be “a leap in the real estate and urban development map in Egypt.”[21] Like all other projects of similar magnitude, the announcement of the new desert development was followed by a vigorous advertising campaign, which included street billboards that one finds today on most major roads and highways in and around Cairo (see Fig. 3 and 4). Like Emaar’s carefully planned showroom objectives, these billboards carry a similar message establishing the

20 See Huron, 1989.
21 Talaat Mostafa Group, 2021; see also this company’s webpage for images of the project.

Fig. 4: Noor City advertisement establishes a memory of the promised future and communicates the financial objectives of the investor
Photo: Khaled Adham, 2021.

memory of the promised future and communicating the financial objectives of the investor.

3.2 Urban Lifestyle Script

If we believe that these images and promotional and advertising materials contain messages about the future they portray, then what are these messages? And how do they connect the future and the present? Consider one representative rendering from the scores of images produced for various desert developments, namely, the iconic Ring Gate, as it is called. Designed as an arch to cross over a three-lane bi-directional highway forming a western gate to the New Administrative City, the Ring, with its unique shape and urban setting, is meant to signify Egyptian innovative capabilities, as the project website tells us.[22] The highway that passes below the building is flanked by service roads in both directions, with generic renderings of high-rise buildings lining up on the sides, and with more high-rise buildings in the far distance. On one side, one sees a metro line, confirming the connectivity of the new city and the availability of rapid transit systems, a hallmark of sustainable urban developments. Lush green areas are dispersed throughout this image, along with various representational images of the future city. The central spine of the city is planned as a continuous stretch of green spaces, which are supposedly double the area of Central Park in New York City. In short, the overall impression that the viewer gets from the various visualisations of the iconic building constructions supports the memory of a future capital city that will be modern, connected, innovative, ordered, green, clean, and spacious.

While it might be argued that the ultra-realistic image is reminiscent of urban environments in other regional cities, particularly Dubai, I contend that any semblance lies in the peculiar way these architectural presentational instruments have been transformed into present-day "urban lifestyle script" materials that can be used to make the future durable and legible for the here and now. By "urban lifestyle script," I mean the loosely shared expectations of a global-oriented class of citizens about the quality of certain lifestyle forms in a prototypical global city.[23] They comprise a framework for a good urban environment in the global city: green parks, fancy houses and loft apartments, sleek restaurants, various cultural venues, music scenes, sports complexes, conference halls, business parks, efficient transportation network, etc.[24] To simulate future urban lifestyle script in the produced visual representations, the makers of these images actually rely on their memories of other environments. This is how the past, the present, and the future are entangled. Let me explain.

Recent studies in cognitive psychology have shown that imagining or simulating the future relies on many of the same cognitive and neural processes as remembering past events and places. "Future simulations," write Daniel Schacter and Kevin Madore, "are built on retrieved details of specific past experiences that are recombined into novel events."[25] All of these details come from our memory of direct past experiences, similar depictions in cultural imageries and events, circulating images in the media, or the shared memories of others. Like remembering an event from the past, when we imagine a place we might experience in the

22 For images of the iconic Ring, see Cube Consultants, 2021.

23 This explanation has its starting point in the concept of "cultural life script." See Schank and Abelson, 1977.

24 See Zukin, 1996.

25 Schacter and Madore, 2016: 245.

future, we are essentially "pre-living" that scene. And just as memories are more detailed the more recent they are, imagined future scenes are more detailed the nearer in the future they are. But when people try to imagine the more distant future (or past), cognitive psychologists tell us, they tend to rely heavily on "cultural life scripts."[26] By this they mean the skeleton or framework of progression of events that a life in a certain culture is expected to contain. In Egypt, for example, the cultural life script for a typical young Egyptian male adult is something like this: go to school, go to college, find a job, get married, move out of one's parents' residence, have kids, retire, ...etc. These are milestones with which young Egyptians will generally tell their life story, using them as a framework. In a similar vein, I will argue that the makers of these developments have relied on prescriptive components (milestones), which order what they collectively have imagined to be the good, modern, global city life. These milestones are the building blocks they have used to construct their urban vision of the future global city in the surrounding deserts of Cairo. From this perspective, the visual connection forged between the iconic Ring and other cities, such as Dubai, can be interpreted in the sense that their makers are using similar urban lifestyle scripts, as both cities aspire to respond to the same global cities' audiences. Moreover, I will argue that there is an important functional aspect that connects the use of visualisations, such as the one described above, with other global cities emerging under the neoliberal economic paradigm. Functionally, the memory that is created with these ultra-realistic visualisations is a memory of the future – seen as a generic global city – in the here and now. This constructed memory of the future matches and is necessary for the workings of an economy that is increasingly turning towards the future, and more precisely, towards extracting economic value from the future.

4 The Future-Oriented Economy

Adam Hanieh tells us that the term "financialisation" has emerged in recent years as a conceptual framework to describe and analyse the transformations taking place within contemporary capitalism.[27] While finance has always been part of capitalism, contends Hanieh, it is in the past three decades that we observe an expansion of the financial sector over the other sectors of the economy and a pronounced shift in the degree and magnitude to which the accumulation of profits

26 See Berntsen and Rubin, 2004.
27 See Hanieh, 2016.

"pivots around financial processes."[28] Moreover, it is argued that since the 1970s land and housing have increasingly become financialised.[29] This is so, because they are considered assets with high-quality collateral that can absorb the surplus capital generated through finance. The expansion of finance, or financialisation, in these analyses corresponds to a particular growing globally dominant form of economic neoliberalism.[30]

One of the important issues raised in the various rising analyses of financialisation of the economy is the temporal dimension and the economic logic and orientation that follow from it. All the instruments, techniques, and innovations in finance are intrinsically time- or future-oriented. For example, finance is a promise of future wealth; a credit is a promise to repay a debt in the future; and a financial asset is a promise of future value.[31] Thus, the logical argument about temporality constructed here revolves around the following statement: because of the increasing financialisation of the global economy, its logic has turned towards the future, towards extracting economic value from the future. David Harvey, for example, argues that this future-oriented wealth extraction was capitalism's response to the politics of wage repression and stagnation in the 1970s in the US and the UK.[32] By pumping up the credit economy, argues Harvey, capitalism overcame the barrier of declining effective demand. And much of this created credit went into the housing market through the ever-expanding financial institutes. It is important to highlight that the financialisation of real estate should not be understood, however, as a process that unfolds uniformly across geographical spaces; rather, it is a process that is fundamentally fragmented, path-dependent, and variegated.[33] This raises the following questions: how is the housing market in Egypt responding to these global trends? Is the housing market in Egypt financialised?

The housing market in Egypt has a set of locally relevant policies, forces, and actors that shape and configure housing provision in general and housing financing in particular, with its associated current or future value extraction mechanism. For over four decades in Egypt, there has been a mismatch between the market prices and the ability of most income groups to purchase a home, particularly given that most of the customers in the market are cash buyers who have no recourse to institutionalised housing financing. True, there have been several attempts during the past two decades to expand the effective demand through the

28 Hanieh, 2016: 1228.
29 See Aalbers, 2016.
30 See Palley, 2013.
31 See Lazzarato, 2012: 45.
32 See Harvey, 2006.
33 See Aalbers 2006: 1–6.

promotion of a mortgage finance market, for example, by establishing in 2001 a regulatory body, the Mortgage Finance Authority. These efforts were even extended further when the Central Bank of Egypt, supported by a fund from the World Bank, launched a nearly 700-million-USD initiative (doubled a year later) to stimulate home financing for low- and middle-income Egyptians.[34] While these initiatives managed to attract a few thousand customers, their reach remains far below their intended target, making the mortgage penetration rate in the country very negligible. Moreover, most of these initiatives do not cover the high-end market category, where listed developers typically operate and to which all new desert developments cater entirely, attested by the prices of houses offered relative to Egyptian average yearly incomes.

The most common financing arrangement in the high-end market in Egypt today is the deferred-instalment system, by which the developer sells a housing unit and receives a down payment of around ten to twenty-five per cent of the total purchasing price, followed by instalments over a period ranging from five to fifteen years.[35] The title is formally transferred when the last instalment is paid. There are three important points to emphasise here: first, developers operating in Egypt tend to begin construction once they secure the necessary number of buyers, meaning that most of their sales are off-plan, hence the importance of visualisations in the making of their projects. Though not legally pending, it is with these visualisations that customers are induced to sign contracts with developers. Second, the instalment system forms a barrier to capital accumulation, as it ties up the funds of developers, who would rather invest in new projects and who can be constrained by an adverse cycle of real estate markets. This is one reason why the mortgage system has been pushed: to resolve this problem of capital. Third, because large-scale developers' offerings are mainly in the high-end housing market, these large instalment plans usually cater only to a specific market segment: upper-middle-income groups of Egyptians and expatriates in the Gulf countries, Arab investors, and speculators, who compose the primary customer targets of developers. In 2015, for example, most listed developers targeted salaried workers who earn an annual average of 600,000 EGP (nearly 40,000 USD as of August 2021) and are willing to pay around forty per cent of this amount on housing – notice that the national average household income during the same time was less than one-tenth of this amount.[36]

34 See Al-Aees 2019.

35 All methods and figures are subject to change, depending on the level of saturation in the housing market and the size and experience of the developer.

36 Compare OBG, 2016.

To sum up this point, the developers of desert developments are using visualisation and promotional techniques to sell their housing units, not at the cost of construction (including profit), but at the discounted value of the instalment payments that they are charging its future occupants or buyers. As Timothy Mitchell argues, since this future revenue exceeds the cost of construction, the difference is presented as the future value of land itself.[37] Today, turning the future into a revenue stream in the present is partially operating through developers and is promoted and maintained by the various visualisations produced for their large-scale desert developments.

5 Parting Thought: The Power of the Speculative Image

The value of any land stems from both its current use and the expectations for its future, its locational potential in relation to its wider economic and political milieu. As an economic asset, its current price reflects these future expectations. By constructing images of a durable, attractive future, these various visualisations and experiential methods intend to create a social interest and raise the expectations for that geographic future in the present and thereby increase, or decrease (if they should be unsuccessful), the lands' economic and political values. But these visualisations are not only about the future; they are also about the present. Because they reflect the design choices of their makers in the present, they collectively function like a mirror. They imply both the construction of a future world and of a way of seeing ourselves in it – at once a window and a mirror. Every visualisation used is therefore a means of choosing, testing, confirming, and constructing a total view of what is considered a good life now. Because these visualisations reflect the way we want to transform our present lives to produce a future, they are indeed cultural artefacts imbricated in the politics of social change. The political economy of the reality, comprehended through these computer-generated visualisations and other promotional materials produced, conjures a window of a future in these particular geographic locations that is limited to a small fraction of society, while millions of other Cairenese can only peek into these promised futures on billboards or TV commercials, living in a reality that the well-to-do struggle to grasp.

37 See Mitchell, 2016.

Bibliography

Aalbers, Manuel. *The Financialization of Housing.* London: Routledge, 2016.

Abo Almajd, Marwa. "Egypt's Talaat Moustafa Group, NUCA Partner for Noor City Project." *Zawya* 6 June 2021. https://www.zawya.com/mena/en/projects/story/PROJECTS_Egypts_Talaat_Moustafa_Group_NUCA_partner_for_Noor_City_project-ZAWYA20210606131405/. Accessed 7 June 2021.

Adham, Khaled. "Cairo's Urban Déjà vu." In *Planning Middle Eastern Cities*, edited by Yasser Elsheshtawy, 134–167. London: Routledge, 2004.

Adham, Khaled. "Modes of Urban Diffusion." In *Under Construction: Logics of Urbanism in the Gulf Region*, edited by Steffen Wippel, Karin Bromber, Christian Steiner, and Birgit Krawietz, 233–245. Farnham, Burlington: Ashgate, 2014.

Adham, Khaled, and Mostafa Fahmy. "Gulfanization of Egypt." In *Al Manakh II*, Vol. 23, edited by AMO and Rem Koolhaas, 468–475. Amsterdam: Archis, 2010.

Adly, Amr. *Cleft Capitalism.* Stanford: Stanford University Press, 2020.

Al-Aees, Shaimaa. "CBE Allocates EGP 50bn for Mortgage Finance for Middle-income People." *Daily News Egypt* 2 June 2019. https://dailynewsegypt.com/2019/06/02/cbe-allocates-egp-50bn-for-mortgage-finance-for-middle-income-people/. Accessed 24 June 2019.

ʻAlama, Ragheb. "Al-ḥayāh ʿalā uṣūlihā." Commercial song. *YouTube* 18 April 2021. https://www.youtube.com/watch?v=ts15rBCzIqo. Accessed 14 May 2021 (link expired).

Asala. "Madinaty." Commercial song. *YouTube* 7 May 2019. https://www.youtube.com/watch?v=EzUYf0uvHvU. Accessed 17 April 2021.

Berntsen, Dorthe, and David Rubin. "Cultural Life Scripts Recall from Autobiographical Memory." *Memory and Cognition* 32.3 (2004): 427–442.

Cairo from Below. "Vision of Cairo 2050 Within a National Vision of Egypt." Blog. https://cairofrombelow.files.wordpress.com/2011/08/cairo-2050-vision-v-2009-gopp-12-mb.pdf. Accessed 20 March 2017.

City Edge Developments. "The Gate Towers." https://cityedgedevelopments.com/projects/the-gate-tower. Accessed 23 April 2021.

Cube Consultants. "The Ring Tower." https://cubeconsultants.org/portfolio/the-ring-the-capital-cairo-2/. Accessed 10 May 2021.

Denis, Eric. "Cairo as Neoliberal Capital?" In *Cairo Cosmopolitan*, edited by Diane Singerman and Paul Amar, 47–71. Cairo: AUC Press, 2006.

Hanieh, Adam. "Absent Regions: Spaces of Financialisation in the Arab World." *Antipode* 48.5 (2016): 1228–1248.

Harvey, David. *The Limits to Capital.* London: Verso, 2006.

Huron, David. "Music in Advertising: An Analytical Paradigm." *The Musical Quarterly* 73.4 (1989): 560–569.

Keeton, Rachel, and Michelle Provoost. "New Cities in the Sand." *The Guardian* 10 July 2019. https://www.theguardian.com/cities/2019/jul/10/new-cities-in-the-sand-inside-egypts-dream-to-conquer-the-desert. Accessed 2 February 2021.

Lazzarato, M. Maurizio. *The Making of the Indebted Man: An Essay on the Neoliberal Condition.* Los Angeles: Semiotext(e), 2012.

Mitchell, Timothy. "The Capital City." In *The Arab City: Architecture and Representation*, edited by Amale Andraos and Nora Akawi. New York: Columbia University Press. https://www.arch.columbia.edu/books/reader/49-the-arab-city-architecture-and-representation#-reader-anchor-24. Accessed 7 August 2021.

OBG. “Challenges and Opportunities for Egypt’s Real Estate Sector.” In *The Report: Egypt 2016*, edited by Oxford Business Group. https://www.oxfordbusinessgroup.com/overview/interesting-times-two-tiered-sector-resulting-diverse-challenges-and-opportunities. Accessed 17 November 2019.

Palley, Thomas I. *Financialization.* New York: Palgrave Macmillan, 2013.

Piketty, Thomas. *Capital in the Twenty-First Century.* Cambridge: Belknap Press, 2014.

Schacter, Daniel L., and Kevin P. Madore. “Remembering the Past and Imagining the Future: Identifying and Enhancing the Contribution of Episodic Memory.” *Memory Studies* 9.3 (2016): 245–255.

Schank, Roger. C., and Robert P. Abelson. “Scripts, Plan, and Knowledge.” In *Thinking: Readings in Cognitive Science,* edited by P. N. Johnson-Laird and P. C. Wason, 421–435. Cambridge: Cambridge University Press, 1977.

Sims, David. *Egypt’s Desert Dreams: Development or Disaster?* Cairo: AUC Press, 2015.

Singerman, Diane, and Paul Ammar. “Introduction.” In *Cairo Cosmopolitan*, edited by Diane Singerman and Paul Amar, 1–45. Cairo: AUC Press, 2006.

Talaat Mostafa Group. “TMG Cities: Noor Capital Gardens.” http://www.talaatmoustafa.com/Cities.aspx?SID=3043. Accessed 15 May 2021.

Zukin, Sharon. *The Cultures of Cities.* New York: Wiley-Blackwell, 1996.

Roman Stadnicki

Branding Backlash: The Erring of Urban Advertising in Gulf Cities

1 Introduction

The Gulf States were quick to feed oil revenue into urbanisation, as early as the 1950s in the case of Kuwait. In just a few decades, new conurbations appeared and feature among today's key players in the region's globalisation. These cities were planned to meet the requirements of economic diversification in a post-petroleum world. They are also the result of an image policy that aims to create an "urban spectacle of modernity."[1] Renowned architects and planners participated in the international promotion of the metropolitan cities that was orchestrated by the governments themselves. Thus, current images of urban projects, often projected as avant-garde and excessive, are heirs to a relatively old policy of creating *showcase cities.*

This strategic urban communication, the theme of this chapter, has been handed down to a plethora of prominent private players in the form of real estate developers and advertisers, making the general approach and strategy of governments less clear. Worse still, the systematic recourse to visual branding (not only in the Gulf) and the proliferation of town planning advertisements on city walls have produced a series of counter-effects. Starting with graphic town planning overload, followed by an increase in the "simulated urban surface"[2] or a process of urban virtualisation, whereby in designing the future, the images of the planned spaces run the risk of being out of synch with the future reality of those very spaces.[3] In the discrepancy between the city as projected and the one finally produced, urban advertising appears as a symptom of the real estate and financial crisis, as a public indicator of unfinished planning, and as a printed representation of what the city should have been. In the end, the very production of images of urban projects reveals a two-fold crisis in communication and in the urban fabric. Architects become producers of visuals (marginalising those who resist the shift), the layering of posters forces the observer to practice an *archaeology of the future,* and billboards on which the visuals are displayed end up in a state of

1 Cf. Elsheshtawy, 2010; Al-Nakib, 2013.

2 Söderström, 2001: 72.

3 Cf. Bailleul and Houllier-Guibert, 2008.

https://doi.org/10.1515/9783110741100-029

decay. This can be seen as the backlash to "the economy of fascination"[4] that consists of building a marketable image from the accumulation of varyingly iconic urban projects.

Urban imagery is approached here as both the method and the object of research. The notion of imagery is preferred to that of image insofar as it refers to the processes of both the design and the distribution of images. We focus more on putting urban objects into image form than on the images themselves. Moreover, imagery is associated with visual aspects, thus to image, to the speech that goes along with it. In seeking to convey a specific representation of a city, district, or project, the way this association occurs helps to shape the imaginary. "More real than you can imagine," in the expression coined by M. Godelier,[5] the imaginary lies at the heart of social science research, particularly with regard to the Arab world.

Our methodology analyses the strategies along with the visual and discursive aspects of urban imagery in order to understand what the latter conveys about contemporary urbanisation. Urban imagery is an appropriate means to understand the political, economic, and social dynamics at work in the urban environment. In short, there is more to this than meets the eye!

Much has been written about what the images actually depict, particularly about how the Gulf cities moved into the international spotlight via abundant images of urban and architectural projects, to the point of saturation of urban landscapes locally.[6] However, as to what the imagery reveals of the town planning production, of the city's materiality (any image, even an artificial one, is generally displayed in a physical place and on a specific medium), of its policy, and of the transnational logic involved (from local production to international distribution), little work has been done on the Middle East. This chapter aims to contribute to reinforcing the legitimacy and the heuristic value of this second approach that involves seeing beyond the image and the ideologies it conveys, by considering it first and foremost as being *in* and *of* the city, one of both its parts and its products.

With regard to imagery being a research subject in its own right, in the age of generalised visual communication, the city as a whole has become a *medium*.[7] Architecture and advertising, for example, are totally intertwined, and imagery is present at every stage of site development. The discipline of urban planning is increasingly based on things visual and virtual. Images that are disseminated by

4 Cf. Schmid, 2009.

5 Godelier, 2015: 81.

6 Cf. Elsheshtawy, 2010; Wippel et al., 2014; Stadnicki, 2019; Steiner and Wippel, 2019.

7 Cf. La Rocca, 2013.

town planning through architecture and construction involve a broad spectrum of urban society, from the designer – whose role in the urban production chain is constantly growing – to the recipient, immersed in a "continual visual suggestion."[8]

2 In the Gulf, Image Takes Precedence over the City… Bringing it Down

In the 1960s, the visibility of the young monarchical powers that still had everything to prove meant promoting their cities internationally. The cities' location between the Indian subcontinent and the Middle East, along with economic globalisation, took care of the rest. We are now witnessing the birth of urban phenomena of a new kind: a global city created from scratch, in a matter of decades for Dubai, and veritable city-states, in the case of Kuwait and Qatar, almost completely urbanised, having agglomerated former Bedouin populations now submerged by expatriate labour.

Image plays a fundamental role in the development of these political urbanisation projects at the service of economic development and of international standing. Without any physical or financial limits, these cities quickly turn into playgrounds for internationally renowned architects and town planners who engage in all kinds of experiments, using American-style master plans, and who receive highly prestigious awards. Each experiment is made legitimate by an iconographic production that is widely distributed nationally and internationally.[9] From the central streets of Kuwait City, where buildings with modernist architecture of the 1960s were set up and inaugurated lavishly even before completion,[10] to the highest tower in the world, *Burj Khalifa*, inaugurated in Dubai in 2010, the constant search for urban spectacle seems to prevail. Major institutions dedicated to urban staging, in both the public and private sectors, are reminiscent of the large international campaigns led by the Chamber of Commerce and Industry in Dubai as early as the 1980s or of the Media & Communication branches of the great multinationals of real estate promotion (Emaar, Nakheel, Qatari Diar, Kipco, etc.), the main authors of the dissemination and the exportation of a "Gulf urban model."[11]

---

8 La Rocca, 2013: 160.
9 Cf. Al-Ragam, 2017.
10 Cf. Al-Nakib, 2013.
11 Sinno, 2018.

The urban communication that is set up enables governments to hide certain internal difficulties. Although Kuwait was in economic stagnation during the 1980s as a result of the oil counter-shock, with a parliamentary crisis into the bargain, it was also then that the Emir most called upon starchitects to produce certain iconic buildings (Parliament, Kuwait Towers, etc.). Likewise, the inauguration of *Burj Khalifa*[12] meant that people forgot dozens of other urban projects that had been abandoned in Dubai after the financial crisis of 2008. When the United Arab Emirates (UAE) appeared as the world's leading CO_2 emitter, Abu Dhabi chose, in a flurry of communication, to launch the construction of the first theoretically "100 % ecological" city, Masdar City. As Doha's Saudi neighbours put it under diplomatic embargo between 2017 and 2020, criticising the Qataris for their proximity to the Muslim Brotherhood and Iran, Qatar continued to build stadiums for the 2022 football World Cup.

Today, the Gulf cities excel in the art of international self-promotion, judging by the mass of investments in events, the promotion of heritage, and iconic architecture, currently the three major domains of city branding.[13] Some projects tick all three boxes, such as the Abu Dhabi Louvre inaugurated in 2017. It satisfies event criteria by staging exhibitions, heritage criteria by celebrating the history of civilisations, and iconic architectural criteria with the Jean Nouvel design. The organisation of "Festivals" in gigantic exhibition centres, the construction of many "Heritage Villages,"[14] and the race for record heights in the skylines are just some of the concrete illustrations of self-promotion. In such domains, cities employ the most advanced visibility strategies to assert their existence in the global market of metropolises.[15] "Showcase projects are therefore a means of existing on a stage increasingly obstructed by metropolitan cities from a range of backgrounds."[16] In a competitive regional game, these strategies try to mark each of the cities with a sophisticated identity: sport for Doha, culture for Abu Dhabi, and entertainment for Dubai are just a few examples. However, this large sectoral division, which has more in common with political marketing strategy[17] than with territorial marketing, reveals little of the fierce architectural and urban competition waged by metropolitan cities vying to take advantage of the other's difficulties. Abu Dhabi, for example, took advantage of the financial crisis that hit Dubai to re-

12 The tower, which was originally to be called *Burj Dubai*, was renamed for the Emir of Abu Dhabi, who paid off the debts of his federal neighbour after the crisis.

13 Cf. Dinnie, 2010.

14 Name given to the new "heritage" neighbourhoods.

15 Cf. Kanna, 2011.

16 Meyronin, 2015: 53.

17 Cf. Piquet, 2013.

assert its authority over the federation of the UAE and to launch a series of major projects, including the museum island of Saadiyat. Kuwait City and Muscat, with a more peripheral position in the Gulf, are seeking to improve their attractiveness at a time when the regional powers, Riyadh and Doha, are politically opposed.

Homogeneous in appearance alone, each of these cities has its own agenda. While colossal means seem to be available everywhere for communication, they are deployed and supervised unequally. Dubai and, to a lesser extent, Doha are each seeking to become a hub of international tourism and to attract millions of foreign visitors. Both cities are increasingly taking on the appearance of what Richard Florida calls a "creative city."[18] To do so, Dubai and Doha have a well-targeted city branding strategy,[19] with their own media, aimed at shaping the image of the city internationally. In other cities, visual communication is omnipresent and overpowering, as in Dubai, whose success is a model for many. In Kuwait City, as we will show later, visual communication appears to be less well organised and more artisanal, having less to do with government strategy than with private actors from an advertising background who are increasingly influential in urban production.

Images are everywhere, proliferating in huge format in front of planned or ongoing construction sites, finding their way into all stages of the urban fabric. They are almost always the product of creative work using 3D design software, producing with results that are both so realistic that they could be mistaken for a photograph and very artificial (smooth surfaces, immaculate flowerbeds, flawless vegetation, and with people positioned geometrically). Advertising for future buildings, neighbourhoods, malls, and resorts represents a considerable share of the advertising market. In marketing terms, "city products" are urban projects of symbolic significance and have taken over from the "product city," aimed at promoting a particular identity trait.[20] Consequently, the interchangeable and de-territorialised dimension of urban projects and their images has been accentuated (Fig. 1).

---

18 Cf. Florida, 2003. According to Florida, a "creative city" is one that adapts to the needs of a category of professionals that he calls the "creative class" (comprising individuals working in the artistic sector, the media, research, computing, architecture, design, and entertainment) and that he regards as necessary for a city's economic development.

19 Cf. Bromber, 2014.

20 Cf. Meyronin, 2015.

Fig. 1: When advertising looks like a city: construction site in Abu Dhabi, UAE
Photo and copyright: Manuel Benchetrit, 2012. Courtesy of the photographer.

3 The "Dubaisation" via Image: When Advertisers Make (and Unmake) the City

The importance of advertising urban projects in the Gulf reflects the increasing role of advertisers in urban production and the regional influence of Dubai. Be they freelance or employees of real estate promoters, the advertising executives are much more than a link in the chain; they exert considerable influence on the content of architectural and urban projects. Sometimes, they provide the initial impetus, as promoters approach them very early on to market a product according to very brief specifications as demonstrated by our surveys in Kuwait.[21] Advertisers have also established themselves in the physical and institutional landscapes of Gulf cities, especially thanks to the Cityscape show. Cityscape began in Dubai in 2002 and is an annual event comprising regional shows in each of the Gulf States and beyond. It was conceived as an event where real estate promoters could present their projects in any imaginable advertising format: flyers, brochures, videos,

21 Cf. Stadnicki, 2019.

3D models. More than a real estate show, Cityscape puts the design of urban marketing spin-off products on centre stage.

City professionals, builders, engineers, architects, and advertisers act as commercial agents, disseminating contact information, logos, and references on the city walls. They are also gaining ground in academic architectural training, which is turned towards graphics and new technologies, while advertising agencies and large real estate developers recruit former architecture students. Architects, at the service of promoters and advertisers, are less creators of space than they are producers of visuals,[22] making more permeable the boundary between the professions of architect and advertiser.

Branding's invasion of the public space, well analysed by Peter Van Ham,[23] is emblematic of the "Dubaisation" process that describes the regional influence of Dubai[24] or, more precisely, the imitation effect seen in neighbouring countries that dream of developing highly symbolic urban mega-projects so that they, too, can become metropolitan cities.[25] The recurrence of the words *pearl* or *dream* on the posters bears witness to how images and their symbols circulate and are reinterpreted, making Dubai one of the region's lasting models. Beyond its pioneering and avant-garde role in urbanisation, inspiration also comes from advertising that is often conceived in Dubai, where the world's biggest agencies have set up regional branches.

This "Dubaisation" can be seen in both the urbanistic-architectural one-upmanship, with Dubai as its figurehead in a quest for technical prowess that actually starts with advertising, and the "topicalisation" of urban projects, which has become a trademark of Dubai.

"Topicalisation" relies upon "territorial ideologies"[26] and produces functional zoning that involves assigning a function to a district, generating what Roland Marchal called "self-regulated enclaves":[27] Media City in Dubai, Education City in Doha, Fun City in Al-Ain, etc. Among the currently trending "territorial ideologies," the urbanistic and communication aspects of heritage receive special treatment. The Gulf cities are in a paradoxical situation, as most of them are so recent that they have no heritage to speak of. Today, however, they are being affected by a

22 Cf. Sommerlad, 2014.

23 Cf. Van Ham, 2002. According to this author, the practice of branding by a growing number of stakeholders increases links between two professional environments that usually little interact: public relations and international relations.

24 Cf. Elsheshtawy, 2010; Steiner and Wippel, 2019.

25 Cf. Aoun and Farah, 2014.

26 Houllier-Guibert, 2011.

27 Marchal, 2001.

"heritage boom"[28] comprising two aspects. The first aspect reflects the two-fold obsession with international attractiveness and the construction of a collective memory, manifested by the frenetic opening of museums.[29] The second aspect fundamentally concerns urban planning and advertising. From the excessive introduction of wind towers as unique vestiges of Bedouin architecture in many projects to the construction of pastiches of medinas fantasising Arab-Islamic civilisation, the representation of a wholly invented heritage through intense use of images is striking. Dubai set the tone once again with *Madinat Jumeirah*, at the foot of its urban icon *Burj al-Arab*, the Gulf's well-known "7-star" hotel, without worrying about having almost antinomic symbolic centralities together on the city's edge. Doha followed suit, replacing its precarious city centre, built in the 1970s and inhabited ever since by foreign workers, with a brand-new souk connected to a new business district (Fig. 2 and 3). Since then, "Heritage Villages" have continued to proliferate, sometimes no sooner imagined than abandoned, as in Kuwait, where only the advertising images remain as an illusion of heritage, confirming yet again the strength of the Dubai model.

In Gulf cities that do not benefit from the same financial and political conditions as Dubai, the virtual nature of the results may surprise by their precariousness and the simplicity of their messages, with a simple frieze by way of architectural content, for example. What works in Dubai does not always work elsewhere, largely due to Sheikh Maktoum's sustained efforts to occupy the main role in shaping Dubai's urban fabric, where other leaders leave the field open to private players.

4 Image as the Project

The place occupied by image in professional town planning and architectural practices, revealing a general and probably irreversible trend towards visualisation and "virtualisation" of projects,[30] has reversed the established order. First the image, then the building and finally the site itself! The image comes before the project. It can even be a project in itself. In Kuwait City, as elsewhere in the Gulf, image sells. In the Tamdeen Square project, according to the developer who proudly displays the point in his office window in a mall of the 6th Ring Road, 50 % of the apartments were sold before the first phase of work, before

28 Nonneman and Valeri, 2017.

29 Cf. Kazerouni, 2017.

30 Cf. Söderström, 2001.

Fig. 2 (left) and 3 (right): Simultaneous destruction and rebuilding: the billboard reassures those who witness the destruction of the Musheireb district (Doha). But immigrant workers who have been driven out are excluded from gentrification
Photos and copyright: Manuel Benchetrit, 2011. Courtesy of the photographer.

the appointment of architects, before the publication of the master plan. The virtual city possesses a real value: the housing of Tamdeen Square was actually negotiated in Kuwaiti dinars.

When the image is associated with a construction site, the dimension of the project is enhanced. This is not specific to Kuwait. Lise Serra has shown that in France the site is no longer considered a simple space to be developed, suspended in the city.[31] It is also a reference in space and time that is perceived and experienced by the inhabitants, which explains why communication about the site is innovative. The palisades of Kuwaiti construction sites illustrate this perfectly. Images, adds Serra, build “the immunity of the construction site,” anchoring it to the urban landscape.

Failing to keep promises does not prevent the project from being “virtualised.” Advertisers usually design posters with a few lines presenting the construction project and the target audience, not always with models or a land use plan. Mohamed Abotera and Safa Ashoub made a similar observation based on urban planning advertising in Egypt: “The developer (or client) only presents facts, the target audience and market differentiators (unique selling proposals) and passes them on to the marketing agency. The agency then creates marketing materials stressing the message, with its slogans and images.”[32] The visual results are often very vague, functioning as trailers highlighting certain aspects of a fantasy lifestyle. Information about the precise location of the project, prices, activity content, site characteristics, etc. seldom appears on the posters. As Felix Sommerlad points out about

31 Cf. Serra, 2017.
32 Abotera and Ashoub, 2017: 14.

Dubai, "the site is no longer a premise for the architecture; and the architecture is no longer the premise on which its image rests."[33] Images therefore seem to have acquired almost total autonomy vis-à-vis the project they support, becoming interchangeable and transportable.

Moreover, the spread of digital tools has accelerated both processes and increased the "virtualisation" process. Proportions and angles that are impossible in reality become possible with digital tools. Radiant suns inhabit the cloudiest skies, ten-storey facades are made from one block of marble, and lawns are immaculate. Instead of blending the "existing city and potential city,"[34] the virtual world seems to have overtaken the real world. At a time of open access and big data, unlimited image banks are used to reproduce any type of urban atmosphere – raw material for urban advertisers. They have produced what Ola Söderström names an "extension of simulated urban surface,"[35] maintaining the illusion of an ideal unchanging world, without conflict. But do these mirage images withstand the test of urban development's reality?

5 The "Virtualisation" of Urban Projects: The Case of Kuwait City

5.1 Image before the Project: The Hessah Al-Mubarak District

The Hessah Al-Mubarak District project is a good example of the deployment of blaring and colossal imagery presiding over the project itself, revealing how project communication sometimes slips through the hands of its developer.[36] The Hessah Al-Mubarak District is presented in the project brochure as "a comprehensive mixed-use development that caters to the country's millennial population and expat residents alike (...). The exemplification of Kuwait's drive into the future;

33 Sommerlad, 2014: 94.

34 Söderström, 2001: 72.

35 Söderström, 2001: 74.

36 The data presented here on Kuwait City are the result of two field trips in June and October 2017. The first one, in the presence of photographer Manuel Benchetrit, enabled us to constitute a corpus of about 3,500 photographs covering more than 150 items of urban advertising. It was also possible to identify the main players in the advertising and the display (promoters, advertising agencies, architectural firms, construction companies, government). On the second field trip, we carried out 13 semi-structured interviews with a sample of those involved and renewed our observations on the project sites, in progress or abandoned, which are the subject of particularly pronounced advertising.

a unique, inclusive community that gives back to its hard-working, ambitious populace." Apart from the fact that these extracts suppose that those who write the texts are probably also those who produce the images, they summarise "the spirit" of the project: a new district of businesses, services, and residences of high standing and leisure at the heart of the city, on the coast road (Da'iya district). The new district will be fully managed by its developer, Kuwait Projects Company (KIPCO),[37] which acquired the 220,000-m^2 tract of land at a state auction. KIPCO is also the "master planner," according to the group's communications director, whom we interviewed. Marketing the project lasted two years, according to the group, with to-ing and fro-ing between the parties: "the American architect,"[38] "consultants in French communication," the international advertising agencies and J. Walter Thompson (JWT) via their Dubai offices, and the Starcom agency that organised the photo sessions of the human subjects in the images.[39] In an interview, the director of communication recognises that "it's a huge machine that cannot be stopped (...). Posters were displayed on all the city's billboards, the campaign was present on YouTube and Instagram, a website was created, a call centre was opened, and a press conference was organised (...).[40] But the product was not in place. Things moved too quickly, and we could have lost our credibility."

On site, communication went through two phases. In the first phase, giant images printed on tarpaulins were hung on the black palisades that surround the site. The second phase consisted of opening a "pavilion" dedicated to a public presentation of the project. Between these phases, the advertising tarpaulins were torn down within a few days by order of the government, which banned advertising on sites after the work had started (Fig. 4). However, the advertising images did not disappear, they simply changed format, shifting to glossy paper brochures available at the entrance to the pavilion and projected in promotional films shown in a constant loop on three flat screens. In the pavilion, a URC employee was in charge of welcoming the public during our stay in October 2017. His main role was to ensure that visitors looked at the leaflets and videos. The man

37 In 2010, KIPCO acquired 30% of the capital of the United Real Estate Company (URC), another real estate development giant in Kuwait.

38 His name escaped the person speaking to us, which speaks volumes about the role played by the architect in the process...

39 According to the director of communication, these sessions are "the most difficult part" because "the models who work in Dubai are not Kuwaiti enough in appearance, nor do they speak Arabic and we see them in too much advertising. I recognised the same face in an advertisement for a bank and a taxi company."

40 See the link to the press conference on the project's official website: Hessah AlMubarak District, 2016. You see people filmed from behind, watching a promotional film of the project, a rather eloquent *mise en abyme*.

introduced himself as a communication officer but knew almost nothing about the project's communication (be it the person or company that had produced the promotional film, published the booklet, or produced the 3D models). In a speech learnt by heart, like a live slogan, he repeated that "the materials are imported from Europe," that "solar energy will be used," and that "the apartments are luxurious and high-priced." All that remained of an internationally orchestrated marketing strategy machine that gets carried away at the start of the advertising campaign were a few truncated and disconnected messages in the words of the official communication officer. This man is at the service of the image he supports and extends. Of course, Kuwaiti architects attempted to alert KIPCO and the URC to problems in the project's plan, such as the major one of residences facing each other, but to no avail. According to one of these whistle-blowers, "the sexier the image, the easier it is to sell, even if it is not liveable!"

Fig. 4: Tearing down advertising tarpaulins in the Hessah Al-Mubarak District before the start of construction work
Photo and copyright: Manuel Benchetrit, 2017. Courtesy of the photographer.

5.2 The Image without a Project: The Heritage Village

The Heritage Village project, located on the coastal tip of the Sharq district, reflects two strong trends in Kuwait that are also found in neighbouring countries: the state's encouragement to increase the number of "public-private partnership" projects[41] and the reinvention of urban heritage from the reconstruction of pastiches of Arab-Islamic cities, signalling a desire to restrict outside identifying influences from the urban landscape. Following a rather singular definition of "tradition," Heritage Village projects have been multiplying in the Gulf since the 2000s. The one in Kuwait was launched in 2009. Its 75,000 m^2 was to include housing, shops, a restaurant, a hotel and, of course, a souk. The building designs were inspired by traditional architectural forms, and the site plan (in a system of alleys and courtyards) was apparently conceived from old maps of Kuwait City. The land belongs to the state (Ministry of Finance), the Municipality carried out the technical studies, the Faculty of Architecture was consulted, and an ad hoc developer, Heritage Village Real Estate Company, was in charge of the financing. But by 2018, little more than a skeletal, reinforced concrete edifice had appeared. The reasons for interrupting work varied according to who was asked. For one of the project's senior executives, it was due to having chosen a "bad investor" who did not follow the Municipality's instructions. The promoter put it down to poor coordination with public authorities that failed to comply with the terms of the public-private partnership (particularly by building on part of the site reserved for the new headquarters of the National Bank of Kuwait). Ironically, genuine antiquities, including at least one wall and the ruins of an old mosque, were discovered. One architect pointed to "glaring design flaws," amongst which were the roof terraces with sea views that were "fine, were it not for hundreds of apartments in the Sharq towers just behind, overlooking them directly." Lastly, according to Omar Al-Khattab (Dean of the Faculty of Architecture), the competition was "more effective when it came to creating artificial heritage" in the form of The Souq, a pastiche of a shopping medina rebuilt within the walls of The Avenues mall, which opened around the same time.

It is not unusual for speculative phenomena to be abandoned, but maintaining the advertising despite incompletion is unusual (Fig. 5). The images are imposing, a mixture of impressions on fencing and large metal panels in the ground. The cocktail of "tradition" and "modernity" lacks subtlety (a man in a *thawb*[42] carrying a briefcase, an aerial view of a 3D model of sand-coloured buildings bearing the slo-

41 Cf. Cadène, 2012.
42 Traditional male clothing.

gan "Inspiration from the past") on posters that are in good condition. According to one source, some of them have been replaced since the work ceased. You can tell that they were not all put up at the same time. Several layers coexist to form a sort of stratification, echoing how the site's archaeological content arose through layers of history. Why would the developer make such changes after having abandoned the project? Is it to maintain the illusion that the work is ongoing? The government is usually quick to remove posters that just take up space. Is it attempting to save face by allowing the town planning fiasco to hide behind flattering images? These questions remain unanswered but support the two-fold thesis of the image rendering something "invisible" and the image as a project. Packaging prevails over content and the absence of images in an *icon-mad* society appears to be more attractive than their presence.

Fig. 5: Advertising stratification and pixilation of the Heritage Village project, discontinued in 2010 Photo and copyright: Manuel Benchetrit, 2017. Courtesy of the photographer.

6 From Mirage Image to Waste Image: When the Gulf Cities Lose Control of their Urban Image(s)

Investigative journalism, researchers, and social networks present counter-images to the spectacular images of urban development, showing the Gulf's "vulnerability of success"[43] in urban planning: frozen construction sites, inhumane living conditions in the workers' camps, automobile crime,[44] etc. Without going behind the scenes, the decor itself bears signs of fragility. Beyond major architectural gestures, urban imagery reveals contradictions and hesitation in production and everyday urban management with oppositions between private and public players (particularly in the case of Kuwait, where the government can arbitrarily order that advertisements be taken down, either to requisition billboards or to reprimand a particular company); power games between architects and designers or advertisers; reinventing tradition after having replaced the vernacular habitat with glass towers…

Saturating the landscape with images of projects suggests an absence of a defined approach or strategy in urban communication, even though some Gulf governments have made significant resources available for city branding. The external image appears to have been better thought through than the internal image, which is unrestrained, deregulated, and rather precarious. As a matter of principle, urban imagery simplifies things as the project portrayed provides something "to see rather than to understand."[45] But the Gulf tends to standardise and to provide little information. Section drawings replaced traditional computer-generated images, advertising slogans did away with factual and technical information…

The relationship between image and construction site also raises questions. Although advertising on fencing generally provides "immunity"[46] against criticism and a bad image, it can also reinforce the fact that the work is unfinished. Advertisements for City of Arabia were still to be found in Dubai three years after the Emir abandoned it after the 2008 financial crisis for lack of funding.

43 Cf. Davidson, 2008.

44 On this point, see Ménoret, 2016. He investigated the *tafhit* in Riyadh, a kind of urban rodeo that involves performing acrobatic figures using vehicles, more often than not rented or stolen, in the asphalt suburbs of the Saudi capital.

45 Bailleul, 2008.

46 Cf. Serra, 2017.

Likewise, ten abandoned or never started Kuwaiti construction sites, such as the Heritage Village, still display their advertising on fencing or ad hoc panels.[47] Aging images accentuate their obsolescence, symbolising urban crises, be they linked to stakeholders' conflicts, corruption, or the financial difficulties of the companies that suspended the projects. Furthermore, the outlandish sums invested in the advertising campaigns of the new Kuwaiti cities of Silk City and Al-Mutlaa, whose images "were never approved by anybody" as the consultant working for the Municipality confided to us at a time when the videos were still available on YouTube,[48] remind us of the failed municipal master plans (promising new cities for the past 30 years) and the fantasies of the advertising agencies working from reports generally drawn up by foreign consultants.

This seems to convey a form of visual communication crisis in town planning. It stands out everywhere, taking root in the urban landscape, and bears signs of precariousness: repeated use of online copyright-free image banks, roughly pixelated photographs, poor-quality printing, pasting, and frail billboards. If we consider these signs along with contemporary trends in the advertising market, is a 4 m x 3 m image posted on a panel the epitome of 20th-century marketing, although still generating a considerable urban micro-economy (Fig. 6)? Nowadays, new budgets go to advertising campaigns in the social networks and on video platforms, as demonstrated by the recent promotional film for the new town of NEOM desired by the crown prince of Saudi Arabia in the Gulf of Aqaba, which has been viewed more than 300,000 times. Dilapidated images, empty billboards, and mirage advertising are symptomatic of a crisis in this outdated visual and material advertising. This raises questions about what is to become of urban advertising and about the place it occupies in urban settings when the field is increasingly digitalised and played out in social networks (Fig. 7).

7 Conclusion

On the one hand, today's marketing of urban projects in the Gulf confirms that images tend to become independent of the projects they support, which accentuates the "virtualisation" process of the city as well as the shift from "project" to "programme."[49] While technical progress has made it possible to produce oversized images as large as buildings and to add human subjects in action, thereby enhancing

47 This was still true in 2019 for the restaurant-club project ShowBiz, the Sahoud Mall, and the Abu Al-Ḥasaniya marina.

48 For Silk City, see YouTube, 2008; Al-Mutlaa City, see YouTube, 2015.

49 Cf. Pignol-Mroczkowski and Mroczkowski, 2017.

Fig. 6: Putting up the image: Advertising is an economy its own right, with its workers and scaffolding, exactly like a construction site, Sharjah, UAE
Photo and copyright: Manuel Benchetrit, 2011. Courtesy of the photographer.

realism, images of urban projects aim less and less to represent reality. Indeed, in the image, the project, including its location, real estate, and architectural and town planning characteristics and activities, gives way to a "programme." And the programme supersedes the scale of the project. It is an urban projection in the broad sense, representing imagined ways of life as well as ideologies.

On the other hand, images of urban projects, whatever their feasibility, enable territorial ideologies to be diffused, including main trends of development that

Fig. 7: Panel lying on the ground, Fintas, Kuwait
Photo and copyright: Manuel Benchetrit, 2017. Courtesy of the photographer.

projects are based upon, and to associate "environments for sale"[50] or distinctive lifestyles. The communication and digital two-fold turning point has therefore considerably modified the role and dimension of town planning imagery.

In town planning imagery, a project is more likely to be abandoned than the traces of its visual promotion are to be taken down. The images then print the obsolescence and preserve the memory of unfinished urban work. Advertising represents and symbolises urban crises. Images of abandoned projects, empty and altered billboards, mirage advertisements selling dreams, are symptomatic of excessive visual communication in the era of globalised urban contexts. However, from a material and global point of view, images convey the extent to which they shape the city. If, as Richard Sennett believes, urbanisation constitutes a society of image,[51] then we have to admit likewise that the image constitutes urbanisation.

---

50 Moreno, Simonnot and Siret, 2013.

51 Cf. Sennett, 2009.

Bibliography

Abotera, Mohamed, and Safa Ashoub. "Billboard Space in Egypt: Reproducing Nature and Dominating Spaces of Representation." *Urban Transcripts* 1.3 (2017). http://journal.urbantranscripts.org/article/billboard-space-egypt-reproducing-nature-dominating-spaces-representation-mohamad-abotera-safa-ashoub/. Accessed 11 May 2021.

Al-Nakib, Farah. "Kuwait's Modern Spectacle: Oil Wealth and the Making of a New Capital City, 1950–90." *Comparative Studies of South Asia, Africa and the Middle East* 33.1 (2013): 7–25.

Al-Ragam, Asseel. "Denial of Coevalness: Discursive Practices in the Representation of Kuwaiti Urban Modernity." *Traditional Dwellings and Settlements Review* 28.2 (2017): 7–20.

Aoun, Oula, and Jihad Farah. "La 'Dubaïsation', une métropolisation du zéro politique." In *Aménager les métropoles: La réponse des urbanistes*, edited by Jérôme Dubois, 117–136. La Tour d'Aigues: Éditions de l'Aube, 2014.

Bailleul, Hélène. "Les nouvelles formes de la communication autour des projets urbains: modalités, impacts, enjeux pour un débat participatif." *Métropoles* 3 (2008). http://journals.openedition.org/metropoles/2202. Accessed 11 May 2021.

Bailleul, Hélène, and Charles-Édouard Houllier-Guibert. "Les limites des politiques de communication territoriale basées sur le visuel." *Studies in Communication Science* 8.1 (2008): 259–280.

Benchetrit, Manuel. "L'épiderme de la ville." *Urbanisme* 409 (2018): 48–49.

Bromber, Katrin. "The Sporting Way: Sport as Branding Strategy in the Gulf States." In *Under Construction: Logics of Urbanism in the Gulf Region*, edited by Steffen Wippel, Katrin Bromber, Christian Steiner, and Birgit Krawietz, 119–130. Farnham, Burlington: Ashgate, 2014.

Cadène, Philippe. "Croissance urbaine, migrations et diversification sociale dans le golfe Arabo-persique." *Espace populations sociétés* 2 (2012). http://journals.openedition.org/eps/4933. Accessed 11 May 2021.

Davidson, Christopher. *Dubai: The Vulnerability of Success.* New York: Columbia University Press, 2008.

Dinnie, Keith. *City Branding: Theory and Cases.* London: Palgrave Macmillan, 2010.

Elsheshtawy, Yasser. *Dubai: Behind an Urban Spectacle.* London: Routledge, 2010.

Florida, Richard. *Cities and the Creative Class.* New York, London: Routledge, 2003.

Godelier, Maurice. *L'imaginé, l'imaginaire et le symbolique.* Paris: CNRS, 2015.

Hessah AlMubarak District. "KIPCO and its partners announce details of Hessah Al Mubarak real estate development project." Kuwait City, 25 September 2016. http://www.hessahalmubarak.com/sub-media.html. Accessed 11 May 2021.

Houllier-Guibert, Charles-Édouard. "La fabrication de l'image officielle de la ville pour un rayonnement européen: Gouvernance, idéologies, coopération territoriale et rayonnement." *Cahiers de Géographie du Québec* 55.154 (2011): 7–36.

Kanna, Ahmed. *Dubai: The City as Corporation.* Minneapolis: University of Minnesota Press, 2011.

La Rocca, Fabio. *La ville dans tous ses états.* Paris: CNRS, 2013.

Kazerouni, Alexandre. *Le miroir des cheikhs: Musée et politique dans les principautés du golfe Persique.* Paris: PUF, 2017.

Marchal, Roland. *Doubaï: Cité globale.* Paris: CNRS, 2001.

Ménoret, Pascal. *Royaume d'asphalte: Jeunesse saoudienne en révolte.* Paris, Marseille: La Découverte, Wildproject, 2016.

Meyronin, Benoît. *Marketing territorial, enjeux et pratiques.* Paris: Vuibert, 2015.

Moreno, Paola, Nathalie Simonnot, and Daniel Siret. "Ambiances à vendre: la représentation des personnages dans les supports de promotion des projets immobiliers." *Cahiers thématiques* 12 (2013): 121–129.

Nonneman, Gabriel, and Marc Valeri. "The 'Heritage' Boom in the Gulf: Critical and Interdisciplinary Perspectives." *Journal of Arabian Studies* 7.2 (2017): 155–156.

Pignol-Mroczkowski, Alexandra, and Stéphane Mroczkowski. "Projet, programme, image: Affichage urbain et promotion immobilière." *Revue des Sciences Sociales* 57 (2017): 122–127.

Piquet, Caroline. *Les pays du Golfe: De la perle à l'économie de la connaissance les nouvelles terres du libéralisme.* Paris: Armand Colin, 2013.

Schmid, Heiko. *Economy of Fascination: Dubai and Las Vegas as Themed Urban Landscapes.* Berlin: Gebrüder Borntraeger, 2009.

Sennett, Richard. *La conscience de l'œil: Urbanisme et société.* Paris: Éditions de la Passion, 1990.

Serra, Lise. "Images de villes, images de chantiers." *Urbanités* 9 (2017). http://www.revue-urbanites.fr/9-images-de-villes-images-de-chantiers/?preview=true. Accessed 11 May 2021.

Sinno, Maïa. "Le modèle urbain du Golfe au Caire." *Urbanisme* 409 (2018): 41–43.

Söderström, Ola. *Des images pour agir: Le visuel en urbanisme.* Paris: Payot, 2001.

Sommerlad, Felix. "Promise and Reality in Dubai's Architectural Design." In *Under Construction: Logics of Urbanism in the Gulf Region*, edited by Steffen Wippel, Katrin Bromber, Christian Steiner, and Birgit Krawietz, 91–100. Farnham, Burlington: Ashgate, 2014.

Stadnicki, Roman. "La publicité urbanistique à Koweït: De l'image de ville à l'image-ville." *Arabian Humanities* 11 (2019). http://journals.openedition.org/cy/4180. Accessed 11 May 2021.

Steiner, Christian, and Steffen Wippel, eds. "Urban Development." *Middle East–Topics & Arguments* 12.1 (2019). https://archiv.ub.uni-marburg.de/ep/0003/issue/view/230. Accessed 11 May 2021.

Van Ham, Peter. "Branding Territory: Inside the Wonderful Worlds of PR and IR Theory." *Millennium: Journal of International Studies* 31.2 (2002): 249–269.

Wippel, Steffen, Katrin Bromber, Christian Steiner, and Birgit Krawietz, eds. *Under Construction: Logics of Urbanism in the Gulf Region.* Farnham, Burlington: Ashgate, 2014.

YouTube. *Kuwait Future City – City of Silk* – Madīnat al-ḥarīr. Video. 26 June 2008. https://www.youtube.com/watch?v=1A0u2Y10G1w. Accessed 11 May 2021.

YouTube. *South AL-Mutlaa City Project.* Video. 11 October 2015. https://www.youtube.com/watch?v=6N4rMGlVfpI. Accessed 11 May 2021.

Kamaluddin Duaei

Qom to Tehran and Back, Express: Branding a "Suburb"?

As I stood at the Qom Railway Station awaiting the high-speed train to Tehran, a banner on the wall caught my attention. "Suburban Rail," read the title, "Qatār-hā-ye Ḥūmeh-ī" in Persian, followed by a brief definition of the term, for which, I later learned, "regional rail" was a more suitable equivalent in English. As explained methodically on the website of Iran Railways, in addition to regular intercity train services, the capital Tehran is also connected to a few medium-sized and small cities by commuter/suburban rail and regional rail. While the Tehran-Pīshvā and Tehran-Parand lines are categorised as commuter/suburban, the services from Tehran to Qom and Karaj are called regional rails.[1]

On that day, however, the designation "Suburban Rail" engaged my attention beyond technicality. Despite the 140-kilometre distance between Qom and Tehran, the fare was like a giveaway. It is still notoriously low-cost, perhaps the lowest among intercity services in Iran, carrying around 300 passengers in each direction five times a day. In terms of price, it does sound like a suburban rail service, implying that it is heavily, distinctively subsidised.

This observation leads us to two important facts.

First, as the well-known economic adage goes, "There is no such thing as a free lunch." The relatively low cost of living in Qom, benefiting from massive developmental plans, and being branded, albeit unwittingly, as a "suburb" of the capital have ironically contributed to a steady rise in the cost of living in Qom over the last decade. Along with Karaj, Arāk, and other newly developing cities at commuting distances from Tehran, Qom currently serves as a reserve area for the influx of surplus population from rural and less-developed regions of Iran who cannot afford to migrate to their traditional destination, Tehran.[2]

Second, and on an expressively cultural level, the Tehran-induced vivacity has triggered conflicting branding trends and, consequentially, contradictory social developments.

On the one hand, Qom, historically renowned as a religiously orthodox place, is receiving officially organised branding treatments to revitalise its traditional

1 Cf. Labbāfī and Shokūhī, n.d.

2 The head of the Housing Foundation of Islamic Revolution proposed in 2015 that cities like Arāk and Qom can become "satellite cities" of Tehran and receive the latter's "surplus population." Quoted in Dana, 2015.

https://doi.org/10.1515/9783110741100-030

identity. In public, municipal designations, Qom is referred to as "Shahr-e Karīmeh," meaning the city of *Ḥażrat-e Maʿṣūmeh*, the holy sister of Imam ʿAlī ibn Mūsā ar-Reżā, the eighth Shiʿite Imam, whose tomb in Mashhad, is one of the Shia world's most prominent religious epicentres, along with Qom. Qom is also globally famous for housing the greatest Shia scholarly hub that, apart from the mark on its identity, has secured a sizable, consistent religious stratum in the population.

In light of these historical factors, governmental (re-)branding initiatives have moved in a direction that concurrently seeks to boost the city's economy while also appealing to its traditional profile. For instance, Iran's Ministry of Cultural Heritage, Tourism, and Handicrafts has designated Qom the "National City of Ring-Making."[3] A beautiful, valuable item of personal possession and souvenir, the handmade Persian silver ring has often been a cultural sign with significations of religiosity and piety. The Governor General of Qom has also emphasised the necessity for Qom to become a "branding centre in the production of black *Chādor*,"[4] the traditional cloak worn by women. A Deputy of Qom Governor's Office called the city "a paradise for investment" with a specific eye to its potentials in "[religious] tourism."[5]

On the other hand, the favoured push towards urban evolution has led to developments disrupting the very official line of branding. Gentrification, the expansion of consumption venues and facilities, and the general restructuring of habits of thought and performance instigated by the new media do not appear to be conducive to the ideological purpose of such infrastructural developments.

The modernisation of Qom was perhaps meant to provide the people of Qom with a "safe" Tehran, one free of its excesses. The move, however, has led to the production/satisfaction of unintended, unexpected desires. The complete renovation of major parts of the city, both residential and commercial, has made it difficult to tell the difference between Qom and Tehran.[6] The new citizens of Qom are increasingly moving away from their former persona and resembling their Tehrani counterparts. They are actively rebranding themselves in consumer terms adopted from Tehran.

Consider the feedback loop that exists between eateries and social networking platforms. Every week, new fast-food joints and cafes open in Qom, unmistakably modelled after similar places in Tehran. Instagram pages known for reviewing and promoting such businesses are then employed, spreading content that in turn fol-

3 Cf. Tehran Times, 2021.
4 IQNA, 2020. Translated by the author.
5 ILNA, 2019. Translated by the author.
6 For the neoliberalisation and "Tehranisation" of Qom, cf. also Duaei, 2019.

lows in the footsteps of those active in Tehran cyberspace. The cycle comes full circle when customers eat there and post about their moments, confirming that the purpose of the sequence was met. More than material fulfilment, these new consumers seem to seek the aesthetic aspect of the experience, and Tehran appears to be the deciding factor.

In this way, Qom is progressively being reconfigured into a less excessive Tehran, a Tehran that feels at home in Qom, influenced by and attuned to religious and secular factors alike. And the figure of the middle-class religious individual finds herself or himself at the crossroads of these clashing waves: they enjoy the modern urban amenities while being liberated from the undesirable aspects of the capital, and at the same time they experience the surge of socio-cultural change that tightens the boundaries of religiosity and undermines the very traditional identity whose maintenance has attracted such sources of change.

Bibliography

Dana. "Arāk Shahr-e Aqmārī-ye Tehrān mī Shavad [Arāk Becomes Tehran's Satellite City]." *Dana Information Network* 20 October 2015. https://www.dana.ir/news/506828.html. Accessed 1 October 2021.

Duaei, Kamaluddin. "Qom after Islamic Neoliberalism: A Narrative of the City in Limbo." *Middle East–Topics and Argument* 12.1 (2019): 55–65. https://archiv.ub.uni-marburg.de/ep/0003/article/view/7932. Accessed 19 July 2019.

ILNA. "Qom, Behesht-e Sarmāyeh Goẕārī-ye Īrān dar Bakhsh-e Gardeshgarī [Qom, the Paradise for Investment in the Tourism Sector]." *Iranian Labour News Agency* 16 December 2019. https://www.ilna.news/fa/tiny/news-847213. Accessed 1 October 2021.

IQNA. "Tākīd-e Ostāndār-e Qom bar Markazīat-e Qom dar Brand-Sāzī-ye Chādor-e Meshkī [Qom Governor General Emphasises the Centrality of Qom in Black Chador Branding]." *International Quran News Agency* 16 July 2020. https://qom.iqna.ir/fa/news/3910908. Accessed 1 October 2021.

Labbāfī, ʿAlī Akbar, and Saʿīdeh Shokūhī. "Ṭabaqeh-Bandī Anvāʿ-e Sīstem-hā-ye Reylī [Classification of Railway Systems]." *The Railways of the Islamic Republic of Iran.* n.d. https://commuterrail.rai.ir/page-RaiCommuter/fa/2039/form/pId10182#. Accessed 1 August 2021.

Tehran Times. "Qom named national city of handmade rings." 12 January 2021. https://www.tehrantimes.com/news/456907/Qom-named-national-city-of-handmade-rings. Accessed 1 October 2021.

Pekka Tuominen

Who is Branding Beyoğlu? Commodification and Surveillance of Public Space in Istanbul

1 Introduction

The sense of belonging in the public space, depending on practices of inclusion and exclusion, lies at the heart of the spatial politics of Istanbul: a city divided into spaces that call for different standards of behaviour. These spaces can be central to national identification, like Taksim Square with its troubled relationship with various shades of Republican and Ottoman histories, or emerge in quotidian locations where inhabitants from all walks of life meet on busy Istiklal Street. In the urban environment, the variety of reference points, anchored to specific periods and different spaces, creates multiplicity, but not chaos. With its pluralisation of life worlds, the city acts, in the words of David Harvey, "as a theatre, a series of stages upon which individuals could work their own distinctive magic while performing a multiplicity of roles."[1] Accordingly, in Istanbul, the urban space reflects a mosaic of overlapping facets of city branding, based on historically grounded notions of individual freedom, agency, solidarity, and community.

I illustrate here the dynamics of city branding in the everyday lives of Istanbul's inhabitants. I argue that, despite constant attempts to create a widely shared city brand, it does not exist. Rather, inhabitants contribute to the various aspects of the city brand through their everyday practices, often contesting the official narratives of its urban development. At the same time, there is a powerful emphasis on the uniqueness of the city and its fundamental difference from every other city. No one living in Istanbul denies that the past of the city is constantly appropriated and manipulated for both internal and external consumers[2] and that place branding in Istanbul furthers both economic development and its residents' identification with their city.[3] However, a sense of a unified city brand remains at a superficial and clichéd level with slogans like "the meeting point of Asia and Europe."

I am interested here in city branding situated within everyday practices, with no single dominant actor in charge. I study how the image of Istanbul is a "result of various, different and often conflicting messages sent by the city and is formed in

1 Harvey, 1990: 5.
2 See also Hall, 1997.
3 See Kavaratzis, 2004.

https://doi.org/10.1515/9783110741100-031

the mind of each individual receiver of these messages separately."[4] I emphasise the symbolic features incorporated into its city brand[5] and focus on how its competing dimensions "incite beliefs, evoke emotions, and prompt behaviours".[6] In my ethnographic case studies, authenticity is posited in relation to its various reinterpretations, urban anonymity is contrasted with powerful senses of intimacy, and expressions of individual freedom are countered with repression in the name of security. What unites these very different examples is their intimate relationship to public space.

What caught my attention early on during my ethnographic fieldwork was the remarkable ease that the inhabitants of Istanbul expressed when adapting to new situations, their detailed knowledge of how the competing aspects of the city brand were advanced and contested, and how the range of appropriate practices could be analysed. My focus here will be on diverse phenomena that illustrate the recent transformations of urban Istanbul: how public and private spaces have been reconfigured, how public space is related to the commodification and branding of the urban sphere in the district of Beyoğlu, and how the notion of "public" is reframed in encounters with state power.

The ethnographic analysis, based on 13 months of participant observation and in-depth interviews in Istanbul between 2008 and 2015, approaches public space and city branding in Istanbul from the position of everyday life, moving from appearances in the immediate environment to complex entanglements of historical narratives.[7] Together they form a sense of historical consciousness of urban space that cannot be formalised perfectly.[8] This lived embodiment of the unique but contested brand of Beyoğlu is crucial for understanding the subtle dynamics of its urban transformation. The analysis proceeds from debates around historically branded commercial appearances in Beyoğlu to how coffeehouses in the area reflect urban solidarities among their clientele and continues with questions of the surveillance and control of public space, especially in the context of Istanbul's public squares, which harness powerful political sensibilities.

4 Kavaratzis, 2004: 62.

5 See Freire, 2005.

6 Kotler and Gertner, 2011: 35.

7 This chapter is based on Chapter 8: "Morality, Public Space and Urban Transformation: New Solidarities in Beyoğlu" of my doctoral thesis (Tuominen, 2016).

8 See Faubion, 1994.

2 Public Space in Istanbul

In the social sciences, discussion of "publicness" has centred on Jürgen Habermas'[9] remarkably influential theory of the modern public sphere and its critiques or reinterpretations.[10] In the historical context of Turkey, its application poses several problems. These range from very different ideas of privacy in Ottoman times,[11] to the Republican ideologies of public space, regulated by the extremely detailed control by the state.[12] I prefer to use the term "public space" rather than "public sphere" because of the latter's close connections with specifically Western European liberal modernity, but I acknowledge the overlap between the terms.

Following Charles Taylor, my study focuses on "a common space in which the members of society are deemed to meet through a variety of media: print, electronic, and also face-to-face encounters; to discuss matters of common interest; and thus to be able to form a common mind about these."[13] I emphasise the lived character of public space, bringing together the historical formation of mediated encounters, civil society, and gendered space with the pragmatic realities, ongoing life, and commentary on what publicness means.[14] I argue that these quotidian practices form the sociocultural basis for the branding of the quarter.

As a theoretical or political concept, public space/sphere (*kamu alanı, kamusal alan*) was not as regularly used in public debates in Turkey at the time I began my ethnographic fieldwork in 2008 as it has increasingly been after the Gezi Park protests. However, many of its integral principles have been central to my ethnographic cases, especially those concerning boundaries regulating movement in the city and the right to occupy particular locations.[15] From the early 2000s onwards, there has been a clear and growing feeling that public space is becoming increas-

---

9 See Habermas, 1989.

10 See e.g. Mitchell, 1988, 2002; Taylor, 1989; Warner, 2002.

11 Detailed discussion of the Ottoman notions of public space, which were subject to profound changes at different stages of the Empire, is outside the scope of this study. Murphey suggests that the principles of Islamic law played a major role in designating the character of spaces: "Because of the strongly developed sense of social welfare expressed in concepts such as *mashala* or 'public benefit,' the spheres in which private and individual rights could prevail were strictly delimited. Nonetheless, the sanctity of those spheres was all the more jealously guarded precisely because it was so exceptional" (Murphey, 1990: 119).

12 See Altınay, 2004; Özyürek, 2006.

13 Taylor, 1992: 220.

14 See Dahlgren, 2010: 4.

15 See Low, 2000.

ingly restricted for several new reasons, not always originating from the same sources of power.

2.1 Beyoğlu and Istiklal Street: Spaces of Experimentation and Freedom

The district of Beyoğlu[16] is connected with Turkey's encounter with modernity more than any other space in Istanbul.[17] Its grand themes, as well as its ephemeral peculiarities, are aesthetically present in the environment and subject to endless debates and reinterpretations, often contrasted with the city's Historical Peninsula, across the Galata Bridge. They are reflected in contemporary Turkish literature, cinema, and fine arts and find more quotidian expressions in homes, on street corners, and at the tables of the tea and coffee houses. Yet, they refer simultaneously to political ideologies, individual desires, and senses of communal affiliations with very differently grounded connotations.

In Beyoğlu's lived environment, nostalgia for the cosmopolitan past or for the early Republican modernity coexists with traits from different eras: early Republican taverns (*meyhane*) serving fish with *rakı*, *Türkü Evi* clubs showcasing Turkish folk music often accompanied by synthesisers, and the hypermodern cinema multiplexes that have sprung up in the area. Perhaps the past of Beyoğlu is uncomplicated only in the souvenir stalls, representing reflective nostalgia that thrives in longing itself, without any serious attempt to restore past conditions.[18]

The pre-Ottoman history of Beyoğlu is scattered around the area in the form of the ruins of the old city walls and a few buildings, most notably the Galata Tower (*Galata Kulesi*), built by the Genoese colony of the area in 1348 and still the most famous landmark in the district.[19] Throughout Ottoman times, the area was mostly called Pera and was home to the Empire's non-Muslim minorities; nowadays those populations have dwindled to remnants, but their historical presence is evoked by the numerous churches of various denominations and the historical embassies of

16 Beyoğlu municipality covers Tophane and Tarlabaşı and stretches into a very wide area. However, the word Beyoğlu is also used to refer to the urban core around Istiklal Street. Also used are sometimes Taksim (referring to either the square at the end of Istiklal Street or a slightly larger area), Istiklal (referring also to its side streets), or even the old Greek name Pera (when referring to the nostalgic character of the area).

17 See e.g. Navaro-Yashin, 2002; Özyürek, 2006; Sumner-Boyd and Freely, 2000: 427–447.

18 See Boym, 2001: xviii; also Navaro-Yashin, 2009.

19 See Sumner-Boyd and Freely, 2000: 438–440.

various European nations, now reduced to consulates, as the status of embassy has been transferred to offices in Ankara.

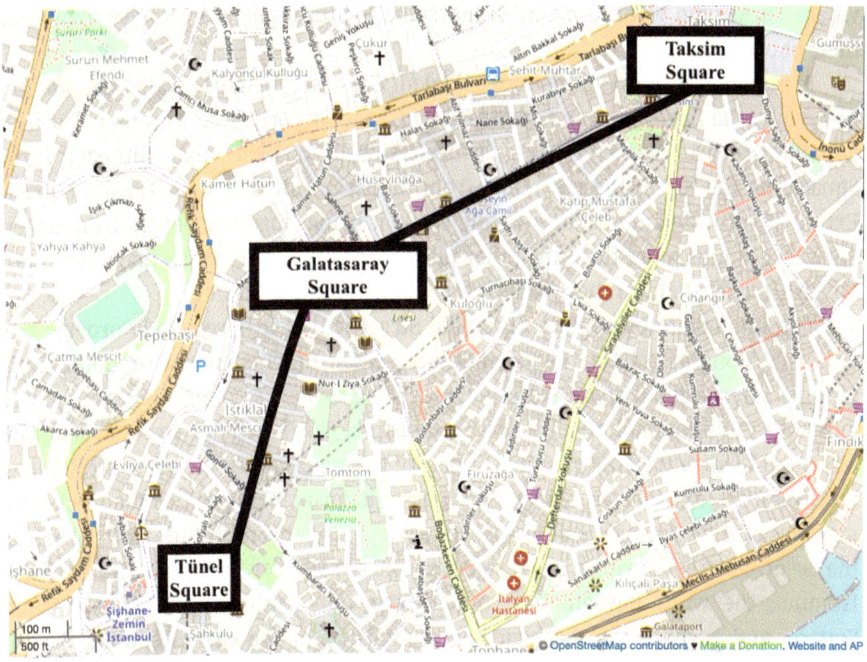

Fig. 1: Istiklal Street and its public squares
Source: OpenStreetMap. https://www.openstreetmap.org. Accessed 30 November 2021, adapted by the author.

For the whole of its history, Beyoğlu has been a space of experimentation with alien elements. There are stories of sultans visiting its taverns in disguise[20] and of Atatürk and the other Republican revolutionaries immersing themselves in the cosmopolitan atmosphere of its establishments;[21] even nowadays, it would be difficult to imagine the Gezi Park protests, uniting people from very different backgrounds, occurring in any other part of the city. At the heart of Beyoğlu lies Istiklal Street, connecting Tünel and Taksim squares (Fig. 1).

Istiklal Street is a world-famous boulevard, an egalitarian urban space, a site of self-expression, self-realisation, and tolerance, in contrast to the surrounding neighbourhoods, where people have been defined as a part of community by

---

20 See Boyar and Fleet, 2010: 40.
21 See Mango, 2002: 52–53.

their similarity and uniform ways of life.[22] Moreover, in Turkey there is a significant difference that makes Istiklal Street unique: "Neither a street, nor a neighbourhood (…). For at least two centuries it has been the most significant space where Turks who want to make an individual cultural preference have expressed their choice."[23]

In concrete terms, Istiklal Street (*İstiklâl Caddesi*), formerly called *Grande Rue de Péra* by the Europeans or *Cadde-i Kebir* (Grand Street) by the Ottoman Turks, is a boulevard 1.4 kilometres long, pedestrianised in 1988, that connects Tünel Square, on the top of the hill rising from the Galata Bridge, with Taksim Square. Extremely crowded almost around the clock, it brings together people from different backgrounds more than any other place in Istanbul. It is also a place that most Turkish tourists add to their itineraries when visiting Istanbul.

The immediate perception of Istiklal Street is that it is relatively orderly and uniform. Along its course, the ground-floor establishments consist predominantly of large international chain stores such as Nike or Levi's, alongside coffeehouses and both multinational and Turkish restaurants. This is Istiklal Street in its quintessential form, attracting all kinds of people to spend money or just to stroll along the street. The extreme crowdedness is one of its principal features: the stock photographs of the street come across as either depicting this multitude or its absence, the deserted street during a snow storm or heavy rain. For Turks not familiar with Istanbul, the word Beyoğlu has connotations only with Istiklal Street, Taksim Square, and perhaps the nostalgic representations of the early Republican past. The organisation of its more detailed contours is easily lost amidst the dominant currents. At the same time, many of the significant contestations of today draw heavily on its brand of urbanity and take place in the quotidian sphere of the street.

2.2 Branding Simit Carts and Shop Signs in Beyoğlu

The commodification of the famous *simit* bagel tells a detailed story of the historically changing geography and the reconfiguration of boundaries in Beyoğlu. The well-known *simit* carts, selling fresh bagels cheaply to passers-by, have been subject to regulations about their appearance, in a way that reflects the wider trends of urban development. For many Istanbulites, these were not trivial matters, but

22 See Özyürek, 2006: 76; Robins and Aksoy, 1995: 229.
23 Özgüven, quoted in Tanju, 2008: 156.

integral features of Beyoğlu's urbanity, ways to establish intimate connections with specific spaces and to engage with practices of city branding.

The comparison of different bakeries and the perfect consistency of their products, the crunch and freshness of the bagel, usually served plain, is one of the definitive Istanbul experiences, something that can be elaborated to great heights. Many *simit* salesmen were also distinctive personalities who got to know their customers across class boundaries and provided news and gossip of the area. The encounters were usually brief but became meaningful when repeated over the years, in some cases decades.

At first glance, the most recent transformation of Beyoğlu is apparent in the large-scale renovation of the buildings lining Istiklal Street and the march of international retail chains. However, on closer examination, there are other forces at work in the change of its historically defined ambience. The local municipality has been active in initiating new policies to make it a distinctive and positively perceived brand referring to their depiction of the "golden age" of Beyoğlu. In the beginning of the 2000s, the *simit* carts were redesigned to fit into the widely recognised nostalgic image of the street (Fig. 2), and all the stores were instructed to change their signs to ones with brass lettering on a wooden background, following the style of many of the older establishments (Fig. 3).[24] This practice of city branding, again, was deeply ingrained with history.

The glorious Istiklal Street of the post-war era had been lost in the 1980s and the early 1990s to an environment plagued by derelicts and drug addicts, with many businesses leaving the area.[25] The aesthetic interventions that followed were part of "The Beautiful Beyoğlu Project" (*Güzel Beyoğlu Projesi*), initiated to bring back the former glory of the area.[26] It is noteworthy that the 1980s, generally depicted as the rebirth of a more open, international, and liberal Turkey, were experienced in Beyoğlu as the loss of its status as the apex of modernity and urbanity.

When discussing the uniform appearance of the carts, the *simit* vendors were initially cautious with their choice of words and spoke of the changes as "signs of the times," but after some encouragement, unvaryingly expressed offence at the intrusion and the regulation of something that they had established and developed and had now become homogeneous and regulated. Of course, many of the younger ones had only worked with the new carts, but they also acknowledged the change, as it reflected the wider considerations of the cityscape and the role of the *simit*

24 See Ertep, 2009; Esen, 2008: 267.

25 See Ertep, 2009.

26 See Adanalı, 2011.

Fig. 2: The uniform appearance of the simit carts reflects the desired historical markers of the municipal beautification project
Photo: Ayşe Erek, 2022. Courtesy of the photographer.

vendors as unique individuals, commentators on the neighbourhood's news and broader issues concerning Turkey and the world.

Ümit[27] had been working for decades close to Galatasaray Square, halfway between Taksim and Tünel Squares, and was renting out his *simit* cart to his brother's grandson more often, blaming his old age and frail health, especially on hot summer days. He was very proud of his personal history in connection with Istanbul's changes and explained in detail how he had seen several demonstrations around the square, many of them culminating in violence, and the character of the area changing into a rundown and even dangerous enclave before it started

27 The names have been changed to protect the privacy of the people appearing in the text.

Fig. 3: Some multinational chains have adopted the classic presentation of brass lettering on a wooden surface
Photo: Pekka Tuominen, 2014.

to attract masses of people again. Back then, he said, you would not see families strolling in the street; and especially in the evenings, the space was exclusively male, except for the prostitutes. Following the populist narrative of failures in Turkish modernity, he, as a born Istanbulite, associated the deterioration of Beyoğlu with the influx of Anatolian migrants, bringing *arabesk* culture to the area with dreadful consequences. Now, according to him, the area had become "cultured" (*kültürlü*) again, and people were behaving in a more sophisticated manner.

The commodification of the desired historical elements in Beyoğlu reflected a widely acknowledged hierarchy of modernisation in a double sense, from above and below,[28] alternating between the Republican and populist registers. The top-down modernisation of public space in the years of the early Republic is still visible in the street and square names: *İstiklâl* (Independence), *Meşrutiyet* (Constitution) and *Tünel* (Tunnel – from the world's third oldest subterranean urban rail line, connecting the square with the northern shore of the Golden Horn), and its populist modernity is associated with the informal *arabesk* culture of the

28 See Hebbert, 2005.

area. Now the commodification and branding strategies selectively associate the hypermodern centre of shopping malls as well as the modest *simit* carts with the nostalgic past of Republican modernity.

In the locally framed context, the diverse designs of the carts, still found in other areas of Istanbul, were seen as a distraction from the uniform image of the nostalgic depiction. The same applies to the regulations on the shop signs. It seemed that the regulation of wood-and-brass signs applied only to companies that are somehow connected to Turkey or the supposed spirit of the street. Later, the international brands were allowed to have their own signs with no clear rules, and many of the global Turkish brands, not specifically associated with the nostalgic spirit of Beyoğlu, also operated without restriction. The seemingly innocent rebranding of the district, based on the nostalgic images of its past, brought to mind the freedom of its past, with its famous cultural figures and intelligentsia. However, this commodification of public space was not restricted to appearances, but also affected the everyday practices of the inhabitants.

2.3 Coffeehouse Solidarities

Istiklal Street, all the way from Tünel to Taksim Square, has no public benches. The nearest ones are at Gezi Park, which was an insignificant and abandoned place[29] behind Taksim Square when I began my fieldwork, with just a few lonely characters spending their days in the grey park. For a place to sit down for free, one could go down the hill to the seafront of Karaköy, to the squares of the Historical Peninsula, or alternatively to Kadıköy, a substantial urban centre on the Asian side of Istanbul. In the Istiklal area, you either paid for a seat in a commercial establishment or occupied a street corner.[30] This left people to choose between various teahouses, cafes, bars, and restaurants or just to walk around, stopping on street corners; the preferences here varied considerably, related to degrees of publicness of space, access, and desired activities. Many were semi-public spaces that played an important role in establishing social links.

29 In light of more recent events, the isolation of Gezi Park might seem odd. It was, nonetheless, confirmed to me in many occasions. The park carried next to no connotations before it became a focus of the massive protest movement.

30 Interesting exceptions to this pattern were some staircases where people would congregate to sit. At the time of my fieldwork, the one behind Galatasaray Lycée attracted a slightly sinister crowd, with some groups sniffing glue. The other famous one, in the middle of the Cihangir neighbourhood with a beautiful view of the sea from the hill, pulled a crowd of people drinking beer and wine bought from the shops nearby.

I found it interesting how people in Beyoğlu would discuss their choice of a teahouse or a coffee bar at length, employing ideas of sociality and solidarity in addition to the looks of the place and the quality of its products. These questions lie at the heart of branding the district. In these descriptions, notions of urbanity, class, and differently framed senses of belonging distinguished Beyoğlu from the other districts of Istanbul. The variety of establishments corresponded to the variety of people found in the area, a microcosm of Turkey's social relations.

The establishments were also ordered spatially – many cafes along Istiklal Street were decorated in the classic French style, reminiscent of the Golden Age of the cosmopolitan urbanity of the area, but they were rapidly giving way to multinational coffee chains and fast-food joints. To supplement these, there were a few simple teahouses that catered mostly to people who wanted to sit down for a quick glass of tea on their way somewhere else. In the side streets, the situation changed considerably; the number of multinational franchises diminished radically, and the cafes and bars expressed much wider variety in narrow but busy streets, with many of the establishments tucked into the upper floors of the buildings and extending to their roof terraces. This classification provided a framework for understanding how the image of Beyoğlu, a cherished mosaic of variable senses of belonging, was built in an environment where truly public space was not a permanent condition.

In addition to tea and coffee, the establishments provided various encounters that corresponded to the brand of the district in different ways. Although the brand of Beyoğlu, visible in the ubiquitous representations of artistry and experimentation, celebrated the trajectory of tolerance in the district, encounters with others were often marked by suspicion. The globally familiar coffeehouse and restaurant chains lining Istiklal Street offered a sense of anonymity and much of the clientele consisted of irregular visitors and tourists. Sometimes the anonymity could be made to serve a purpose; many wanted to have a snack or a drink with minimal social interaction and these places were perfect for that.

At the other extreme, there were places where entry was restricted, although not in an explicit manner. The restrictions were internalised and rarely challenged because people did not want to push the boundaries. The question had much more to do with nuances of recognition and acceptance: the degree to which places were welcoming played a huge role. At the same time, the city was seductive in the possibilities it offered to establish a wide range of contacts in different spaces.

Most of the teahouses (*çay evi, çay bahçesi*), reading cafes (*kıraathane*), modest cafes (*kahve*), and European-style cafes (*cafe*) had strong connotations with different senses of sociality, intimately interwoven with the notions of modernity and publicness in Beyoğlu, forming spaces within the area that connected – as well as excluded – people in various ways. Here, it is important to remember the exceptional quality of the urban sphere of Beyoğlu as a melting pot and a meeting point; there are, of course, cafes and teahouses all over Istanbul. However, in most of the neighbourhoods they retain a very private character and are only extremely rarely visited by people who are not part of the daily clientele.

If Şivan, a friend of mine living in the rundown Tarlabaşı district, just five minutes' walk from Istiklal Street, was not spending his evenings in the Istiklal area, he went to play *tavla*[31] in the Özdemir *kıraathanesi* in his neighbourhood. He often told me that the place reminded him of his childhood in Mardin, a city in the Southeast of Turkey, where he had spent his childhood before moving to Istanbul ten years ago. The place was filled with people from the immediate area, all of them male, some playing games and others reading newspapers. At first, I felt somewhat hesitant to enter this place, almost next door to where I lived, and wanted to have Şivan accompany me.

He seemed to know everyone present and wanted me to shake hands with them on our first visit. That was enough to make me welcome in a space that had felt extremely private before. It was frequented mostly by Kurds and acted as an extension to their homes, with the same faces at their regular tables every day. Şivan joked to me that everybody also came to read the papers in the daytime during the Ramadan fast, even though tea was not served, a fact that I had encountered in teahouses during my earlier trips to rural Turkey. Now cigarette smoke filled the air and people were discussing politics and the latest gossip freely across the tables. This was the perfect combination of hominess and acceptance for a neighbourhood cafe. However, for the clientele, this was not what Beyoğlu stood for. The establishments around Istiklal Street represented different kinds of solidarities.

Another friend of mine, Ozan, was a true connoisseur of cafe culture of Istanbul. He was employed in a gallery exhibiting the work of Turkey's upcoming artists and often worked remotely on his laptop in the coffeehouses nearby. For him, Beyoğlu's cafes were a unique phenomenon, something that he had not come across elsewhere. The finely tuned distinctions were important: he loathed the coffee chains lining Istiklal Street and preferred *kahves*. This is a general name for modest coffeehouses, known for their informal atmosphere and sometimes heated debates on politics and other matters. There were several of them in the side streets of Istiklal, and he liked to alternate between a couple of favourites.

When I joined him, I entered an atmosphere resembling Habermas' definition of the public sphere[32] in the early 18th century, transposed into present-day Istan-

31 A game very similar to backgammon.
32 See Habermas, 1989.

bul. Our *kahve* attracted a wide variety of people: men and women; construction workers on a coffee break; retired academics who spent most of their days around the same table; students preparing for exams; and people working in media industries. No one was obliged to take part in discussion – some concentrated on their books, and some just smoked cigarettes and listened to the others. The discussions did not centre on one topic, but flowed from one to another with constantly changing groups of participants. This was the most authentic pocket in Istanbul's urbanity that Ozan cherished the most: he said with pride that it was only here that you could meet people from all walks of life in an atmosphere of mutual respect. For him, it represented a brand of urban life that was nowadays under threat from the homogeneous coffeehouse chains. After my first visit, I asked Şivan about this *kahve*; he said that it was a good place; he would sometimes stop by, but he felt too shy to talk with all the educated people around.

The publicness of cafes and teahouses was a highly valued characteristic, especially for those who lived in cramped conditions with extended families, sometimes felt suffocated by the watchful atmosphere of their neighbourhoods, and wanted to enjoy the freedom offered by Beyoğlu. In addition, these places provided opportunities to test the boundaries of conservative culture and to try out new ways to participate in urbanity and modernity. I regard crossing boundaries and testing the degrees of access as intimately associated with reproducing the specific brand of Beyoğlu's urbanity in significant ways through everyday practices. However, consumption is just one variant of sociality. With the lack of a truly public space, squares have become extremely important and resonate with the central questions of publicness and participation.

3 City Squares of Beyoğlu

Boulevards and squares lie at the heart of urbanity and are in many cities distinctive elements of their brand. Open boulevards have been seen as moral projects from the times of Baron von Haussmann, who sought to eliminate the filth and the squalor of the inaccessible slums of 19th-century Paris,[33] but also as urban places where various elements of society can mix freely. In turn, squares have even stronger connotations of political action, often related to their specific histories. Especially in the case of political protests, these meanings are embodied in the space

33 See Mitchell, 1988: 65.

itself, placing demands on the symbolic centres of society and capturing greater national attention.[34]

The concept of the square was very different in the Ottoman city from its modern sense. The spaces where public and private would intersect were not emphasised in the architecture of the times; open spaces, if they existed, were used for pitching tents or for sports.[35] The large public squares in Turkey are a specifically modern phenomenon with strong connections to Republican history. They are also intimately tied to the international developments of the times; the opening of large spaces in the master plan of Henri Prost, an enormous project initiated by an invitation from Atatürk in 1936 and implemented beginning in 1939, was in line with the modernist planning principles of the times – the ideas of conserving the vernacular heritage were not valued, not just in Turkey, but also more widely.[36] Prost saw the future of Istanbul as "a city of public squares."[37]

Like boulevards, the squares also act as catalysts for establishing solidarities: people who would otherwise have little to do with each other, and whose encounters are limited to short exchanges, have found common points of interest by participating in politics in the shared space of a square. In Beyoğlu, Taksim Square is the apex of the politicised spaces in Turkey, intensifying the questions of freedom, liberalism, and democracy, but there are other squares along Istiklal Street that present different constellations.

3.1 Street Corner Life and Demonstrations at Galatasaray Square

The events that sometimes explode in Taksim Square are repeated on a smaller scale on Galatasaray Square. Taking its name from *Galatasaray Lycée*, a revered institution that has played a crucial role in educating many of Turkey's intellectuals and political leaders,[38] its massive gates still dominate the location and create a discernible ambience. It is no wonder that Ümit, selling *simit* bagels outside the gates, portrayed his location as the best to observe all kinds of changes in Beyoğlu. The Square is a location to arrange meetings and to find a quick snack around the clock, but also a space for political action.

34 See Low, 2000: 184.

35 See Goodwin, 1998: 111.

36 See Gül, 2006: 174.

37 Yıldırım, 2012: 1.

38 See Sumner-Boyd and Freely, 2000: 431.

Most of the activities have only a few participants, reflecting a wide spectrum of political actors: alongside the LGBTQ+, animal rights, and environmental protection activists, the trade unions and small leftist parties are often present in the almost daily demonstrations. Sometimes the political events of the day spontaneously bring people from different groups to the Square to protest or to celebrate.

Galatasaray Square has no public benches, and the nearby cafes also work chiefly as takeaways. As a result, most of the people stand around in groups, lean against the walls, or sit on the ground. The atmosphere is generally very relaxed and informal, with a diverse mix of people. This was where I often came to spend time with Şivan. He and his friends frequented a street corner next to a small grocery store (*bakkal*) close to the square. The group did not have a precise composition; people would come, say hello to others, and take part in the current discussions; some would buy a small glass of tea from a vendor nearby, often to drink it standing, and continue somewhere else, only to come back soon to repeat the pattern. Most of the participants were males between twenty and thirty years of age, but often their friends and relatives, or women married to or dating the regulars, would stop by, exchange the latest gossip, and move on.

They described this activity using spatially defined terms that separated Beyoğlu from their home neighbourhoods. It was referred to as going to Istiklal or Taksim; many evenings consisted of wandering around the area, with the *bakkal* as the focal point. Şivan styled this as life in Beyoğlu, a quintessentially urban way to spend time for those who claimed the area as theirs. Şivan and his friends distinguished themselves from tourists and casual visitors in harsh terms. According to them, these would walk Istiklal Street from one end to another like a flock of sheep, with their mouths open in amazement. Here, the criterion was streetwise knowledge, shared by people from all social classes, but not tied to class. It was a specific quality possessed by the Istanbulites who spent their time on the streets in constant interaction with very different people.

Most of Şivan's friends originated from remote villages in the Southeast: many of them had a poor command of formal Turkish and no foundation in the sophisticated manners conventionally associated with modern life in metropolitan centres. Nonetheless, they felt at home in the area and explicitly claimed to belong to Beyoğlu just as much as anyone else. In addition, in a manner reminiscent of the higher-class urbanites, they shared the pride in having in-depth knowledge of the city and situated their discussions in very familiar sociopolitical frameworks, the dynamics that have animated discussions of modernity and urbanity in Istanbul for over a century.

In addition to being a conventional place to hang around, Galatasaray Square functions as a scene for encounters between the police and people who want to raise awareness of political issues. Many of the battles concerning the brand of

Beyoğlu are conducted in front of the people passing by. In the street protests, the presence of the state is always overpowering; the police wear helmets and carry shields and automatic weapons, with intervention vehicles equipped with water cannon in the immediate vicinity.

Sometimes this led to comical situations. Şivan told me that he had witnessed a demonstration on behalf of the rights of the blind on the Square some time ago. There had been a group of protesters, mostly blind and elderly, carrying white canes, distributing leaflets and occupying the square in very small numbers. All the same, in front of the giant doors of *Galatasaray Lycée*, they were met by the police in full riot gear. Şivan said that he felt that even some of the police officers were rather ashamed of the situation. Unsurprisingly, sympathy had turned to the side of the blind.

The frequent protests around Galatasaray Square uphold the tradition of free expression associated with the image of Beyoğlu. If many of the commercial appearances in Istiklal Street are controlled by the municipality and the negotiation of the image of Beyoğlu often happens through the choice of an establishment to eat or drink in, Galatasaray Square acts as a public space for citizens to point out their concerns – or to take part in its specific urbanity by frequenting the street corners. However, at this level, the liberal image of Beyoğlu often comes into direct confrontation with state power, and the protests often seem like showcases of the state forces. It is also possible that the citizens' selective history of the image of Beyoğlu comes into open conflict with the one proposed by the state. The exemplary case of this is the yearly May Day protests on Taksim Square.

3.2 Contestation over Taksim Square

The yearly event of May Day radically transforms the urban space of Beyoğlu and is especially interesting in how it deviates from everyday life and demonstrates cracks in the order of symbolic spaces, which normally reproduce and enforce widely shared stereotypes. In Istanbul, May Day has strong connotations of what is referred to as the Taksim Square Massacre of 1977. The Confederation of Revolutionary Trade Unions (*Türkiye Devrimci İşçi Sendikaları Konfederasyonu*, DİSK) had organised the first big rally on Taksim Square in 1976, and the bloody events of the following year were anticipated in Turkey amidst violent confrontations along politically divided lines, culminating in the military coup of 1980. It is still uncertain who opened fire from the roof of the Intercontinental Hotel, now called Marmara, killing four people and resulting in a chaos that caused the death of 34 people and injured hundreds.[39]

Here, I will focus on how the present-day protests reflect the qualities associated with Beyoğlu and manage to create solidarities among people from different backgrounds; I consider the May Day protests as extracting material from historical events and using their significance creatively in the yearly reproduction of ephemeral solidarities. The rhythms of the May Day activities redraw the boundaries of the city in unusual ways and provide an outlet to express tensions in public space, especially in relation to Beyoğlu's most politicised sites.

At the time of my fieldwork, there was nervous expectation of what was going to happen: May Day had been declared a holiday in April but people had not been allowed to gather on Taksim Square in 2008, the year before. Now various leftist parties had received permission for 5,000 people to march into the square under heavy police presence.[40] In local *bakkals*, cafes, and teahouses, there was a fair amount of speculation on the security situation: how the security forces would be positioned and whether people would be allowed to enter Istiklal Street or Taksim Square freely. The preparations were already underway with increased police presence in the streets, and people were discussing the different signals in the cityscape.

While much of the speculation was done in a curious, even joking manner, there were instances that portrayed more serious tensions over the spatial order of Beyoğlu. Ridvan, a young waiter and a grocery store worker living close to Şivan in Tarlabaşı, came to visit me, furious at what had happened to him two days before May Day. As usual, he had been spending time with his friends around Taksim Square, when a policeman had approached them. The officer had told the group of five to go back to Tarlabaşı.[41] I could not be sure if this was just a way to offend them by designating their place in a derogatory way, but in this case the words had really hit home. He told me that one of his friends had argued for their right to be in the public space of the square as citizens (*vatandaş*) and this had led to policeman slapping him, arresting the whole group, and taking them to be verbally disciplined beside the nearby police van.

The message from the police had been that they were prohibited from being near the square on May Day and should do their rioting in their own neighbourhood. It was hard to establish which was more offensive to him: depriving him of his right as a Turkish citizen to be in a public space or alienating him from urban

39 See Baykan and Hatuka, 2010.

40 See Timur, 2009.

41 See also Secor, 2004: 358 on regular ID checks on Taksim.

space by suggesting he should instead cause trouble in his own neighbourhood, a space that the police would not be interested in. His version of what had happened fluctuated between contempt for the state that would discriminate against the poor and the Kurds, and pride in supporting himself financially and contributing to Turkish society with his store and his job as a waiter. The recurring confrontations with the police seemed like repetitions of the same pattern; constant regulatory work to remind the undesirable elements of their place in the supposed freedom of Beyoğlu.

May Day brought numerous policemen who seemed bored patrolling the street on a hot day in full riot gear. Again, it felt like a staged drama: the police cordons encircled the symbolically significant spaces of Istiklal Street and Taksim Square to protect them from undesirable elements. This was the performance of upholding the desired brand of Beyoğlu in changing times. The intrusion of dangerous people causing mayhem in the city centre was not specified, but followed the familiar spatial logic of the egalitarian centre of Beyoğlu belonging to responsible citizens and their incommensurability with inner-city populations, who could be controlled only by the strong state. The annual drama seemed to yield the same results and remind the people of the boundaries in the area.

4 Conclusion

The ethnographic vignettes above point to transformations of public and private spaces at very different scales. They point to the serious work of redetermining one's place in Beyoğlu through Low's categories of access, freedom of action, taking over space, ability to modify the environment, and ownership of public space.[42] In Istanbul, the definition of "public" resides within a rich semantic network, consisting of several oppositions and complementary relations with concepts such as "privacy, secrecy, domesticity, isolation, individualism, sectarianism, market, state,"[43] all built on top of earlier historical formations.

I maintain that different definitions of publicness play a very significant role in the geographical, conceptual, and symbolic reworking of the urban topography of present-day Istanbul. Beyoğlu's specific brand of urbanity consists in following complex historical trajectories, with their contested emphases and disguised meanings. The brand of the district is constantly reworked and transformed with no sin-

42 See Low, 2002.
43 Starrett, 2008: 1036.

gle dominant actor in charge. The resulting actions range from the choice of a particular typeface to large-scale police interventions; both can yield powerful results.

Bibliography

Adanalı, Yaşar Adnan. "De-spatialized Space as Neoliberal Utopia: Gentrified İstiklal Street and Commercialized Urban Spaces." *Red Thread* 3 (2011): 1–13.

Altınay, Ayşe Gül. *The Myth of the Military-Nation: Militarism, Gender, and Education in Turkey.* New York: Palgrave Macmillian, 2004.

Baykan, Aysegul, and Tali Hatuka. "Politics and Culture in the Making of Public Space: Taksim Square, 1 May 1977, Istanbul." *Planning Perspectives* 25.1 (2010): 49–68.

Boyar, Ebru, and Kate Fleet. *A Social History of Ottoman Istanbul.* Cambridge: Cambridge University Press, 2010.

Boym, Svetlana. *The Future of Nostalgia.* New York: Basic Books, 2001.

Dahlgren, Susanne. *Contesting Realities: The Public Sphere and Morality in Southern Yemen.* New York: Syracuse University Press, 2010.

Ertep, Hakan. "Chaos or Homogenization? The Role of Shop Signs in Transforming Urban Fabric in Beyoğlu, Istanbul." *Visual Communication* 8.3 (2009): 263–272.

Esen, Orhan. 2008. "Simit." In *Becoming Istanbul: An Encyclopedia*, edited by Pelin Derviş, Bülent Tanju, and Uğur Tanyeli. Istanbul: Garanti Gallery, 2008: 315–317.

Faubion, James D. *Modern Greek Lessons: A Primer in Historical Constructivism.* Princeton: Princeton University Press, 1993.

Freire, Joao R. "Geo-branding, Are we Talking Nonsense? A Theoretical Reflection on Brands Applied to Places." *Place Branding* 1.4 (2005): 347–362.

Goodwin, Jason. *Lords of the Horizon.* London: Chatto & Windus, 1998.

Gül, Murat. *The Emergence of Modern Istanbul: Transformation and Modernisation of a City.* London: Tauris Academic Studies, 2006.

Habermas, Jürgen. *The Structural Transformation of the Public Sphere: An Inquiry into a Category of Bourgeois Society.* Cambridge, MA: Polity Press, 1989.

Hall, C. Michael. 1997. "Geography, Marketing and the Selling of Places." *Journal of Travel & Tourism Marketing* 6.3–4 (1997): 61–84.

Harvey, David. *The Condition of Postmodernity.* Malden: Blackwell Publishers, 1990.

Hebbert, Michael. "The Street as Locus of Collective Memory." *Environment and Planning D: Society and Space* 23.4 (2005): 581–596.

Kavaratzis, Michalis. "From City Marketing to City Branding: Towards a Theoretical Framework for Developing City Brands." *Place Branding* 1.1 (2004): 58–73.

Kotler, Philip, and David Gertner. "A Place Marketing and Place Branding Perspective Revisited." *Destination Brands: Managing Place Reputation* 3 (2011): 33–53.

Low, Setha M. *On the Plaza: The Politics of Public Space and Culture.* Austin: University of Texas Press, 2000.

Mango, Andrew. *Atatürk: The Biography of the Founder of Modern Turkey.* Woodstock, New York: Overlook Press, 2002.

Mitchell, Timothy. *Colonizing Egypt.* Cambridge: Cambridge University Press, 1988.

Murphey, Rhoads. "Communal Living in Ottoman Istanbul: Searching for the Foundations of an Urban Tradition." *Journal of Urban History* 16.2 (1990): 115–131.

Navaro-Yashin, Yael. *Faces of the State: Secularism and Public Life in Turkey.* Princeton: Princeton University Press, 2002.

Navaro-Yashin, Yael. "Affective Spaces, Melancholic Objects: Ruination and the Production of Anthropological Knowledge." *Journal of the Royal Anthropological Institute* 15.1 (2009): 1–18.

Özyürek, Esra. *Nostalgia for the Modern: State Secularism and Everyday Politics in Turkey.* Durham: Duke University Press, 2006.

Robins, Kevin, and Asu Aksoy. "Istanbul Rising: Returning the Repressed to Urban Culture." *European Urban and Regional Studies* 2.3 (1995): 223–235.

Secor, Anna. "'There Is an Istanbul That Belongs to Me': Citizenship, Space, and Identity in the City." *Annals of the Association of American Geographers* 94.2 (2004): 352–368.

Starrett, Gregory. "Authentication and Affect: Why the Turks Don't Like Enchanted Counterpublics. A Review Essay." *Comparative Studies in Society and History* 50.4 (2008): 1036–1046.

Sumner-Boyd, Hilary, and John Freely. *Strolling Through Istanbul: A Guide to the City.* 2nd edition. Istanbul: SEV Matbaacılık ve Yayıncılık – Eğitim Ticaret A.Ş., 2000 [1972].

Tanju, Bülent. "Public Space (I)." In *Becoming Istanbul: An Encyclopedia*, edited by Pelin Derviş, Bülent Tanju, and Uğur Tanyeli, Istanbul: Garanti Gallery. 2008: 272–274.

Taylor, Charles. *Sources of the Self: The Making of the Modern Identity.* Cambridge MA: Harvard University Press, 1989.

Taylor, Charles. *Modernity and the Rise of the Public Sphere.* The Tanner Lectures on Human Values. Stanford University, 25 February 1992.

Timur, Şafak. "Back at Taksim in Peaceful Rally." *Hürriyet Daily News* 2 May 2009. http://www.hurriyet.com.tr/english/domestic/11560107.asp?gid=244. Accessed 12 February 2015.

Tuominen, Pekka. *Moral Qualities of Space, Historical Consciousness and Symbolic Boundaries in the Beyoğlu District of Istanbul.* Publications of the Faculty of Social Sciences, University of Helsinki, 2016. http://hdl.handle.net/10138/160017. Accessed 30 November 2021.

Warner, Michael. Publics and Counterpublics. *Public Culture* 14.1 (2002): 49–90.

Yıldırım, Birge. *Transformation of Public Squares of Istanbul between 1938–1949.* Paper presented at the 15th International Planning History Society Conference. São Paulo, 15–18 July 2012. http://www.usp.br/fau/iphs/abstractsAndPapersFiles/Sessions/10/YILDIRIM.pdf..pdf. Accessed 4 February 2014.

Part V: **Place Branding**

Hend Aly

Place Branding as a Political Act: Approaching Saudi Arabia's NEOM beyond its Shiny Façade

1 Introduction

NEOM is a Saudi mega-project. It extends over an area of 26,500 km^2 beside the Red Sea, adjacent to the Egyptian and the Jordanian border. NEOM is short for "new future": *neo* is Latin for new and m is the first letter of *mustaqbal*, Arabic for future. The mega-city was first announced in 2017 by the Saudi Crown Prince Mohammed bin Salman (MBS). This chapter shows that NEOM, as the Crown Prince's brainchild, cannot be understood in isolation from his aspirations and argues that NEOM's place branding is utilised by MBS as a spatial realisation of self-branding and power reaffirmation. Hence, the chapter foregrounds place branding as a political act composed of processes, actors, and narratives and triggered by its creator's aspirations and local and international dynamics and implies political and socioeconomic consequences. The chapter asserts the importance of broadly approaching place branding as a political act by systematically viewing NEOM's branding through this lens.

NEOM is one of the national Vision 2030's most prominent projects and is envisioned to grow and diversify the economy.[1] While the project has slowed due to reputational reverses connected to the killing of the Saudi journalist Jamal Khashoqji and economic challenges, in early 2021, MBS announced "The Line" as NEOM's first city to be constructed. The city of one million inhabitants is envisioned to be "a revolution in urban living," free of cars, streets, and carbon emissions. It is defined as "an economic engine for the Kingdom, it will drive diversification and aims to contribute 380,000 jobs of the future and 180 billion SAR (48 bn USD) to domestic GDP by 2030."[2]

Notably, NEOM is not the Kingdom's first new city. It was preceded by four economic cities, including the King Abdullah Economic City (KAEC).[3] Their main aims

1 For more information, see the official website of Vision 2030, 2021.

2 MBS' announcement of The Line on NEOM, 2021b.

3 KAEC is considered one of the success stories, despite falling far short of the two million targeted population; in 2018, its official statistics showed that the population slightly exceeds 5,000. See King Abdullah Economic City, 2018.

https://doi.org/10.1515/9783110741100-032

are diversifying and boosting the Saudi economy and enhancing Saudi cities' competitiveness. It is seen as imperative that the Kingdom acquire a competitive advantage in a world of booming new urban areas and a region where Dubai long ago succeeded in diversifying its economy away from oil, has qualified as a global city, and became a model replicated around the world.[4] For that reason, the Kingdom became the most active member of CityQuest, an annual international "elite, nonacademic new-cities-themed meeting,"[5] launched in 2013 and hosted since then by the Kingdom in KAEC. CityQuest provides the Kingdom with an opportunity to claim a leading role in the world of new cities. According to Moser, CityQuest establishes a "hierarchy of new cities" among emerging economies in which the Kingdom plays the role of a mentor.[6]

This chapter analyses NEOM's branding documents and platforms, including the launch event, official website neom.com, NEOM YouTube channel, and statements by the involved actors. It first engages with academic debates on branding the city in a neoliberal context. It then explores NEOM's branding processes, the actors involved, and the main branding narratives as constituent pillars of the political act of place branding. The last section gives two solid examples of how NEOM's branding narratives reflect the Crown Prince's power aspirations and spatially realise his self-branding.

2 Branding the City in a Competitive Context

Various shifts in cities' roles and forms of governance accompanied the rise of neoliberalism. As early as the 1980s, Harvey initiated a debate on the shift of city governance from managerialism towards entrepreneurialism.[7] Fostering economic growth and capital accumulation became the most prominent functions of the city as an economic engine. This shift went hand in hand with the rise of competition among places, creating a hierarchy of cities, or as Sassen refers to it, "new geographies of centrality,"[8] in which some cities are located in the core and others in the periphery. Cities' connectivity within the network of cities and their location within its spatial hierarchy are defined by various factors, including their shares of global circuits, transactions, workflows, businesses, and professionals. Cities that score high are identified as "global" or "world cities"; various indices have

4 Cf. Moser, 2018; Elsheshtawy, 2009.

5 Moser, 2019: 413.

6 Moser, 2019: 429.

7 See Harvey, 1989.

8 Sassen, 2002:13.

emerged to rank them, including the Global City Index, the Global Power City Index, and datasets compiled by the Globalisation and World Cities Research Network (GaWC). The world and global city concepts have attracted the attention of a huge number of scholars.[9] While cities at the global periphery were left out, the "worlding city" concept emerged to address their aspirations to move closer to the core.[10]

Such competitive worlding aspirations are echoed in new cities' branding. According to Moser and Côté-Roy, at least 150 new cities were announced over the past two decades, mostly in emerging economies.[11] Remarkably, a huge number of these new cities have not yet made progress out of branding documents and urban plans towards construction on the ground. Branding documents, unlike construction, make it possible to elaborate fantasies and utopias – earning these cities the deserved title "PowerPoint cities." Fostering economic growth is a main motive for founding new cities. Accordingly, in their branding, they focus on having an enabling business environment, and many are announced as Special Economic Zones. Moser and Côté-Roy argue that, unlike the previous waves of state-driven new cities that emerged in the post-Second World War and post-colonial eras, new cities of the past two decades have been notably characterised by an urban entrepreneurial rationale in which the national and international private sector plays a major role. Datta also tackled the shifting role of the state in mega-urban development, which she has called the "entrepreneurial state" and that provides new cities with the necessary legitimacy by adapting laws and regulations and plays a major role in new cities' promotion.[12]

New cities promise utopias that realise a new future and offer universal solutions to all urban challenges. Academic literature has explored the utopian claims of new cities, analysing discourses of sustainability and economic growth by "building big and fast" in the Global South,[13] the rhetoric of the smart city and the eco-city and promises of modernisation in sub-Saharan Africa,[14] and claims of prosperity in the post-oil economy in the Gulf.[15] Importantly, new cities are considered developmental necessities and prerequisites for economic growth for developing economies. This drive and this speed in establishing new cities are reflected in academic writings, most notably in Cugurullo's "Speed Kills" and Côté-Roy

9 Cf., most prominently, Friedmann, 1986; Sassen, 2005; Taylor, 2010.
10 Cf. Roy and Ong, 2011.
11 Cf. Moser and Côté-Roy, 2021.
12 Cf. Datta, 2017.
13 Cf. Datta and Shaban, 2017.
14 Cf. Watson, 2014.
15 Cf. Molotch and Ponzini, 2019.

and Moser's "Does Africa not deserve shiny new cities?", which quotes African leaders and elite.[16]

Global cities, worlding cities, and PowerPoint cities continuously work on enhancing their competitiveness to adjust, maintain, or acquire a position in the geography of centrality. In such a competitive framework, city branding became one of the most necessary tools to improve city attractiveness. Cities, like corporations, started to have their own logos, slogans, visions, missions, branding strategies, etc. Corporate branding constitutes the main way to produce a place brand. This is expressed in various consultations and academic works, such as Govers' academic productions as an editor of the *Place Branding and Public Diplomacy* journal and consultancies through different platforms including the *International Place Branding Association* and *Apolitical*, as well as Florida's academic writings on the creative class and his role in advising businesses and local governments through his consultancy firm, Creative Class Group.

Adopting a corporate branding approach, Govers defines place branding as a strategy to constitute positive image "associations" with and a "distinctive identity" of places.[17] Dinnie, a business scholar, argues that place competition establishes a strong relation between a city's image and reputation and its attractiveness. He affirms that branding strategies are necessary to connect cities to their "customers."[18] This approach packages place branding as a purely technical, apolitical process. For instance, Govers and Go use project management fundamentals in place branding and break the process down into five steps, starting from setting goals and arriving at implementing and monitoring the brand.[19] Importantly, variations of this package have been successfully recycled and sold by consultancies and experts as a one-size-fits-all product.

In contrast, Vanolo defines place branding as a political act triggered by power relations, rather than a mere technical tool. He writes, "The construction and manipulation of urban images trigger a complex politics of representation, modifying the visibility and invisibility of spaces, subjects, problems and discourses."[20] He notes that since branding defines what is visible (e.g., diversity and inclusion in public space) and what should remain invisible (e.g., homelessness), analysing the "invisible and the untold" is as important as studying what the brand makes visible. He also argues that the replicability of place branding makes it a tool for the "subjectification of cities," as it defines and globally reproduces specific vis-

16 Cf. Cugurullo, 2017; Côté-Roy and Moser, 2019.

17 Cf. Govers, 2011.

18 Cf. Dinnie, 2011.

19 Cf. Govers and Go, 2009.

20 Vanolo, 2017: i.

ual elements, vocabularies, adjectives, and aesthetics that any attractive city should possess. So, aspects of modernity, skyscrapers, waterfronts, diverse people enjoying public spaces, and adjectives such as vibrant and global become default imageries and rhetoric for brands of cities around the world, regardless of the local context. He also asks who has the right to the brand and to what degree does it connect with local aspirations and self-representation. Moreover, the production of place branding through top-down processes and the domination of consultancy firms simply commodifies the city and inhibits any sort of collective agency and ownership of the city brand.[21]

3 Branding NEOM: Scratching Beyond the Surface

This section provides a practical application of approaching place branding as a political act composed of processes, actors, and narratives. It first explores the main features shaping the branding process and maps the involved actors and then dives deep into the rhetoric and imageries of NEOM's main branding narratives: the future, the environment, and people. This is done by analysing both positive image associations that the brand makes visible, such as inclusion and diversity, as well as untold and invisible aspects, including forced evictions. It argues that the choice of what is told and what is untold is purely political in nature. The section provides a contextualised analysis of NEOM by locating it within academic debates, international trends, local dynamics, and power relations.

3.1 Processes and Actors

Although the private sector plays a major role in NEOM, it is still clearly a state-led project. The Saudi state, represented here by the Crown Prince, indeed fulfils the functions of the entrepreneurial state, as defined in the previous section, which facilitates the project by allowing NEOM to function outside of Saudi jurisdictions and enthusiastically promotes NEOM. However, the role of MBS expands beyond the typical function of the entrepreneurial state. He is the Chairman of the NEOM Company Board of Directors, and the project is considered his personal legacy. It is also partially financed by the Saudi Public Investment Fund (PIF), which

21 Cf. Vanolo, 2017: 92–98, 109–110.

he has headed since 2015.[22] The complex roles and relations between the actors involved in the project are reflected in managing the brand. Unfortunately, it is not possible to fully grasp the nature of the interactions, the actors involved, and their exact roles, because of the project's top-down, secretive approach to producing the brand. NEOM and more recently The Line were publicly announced only at the moment of their launch, and no public debates preceded this moment. However, this chapter draws on the available data to develop a better understanding of who contributes to the brand and how it is being developed.

So far, the process of constructing the brand has not involved public consultations. It relies mainly on the political leadership, represented by the Crown Prince, business figures, consultancy firms, and experts. The branding process has witnessed various shifts since its launch in 2017. During the period between the launch event and Khashoqji's murder in the Saudi Consulate in Istanbul in 2018, international stars of the business world were in the forefront of the brand.[23] This changed quickly by the end of 2018, as various public figures have pulled out of the project due to the killing.[24] The brand shifted to be more connected to the faces of experts in NEOM's fields, such as water, energy, and health. The website lists their names and quotes some of them, while the YouTube channel contains a list of short videos of the experts sharing their experience of working and living in NEOM and a series of short expert interviews under the title *Discuss the Future.*

A broad range of international consultancies are also involved in the project, including the Boston Consulting Group, McKinsey & Company, and Oliver Wyman. Their participation in the project has never been publicly announced, and it is not entirely clear what their roles and costs are. However, their engagement became evident after the *Wall Street Journal* (WSJ) published a report in 2019 based on leaked confidential documents encompassing 2,300 pages by the three consultancies planning NEOM. Other consultancies were contracted by NEOM and announced by media outlets and the US-Saudi Business Council.

Although public knowledge about the brand-making process is limited, what has been made public triggers three important observations. First, the actors involved in the project, regardless of their roles, be it constructing the city or the

22 PIF is a sovereign wealth fund. MBS reformed it in 2015.

23 The main launch event included a selection of the brightest names in business and technology as panellists, alongside the Crown Prince: Klaus Kleinfeld, the former CEO of NEOM and former CEO of Siemens; Masayoshi Son, CEO of Softbank Vision Fund and the richest person in Japan at that time; Stephen Schwarzman, ranked among the richest 400 people in the US and the cofounder of Blackstone; and Marc Raibert, the CEO of Boston Dynamics, a leading company in the robot industry in the US.

24 Cf. Perper, 2018; Block, 2018.

brand, became themselves part of the brand, as discussed in further detail below. Second, the top-down approach that the branding process relies on completely excludes any kind of public engagement and eliminates data accessibility. Third, branding relies predominantly on experts and excludes any sort of public input. This technical, apolitical approach is noticeably taken in a huge number of urban mega-developments around the world, and, according to various studies, this approach aims to depoliticise urban development and presents it as a purely technical issue that needs technical expertise rather than a political decision that requires public engagement.[25]

3.2 Branding Narratives

NEOM's branding materials present it as an "economic engine" that fosters economic growth and diversifies the Saudi economy. This is to be accomplished by leading the future of 14 economic sectors, including energy, water, mobility, media, design, and construction. It seeks to attract creative people, businesses, and investments through "unmatched liveability," a "profitable economy," and "progressive laws conducive to economic growth." Moreover, already by its name, NEOM promises the future. Its constant invocation is reflected in its branding material under such slogans as "building the future," "a roadmap for the future of civilisation," "a new future on earth like nothing on earth," and the "most future-oriented place."[26]

Promising the future, economic growth, and profit represents a motive to reaffirm NEOM's novelty and uniqueness on every possible occasion. For instance, during NEOM's launch event, MBS compared a smartphone to an old cell phone, saying that "the difference between the two devices is exactly what NEOM will achieve."[27] Furthermore, the website presents The Line as a "never-before-seen approach to urbanisation."[28] The website pushes the novelty rhetoric further by adopting a fictional story to explain how "astounding" NEOM is, stating, "Nikola Tesla, Jules Verne, Thomas Edison and Gustave Eiffel shared a vision – to create a place on earth where nothing would be impossible. If they saw our plans for

25 Cf. Swyngedouw, Moulaert, and Rodriguez, 2002; Aly, 2020.

26 All quotes on the future in this paragraph are taken from NEOM's official website NEOM, 2021a and its subpages.

27 NEOM, 2017.

28 NEOM, 2021b.

NEOM today, they'd be astounded."[29] This urge to astound drives NEOM's creators to sell unrealistic visions to their customers, meanwhile buying absurd imaginaries from international consultancies. NEOM's consultancies leaked documents that, according to the WSJ, were adopted by NEOM's Board; they mention plans to have flying cars, robot dinosaurs, and a giant artificial moon.[30] Later, in early 2021, MBS announced The Line, which offers a more realistic vision, but there is still much doubt whether it can be funded and implemented.

Tech-utopias are not uncommon among new cities. According to its official website, NEOM promises an "acceleration to human progress." The website also states: "We are building the world's first cognitive cities. Through the use of real-time data and intelligence, NEOM will fundamentally change the way people interact and work."[31] Furthermore, during the launch event, it was announced that NEOM will have more robots than human residents. The latest technology was promised in 14 fields, including "real-time assessments and 'digital twins' for each resident" in the field of health and well-being. Technology is represented as a solution to global problems and a way to create a more sustainable and liveable future. Aside from these buzzwords, no information is available about the cost of such technologies, technological limitations, and, most importantly, privacy. In its report, the WSJ has quoted MBS, based on the leaked documents, explaining "this should be an automated city where we can watch everything (...) where a computer can notify [sic!] crimes without having to report them or where all citizens can be tracked."[32] Although this vision has never been publicly announced, it is within the scope of the current branding narrative on technology. NEOM's branding is very explicit about the major and desirable change technology will bring to people's interactions, relations, life, and work. Importantly, NEOM offers technology as a solution to all the problems existing cities are encountering, ignoring the socioeconomic and political root causes of urban issues and reducing them to technical matters. Academic literature has explored and titled this phenomenon "tech-driven urbanism."[33]

NEOM's branding views it as a no man's land that provides a unique opportunity for experimenting. The website reaffirms this narrative by calling NEOM "a

29 Ironically, this vision shared by Tesla, Verne, Edison, and Eiffel as referenced in NEOM marketing never existed in reality, but it is part of the back-story of Disney's *Tomorrowland* film. The story was presented in NEOM, 2018.

30 Cf. Scheck, Jones, and Said, 2019.

31 For more on the future of technology and digital technology in NEOM, see NEOM, 2021d.

32 Scheck, Jones, and Said, 2019.

33 Cf. for example Cugurullo, 2013; Moser and Côté-Roy, 2021.

living laboratory."[34] To a great extent, this discourse, based on a broader narrative that NEOM is "a virgin area"[35] and will be built "from scratch,"[36] is frequently repeated by the professionals involved in the project and featured by the YouTube channel. The promotional video *Pioneers* confirms this rhetoric and pushes it further by featuring one of NEOM's pioneers stating: "we were the first ones to come here in the middle of nowhere,"[37] while another video is titled *The Settlers.*[38] This rhetoric was supported by the image of settlers walking through the desert, passing a plane wreck and swimming beside an abandoned sunken ship – evoking the imagery of the periphery of civilisation from movies like *Indiana Jones* and series like *Lost.* Importantly, not far from where these videos were filmed, forced evictions took place to pave the way for the new "giga"-development. Viewing NEOM as a no man's land of opportunities and presenting the new residents as settlers who bring civilisation to the empty desert is a poor replication of colonial discourses. It also exemplifies an utter dichotomy between reality and the narratives of the newcomers, which is also a feature of colonial discourse.

Initially, NEOM's branding paid minimal attention to the environment. The early branding material, such as a NEOM brochure of 2018, did not mention any related keywords even a single time, while the NEOM press release limited the issue to "net-zero carbon houses," "walking and cycling," and "renewable energy."[39] However, 2021 witnessed a huge shift as the updated NEOM brochure mentioned environmental issues in two of the five newly formulated principles, namely sustainability and nature.[40] The environment also became a defining element of The Line, which is presented as "a blueprint for how people and planet can co-exist in harmony."[41] In The Line launch video, MBS defines it as "a city of a million residents with a length of 170 km that preserves 95% of nature within NEOM, with zero cars, zero streets, and zero carbon emissions." In the meantime, Saudi Arabia, the largest oil exporter in the world, announced it was increasing its oil production.[42] This paradox between NEOM's branding discourse and practices connected

34 NEOM, 2021b.
35 NEOM, 2019b and 2020a.
36 This expression appeared in various videos on the NEOM YouTube channel, for example NEOM, 2019c, 2020a, and 2020b.
37 NEOM, 2019b.
38 NEOM, 2020a.
39 NEOM, 2017 and 2018.
40 NEOM, 2021c.
41 This quote and the following one are parts of MBS' announcement of The Line on NEOM, 2021b.
42 Cf. Faucon and Said, 2021.

to the oil industry and the Saudi share in carbon emissions can be understood at best as economic diversification, rather than transformation towards a post-carbon future. Notably, this leads to charges of greenwashing.[43]

"People" is one of the most frequently recurring words in branding NEOM. A set of other terms have been used to refer to the "Neomians," as well, including settlers, global pioneers, dreamers, thinkers, doers, world's greatest minds, and best talents. Although these labels do not imply diversity and inclusion, branding material still stresses both as defining characteristics of its community and mentions, "NEOM is for everybody." What NEOM actually offers is an exclusive inclusivity to those who qualify to be Neomians. MBS stressed this point during the launch event, saying: "This place is not the place for conventional people or conventional companies, this is a place for dreamers that want to create something new in the world."[44] NEOM's strategy of defining and attracting the dreamers resembles Florida's conception of the creative class and the irresistible 3Ts, talent, technology, and tolerance.[45] This rationale assumes a strong correlation between attracting the creatives and fostering the economy. Although this assumption has never been proven and remains debated in academia[46] even two decades after its introduction, political leadership still buys into it.

As I briefly mentioned before, the people who are involved in constructing NEOM as a city or as a brand became themselves part of the brand. In particular, since 2019, the YouTube channel has produced a huge number of promotional videos, including but not limited to two series. The first is presented under the hashtag *Discuss the Future* and is dedicated to interviews with professionals/dreamers who have been recruited by NEOM. The interviews present NEOM as a breakthrough in each and every area of expertise of the affiliated professionals. The second hashtag is *Discover NEOM.* It features the professionals' unique living and work experience in NEOM. The selection of the featured professionals can be described as gender-balanced and diverse in terms of age, nationality, profession, and cultural background. The two videos display a "real life" already taking place in NEOM, where the settlers are enjoying quality time with their families, engaging in sports, arriving at the airport, and working hard. The brand creates the imaginary of a fully functioning city out of what is primarily a construction site.

43 Boykoff and Mascarenhas, 2016: 2 define greenwashing as "the duplicitous practice of voicing concern for the environment and claiming credit for providing solutions while doing the bare minimum, if anything at all."

44 For more information, watch the launch event on Al Arabiya, 2017.

45 Cf. Florida, 2003. The parallels between NEOM's dreamers and Florida's creative class are discussed in detail in Aly, 2019.

46 Cf. Peck, 2005.

The generous production of imageries and rhetoric around Neomians contributes to creating a corporate identity, which directs consumers' imaginations towards positive associations with the brand. In other words, once a consumer hears the word NEOM, visuals of creative people enjoying their lives should immediately appear. However, scratching beyond the surface shows that other groups actually exist and are intentionally kept invisible. The only difference is that, unlike the "dreamers," they are not "Welcome to NEOM."[47] Two groups can be identified. The first is the working and service classes. It was announced during the launch event that robots will outnumber human residents and will provide all kinds of services, including care. Regardless of how realistic this idea is, it contradicts the existing reality of NEOM, as human workers are involved in the construction and vastly outnumber the settlers in NEOM. Their exclusion in the brand does not change the fact that they exist in NEOM and will continue to do so.

The second group is the tribes that were already living in the area for a long time before the idea of NEOM was even proposed. NEOM is very specific about whom it will accommodate, and the existing tribes clearly did not fit the criteria. In 2020, the Saudi authorities forcibly evicted the al-Huwaitat tribe from areas it has occupied for hundreds of years. During the evictions, an outspoken opponent and a member of the tribe, Abd al-Rahman al-Huwaiti, was killed.[48] While this killing case was well documented and covered by the international media, no further news about forced evictions connected to NEOM have been reported since then. Despite the documented evictions and killing, branding has persisted in claiming the virginity of the land. Ironically, this is an indication that branding imaginaries, even if based on deceptions, matter more than realities, as long as they are neatly and widely presented to the right audience.

4 Spatial Realisation of Self-Branding

Branding material has repeatedly and consistently presented NEOM as the legacy of MBS. Hence, it cannot be fully understood in isolation from his power aspirations and self-branding. Moser and Côté-Roy define new cities by "the aspirations of their builders."[49] The case of NEOM is an ideal fulfilment of this statement. This section builds on the previous section by contextualising NEOM's branding narratives and connecting them with the aspirations of its creator. Essentially, the chap-

47 NEOM, 2019a.

48 Cf. Daragahi and Trew, 2020.

49 Moser and Côté-Roy, 2021: 2.

ter analyses place branding as a political act, which implies a specific choice by ruling institutions and the political elite – in the case of NEOM, the Crown Prince. It further unpacks the chapter's argument that NEOM is a spatial realisation of the Crown Prince's self-branding and power reaffirmation.

In 2017, King Salman bin Abd al-Aziz Al Saud, who had acceded to the throne two years earlier, decided to replace the former Crown Prince Mohammed bin Nayef, his nephew, with his son MBS. In the same year, 200 princes and prominent business figures were arrested in a bloodless palace coup.[50] The power of MBS has increased tremendously since then, and he is strongly perceived as the "power behind the throne."[51] He carried out transformations in a number of fields that were previously considered taboo, including religious and social reforms. MBS presents himself as the champion of transforming the Saudi economy away from oil towards knowledge. He ambitiously announced in 2016, "[W]e can live without oil by 2020."[52] Remarkably, his progressive stance is strongly based on authoritarian rule and repression.

NEOM was launched in the same year as MBS was proclaimed the Crown Prince. All state capacities were harnessed to make NEOM possible. It is the Crown Prince's physical and spatial realisation of his self-brand and power reaffirmation internally and internationally. As a city built from scratch, NEOM is viewed as a unique opportunity to materialise his "progressive" ideas, which are close to impossible to implement in existing cities. Internally, NEOM has been introduced to the society as an economic engine of the post-oil transition that will bring prosperity to the Saudis and will maintain their quality of life. NEOM is also represented as a factor of national pride, arguing that the Kingdom deserves to have an advanced city that leads the future. NEOM also exemplifies MBS' social reforms. This is demonstrated on a wide scale by the branding material. *The Settlers'* promotional video stars Fayza al-Shaalan, a London-educated architect, who belongs to Saudi Arabia's growing class of young, well-educated professionals, to whom relaxing the control of the religious apparatus is an important promise. In the video, al-Shaalan is featured as a modern woman on a professional adventure, driving her car by the sea beside the mountains. Al-Shaalan not only drives herself to NEOM, which would not have been possible a couple of years ago, but also symbolically takes off her veil when she arrives in NEOM and steps out of her car. The transition from Saudi Arabia to NEOM, the new future, serves as an allegory of MBS succeed-

50 Cf. Gardner, 2019.

51 BBC, 2020.

52 Quoted by BBC, 2016.

ing Abdullah to become King. Importantly, NEOM spatially reflects not only a post-oil economic transition, but also an evolution of the social contract.

Internationally, NEOM has been used as a medium to formulate foreign policies that strategically strengthen relations to superpowers such as the United States. Saudi attention to environmental and climate issues increased abruptly, coinciding with US President Biden's inauguration in early 2021, as The Line's branding material shows. After his inauguration, Biden initiated a Leader Summit on Climate, and King Salman was among the 40 invited leaders. Coincidently, one day after the invitation, the Crown Prince publicly announced the "Saudi Arabia Green Initiative" and the "Middle East Green Initiative."[53] Notably, NEOM is employed to help Saudi Arabia build an international image that blocks out the paradox of being the biggest petrol exporter while simultaneously claiming to be a leading international actor in climate-protecting measures. Personalising the green initiatives, NEOM, and The Line as the brainchildren of the Crown Prince is one of the ways to re-establish positive international associations with him, after his image suffered in the aftermath of the killing of Khashoqji and the Yemen War. This personalisation affirms his power as a world-class leader. Importantly, contextualising NEOM's environmental branding also raises questions about the path MBS is following: is he taking solid steps towards green urbanism and low emissions, or rather merely greenwashing? Globally, such state-led greenwashing raises concerns about current efforts and future climate-protecting measures, as it could aggravate the effects of climate change and hinder, rather than boost, mitigation and prevention efforts.

5 Conclusion

NEOM provides this chapter with a very fertile soil to unpack a variety of issues and pose both analytical and conceptual questions. The chapter approaches branding as a political act that implies a political choice and is shaped by power dynamics. The stakes of the political leadership and other actors, including consultancies, the construction sector, and tech companies, shape NEOM as a city and a brand and decide which narratives are to be told and which ones are to stay untold. In other words, branding is not just images and slogans. Like any other political act, it has consequences that do not affect everybody in the same way: while some are included, other are left out; while certain groups are advantaged, others are disadvantaged.

53 Cf. Naar, 2021.

The chapter has shown that NEOM is not just a bright image of the future, but also a reflection of present realities. In more general terms, it asserts that studying the place branding of new cities is essential for comprehending their complexities, conflicting interests, and power relations. Bringing NEOM's branding narratives and MBS' power aspirations close together under one analytical framework exemplifies how place branding can be used to strengthen MBS' power ambitions, both nationally and internationally. NEOM's branding narratives systematically reflect MBS' views of how the future should be, who should be allowed to contribute to the making of the future, and who is invited to it. This chapter thus argues that NEOM is a spatial realisation of present Saudi political dynamics orchestrated by MBS and his future power ambitions.

Essentially, the chapter argues that future studies of branding should approach it as a political act. Depoliticising urban development in general and place branding specifically contributes to further excluding large parts of the population from city politics, fosters the dominance of experts and technocrats at the expense of citizens, and normalises the absence of accountability. Hence, the questions how and who creates the brand are very important. The role that international consultancies play in widely replicating and selling brands around the world is definitely worth our attention. The first reason is so that we can understand their stake in building the new urban imaginary. The second reason is so that we can recognise the extent to which, by overemphasising fantasies and fiction as the prototype for the future, they hinder the emergence of any possible collective alternative imaginaries. The last reason is so that we can realise how such consultancies serve the political ambitions of an authoritarian ruler, while impeding any sort of democratic practices in the city.

Bibliography

Al Arabiya. "Day1 Coverage: Saudi Arabia Hosts Landmark Investment Conference." *YouTube* 24 October 2017. https://www.youtube.com/watch?v=TdtaNpevCVg. Accessed 10 April 2018.

Aly, Hend. "Royal Dream: City Branding and Saudi Arabia's NEOM." *Middle East–Topics & Arguments* 12.1 (2019): 99–109. https://archiv.ub.uni-marburg.de/ep/0003/article/view/7937. Accessed 9 May 2021.

Aly, Hend. "Global City Mirage: Depoliticising Urban Transformation in Belgrade and Tirana." *Mitteilungen der Österreichischen Geographischen Gesellschaft* 162 (2020): 43–63.

BBC. "Saudi Arabia Agrees Plans to Move Away from Oil Profits." 25 April 2016. https://www.bbc.com/news/world-middle-east-36131391. Accessed 4 May 2021.

BBC. "Saudi Crown Prince Mohammed Bin Salman, Power behind the Throne." 6 October 2020. https://www.bbc.com/news/world-middle-east-40354415. Accessed 2 May 2021.

Block, India. "Norman Foster Steps Back from Saudi Tech City over Journalist's Murder." *Dezeen* 23 October 2018. https://www.dezeen.com/2018/10/23/norman-foster-partners-neom-city-khashoggi-murder-news/. Accessed 9 May 2019.

Boykoff, Jules, and Gilmar Mascarenhas. "The Olympics, Sustainability, and Greenwashing: The Rio 2016 Summer Games." *Capitalism Nature Socialism* 27.2 (2016): 1–11.

Côté-Roy, Laurence, and Sarah Moser. "'Does Africa Not Deserve Shiny New Cities?' The Power of Seductive Rhetoric around New Cities in Africa." *Urban Studies* 56.12 (2019): 2391–2407.

Cugurullo, Federico. "Speed Kills: Fast Urbanism and Endangered Sustainability in the Masdar City Project." In *Mega-Urbanization in the Global South: Fast Cities and New Urban Utopias of the Postcolonial State*, edited by Ayona Datta and Abdul Shaban, 66–80. London, New York: Routledge, 2017.

Cugurullo, Federico. "How to Build a Sandcastle: An Analysis of the Genesis and Development of Masdar City." *Journal of Urban Technology* 20.1 (2013): 23–37.

Daragahi, Borzou, and Bel Trew. "Neom: Ancient Saudi Tribe in Danger of 'Disappearing off Face of the Earth' to Make Way for Vanity Project." *The Independent* 5 October 2020. https://www.independent.co.uk/news/world/middle-east/neom-saudi-arabia-city-mbs-huwaitat-b809153.html#/comments. Accessed 5 May 2021.

Datta, Ayona. "Introduction: Fast Cities in an Urban Age." In *Mega-Urbanization in the Global South: Fast Cities and New Urban Utopias of the Postcolonial State*, edited by Ayona Datta and Abdul Shaban, 1–28. London, New York: Routledge, 2017.

Datta, Ayona, and Abdul Shaban, eds. *Mega-Urbanization in the Global South: Fast Cities and New Urban Utopias of the Postcolonial State.* London, New York: Routledge, 2017.

Dinnie, Keith, ed. *City Branding: Theory and Cases.* Basingstoke: Palgrave Macmillan, 2011.

Elsheshtawy, Yasser. "Redrawing Boundaries: Dubai, an Emerging World City." In *Planning Middle Eastern Cities: An Urban Kaleidoscope in a Globalizing World*, edited by Yasser Elsheshtawy, 169–199. London, New York: Routledge, 2009.

Faucon, Benoit, and Summer Said. "Saudi Arabia Set to Raise Oil Output Amid Recovery in Prices." *Wall Street Journal* 17 February 2021. https://www.wsj.com/articles/saudi-arabia-set-to-raise-oil-output-amid-recovery-in-prices-11613570923. Accessed 1 May 2021.

Florida, Richard. "Cities and the Creative Class." *City & Community* 2.1 (2003): 3–19.

Friedmann, John. "The World City Hypothesis." *Development and Change* 17.1 (1986): 69–83.

Gardner, Frank. "Mohammed Bin Salman: How Saudi Arabia's Crown Prince Rose to Power." *BBC* 2019. https://www.bbc.co.uk/news/extra/ILGBQVCUCZ/mohammed_bin_salman. Accessed 1 May 2021.

Govers, Robert. "From Place Marketing to Place Branding and Back." *Place Branding and Public Diplomacy* 7.4 (2011): 227–231.

Govers, Robert, and Frank M. Go. *Place Branding: Glocal, Virtual and Physical Identities, Constructed, Imagined and Experienced.* Basingstoke: Palgrave Macmillan, 2009.

Harvey, David. "From Managerialism to Entrepreneurialism: The Transformation in Urban Governance in Late Capitalism." *Geografiska Annaler: Series B, Human Geography* 71.1 (1989): 3–17.

King Abdullah Economic City. *Annual Report 2018: King Abdullah Economic City.* 2018. https://www.kaec.net/wp-content/uploads/2020/12/KAEC-Annual-Report-2018-English.pdf. Accessed 2 April 2021.

Molotch, Harvey Luskin, and Davide Ponzini, eds. *The New Arab Urban: Gulf Cities of Wealth, Ambition, and Distress.* New York: New York University Press, 2019.

Moser, Sarah. "'Two Days to Shape the Future': A Saudi Arabian Node in the Transnational Circulation of Ideas about New Cities." In *The New Arab Urban: Gulf Cities of Wealth, Ambition, and Distress*, edited by Harvey Luskin Molotch and Davide Ponzini, 412–448. New York: New York University Press, 2019.

Moser, Sarah, and Laurence Côté-Roy. "New Cities: Power, Profit, and Prestige." *Geography Compass* 15.1 (2021): 1–15.

Naar, Ismaeel. "Saudi Crown Prince Announces Saudi Green Initiative, Middle East Green Initiative." *Alarabiya News* 27 March 2021. https://english.alarabiya.net/News/gulf/2021/03/27/Saudi-Crown-Prince-announces-Saudi-Green-Initiative-Green-Middle-East-Initiative. Accessed 1 May 2019.

NEOM. *HRH the Crown Prince Mohammed bin Salman Announces: NEOM – The Destination for the Future.* Press Release. Riyadh, 24 October 2017. http://www.neom.com/content/pdfs/NEOM_press_release_English_2017.10.24.pdf. Accessed 23 August 2018.

NEOM. *NEOM: New Way. New Era.* Brochure. 2018. https://neomdevelope.com/assets/neom/pdfs/NEOM-Brochure-en.pdf. Accessed 1 September 2021.

NEOM. "Welcome to NEOM – A New Destination for Extreme Sports." *YouTube* 22 May 2019a. https://www.youtube.com/watch?v=APaL2DBfHOU. Accessed 5 May 2021.

NEOM. "NEOM Pioneers." *YouTube* 6 December 2019b. https://www.youtube.com/watch?v=AcneFdW3cG4. Accessed 5 May 2021.

NEOM. "Discover more about #NEOM's Health, Well-being and Biotech Sector." *YouTube* 22 December 2019c. https://www.youtube.com/watch?v=Gdd-DYh6TeA. Accessed 7 May 2021.

NEOM. "NEOM: The Settlers." *YouTube* 26 January 2020a. https://www.youtube.com/watch?v=e7PIhIh3LTg. Accessed 5 May 2021.

NEOM. "Life in NEOM – Episode 02 – Education." *YouTube* 3 April 2020b. https://www.youtube.com/watch?v=8T9GvsS4bw0. Accessed 8 May 2021.

NEOM. "NEOM: An Accelerator of Human Progress." https://www.neom.com/en-us. Accessed 1 September 2021a.

NEOM. "HRH Prince Mohammed bin Salman Announces The Line at NEOM." 10 January 2021b. https://www.neom.com/en-us/newsroom/hrh-prince-announces-the-line. Accessed 2 April 2021.

NEOM. *An Accelerator for Human Progress.* Brochure. 2021c. https://www.neom.com/content/dam/neom/downloads/NEOM%20Information%20Pack-20210512T073913Z-001.zip. Accessed 12 April 2021.

NEOM. "The Future of Technology and Digital." https://www.neom.com/en-us/sectors/technology-and-digital. Accessed 1 September 2021d.

Peck, Jamie. "Struggling with the Creative Class." *International Journal of Urban and Regional Research* 29.4 (2005): 740–770.

Perper, Rosie. "Individuals and Businesses are Distancing Themselves from Saudi Arabia Following the Disappearance of Journalist Jamal Khashoggi." *Business Insider* 19 October 2018. https://www.businessinsider.com/businesses-cutting-ties-with-saudi-arabia-over-jamal-khashoggi-disappearance-2018-10. Accessed 1 May 2019.

Roy, Ananya, and Aihwa Ong, eds. *Worlding Cities: Asian Experiments and the Art of Being Global.* Oxford: Wiley-Blackwell, 2011.

Sassen, Saskia. "Locating Cities on Global Circuits." *Environment and Urbanization* 14.1 (2002): 13–30.

Sassen, Saskia. "The Global City: Introducing a Concept." *The Brown Journal of World Affairs* 11.2 (2005): 18.

Scheck, Justin, Rory Jones, and Summer Said. "A Prince's $500 Billion Desert Dream: Flying Cars, Robot Dinosaurs and a Giant Artificial Moon." *Wall Street Journal* 25 July 2019. https://www.wsj.com/articles/a-princes-500-billion-desert-dream-flying-cars-robot-dinosaurs-and-a-giant-artificial-moon-11564097568. Accessed 1 May 2020.

Swyngedouw, Erik, Frank Moulaert, and Arantxa Rodriguez. "Neoliberal Urbanization in Europe: Large-Scale Urban Development Projects and the New Urban Policy." In *Spaces of Neoliberalism: Urban Reconstructing in North American and Western Europe*, edited by Neil Brenner and Nik Theodore, 194–229. Malden: Blackwell, 2002.

Taylor, Peter J. "Specification of the World City Network." *Geographical Analysis* 33.2 (2001): 181–194.

Vanolo, Alberto. *City Branding: The Ghostly Politics of Representation in Globalising Cities.* London, New York: Routledge, 2017.

Vision 2030. *Home.* https://www.vision2030.gov.sa. Accessed 1 September 2021.

Watson, Vanessa. "African Urban Fantasies: Dreams or Nightmares?" *Environment and Urbanization* 26.1 (2014): 215–231.

Annegret Roelcke

Two Politicians and a Shrine: Competing Personal Brands around Eyüpsultan in Istanbul

Shortly before Istanbul's mayoral elections in March 2019, Ekrem İmamoğlu, the candidate of the oppositional secularist Republican People's Party (*Cumhuriyet Halk Partisi*, CHP), publicly recited the Quranic Yāsīn Surah in Istanbul's Eyüpsultan Mosque, which many regard as the most sacred Islamic place in Turkey. The media have routinely covered the frequent prayers there by Turkish president Recep Tayyip Erdoğan of the ruling Justice and Development Party (*Adalet ve Kalkınma Partisi*, AKP), but İmamoğlu's visit sparked controversies across the political factions. On Twitter, journalist Orhan Gökdemir declared the death of secularism,[1] while others accused the CHP candidate of pre-election hypocrisy.[2]

1 Branding Politicians with Shrines

In the following, I discuss how rival politicians in Turkey have branded themselves by visiting Eyüpsultan within the recent context of the increasingly tense polarisation between so-called Islamic-religious and secular groups. The AKP, having ruled with its predecessors locally since 1994 and nationally since 2002, claims to represent society's religious segments, while the CHP portrays itself as promoting secular, republican values. I also investigate how these branding activities may transform Eyüpsultan's dominant Islamist image. In doing so, I analyse the interplay between personal branding and place branding. The research focuses on both traditional and social media as the main arenas in which the visits are communicated to and commented on by the public.

Iulia Medveschi and Sandu Frunză have discussed the ways in which politicians are frequently branded with an "aura of sacredness,"[3] at times even in a messianic manner, that mobilises transcendent motifs.[4] Likewise, Erdoğan is venerated by his supporters as taking a stand against the secularist policies of the

1 See Gökdemir, 2019.

2 See halkweb.com.tr, 2019.

3 Medveschi and Frunză, 2018: 148.

4 See Medveschi and Frunză, 2018: 141–144.

https://doi.org/10.1515/9783110741100-033

elite, while İmamoğlu is seen – even by people outside the CHP's core supporters – as a potential saviour from what they perceive as the AKP's increasingly authoritarian rule.[5] Targeting pious Sunni groups in particular, both politicians use religious elements such as visits to shrines in order to brand themselves. The ways in which they do this differ, however, based on their personal and party backgrounds. For example, by combining their Eyüpsultan visits with visits to other shrines, they are able to symbolise their competing identity narratives.

2 Eyüpsultan as a Symbol of Islamic-Ottoman Rule

The Eyüpsultan Shrine is a central feature in Turkey's religious topography. With the adjacent mosque and the surrounding Eyüpsultan neighbourhood, it has for centuries been a popular pilgrimage site (cf. Fig. 1) and a symbol of Sunni Islam's connection to political rule. It is named after a companion of the Prophet Muhammad whose grave, legend has it, was rediscovered during the Ottoman conquest of Istanbul in 1453. Ottoman sultans later connected their power to the saint by visiting the shrine during enthronement ceremonies and before military campaigns.

Recently, the AKP has branded Eyüpsultan as a symbolic place in its revivalist Ottoman and Islamist rhetoric.[6] Erdoğan has held numerous public meetings and prayed there at events crucial to his career. After winning the constitutional referendum in 2017, which was intended to augment his power in a new presidential system, he performed a prayer of gratitude in the Eyüpsultan Mosque. Journalist Erk Acarer interpreted this as Erdoğan imitating Ottoman enthronement ceremonies for his legitimation rather than responding to the protests about the referendum's rightfulness.[7] Erdoğan's subsequent prayer at the shrine of Mehmed II, the sultan who had led the Ottoman conquest of Istanbul, was a further reference to Ottoman state rituals.

5 See Gottschlich, 2019.

6 For more details, see Roelcke, 2019.

7 See Acarer, 2017.

Fig. 1: Eyüpsultan Shrine
Photo: Annegret Roelcke, 2016.

3 Using a Sacred Place to Brand the Secularist Party Candidate

Since many who consider themselves secular have viewed Erdoğan's public prayers as aggressive demonstrations of the Islamisation of politics, they have also felt uneasy about the prayers of the secularist party candidate in Eyüpsultan. However, İmamoğlu's pious behaviour has posed a serious threat to the AKP's image as the main protector of Islam. By using his conservative Sunni origins and childhood in a rural Black Sea area to brand himself, İmamoğlu presents a social background shared by many AKP supporters, in contrast to other CHP politicians who are viewed as secular urban elites. His image as a pious Muslim promoting secular values has been central to his reconciliatory discourse. When İmamoğlu won the election, it was seen by many as a victory beyond Istanbul and especially against Erdoğan, due to the city's economic, cultural, and symbolic significance. Under the pressure of the AKP, the election was repeated, which only made İmamoğlu's victory even clearer.[8]

In 2021, after two years in office and polls indicating İmamoğlu's popularity vis-à-vis Erdoğan and thus suggesting his future as the country's president, the AKP is increasingly viewing him as a threat.[9] AKP-ruled institutions' interference with İmamoğlu's visits to shrines only confirm their importance in the success of his personal branding. In 2019, he was denied access to pray at Eyüpsultan Shrine.[10] While this was possibly aimed at preventing pictures of him from being taken at the symbolic Islamic site, media coverage instead portrayed him as having been wronged by the AKP, which only increased his popularity.[11] In 2021, the Interior Ministry sued İmamoğlu for disrespectful behaviour simply because he had walked with his hands folded behind his back in the courtyard of the shrine of Mehmed II.[12]

4 Eyüpsultan as a Symbol of Islamic Diversity

Apart from his own personal branding, visits to Eyüpsultan have also helped İmamoğlu identify the place with narratives that differ from the dominant revivalist Ottoman and Islamist ones promoted by the AKP. Thus, on 19 May 2020, he observed both secular-republican and Islamic holidays there. In addition to Eyüpsultan Shrine, he also visited the nearby shrines of Ümmi Sinan and Karyağdı Baba. The first represents a narrative celebrating early republican politics involving a member of the convent connected to the shrine. While the CHP cherishes the early republican era of the 1920s for its modernising and secularising reforms, revivalist narratives portray it negatively for having broken with Ottoman traditions. The second shrine belongs to the Bektaşi order, whose heritage is nowadays claimed by Alevis. This heterogenous, religious-ethnic community has been often discri-

8 See Gottschlich, 2019.

9 See Gottschlich, 2021.

10 İmamoğlu refrained from naming the individual who denied him access. The Istanbul Directorate for Shrines and Museums, which belongs to the AKP-ruled Ministry of Culture and Tourism, is officially responsible for the administration of Eyüpsultan Shrine.

11 See iyigunler.net, 2019.

12 See Gottschlich, 2021.

minated against in Turkey's Sunni-majority society. Many of them support the CHP.[13]

The two politicians' visits to Eyüpsultan clearly illustrate the reciprocal relationship between personal branding and place branding. Both use the place as a symbol of Islam in society, but by incorporating it into their individual brand images, they frame it – and therefore Islam – with different identity narratives. Erdoğan legitimates his power by claiming to revive an Islamic-Ottoman heritage and, more implicitly, as Islamically sanctioned by the saint. As a politician of the secularist CHP, İmamoğlu aims to prove his Muslim integrity in order to attract religious voters as well. His visits are central to his rhetoric of reconciling society, especially his secularist party with pious groups. By highlighting the presence of groups not commonly associated with Eyüpsultan, he constructs it as a place of diversity, thereby symbolising his respect for the various members of society. Since only those familiar with religious places in Eyüpsultan can understand the symbolism of the different shrines, the second message targets mainly religious segments. However, the diversity within İmamoğlu's image of Eyüpsultan remains within an Islamically influenced framework, and the centrality of Islam in Eyüpsultan's image is crucial for the construction of İmamoğlu's own image.

Bibliography

Acarer, Erk. "Erdoğan'ın Eyüp Sultan'da kıldığı şükür namazının anlamı: 'Saltanatımı ilan ettim' mesajı [The Meaning of Erdoğan's Prayer of Gratitude in Eyüp Sultan: A Message of 'I Have Announced My Sultanate']." *Birgün.net* 17 April 2017. https://www.birgun.net/haber/erdogan-in-eyup-sultan-da-kildigi-sukur-namazinin-anlami-saltanatimi-ilan-ettim-mesaji-155852. Accessed 8 September 2021.

Dreßler, Markus. "Was ist das Alevitum? Die aktuelle Diskussion und historische Traditionslinien." In *Ocak und Dedelik: Institutionen religiösen Spezialistentums bei den Aleviten*, edited by Janina Karolewski, Hüseyin Ağuiçenoğlu, Robert Langer, and Raoul Motika, 13–35. Frankfurt am Main: Peter Lang, 2013.

Gökdemir, Orhan. "Ekremeddin İmamoğlu laikliğin ölüsünü cami avlusuna bırakıp kaçarken... Bunlar akp'nin askerleridir! [Ekremeddin İmamoğlu Fled and Left the Dead Body of Secularism in the Mosque Yard... These Are the Soldiers of the AKP!]" *Twitter* 17 March 2019. https://twitter.com/gokdemirorhan/status/1107343170273202179. Accessed 23 March 2021.

Gottschlich, Jürgen. "Bürgermeisterwahl in Istanbul: 'Alles wird sehr schön werden.'" *Taz* 26 June 2019. https://taz.de/Buergermeisterwahl-in-Istanbul/!5601833/. Accessed 22 March 2021.

Gottschlich, Jürgen. "Politische Justiz in der Türkei: Verfahren gegen Erdoğans Rivalen." *Taz* 5 May 2021. https://taz.de/Politische-Justiz-in-der-Tuerkei/!5765513/. Accessed 6 May 2021.

13 See Dreßler, 2013: 16–30.

halkweb.com.tr. “Yandaş yazardan Ekrem İmamoğlu’nun Yasin okumasına şaşırtan tepki [Partisan Writer’s Surprising Reaction to Ekrem İmamoğlu Reading the Yāsīn Surah].” 17 March 2019. https://halkweb.com.tr/yandas-yazardan-ekrem-imamoglunun-yasin-okumasina-sasirtan-tepki/. Accessed 24 March 2021.

iyigunler.net. “Ekrem İmamoğlu’nu Eyüp Sultan Türbesi’ne almadılar [They Did Not Take Ekrem İmamoğlu Into Eyüp Sultan Shrine].” 5 April 2019. https://www.iyigunler.net/gundem/ekrem-imamoglu-nu-eyup-sultan-turbesi-ne-almadi-lar-h333414.html. Accessed 12 February 2021.

Medveschi, Iulia, and Sandu Frunză. “Political Brand, Symbolic Construction and Public Image Communication.” *Journal for the Study of Religions and Ideologies* 17.49 (2018): 137–152.

Roelcke, Annegret. “Constructing the Capital of Peace: Changing Branding Strategies for Istanbul’s Eyüp Quarter.” *Middle East–Topics & Arguments* 12.1 (2019): 110–120. https://archiv.ub.uni-marburg.de/ep/0003/article/view/7931. Accessed 12 February 2021.

Melissa Gatter

Who Labels the Camp? Claiming Ownership through Visibility in Jordan

1 Introduction

"They stole our women's bathroom," a resident of Azraq refugee camp in Jordan told an aid worker and me during an outreach visit in Village 6 in 2017. "Some people came in the night and stole the bathroom."

For every three caravans in the camp, there is one women's and one men's bathroom unit. The units are made from the same white aluminium sheets as the caravans and propped up on a 15-centimetre-tall cement foundation. Each unit contains one squat toilet and a shower on a concrete floor. In this unit in Village 6, the toilet was missing. The stolen toilet was likely intended to be installed in a caravan for private use, as the communal facilities of Azraq are an uncomfortable experience for most residents. Citing issues of safety, hygiene, inaccessibility, and inconvenience, many in the camp have taken to showering inside their residence using a bucket and water.[1]

Prominently stamped on each door of the bathroom units are the blue logos of UNICEF and World Vision (Fig. 1), the sponsors of the facilities that its users have deemed less preferable to a bucket and water. From toilets to backpacks to tents, "humanitarian organizations always sign their works."[2] This is the case in Za'tari and Azraq, the two main camps for Syrian refugees in Jordan run by the United Nations High Commissioner for Refugees (UNHCR). A colourful mix of logos and flags decorates the beige landscape of each camp. While the Jordanian flag at the entrance and blazoned on the arms of Jordanian military officials throughout both camps asserts Jordan's authority over all, it is greatly outnumbered by the flags of United Nations organisations (UNOs), international nongovernmental organisations (INGOs), and donor states in the Global North and the Gulf. In Za'tari, Saudi Arabia is especially visible, having marked caravans, winter coats, and clothes with its bright green sword and palm tree emblem. These flags and logos establish the camps as pseudo-"surrogate states"[3] of cosmopolitan aid – and increasingly corporatised humanitarianism.

---

1 See Alshawawreh, 2019: 112.

2 Martinez Mansell, 2016.

3 Slaughter and Crisp, 2009. See also Hoffmann, 2016.

https://doi.org/10.1515/9783110741100-034

The flag that does not fly in either camp is the Syrian flag. In Za'tari's first year in 2012, flags and symbols of the Syrian revolution were prominent in the camp. However, when the UNHCR assumed camp management the following year, the agency implemented a strict push for depoliticisation.[4] Syrian revolution flags were taken down, spaces of political discussion such as coffee shops and shisha bars were closed, and youth being photographed in NGO centres were instructed to change peace signs to thumbs up. When Azraq opened the following year, the space was depoliticised before refugees even moved in.

Fearful of security issues and a repeat of the Palestinian case of empowered displaced people, the Jordanian state drives the depoliticisation of its Syrian refugee camps. Aid agencies must adhere to Jordan's mandate in order to operate in the country, and they are also motivated by humanitarian ideals of political neutrality.[5] Liisa Malkki has framed the forced neutralisation of humanitarian space as a "leaching out"[6] of refugees' rich political histories. Recent scholarship points out that depoliticisation in refugee camps actually constitutes a new form of politics,[7] namely, a *humanitarian* politics that shapes the boundaries of the governed within the physical camp borders set by the host state. The camp space is thus neither neutral nor depoliticised, but rather "hyperpoliticised,"[8] "explicitly political, even as humanitarian organizations reject the political contours of the space in which they work."[9] The spirit of humanitarianism in Azraq and Za'tari reinforces a non-state regime under which politics, aid, histories, and regulation converge to shape both camp spaces.

One of the new kinds of politics created through depoliticisation is a politics of visibility. Jordan employs both Azraq and Za'tari as its own "emblems of visibility"[10] that provide evidence of its hospitality, but actually work to contain refugees. Corporatised aid agencies in the camps "rent the essence of [their] particular brand value – trust, respect, ethical motivation"[11] to Jordan in exchange for business in the world's largest refugee crisis. The branding of aid space establishes the organisations operating in the camps as forming a legitimate apparatus with authority over the camp territories. The camps' aid organisations must maintain a regime of visibility to sustain legitimacy in the eyes of the host state and an inter-

4 See UNHCR, 2013.

5 See Audet, 2015; Terry, 2002; Weiss and Barnett, 2008; Yanacopulos, 2015.

6 Malkki, 1996: 378.

7 See Turner, 2016; Stein, 2008.

8 See Turner, 2016: 145.

9 Stein, 2008: 129.

10 Ali, 2021: 9. See also Gatter, 2021; Pasha, 2021; Tsourapas, 2019; Turner, 2015.

11 Hopgood, 2008: 106.

Fig. 1: The branded toilets of Azraq camp
Photo: Melissa Gatter, 2018, with faces blurred out.

national audience. Thus, the visible insignia of the camps – the flags and logos of humanitarian organisations and donor states – are part and parcel of Azraq's and Za'tari's hyperpoliticised space.

While the literature on refugee camps is replete with studies of space,[12] scarce attention has been paid to the politics of visibility created by humanitarian organisations and donor states *within* camp spaces. With a particular focus on UNOs, (I)NGOs, and donor states of the Gulf Cooperation Council (GCC),[13] this chapter aims to highlight the strikingly visible but often overlooked branding that not only labels the camps, but also shapes their everyday operations. I do not intend to generalise the motivations of humanitarian organisations; rather, the chapter explores how the collective visual presence of logos and flags influences both camp spaces, based on ethnographic fieldwork conducted in Za'tari in 2016 and

12 See Agier, 2011; Katz, Martin, and Minca, 2018; Malkki, 1992; Ramadan, 2013; Sigona, 2015.
13 The GCC consists of six Gulf countries: Bahrain, Kuwait, Oman, Qatar, Saudi Arabia, and the United Arab Emirates.

in Azraq from 2017 to 2018.[14] It argues that these symbols have marked the camps as belonging not to their residents, but instead to their humanitarian governors. Aid agencies and Gulf donor states use visibility to claim credit and ownership over physical spaces and operations in the camp, and aid workers and refugees become extensions of these brands to a global audience. Furthermore, this chapter challenges the implication that the visibility of branding signifies accountability for action tied to these logos and asks: accountability *to whom?* Just as Jordan uses the camps as "emblems of visibility" for a global audience, aid agencies and Gulf donor states use emblems within the camps as indicators of accountability deferred either onto the individual donor of the Global North, in the case of humanitarian organisations, or onto the host country, in the case of GCC donors.

2 "NGOization" and Gulf Philanthropy

In the last century, aid assistance has transformed from the "pure" altruism of *Médecins Sans Frontières* to a now globalised market of international organisations, INGOs, and NGOs that have relieved states of their obligations to humanitarian response and responsibility. As states withdrew from the aid arena, their focus shifted from carrying out service provision to funding it through donations to humanitarian organisations.[15] This trend led the way for the professionalisation and corporatisation of humanitarian organisations, a phenomenon scholars and activists have referred to as "NGOization."[16] Humanitarian agencies developed "strategies"[17] to maximise competitiveness as donors shifted to project-focused funding. Increasing competition in the market has pushed aid organisations to "copy the structures, interests, and procedures of their for-profit counterparts."[18]

Since 2012, Jordan has witnessed particularly acute NGOisation – driven by more than 450 local and international NGOs[19] – that has "shaped the Jordan response to Syrian refugees."[20] The creation of Azraq and Za'tari, as well as the

14 To access the camps, I joined three reputable INGOs as an aid worker supporting their communications teams. This port of access provided insight into the internal and external communications strategies of aid agencies in the camps, how their implementation shapes refugee lives in the camps, and how residents respond to the visible marking of their space.

15 See Stein, 2008.

16 See Choudry and Kapoor, 2013; Farah, 2020.

17 See Barnett and Snyder, 2008.

18 Cooley and Ron, 2002: 13.

19 See Jordan Times, 2017.

20 Farah, 2020: 133. See also Campbell and Tobin, 2016.

needs of the 80 per cent of Syrian refugees who live in urban settings, brought numerous well-paid employment opportunities for Jordanians in the humanitarian sector. It also brought to Jordan a "specialised cadre of international development professionals who spend the bulk of their working lives on a series of assignments in global metropolises and the capitals of low-income countries";[21] these people are usually referred to as "expats" and are mostly white and from the Global North. These expats occupy management positions and oversee the "local" staff, who are expected to provide a cultural and linguistic bridge between management and refugees.[22] The impact of NGOisation in Jordan can also be seen in the recent introduction of development studies curricula in various Jordanian universities, which will no doubt add to the competitiveness of the local humanitarian job market.

Jordan's neighbours to the south-east, the Gulf states, have made their philanthropic efforts particularly visible in the country's Syrian-refugee response. Together, the members of the GCC have donated billions of dollars to the regional response, including material or financial assistance to the Jordanian government, UNOs, and INGOs, including Islamic charities, operating in the country.[23] This support has focused mainly on funding cash assistance, food, health, education, and caravans in camp and urban settings.[24] The UAE also funds and operates the Emirati Jordanian camp, known as *Mrajeeb al Fhoud*, located just seven kilometres from Azraq camp.[25] Because the Gulf's response has consisted of almost exclusively external aid to refugee-hosting countries, Hitman has argued that the GCC has chosen "charity" over "hospitality," noting that, "in 2015, when Syrians were fleeing to Europe, the Gulf States, trying to respond to criticism for closing their borders to the refugees, recruited their media to highlight the support they provided to the Syrians."[26]

The Gulf states, none of which are signatories of the 1951 Refugee Convention, have admitted Syrian citizens but not recognised them as refugees or granted them the legal rights that the refugee label would afford them.[27] Hitman cites demographic tensions as a main reason Gulf states have kept their doors closed to Syrian refugees, as foreigners in some states already equal or outnumber national

21 Jad, 2007: 627.

22 See Ward, 2020; Farah, 2020.

23 See BBC, 2021; UNHCR, 2014b: 20.

24 See UNHCR, 2014b: 24.

25 Host to around 6,000 Syrian refugees, the camp admits only the most vulnerable, defined as widowed mothers, single women, the elderly, and people with disabilities; see UNHCR, 2021.

26 Hitman, 2019: 92.

27 See Al-Jabri, 2016.

citizens; the regimes consider this a threat to national stability. The UAE – the world's overall largest aid donor – has actively deported Syrians on numerous occasions over the years.[28] Most of the UAE's aid is coordinated through Dubai's International Humanitarian City (IHC), "the largest humanitarian logistics hub in the world."[29] The UAE promotes the IHC as the "future of humanitarian assistance"[30] and situates it favourably within a competitive market, promising humanitarian member organisations advantageous visibility and strategy. Ziadah argues that the UAE's humanitarian endeavours have been a way of projecting regional power, "bolstered by a branding campaign that presents the UAE as a stable commercial hub and 'giving nation.'"[31] In addition to demographic pressures, national security, and political prowess, Jawad adds vanity to the reasons behind the Gulf's inhospitality: keeping its refugee response external allows the Gulf to uphold its reputation as a "consumerist heaven" with "spotless highways, sports cars, [and] massive malls"[32] – refugee camps would only taint this image.

By externalising its aid efforts in Jordan, the Gulf has managed to divert attention from its unwelcoming position towards Syrian refugees. Both the humanitarian sector and GCC states have played into the visibility of Jordan's refugee camps to further their corporatised strategies. The next section explores this in the context of Azraq and Za'tari.

3 A Regime of Visibility

Aid agencies have developed and re-articulated branding strategies and mission statements to maintain their competitiveness in a globalised market and appeal to corporate donors.[33] As Hopgood notes, humanitarian organisations now sell a "product" – "a moral brand with feel-good associations"[34] – to donor institutions and corporations. These "feel-good associations" are captured and communicated most effectively in humanitarian logos and emblems. The classic humanitarian symbology of hands, people, olive branches – the UNHCR logo has all three – has become a tired trope in today's aid branding landscape. However, while humanitarian logos shamelessly play into this cliché, they are effective. For example,

28 See Hitman, 2019.
29 Ziadah, 2019: 1685.
30 UAE Federal Competitiveness and Statistics Authority, 2017: 21.
31 Ziadah, 2019: 1686.
32 Jawad, 2015.
33 See Quelch and Laidler-Kylander, 2005.
34 Hopgood, 2008: 106.

with its trademark red circle and highlighted sans serif text, Save the Children is arguably one of the most recognisable brands in the humanitarian sector.

Both Za'tari and Azraq camps are awash with variations of the stereotypical hand-person-olive branch combination. And yet, little has been written about how this visual politics has played out in displacement and camp settings. In the Lebanese context, Carpi has commented on the "war of logos"[35] among humanitarian actors and Gulf donors in non-camp aid spaces, situating the visuality of branding within a politics of space. Aid-marked spaces in Lebanon, she argued, "become stable hubs of human trust and reciprocity, a normal part of everyday life, inviting dwellers to rethink these spaces of coexistence." In many of these spaces, however, refugees described an "ephemeral" humanitarian presence in which the logos and symbols remain even though aid is not consistently physically available through aid workers. Martinez Mansell has reflected on the visible symbols of militant groups, political factions, and humanitarian organisations in the Palestinian *Bourj Al Shamali* refugee camp in Lebanon. She argued that these symbols "code" the camp as a "paradoxical space" in which "the politics of humanitarianism enable leaders to treat the refugee situation as forever temporary… even as they invest in infrastructure and housing upgrades that make the camp more permanent in real terms."[36] This section considers these themes in light of Azraq and Za'tari's everyday socio-spatial politics.

3.1 The Semi-Public Humanitarian Spaces of Azraq and Za'tari

In January 2012, thousands fleeing escalating violence in the southern Syrian province of Dar'a set up a camp near the northern Jordanian city of Mafraq, where they were met by the UNHCR and other humanitarian agencies providing tents and basic provisions. In a matter of weeks, this aid space developed into Za'tari camp, which would reach 200,000 residents by mid-2013. Today, 80,000 residents live in twelve districts within five square kilometres and have appropriated much of the camp space, with an estimated 50 per cent of the camp "effectively re-made by refugees themselves."[37] Most notable is the emergence of a micro-economy in Za'tari generated through a refugee-run market along two main streets of humanitarian services.[38] Refugee spatial appropriation prompted the UNHCR to negotiate with residents about space, electricity use, and commercial activity.[39]

35 Carpi, 2020.
36 Martinez Mansell, 2016.
37 Paszkiewicz and Fosas, 2019: 4.
38 See Al Nassir, 2020.

Political demonstrations against the Assad regime in Syria and against the camp management were frequent during Za'tari's first years.[40] The UNHCR framed demonstrations and spatial appropriation as justification for implementing intense security measures in the camp as well as in Azraq, which was being constructed at that time in 2013 and officially opened in 2014.[41] Covering 15 square kilometres in the middle of the desert east of Amman, Azraq's four villages host 40,000 residents from across Syria. The expanse of space has been used to prevent social mobilisation. Caravans are cemented into the ground, rendering their movement or expansion impossible. Azraq's micro-economy is muted in comparison to Za'tari's, as marketplaces are owned by aid agencies. As a result of the camp's securitised humanitarianism, Azraq lacks Za'tari's lived-in feel.

Both camps are managed by the UNHCR and the Syrian Refugee Affairs Directorate, the Jordanian government agency in charge of camp coordination. Security is enforced by the Jordanian military. The military operates entrance checkpoints for both camps, where aid workers must show official badges and all other visitors are required to carry permits obtained via the Ministry of the Interior. Around 24 INGOs and NGOs are active in Za'tari[42] and 22 in Azraq,[43] many of which are the implementing partners of UNOs and other international organisations. While the two camps are very different spaces, one aspect that remains consistent is their branding landscape. NGO centres throughout the camps feature logos and flags of NGOs and their UN partners. The caravans in these centres are decorated in the NGO's brand colours and aid workers don t-shirts, vests, or badges displaying their affiliation. While almost all the camp's humanitarian staff are employed at the national grade level in NGO country offices, the logos do not represent to visitors and outsiders the local teams, but rather the international corporatised brand itself.

These logos mark a network of semi-public, humanitarian-run spaces in both camps. The centres can be envisaged as exclusive gated publics, requiring registration for specific programmes with limited capacity. Some NGO centres are accessible only to certain groups in the community; for example, kindergarten spaces permit only three- to five-year-old "students" on the premises, and parents and unregistered children are not allowed entrance. One NGO working with youth allows either only boys or girls in their centres at scheduled times of the day. NGO centres also follow set hours of operation. For example, the community centres at

39 See Beehner, 2015; Dalal, 2015.

40 See Clarke, 2018.

41 See UNHCR, 2014a. See also Gatter, 2018, 2021; Hoffmann, 2017; Pasha, 2021.

42 See UNHCR, 2020a.

43 See UNHCR, 2020b.

Azraq camp – spaces open to all – admit residents between 8 a.m. and 2:30 p.m. Sunday through Thursday. These spatial and temporal boundaries are enforced by camp residents employed by the NGOs as security guards. While traditionally symbols of protection and defence, the guards simultaneously serve as links between the enclosed NGO spaces and their residential surroundings within the camps. In this way, the semi-public spaces of the centres extend into the public space outside of official NGO territory.

Just as the logos that mark these territories communicate to an international audience the presence of aid agencies in the Syrian refugee response, the logos also communicate to a refugee audience the humanitarian ownership of designated spaces within the camps. In other words, the centres are branded as belonging to the aid agencies that operate them more than to the residents who visit these spaces. The logos remind their beneficiaries of the NGO's rules and norms to be followed within the space. Especially for Azraq, where there is almost no refugee-run or unregulated public space, the overt labelling of space by humanitarian actors has left little room for recognised refugee ownership of the physical terrain.

3.2 The Brand-Refugee Relationship

Most humanitarian organisations operating in these camps adhere to a branding strategy designed in Northern headquarters. These communications strategies, updated every few years, include colour palettes, font styles, photography, social media hashtags, and tone of voice to be used in all visible materials to cultivate a consistent brand identity across numerous humanitarian contexts. The main objectives of communications teams working in the camps are to keep donors happy and to increase brand visibility. Logo placement in photographs is a key aspect of this: "A photo of a beneficiary is good, but a photo of a beneficiary with our logo somewhere in the background is always better," a communications aid worker instructed me.

I observed this in action when a small crew of filmmakers joined Jordan's communications team at Save the Children in Za'tari to film an advertisement for the organisation's new global campaign.[44] The objective was to exhibit aid workers helping children in one-second shots. As the crew visited numerous Save the Children centres around the camp, the communications team handed out red t-shirts with the organisation's logo to any aid workers who were to be filmed. All filming was done behind the shoulder of an aid worker physically as-

44 See Save the Children, 2016.

sisting a vulnerable-looking child – picking up a crying child, extending a hand, or providing one with a football for play. The camera crew calculated each shot so as to film only the back of the shirt, which displays the logo, literally juxtaposed onto the act of aiding a child in need. The ad focuses on the face of the child while the aid workers become faceless t-shirts. In the ad, the NGO was thus not composed of individual aid workers, as is the reality for camp residents, but was rather an omnipresence in a generic vulnerable community. This branding strategy fits within a corporatised humanitarianism that produces images that bring global attention to the "state of emergency more than they depict particular places."[45] The faces of refugee beneficiaries are portrayed, but their stories are decontextualised.[46] "Inexplicably clean T-shirts"[47] are paired with nameless "victims."

Fig. 2: Malek's favourite photograph, showing the Save the Children centre's signpost
Photo: Malek, 2016. Courtesy of the photographer.

The logos that illustrate the presence of aid to a global audience hold a more complex significance for camp residents. Refugees come to associate meaning with brands throughout the camp, as these symbols mark their everyday spaces. Returning to the case of Save the Children in Za'tari, I observed that many children reacted positively to seeing the logo on aid workers' uniforms or around the centres, often volunteering to pose in front of the logos for pictures. When provided with a camera for a day, a young boy named Malek photographed every logo in the NGO's centre from multiple angles, even squeezing between the fence and sign-

45 Calhoun, 2010: 33.
46 See Brun, 2016.
47 Malkki, 2015: 26.

post to capture the large sign that listed Save the Children and its donor country partners (Fig. 2). Malek picked this photo of the signpost as his favourite, saying, "It's a large sign, so I can see it from my house. Whenever I see it, I feel calm." Malek associated positive emotions with the humanitarian brand, but the meanings camp residents ascribe to aid emblems are not always positive. An aid worker noted that the Gulf emblems and flags stamped on the exterior and interior of caravans in Za'tari were unpopular among residents, who are fully aware of the problematic role Gulf politics has played in the Syrian conflict.[48]

Furthermore, the meanings residents associate with humanitarian and Gulf emblems can "migrate"[49] with brands from centre to centre. For example, while Malek frequents Save the Children's centre in his neighbourhood, he could identify a familiar space in the NGO's centres in any other district through its branding. But this is not always the case. In Azraq, where physical isolation is integral to everyday lived experience, meanings associated with brands do not necessarily migrate from one area of the camp to another. Noor, a youth attendee of an NGO centre in the locked-down Village 5, struggled to find social networks when her family was transferred to a different village. While the Village 5 centre had assisted Noor in feeling socially grounded, the branding of the same NGO in an adjacent village's centre did not feel familiar to her. For Noor, it was the individual aid workers and attendees of the Village 5 centre who gave the NGO logo its meaning. The positive associations she held with the NGO's brand in Village 5 simply did not apply to other instances of the logo elsewhere in the camp.

Moreover, just as aid workers are branded by their employer, beneficiaries also represent their "benefactors." Young residents attending schools in the camps are provided with backpacks displaying Saudi or NGO logos. The winter market thoroughfare in Za'tari is noticeably greener than usual, as many wear the bright green winter jackets provided by Saudi Arabia. Youth attendees of a World Refugee Day carnival in Azraq were given balloons with the sponsoring NGO's logo on it.

Hence, the relationship between aid emblems and their beneficiaries is much more complicated than that between aid emblems and their intended global audience. But regardless of the relationship camp residents have with various humanitarian and philanthropic brands, the main significance of these items lies in their visibility to an external audience, who will see the logos prominently displayed in pamphlets and ads like the one described at the beginning of this section. The or-

---

48 Estella Carpi, 2020, reported a similar sentiment among Syrian refugees in Lebanon, who told her, "We're using the plates with the Saudi logo to show you we are given this stuff… but we normally don't like using them as we don't think Saudi politics helped Syrians in any way."

49 Hopgood, 2008: 107.

ganisations become their logos, a symbol of both the agencies' good will and their need for donor backing to ensure their continued operation, and aid workers and camp residents become visual representations of these brands to a global audience via logos and other branded merchandise. The following section discusses the implications of this ownership-through-branding.

4 Ownership, But Not Accountability

An aid worker recounted the story of a family from one of the camps who had begun the journey to Europe but did not survive crossing the Mediterranean: "Their child drowned wearing our NGO's t-shirt," he told me. This image drastically contrasts with those circulated by NGOs in which they are "'doing good,' unencumbered, and untainted."[50] It is a sobering reminder that brand visibility does not necessarily signify accountability towards refugee beneficiaries.

The corporatisation of humanitarianism generated not only branding strategies, but also a rise in monitoring and evaluation, prompting an "emergence of a language of accountability."[51] But, as scholars have shown, NGOisation "produces upward rather than downward accountability"[52] – that is, accountability towards donors or the states that fund agencies, but rarely to the beneficiaries themselves.[53] Aid workers regularly collect "success stories" (*qiṣaṣ al-najāḥ*) – profiles of beneficiaries who have benefitted from their organisation – to include in reports to the programme's donors. In some instances, aid workers must find a positive spin to a beneficiary's story to fulfil the requested number of success stories. This was the case in the previous example of Noor, who had been transferred out of Village 5 and missed the NGO centre there. Even though Noor did not feel comfortable enough to attend the same NGO's centre in neighbouring Village 3, the NGO's communications team focused instead on her attachment to their centre in Village 5. The resulting success story emphasised to the donor the need for continued financial support to be able to aid Noor's transition to her new village. For the success story interview, aid workers brought Noor to their Village 3 centre to take her photograph; the final report featured a photo of Noor smiling in front of the NGO's logo at the centre she had no desire to attend.

50 Fisher, 1997: 442.
51 Stein, 2008: 128.
52 Jad, 2007: 625.
53 See Slim, 2002; Cunningham, 2012.

This meticulous shaping of optics reflects donor-driven prioritisation of programmatic performance and outcome over the lived experiences of programme beneficiaries. This results in a system in which refugees are spoken "for" or "about," but rarely "with."[54] For example, while Noor was quoted in her success story, her words were used to communicate the *NGO's* message to the donor. In the camps, humanitarian and philanthropic branding focuses on the emergency, rendering aid agencies visible at the expense of refugee histories.

This regime of visibility in the camps works to deflect responsibility either onto donors in the Global North, in the case of aid agencies, or onto the host country itself, in the case of Gulf donor states. By directing beneficiary messages set against humanitarian branding to external audiences, aid agencies communicate a dire need for the international community to step up and assume individual responsibility where states and transnational structures have failed. By externalising their aid efforts – and visibly branding each of these efforts – in the Jordanian host country, Gulf donor states have managed to avoid having to take in Syrian refugees or assume responsibility for Syrians already in their own countries.

5 Conclusion

Branding strategies of humanitarian organisations have increasingly mirrored corporate branding strategies in recent decades, and these strategies have extended into the two main camps for Syrian refugees in Jordan. While refugees form their own associations with the logos in their everyday spaces, as seen in the examples of Malek and Noor above, they also become extensions of these brands through branded provisions and strategic brand placement. Such visibility works to claim spatial ownership in the camp on behalf of aid agencies and donor states, but it does not indicate accountability towards camp residents. Still, this chapter does not intend to negate the important work that humanitarianism and philanthropy have done in the camps, but rather to understand the influence of this politics of visibility on spaces in the camps and those who use them.

To be sure, camp residents have also used symbols and other insignia to reclaim their space. In Za'tari, residents have painted street signs onto the sides of caravans, and artists in Azraq have painted murals. Caravan interiors are often decorated with Islamic calligraphy. Subtle signs of ongoing support for the Syrian revolution exist in small or deconstructed forms: a bracelet with the Syrian colours (red, white, black, and green), a small flag hand-painted on a child's hand at a car-

54 See Stein, 2008: 131.

nival, a graffitied message on the side of a restroom in an NGO centre reading, "*rā-ji'īn yā waṭan* [we're returning, oh homeland]," soon to be erased. These are signs not just of refugee agency but of their histories, and for this reason, their marking of the space is deemed political. In the same vein, how can branded toilets be considered any less political?

Bibliography

Agier, Michel. *Managing the Undesirables: Refugee Camps and Humanitarian Government.* Cambridge, UK: Polity Press, 2011.

Ali, Ali. "Disaggregating Jordan's Syrian Refugee Response: The 'Many Hands' of the Jordanian State." *Mediterranean Politics* (2021): 1–24.

Al-Jabri, Tala. "The GCC 'Must Rethink Its Refugee Strategy.'" *Refugees Deeply* 20 June 2016. https://deeply.thenewhumanitarian.org/refugees/community/2016/06/20/the-gcc-must-rethink-its-refugee-strategy. Accessed 7 August 2021.

Al Nassir, Sara. "Constructive Exceptionality: Spontaneous Urbanization and Recovered Agency in Zaatari Refugee Camp." *Research in Urbanism Series* 6 (2020): 81–98.

Alshawawreh, Lara. *Architecture of Emergencies in the Middle East: Proposed Shelter Design Criteria.* PhD thesis, Edinburgh Napier University, 2019.

Audet, Francois. "Humanitarian Space." In *The Routledge Companion to Humanitarian Action*, edited by Jenny H. Peterson and Roger MacGinty, 141–152. Abingdon, Oxon: Routledge, 2015.

Barnett, Michael, and Jack Snyder. "The Grand Strategies of Humanitarianism." In *Humanitarianism in Question: Politics, Power, Ethics*, edited by Thomas Weiss and Michael Barnett, 143–171. Ithaca: Cornell University Press, 2008.

BBC. "Mu'tamar al-Kuwait: Ta'ahhudāt tatajāwaz milyār dūlār lil-lāji'īn al-sūriyyīn (Kuwait Conference Pledges to Provide More Than 2 Billion USD for the Syrian Refugees)." *BBC News Arabic* 30 January 2013. https://www.bbc.com/arabic/middleeast/2013/01/130130_syria_kuwait. Accessed 19 August 2021.

Beehner, Lionel. "Are Syria's Do-It-Yourself Refugees Outliers or Examples of a New Norm?" *Journal of International Affairs* 68.2 (2015): 157–175.

Brun, Cathrine. "There Is No Future in Humanitarianism: Emergency, Temporality and Protracted Displacement." *History and Anthropology* 27.4 (2016): 393–410.

Calhoun, Craig. "The Idea of Emergency: Humanitarian Action and Global (Dis)Order." In *Contemporary States of Emergency: The Politics of Military and Humanitarian Interventions*, edited by Didier Fassin and Mariella Pandolfi, 29–58. New York: Zone Books, 2010.

Campbell, Madeline Otis, and Sarah Tobin. "NGO Governance and Syrian Refugee 'Subjects' in Jordan." *Middle East Research and Information Project* 278 (2016). https://merip.org/2016/04/ngo-governance-and-syrian-refugee-subjects-in-jordan/. Accessed 3 January 2017.

Carpi, Estella. "Spaces of Transregional Aid and Visual Politics in Lebanon." *Refugee Outreach & Research Network* 23 November 2020. http://www.ror-n.org/2/post/2020/11/spaces-of-transregional-aid-and-visual-politics-in-lebanon.html. Accessed 24 November 2020.

Choudry, Aziz, and Dip Kapoor, eds. *NGOization: Complicity, Contradictions and Prospects.* London: Zed Books, 2013.

Clarke, Killian. “When Do the Dispossessed Protest? Informal Leadership and Mobilization in Syrian Refugee Camps.” *Perspectives on Politics* 16.3 (2018): 617–633.

Cooley, Alexander, and James Ron. “The NGO Scramble: Organizational Insecurity and the Political Economy of Transnational Action.” *International Security* 27.1 (2002): 5–39.

Cunningham, Oliver. “The Humanitarian Aid Regime in the Republic of NGOs: The Fallacy of ‘Building Back Better.’” *Josef Korbel Journal of Advanced International Studies* 4 (2012): 101–126.

Dalal, Ayham. “A Socio-Economic Perspective on the Urbanisation of Zaatari Camp in Jordan.” *Migration Letters* 12.3 (2015): 263–278.

Farah, Reem. “Expat, Local, and Refugee: ‘Studying up’ the Global Division of Labor and Mobility in the Humanitarian Industry in Jordan.” *Migration and Society* 3 (2020): 130–144.

Fisher, William. “Doing Good? The Politics and Antipolitics of NGO Practices.” *Annual Review of Anthropology* 26 (1997): 439–464.

Gatter, Melissa. “Rethinking the Lessons from Za’atari Refugee Camp.” *Forced Migration Review* 57 (2018): 22–24.

Gatter, Melissa. “Preserving Order: Narrating Resilience as Threat in Jordan’s Azraq Refugee Camp.” *Territory, Politics, Governance* (2021): 1–17.

Hitman, Gadi. “Gulf States’ Policy towards Syrian Refugees: Charity before Hospitality.” *Asian Affairs* 50.1 (2019): 80–101.

Hoffmann, Sophia. “A Sovereign for All: The Management of Refugees as Nation-State Politics.” In *The Politics of Humanitarianism: Power, Ideology and Aid*, edited by Antonio De Lauri, 147–174. London: I.B. Tauris, 2016.

Hoffmann, Sophia. “Humanitarian Security in Jordan’s Azraq Camp.” *Security Dialogue* 48.2 (2017): 97–112.

Hopgood, Stephen. “Saying ‘No’ To Walmart? Money and Morality in Professional Humanitarianism.” In *Humanitarianism in Question: Politics, Power, Ethics*, edited by Thomas Weiss and Michael Barnett, 98–123. Ithaca: Cornell University Press, 2008.

Jad, Islah. “NGOs: Between Buzzwords and Social Movements.” *Development in Practice* 17 (2007): 622–629.

Jawad, Rana. “Why Are the Gulf States so Reluctant to Take in Refugees?” *The Conversation* 25 September 2015. http://theconversation.com/why-are-the-gulf-states-so-reluctant-to-take-in-refugees-47394. Accessed 7 August 2021.

Jordan Times. “450 Associations Registered at Social Development Ministry This Year.” 19 September 2017. http://jordantimes.com/news/local/450-associations-registered-social-development-ministry-year. Accessed 5 July 2020.

Katz, Irit, Diana Martin, and Claudio Minca, eds. *Camps Revisited: Multifaceted Spatialities of a Modern Political Technology.* London: Rowman & Littlefield Publishing Group, 2018.

Malkki, Liisa. “National Geographic: The Rooting of Peoples and the Territorialization of National Identity among Scholars and Refugees.” *Cultural Anthropology* 7.1 (1992): 24–44.

Malkki, Liisa. “Speechless Emissaries: Refugees, Humanitarianism, and Dehistoricization.” *Cultural Anthropology* 11.3 (1996): 377–404.

Malkki, Liisa. *The Need to Help: The Domestic Arts of International Humanitarianism.* Durham: Duke University Press, 2015.

Martinez Mansell, Claudia. “How to Navigate a Refugee Settlement.” *Places Journal* (2016). https://placesjournal.org/article/camp-code/. Accessed 1 May 2016.

Pasha, Suraina. "Humanitarianism, Securitization, and Containment in Jordan's Za'atari Refugee Camp." *British Journal of Sociology* (2021): 1–15.

Paszkiewicz, Natalia, and Daniel Fosas. *Reclaiming Refugee Agency and Its Implications for Shelter Design in Refugee Camps.* Conference Paper. Comfort at the Extremes Conference, Dubai, 2019.

Quelch, John, and Nathalie Laidler-Kylander, eds. *The New Global Brands: Managing Non-Governmental Organizations in the 21st Century.* Toronto: Southwestern Publishing, 2005.

Ramadan, Adam. "Spatialising the Refugee Camp." *Transactions of the Institute of British Geographers* 38 (2013): 65–77.

Save the Children. "Doing Whatever It Takes to Save Every Last Child." *YouTube* 25 April 2016. https://www.youtube.com/watch?v=Cmtg7v9I2JQ&ab_channel=SavetheChildrenUSA. Accessed 1 May 2016.

Sigona, Nando. "Campzenship: Reimagining the Camp as a Social and Political Space." *Citizenship Studies* 19.1 (2015): 1–15.

Slaughter, Amy, and Jeff Crisp. *A Surrogate State? The Role of UNHCR in Protracted Refugee Situations.* New Issues in Refugee Research, Research Paper 168. Geneva: UNHCR, 2009.

Slim, Hugo. "By What Authority? The Legitimacy and Accountability of Non-Governmental Organisations." *Journal of Humanitarian Aid* (2002). https://www.jha.ac/a082/. Accessed 19 July 2021.

Stein, Janice. "Humanitarian Organizations: Accountable – Why, to Whom, for What, and How?" In *Humanitarianism in Question: Politics, Power, Ethics*, edited by Thomas Weiss and Michael Barnett, 124–142. Ithaca: Cornell University Press, 2008.

Terry, Fiona. *Condemned to Repeat? The Paradox of Humanitarian Action.* Ithaca: Cornell University Press, 2002.

Tsourapas, Gerasimos. "The Syrian Refugee Crisis and Foreign Policy Decision-Making in Jordan, Lebanon, and Turkey." *Journal of Global Security Studies* 4.4 (2019): 464–481.

Turner, Lewis. "Explaining the (Non-)Encampment of Syrian Refugees: Security, Class and the Labour Market in Lebanon and Jordan." *Mediterranean Politics* 20.3 (2015): 386–404.

Turner, Simon. "What Is a Refugee Camp? Explorations of the Limits and Effects of the Camp." *Journal of Refugee Studies* 29.2 (2016): 139–148.

UAE Federal Competitiveness and Statistics Authority. *International Humanitarian City: The Competitiveness of Compassion.* Policy in Action Series 10. Dubai, 2017.

UNHCR (United Nations High Commissioner for Refugees). *Zaatari Governance Plan.* 9 June 2013. https://reliefweb.int/sites/reliefweb.int/files/resources/ZaatariGovernancePlan%20June2013.pdf. Accessed 1 July 2020.

UNHCR. *Za'atari Refugee Camp: 2013 Safety and Security Report.* Mafraq, March 2014a. https://reliefweb.int/sites/reliefweb.int/files/resources/1403-ZaatariSafetySecurityReport%282013-final%29.pdf. Accessed 1 July 2020.

UNHCR. *Gulf Donors and NGOs Assistance to Syrian Refugees in Jordan.* Amman: UNHCR Jordan Operation, June 2014b. https://reliefweb.int/sites/reliefweb.int/files/resources/GULFreportdesign14.pdf. Accessed 5 July 2021.

UNHCR. *Jordan – Zaatari Refugee Camp.* UNHCR Factsheet. January 2020a. https://data2.unhcr.org/en/documents/download/73845. Accessed 7 July 2021.

UNHCR. *Jordan: Azraq Refugee Camp.* Azraq Camp Fact Sheet. July 2020b. https://reliefweb.int/sites/reliefweb.int/files/resources/78179.pdf. Accessed 7 July 2021.

UNHCR. "Syria Regional Refugee Response: Emirati Jordanian Camp." Operational Data Portal. 2021. https://data2.unhcr.org/en/situations/syria/location/41. Accessed 1 August 2021.

Ward, Patricia. "'What Do They Want From Us?': How Locals Work to Meet Their Employers' Expectations in Jordan's Aid Sector." *Sociology of Development* 6.3 (2020): 318–337.

Weiss, Thomas, and Michael Barnett. *Humanitarianism in Question: Politics, Power, Ethics.* Ithaca: Cornell University Press, 2008.

Yanacopulos, Helen. *International NGO Engagement, Advocacy, Activism: The Faces and Spaces of Change.* Basingstoke, New York: Palgrave Macmillan, 2015.

Ziadah, Rafeef. "Circulating Power: Humanitarian Logistics, Militarism, and the United Arab Emirates." *Antipode* 51.5 (2019): 1684–1702.

Helle Lykke Nielsen

Branding the Middle East in the Diaspora: Names of Mosques in Denmark

1 Introduction

In 2019, the Egyptian Minister of Religious Endowment, Mohamed Gomaa, decided that several of the country's mosques should be renamed. This applied especially to mosques bearing the names of persons related to the Muslim Brotherhood: the Hassan al-Banna Mosque in Beni Suef, named after the founder of the Brotherhood, is today called *al-Huda* or "the Mosque of True Religion," and the al-Qaradawi and al-Hudaibi mosques in Kafr al-Sheikh and al-Qalyubiya, both named after other Brotherhood leaders, were also renamed. According to a March 2019 report from the Ministry of Religious Endowment, more than 100 of Egypt's mosques were renamed to make their titles devoid of references to Brotherhood ideologies.[1] The renaming process was part of a larger political plan to gain control of the country's mosques and a clear sign that names of mosques in Egypt have great symbolic value, religiously as well as politically.

Mosque names in Denmark and other European countries do not have the same political potential as in Egypt, but there may still be good reason to take an interest in them. In a recent article, Öcal argues for the need to approach mosques in Europe as sites of everyday geopolitics where "interstate matters, religion, identity, and territoriality coexist, align, and intertwine"[2] and where discussions about mosques' alleged transnational ties with Muslim-majority countries and their transnational Islamic networks question their sense of belonging to "either here or there."[3] This is a recurring theme in public debates in most European countries. In January 2020, for example, Danish politicians and journalists publicly criticised imams and board members from the Shia Imam Ali Mosque in Copenhagen for supporting the Iranian regime, because they allegedly participated in a memorial service for the Iranian General Qassem Soleimani, killed in a US drone attack in Baghdad.[4] And in October 2019, Danish politicians criticised the Turkish *Selimiye* Mosque in Odense, Denmark's third-largest city, for being the extended

1 See Mostafa, 2019: 9.
2 Öcal, 2020: 20.
3 Öcal, 2020: 2.
4 See Birk, 2020.

https://doi.org/10.1515/9783110741100-035

arm of Turkish President Erdoğan, because they congratulated him on Facebook and Twitter for his attack on Syrian Kurds, using the hashtag for the name of the Turkish offensive, "Operation Peace Spring."[5]

However, everyday geopolitics manifests itself not only through single political events. If we accept Öcal's premise that mosques in Europe are *also* sites of geopolitical conflict, there may be good reason to take an interest in the names of mosques in the diaspora, because they have the potential to express a sense of belonging and thus to brand mosque affiliations with various states, ideologies, and actors in the Middle East. This potential is based on (at least) three assumptions: firstly, in onomastics, the naming of a place is seen as a "socially embedded act, one that involves power relations,"[6] and consequently, toponyms (place names) are neither accidental nor politically or religiously neutral, but "are chosen and foregrounded as being somehow 'appropriate,' while other, less acceptable, names are overlooked or marginalized."[7] Secondly, names of mosques, like other toponyms, can be used as a tool to position them in the urban landscape. From an onomastic point of view, a toponym is understood as a discursive construction of narratives that are compressed and materialised in a short form and thereby becomes the outermost visible sign of a business's or an organisation's identity in public space. This makes toponyms an easily accessible and indisputable resource of empirical data that contains valuable information about the way mosques situate themselves in the public space. And thirdly, it has become increasingly common for toponyms to serve as a commodity that can be bought for money. This is especially well-known in sport, where clubs sell the rights to name sports stadiums to big brands, which then use a chosen name to brand themselves in the public space. A toponym can thus function as a commodity in the form of economic, political, or religious capital, which can be converted into symbolic capital.[8]

In this chapter, I illustrate how mosques can express a sense of belonging and (self-) positioning in everyday geopolitics and thus brand Middle Eastern actors in the European diaspora. The analysis takes Giraut and Houssay-Holzschuch's theoretical framework for naming and naming processes as a starting point[9] and combines it with the concept of *scaling*, taken from the research literature of human geography, but today also widely used in sociolinguistics.[10] Following a brief overview of the complex naming practices of mosques in Denmark and a few methodo-

5 See Birk, 2019.
6 Vuolteenaho and Berg, 2009: 9.
7 Light and Young, 2015: 436.
8 See Light and Young, 2015; Medway et al., 2018.
9 See Giraut and Houssay-Holzschuch, 2016.
10 See Blommaert, 2007; Medway et al., 2018; Radil, 2017.

logical reflections, two mosque names are analysed, each illustrating how the choice of names situates the mosques in the geopolitical landscape. Based on this analysis and the conclusions drawn from it, I hope to illustrate how onomastics can inform research in geopolitics and branding and can thus contribute to a better understanding of how branding the Middle East – and in this case: *through* Middle Eastern actors – *also* takes place in the European diaspora.

2 Place Names and Place Naming-Processes

Research in onomastics has often been criticised for lacking theoretical underpinning,[11] but in recent years the field has witnessed a critical turn that emphasises the use of theories that can unpack the political power relations often involved in place-naming processes.[12] Some of these studies use Bourdieu's concepts of capital as their theoretical starting point: they see toponyms as symbolic capital that businesses, organisations, and individuals use to achieve social status, legitimacy, and influence and that in some cases can even be exchanged for economic profit.[13] Other critical studies are based on the multifaceted theoretical framework of Giraut and Houssay-Holzschuch,[14] which distinguishes among three aspects of the naming process, as seen in the triangle in Fig. 1. Here, names are seen in their geopolitical context (with a focus on time and place), from an actor perspective (who influences the naming processes), and in a (Foucauldian) name-technology perspective (what functions a toponomy fulfils). In this way, the framework aims to capture as many of the complex processes involved in place naming as possible.

If we look at mosque names in Denmark through this framework, they fall, in the geopolitical context, either under the concept of *emergence*, which designates the naming of new places (also termed neotoponyms), or under *commodification*, which covers all contexts in which individuals, organisations, or businesses with money and power can decide how a public place should be named. The actors involved typically represent *civil society* in the form of cultural associations and mosque boards, as well as *state power* in cases where, for example, Middle Eastern states contribute to the establishment of a mosque in the diaspora. If we look at

11 See Alderman, 2008; Light and Young, 2015; Puzey, 2011.

12 See Giraut and Houssay-Holzschuch, 2016: 3–5; Puzey, 2011: 216; Rose-Redwood, Alderman, and Azaryahu, 2017: 7.

13 See Alderman, 2008; Rose-Redwood, Alderman, and Azaryahu, 2010; Light and Young, 2015; Medway et al., 2018.

14 See Giraut and Houssay-Holzschuch, 2016.

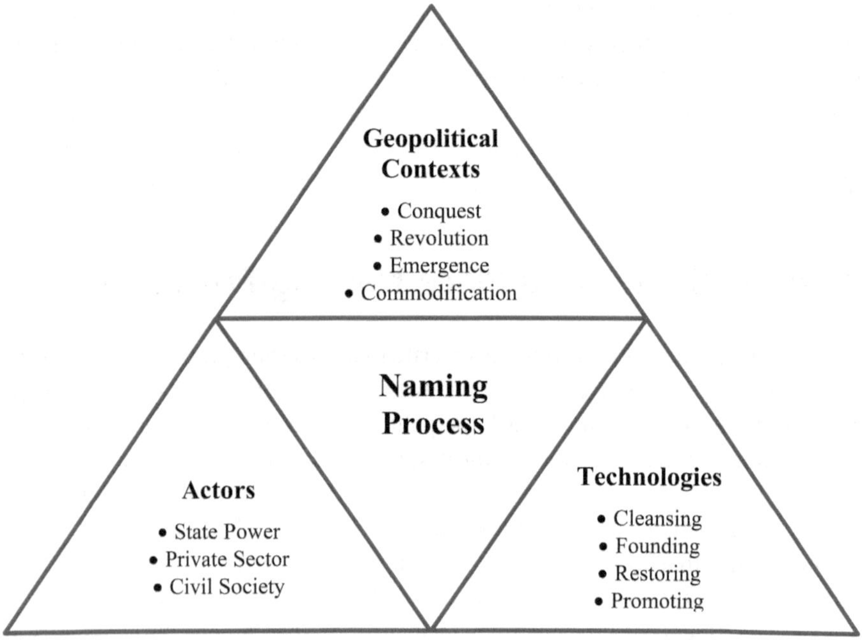

Fig. 1: A framework for interpreting place-naming processes
Source: Redrawn after Giraut and Houssay-Holzschuch, 2016: 8.

the naming technologies that may be relevant for an analysis of mosque names, the concepts of *founding*, *restoring*, and *promoting* are essential: *founding* denotes toponyms that contain cultural or political references to certain historical, ideological, or value-based features with the aim to "create, legitimize, and, ultimately, sustain a new political and cultural order at the local, or the national, level" among those who move and reside in a given area. *Restoring* aims at reinstituting memories of past cultural or political conditions or events by "deploying previous toponyms from such a culture in order to atone for (newly considered) historical injustices, or to legitimize territorial claims";[15] an example of this could be a US city council with a Republican majority that decides to name a street after Trump following his electoral defeat in November 2020. *Promoting* is the use of toponyms to brand a place so that it generates symbolic and economic capital, thereby positioning the place in the best way possible in the local, national, or international competition to attract citizens, businesses, and capital. To give but one example: in 2011, the City of Manchester Stadium, home of the Premier League

15 Giraut and Houssay-Holzschuch, 2016: 9.

football club Manchester City FC, was renamed the *Etihad* Stadium because of a ten-year deal with the international airline *Etihad*, owned by Abu Dhabi's ruling Al Nahyan family.[16]

The concept of scale, which will also be used in the analysis, is based on the notion that there are "different levels or layers that interact in order to produce particular sociospatial dynamics."[17] In our context, the concept takes the form of spatial and temporal scaling. *Spatial scale* is defined, *inter alia*, as "a nested hierarchy of differentially sized and bounded spaces,"[18] which makes it suitable for examining how a place is connected to other spaces, whereas *time scale* relates to how the spatial hierarchy is embedded into different points in time. Spatial scaling is at stake if, for instance, a family chooses to name their cottage the "Garden of Eden," thus attributing paradisiac features to the house and implicitly tying it to "eternity," or if a mosque in a small provincial town, which in everyday life goes by the name of, e.g., "the Mosque at Graham Road," chooses to name itself the "Islamic Centre for Muslims in the South of England" in Arabic, thus upscaling the mosque's catchment area and attributing increased political significance to it for an Arabic-speaking audience.

3 The Complex Naming Practices of Mosques – Some Methodological Reflections

Examining the naming practices of mosques in the diaspora poses several challenges that mainly have to do with the fact that mosques are a relatively new phenomenon in the European context, both organisationally and linguistically. It is, for example, a prerequisite that the name of a mosque has materialised: according to Giraut and Houssay-Holzschuch, toponyms are considered the end result of a naming process, after which – as a confirmation that an agreement on the name has been reached, at least among those who have the power to make the decision – names generally assume a material expression in the sense that they are inscribed on signs and maps, in documents, on web pages, etc.[19] This materialisation also has an impact on the visibility of mosques: the vast majority of Denmark's more than 170 mosques are housed in buildings that were originally built for other purposes[20]

16 See Medway et al., 2018: 789.
17 Soler-Carbonell, 2016: 3.
18 Radil, 2017: 76.
19 See Giraut and Houssay-Holzschuch, 2016: 6; Light and Young, 2015: 444.
20 See Kühle and Larsen, 2019: 61–62.

and are therefore not linked to Islam through their architecture; hence, the materialised name in the form of a sign, a web page, or otherwise becomes an important tool for locating them. A second challenge is that the word "mosque" is not necessarily included in the materialised name. Many mosques choose instead to use "cultural centre" or "association" as a part of their names, either in what they perceive as respect for the non-Muslim majority or because they do not want to attract unwanted attention[21] or because they want to send the message that not only religious but also social, cultural, and educational activities take place in their mosque.[22] And as a third major challenge, mosque names in Denmark – and in the Islamic diaspora in general – typically appear in several languages, since the mosques use both a religious language (Arabic), a majority language (in this case, Danish), and one or more minority languages (typically those used for communication by the ethnic groups attending the mosque). These names might be identical, (partly) overlapping, or sometimes completely different,[23] and this makes it important to include all the names in an analysis to highlight the dynamics that unfold around the interplay between the different names.

This chapter analyses the names of two large Danish mosques, a purpose-built and a non-purpose-built one, in Copenhagen and Odense, respectively. Large mosques in large cities involve numerous actors, in terms of both establishing and running the mosque, and thus provide a good empirical basis for understanding the actors' choice of names.[24] To illustrate different aspects of naming and branding the Middle East in the diaspora, I have chosen mosques that are frequented by different ethnic or national groups and whose names demonstrate different naming technologies. Together, these criteria have led to the choice of the *Khayr el-Barriya* mosque in the Hamad Bin Khalifa Civilisation Center in Copenhagen, also known as the Copenhagen Grand Mosque, which is probably the biggest purpose-built mosque in Denmark, and the Turkish *Selimiye* Mosque in Odense, one of the most well-attended mosques in the city, housed in a former factory building.

The data set for the analysis consists of photos of the nameplates on and around the mosques and of the names used by the mosques on their website, Facebook, and Instagram profiles. In addition to the mosques' own use of names, I also investigated what names were used in the media (through the Danish media database Infomedia) to get as complete a picture of the mosques' name practices as possible. In cases where the mosques used multiple names, I hierarchised these

21 See Monnot, 2016: 50–52.

22 See Verkaaik, 2012: 170.

23 See Reh, 2004.

24 See Kühle and Larsen, 2019: 266–267.

based on frequency, media, typography, colour, location, etc., as is usually done in the field of linguistic landscape.[25] Using these tools made it possible to determine what functions the materialised names fulfil, whom they address, what types of naming technologies are used, and hence, how the names are used to brand Middle Eastern actors.

4 The Khayr el-Barriya Mosque

The *Khayr el-Barriya* mosque (*khayr* means "good" or "charity," and *el-barriya* means "creation" or "creature(s),"[26] approx. "the Mosque for the Best of Creatures") is located in Rovsinggade at Nørrebro in Copenhagen, one of the capital's most culturally diverse neighbourhoods. The name refers to sura 98, verse 7 of the Qur'an, which states, "Indeed, they who have believed and done righteous deeds – those are the best of creatures," as opposed to the unbelievers who, cf. verse 6 in the same sura, "will be in the fire of Hell, abiding eternally therein. Those are the worst of creatures." The Mosque for the Best of Creatures, a term that might refer specifically to the Prophet Muhammad,[27] was inaugurated as a part of the Hamad Bin Khalifa Civilisation Center in June 2014, thanks to a donation of 150 million DKK (approx. 20 million EUR) from the former Emir of Qatar, Hamad Bin Khalifa (r. 1995–2013).

As can be seen in Fig. 2, the mosque and the cultural centre consist of two large, interconnected buildings – the mosque to the left and the cultural centre to the right. On the wall of the building to the right, facing the busy Rovsinggade, the name of the place is written in Arabic (at the top) and English (below) – *Markaz Ḥamad bin Khalīfa al-Ḥaḍārī* (*markaz* is Arabic for centre; *ḥaḍārī* means civilisational or cultural), corresponding to its English name. Fig. 3 shows that the name Hamad Bin Khalifa in Arabic appears in larger letters than the rest of the name and hence highlights the donor's name. There is no other signage on or around the buildings, so the name of the mosque is not stated anywhere in public space, neither in Arabic nor in Danish or English.

25 See e.g. Kress and van Leeuwen, 2001; Puzey, 2011; Rose-Redwood, Alderman, and Azaryahu, 2017.

26 The English translations of the Qur'an, such as https://quran.com/98 (which is used here) and the Saudi version of *Dar al-Arabiya* (Ali, n.d.), translate *al-barriyya* in the plural (creatures), while Wulff's Danish translation construes the term as a verbal noun and thus in the singular (Wulff, 2006: 504).

27 See Kühle, 2020: 2.

Fig. 2: The cultural centre (to the right) and the mosque (to the left) on Facebook
"Stormoskeen" mentioned in Danish below the name of the cultural centre means "the Grand Mosque."
Source: Facebook, 2021a.

Fig. 3: Hamad Bin Khalifa Civilisation Center, in Arabic and English, on the wall facing Rovsinggade in Copenhagen
Photo: Helle Lykke Nielsen, July 2020.

The name of the mosque can be found online, but only as a part of texts written in Arabic. In a Danish-language context, the mosque is most often referred to as "the Grand Mosque," and no distinction is made between the cultural centre and the mosque. In other words, the use of the name *Khayr el-Barriya* is scaled down to the extent that it is visible only in Arabic script and hence aimed at Arabic-speaking Muslims who either attend the mosque or follow its activities on social media. On the other hand, the mosque has a number of bynames in Danish: in addition to "Copenhagen's Grand Mosque," in practice often just "the Grand Mosque" (cf. Fig. 2), it also goes by names such as "the Qatar Mosque," "the Khalifa Mosque," and "the Mosque in Rovsinggade."[28] In the Danish media, "Copenhagen's Grand Mosque" is by far the most widely used: a search for this name in Infomedia yielded almost 500 hits in national newspapers and dailies, followed by 60 hits for "the Mosque in Rovsinggade" and only three for *Khayr el-Barriya.*[29]

There is little doubt that the naming of the Hamad Bin Khalifa Civilisation Center is due to the large donation from Qatar's former emir. The name thus belongs to the context that Giraut and Houssay-Holzschuch label *commodification*, and in terms of name technology, the name of the cultural centre seems to fall under the concept of *promoting*. Hence, the name serves to brand the Khalifa family in an area of the capital that has a significant number of mosques and cultural associations,[30] while at the same time positioning the Khalifa family and Qatar clearly in a Danish geopolitical context.

As for the name of the mosque, *Khayr el-Barriya* is a religious neotoponym. The meaning of the name and the way it is used here make it interesting in at least three ways: firstly, the name is almost invisible, and certainly incomprehensible, to the Danish-speaking majority. Secondly, the name can be interpreted in (at least) two ways: either as a name that conveys religious and value-based qualities, thus legitimising Islam in a Danish context, corresponding to Giraut and Houssay-Holzschuch's term *founding*; or as a reference to the Prophet Muhammad, whereby the mosque is scaled back in time and place, falling under the category of *restoring*, hence indirectly paying homage to Islam in the way it was practiced at the time of the Prophet. This reference is often used today by various Sunni Muslim groups, from traditionally fundamentalist Muslims to more extreme jihadists. And thirdly, the religious connotations of the name create a clear and functional demarcation from the cultural centre's secular and political name. It may well be, however, that the name of the mosque thus serves to distinguish the Centre's religious from the more cultural and political activities – but at the same time, the name also allows for linking to the Khalifa family, so that they will be the ones who appear to be "the best of creatures."

For the Danish-speaking majority, on the other hand, that the Arabic name is almost invisible means that they are unaware of the strong religious connotations associated with the mosque building. But since the mosque is physically visible in the urban landscape, it is hardly surprising that it goes by a number of Danish bynames, which are semantically legible to the majority (cf. "the Mosque in Rovsinggade") and that merge, conceptually and semantically, with the name of the cultur-

28 See Kühle, 2020: 2.

29 See Infomedia, 2020.

30 Of Denmark's approx. 170 mosques, 20 are located in the neighbourhood of Nørrebro in Copenhagen, cf. Kühle and Larsen, 2019: 368–371.

al centre (cf. "The Khalifa Mosque," "the Qatar Mosque"). The latter in particular reinforces the way the Khalifa family and Qatar are branded in the mosque landscape of Nørrebro, where this mosque contrasts with the other large purpose-built mosque in Copenhagen, the Shia Imam Ali Mosque, funded by Iran: when both the mosque and the cultural centre are known by the names of Khalifa and Qatar, the family and the country are branded strongly, religiously as well as politically, making both names highly visible in the underlying struggle for Danish Muslims among the many mosques and Muslim donor countries in the area.

5 The Odense *Selimiye* Mosque

Odense Selimiye Cami (*cami* is Turkish for mosque) has its roots in the Turkish Islamic Cultural Association, which was established in 1980 by a group of Turkish immigrants who raised funds to buy a residential property in Pjentedamsgade in central Odense. In 1990, the building's prayer room was replaced by a mosque in the backyard of the building, and the *Selimiye* Mosque was located here until 2016, when the cultural association bought a significantly larger (former factory) building at Odense harbour and gradually relocated all religious and social activities to the new premises.

In the nearly 30 years that the mosque was located in Pjentedamsgade, it was visible only to those passers-by who knew Turkish. The sign above the gate, which is seen in Fig. 4, reads "*Türk Islam Kültür Derneği* (*dernek* is the Turkish word for association), *Odense Selimiye Cami*," followed by "Tyrkisk Islamisk Kultur Forening," the Danish name of the cultural association. One had to enter the gate and walk into the backyard to understand the religious significance of the place: on the wall of the neighbouring building, which can be seen only from the backyard, is a large painting of the famous *Selimiye* Mosque in Edirne in northwestern Turkey, considered one of the country's most important historical mosques and a highlight of Islamic architecture (Fig. 5). The mosque in Edirne, which dates back to 1575, is named after the Ottoman Sultan Selim II, who, according to tradition, met the Prophet Muhammed in a dream and was asked by him to build the mosque. Today, it is one of the country's 13 properties inscribed on the UNESCO World Heritage List. The name of the mosque is thus associated with historical, religious, and political prestige, which is probably the reason why the name is often used for mosques in the diaspora – in Germany alone, more than 33 Turkish mosques bear the name *Selimiye*.[31]

31 For a list of *Selimiye* mosques in Germany, see Wikipedia 2021.

Fig. 4: The entrance to the *Selimiye* Mosque and the Turkish Islamic Cultural Association in Pjentedamsgade in Odense
Photos: Helle Lykke Nielsen, July 2016.

Fig. 5: The mural on the *Selimiye* Mosque in Edirne, in the courtyard behind the Turkish Islamic Cultural Association in Pjentedamsgade, Odense
Photo: Helle Lykke Nielsen, July 2016.

The relocation of the *Selimiye* Mosque from Pjentedamsgade to the harbour area has led to more legible signage for the Danish majority. Large signs have been placed on the front and back of the building with the name of the cultural association in Danish, as seen in Fig. 6, but neither the word mosque nor the name *Selimiye* appears on the signs. However, the association's link with Islam is still obvious, as can be seen from the logo with the crescent, which embraces four minarets and the mimicry of minarets that appears in the two d's in the abbreviation "dtdv" at the top corners of the signs. The abbreviation stands for *Danimarka Türk Diyanet Vakfi* or "Danish Turkish Islamic Foundation," which is an umbrella organisation for about 30 Turkish mosques in Denmark that cooperate with the Turkish state through the *Diyanet*, its Directorate of Religious Affairs.[32]

Fig. 6: The sign at the main entrance to the Turkish Islamic Cultural Association and the *Selimiye* Mosque in Helsingborggade at Odense Harbour
Photo: Helle Lykke Nielsen, July 2019.

On the Internet, things differ. Both on the association's website, which is almost entirely in Danish, and on its Facebook profile, which communicates almost exclusively in Turkish, the *Selimiye* Mosque appears in text and headings, though very rarely so on the website, whereas on Facebook the name is used consistently and always textually in a position equal to that of the cultural association when it comes to colour, font size, and shape (cf. Fig. 7). The use of the mosque name thus seems to have evolved over time in the sense that it was toned down and completely disappeared from the physical signages, while it appears on an equal footing with the name of the cultural association in Turkish on Facebook.

Naming a Turkish mosque located in a Danish provincial town after one of Turkey's largest and most famous historical mosques and providing a large

32 See Kühle and Larsen, 2019: 205–207.

Fig. 7: The Turkish Islamic Cultural Association and Odense *Selimiye* Mosque on Facebook
Source: Facebook, 2021b.

mural of the latter in the backyard of Pjentedamsgade is an example of *scaling*, not only in space, but also in time. The scaling is most certainly intended to remind those who attend the mosque of Turkey's great cultural and religious heritage and its glorious political past during Ottoman rule. Using Giraut and Houssay-Holzschuch's framework, it would be the Turkish Islamic Cultural Association together with *Diyanet* who are behind the naming process,[33] and in a geopolitical context the name is a neotoponym that can be categorised either as *emergence* or, referring to the role played by the Turkish *Diyanet*, as *commodification*. The categories of the geopolitical context are not mutually exclusive, and it is not unusual that they overlap. The name technology used can be described as either *founding* – i. e. a neotoponym that signals certain ideological or value-based features, in this case an attempt to associate the Turkish mosque in Odense with Turkish national history and Ottoman greatness – or as *restoring*, where the name serves to reinstitute ancient memories by using previous toponyms as a reminder of the historical or political injustices that Turkey has suffered as a result of the fall of the Ottoman Empire. The use of this naming technology does not relate primarily to the place-making strategies of Turkish migrants in Denmark, but rather serves to establish a collective memory of the country they left and is thus linked to a narrative of

33 The Turkish mosque, which opened in 2008 in Aarhus, Denmark's second largest city, as a result of a merger of several smaller Turkish mosques, was purchased by dtdv and was also named *Selimiye* Mosque, cf. Aarhus Wiki 2020.

Turkish national history. Hence, the mosque presents itself quite differently to the minority group of Turkish Muslims and to the Danish majority: to a Turkish-speaking public, the Odense *Selimiye* Mosque evokes historical, cultural, and religious prestige related to the Ottoman Empire, whereas it is portrayed almost exclusively as a Turkish cultural association to the Danish-speaking majority.

6 Mosque Names as a Branding Device

If we accept the onomastic precondition that a toponym is to be understood as a compressed narrative that is the outermost visible sign of a mosque's identity in public space, whom does the name of the mosque then target, and what does this tell us about everyday geopolitics and about mosque names used as a branding device?

The two mosques under scrutiny here have a number of characteristics in common: in both cases, a civil society (the local mosque boards) and a state power actor (the ruling Khalifa family in Qatar and the Turkish *Diyanet*) are involved in the place-naming process. Both mosques position themselves differently towards the in-group (the Muslims) and the out-group (the Danish majority): in the public space, the mosques identify themselves to the Danish majority as cultural associations, whether on large signs or on their websites, which are primarily used to inform a Danish-speaking audience. The names of the mosques, however, have very low visibility for the Danish majority, as the names do not appear in the physical space, but occur almost exclusively in Turkish and Arabic texts in the social media and, even in the few cases in which they appear in a Danish (con)text, are semantically opaque. Hence, the mosques outwardly present themselves as cultural associations, while inwardly they are clearly mosques. For the Muslim in-group, on the other hand, the mosque names carry clear religious, cultural, and political connotations, and the fact that there seems to be no clear distinction, either organisationally or linguistically, between the cultural associations and the mosques makes culture and religion merge. This can also be seen, for example, in Khayr el-Barriya's architecture (cf. Fig. 2), where the minaret is located in front of the building of the cultural association and not in front of the mosque, and in the Facebook profiles (Fig. 2 and 7), where the names of the mosques and the cultural associations merge. Taken together, this seems to suggest that the mosques want to avoid, or at least play down, the risk of triggering discussions of geopolitical issues.

There are, however, also differences between the place-naming practices of the two mosques. Through their use of naming technology, they both scale back in time and space, but in different ways: the name *Khayr el-Barriya* is rooted in the religious space of the Qur'an and intertwines semantically with Qatar's ruling Khalifa family as "the best of creatures." *Selimiye*, on the other hand, scales back to the glorious times of Ottoman rule under Selim II and hence sends a message of the "compelling national history" on which the modern Turkish nation state is built, and which (are we led to believe?) should be restored. The symbolic nature of both names thus differs in content and therefore, too, in the way they are used as a branding device: they are not bound up with the economic logic of capital accumulation and maximising profit, but rather, in the case of *Khayr el-Barriya*, with a place branding that indexes Islamic tradition to obtain religious fame that eventually can be exchanged to political fame, while the *Selimiye* Mosque, which indexes cultural prestige and political greatness, is used as a branding device for recognition and heritage.

Toponyms often serve as an indication to tell people what is historically, culturally, or politically important. Therefore, place-naming processes are considered a kind of identity work,[34] in which the transformation or "translation" of a (physical) space into a text can show us something about a phenomenon that we might not otherwise have spotted. The different ways the two mosques present themselves to the in-group and the out-group and the different naming technology used give us a glimpse into the everyday geopolitics of mosques and help us understand how historical and religious narratives in the form of names can be used as branding devices in the diaspora.

Bibliography

Aarhus Wiki. "Århus Selimiye Stiftelse/Århus Dansk-Tyrkisk Kulturforening." Aarhus Stadsarkiv. https://aarhuswiki.dk/wiki/%C3%85rhus_Selimiye_Stiftelse/%C3%85rhus_Dansk-Tyrkisk_Kulturforening. Accessed 12 September 2021.

Alderman, Derek H. "Place, Naming, and the Interpretation of Cultural Landscapes." In *The Ashqate Research Companion to Heritage and Identity*, edited by Brian Graham and Peter Howard, 195–213. Hampshire: Ashgate, 2008.

Ali, Abdullah Yusuf. *The Holy Qur'an. Meanings translated by Abdullah Yusuf Ali.* Beirut: Dar al-Arabiya, n.d.

Birk, Christian. "Tyrkisk moské svarer på kritik: Vi skal ikke forbindes med politik." *Berlingske* 15 October 2019.

Birk, Christian. "Omstridt moske knyttes tættere til Irans præstestyre." *Berlingske* 18 January 2020.

Blommaert, Jan. "Sociolinguistic Scales." *Intercultural Pragmatics* 4.1 (2007): 1–19.

Facebook. "Hamad Bin Khalifa Civilisation Center." https://www.facebook.com/Stormoskeen/. Accessed 10 July 2021a.

34 Rose-Redwood, Alderman, and Azaryahu, 2017: 6.

Facebook. "Türk-İslam Kültür Derneği/Odense Selimiye Camii." https://www.facebook.com/turkcamiiodense/. Accessed 12 September 2021b.

Giraut, Frédéric, and Myriam Houssay-Holzschuch. "Place Naming as Dispositif: Toward a Theoretical Framework." *Geopolitics* 21.1 (2016): 1–21.

Infomedia. *Medieovervågning, analyser og rådgiving: Global Media Intelligence.* Danish Media Archive. https://infomedia.dk. Accessed 20 September 2020.

Kress, Gunther, and Theo van Leeuwen. *Multimodal Discourse: The Modes and Media of Contemporary Communication.* London: Arnold, 2001.

Kühle, Lene. "Konflikten i Hamad bin Kalifa Civilization Center." In *Årbogen Religion i Danmark 2020*, 1–19. Afdeling for Religionsvidenskab: Aarhus Universitet, 2020.

Kühle, Lene, and Malik C. R. Larsen. *Danmarks moskeer: Mangfoldighed og samspil.* Aarhus: Aarhus Universitetsforlag, 2019.

Light, Duncan, and Craig Young. "Toponymy as Commodity: Exploring the Economic Dimensions of Urban Place Names." *International Journal of Urban and Regional Research* 39.3 (2015): 435–450.

Medway, Dominic, Gary Warnaby, Leah Gillooly, and Steve Millington. "Scalar Tensions in Urban Toponymic Inscription: The Corporate (Re)naming of Football Stadia." *Urban Geography* 40.6 (2018): 784–804.

Monnot, Christophe. "Visibility or Invisibility: The Dilemma of the Muslim Associations of Switzerland." *Journal of Religion in Europe* 9.1 (2016): 44–65.

Mostafa, Amr. "Ministry of Religious Endowment Renaming Mosques across Egypt." *Al-Monitor* 23 April 2019. https://www.al-monitor.com/originals/2019/04/egypt-endowments-changing-names-political-muslim-brotherhood.html. Accessed 4 June 2019.

Öcal, Devran Koray. "Mosques as Spaces of Everyday Geopolitical Tensions." *Geopolitics* (preprint), published online 23 September 2020. https://doi.org/10.1080/14650045.2020.1820485.

Puzey, Guy. "New Research Directions in Toponomastics and Linguistic Landscapes." *Onoma* 46 (2011): 211–226.

Radil, Steven M. "The Multi-Scalar Geographies of Place Naming: The Case of Cyprus." *Journal of Territorial and Maritime Studies* 4.1 (2017): 72–85.

Reh, Mechthild. "Multilingual Writing: A Reader-Oriented Typology – with Examples from Lira Municipality (Uganda)." *International Journal of the Sociology of Language* 170 (2004): 1–41.

Rose-Redwood, Reuben, Derek Alderman, and Maoz Azaryahu. "Geographies of Toponymic Inscription: New Directions in Critical Place-Name Studies." *Progress in Human Geography* 34.4 (2010): 453–470.

Rose-Redwood, Reuben, Derek Alderman, and Maoz Azaryahu. *The Political Life of Urban Streetscapes.* London: Routledge, 2017.

Soler-Carbonell, Josep. "Complexity Perspectives on Linguistic Landscapes." *Linguistic Landscape: An International Journal* 2.1 (2016): 1–25.

Verkaaik, Oskar. "Designing the 'Anti-Mosque': Identity, Religion and Affect in Contemporary European Mosque Design." *Social Anthropology* 20.2 (2012): 161–176.

Vuolteenaho, Jani, and Lawrence D. Berg. "Towards Critical Toponymies." In *Critical Toponymies: Contested Politics of Place Naming*, edited by Jani Vuolteenaho and Lawrence D. Berg, 1–18. Ashgate: Routledge, 2009.

Wikipedia. "Liste von Selimiye-Moscheen." https://de.wikipedia.org/wiki/Liste_von_Selimiye-Moscheen. Accessed 12 September 2021.

Wulff, Ellen. *Koranen i ny dansk oversættelse.* Copenhagen: Vandkunsten, 2006.

Birgit Krawietz

Showcasing Tulips in Istanbul

The *Read National* Internet portal identifies certain flowers, animals, and birds with nations around the globe. It declares the tulip *the* "National Flower of Turkey."[1] However, from a longer historical perspective, concrete associations with this flower are primarily associated with, on the one hand, Islamicate[2] culture, notably the Ottoman Empire, and, on the other, the Netherlands. On closer inspection of the secondary literature, some newspaper articles, a few Turkish MA theses, and a number of visuals, and after several field visits especially to the metropolis Istanbul, which is no longer the capital but economically and culturally powerfully back again, the tulip emerges as a highly "polyvalent symbol"[3] that defies close confinement. In utterly rough strokes, this chapter takes stock of various interpretations in history and of some current trends. It cannot rely on a comprehensive critical cultural history of tulips[4] in the "world of Islam," but rather on bits and pieces from different angles and entanglements. Available scholarship is taken as an invitation to diagnose here a certain branding strategy as early as in the so-called Tulip Age of the 18th century. Moreover, focusing on the first two decades of the 21st century makes it evident that even an ancient metropolis like Istanbul with immense multilayered historical treasures feels compelled – under the conditions of the media society and city/place competition – to reframe its old worthies and new assets in a thoroughly branded fashion. The tulip plays a major role in both these periods of enhanced global outreach, although they are separated by up to three centuries. The first part of the chapter will demonstrate the extreme variability of tulip messages and the rather limited religious or religiously ambivalent profile of this flower.

1 Khan, 2017. The same applies to the Netherlands and Afghanistan. I thank BGSMCS doctoral students Aslı Altınışık and Muhammed Vural for helping me prepare this chapter.
2 The term "Islamicate" follows Marshal Hodgson, who used the term in *The Venture of Islam* to set expressions of the religion of Islam apart from more cultural forms; cf. Morrissey, 2021.
3 Salzmann, 2000: 88.
4 However, what comes closest to that is the excellent book by İrepoglu, 2012, that focuses on the Ottoman Empire and assembles many visuals.

https://doi.org/10.1515/9783110741100-036

1 Ex Oriente Tulip

The word "tulip" is alien to both Turkish and European languages. As *dülbent* or *tülbent*, it entered Ottoman Turkish via the Persian *dolband*, which denotes a turban.[5] Yet, the likewise adopted Persian expression *lâle* became a much more widespread and in fact the standard Turkish term for tulip. According to the *Book of Kings* written by the "national" Iranian poet al-Ferdowsi around the year 1,000 CE and that presents Iranian history before the Islamic conquest, *gol* (flower, rose) denoted cultivated flowers, whereas *lāla* meant wild-growing, usually red plants.[6] Hamidifard-Graber points out that the fresh redness of this spring flower symbolised human beauty and splendour in nature; besides, it was used in poetry as a stand-in for blood, wine, dawn, shining lances, and death.

Already in the 10th century, tulips started to be cultivated in Iranian gardens, but notably during the Seljuk dynasty, various sorts of tulips were brought westward to Asia Minor, which already hosted some indigenous wild types. In its cultivated form, the flower was enthusiastically embraced by the Ottomans. The Turkish newspaper *Daily Sabah* states: "While the flower was relatively unknown during the Roman and Byzantine periods, it started being used as an ornamental flower in Anatolia in the 12th century. The flower made its artistic debut in the artworks of the Seljuk Sultanate of Rum and continues to this day."[7] Afterwards, it turned into *the* flower of Ottoman high culture, as shall be shown, not only during the Tulip Period (*lâle devri*) of 1718–1730 (according to others 1703–1730), but over a much longer time.

As an originally mainly Central Asian wildflower that became extensively cultivated and crossbred, the tulip is mentioned neither in the *Qur'ān* that emerged in the Arabian Peninsula in the 7th century CE, nor in early Arabic poetry. Over time, the tulip did acquire diverse religious and poetic meanings: Sufis highlighted that the Arabic words God (*allāh*), crescent (*hilāl*), and tulip (*lālah*) all consist of the same letters and reveal, transposed in anagrams, their inner spiritual linkage.[8] The tulip serves also as a mystic symbol of unity, because each bulb produces one flower only. In addition, it was hailed for its widespread gesture of true devotion, so that some "held it to be the symbol for modesty before the Almighty, be-

5 See Mélikoff, 1967: 346. Ther, 1993: 15–16, mentions a kind of delicate cotton cloth that was used to wind up high turbans to resemble wild tulips. See also Baytop and Kurnaz, 2003: 79.

6 See Hamidifard-Graber, 2009: 74; Mélikoff, 1967: 345–346.

7 Tüfekçi, 2021.

8 See İrepoglu, 2012: 33; Baytop and Kurnaz, 2003: 80.

cause when the tulip is in full bloom it usually bows its head."[9] In the Persianate[10] realm, it was one of the favourite flowers of poetry, but often at variance with more piously imbued interpretations.[11] In various versions of a famous Persian folk story, Farhad, who is madly in love with princess Shirin, dies a tragic death or commits suicide. A red tulip emerges wherever a drop of his blood falls.[12]

The tulip variously denotes passionate but unfulfilled love.[13] There is considerable symbolic overlap between the manifold martyrs of love and the religious and political martyrs, especially those in Kerbela in what is now Iraq, where in 680 CE the Umayyad troops killed the Prophet's grandson Husain ibn Ali and many others. Hence, this flower evolved into a widespread trope for different sorts of – not only Shiite – Holy War (*jihād*) contexts, in which the tulip has functioned as a widespread marker of blood spilled for a higher cause. To this day, tulip imagery can be spotted variously in this sacrificial and folk tradition. For instance, a number of announcement posters (and related material) for the Turkish martial arts oil wrestling in Edirne mark this connection between blood and the tulip (Fig. 1).

2 The Dutch Tulip Mania of 1636/37

In the 16th century, tulips taken from the Ottoman Empire reached Western Europe. Travellers who had passed the tulip fields then existing between Edirne and Istanbul used to be very impressed by the floral splendour they witnessed.[14] Fostered by colonial trade, the European enthusiasm for tulips increased in the first quarter of the 17th century.[15] A Dutch "tulip mania" (some call it Tulipomania) has been diagnosed for the time around 1636/37 and compared to the contemporary "Bitcoin craze."[16] However, the Netherlands have long since established a profitable tulip industry on a very rational basis. In her diligent and erudite historical analysis of Dutch and other documents, Anne Goldgar shows that "there

9 Demiriz, 1993: 57.
10 "Persianate" denotes Persian as a cultural *lingua franca* in a wide-ranging geographical realm imbued with the Iranian cultural imaginary.
11 See Schimmel, 2001: 90–95. It seems to have entered Turkish poetry in the 14th century, see Baytop and Kurnaz, 2003: 80.
12 See Baytop, 1993: 51.
13 See Mélikoff, 1967: 357 et passim.
14 See Baytop, 1993: 52. Nowadays this corridor is full of sunflower plantations.
15 Cf. Afyoncu, 2018.
16 Afyoncu, 2018.

Fig. 1: Edirne oil wrestling poster
Photo: Birgit Krawietz, 2009.

was nothing intrinsically crazy"[17] in the rise of the tulip trade in the Netherlands, and she has systematically deconstructed the allegation of some kind of a collective suicidal mania for investing in illusionary projects. Analysing developments in some important Dutch towns, she explains how "money intersected with aesthetics" and that "tulips fit well into a culture of both abundant capital and a new cosmopolitanism."[18] Goldgar unearthed the very logic of the events in the Netherlands over time and in view of wider societal developments and markets. Although the state of shock resulted from impaired trustworthiness in carefully balanced societal relationships, the legend of a collective craze is nevertheless still very popular.[19]

17 Goldgar, 2007: 227.
18 Goldgar, 2007: 11.
19 Cf. Hock, 2018.

3 The Tulip Era of Ottoman Istanbul

The “Tulip Era” of early 18th-century Ottoman Istanbul corresponds to the Dutch “Tulipomania,” because in both realms “professionals and amateurs grew tulips” fervently.[20] And they were somehow disrupted in their enthusiasm by historical events, one could add. However, these two prominent currents are not only to be distinguished by the gap of nearly a century between them. İsmail Hakkı Gülal from the Istanbul Tulip Foundation’s science committee claims quite condescendingly that the tulip “became a trade good in the Netherlands” whereas in Turkey “it has more of a cultural meaning,” so that: “You can see tulip patterns on Turkish banknotes and on Turkey’s logo for its 2020 Olympics candidacy. You can see it everywhere, from fountains to tombstones. It became part of Ottoman royal culture but it’s really also part of the culture of the people.”[21]

Not going any further into the problematic issue of the comparability of the two countries in terms of mammon versus culture (and for that matter, e.g., the role of the tulip in European still life paintings), it is important for our purposes here merely to stress with Shirine Hamadeh’s eye-opening study that the Ottoman Tulip Era with its central design and aesthetic underpinnings should not be restricted “to the period in office of Grand-Vizier Nevşehirli Damad İbrahim Pasha from 1718 to 1730,”[22] the son-in-law of Sultan Ahmed III. Hamadeh has to be credited for her insistence on a whole century of new ostentatious garden culture and sensibility that ensued after the court came to Istanbul in 1703, finally returning from the city of Edirne where Ahmed III had grown up in the palace and where the Ottoman court had resided for decades.[23] She diligently demonstrates how a splendid garden and park space emerged not only in and around the court, but especially in extramural Istanbul alongside the shores of the Golden Horn inlet and the Bosphorus in general. In a multifaceted process of “décloisonnement,”[24] Ottoman court culture started to engulf wider spaces within the city and to appeal to broader segments of society. According to Murat Gül, the “tulip was the preferred symbol and cultivar of the era,” and the market for tulips heated

20 Demiriz, 1993: 57. The Turkish term *lâle devri* was popularised only much later by the 20th-century Turkish historian Ahmed Refik; see Özcan, 2003: 81–82.

21 Hürriyet Daily News, 2018a. The mission statement of the institution, the *İstanbul Lale Vakfı*, reads: “promoting the case that the tulip is a Turkish flower, tracing the tulip as a figure in Turkish culture and arts, conducting research together with universities and professional associations and raising awareness about the tulip in the public”; İLAV, 2022 (translated by the author).

22 Hamadeh, 2008: 13.

23 For the inspirational background of riverside *villeggiatura* in Edirne, see Scollay, 2019.

24 Cf. Hamadeh 2008: 12–14, 56, 75, 170.

up, so that an imperial decree tried to calm things down in 1722 through price regulation.[25] It was also a period of tremendous peaceful economic, political, and cultural opening.[26]

The flower's popularity in Ottoman Istanbul grew steadily throughout the 16th and 17th centuries.[27] In that period, around 2,000 different types of tulips were already circulating in the city; some local variants were characterised by elongated almond-shaped blossoms.[28] During the 16th century, tulips had also been exported to, notably, the Netherlands; and, in the quest for all sorts of crossbred tulips, in the 18th century they were "re-imported from Holland to their native country,"[29] but also ordered from Iran. In times of relatively peaceful relations, the tulip as *the* Ottoman signature flower already constituted a transcultural commodity propelled by growing long-distance trade and rising mass consumption. According to Ariel Salzmann, "Given these crosscurrents in the flow of goods, terms like 'occidental' and 'oriental' fail to qualify a cosmopolitan taste that followed transcultural commodity trends."[30] Furthermore, these flows not only affected outdoor spaces; floral designs also appeared in homes and on objects all over the place.[31]

4 A Quick Glance at the Ottoman Tulip Cosmos

The tulip is the most prominent[32] flower that imprints Ottoman visual representations and commodities across the board, even though at times it "shared an equal level of importance with other motifs."[33] It decorates Ottoman architectural structures, tiles and ceramics, textiles, embroidery, carpets, glasswork, woodwork, metal objects including weaponry, miniatures, paper marbling, jewellery, and even book covers and tombstones.

25 Gül, 2009: 183.

26 See Özcan, 2003: 82.

27 According to Öztürk, 2019: 16, the tulip was introduced to Ottoman culture especially via illustrated manuscripts.

28 Cf. Baytop and Kurnaz, 2003: 79–80.

29 Demiriz, 1993: 58.

30 Salzmann, 2000: 91.

31 See Salzmann, 2000: 90.

32 The other popular flowers are the clove, hyacinth, and rose; see Öztürk, 2019: 107. Such motifs can be combined with animals or other things.

33 Krody, 2000: 58. However, as the author further mentions, the "tulip as a motif sometimes played a major role, sometimes a secondary role, but it was ever-present on embroidered textiles from the sixteenth to the eighteenth century", although "it lost favour to the rose in the late eighteenth and nineteenth centuries."

Although tulip motifs had already been used on tiles and ceramics under the Seljuks, in the Ottoman Empire during the 16th to 18th centuries, various pottery studios brought them to their full artistic bloom.[34] İznik ceramics were developed in close relation and cooperation with the court, so that one can regard the tuliped floral world as an official avenue of Ottoman imperial branding. As mentioned above, tulips very much signal and naturalise the cultural opening and broad trade relations that allowed for widely circulating goods between various Asian and European cities. Following Salzmann again, "The Istanbul tulip was itself the product of confluence in early modern consumer markets."[35] Especially İznik tiles and dishes, displaying that message with utmost refinement, became world-famous, and manifold vessels were produced.[36] During the 16th century, the "tulip was the most prevalent flower in wall tiles."[37] The Rüstem Pasha Mosque built by Mimar Sinan (d. 1588) in Istanbul's Fatih district displays no fewer than 37 different tulip motifs.[38] Furthermore, the Topkapı Palace and the Selimiye Mosque in Edirne are also central imperial highlights of this type of tulip design artistry. In the second half of the 16th and in the 17th century, the art of creating splendid ceremonial Sultanic caftans flourished with the motifs of the Tulip, spiralling Golden Horn Work (*Haliç İşi*), and Far Eastern Chintamani (*Çintemani*, consisting of three balls and two tiger-stripes) as their most common design patterns.[39] In sum, the most important insignia of Ottoman sultanic rule were strategically tulip-branded.

5 From the Modern Break with the Ottoman Past to Contemporary Competitive Identity

According to the journalist Kai Strittmatter, the Turks themselves are responsible that their merits concerning the tulip became forgotten in Europe: the young Turkish Republic framed the Tulip Era in terms of decadence and decay and those in

34 See Çekinmez, 2010: 29, et passim, who gives various schematic examples of the three-digit number of different tulip motifs on wall ceramics in Istanbul.

35 Salzmann, 2000: 84.

36 İznik pottery can be admired in famous museums worldwide. Öztürk, 2019: 21–94, identifies design specificities of tulip representations during the 15th to 17th centuries and takes a close look at dishes, bowls, drinking vessels, vases, carafes, glass jars, mugs, bottles, flasks, and candlesticks. Kütahya pottery stepped in when the İznik production declined in the 18th century.

37 Ünver, 2021.

38 See Schimmel, 2001: 94. Çekinmez, 2010: 30, exhibits many spectacular ceramics and tiles and lists their locations in certain Istanbul mosques and *türbe*s.

39 See Cihan, 2012: 2, 30.

charge systematically prescribed oblivion to all things Ottoman.[40] Authors like Begüm Adalet and Sibel Bozdoğan demonstrate the impact of architectural modernism and international style on urban Turkey.[41] To this day, a strong current of hyper-modernist architecture avoids organic appeal; but modern functional architecture is not what tourists are looking for.

In his monograph on what he calls "Competitive Identity," Simon Anholt emphasises that today "the world is one market"[42] and explains, "[T]he real meaning of globalization: almost every nation and culture on earth is now sharing elbow-room in a single information space."[43] His book therefore analyses the conditions for constructing "a positive, famous, well-rounded national reputation, one that stimulates attention, respect, good relations and good business."[44] When Turkey finally wanted to transform itself into an international tourist destination, visitors yearned for typical characteristics and especially Ottoman traditions. The title of a chapter of Strittmatter's German book on Istanbul can be translated as "The return of the tulip. The Turks discover their past. How the palace director İlber Ortaylı and the art historian Serdar Gülgün enable a renaissance of everything Ottoman."[45] Yet, what has happened is not a full-fledged reintroduction of Ottoman culture, but very selective and differing forms of self-Orientalisation.[46] While touristy spaces like restaurants and products of the souvenir industry, with its manifold miniaturised knick-knacks, decorated notably with the tulip motif, openly indulge in nostalgia, there are more-nuanced official ways that actors in Turkey engage with the Ottoman floral past, such as including a tulip in the name *Türkiye* in official tourism logos or occasionally intertwining tulip design with contemporary transportation infrastructure (cf. Fig. 2).

Furthermore, there seems to be a tendency that younger Turkish people are very open to the Ottoman pool of design and meanwhile combine it creatively with (other) global image flows. Universities have readmitted considerations of Ottoman culture to the scholarly debate. In the year 2008, the *Anadolu Üniversitesi* in Eskişehir organised a student exhibition of contemporary art showcasing tulips.[47]

---

40 See Strittmatter, 2008: 21–22.

41 See Adalet, 2018; Bozdoğan, 2001.

42 Anholt, 2007: 1.

43 Anholt, 2007: 52.

44 Anholt, 2007: 31.

45 Strittmatter, 2008: 21.

46 Here, I leave out the discussion of explicit political (Neo-)Ottomanism.

47 See Ak, 2008: 75–76. Her thesis offers a broad array of visuals concerning the historical depiction of flowers and especially the tulip in various genres of art and material culture. She then presents modern tulip art or ceramics design, notably in her own work.

Fig. 2: Istanbul metro wagon with tulip motif
Photo: Birgit Krawietz, 2022.

In her thesis on modern applications of the tulip motif, Canan Ak expresses genuine interest in and inspirational joy about the refined naturalism encountered in Ottoman material culture and the thrust to link past and present is perceptible in the dual collocation of real flower photographs and selected comparable pieces of artwork. To mention another example, in his thesis on the tulip in Turkish ceramic art and ceramic tiles, Sevgi Çekinmez presents production pieces by some designers of recent decades.[48] Nurcihan Cihan's thesis in Fine Arts tries to actively revive these motifs and transfer them to modern pottery design.[49] Yet another Fine Arts thesis on the tulip motif in fabrics and cloth looks at the period of the 16th to 18th centuries and uses them in 2019 as a resource for computerised modern textile patterns.[50] Such graduation works convey a keen sense of actively revisiting

48 Cf. Çekinmez, 2010.

49 See also the many caftan pictures that illustrate the vivacity of flowers in Ottoman textile court culture. Starting with design sketches, Cihan, 2012, presents the ceramics thereby inspired and then moves to their material implementation.

50 Cf. Yavuz, 2019.

and creatively exploring the Ottoman floral heritage. Hence, a number of Turks themselves seem to be increasingly willing, even proud, to curiously engage and experiment with Ottoman-style design items in their surroundings and not only to join international tourists in the hedonistic realms of recreational Ottoman Orientalism. In the following section, two significant examples of celebratory appropriation by state authorities shall be highlighted.

6 The Istanbul Tulip Festival

Tulips were ostentatiously displayed in the park- and streetscape of Istanbul in the first two decades of the 21st century. The major event that produces this splendour was the annual Istanbul Tulip Festival established in 2006 by the Istanbul Metropolitan Municipality.[51] Since then, it has been staged in April in a number of historical plant locations, such as Çamlıca Hill, the 60th Anniversary Göztepe Park, Gülhane Park, Sultanahmet, Yıldız Park, and especially Emirgan Grove, although tulips are presented on a smaller scale also elsewhere alongside major roads. The *Istanbul City Bulletin* of July 2007 explains this initiative by the long-time AKP mayor Kadir Topbaş (2004–2017)[52] with the slogan: "Istanbul has started to make itself felt in the world." The mayor added that the Internet is crucial to publicise the city. Given that everybody loves flowers and due to the decorative ubiquity of tulips in Turkish material culture – along with the additionally planted hyacinth, narcissus, and grape hyacinth – the tulip in particular "treats the soul by giving people a kind of psychotherapy."[53]

Hence, millions of tulips (imported mainly from other parts of the country) temporarily adorn the city, welcoming visitors with a burst of colours. Each year, press reports emphasise the great numbers of tulips planted. Tourists from abroad and from within Turkey, as well as inhabitants of Istanbul themselves, are drawn to visit such places. They respond actively and post about their trips on social media. According to Magdalena Florek, "Nowadays, in order to say something about themselves, cities do not have to count solely on journalists. Today,

51 See the programmes and pertinent pictures at İBB, 2006–2022. Many tulips had been planted already in 2005, so that statements diverge on whether the festival actually started in 2005 or 2006.
52 The AKP (*Adalet ve Kalkınma Partisi*, Justice and Development Party) has reigned in Istanbul since 2004, whereas since 2019, the city's mayor has come from the oppositional coalition Nation Alliance headed by CHP (*Cumhuriyet Halk Partisi*, Republican People's Party) member Ekrem İmamoğlu. The general policy of the latter, but also the impact of the earthquake disaster in Turkey in 2023, led to a significant reduction in the tulip/flower budget.
53 Istanbul City Bulletin, 2007: 39 (translated by the author).

everyone has become not only the receiver but also the sender of messages."[54] Therefore, pictures of such temporary floral installations are easily displayed and multiplied. Furthermore, "the annual festival, art and cultural life is reinvigorated through a wave of tulip-themed exhibitions and various other events."[55] Mayor Topbaş depicted this as a homecoming for the tulip.[56] While the 18th-century tulip grown in Istanbul went extinct, this narrative can be understood as an obviously wider claim of socioeconomic grandeur, early modern cosmopolitanism, and the circulation of luxury commodities, which unfolds an attractive message. In her study of Istanbul's Ottoman heritage through the lens of a newly established theme park showcasing famous Ottoman buildings in miniature, Ayşe Öncü explains such efforts "to reinvent the Tulip Era as an imaginative point of reference," which began, notably along the shores of the Golden Horn, at a time "when the Muslim populations of Istanbul occupied a privileged status and Islam was the locus of authority merging both religious and political power."[57] In that sense, the new tulip boom since 2005 can be regarded as expressing an upbeat attitude, a feeling of entitlement, and a quest for visibility in an increasingly globalised world by showcasing Ottoman religious and Islamicate icons.

Other towns in Turkey and worldwide have initiated their own tulip festivals. In 2013, Istanbul hosted the Fifth World Tulip Summit. During the World Tulip Summit held in the Canadian capital Ottawa in 2017, the Istanbul Metropolitan Municipality received an award for its Tulip Festival.[58] Although the Amsterdam Tulip Festival is (still) the best known, an Ottoman narrative framing the tulip as Turkey's "gift to the world"[59] seems to be of paramount concern to the organisers. A particular forum to showcase this flower from the historical perspective of Istanbul is the 2015-inaugurated "biggest tulip museum in the world," the Tulip Museum and Research Center.[60] This institution seems to emulate the Amsterdam Tulip Museum, but it is no coincidence that this place for permanent and temporary exhibitions is located in a renovated historical building in Emirgan Park and that, due to its potential to boost national pride, its outreach activities are coordinated with the Ministry of National Education. The general aesthetics of the Istanbul Tulip Festival seem to follow contemporary globalised standard models rather than genuine Ottoman prototypes: "Tulip blooms are planted in the shape of waves, tulips,

54 Florek, 2011: 83.
55 Tüfekçi, 2021.
56 Cf. Öncü, 2007: 244–245.
57 Öncü, 2007: 246.
58 See Anadolu Agency, 2017a; Visit Istanbul, 2022.
59 Hürriyet Daily News, 2018a.
60 Anadolu Agency, 2018.

the Turkish flag, butterflies, ladybugs, and rainbows along the paths. The tulip motif is carried throughout the park and is seen in the site amenities, such as the light fixtures, paving pattern, trash receptacles, benches, and fencing."[61] Statements of this type also convey an understanding of the material translation of the tulip motif into something different from its Ottoman predecessors. Such settings clearly address the gaze of domestic and foreign tourists, but their reading and aesthetic appreciation do not require any specific cultural knowledge and sensitivity.

A special highlight of the festival is the gigantic rectangular carpet of planted real tulips put together for ephemeral pleasure. It gets "rolled out" on Sultanahmet Square in front of the Hagia Sophia,[62] thereby offering an ornamental addition to this already most prominent touristic location in Istanbul, turning it even more instagrammable (Fig. 3). A blog that refers to the 2018 edition informs us: "The carpet was made up of 565 thousand colored Tulip flowers, symbolically marking the 565-year-old opening of the city of Istanbul by the Ottoman Sultan Fatıh Mehmet in 1453,"[63] i. e. it is advocated as yet another feature of Ottomanism. Furthermore, the 1,734-square-meter rectangular tulip field "creates a traditional Turkish carpet motif."[64] In this installation, set up for remote sensing purposes, one icon mimics another, or several icons are merged. In 2022, Istanbul Governor Vasip Şahin spoke at the opening, "The tulip was born in this country, but it spread across the globe, especially in Western Europe. We are a nation that has been sharing our beauties since long and we are not a jealous nation."[65] While this is claimed to be the "world's largest live tulip carpet,"[66] it follows certain role models of spectacle and eventisation practices, sending a message to a worldwide audience about Istanbul's new confidence as an utterly important global hub for tourism and hedonistic leisure, confidently relying on its rich heritage.

The organisers manage to do things by the book so that the tulip with its Ottoman underpinnings, as a branding expert postulated, "can operate as an umbrella that can cover a multitude of stakeholders and audiences."[67] The costly overall flower initiatives of Istanbul under AKP mayor Topbaş and his successor Mevlüt Uysal have already been criticised by the opposition led by Ekrem İmamoğlu, who became mayor in 2019. The tulip proponents in the Istanbul Metropolitan Mu-

---

61 Kopinski, 2012.
62 Anadolu Agency, 2017b.
63 Proact, 2018.
64 Anadolu Agency, 2018.
65 Quoted in ILKHA, 2018.
66 ILKHA, 2018.
67 Kavaratzis, 2004: 71.

Fig. 3: Tulip Carpet in Sultanahmet Square, Istanbul
Photo: Feridun F. Alkaya. "2019 Istanbul Tulip Festival." 2019. Courtesy of the photographer.

nicipality seem to be aware of the fact that – according to leading branding literature – a "single symbolic action will seldom achieve any lasting effect: multiple actions should emanate from as many different sectors as possible in order to build a rounded and believable image for the place; they must also continue in unbroken succession for many years."[68]

In 2019, after the enforced annulment of the first round, the Istanbul municipality elections had to be repeated, which probably explains why not much was organised for the tulip festival, although the famous carpet was still provided.[69] In 2020, the Tulip Festival was cancelled due to Covid-19. In the following two years, the new city administration drastically cut its funds so that "only" eight[70] and then seven million tulips could be planted (and afterwards, as usual, quickly removed), but the carpet was nevertheless staged in the familiar fashion. İmamoğlu even rebranded the *Lale Festivali* event *Lale Bayramı*, possibly in yet another symbolic attempt to distinguish his rule as mayor of Istanbul and label it as closer to the local people.[71] Political orientations and internal frictions over spending and

68 Anholt, 2011: 292.

69 See Aksu, 2019. However, in 2023, the year of the earthquake catastrophe, there was no such carpet of tulips.

70 Aksoyer and Okur, 2021. In 2013, for example, the planting of 30 million tulips is reported for Istanbul; see Hürriyet Daily News, 2018b.

71 See Show Ana Haber, 2022. However, he usually does not act disruptively, but aims at inclusion.

budget calculation aside, the return of the tulip to the city of Istanbul to especially but not exclusively celebrate the annual start of outdoor consumption and the tourist season seems to be an established branding practice under different mayors. And the material translation into permanent design solutions in public space, often tied to infrastructure, is sometimes even conspicuous, as the next example will demonstrate.

7 Air Traffic Control Tower at Istanbul Airport

Istanbul Airport, officially newly opened in 2018 in the north of the metropolis, is designed as a gigantic international aviation hub with an extremely high turnover, especially of international passengers. It has a unique welcoming building: approaching visitors are already visually guided from afar by a 95-metre standalone tower, a functional sculpture shaped like a tulip (Fig. 4).[72] The elliptical structure is built of sturdy grey concrete, and the tower is flanked by two longish "leaves," while the control centre at the top represents the head of this "flower." A complex lighting system sublimely modifies the colours of this novel 24-hour landmark. Together with the international American engineering firm AECOM (Architecture, Engineering, Consulting, Operations, and Maintenance), the North Italian car design and transportation infrastructure firm *Pininfarina* that is famous for high-speed luxury vehicles won the competition to build this futuristic architectural object. According to Yusuf Akçayoğlu, the CEO of the responsible airport managing firm İGA, this "iconic structure" offers "a striking design fit for a 21st century airport while remaining sensitive to Istanbul's unique heritage."[73] Likewise Bernardo Gogna (associated with AECOM), who has long-standing expertise in aviation architecture and management, depicts the tulip as "the symbol of Istanbul for many centuries" and as "an important cultural reference in Turkish history."[74] This design choice pushed aside the five other invited proposals, among them one by the architectural office of Zaha Hadid. The international competitors had all been "inspired" by "authentic Turkish symbols," namely "whirling dervishes," "Ottoman geometrical patterns," "minarets," and the "seagulls of Istanbul."[75] Although public infrastructure at times exhibits only a rather subtle tulip design, the new Air Traffic Control Tower at Istanbul Airport is an unprecedented exam-

72 Not everybody is convinced by this design. One twitter user feels reminded instead of a cobra; see Uslu, 2018.

73 Quoted in Rosenfield, 2015.

74 Quoted in Rosenfield, 2015.

75 Jain, 2017.

ple of ostentatiously showcasing this Ottoman, yet, through its modern and hyper-technological style, strongly de-Ottomanised heritage. At the same time, it brings to bloom a certain logic and pride in heritage that has been around for quite a while now. This type of tulip connoisseurship conveys that Turks are no newcomers to high-level consumer goods and their circulation among empires and nations and links this to the bustling, worldwide-connected airport.[76]

Fig. 4: Advertisement at Istanbul Airport
Photo: Birgit Krawietz, 2022.

Besides the signature colours red and white (not to mention letters in blue) of Turkish Airlines (TA), there is another one, namely grey. TA planes carry an anthracite-coloured, elongated tulip head, placed lopsidedly behind the wings, so that it is easily overlooked (Fig. 5a). It pales in comparison with the most attention-grabbing element, namely the white bird symbol on a blood-red background.[77] A retained tulip motif can be found also inside a TA plane, for instance perforated in the greyish curtains that obstruct the view of economy-class passengers. Images of tulips emerge among the sharply creased folds (Fig. 5b). Not only the outward appearance of the TA fleet as the Turkish national and globally operating carrier, but also the interior design of the planes allows for restrained depiction of tulips. However, any impressions of nostalgic backwardness are carefully avoided within the

76 Ranked 14th on the global list of the busiest airports in 2021; cf. Wikipedia, 2022.

77 On the "Meet our Fleet" website of Turkish Airlines, 2022, all 13 plane types display the stylised grey tulip.

modern space of transport infrastructure. Turkish Airlines, which started in 1933 with only five machines, has meanwhile turned into the flagship enterprise of the country. As reported in 2022, Turkish Airlines appears "for the fifth time in a row" on BrandFinance's "Turkey 100" list; as "the country's most valuable brand," the carrier "flies to 128 countries in 334 destinations with a fleet of 372 aircraft."[78] Mithat Yılmaz and Hakan Mazlum demonstrate that TA has used tulip imagery variously in its image campaigns.[79] This brand choice is supposed to convey the perfect global service performance and international outreach of the flight carrier. Against the background of especially infrastructural success stories, tulips are blooming, embellishing particularly international mobility as the road to success.

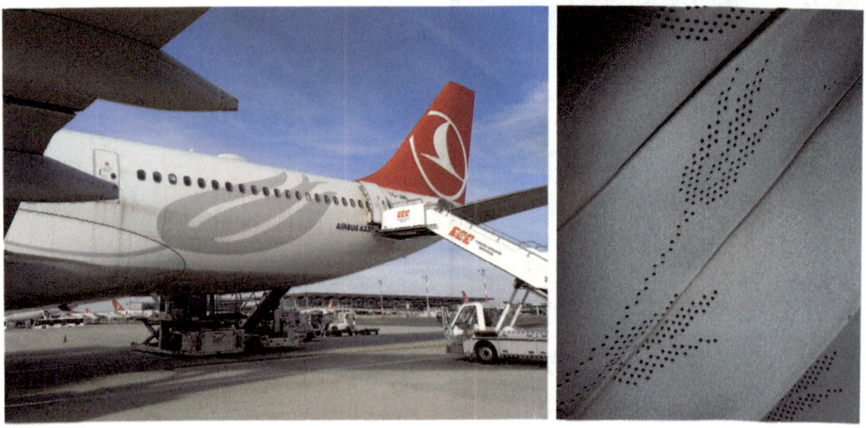

Fig. 5: Turkish Airlines airbus and curtain
Photos: Birgit Krawietz, 2022.

8 Concluding Remarks

The tulip has a variegated historical genealogy. Due to its rich cultural associations and malleability, it was already developed into the brand flower of high Ottomanism.[80] The pervasiveness and transmediality of tulip design in the Ottoman Empire, emanating from Istanbul as its main stage, has been described in the scholarly literature. As much as a particular architectural style of Ottoman Imperialism can be discerned, the interior decoration of mosques was at times marked by

78 Hürriyet Daily News, 2022.
79 See Yılmaz and Mazlum, 2019.
80 At least up until the emergence of Rococo style, which favoured the rose; see Demiriz, 1993: 58.

many tiles exhibiting tulip motifs alluding to Paradise. Usually, tulips were presented in interplay with additional floral or other motifs. Such decorative patterns were interlinked with wider realms of society, including private homes that likewise displayed hedonistic amenities showing tulips or using tulip shapes. The polyvalence of the tulip with its highly ambivalent underpinnings provided a perfect means to create powerful and deliberately blurred linkages between paradisiac and inner-worldly imaginings. Ottoman tulip design combined religious gratification, theologically in principle postponed to the Hereafter, with conspicuous consumption as materialised in the wider Bosphorian realm, especially since Ahmed III.

The drawn-out process of territorial losses, belated reforms, economic decline, imperial dismemberment, and the general demise of influence finally culminated in the abolition of the Ottoman Empire in 1922. The ensuing political, architectural, and wider cultural developments of Kemalist Turkey brought a systematic rejection of most things Ottoman. Yet, the tulip has (re-)emerged as the brand flower of contemporary Turkey, as well. The years especially since the 2000s show a conscious selective reintroduction of Ottoman elements, notably of the tulip. It is no coincidence that this period has been marked by the rise and dominance of the AKP, which won the Turkish general election in 2002 and provided the mayor of Istanbul until 2018/19. This ruling party has persistently criticised Kemalism for its iron-fisted banning of visible religion and its eradication of Islamic and Ottoman cultural memory. However, the process of a new cultural flourishing that this chapter traces in the example of the tulip cannot be explained merely with changed national policy or party politics that readmit religion and Ottoman memory, if not pride. It must also be interpreted against the background of global neoliberal city competition, which forces even old metropolises worldwide to systematically re-inspect their historical resources for capitalistic promotional purposes. Those cities that can count on a rich heritage are blessed in contemporary media society,[81] but full-fledged promotional strategies are deemed indispensable.

What takes place in Istanbul, represented here by the Tulip Festival, and is sketched as the national policy of Turkey, taking Turkish Airlines as the major example, is not a full embrace of Ottomanica as such, but a deliberately controlled, selective reframing that constructs certain trajectories, in line with overall development plans. The ex oriente tulip narrative has the strategic advantage of expressing an upbeat attitude. The return of this signature flower is not only a keeping up with the Joneses in Amsterdam, Ottawa, and Tokyo, but also cutting-edge global city competition. It reminds the world that it was the Ottomans who first

81 Compare Hospers, 2011: 35.

infused cosmopolitan trade with the tulip. This colourful "gift to the world" bears beautiful living testimony that Turkey (in a recent campaign rebranded as "Türkiye," to set it apart from the animal) is not just an emerging industrialising country that merely aspires to have a share in new riches, but that it already operated on equal terms with other empires in the East and West in early modernity. It can also be gauged that this development is not just a top-down strategy for branding purposes. A number of people, from young design students to selfie-taking Istanbulites and domestic visitors – i. e. not only international tourists – obviously respond to such offerings. Therefore, the tulip is not merely employed as a promotional country logo, but has meanwhile taken root, so that the Istanbul Airport tulip tower was set up to orient visitors from all around the globe.

Bibliography

Adalet, Begüm. *Hotels and Highways: The Construction of Modernization Theory in Cold War Turkey.* Stanford: Stanford University Press, 2018.

Afyoncu, Erhan. "Tulip Mania: The 17th Century Bitcoin Craze." Daily Sabah 2 March 2018. https://www.dailysabah.com/feature/2018/03/02/tulip-mania-the-17th-century-bitcoin-craze. Accessed 2 March 2018

Ak, Canan Gürel. *Geleneksel Türk seramik sanatında çicek: Bir tasarım ögesi olarak ele alınışı ve kişisel yorumlar.* Yüksek Lisans Tezi, Afyon Kocatepe Üniversitesi, Afyonkarahisar, 2008.

Aksoyer, Ali, and Yılmaz Okur. "İstanbul'un parklarında görsel şölen! 8 milyon lale." *Hürriyet* 20 April 2021. https://www.hurriyet.com.tr/gundem/istanbulun-parklarinda-gorsel-solen-8-milyon-lale-41792889. Accessed 22 July 2022.

Aksu, Fatma. "Sultanahmet'e 570 bin lalelik halı." *Hürriyet* 26 April 2019. https://www.hurriyet.com.tr/gundem/sultanahmete-570-bin-lalelik-hali-41194523. Accessed 22 July 2022.

Anadolu Agency. "Istanbul Municipality Awarded at World Tulip Summit." *Daily Sabah* 9 October 2017a. https://www.dailysabah.com/istanbul/2017/10/09/istanbul-municipality-awarded-at-world-tulip-summit. Accessed 18 October 2017.

Anadolu Agency. "World's Biggest 'Tulip Carpet' in Istanbul." 20 April 2017b. https://www.aa.com.tr/en/pg/photo-gallery/worlds-biggest-tulip-carpet-in-istanbul. Accessed 23 March 2022.

Anadolu Agency. "Istanbul Tulip Museum Traces History of the Flower." *Daily Sabah* 19 April 2018. https://www.dailysabah.com/history/2018/04/19/istanbul-tulip-museum-traces-history-of-the-flower. Accessed 25 March 2022.

Anholt, Simon. *Competitive Identity: The New Brand Management for Nations, Cities and Regions.* London: Palgrave Macmillan, 2007.

Anholt, Simon. "Beyond the Nation Brand: The Role of Image and Identity in International Relations." In *Brands and Branding Geographies*, edited by Andy Pike, 289–301. Cheltenham, Northampton: Edward Elgar Publishing, 2011.

Baytop, Turhan. "The Tulip in Istanbul during the Ottoman Period." In *The Tulip: A Symbol of Two Nations*, edited by Michiel Roding and Hans Theunissen, 51–56, 82. Utrecht, Istanbul: M.T. Houtsma Stichting, Turkish-Netherlands Association, 1993.

Baytop, Turhan, and Cemal Kurnaz: "Lâle." In *Islam Ansiklopedisi*, Vol. 27, edited by Türkiye Diyanet Vakfı, 79–81. İstanbul: Islâm Araştımaları Merkezi, İslâm Ansiklopedisi Genel Müdürlüğü, 2003.

Bozdoğan, Sibel. *Modernism and Nation Building: Turkish Architectural Culture in the Early Republic.* Seattle, London: University of Washington Press, 2001.

Carswell, John: "From the Tulip to the Rose." In *Studies in Eighteenth Century Islamic History*, edited by Thomas Naff and Roger Owen, 328–355, 404–405. Carbondale, Edwardsville: Southern Illinois University Press, 1977.

Çekinmez, Sevgi. *Türk çini ve seramik sanatında lale.* Yüksek Lisans Tezi, Anadolu Universitesi, Eskişehir, 2010.

Cihan, Nurcihan. *17. yüzyıl Osmanlı kaftalarında yer alan (Lale, Haliç İşi ve Çintemâni) motiflerden yola çıkarak seramik yüzlere yeni tasarım onerileri.* Yüksek Lisans Tesi, Ericiyes Üniversitesi, Kayseri, 2012.

Demiriz, Yildiz. "Tulips in Ottoman Turkish Culture and Art." In *The Tulip: A Symbol of Two Nations*, edited by Michiel Roding and Hans Theunissen, 57–75, 83. Utrecht, Istanbul: M.T. Houtsma Stichting, Turkish-Netherlands Association, 1993.

Florek, Magdalena. "Online City Branding." In *City Branding: Theory and Cases*, edited by Keith Dinnie, 82–90. Houndmills, New York: Palgrave Macmillan, 2011.

Goldgar, Anne. *Tulipmania: Money, Honor, and Knowledge in the Dutch Golden Age.* Chicago: University of Chicago Press, 2007.

Gül, Murat. *The Emergence of Modern Istanbul.* London, New York: Tauris, 2009.

Hamadeh, Shirine. *The City's Pleasures: Istanbul in the Eighteenth Century.* Seattle: University of Washington Press, 2008.

Hamidifard-Graber, Fatemeh. *Von Ackerwinde bis Zypresse: Das Pflanzenreich im "Königsbuch" des Ferdousı.* Berlin: Klaus Schwarz Verlag, 2009.

Hock, Martin. "Spekulationslegende: Die Tulpenblase, die keine war." *Frankfurter Allgemeine Zeitung* 21 February 2018. http://www.faz.net/aktuell/finanzen/finanzmarkt/die-tulpenblase-eine-historische-legende-15460972.html. Accessed 22 February 2018.

Hospers, Gert-Jan. "City Branding and the Tourist Gaze." In *City Branding: Theory and Cases*, edited by Keith Dinnie, 27–35. Houndmills, New York: Palgrave Macmillan, 2011.

Hürriyet Daily News. "Turkey's Gift to the World: Tulips." 7 April 2018a. http://www.hurriyetdailynews.com/turkeys-gift-to-the-world-tulips-129905. Accessed 8 April 2018.

Hürriyet Daily News. "Tulip Festival Kicks off in Istanbul." 4 April 2018b. http://www.hurriyetdailynews.com/tulip-festival-kicks-off-in-istanbul-129766. Accessed 5 April 2018.

Hürriyet Daily News. "Turkish Airlines Named 'Most Valuable Brand'." 10 June 2022. https://www.hurriyetdailynews.com/turkish-airlines-named-most-valuable-brand-174449. Accessed 10 June 2022.

İBB (İstanbul Büyükşehir Belediyesi). 2006–2022. https://istanbulunlalesi.ibb.istanbul/festival-programi/lale-festivali-programi. Accessed 26 March 2022 (link expired).

İLAV (İstanbul Lale Vakfı). "Vizyon ve misyon." 2022. https://www.ilav.org/vizyon-ve-misyon.php. Accessed 3 July 2022.

ILKHA (İlke Haber Ajansı). "The world's Largest Live Tulip Carpet in Istanbul." 13 April 2018. https://ilkha.com/english/latest/the-worlds-largest-live-tulip-carpet-in-istanbul-3652. Accessed 26 March 2022.

İrepoglu, Gül. *Lâle: Doğada, tarihte, sanatta.* Istanbul: Yapı Kredi Yayınları, 2012.

Istanbul City Bulletin. "Istanbul yeniden lalesiyle buluştu." July 2007: 38–39.

Jain, Kushal. "Traffic Control Tower at Istanbul Airport." *Arch20* 2017. https://www.arch2o.com/air-traffic-control-tower-istanbul-airport/. Accessed 21 March 2022.

Kavaratzis, Michalis. "From City Marketing to City Branding: Towards a Theoretical Framework for Developing City Brands." *Place Branding* 1.1 (2004): 58–73.

Khan, Waseem. "Tulip: The National Flower of Turkey." *Read National* 2017. https://readnational.com/tulip-national-flower-of-turkey/. Accessed 17 September 2022.

Kopinski, Eric. "Tulip Paradise: The History of the Tulip and Emirgan Park." *The Field, American Society of Landscape Architects' Professional Practice Networks' Blog* 7 November 2012. https://thefield.asla.org/2012/11/07/tulip-paradise-the-history-of-the-tulip-and-emirgan-park/. Accessed 25 March 2022.

Krody, Sumru Belger. *Flowers of Silk and Gold: Four Centuries of Ottoman Embroidery.* Washington, DC: Merrell Publishers, 2000.

Mélikoff, Irène. "La fleur de la souffrance: Recherche sur le sens symbolique de *lâle* dans la poésie mystique turco-iranienne." *Journal Asiatique* 255 (1967): 341–360.

Morrissey, Fitzroy. "The Venture of the Islamicate: The History of a Key Concept in Islamic Intellectual History." Centre for Intellectual History, University of Oxford, 29 July 2021. https://intellectualhistory.web.ox.ac.uk/article/venture-islamicate-history-key-concept-islamic-intellectual-history. Accessed 6 May 2022.

Öncü, Ayşe. "The Politics of Istanbul's Ottoman Heritage in the Era of Globalism: Refractions through the Prism of a Theme Park." In *Cities of the South: Citizenship and Exclusion in the 21st Century*, edited by Barbara Drieskens, Franck Mermier, and Heiko Wimmen, 233–264. London, Beirut: Saqi Books, 2007.

Özcan, Abdülkadir."Lâle devri." In *Islam Ansiklopedisi*, Vol. 27, edited by Türkiye Diyanet Vakfı, 81–84. İstanbul: Islâm Araştımaları Merkezi, İslâm Ansiklopedisi Genel Müdürlüğü, 2003.

Öztürk, Emin Emre. *15.–17. yy İznik seramiklerinde lale motifinin tasarım özellikleri.* Yüksek Lisans Tezi, Selçuk Universitesi, Tasarım Anabilim Dalı, Konya, 2019.

Proact. "The World's Largest Tulips Carpet in Sultan Ahmet Square Now." 13 April 2018. https://www.proact-group.com/blog/worlds-largest-tulips-carpet-sultan-ahmet-square-now/. Accessed 26 March 2022.

Rosenfield, Karissa. "AECOM and Pininfarina Selected to Design Istanbul New Airport's Traffic Control Tower." *ArchDaily* 24 December 2015. https://www.archdaily.com/779422/aecom-and-pininfarina-selected-to-design-istanbul-new-airports-traffic-control-tower. Accessed 28 February 2022.

Salzmann, Ariel. "The Age of Tulips: Confluence and Conflict in Early Modern Consumer Culture (1550–1730)." In *Consumption Studies and the History of the Ottoman Empire, 1550–1922: An Introduction*, edited by Donald Quataert, 83–106. Albany: State University of New York Press, 2000.

Schimmel, Annemarie. *Kleine Paradiese: Blumen und Gärten im Islam.* Freiburg im Breisgau: Herder, 2001.

Scollay, Susan. "*ʿIlm* and the 'Architecture of Happiness': The Ottoman Imperial Palace at Edirne/Adrianople, 1451–1877." In *ʿIlm: Science, Religion and Art in Islam*, edited by Samer Akkach, 141–156. Adelaide: University of Adelaide Press, 2019.

Show Ana Haber. "Lale bayramı başladı." YouTube 24 April 2022. https://www.youtube.com/watch?v=glzvD_QZLLo. Accessed 22 July 2022.

Strittmatter, Kai. *Istanbul: Metropole zwischen den Welten.* Munich: Knesebeck, 2008.

Ther, Ulla. *Floral Messages: From Ottoman Court Embroidery to Anatolian Trousseau Chests.* Bremen: Edition Temmen, 1993.

Tüfekçi, Ali. "Tulip: The Flower Lending its Name to an Ottoman Period." *Daily Sabah* 13 April 2021. https://www.dailysabah.com/arts/tulip-the-flower-lending-its-name-to-an-ottoman-period/news. Accessed 14 April 2021.

Turkish Airlines. "Meet our Fleet." 2022. https://www.turkishairlines.com/de-de/flights/fly-different/fleet/. Accessed 3 July 2022.

Ünver, Süheyl. "History of Tulip in Turkey." http://trdergisi.com/en/history-of-tulip-in-turkey/. Accessed 19 July 2021.

Uslu, Emre. "İstanbul Havalimanı kulesi: İstanbul'un simgesi lale olarak dizayn edilmişdi. Bu açıdan daha çok kobra'ya benziyor gibime geldi ne dersiniz?" *Twitter* 29 October 2018. https://twitter.com/emreuslu/status/1056973190038204424?lang=de. Accessed 22 July 2022.

Wikipedia. "List of Busiest Airports by Passenger Traffic." 2022. https://en.wikipedia.org/wiki/List_of_busiest_airports_by_passenger_traffic. Accessed 3 August 2022.

Visit Istanbul. https://www.visitistanbul.com. Accessed 18 September 2022.

Yavuz, Cemalettin. *Lâle motifinin 16.–18. yüzyıl Osmanlı'da kullanımı ve bilgiyasar ortamında armürlü dokuma tasarım örnekleri.* Yüksek Lisans Tezi, Süleyman Demirel Üniversitesi, Güzel Sanatlar Enstitüsü Geleneksel Türk Sanatları Anasanat Dalı, Isparta, 2019.

Yılmaz, Mithat, and Hakan Mazlum. "Kültürel motiflerin reklam üzerinde kullanımı: Türk Hava Yolları lale motifi örneği." *Akdeniz Sanat Dergisi* 13.23 (2019): 59–69.

Philip Geisler

Architecture and the Myth of Immaculate Form in Dubai

1 Introduction

Dubai is a place of fractures and frictions. These play out most urgently in the Emirate's exclusionary social configuration based on ethnic discrimination against foreign workers, who are exploited for the benefits of a system of autocratic rule that projects a global image as a cosmopolitan hub of sports, shopping, and indulgence.[1] Hence, for many, Dubai embodies a utopian promise of happiness, freedom, and material affluence. This view was recently exemplified by dozens of social media influencers relocating to the Emirate. To evade tax payments, many of them left Germany in Winter 2021 to find a new home in Dubai that promised them cash incentives, a density of global brands, and free products – as long as they would promote the totalitarian state as part of their professional activities and censor any critique. "Dubai (…) has become the ideal Instagram city,"[2] the Guardian wrote a few months later.

The perceived ideal status of this urban space, gained through official representation, global (digital) image circulation, and cultural myth is the subject of this contribution.[3] Architecture, this chapter maintains, is the major strategic instrument with which Dubai glosses over its inner contradictions and brands itself as such an idealised place. The spectacle of architectural spaces and their event qualities are merely one part of a more comprehensive constitutive myth that comes to the fore when assessing branding as a system of aesthetics. Taking the case studies of residential master plan projects, namely the Dubai Marina towers and the Palm Jumeirah villas, as well as of the multifunctional spaces of the Mall of the Emirates (MOE) and the *Burj Khalifa*, I will explore how the depoliticised myth of immaculate form is at the heart of Dubai's architectural culture in the early 21st century. Vis-à-vis the Emirate's flawed socio-political realities, immaculateness epitomises the quintessential counter-narrative. It is an aesthetic echo of Dubai's investment, thematic shopping, and tourism strategy outlined in the early 2000s that resonates appositely with the proliferation of positive social media imagery

1 See Kanna, 2011: 38.

2 Michaelson, 2021.

3 Major parts of this chapter are based on my master's thesis, see Geisler, 2017.

https://doi.org/10.1515/9783110741100-037

and with international middle classes desiring social beneficiation.[4] By connecting mid-century cultural associations of architecture with hypermodern form, Dubai's architectural branding efforts blur clear-cut distinctions between modern and postmodern aesthetics.[5]

2 Approaching Dubai through its Cracks

Dubai has become a place that continuously breaks architectural records. Yet, mega-dimensions are only one tangible basis for architectural and urban development operating as socio-spatial refinement. Many of Dubai's architectural showpieces evince material fractures and spatial contradictions – "cracks in the façade,"[6] as Chad Haines puts it. The structure of the *Burj Khalifa* (Fig. 1) is built of optimised concrete that constantly shrinks and has to be monitored continuously. Years after their completion, the residential towers of the master plan district of Dubai Marina (Fig. 2)[7] were virtually uninhabited, creating an enormous oversupply of exclusive real estate, while Dubai's working class population lives in ghettoised labour camps off the dominant and formal highways (Fig. 3). Palm Jumeirah (Fig. 4) is characterised by an extreme density of residential buildings due to high development costs, so that the luxurious villas hardly allow for any feeling of privacy. The island's fronds entail stagnant, stinking water and the destruction of marine habitats. The MOE (Fig. 5), a place for luxury shopping and sports entertainment, orchestrates a spatial imagery of interiorised publicness, while being a highly exclusionary private space in which security forces control access and enforce social homogeneity.

3 Geometry

Such ruptures are effectively countered by branding Dubai through mythologically charged design principles, both in physical reality and in manipulated photographs. Architecture objectifies flawlessness through colossal geometric figures.

4 On Dubai's investor and tourism strategy from the late 1990s until 2000, see Hazbun, 2008: 189–207.

5 The strong continuity between the two has been discussed previously for the case of Kuwait's petro-modernity, see Hindelang, 2022: 23. See also Jameson, 1991; Huyssen, 1984.

6 Haines, 2011: 160.

7 I would like to thank Felix Torkar for generously supporting my work on this article by giving me permission to include his photographs.

Fig. 1: *Burj Khalifa*, Architect: Adrian Smith/Developer: Emaar, 2004–2010
Photo: Guilhem Vellut. "*Burj Khalifa* @ Dubai." *Flickr* 13 November 2014. CC BY 2.0, https://flic.kr/p/pP55CJ. Accessed 11 March 2022.

A structure like the pyramidal *Burj Khalifa* thereby acquires an immense spatial presence and aura. The corporeality of geometric cuboids, cones, and pyramids not only references design concepts easily seen as timeless and ancient, but also raises these structures' photogenic potential as immaculate sculptural icons.

Dubai's master plan regime foregrounds the symmetry of circles, squares, and triangles. This highlights centres through structural or functional emphases: the Palm Jumeirah's contour forms an idealised circle, with the Nakheel Mall accentuating its focal point. Similarly, the cuboid Dubai Marina towers and the ground plan of the *Burj Khalifa* are based on mirror-symmetrical designs, whose centres are statically and functionally highlighted. How Dubai Marina navigates spatial dis-

Fig. 2: Dubai Marina, HOK Canada/Emaar, 2003–today
Photo: Felix Torkar, 2014. Courtesy of the photographer.

Fig. 3: Al Quoz Labour Camp
Photo: Philip Geisler, 2017.

ruptions is especially instructive. Here, the shoreline of the district's artificial Marina Canal serves as a point of reference for subsequent buildings and generates spatial coherence. Master plans incorporate infrastructure into symmetrical spatial design, too. The road systems of the Palm Jumeirah and Dubai Marina allow for easy accessibility and integrated parking in a city conceived for automobile traffic. The seamless infrastructural connection of the MOE, Dubai Marina, the *Burj Khalifa*, and the Palm Jumeirah is essential to the perception of the availability of the abundance on offer and to the relational exclusion of places deemed undesirable.[8]

4 Reflection

In contrast to Dubai's concrete architecture of the 1960s to 1980s, its post-2000 signature buildings like the *Burj Khalifa* and the Marina towers use smooth surfaces to emphasise immaculate form. To prevent sand deposits, the *Burj Khalifa*'s glass curtain wall has no cornices or projections. It employs aerodynamic engineering technology to resist wind forces. As a mirrored glass building, it consumes its exterior space by means of reflection. This visual operation of Dubai's sleek glass façades effectively draws on the established architectural tropes of American corporate modernism of the post-war period. Jeffrey Lieber observed the obsession with immaculate form in this era, in which glass curtain walls acquired their meaning of "ideal systems with universal application offering the world an endless series of representations of itself."[9]

Taking up such tropes, Dubai's signature buildings integrate shining, luxurious materials like gold, oiled wood panelling, and marble in their interior designs, illustrated well by the section of the *Burj Khalifa* that houses the Armani Hotel. Here, the visual spectacle of luxurious materials generates a strong immersive power. With its minimalist elegance and association with Armani, the hotel architecture conveys the brand's impeccable exclusivity. Its emphasis on reflecting materials and sharp impeccability as an aesthetic aspiration is another echo of cultural debates in the aftermath of the Second World War. In her study of French consumer culture of the 1950s, Kristin Ross highlights that "there is no give to the surfaces, no tactile dimension, even an imagined one – just smooth shine. The narcissistic satisfaction offered is one of possession and self-possession: clean surfaces and sharp angles."[10]

This aesthetic narcissism is expressed through the trope of reflection: in the joint venture of Armani and the *Burj Khalifa*, two brand images mirror each

8 On infrastructure as a relational concept and signifying form, see Star, 1999.
9 Lieber, 2018: 34.
10 Ross, 1996: 84–85. Ross also points out that in the same decade, the ideological concept of communication began to refer not only to the mass media newly developed at that time and information technologies like the TV, but also to idealised spatial arrangements.

Fig. 4: Villas along the Palm Jumeirah Island fronds, HHCP/Nakheel, 2001–today
Photo: Alexander Heilner. "The Center Core of the Palm Jumeirah." *Wikimedia Commons* 11 March 2008. CC BY-SA 4.0, https://commons.wikimedia.org/wiki/File:Palm_jumeirah_core.jpg. Accessed 11 March 2022.

other. Each trademark reflects the other's polished brand surface and thereby strengthens its own attractiveness. Much like the canals in Palm Jumeirah and Dubai Marina, the many water pools and decorative fountains in the Burj's compound underline the purity of this reflection. As the *Burj Khalifa*'s surface dissolves in mirror images of its surroundings, including the blue sky, water pools, green spaces, other high-rises, and traditionalised low-scale buildings, the tower becomes an icon of capitalist consumption. As a reflecting investment object, whose surface exists by visually consuming its surroundings, the *Burj Khalifa* transitions from architecture to what Lieber terms an all-encompassing eye of enterprise.[11]

11 See Lieber, 2018: 9.

5 Air Conditioning

In its ideological absorption, this consumerism also reduces nature to a commodified motif. The MOE's glass barrel vault, referencing Paris' famous passages, integrates pleasant aspects of outdoor space, such as bright light and the blue sky, in the mall's interior. The interior operates as refined outdoor space, simulating an open-air yet climatically cooled street with house façades. Its main entertainment facility, Ski Dubai, likewise offers a skiing experience under ideal climatic conditions, void of any inclement weather. Such systems of technological control illustrate the overcoming of nature. They are also reflected in the engineering technologies used to stabilise the *Burj Khalifa* and are particularly evident in the case of the artificially created Palm Jumeirah.

Fig. 5: Shops, outdoor elements, and security camera inside the Mall of the Emirates, F+A Architects/Khansaheb, 2003–2005
Photo: Philip Geisler, 2017.

Significantly, the island's palm tree motif is highly stylised and resembles a logo. In this way, form itself conveys the overcoming of nature as the successfully fulfilled vision of Sheikh Mohammed bin Rashid Al Maktoum himself, who brands the Emirate as a climatically human-friendly, liveable habitat.[12] As a stylised motif, the palm tree iconographically epitomises a shift through which nature has become

12 The Sheikh's utopian vision, see Al Maktoum, 2012, considerably attests to Dubai's branding strategy of immaculate form.

a flexible resource for commodified residential development planning. This narrative is supplemented by advertising photography that stages the Palm's villas as part of an immaculate and idyllic geo-pictography.[13]

6 Closure

Together with glass façades, gated communities, infrastructural exclusions, and visual culture, the master plan is a major instrument in Dubai's capitalist and autocratic spatial regime. By foregrounding geometric spatial design, urban megaprojects, and climatic fortification, Dubai's master plan architecture operates as an aesthetic closure that resonates with the Emirate's social organisation.[14] Dubai's topos of enjoyment and open cosmopolitanism is based on strict spatial and social segregation. The MOE implements this through decorative store fronts, stage-like lighting, and mirror-bright marble flooring in its interior space. Similar to residential districts, the mall functions as a form of gated community by regulating the social groups who gain access to it. By keeping milieus among themselves, the consumer spaces at the heart of Dubai's global brand marketing tend to establish places of homogeneous, class-based gathering. Despite cultural differences, these milieus are united in an immaculate, narcissistic social self by Dubai's thematic consumerism.

This socio-aesthetic closure is at the same time a political closure. Dubai's architectural icons embody the vision of a local ruling class for the high-speed modernisation of an emirate that until the 1960s was a pre-oil trade hub unknown to a more general global public. Contrasting with earlier local architecture and heritage, the aesthetic closure of the MOE, Palm Jumeirah, and *Burj Khalifa* projects an imagined community that transcends its earlier history through capitalist globalisation. The Emirate's seamless, futuristic architectural form testifies to the anticipation of progress and thereby corresponds to Dubai's specific temporality of modernisation marked by extraordinary swiftness and abrupt transformation.[15] Such futuristic brand aesthetics, master plan compounds, and specialised social, commercial, and legal zones as Dubai's Media and Internet Cities result in a spatial configuration of architectural solitaries (Fig. 6). Their binary of highlighted, seamless surface/outside space and interiorised regime/inside space tends to sustain power dynamics that build on architectural production. By directly generating fi-

13 On promoting the Palm through photography, see Burs, 2016: 318–327.

14 With closure, I use a term coined in Marxist interpretations of utopian and science fiction aesthetics, see Jameson, 2007: 202.

15 This phenomenon of modernisation in the case of France was first noted by Ross, 1996: 4–5, 27.

Fig. 6: View of plots from the *Burj Khalifa*
Photo: Felix Torkar, 2014. Courtesy of the photographer.

nancial revenue and by privatising space, building projects consolidate local power. The closed interiority that these structures foreground thus offers metaphorical and very real protection from the contagion of other political systems and of an overcome past.[16]

7 Purification

This closure of space, conveying at once a temporal and social closure, can be read as growing out of the history of utopian form and its dogma of purification.[17] Master plans and social exclusion enable a clear ordering of space and orchestrate views as a visual pleasure. This is particularly evident in residential spaces: organic shorelines organise space in Dubai Marina; standardised villas behind curved waterfronts evoke ordered rhythm on the Palm Jumeirah. The immaculate luxury of living is fulfilled not only by affluence manifesting itself in an unrestricted view.

16 For the concept of interiority in Dubai's spatial configuration, see Hazbun, 2008: 216.
17 On the notion of utopia in Dubai's image production, see Kanna, 2005.

Water basins and great height allow for residential units that permit views dominated by the distance from and absence of other people in their panoramas.

Again, this notion of a purified individualistic civilisation resonates with American mid-century narratives of corporate modernism as embodying Edenic purity. At the time, this was a new ideal in architectural, fashion, and cosmetics discourses, as well as in film, which liberated the United States' cultural discourse from the turmoil of war and the limitations of tradition and which matched its economic domination with a new monumentality.[18] This modernist current associated mirrored glazed skyscrapers, shiny materials, water-related lifestyles, and mass-produced residential units with flawless advertising aesthetics promising individual perfection. As the steel-and-glass façade came to signify values of self-maintenance and new cultural tropes of shimmering metallic beauty, Lieber convincingly argues that we can read this architectural mid-century era as forging a socio-political allegory for the purified post-war nation claiming a new hegemonic position. Dubai's branding in the early 21st century seems to take advantage of this established signification of architecture exemplifying a new golden age of hegemonic nationalism after undergoing substantial transformation. Adapting Lieber's reading of earlier American architecture for the Gulf, I suggest that it foregrounds an idealised representation of a modernised, self-sustaining autocracy under glass, purified of its racist, exploitative, and ethnocratic logic.[19]

8 Conclusion: A Combined and Uneven Mythology

The adoption of a mid-century corporate repertoire in 21st-century Dubai by no means configures a congruent spatial aesthetics. With shifted engineering technology, postmodern symbolic forms, and a hypercapitalist autocratic context, Dubai's architecture is as much part of a universal capitalist world system as it is temporally and culturally specific. One might presume that this local specificity primarily concerns how the Emirate stages cultural difference through modern reinterpretations of architectural tradition in cases like its heritage village and the repeated emphasis on its wind towers as a way to disentangle its identity from the West. In their brightly polished spatial realisation, though, such traditionalised buildings and sites add to the spotless, hypermodern contours of Dubai in much the same way as the Emirate's more recent architecture of spectacle. The desire to uphold

18 See here and in the following Lieber, 2018: 9, 35.

19 On modern spatial organisation as a tool to disguise unevenness, see Ross, 1996: 13.

Dubai's identity as an Islamic and Arab city in order to distinguish the local from the universal is still inherently produced through and within a late-stage capitalist system. Rather than its heritage inventions, the Emirate's particular model of development and symbolic spatial aesthetics seems to be the key to its differentiation from American, European, and Asian precursors. It primarily includes the immense availability of financial resources in the early 2000s, the lack of democratic structures, the extraordinary swiftness of abrupt urban transformation, and the unity of political regime, state-owned architectural production, and global marketing.[20] Topoi of the ideal city in modern Arab intellectual history might further contribute to such a nuanced cultural understanding.[21]

In this sense, Dubai is at the same time a connected and a different kind of iteration of the capitalist dream city. Through its aesthetic regime of immaculate hypermodernity, it outmoderns the modern. With this conclusion, one key for noticing cultural nuance in the corporate arenas of spatial production and branding in the Middle East lies in the Marxist approach of combined and uneven development that recently resurfaced in the social sciences and humanities. While acknowledging that capitalism is one singular world system, this perspective refocuses on the circumstance that modernity has not assumed the same shape everywhere. Dubai's appropriation of the immaculate aesthetics of lifestyle branding regimes underlines that modernisation is inherently site-specific because no two social and cultural instances are the same.[22]

The philosopher Byung-Chul Han sees sleekness as the signature of our neoliberal present, its digital apparatus, and its optimised, positivised communication.[23] Dubai's commodification of life builds on such smooth communicability and flawless, instagrammable photogenicity that allow for the dramatisation of early 21st-century lifestyles through the local reworking and adaptation of cultural tropes of the 1950s and '60s. Yet, by combining established significations of corporate modernism with a postmodern formal repertoire, Gulf architecture complicates streamlined narratives of neatly separated modern versus postmodern archi-

20 See Kanna, 2011: 8, 40. On iconic architecture as an instrument of power employed by the transnational corporate class, see Sklair, 2017. On Dubai's connection to Asian models of urban branding and globalisation, see Haines, 2011; Lowry and McCann, 2011.

21 This would include examining the extent to which premodern conceptualisations of idealised urban form were reformulated or abandoned in modern theories of the ideal city. In the larger context of the Middle East, modern Arab intellectual history focused on concepts that came from European ideals of urban modernisation, supplemented by vernacular elements. In some cases, European architects implemented these visions. See for example the various contributions on Baghdad and larger dynamics of modernisation in the Middle East in Isenstadt and Rizvi, 2008.

22 See Warwick Research Collective, 2015: 12.

23 See Han, 2015: 9–10.

tectural aesthetics. The Emirate's immaculate promise is a branded utopia void of the utopian genre's aspirational political content. Dubai's architectural branding instead exploits the surface image of utopia's poetic form to consolidate the revenue-driven power of autocratic rule. As the Emirate uses architecture to brand its place through the mythology of immaculate form, its buildings function as a promise of partaking in their aesthetic principles: of becoming immaculate consumers.

Bibliography

Al Maktoum, Mohammed Bin Rashid. *My Vision: Challenges in the Race for Excellence.* Dubai: Motivate Publishing, 2012.

Burs, Gerhard Martin. *Mediale Präsentation in der Gegenwartsarchitektur: Das Beispiel der Vereinigten Arabischen Emirate.* Bielefeld: Transcript, 2016.

Geisler, Philip. *Die Höchste Form des Glücks: Architektur, Urbaner Raum und Utopische Gestalt in Dubai, 2001–2017.* MA Thesis, Freie Universität Berlin, Kunsthistorisches Institut, 2017.

Haines, Chad. "Cracks in the Façade: Landscapes of Hope and Desire in Dubai." In *Worlding Cities: Asian Experiments and the Art of Being Global,* edited by Ananya Roy and Aihwa Ong, 160–181. Chichester: John Wiley & Sons, 2011.

Han, Byung-Chul. *Die Errettung des Schönen.* Frankfurt am Main: S. Fischer, 2015.

Hazbun, Waleed. *Beaches, Ruins, Resorts: The Politics of Tourism in the Arab World.* Minneapolis: University of Minnesota Press, 2008.

Hindelang, Laura. *Iridescent Kuwait: Petro-Modernity and Urban Visual Culture since the Mid-Twentieth Century.* Berlin, Boston: De Gruyter, 2022.

Huyssen, Andreas. "Mapping the Postmodern." *New German Critique* 33 (1984): 5–52.

Isenstadt, Sandy, and Kishwar Rizvi. *Modernism and the Middle East: Architecture and Politics in the Twentieth Century.* Seattle, London: University of Washington Press, 2008.

Jameson, Fredric. *Postmodernism, or, the Cultural Logic of Late Capitalism.* Durham: Duke University Press, 1991.

Jameson, Fredric. *Archaeologies of the Future: The Desire Called Utopia and Other Science Fictions.* London, New York: Verso, 2007.

Kanna, Ahmed. "The 'State Philosophical' in the 'Land without Philosophy': Shopping Malls, Interior Cities, and the Image of Utopia in Dubai." *Traditional Dwellings and Settlements Review* 16.2 (2005): 59–73.

Kanna, Ahmed. *Dubai: The City as Corporation.* Minneapolis: University of Minnesota Press, 2011.

Lieber, Jeffrey. *Flintstone Modernism or The Crisis in Postwar American Culture.* Cambridge, MA, London: The MIT Press, 2018.

Lowry, Glen, and Eugene McCann. "Asia in the Mix: Hong Kong, Vancouver, Dubai." In *Worlding Cities: Asian Experiments and the Art of Being Global,* edited by Ananya Roy and Aihwa Ong, 182–204. Chichester: John Wiley & Sons, 2011.

Michaelson, Ruth. "'In this World, Social Media is Everything': How Dubai Became the Planet's Influencer Capital." *The Guardian* 17 April 2021. https://www.theguardian.com/world/2021/apr/17/in-this-world-social-media-is-everything-how-dubai-became-the-planets-influencer-capital. Accessed 15 January 2022.

Ross, Kristin. *Fast Cars, Clean Bodies: Decolonization and the Reordering of French Culture.* Cambridge, MA, London: The MIT Press, 1996.

Sklair, Leslie. *The Icon Project: Architecture, Cities, and Capitalist Globalization.* New York: Oxford University Press, 2017.

Star, Susan Leigh. "The Ethnography of Infrastructure." *American Behavioral Scientist* 43 (1999): 377–391.

Warwick Research Collective. *Combined and Uneven Development: Towards a New Theory of World-Literature.* Liverpool: Liverpool University Press, 2015.

List of Contributors

Khaled Nezar Adham is an Associate Professor of Architecture and Urban Planning. He received his bachelor degree in Architecture from Cairo University, his MA from Kent State University, and his PhD from Texas A&M University. He has taught in universities in the USA, Egypt, and the United Arab Emirates (UAE). Currently, he is an affiliate researcher at the Leibniz-Zentrum Moderner Orient (ZMO) Berlin, Germany. His publications and recent research activities focus on the impact of late capitalism on the architectural and urban transformations of Cairo and selected Arab Gulf Cities.

Karin Ahlberg is a social anthropologist. She is a researcher at the Department of Social Anthropology, Stockholm University, Sweden, and a postdoctoral fellow at the *Institut für Ethnologie und Kulturwissenschaft*, Universität Bremen, Germany. Previously, she worked at the Department of Social Anthropology, University of Oslo, Norway. In 2017, she received her PhD from the School of Oriental and African Studies (SOAS), University of London. Her PhD thesis examines entanglements between tourism, statecraft, and national image curation in contemporary Egypt. Ahlberg's current research explores the environmental afterlife of the Suez Canal and the effects of Lessepsian migration in the Mediterranean Sea from a more-than-human perspective.

Hend Aly is an Economic and Social Research Council (ESRC) doctoral fellow and a PhD student at the University College London, UK. She has held various positions in international development and academic institutions including the University of Cambridge and the United Nations. Aly received an interdisciplinary education with two post-graduate degrees in political science and urban studies. Her doctoral research focuses on rethinking integration in urban contexts. She has previously published on urban inequalities and citizenship, neoliberal urbanism, authoritarianism, urban branding, urban governance, and urban activism. Her research covers diverse cities including Cairo, Brussels, Madrid, Belgrade, Tirana, and new cities, namely NEOM.

Gergana Alzeer is an Assistant Professor in the College of Humanities and Social Sciences at Zayed University, Dubai Campus, UAE, and a fellow at the Higher Education Academy in the UK. She has over 14 years' experience in teaching and advising Emirati women students at Zayed University, including her previous administrative role as the Assistant Dean of Student Affairs. Alzeer has an interdisciplinary background in Architecture, Social Science, and Education and is a specialist in studying women's spatial experiences in education with a focus on the intersection of culture, place, gender, and learning.

Raffael Beier is an urban geographer working as a postdoctoral research fellow in the research group "International Planning Studies" at the Department of Spatial Planning, TU Dortmund University, Germany. Previously, he coordinated the PhD programme in International Development Studies at the Institute of Development Research and Development Policy, Ruhr University Bochum and was associated with the Centre for Built Environment Studies (CUBES) at the University of the Witwatersrand, Johannesburg, South Africa. Currently, he is leading a research project on dropout and post-resettlement mobilities in state-led affordable housing projects in Africa, funded by the German Research Foundation (DFG).

https://doi.org/10.1515/9783110741100-038

Marie Bonte is a geographer and associate professor at the *Laboratoire Dynamiques Sociales et Recomposition des Espaces* (LADYSS) and at Université Paris 8, France, where she teaches in the Department of Social Sciences of the Mediterranean Area. She defended a thesis on Beirut's nightscape and its recreational uses in post-conflict Lebanon. Her research explores the moral, social, and political dimensions of urban nights in the Middle East, including the production, marketing, and consumption of alcohol. Her publications are about gay places at night, urban rhythms, drinking patterns in Rabat and Beirut, and the geography of ghosts and alcohol practices in the Global South.

Kamaluddin Duaei holds an MA in North American Studies from the University of Tehran, Iran. His academic interests include urban studies, visual culture, and political economy. His thesis, a cultural analysis of Alabama's depression murals, addressed the ways dominant ideological discourses moulded the landscapes of identity in the New South during the 1930s. Duaei is the author of *Chernobyl: Lying to Solicit Truth* (Iran, 2020), which provides a comprehensive treatment of an HBO-Sky miniseries, and of a critique of the animated film *Inside Out*, published in the *European Journal of American Culture* (2020). He works as an independent researcher and freelance translator in Iran.

Hicham El Bayed has been a Professor of Economics at the *Université Hassan 1er* at Settat, Morocco since 2004. He holds a doctorate in International Economics from the *Université Grenoble-Alpes*, France, a *Diplôme d'études supérieures spécialisées* (DESS) in Business Diagnostics from the same university, and a Doctorate in Economics from the Université Mohammed V de Rabat, Morocco. El Bayed is currently working on a book about "Branding and the world of brands," to be published at the end of 2022. In addition, he is a senior trainer in strategy and organisation, with a multitude of missions conducted in Morocco and Africa.

Hassan Elmouelhi is an architect and urban planner and works as a senior researcher and project leader at the Department of Urban Development, Campus El Gouna, Egypt and the Habitat Unit – International Urbanism and Design at the TU Berlin, Germany. His interests include culture and urban informality in relation to aspects of urban development and governance in the Global South. He is involved in several cooperation and research projects on informal urbanism, urban management, urban mobility, new settlements, and the localising global agendas. He has participated as an expert and consultant for international organisations and academic research projects in Germany and in African and Asian countries.

Lisa Maria Franke is specialised in Arabic and Islamic Studies, as well as in Social and Cultural Anthropology. Currently, she works as an assistant professor in the field of Anthropology of Islam at the Institute of Social and Cultural Anthropology, University of Göttingen, Germany. Franke graduated from Bayreuth University and SOAS, London. Her PhD from Leipzig University focused on martyrdom, gender constructions, and social discourses in Palestine; at the University of Cologne, she dealt with the religious, social, and political content of colloquial poetry in Egypt. Her interests include everyday history, eschatology, belief and identity, and emotions, as well as individualisation processes, religious transformations, and social dynamics.

Melissa Gatter is a Lecturer in Anthropology and International Development at the University of Sussex, UK. At the Sheffield Institute for International Development, she conducted research on the impact of the Covid-19 pandemic on livelihoods in the Za'tari camp, Jordan. She completed her PhD in Middle East Studies at the University of Cambridge, for which she carried out ethnographic fieldwork in the Azraq camp. Gatter has consulted on development programs across the Middle East and worked for leading aid agencies in Jordan. Her research centres on forced migration and development in the Middle East, particularly the intersection of time, space, and aid in refugee camps.

Richard Gauvain has lived and worked in Egypt and the UAE for nearly twenty years. He has taught courses in the fields of political science, sociology, cultural studies, anthropology, and comparative religion. He has published books and articles relating to Islamic reform movements, but also on religious ritual, gender, and social media. In addition to working at a number of American universities in the Middle East, he has been a research fellow at the Universities of Heidelberg and Durham. His current research focuses on the workings of Egyptian Anglicanism, past and present. Gauvain presently teaches at the British University in Egypt.

Philip Geisler is a PhD candidate at the Berlin Graduate School Muslim Cultures and Societies, Germany. In his dissertation, he assesses the history of performance in material exhibitions of the Islamic world. After obtaining a degree in journalism and media economics at the *Medienakademie Berlin*, he studied Art History, Islamic Studies, and Political Science at the *Freie Universität Berlin* and Harvard University. He has published on Ottoman imperial architecture, Islamic heritage constructions, and transcultural craft making. He is a former fellow of the *Studienstiftung des Deutschen Volkes* and the *Kunsthistorisches Institut in Florenz – Max-Planck-Institut*, Italy, and is currently a Krupp-Foundation Fellow at Stanford University, USA.

Dieter Haller has been Professor for Ethnology (Cultural and Social Anthropology) at the Ruhr University Bochum, Germany since 2005. His main fields of interest include studies of borderlands, port cities, transgressions, possession, cosmopolitanism, diaspora, and corruption; he has been working on Morocco, Gibraltar, Spain, and the Mediterranean. Among his publications are ethnographic monographs (like *Gelebte Grenze Gibraltar*, 2000; *Lone Star Texas*, 2007; *Tanger: Der Hafen, die Geister, die Lust*, 2016; and *Tangier/Gibraltar: A Tale of One City – An Ethnography*, 2021); and other books (including *Corruption*, 2005, coedited with Cris Shore; *DTV-Atlas Ethnologie*, 2005; and *Die Suche nach dem Fremden*, 2012).

Laura Hindelang is an Assistant Professor at the Institute of Art History, University of Bern, Switzerland. Her book *Iridescent Kuwait: Petro-Modernity and Urban Visual Culture Since the Mid-Twentieth Century* (2022) studies the (in)visibilities of petroleum in Kuwait's visual culture. She coedited the anthology *Into the Wild: Art and Architecture in a Global Context* (2018) and has published on the magazine culture, architecture, and contemporary art of the Gulf States. Her current interests are nostalgia and glass in art and architecture. She is a committee member of *Manazir–Swiss Platform for the Study of Visual Arts, Architecture and Heritage in the MENA Region* and an editorial member of *Manazir Journal*.

Thibaut Klinger holds a PhD in Geography from the University of Tours, France, is a graduate of the Ecole Normale Supérieure in Paris, and has an "agrégation" in history. He is an associated researcher of the Equipe Monde Arabe et Méditerranée (EMAM) at the University of Tours. His doctoral thesis on "Spatial Planning and National Identity in Oman" shows the key role of housing policy in land-use planning under Sultan Qaboos from 1970 onwards and the recomposition of the territory that it brought about. It demonstrates how regional planning also sought to redefine national identity to allow the country to integrate globalisation.

Natalie Koch is Professor of Geography at Syracuse University's Maxwell School of Citizenship and Public Affairs, USA. Before, she was Professor at Heidelberg University, Germany, and Associate Professor in the Department of Geography and the Environment in Syracuse. She is a political geographer working on geopolitics, empire, nationalism, identity politics, and resource governance. Her research focuses on alternative sites of geopolitical analysis such as spectacle, sport, science and higher education, environmental policy, and urban planning. She is the author of *The Geopolitics of Spectacle: Space, Synecdoche, and the New Capitals of Asia* (2018) and *Arid Empire: The Entangled Fates of Arizona and Arabia* (2023).

Alina Kokoschka, who holds a PhD in Islamic Studies from the *Freie Universität Berlin*, Germany, investigates contemporary Islam at the intersection of things, images, and script. Beyond her philosophically informed approach, Kokoschka has a keen interest in documentation. For this, she founded the contemporary archive, virtual showroom, and open research network "Hawass: Contemporary Islamic Aesthetics" (http://www.hawass.org/). As a curator, she currently works for the museum and columbarium *Die Eiche* in the North German town of Lübeck, focusing on the relations between art and grief, objects and loss.

Birgit Krawietz is Professor for Islamic Studies at the *Freie Universität Berlin*, Germany and involved in the Berlin Graduate School Muslim Cultures and Societies. She earned her PhD in Islamic Studies from the University of Freiburg in 1990 with a PhD thesis on the human body in Arabic Islamic medical fatwas of the 20th century. Her second book, for her habilitation from Tübingen University, deals with Sunni Islamic legal theory. Her research interests comprise Islamic normativity and the cultural history of the Muslim societies. Krawietz's publications have hitherto focused on medical ethics, traditional sports, urbanism in Turkey and the Gulf, and heritage studies.

Helle Lykke Nielsen is an Associate Professor at the Center for Contemporary Middle East Studies, University of Southern Denmark in Odense. She holds a PhD in Applied Linguistics; for a number of years, her research focused on the acquisition of Arabic as a foreign language, educational linguistics, and minority language policies in Denmark. Her current research includes the linguistic and semiotic urban landscapes of immigrant neighbourhoods, of Muslim cemeteries and mosques, and of political and religious graffiti. She is presently involved in the project "The Role of Language in Segregation and Gentrification Processes: Linguistic Landscapes in Gothenburg," which is funded by The Swedish Research Council.

Moritz A. Mihatsch is a global historian interested in nationalism, self-determination, and sovereignty. He is currently a Lecturer for World History at the History Faculty of the University of Cambridge, UK and at the Political Science Department of the British University in Egypt. He wrote his D.Phil. dissertation at the University of Oxford on political parties and the concept of the nation in Sudan in the 1950s and 1960s. He is in process of completing a book on the global history of sovereignty. His latest research focuses on decolonisation and the epistemologies of global history at UNESCO.

Ghassan Moussawi is Assistant Professor of Gender and Women's Studies and Sociology with an affiliate faculty appointment in the Unit for Criticism and Interpretive Theory at the University of Illinois, Urbana Champaign, USA. His research and teaching lies at the intersections of transnational gender and sexuality studies, everyday life precariousness and violence, urban studies, queer theory, queer of colour critique, and postcolonial feminisms – with keen attention to nation and empire. His book *Disruptive Situations: Fractal Orientalism and Queer Strategies in Beirut* (2020) examines queer strategies of survival amidst everyday life violence and disruptions.

Annegret Roelcke is a PhD candidate at the *Institut für Islamwissenschaft, Freie Universität Berlin* and a research affiliate at the ZMO Berlin, Germany. Her research investigates identity politics in urban settings in Turkey and the Middle East, combining anthropological and historical approaches. She focuses on the social construction of cultural heritage and religious places and their negotiation between diverse stakeholders in contexts of social inequality and change. Currently, she is working on her dissertation on contemporary urban heritage politics in Istanbul. She studied Arab and Islamic Studies at Leipzig University, Boğaziçi University Istanbul, and the *Freie Universität Berlin* and holds an MA in Islamic Studies.

Ute Röschenthaler is extracurricular professor at Johannes Gutenberg University Mainz, Germany. She is Principal Investigator in the project "Cultural Entrepreneurship and Digital Transformation in Africa and Asia" at the Universities of Frankfurt and Mainz. In 2019/20, she was Senior Fellow at the *Internationales Forschungszentrum Kulturwissenschaften*, Vienna, Austria and a fellow at the African Studies Centre, Leiden, Netherlands. As a member of the project "Africa's Asian Options" at Goethe University Frankfurt, she researched the trade in Chinese green tea to African countries. Recent coedited publications include a special issue "Brokerage from Within" (*Cultural Dynamics*, 2021), *Mobility between African, Asia and Latin America* (2017), and *Cultural Entrepreneurship in Africa* (2016).

Tilde Rosmer is an Assistant Professor at the Department of Social Science at Zayed University, Dubai Academic City, UAE with a PhD in Middle Eastern Studies from the University of Oslo, Norway. She teaches courses on critical thinking, Middle Eastern history, and culture and sustainability. Rosmer's research has been mainly on collective identity formation and religious-political movements, with a particular focus on Israel and Palestine. Her book on the Islamic Movement in Israel was published in 2022. Currently her research in the emerging field of Environmental Humanities focuses on awareness and knowledge of sustainability among Emirati youth.

Heiko Schuss received both his Diploma in Economics and Business Administration and his MA in Oriental Philology, Islamic Studies, and Economics from Ruhr University Bochum, Germany. He worked as an assistant at the *Friedrich-Alexander-Universität Erlangen-Nürnberg*, Germany, from which he also acquired his doctoral degree in 2006. In 2014, he joined the Department of Economics of Abdullah Gül University in Kayseri, Turkey as Assistant Professor. His research focuses on the economic development of Turkey and the Middle East, taking into consideration historical, social, and cultural aspects. Within this context, he also conducts research on Islamic finance and Islamic economics.

Dounia Sedra has a master's degree in financial engineering from the *Ecole Nationale de Commerce et de Gestion de Settat* (ENCG Settat), Morocco and another master's degree in Marketing from the Faculty of Economics and Management, *Université Hassan 1er*, also in Settat. She is Senior Project Manager in place marketing, with more than 15 years of experience in the field. Currently, she is completing a PhD at the *Université Hassan 1er* on the place branding of the city of Casablanca and its impact on foreign direct investments.

Roman Stadnicki, PhD, is an Associate Professor in Urban Geography at the University of Tours, France. He is a member of the *Equipe Monde Arabe et Méditerannée* (EMAM) at the *Laboratoire Cités,*

TERritoires, Environnement et Sociétés (CITERES) and associated with the French Centre for Research in the Arabian Peninsula (CEFREPA). His research focuses on contemporary urbanisation in the Middle East in general and on spatial politics, social practices, and urbanistic imagery in particular. He has done fieldwork in Yemen, Egypt, and, more recently, Kuwait and the UAE. He is co-editor of his last book, titled *Abécédaire de la ville au Maghreb et au Moyen-Orient* (2020).

Nina S. Studer is a historian and Arabist with a strong focus on gender and the history of psychiatry in colonial contexts. Her PhD, which she wrote at the Universities of Zurich, Switzerland and Oxford, UK, concerning descriptions of Muslim North African women by French colonial psychiatrists, was published in 2016. Since then, she has conducted research into medical and psychiatric descriptions of drinking habits in the colonial Maghreb, and has published both academic and popular history articles on coffee, tea, wine, champagne, traditional Maghrebi alcohol, Orangina, and Fanta. She is currently writing a book on the history of absinthe.

Sophie-Therese Trenka-Dalton lives in Berlin, Germany, where she studied Visual Art at the University of the Arts. In her work, she examines the continuous migration of cultural motifs and stories, following the cultural shifts that occur when centres of power dissolve and form anew. For exhibitions, she develops architectural displays that present collected artefacts along with sculptures, photography, and video works. Her work has been exhibited at the *Neuer Berliner Kunstverein*, Berlin; KW Institute for Contemporary Art, Berlin; basso, Berlin; Alserkal Avenue, Dubai; Serpentine Gallery, London; Klaus von Nichtssagend Gallery, New York; Kunstraum Michael Barthel, Leipzig; and the *Heidelberger Kunstverein*, Heidelberg, amongst other places.

Pekka Tuominen is a social and cultural anthropologist specialising in urban transformation, sociocultural qualities of space, and moral dimensions of urbanity. He is a Postdoctoral Researcher at the University of Helsinki, Finland for the Tackling Biases and Bubbles in Participation (BIBU) consortium. His research concentrates on changing urban spheres in Istanbul and on peripheral areas of his native Helsinki. His PhD (2016) studied the relations between urban spaces and the moral frameworks of Istanbul's inhabitants, especially in some run-down but gentrifying neighbourhoods. Tuominen has also led a multidisciplinary research project in a stigmatised suburban estate in Helsinki that is commonly associated with social problems and failed immigration policies.

Steffen Wippel is currently publications manager at the German Institute for Global and Area Studies (GIGA) in Hamburg for the Merian Centre for Advanced Studies in the Maghreb (MECAM), Tunis; he previously coordinated an interdisciplinary group of fellows at MECAM for the *Philipps-Universität Marburg*, Germany. Before that, he worked at the ZMO in Berlin, several German universities, and the University of Southern Denmark in Odense. He holds a PhD in economics from the *Freie Universität Berlin* and a habilitation degree (Dr. habil.) from Erlangen University. His interdisciplinary research focuses on regionalisation and urban development in the MENA region, particularly in Morocco and Oman.

Index

Note: Entries for members of dynastic rulers' families from Gulf countries begin with their personal name; titles such as "Sheikh" are placed after the name. For "al-" and "Al," also search for the entry without the article.

https://doi.org/10.1515/9783110741100-039